Christ
The Destiny of the Human Person

Christ
The Destiny of the Human Person

A Journey into Filial Anthropology

His Excellency Bishop Jean Laffitte
Prelate of the Sovereign Order of Malta

Translated into English by G. J. Woodall

Gracewing

Le Christ destin de l'homme. Itinéraires d'anthropolgie filiale first published by Mame, 2012.

English translation by Canon G. J. Woodall

First published in England in 2023
by
Gracewing
2 Southern Avenue
Leominster
Herefordshire HR6 0QF
United Kingdom
www.gracewing.co.uk

No part of this publication may be reproduced, stored in a retrieval system, or transmitted in any form or by any means, electronic, mechanical, photocopying, recording or otherwise, without the written permission of the publisher.

The right of Bishop Jean Laffitte to be identified as the author of this work has been asserted in accordance with the Copyright, Designs and Patents Act 1988.

English language text © 2023 Bishop Jean Laffitte
French language edition © 2012 Mame, Paris (France)

ISBN 9780852447086

Typeset by Gracewing

Cover design by Bernardita Peña Hurtado

Contents

Acknowledgements vii
Introduction to the French Edition of 2012 ix
Introduction to the English translation of 2020 xxi
Preface by Archbishop Anthony Fisher xxiii

I. Life, Family, and Society

Life

1. The Embryo According to the Plan of God 5
2. *Evangelium Vitae* 37
3. Health as an Ethical Issue: The Donation of Organs 65
4. The Church's Concern for Those Sick with AIDS 89
5. Is There a Christian Way to Die? *Ars Pagana et Ars Christiana Moriendi* 105

The Family

6. The Irreplaceable Role of Marriage and of the Family 141
7. Created in Order to Love 157
8. The Body and Natural Law 191
9. The Eucharistic Body and the Body of the Church 207
10. Conjugal Holiness 233

Society

11. The Family and Society 249
12. The Effects of the Sexual Revolution 259

13. The Demographic Situation in Europe............................ 269

14. Conscience as Inviolable 285

15. The Social Dimension of Human Existence: The Status of the Social Doctrine of the Church... 321

II. Christian Action, Forgiveness, and the Heart of Christ

Christian Action

16. What is a Filial Anthropology? 349

17. Christ: the Contemporary of all People of all Times 373

18. Knowledge of God; Knowledge of the Truth 385

19. The Rational Conduct of the Believer............................ 395

20. The *Sequela Christi* 415

Forgiveness

21. Love and Forgiveness 433

22. The Structure of Sacramental Confession 453

23. The Church and Forgiveness 469

24. The Forgiveness of Sins According to St Augustine ... 487

The Heart of Christ

25. Gratitude and Grace.. 519

26. The Mystery of the Heart in St Bonaventure 529

27. Configuration to the Heart of Christ............................ 543

Acknowledgements

I would like to thank all those who, in one way or another, have made possible this publication, both in the case where the texts assembled here have been edited, and in the course of the final elaboration of this work: the John Paul II Institute for Studies on Marriage and the Family, those who have been my professors, my colleagues, and all the students who, over these last twenty years, have orientated and stimulated my research. I thank also those who have provided me with the support of their encouragement and their affection, in particular Hervé-Marie and Martine Catta, François and Marie-Claude Laffitte, Fr Jean-Baptiste Édart, Robert and Jean Halley, Carl and Dorian Anderson, Stanislaw and Ludmilla Grygiel, Jean-Maire and Anouk Meyer, Mgr Karl Josef Romer, and André Ajoux. My gratitude is directed also to my friends, theologians and philosophers, who, by their writings or in innumerable conversations between friends, have been a source of inspiration to me; among these are Frs Denis Biju-Duval, Olivier Bonnewiyn, Pierre-Marie Hombert, Pascal Ide, and Mgr Livio Melina, as also Fr William Santiago. In union with its founder, the servant of God, Pierre Goursat, I thank the Community of Emmanuel and most especially Mgr Yves le Saux, Laurent Landete, Dominique Vermersch, Fr Dominique de Chantérac, Mauro and Lucia Versari. Finally, I am very thankful to Maxime Nogier for the patient care with which he has contributed to the practical realization of this project, as also to the original publishers of the French edition, Mame, for having given an enthusiastic welcome to the project.

Introduction

(to the original French edition of 2012)

To gather together in a single volume texts, which have been written on a large number of topics and in varying circumstances, over a period of fifteen years, is a dangerous exercise and constitutes a real challenge: how is it possible to provide a unity for the whole? Simply structuring them into parts, into chapters, and into focuses of interest is not enough. If a unity among them exists, it must emerge of itself as something obvious; moreover, it must have its origin elsewhere, in a source of inspiration, a style, or a method. It is necessary, too, that each of the texts in some way be related to the others. Once the classification of these articles had been made, it came as a great surprise to the editor and to myself to notice that a formal unity arose from the whole, a unity which was not contradicted in the course of the months of reflection and of rereading which followed. In my opinion, two factors contributed to this impression of unity; the first stems from the nature of Christian anthropology and the second arises from the thought of John Paul II, who, directly and indirectly, has inspired the research and the teaching, which have been conducted at the Institute for Studies on Marriage and Family, which bears his name.

Theological anthropology, in over half a century, has earned the right to be recognized as a specific discipline; it is taught in numerous Catholic universities throughout the world and has given rise to theological contributions of high quality. At some time or another, all of the authors have referred to the following phrase of the Pastoral Constitution, *Gaudium et Spes* of the Second Vatican Council, which, in some way, has become the foundation stone of a subject that has become a theological specialization in its own right:

> The truth is that only in the mystery of the incarnate Word is the mystery of the human being brought to light. For Adam, the first man, was a figure of him Who was to come, namely Christ the Lord. Christ, the New Adam, by the revelation of the mystery of the Father and his love, fully reveals the human being to himself and discloses to him the sublime nature of his calling.[1]

The perspective which theological anthropology offers on the nature of the human person, on who this being, unique within the created order, really is, on his aspirations, on the meaning which he gives to his own existence and to his future, on his actions and on his choices, is never limited to the horizons of this world; on the contrary, it integrates that which, in the domain of human love, St John Paul II called the "plan of God," a kind of divine deliberation, which is a happy translation of the Latin expression. In fact, the *consilium Dei* evokes everything which specifies the intelligence and the coherence of the plan of God, which are revealed to people of good will only little by little, through those fundamental experiences which are their own: love, self-giving, the gift of life, suffering, the death of dear ones and the prospect of their own death, their deepest desires, the intense joy which they sometimes experience, their relationships with others, their existential choices, their moral decisions, their capacity for sympathy and for compassion, their participation in the good of all; but it encompasses also the relationship of human beings with God, implicit and explicit, their theological life, their belonging to the Church, their awareness of the salvation effected by Christ, their concern for souls and their supernatural charity. They are led to discover that God is bound to everything which concerns their deepest aspirations, and in particular, their desire for a happiness that does not come to an end. Christian vision and Christian dynamism offer a unified intelligibility of the human condition, always on the condition that

---

1. Vatican II, *Gaudium et Spes*, 22.

Introduction

they do not reduce in any way the sovereign character of God, his omnipotence, his unfathomable justice, and his infinite mercy.

The totality of the texts presented here is situated within the context of research conducted in the course of two decades of teaching at the Pontifical Institute of John Paul II in Rome and in the different sessions of the Institute in the five continents. We must recall, even if only briefly, the history of a university institute which was wanted and decided upon by Pope John Paul II. The announcement of its foundation, together with that of the erection of the Pontifical Council for the Family, should have been made during the course of the audience of May 13, 1981, the day on which Ali Agça made an attack on the Holy Father's life. In order to understand well the Pope's intention, it will be useful to remind ourselves of the context at the beginning of the 1980s. The moral philosopher who had become the successor of Peter could not but be alarmed at the spread within the Christian world of cultural tendencies and of ethical systems, some of which appeared to him to be incompatible with Revelation. Among their characteristic features, several could be cited without particular order: the rejection of natural law, the contestation of the competence of the Magisterium of the Church in moral matters, the different variants of utilitarian and of consequentialist theories, the affirmation of a radical autonomy of moral conscience, attributing to itself the power to create its own values and norms of discernment, completely forgetting the object of the human act in moral judgment and, in regard to Christian ethics, the radical separation between Christology and morals, to quote only the most well-known of these tendencies. This debate was not only an intellectual question, disputed among experts; several of these ideas had spread among Christians, having in those years to face up to new challenges in their daily lives. In the area of conjugal life, people had not made their own the teaching of the encyclical *Humanae Vitae* and this remained the object of violent contestation. The stability of the cell of the family unit was going from bad to worse. The eighties were the years in which divorce by mutual consent appeared, thereby rendering commonplace the juridical choice of an alternative to maintaining the conjugal bond. John Paul II was aware that the issues for the coming decades would center upon questions of ethics and of anthropology. Some years later, new moral problems came to the light of day, involving the increasing application of scientific techniques: developments in the procedures of *in vitro* fertilization, prospects of cloning, invasive techniques of pre-natal diagnosis together with, as a corollary, the ever-clearer marginalization, and then the suppression in the wombs of their mothers, of handicapped babies, the justification of euthanasia and, in some places, of assisted suicide. The de-penalization of abortion in many counties and the spread of ever more sophisticated techniques of contraception did not contribute in any way to the reduction in the actual number of voluntary terminations of pregnancy and especially of clandestine abortions. To problems connected to the fundamental moral theology of the seventies and eighties, there were thus added ever more numerous problems of bioethics. John Paul II was persuaded very quickly that a gigantic complex of reconstruction was opening up and that a great mobilization of Christians would be necessary. We call to mind once more that in 1994 he founded the Pontifical Academy for Life, entrusting its presidency in the first instance to Professor Jérome Lejeune.

It was within this constantly evolving context that the Institute for Marriage and the Family, under the impulse of its first presidents, the theologians who then became cardinals, Carlo Caffarra and Angelo Scola, undertook its activity of research and of teaching around these two axes which were its priorities: morality (fundamental and special) and anthropology (theological and philosophical). From the beginning, however, the Institute was careful to avoid neglecting the contribution of the human sciences on the one hand and of biblical and sacramental theology on the other. This brief historical reminder would be incomplete, if we were to forget the capital importance repres-

Introduction

ented by the Wednesday "Catecheses on Human Love," proclaimed by the Pope between 1979 and 1984. The Institute was charged with the responsibility for the first publication of a critical edition which appeared in 1985 in Italian and which is now in its eighteenth edition. To be sure, it is still impossible to measure the prodigious impact that these texts have had and that they continue to have upon couples and families in the countries in which they have been taught. In particular, they have given birth to scores of associations of spouses and of families, notably in the English and Spanish-speaking worlds. Critical editions exist in several languages (English, Spanish, Portuguese, Czech). This scientific work, both of deeper study and of transmitting its fruits, remains to be undertaken in the French-speaking world.

The John Paul II Institute has also been led to examine more deeply, in a scientific fashion and from a pastoral perspective, certain problematic issues that, in the course of recent years, have come to articulate a real anthropological and social revolution, of which the most recent and the most spectacular feature is the diffusion of the ideology of gender. At the level of legislation, numerous measures have been taken which have contributed to the weakening of the cell of marriage and of the family, generally through the juridical recognition granted to *de facto* unions, alternative to marriage. These rather alarming circumstances, however, have offered the Institute an opportunity to deepen tirelessly our understanding of the richness of the contributions of the Magisterium of the Church and the anthropology of the Polish Pope. It will be remembered that, within the space of very few years, magisterial texts were published which today are held to be of fundamental importance: the instruction *Donum Vitae*, the moral part of the *Catechism of the Catholic Church*, the apostolic letter *Mulieris Dignitatem*, the encyclicals, *Veritatis Splendor* and *Evangelium Vitae*, the *Letter to Families*, etc.

To this we add that, within a few years, the John Paul II Institute was asked by numerous episcopal conferences and universities to erect sessions in different countries, which would be capable of formulating in different languages and cultures the riches of such a patrimony.

This historical survey of these years, then, was the context in which the texts presented in this volume were written or proclaimed. More precisely, they relate to themes linked more to general ethics than to conjugal and family morality, though without forgetting specific aspects of Christian conduct, such as forgiveness. This last topic is of very particular importance, by reason of the bond between forgiveness and conjugal and family communion, and also by reason of the imminence of the Jubilee of the Year 2000 which was approaching and which saw the whole Church engaged in a process of purification of memory, which implies the request for forgiveness and steps towards penitence.

The texts presented here constitute a selection of twenty-seven articles, chosen from seventy published in the course of those twenty years. A brief note is appended which notes the different reviews in which most of them were published. With the passing of these years, it seems to me to be appropriate to state once more how much the reflection of John Paul II has shown itself to be capable of penetrating the different expressions of Christian thought in the most varied cultural contexts. First of all, there was the interest aroused by this ethical and anthropological research among the many particular Churches, which sent lay people and clerics, coming from ever more numerous countries, to study in Rome. This cultural embrace has shown itself to be particularly fruitful, if we think of the rhythm with which the different sessions of the Institute were erected canonically throughout the world: Washington D.C. in 1988, Valencia in 1994, Mexico City in 1996, Salvador de Bahia in 2001, Cotonou in 2001, Changanacherry in 2001, without counting the associated institutes and the plans for the erection of new sessions in the future: Melbourne, Beirut, Incheon (South Korea). Hundreds upon hundreds of students for the licence, the doctorate, and the various master's degree programs have been formed in the unity that is constituted by these cen-

Introduction

ters. In the course of the years, many of these have proceeded to discharge major responsibilities in the Church, in universities, or in different associations. Very many lay people have created teaching structures and have developed pastoral programmes designed for couples and for families. The production of books also has been prolific, both in the session in Rome and in the other sessions. For my part, I have had the opportunity to appreciate the fecundity of the thought of Karol Wojtyla in non-Christian contexts. In particular, I think of countries such as Japan or, again, of various international political encounters. This capacity of the Wojtylian approach to penetrate into differing cultures and to capture the attention of audiences of young people stems from the method of John Paul II, who, in order to speak to all people of good will, started systematically from what he described as the basic human experiences in the heart of the human person, experiences common to all people. It is often forgotten that the fruits of the Magisterium of his pontificate were prepared in the course of decades of work in philosophy and in anthropology, undertaken from an authentically Christian pastoral perspective, that is to say, one which embraced all the dimensions of the human person: intelligence, the search for God, the acceptance of his grace, affectivity.

One or other of the texts provided here will evoke the philosophical heritage which was his and, in particular, his desire to integrate into the realism of Christian thought the contributions of modern philosophical reflection on conscience and on the interiority of the person. In one sense, the philosopher Karol Wojtyla can well be located along the path traced by Max Scheler, Edith Stein, and Dietrich von Hildebrand, apparently borrowing from the latter the concern to penetrate more deeply, and in a Christian sense, into the meaning of the communion of persons. The *communio personarum*, which he unfolded in all sorts of ways, was for him the way to live out the Christian experience. The special climate that there has always been in the Institute between professors, students, and personnel, in a certain way is an expression of such an experience of communion.

Over and above one or other particular school of thought, one of the characteristics of Wojtyla's method has been never to shy away from the existential and the spiritual significance of a moral choice, avoiding any literary artifice in the argumentation employed, which constantly sought to bring the human being face to face with his responsibilities, towards himself, towards others, and towards God. This was particularly evident in his approach to human love, from which any kind of superficiality or of reductionism was banished. He never toned down the nature of faith as an event, always, according to him, to be understood as an encounter between the human person and Christ. Two examples are revealing: he saw to it that, before plunging into *Veritatis Splendor*, difficult for people to access, there was a long chapter on the encounter between Jesus and the rich young man. The whole content of the text was thereby illuminated. In *Dives in Misericordia*, he compared the prodigal son of the parable to all human beings of every age, but later on he elaborated his thinking by observing, in *Reconciliatio et Paenitentia*, that every one of us human beings is also, in fact, present in the figure of the elder brother of the prodigal son, he who is not ready to accept the mercy of the Father when it is directed to his brother. We could multiply these examples, but let us say that the philosopher always gave way to the pastor, who himself never forgot the often dramatic nature of the questions which a person who is distant from God poses to himself.

Throughout his pontificate, John Paul II accompanied solicitously the history of the Institute that bears his name, receiving professors and students in audience on eleven occasions. Every one of these recognizes with gratitude what they owe to such a master. To this debt, to which I can see many reasons to unite myself, I would like to add, for my part, what I owe to his first disciple, the philosopher, Stanislaw Grygiel, who did me the honor, in friendship, of agreeing to direct my own research into forgiveness.

Introduction

The beatification of John Paul II, in some way, lends a new status to what he has transmitted. In fact, it confers upon all those who have benefitted from his teachings an even greater responsibility to give witness to and to transmit the patrimony that has been received. The question that arises now for each one of us is to come to know what it means today to be a *disciple* of St John Paul II. His contribution is no longer limited either to philosophical thought or to analyses of personalism or of ethics. He is the proof that there exists a sanctification of the intelligence, completely directed to the untiring search for the truth, the good of our neighbor, our personal growth, and progress towards our eternal destiny. Without any doubt, the years and the generations to come will offer answers to these questions.

The early years after the death of Pope John Paul II have provided an opportunity for a new enrichment of our understanding of human love. The first encyclical of Pope Benedict XVI, *Deus Caritas Est*, was not intended in the first place to be an analysis of human love. The object of the text concerns above all divine charity. Yet, everyone has been able to notice the renewed reflection on the dialectic between *eros* and *agape* in the first part of the text. The love between man and woman appears as the figure of love *par excellence*. Both dimensions of love are to be integrated, one with the other, in a harmonious whole, in such a way that "spirit and matter are newly ennobled." The two dimensions are inseparable. The Pope observes that what is true for human beings is true also for God. To the extent that the love of Yahweh for his chosen people is at the same time both *eros* and *agape*, exactly as is the case also with the love of Christ for human beings, a two-way movement is obtained."Marriage, founded upon a love that is exclusive and definitive becomes the icon for the relationship of God with his people and vice versa; the way in which God loves becomes the standard for human love." We can say that *Deus Caritas Est* offers an essential hermeneutical key for the interpretation of God's plan in regard to human love, even if that was not the primary purpose of the text.

Christ the Destiny of the Human Person

The magisterium of Benedict XVI includes already a large number of texts that, in this way, place his pontificate in a line of continuity with the specific contribution of Saint John Paul II. This is not the place to survey them all, but, apart from *Deus Caritas Est*, we may cite the encyclical *Caritas in Veritate* and its concern to underline the bond between family and society, the allocutions proclaimed in January of 2006 and 2007 to the members of the Tribunal of the Rota on the occasion of the opening of the judicial year, the allocution proclaimed on the occasion of the twenty-fifth anniversary of the foundation of the John Paul II Institute on May 11, 2006, the post-synodal exhortation, *Sacramentum Caritatis*, as well as several homilies, that of July 9, 2006 at Valencia, or again, that of June 5, 2011 at Zagreb. Besides, it was in front of the participants in the international meeting organized by the Pontifical Institute of John Paul II on the occasion of the twenty-fifth anniversary of the apostolic exhortation, *Familiaris Consortio*, on May 13, 2011, that the Pope spoke at length about the human body. He emphasized its constitutive relationship with the Creator and observed that it is when it is amputated from this filial dimension that the body rebels against the person. In the eyes of Benedict XVI, the family is the place where, quite rightly, the theology of the body and the theology of love truly enter into each other.

As we can see, new paths of research are opening up for those who wish to deepen their understanding of issues concerning marriage and the family.

The way Benedict XVI incessantly referred to divine paternity reinforces the conviction of the author of these pages that there is an urgent necessity today to draw up the contours of a genuinely *filial anthropology*. At a time when, one by one, the columns which support the structuring of the human being as a complex whole are being removed and when especially the bonds of filiation and of paternity are being weakened, such an approach is the only one capable of giving us human beings an understanding of the meaning of our lives and, at the same time,

Introduction

of providing answers to the questions and anxieties which are to be found in our spirits and in our hearts. The confirmation of the fact of this urgent necessity was afforded in the course of a homily of Benedict XVI, proclaimed on January 6, 2012, on the occasion of the solemnity of the Epiphany. After recalling the *cor inquietum* of St Augustine, which would not be content with anything less than God, the Pope audaciously made an amazing parallel with the heart of God in search of the human person:

It is not just us, human beings, who are restless in relation to God. The Heart of God is restless for the human person. God is waiting for us. He is searching for us. Neither is he at peace, until he has found us. The Heart of God is restless, and it is for this reason that he set out on the road towards us—towards Bethlehem, towards Calvary, from Jerusalem to Galilee and even to the ends of the world. God is restless out of concern for us. He is searching for persons who will allow themselves to be won over by his restlessness, by his passion for us. Persons who carry out within themselves the search which is within their hearts and, at the same time, who allow themselves to be touched in their hearts by God´s search for us.

The eternal Son reveals to each one of us the secret of our created being; each one is son in the Son, chosen and loved from all eternity and destined to live eternally by the love of the Father. God is waiting for us. The Father is waiting for us.

✠ Jean Laffitte
Titular bishop of Entrevaux
Prelate of the Sovereign Order of Malta

Introduction to the English translation of 2020

This book comprises a selection of twenty-seven articles, written by Mgr Jean Laffitte over a number of years and for different publications. He has grouped them into six parts, each around a particular theme. The first half of the book treats human life, the family, and society in turn, with five articles on each of those themes. The second part treats Christian action, forgiveness, and the heart of Christ, containing five, four, and three articles respectively. The underlying thread that unites the book as a whole is that of a filial anthropology, a theological and specifically Christological understanding of the human being, of our vocation, and of our moral life.

The individual articles were written for different audiences, on varying occasions, across a number of years. A lecture prepared for the opening of an academic year, lectures delivered in the context of international congresses, and addresses to groups of faithful in different circumstances inevitably means that they are marked by a variety of style or of emphasis. In addition, as the notes at the end of the book demonstrate in an eloquent manner, they were published at different times, in various languages, and in a range of books or journals, all with their own specific methodologies and systems. The publication of so many articles on such a range of important topics, as relevant in their content and in their implications today as when they were delivered or written, and now available in English as well as in French and in Spanish, requires a certain level of cohesion in format to reflect the cohesion of content which such a book has to offer.

For this reason, an attempt has been made to standardize the presentation in this book of this collection of articles. In particular, in the footnotes and, also, where they appear in the main text, the practice of the French edition of referring to the numbered paragraphs of Magisterial texts with the symbol § has been retained. For the most part, references have been placed into footnotes, except where a particular article analyzed a specific Magisterial document and where, therefore, it made more sense to leave the references in the body of the main text. The references to John Paul II's "Catechesis on Human Love," often known in English by the expression "A Theology of the Body," have been presented with the title, with the number of the catechesis in Latin numerals and with page references to the Italian edition of those catecheses (as in the original French edition); page references from the 1985 Italian edition have been inserted into this translation also on those occasions where these were not provided in the French text. Where I have been able to access them, references to English translations of major works cited in the footnotes of the French text have been included.

Every attempt has been made to render faithfully the thinking of Mgr Laffitte on these critical areas of theology and of philosophy that he has examined. This is a basic requirement of honesty, but it is also necessary in order for the consistency and depth of his analysis to emerge clearly also in translation, so that the reader may appreciate the rich theological insights, the cogency of the moral positions adopted and defended, and the invaluable indications for spiritual reflection and development for the adoptive sons and daughters of Christ which are provided.

G. J. Woodall
February, 2020.

Preface

I once witnessed a man in a hospital café who was profoundly physically impaired. He was wheelchair bound, and it was pretty clear his hands and arms weren't up to much—certainly not up to holding a cup in his hand and lifting it to his lips. He was trying to drink coffee through a straw, but, comically, the straw kept floating to the top of his drink and falling out of the cup. He would get it back in with his teeth, but the straw would just sit flat on the top of his coffee. So he put his head flat on the table and slurped the coffee from that position through the straw. It was obviously very frustrating for him. People at surrounding tables could easily have helped him, simply holding the straw to his mouth for him. But no one did. Maybe they thought noticing his troubles and offering to help would embarrass him. Maybe they were afraid there was an intellectual or emotional impairment to match his obvious physical ones. Maybe disability somehow made him invisible.

Why didn't I help? Because I was the guy desperately trying to get his caffeine fix but too crippled to do so. During my episode of Guillain-Barré Syndrome in 2016 I suffered terrible pain, crippling paralysis, and other disabilities, including a decided lack of coffee. But I was one of the lucky ones with a condition from which I would recover. The five months in hospital gave me a window into the lives of those whose physical or intellectual impairments would be permanent or likely to worsen. I experienced first-hand the paradox of the human body unresponsive to the human spirit. I knew the grief and frustration, the challenge to patience, courage and hope. I experienced uninformative pain and the humiliation of baby-like dependency. But I also witnessed the triumph of human spirits in the care people gave and received, in the determination of some to conquer their disability or at least manage it, and in the camaraderie amongst the patients as we shared our limitations and frustrations, tried to keep each other's spirits up, and pushed each other to maintain the struggle for rehabilitation.

What sense did I make of all this? Well, I came to these challenges armed with a particular view of the essential nature, identity, and destiny of the human person. I knew "in my bones" that we are essentially bodily, free, rational, emotional, social, immortal creatures, vulnerable and interdependent, made for truth, beauty, and goodness—images of God capable of living his noble plan in genuine communion. We are so much more, then, than our culture usually acknowledges, so much more than complex biochemical systems or minds directing biomechanical prostheses, or producer-consumers, or sites and agents for preference fulfilment, or hostages of our culture. My response was rooted in a theological anthropology with which I had been imbued since childhood by my Christian culture and in my adult years through, amongst other things, the teachings of St John Paul II and the work of his Institute for Studies in Marriage and the Family. It was through that John Paul Institute that I met the Reverend Professor, later Bishop, Jean Laffitte. *Christ the Destiny of the Human Person: A Journey into Filial Anthropology* is the latest gift from that learned prelate, and it articulates a powerful and empowering vision of what it is to be human under grace.

Any Catholic anthropology must start and finish with Christ as both inspiration and goal. By embracing our humanity, as the Second Vatican Council observed, Christ revealed the divine to humanity, but he also he revealed man to himself.[1] He is the basis of our understanding, not only of the Totally Other, God, but of ourselves. Part One of Laffitte's work therefore addresses the insistence that *everyone counts,* from the newly conceived to the nearly dead, from every part of life and its nursery, the family, and from every aggregation such as marriage, society, and cul-

---

1. Vatican Council II, *Gaudium et Spes: Pastoral Constitution on the Church in the Modern World* (1965), §22.

ture. This insistence is comes from Christ himself. "Let the little children come to me," said Jesus, "for it is to such as these that the kingdom of God belongs." Let blind Bartimeus come, let the leprous, fevered or disabled, the bleeding, deaf and dumb. Let the mentally impaired and devil-possessed come, the sinners and outcasts, the hungry, poor and lowly, the trampled or lost. Let even the dead Lazarus come. Let the man paralysed with Guillain-Barré Syndrome be lowered through the roof that he too might come to Jesus.[2] For Christ, as Monsignor Laffitte teaches, is 'the destiny of the human person'.

In those many stories of Christ healing and forgiving, he doesn't exercise power from a distance. He comes close and brings people closer. He welcomes. And he frames his own action and that of his disciples in terms of relationship, communion, and love.[3] Yet in the manualist tradition there was a real caution, even fear, that powerful passions and subjective emotions can distort moral judgment and corrupt moral life.[4] All virtues, even theological charity, were diminished in this desire for rational clarity and universalizability, as theologians and pastors sought to protect their discipline (and flock) from moral subjectivism and cultural relativism. In the process, Christ, the person most central to Christian life, was side-lined.[5] The rule was emphasized above the Ruler, the What of duty without attention to the Who and Why. In response to which we might hear St Paul echoing down the centuries: if I tick all the boxes, but have not love, it's all for nothing! (1 Cor: 13)

---

2. Lk 4:31–41; 5:12–26, 30–2; 6:6–10, 6:17–19; 7:1–17, 36–50; 8:26–56; 9:10–17, 37–43; 10:25–37; 11:14–23; 13:10–17; 14:1–6, 21–23; 15:1–32; 17:11–19; 18:15–17, 35–43; 19:7; 21:1–4; 22:24–7; 23:39–43 etc
3. Mt 5:43–6; 19:19; 22:37–9; Lk 6:27–35; 7:47; 10:27; Jn 3:16,35; 5:20,42; 8:42; 10:17; 11:3,5,36; 13:1,23,34–5; 14:15–31; 15:9–19; 16:27; 17:23–6; 19:26; 20:2; 21:7,15–17, 20.
4. Livio Melina, "Desire for happiness and the commandments in the first chapter of *Veritatis Splendor*", *Thomist* 60(3) (July 1996), pp. 341–59.
5. See chs 16–20 of the present volume.

The fathers of the Second Vatican Council sought both to reemphasise what was perennial in traditional Catholic teaching and to update it in response to the needs and insights of modernity. With respect to moral theology, they diagnosed a serious ailment. Their prescription for renewal was "livelier contact with the mystery of Christ and the history of salvation," a firmer grounding in Scripture and tradition, and a clearer recognition that the Christian calling is heavenward in direction but earthly in enactment. They thus invited, on the one hand, a renewed Scriptural, Christocentric, and eschatological focus and, on the other, an openness to contemporary experience, scientific exegesis, and the human sciences. And they exhorted theologians to look for more appropriate ways of communicating moral truth to the people of our time.[6]

In the "out with the manuals" mood of the post-conciliar period, "beatitude theology" seemed to trump "decalogue theology." But the attempted renewal came at a particularly difficult time. Many preferred the Council's words on the dignity of conscience and the proper liberties of the individual to its emphases on Scripture and tradition, community, and authority in the Christian life. Amidst the advancing sexual revolution and the anti-authoritarianism of "the me generation," Paul VI's *Humanæ vitæ* met incomprehension or dissent in many quarters. This set the stage for the polarisation of moral theology, as contending schools responded to the crisis of '68, and for confusion as well as authentic developments in moral theology. Instead of finding a new vernacular by which to call people to "put on Christ," some acquiesced in the spirit of the age. The "new moralities" of situationism, proportionalism, and liberationism dispensed with inconvenient moral absolutes, especially in sexual and life ethics, reduced conscience to sincerity in pursuit of preferences, and pushed Christ even more to the periphery of Christian morality.

---

6. Vatican Council II, *Dei Verbum: Dogmatic Constitution on Divine Revelation* (1964);*Presbyterorum Ordinis: Decree on the Ministry and Life of Priests* (1965), §19; *Optatam Totius: Decree on Priestly Training* (1965), §16.

Preface

To combat this trend, in the decades after Vatican II, Roman dicasteries published important correctives on various moral questions including those in the area of sexuality, family, and life.[7] These included the Pontifical Council for the Family of which Jean Laffitte was at one time Secretary, the Pontifical Academy for Life of which he was Vice-President, and the Congregation for the Doctrine of the Faith to which he was a Consultor. But these important documents only considered the underlying anthropology and moral methodology *en passant* if at all. Pope John Paul II tended to teach at both levels, elaborating a fundamental vision of the human person and his or her vocation, and some crucial moral principles, before applying them to particular questions. This was especially true of *Veritatis Splendor*. The first-ever encyclical on moral theory, it represented the climax of a lifetime's engagement with the challenges of modernity, especially those to marriage and family life. This engagement included ground-breaking works such as *Love and Responsibility* before he was pope, *Familiaris Consortio* soon after, the long series of catecheses now collected together as *The Theology of the Body*, the encyclical on bioethics *Evangelium Vitae*, and many letters and addresses.[8] In addition to his own enormous

---

7. For example Congregation for the Doctrine of the Faith, *On Procured Abortion* (1974); *On Sterilisation* (1975); *On Sexual Ethics* (1975); *On Euthanasia* (1980); *On the Pastoral Care of Homosexual Persons* (1986); *On Respect for Early Human life and IVF* (1987); *On Artificial Nutrition and Hydration* (2007); *On Certain Bioethical Questions* (2008); Pontical Council for the Family, *Marriage and Family* (San Francisco: Ignatius Press, 1989); *The Truth and Meaning of Human Sexuality* (1995); *Preparation for the Sacrament of Matrimony* (1996); *Vademecum for Confessors on Some Aspects of Conjugal Morality* (1997); *The Family and Human Rights* (1999); *Family, Marriage and* De Facto *Unions* (2000); Pontical Academy for Life, *On Cloning* (1997); *On the Morning After Pill* (2000); *On the Use of Human Embryonic Stem Cells* (2000); *On the Dying Person* (2000); *On Xenotransplantation* (2001).
8. Karol Wojtyla, *Love and Responsibility* (1960; trans. H. T. Willetts, Ignatius Press, 1981); John Paul II, *Theology of the Body* (1979–84; transl. Michael Waldstein, 2nd edn., Pauline Books, 2006) which generated an extraordinary secondary literature; *Familiaris Consortio: Apostolic*

philosophical, theological, and pastoral endeavours, John Paull II initiated and inspired many others, catalysing the bishops of the world to be engaged in family and pro-life ministries, convoking the first Synod on the Family and many other meetings with families themselves, establishing the Pontifical Council for the Family and, perhaps most inspired of all, founding the worldwide John Paul II Institute for Studies on Marriage and the Family at which Bishop Laffitte was destined to be one of the most distinguished contributors.

Pope John Paul, the professors on the various campuses of his Institute, and many fellow-travellers, led the way in developing a distinctively Christian rhetoric with which to describe the mysteries of the human person, sexuality, marriage, and the family, such as "identity-difference" and "subjectivity-alterity" of the person, the "horizon" and "ground" of beings in Being, "the nuptial significance of body" and its "body language" of sex, the family as "a school of virtue" and "site and vehicle of evangelization," the "theo-drama" of the moral life of each actor, and so on. By elaborating an anthropology that is unashamedly Christian in its foundations, contemporary in its language, and orthopractical in its conclusions, these writers pointed a way forward for those engaged in the Church's internal task of theological understanding and catechesis and external task of cultural engagement and evangelisation. *Christ the Destiny of the Human Person* is situated firmly within this project.

Jean Clément Marie Gérard Joseph Françoise Georges Laffitte was, in fact, uniquely well-suited to contribute to this endeavour. A pastor of intellect and charm, widely read and in many languages, he is a member of the Emmanuel Community and priest of the Diocese of Autun. He studied in Toulouse, Cambridge, Salamanca, and the Gregorian University. He gained

---

Exhortation on the Christian Family in the Modern World (1981); *Veritatis Splendor: Encyclical on Fundamental Questions of the Church's Moral Teaching* (1993); *Gratissimam Sane: Letter to Families* (1994); *Evangelium Vitae: Encyclical on the Value and Inviolability of Human Life* (1995).

Preface

his doctorate in Moral Theology from the John Paul II Institute at the Lateran University. Since 1994 he has been a Professor on the Roman campus of that Institute and a visiting professor at the other campuses worldwide. He has served in the several Roman dicasteries already noted, has been an invited speaker at many international gatherings, is now Prelate of the Order of Malta. So he speaks from broad experience and deep expertise. He has already published important works on the theology of marriage, family and sexuality, the spirituality of the heart, justice and mercy, conscience, liberal culture, and religious freedom, and, here on "filial anthropology" and moral theology.

The present workis divided into two broad categories: Life, Family and Society, on the one hand, and Christian Action, Forgiveness, and the Heart of Christ on the other. Beginning with some of the "neuralgic" questions of our day—abortion, laboratory reproduction and euthanasia—Laffitte surfaces their implications for conceptions of the human person and community, as well as for the ethics of healthcare. Here he draws upon the work of a wide range of theological authorities, including St John Paul, and masterfully draws them back to the vision of the Second Vatican Council. In Part Two, he shows how Christian wisdom about the human person enormously enriches our answers not just to particular moral puzzles but to the big questions of *who* and *why* and *for what* that lie behind them. At each point, he delicately moves the discussion from the human to the divine, the concrete to the more theoretical, the personal to the universal. So, for example, the question of forgiveness in Chapter 21 that begins with the individual experience of human forgiveness, leads us eventually into understanding divine forgiveness, and from there, to "the logic of the Eucharist."

In this way, our thinking about concrete matters can lead us to encounter Christ, and that encounter, in turn, reforms our thinking on those concrete matters. As revelation affects the whole way we understand God, each other, the world, and ourselves, it will thus inevitably colour any application by the believer even of "natural" principles, and perhaps bring some additional norms as well. If being a Catholic-Christian brings with it a particular theological anthropology, then there will inevitably be an ongoing dialectic between the human and the divine, the reasoned, philosophical natural law and the faith-given divine law, the natural virtues and the supernatural ones. So Christian faith and love operate not merely at some abstract "transcendental" level of intentionality or motivation, the *why* level, but also in concrete virtues, norms, and actions, the *what* level. Christian character is thus more than "spirituality" narrowly understood. While Christian faith does not annul or contradict sound human principles and virtues, it inwardly transforms them and calls the disciple to be what they can be, and to do what they can do, by virtue of being not only human but also a child of God. Christian beliefs about a loving, provident God, about creation and redemption, sin and salvation, anthropology and sanctity, and all the rest, should be told, not just in formal theological debate, but in the lived drama of its performance.

As each thread is drawn delicately into the one tapestry by Bishop Laffitte, it becomes clear that the book is intended as a gradual encounter with Christ, like St Bonaventure's *Itinerarium Mentis ad Deum*[9] or an embodiment of the thesis of the twelfth-century monk, William of St-Thierry: "Love of truth drives us from the world (to God) and the truth of love drives us back again"[10] *Christ the Destiny of the Human Person* is a reliable guide to that exciting journey.

✠ Most Rev. Anthony Fisher,
Archbishop of Sydney

---

9. St Bonaventure, *Journey of the Mind to God* (transl. Philotheus Boehner, Indianapolis: Hackett, 1956).
10. William of Saint-Thierry, *Meditations*, in Cistercian Fathers, *The Works of William of St Thierry*, vol. 1 (Cistercian Publications, 1971), 11:13.

I

LIFE

FAMILY

SOCIETY

LIFE

1 The Embryo According to the Plan of God[1]

The God in whom we believe, or, more precisely, as the Credo expresses it, the God in whom I believe, is the one who has created me. God has no need of me.

He could exist without me; that is certain. But, this God who is, is inseparable from the God who created me. And that is why, preserving our faith in the supreme sovereignty of God, we must affirm—and no pantheism may be allowed entry here—that, in a certain sense, I participate in the word 'God', insofar as God is the Creator. I am part, so to say, of God's halo, of his context.

Romano Guardini, *The Life of Faith*[2]

This penetrating remark of Romano Guardini sought to demonstrate the personal dynamism of the act of faith, its existential dimension: whoever poses to himself the question of God as the origin of all that exists cannot do so for very long while adopting a neutral stance, as if contemplating a panorama looking down from a precipice. If God exists, and if he is the Creator of all that exists, then even the humblest of his creatures constitutes part of his creative thought; hence, every such creature, whether conscious of this or not, is bound to him by the very fact that it exists.

To be part of "God's halo": this expression greatly surpasses the marvellous discovery that the person of faith can make about himself, a wonder that includes the all-powerful benevolence of

---

1. "Is there a Christian Way to Die? Ars Pagana et Ars Christiana Moriendi" was published under the title «Ars pagana et ars christiana moriendi» in *Anthropotes*, n. 13/2, 1997, pp. 273–295.
2. Cf. Romani Guardini, *La vie de la foi* (Paris: Cerf, 1968), p. 48.

him who created him. "God's halo" gathers within itself all the orders of Creation, that which is visible to our eyes and that which is not. The existence of what is invisible we may come to know at times through an act of faith—for example, the existence of heavenly creatures—and, at times through scientific knowledge. It is by means of science that we know anything, or almost anything, about the embryo, about the stages of its growth and about the innumerable purposes inscribed in the physiological and hormonal phenomena that accompany its formation in the womb of its mother. Hence, the embryo is never limited just to observable phenomena. We need to adopt a particular position on this, to affirm the identity of the embryo at its deepest level, beyond the aspect of the biological matter involved. In a way that is analogous to what Guardini pointed out above in the domain of faith, with respect to the personal participation of every human being in the meaning of the word "God," it is appropriate, in regard to the embryo, that we affirm the need for its *recognition*.

To bestow recognition is a personal way of knowing, that is to be applied above all to objects of a personal nature. For example, we recognize a person whom we love or who is well-known to us according to his or her specific attributes, and by extension we can identify a person from afar according to certain characteristics, and, finally, in a derivative sense, we can recognize, by detecting a silhouette, by some particular mark, by certain pointers, that a person is present.

The embryo demands recognition, even if its characteristics are hidden from us, even if there is no parental bond that would make it a person who is loved, and even if there has not yet appeared any visible trace of its presence.

In the wake of Guardini and still on the matter of the act of faith, Jean Mouroux wrote that, as long as a person does not make the question of faith into a personal issue, he will never succeed in grasping its credibility. As long as his soul does not open itself up with desire, credibility remains for that person purely and simply a matter external to him, without engaging him in a personal way; it remains no more than a simple problem. Our reflection intends to show that the embryo has a credibility that can be grasped in any appropriate way only by someone who makes it into a question that engages him in a personal way.

Now, to consider the embryo as a question that engages us personally is to adopt a stance in its regard that is close to that of faith; in other words, it is to make the choice for a specific hermeneutic. Can faith, perhaps, teach us something about this being, whom we would often wish to withdraw from the theological perspective? Faith recognizes in the human being a contingent ontological reality, who is absolutely dependent upon the principle of a personal creator.

It is worthwhile recalling what it is that constitutes a certitude of faith, namely, the truthfulness and the credibility of a witness, to which we give credence. In order to make clear his distinction between the material object of the act of faith (*"id quod creditur"*) and its formal object (*"id quo creditur"*), St Thomas makes use of the analogy of science and, more precisely, that of geometry: the formal object of geometry is constituted by the means by which the conclusions which are known are actually demonstrated. What guarantee can there be for the knowledge of faith?

"If we look at the formal knowledge of faith," St Thomas answers, "it is nothing other than the first truth; the faith of which we speak, in fact, only gives its assent to something because it is God who reveals it; that amounts to saying that it is divine truth itself which is the basis upon which this faith relies.[3]

God guarantees the truth of every element of the content of faith. He is the foundation of all knowledge of faith, the ultimate and fundamental criterion of everything that we can know about him. It is precisely because we judge the credibility of God to be that which gives total certitude that we are not making a mistake—quite simply, because we cannot be led into error by him

---

3. "Sic igitur in fide, si consideremus formalem rationem objecti, nihil est aliud quam veritas prima; non enim fides de qua loquimur assentit alicui nisi quia est a Deo revelatum; unde, ipsi veritati divinae inititur tamquam medio." (St Thomas Aquinas, *Summa Theologiae*, Ia IIae, q.1 a.1).

who never errs —that the act of faith is a personal act, a real encounter between God and the human person. It is the reason why all the knowledge that human beings will ever have of the world and of the realities that are to be found in the world will be for them the particular place of the disclosure and revelation of God. God is Creator; hence, he is the One through whom all things exist.

Thus, to ask ourselves about the nature and the origin of beings, and in the first place about our own origins, is more than a search for our own identity; it is a reading of the plan of God. This is why a theological reflection upon the embryo demands that the relationship between faith and science be well understood.

Once again, it is necessary that the act of faith be understood according to its proper nature; it is an act of the spirit and, consequently, it must not be put in opposition to the mental operations of scientific knowledge. The act of faith, which sees in God the origin of the whole of human life, is not in any way perturbed by the autonomy of the medical, biological, or genetic sciences.[4]

If faith leads us to make formulations about the world and about human beings, if it does not concern itself directly with the contributions of science as such, yet it cannot be reduced to being a simple answer to the quest for meaning,[5] since faith itself is desirous of knowledge and desires to have knowledge in a way that is coherent. There are occasions when it may furnish philosophical discourse with its own categories.[6]

---

4. "It is by virtue of creation itself that all things are established according to their proper ordinances, laws and values....The human being must respect all of that and must recognise the particular methods proper to each of the sciences and technologies. This is why methodical research, in every domain of knowledge, if it is conducted in a truly scientific manner and if it follows the norms of morality, can never truly be opposed to the faith; profane realities and the realities of faith find their origin in one and the same God" (Vatican Council II, *Gaudium et Spes* § 36).
5. Cf. D. Biju-Duval, "Pour dépasser le complexe de Galilée" in *Nuntium* I, Rome, 1996.
6. In this sense, it is important to note, for example, that the need to define

The Embryo According to the Plan of God

In the Christian faith, the clarification of the status of the embryo can be found in the light of the creative and salvific plan of God for mankind, and hence, necessarily it is to be found in the light of Christ, who reveals and fulfils this plan of salvation.[7]

In every human life, there is present the creative intention of the Creator, that all human beings come to participate in the mystery of Christ:

> By means of a disposition of his wisdom and of his goodness that was completely free and mysterious, the eternal Father created the universe. He wanted to raise up human beings to the point of sharing in the divine life. And once they had sinned in Adam, he did not abandon them, but ceaselessly offered them help so that they might be saved, in view of Christ, the Redeemer, who is "the image of the invisible God, the first-born of all creation" (Col. 1:15).[8]

In order to understand the theological status of the embryo, there are two methodological requirements which are necessary;

> Christological and Trinitarian dogmas made it possible to specify and to conceptualise the term "person" on the philosophical plane. The explanation of the personal mystery of Christ according to St Leo (DS 294) or again at the Council of Chalcedon (DS 301), made it possible to understand that the specific dignity of Christ has been transmitted to the human body. The totality of the acts accomplished by the person of Christ in his humanity has infinite value, if it is true that these acts are imputable to the Word. Since everything in human nature has been assumed by the Word (except sin), there is no dimension of the person that is deprived of the incomparable dignity that arises from the divine action of the Word. We know that St Thomas considered eminently appropriate the analogy between the union of the two natures, human and divine, in Christ and the union in the human being of the rational soul and of the body (*Summa contra Gentiles*, L. IV, C. XLI). The Council of Vienne would come to conceptualize this in a definitive way: "The rational or intellectual soul is, in itself and essentially, the form of the human body" (DS 902).

7. "The Word of God, by whom all things were made, himself became flesh and came to dwell on earth among us. The perfect man, he has entered into the history of the world, taking it upon himself and recapitulating it in himself" (*Gaudium et Spes* § 38).
8. Cf. Vatican Council II, Dogmatic Constitution on the Church, *Lumen Gentium* (21st November, 1964), § 2.

on the one hand, it is a matter of starting from this plan of God in regard to us human beings to arrive at the way in which this plan has been put into action at this precise stage of our development, which is embryonic life; on the other hand, it is a question of demonstrating, at each stage of this process, how the human being comes to participate in what has been brought about in the incarnate Word. Thus, we shall begin from our eternal predestination in Christ in order to show how this is being brought about in history. After drawing certain conclusions with respect to the condition of the embryo, it will be useful, as a third step, to study the delicate problem, on the theological level, of the eternal destiny of those embryos who have not reached the stage of coming to birth.

Our Eternal Predestination in Christ: Its Fulfillment in History

Eternal Predestination

The classical expression of Augustine, according to which everything has been created by the Father, for the Son, in the *Holy Spirit*,[9] and adopted by the whole of the succeeding Tradition, expressed the common action of the three persons within the Blessed Trinity. The Fathers pondered upon the role of the Word and saw in him the exemplary causality of Creation. The Word is the place of divine thought; the Father contemplates in the Son his eternal word, by which all forms of reality which exist outside of God have been named and created. This representation of all things in the Word is the generosity of the Father, who loves them insofar as he loves the Son, eternally. "It is not only his Son whom the Father loves through the Holy Spirit, but equally he loves himself and us too." The reason for this is that "the Word which is generated is sufficient to represent both the Father and also all creatures."[10]

---

9. Cf. St Augustine, *De Trinitate*, I, VI, 12.
10. Cf. St Thomas, *Summa Theologiae* 1a Pars, q. 37, a 2, ad 3um.

Hence, in all creation, there is a finite participation in what the Father contemplates in his Word. It is in this sense that everything has been created *in view of* the Son, *for* the Son and *by means of* the Son. The Christ is the Chosen One, predestined from all eternity. In fact, everything that can be said about the Word within the indivisible Trinity remains true of the Word insofar as he is Son of God made man.

Without entering into the reasons for the Incarnation of the Word, the object of theological reflection across the centuries, we can claim that it constitutes the manifestation in time and in space of God's eternal plan for us human beings:

> When, so to speak, the idea of the human being shone in the Spirit of the Father, this man is his Son; he is the Son who became incarnate and who rose from the dead. He is the One, who is man. The human being whom God has chosen from all eternity is his Son, who became man and who has been constituted Lord.[11]

Through him, every human being is predestined to become an adopted child of God (cf. Eph 1:3–5), and that according to the plan of God himself and according to his grace (cf. 2 Tim 1:9).

The way God looks at the whole human race, as also on every person in particular, is linked to this mystery of predestination. Christ becomes the measure of everything that is human, and, in this way, he establishes a solidarity between all human beings among themselves. He is the central figure, the organic link between each one of them and the Father, to the extent that he brings about this perfect humanity, willed by God from all eternity. At the same time, he is the one who is sent by the Father and the entirety of his mission among us human beings expresses his intimate and unbreakable unity with the Father. In this way, we may say that, although sin has entered into the world, it is the salvation of the whole of mankind that comes into the world in the predestination of the Son. The redeemer of the world is the eternal object of the Father's pleasure. We are aware of how fruit-

---

11. Cf. I. Biffi, *Esistenza cristiana. Principi e prassi*, (Rome: Piemme, 1987), p. 9.

ful such a unified vision of the predestination of the human family in Christ and of our justification can be in moral matters.[12] In terms of the subject which interests us, such a vision allows us to understand better why every human person, the only creature God wanted for himself, can consider that he is under the watchful gaze of God and is the object of the Father's love. Every human being is called by his own name in Christ: "the New Adam, the Christ, in the very revelation of the mystery of the Father and of his love, manifests man fully to himself and enables him to discover the sublime nature of his vocation."[13]

The call of God, directed towards his chosen ones in Israel, is fulfilled in this way. In the biblical tradition, we find those names that were proclaimed by God, to establish a person in his vocation. In this way, called by his name, the prophet perceived that a special mission was being entrusted to him. But God always remains free to offer a more personal relationship to anyone he chooses, giving that person a new name. Sometimes, this name expresses the fact that a mission entrusted to someone has been conducted well; at other times, it points to the fact that the promise made by God is in the course of being fulfilled.[14]

Under the new law, the certitude that every person has of knowing that he is personally loved, chosen, and called is grounded in the fact that the sacrifice of Christ is destined for all human beings universally and for each one personally:

> Since Christ has died for all and since the ultimate vocation of every person is really unique, in fact divine, we must hold that the Holy Spirit offers to everyone, in a way known to God, the possibility of being associated with the paschal mystery."

---

12. Cf. Angelo Scola, *Questioni di antropologia teologica* (Milan: Ares; Rome: PUL, 1995), pp. 110–115.
13. Vatican Council II, *Gaudium et Spes*, § 22.
14. We have also Abram who became Abraham (cf. Gen 17:5), Sarai who becomes Sarah (cf. Gen 17:15) and Jacob who becomes Israel (cf. Gen 32:29).

The Fullness of Time

The fullness of time is the event in time and in history of the plan of God finally becoming revealed to the eyes of us human beings.[15]

In Christ, "God willed that all his Fulness should dwell in him and through him to reconcile to himself all things, those on earth and those in heaven, making peace by the Blood of his Cross" (Col 1:19–20).

It is the whole of the universe that is subjected to this empire of Christ, in whom are to be found all the treasures of Wisdom.[16] These treasures constitute a plenitude of life. In the sapiential Tradition, they have been compared to the waters that irrigate the gardens, which then transform canals into rivers and rivers into the sea.[17] In the same way that there exists a coming of the Son of God in time, a coming that is distinguished by fulfillment, so also the coming into existence of every human being manifests the fulfillment of a work of God.

When a human being is conceived, that human being makes present in some way a fulfillment in time, to the extent that he brings to completion a particular plan of God. Moreover, such an event must not be considered in its individual dimension alone, since it is at the same time a possible enrichment of the Body of Christ.

The birth of every human being depends, in the concrete, upon an infinity of contingent factors. That is true on the biological level, of the encounter between this ovum and that spermatozoon. There, already, is the operation of *chance* to a prodigious degree and, yet, it is a question of a fact of providence. If we consider now the inextricable tangle of created liberties involved, we can understand that, within the totality of the contingent phe-

---

15. "When the fullness of time had come, God sent his Son, born of a woman, born a subject of the Law ... in order to make us adopted sons" (Gal 4:4).
16. Cf. Sir 24:25–31.
17. Cf. P. Lamarche, "Pienezza," in *Dizionario di Teologia Biblica* (Marietti), pp. 920–922.

nomena, there can also be present choices that are sinful (a child conceived within a relationship that is adulterous or as a result of violence). There is here a development, which God brings to a happy end, going to the point, in his Providence, of making use of the sins of human beings, without wishing those sins in any case. In the gospel of St Matthew, the genealogy of Jesus himself does not hide the presence of illegitimate unions, as is witnessed by the mention of the wife of Uriah the Hittite.[18] Even when the child is the fruit of an act deprived of all humanity, God does not shy away from bringing to a good end the maturation of the fruit of such an act.[19] He brings good out of evil, but without willing the evil, and it is for this reason that there is no need to be afraid of affirming that God wants and loves this child eternally, without willing the adultery or the rape that may have been the origin of the conception. In this use of evil with a view to a greater good, the all-powerful mercy of God reveals itself in a very special way, at times through the mastery of contingent events, in their exterior, cosmological, or temporal dimensions. His mercy is exercised especially in regard to those who, at times, are living examples of the fact that the divine law has been violated. It is from this point of view that the newly converted Augustine contemplates his son, Adeodatus: "It was wonderful; in him, there was nothing of me, if we exclude my sin."[20]

This mystery of the encounter between the infinite freedom of God and the finite liberties of human beings is something that we

---

18. This fact must be judged prudently; the coming of Christ into the world did not depend upon this lineage as such, but upon the will of God alone, which had predisposed that the Son of Mary should be situated within this lineage.
19. We do not examine here that affirmation of the Old Testament, apparently contradictory, according to which God exercises his justice by punishing the children for the sins committed by their parents. It is no more than an apparent contradiction to the extent that this action had been a means of divine pedagogy, to prepare the chosen people not only for a just personal retribution for the offences committed, but, above all, to receive the Holy Spirit who sanctifies and who justifies (Ezekiel).
20. St Augustine, *Confessions*, IX.

may ponder even to the point of being at the heart of the event of redemption itself.[21]

Consequences of the Theological Status of the Embryo

From the Love of Parents to Conception

Whatever may be its destiny in the temporal sphere, the embryo is the substantial expression of the love of its parents, who have been the ministers of God in the gift of life. This remark is true in all cases, whatever the duration of the life of the embryo may be. The term *ministers* needs to be taken in its broadest sense.

In the strict sense, the term evokes the special responsibility that rests upon the spouses to engage in acts that are open to life.[22] Already at the sacramental level, they are ministers, in a certain sense, of the sacrament of marriage. To be willing to bestow life in a broader understanding of that responsibility means to act in a way that, for the child, can be a means of revealing the creative love of God. This is a role of absolutely primary importance, which clearly does not limit this divine love in any way, if it is true that God loves all people, including, as we have said, those children who are born from a union which is sinful.

In this sense, the acts of conjugal union that are open to life, *upright and worthy*, as the Second Vatican Council puts it, are acts that, in the order of nature, express fully the creative benevolence of God.

We need to specify further the meaning of this expression: the order of nature is that order which is willed by God, which at the concrete level is translated by those laws which are proper to different beings. To respect the order of nature means to give honor to the Creator because in it we can recognize the traces of

---

21. On Calvary, the very same moment is, at one and the same time, that of the greatest offense possible inflicted upon Jesus, and also that of the greatest act of divine mercy brought about by him.
22. Cf. Paul VI, *Humanae Vitae*, § 11.

his presence and can decipher the providential dispositions of his benevolent will.

As far as human beings are concerned, it is necessary to consider two aspects.

First of all, the natural act of procreation possesses an intimate structure that lies within the indissoluble bond between the two profound meanings that constitute that act, the unitive and the procreative, a bond that the magisterium of the Church calls the *ontological* truth[23] of the conjugal act. The encyclical, *Humanae Vitae*, puts it like this: "The act of marriage, while it associates the husband and the wife in the closest bond, also makes them suitable for generating new life, according to laws inscribed in the nature itself of man and of woman" (§ 12).

On the other hand, the spouses engage in this act in a way which involves the whole of their being; their actions are worthy acts to the extent that they respect the particular dignity of man and woman, and in particular, their nature as spiritual beings (*corpore et anima unus*).

The first implication of these two aspects seems to be obvious; it needs to be seen in the whole of its depth. No individual of the human species, on his own, is the unique principle of procreation, since only the union with another individual, sexually different from the first, is capable of bringing about as its consequence the conception of a child.

A fundamental characteristic of natural human procreation is that it cannot involve an intervention outside of this union; since this union unites two natures, at the same time bodily and spiritual, it cannot but take the form of love and of mutual self-gift. From this perspective, it is possible to understand that the decision to have recourse to other procedures of fecundation, even if taken by both parties, will never be able fully to reflect the creative benevolence of God.

---

23. Cf. John Paul II, *Catechesis* CXVIII (11 July 1984), *Uomo e donna lo creò: catechesi sull'amore umano 1979–1984* (Vatican City: Libreria Editrice Vaticana, 1985), pp. 453–454.

The Embryo According to the Plan of God

It is clear that the love that unites the spouses is extended in the love of the parents, who later will watch over the child, both before and after its birth.

The conjugal act is situated within the coherence of a love which precedes it by a long way and which, when it places itself at the disposition of welcoming a possible new child, offers the best possible conditions for that child to be welcomed. Thus, just as there is a predestination for all human beings to live out a filial love in the Son, so there exists also a sort of predestination for every child to be born of the love of his or her parents and to grow within the framework of this love.

We take note of the fact that, in the case of Christ, we have a situation that is unique by reason of his conception by the Holy Spirit, but that does not alter the fact that there was a true adoption of the Child Jesus on the part of Joseph, who watched over him as a father, to protect him and to attend to his human education.

The role of Mary's spouse goes far beyond that of a simple legal custodian; we can say that, in his humanity, Christ was as if predestined to be welcomed and to grow within the love of the Holy Family, which the Father had predisposed for him from all eternity:[24]

> Oh, true and holy marriage! But in what sense was he a spouse? Because they had one sole spirit and one sole faith. The Spirit who dwelled within them, inspired in them a holy conjugal love; he had entrusted the wife to the faith of this man and, while he was forming the humanity of Christ in the womb of the Virgin, he infused into the adoptive father a love which was total for the child who was going to be born.[25]

---

24. "Let Nazareth teach us what the family is, its communion of love, its austerity and also its simple beauty, its sacred and inviolable nature; let us learn from Nazareth how sweet and how irreplaceable is the formation we receive." Paul VI, *Homily at Nazareth*, June 5, 1964.
25. Cf. R. de Deutz, *De gloria et honore Filii hominis super Mattheum* I, PL, 168, p. 1319, cited by the *Bibbia cristiana* II, pp. 102–103.

The Immediate Creation of the Human Soul and Its Timing

The Church teaches that every spiritual soul is created immediately by God.[26] This truth of faith has not been subjected to any experimental test;[27] hence, it can be neither confirmed nor denied by any positive science.[28] In respect of the subject we are examining here, the fact of the immediate creation of the soul underlines the specific intention of the Creator with regard to our spiritual nature.

In the case of Christ, we are in the presence, from the start, of a real biological miracle, because he was not born of the will of the flesh; on the other hand, his human soul was created. To this, we must add the assumption by the Word of this body and of this soul from their beginning. By contrast, with all other human beings, we have the natural outcome of the fusion of two gametes, that of the father and that of the mother, as well as the immediate creation of the soul by God—all of this together determines the existence of *this unique person*.

The timing of the creation of the soul may perhaps be understood in this way. For Christ, it is a matter of the moment of the Incarnation, which the Tradition has always understood to be the moment immediately following the acceptance by the Virgin Mary of the message of the archangel Gabriel.[29] This is no less the

---

26. "The Catholic faith requires us to hold that souls are immediately created by God." Pius XII, *Humani Generis*, 1950.
27. Cf. John Paul II, Encyclical Letter, *Evangelium Vitae* (March 25, 1995), § 58.
28. This affirmation does not exclude the rational discussion of what is philosophically persuasive; for example, St Thomas inferred the immediate creation of the soul by God from the fact that, since its activity is not circumscribed by the limits of the activity of the body, its individuality cannot be reduced to corporal individuality, so that the act of procreation cannot be a sufficient explanation for the existence of the soul (St Thomas Aquinas, *Summa contra Gentiles*, c. LXXXIII).
29. The immediate animation of Christ was admitted by the Fathers as a whole. St Thomas devotes to this question the four articles of question 33 of the III Pars. For a study of the various positions on this subject and for the analysis of the arguments of the angelic doctor, we refer you to P.

case in the Gospel, which exercises a very great discretion on this subject, limiting itself to an expression of great respect for this ineffable mystery. For all human beings, there is also a mystery to be respected, all the more so because, at the beginning of their existence, it is impossible to accede by way of experimentation to the moment of the creation of the soul; in this sense, what *Evangelium Vitae* transmits to us is not just a judgment of moral prudence but more an attitude of reverential fear.

The Love of God and the History of the Person

Even when Christ is no more than a germ in the womb of the Virgin Mary, yet, by reason of the hypostatic union, he is already the bearer of the whole of the Father's love, and he is marked out for his future mission. This is why the gospels of Matthew and Luke wish to contemplate in this small child the plan of salvation already at work. From the time of the Annunciation, a part of this mystery was revealed to Mary:

> Behold, you will conceive a child in your womb and you will call his name, Jesus. He will be great and will be called the Son of the Most High. The Lord God will give him the throne of his father, David, and he will reign over the house of Jacob for ever, and his kingdom will have no end (Lk 1:31–33).

The visit of Mary to her cousin, Elizabeth, provides the occasion for a revelation of the plan of God, all the more remarkable in that the first witness to it is another child, the one whom Elizabeth is carrying in her womb. John the Baptist is the first to recognize the Lord, because it is at the *very moment* in which Elizabeth extends her greeting to her cousin that he leaps in the womb of his mother. There is more; this leaping for joy is the movement by which Elizabeth, who had thus been mysteriously alerted from the moment when she had been filled with the Holy Spirit, recognizes the hidden dignity of the visit she is receiving.

Caspar, *La saisie du zygote humain par l'esprit* (Namur: Le Sycomore, Lethielleux, 1987).

St Ambrose has expressed this perfectly:

> Elizabeth was the first to hear the voice, John the first to perceive the grace. She heard this through the normal laws of nature, he exulted by virtue of a mystery. She perceived the coming of Mary, he that of the Lord. The woman recognized the woman, the child recognized the child.[30]

In this relationship of child to child, so important for the development of the events of our salvation, there is the most astounding illustration possible of the dignity of unborn children, because it is to them, in the first place, to each one of them, that a unique mission has been entrusted by the Holy Spirit. The one, the Son of Mary and the Son of God, begins his first mission as the one sent by the Father, the other, by recognizing him, begins his mission of being the prophet of the Most High. Thus, every human being is the object of divine predilection from the beginning of his existence; *God contemplates in him everything that he may become, he forms him and he prepares him.*[31] This destiny will be revealed throughout the whole of his life on earth, by means of events, by the sacramental gift of grace, by the moral choices made, by encounters that are providential. It is sure that no one has a perfect knowledge of way in which divine Providence has guided his existence. Such an understanding of the meaning of our own lives we have always *a posteriori*, when we discover that the events which we have experienced had not been directed entirely by the choices of our own freedom.

From a Christian perspective, human beings consider their relationship with God in the light of the great truths of the faith; in

---

30. St Ambrose, *Commentary on the Gospel of Luke*, PL 15, 1460–1461. We note that the author does not hesitate to see, in the signs perceived by John before his mother, the pouring out of the Holy Spirit, who subsequently addresses himself to her: "The child leapt in her, the mother was filled with the Holy Spirit before her son, but, after the son was filled with the Holy Spirit, the mother also felt him; when John leapt in her, she was filled with the Spirit of God."
31. "Before I formed you in the womb, I knew you; before you came to birth, I consecrated you" (Jer. 1:5).

particular, knowing that every human being is the object of a personal act of creation by God, the person of faith is led to rethink the natural event of the beginning of his or her life. This cannot be done, at the human level, without reference to the immediate cause of their existence, the conjugal union between their own parents. To the extent that this union is normally an obvious expression of authentic love between the parents, the dignity of this initial act gives a special meaning to the first moment of the existence of the one who has been conceived. The extraordinary natural event of fertilization necessarily carries with it a certain *dignity*, when it is correctly attributed to the love of the parents and not to some artificial procedure. Then, it is a perfectly human act, just as the life to which it gives rise is perfectly human.

This dignity is not limited to the human level; in fact, at the theological level, conception receives a dignity that is truly eminent, if, at the same time as being the transmission of the love of the parents, it is also the expression of the creative benevolence of God. Thus, it is that then, theologically speaking, the act of procreation and the act of sexual union must be thought of as *a unique and identical* act;[32] in fact, it is in the sexual act that divine causality finds the appropriate place for its being put into effect. More precisely, in this context of divine causality and in the light of faith in God, the Creator—if the person is a substantial unity of body and of soul—how could a creative act of God be imagined which was not, at the same time, an act by which the person's own body was brought into being? And, further, how could the respect that such dignity demands not be guaranteed for the fruit of conception?

It must be observed, further, that there can be no discontinuity in the quality of this nascent life, as appears to be thought possible by those who employ different terms for the unborn child according to whether or not the child is more or less than four-

---

32. Cf. Angelo Scola, "Il principio teologico della procreazione umana" in *Donum Vitae: Istruzione e commenti* (Vatican City: Libreria Editrice Vaticana, 1990).

teen days old (embryo, pre-embryo). How is it possible to imagine an interruption in the dignity of a human person in the course of a particular human existence, once that existence has begun, an interruption that would provide justification for the suppression of that existence? If a conjugal act is such as we have described it, an expression of the love of the parents and the place for the creative act of God, if a child who has been born or who is on the point of being born deserves absolute respect, then, it must be affirmed that, during the whole of the *intervening period*, from conception to birth, the same dignity demands the same respect.[33]

The Child's Vulnerability

The Christ Child, before as well as after his birth, was totally dependent upon his parents. It was at Bethlehem of Judah that he was born, after his parents had made the decision to fulfill their civic duty with regard to the census. Incapable of defending himself against Herod, who was trying to kill him, Jesus, at that time, was entirely subject to the protection of Joseph, who "took with him the child and his mother, by night, and went down to Egypt" (Mt 2:14). It is through these various episodes that the mission of Mary and of Joseph to protect Jesus and to provide for his upbringing is illustrated. This vulnerability of Christ attests to the profound realism of the Incarnation, which concerns all the stages of our Savior's life. It reveals, moreover, in a certain sense, the desire of God that a response be given to his love and, at the same time, that this response be a response of love and a participation in love.

---

33. No one can admit to himself, in fact, the idea that someone else, a parent or a doctor, may attribute to themselves the power of putting a limit to their existence prior to their having been born. This feeling is very clear, when there is a reference to the existence of someone other than oneself, at whatever stage of formation it may be, because such an act, since it constitutes the deliberately provoked death of an innocent human being, demonstrates that the origin and the dignity proper to that being have been misunderstood.

The beginning of the life of every human is marked by the same fragility and by the same vulnerability; it is in this way that the mission of human beings towards their own kind, particularly towards the youngest of them, is brought into perspective.[34] The parents are the depositories of the fragile mystery of their child, and the task of providing for his growth and for his upbringing is entrusted to them. There, too, they operate as the co-operators and interpreters of the love of the Creator.

The Fate of Dead Embryos

The theological status of the embryo is to be comprehended not only from the standpoint of its origin, as a manifestation of the special plan of divine Providence, but also from the standpoint of its destiny. Naturally, we think first of all of its immediate fate. The human embryo is obviously the first visible sign that a human being exists—that he or she is real; it is also the promise, as yet under a veil, of a man or woman to be born.

Beyond this natural aspect, the problem is posed of the embryo's future existence. Every living person is confronted by the question of his or her ultimate future or destiny. It is difficult to see what would prevent people from posing the same question in regard to the embryo. The reason for this is not only theological; in fact, it is a very practical question that is posed by numerous mothers, Christian or non-Christian, often with anguish, when they have had the experience of losing a baby before it has come to term. In a particularly painful way, this question is present in the heart of those mothers who have voluntarily procured an abortion and who have discovered only later the gravity of the act which they have committed. The desire to know where this child

---

34. "He is *weak*, without defence, to the point of being deprived of the most basic means of defence, namely, that of the capacity of the new-born child's groans and tears to plead on his or her behalf. He is entrusted entirely to the protection and to the care of the one who is carrying him in her womb. And yet, at times, it is precisely she, the mother, who decides for and who seeks to have him suppressed, and who goes to the point of procuring his suppression." (John Paul II, *Evangelium Vitae*, § 58.)

may be often accompanies the pathetic desire to rediscover in this child the *partner* in a personal relationship, interrupted by the act of abortion.[35] It happens sometimes that such a need is accompanied by the wish to ask pardon of this being who is absolutely innocent.[36]

It will be helpful to distinguish between different kinds of death that are possible for the embryo: early death, delayed spontaneous abortion (miscarriage), procured abortion. Some of these are no more than biological or medical facts, inherent in the fragility of human nature in a concrete case. Others, by contrast, are the result of acts which can be qualified morally and which correspond to choices to intervene upon the life of the embryo—the choice of the mother, of a doctor, of the situation, or of a combination of different circumstances—which consists in deliberately putting an end to a human existence that has already begun. Every embryo, nevertheless, constitutes an enigma in a given situation; theological reflection can help, if not to resolve this enigma, then at least to formulate it in appropriate terms.

The Death of Embryos

The first biological given observable in the formation of an individual is the penetration by a spermatozoon into the cytoplasm of the oocyte, an event which unleashes a whole series of phenomena, whose culmination is the appearance of a cell endowed with a genetic patrimony that is strictly new and unique,[37] and one which is distinct from those of the parents. Beginning from the very first instant, the program that will characterize this specific individual is fixed. *"From the moment of conception there begins*

---

35. Cf. Vatican Council II, *Gaudium et Spes*, § 50.
36. Cf. S. M Stanford, *Une femme blessée. Le traumatisme de l'avortement*, Avant-propos by A. de Malherbe (Paris: Le Sarment/Fayard, 1989).
37. Monozygotic twins may have an identical genetic patrimony, but their phenotypes and the various influences of the milieu which surrounds them (physical, chemical, biological, etc.), distinguish them completely one from the other. (Cf. R. Colombo, "Statuto biologico e statuto ontologico dell'embrione e del feto umano," in *Anthropotes*, I, 1996, pp. 132–162).

The Embryo According to the Plan of God

an adventure of a human life;"[38] hence, we must consider that, if the vital processes are interrupted after fecundation, we are dealing with the end of a life that has already begun, which we will define, for convenience in our reflection, as the *death of an embryo*. It is impossible for us to argue about the precise moment of the fusion itself or about the normal process of the development of growth. In fact, if we had to conclude that, for reasons of a particular biological difficulty, a fusion between the gametes had not taken place,[39] then, in that case there, we would not be dealing with a death, properly speaking. Spontaneous abortions, on the other hand, even if they pass unobserved, must be defined as accidental deaths of the embryo; there, we have the death of a human being, even if this being has no self-awareness.[40]

The case of procured abortions is very different. The Tradition has always condemned these as acts of homicide, from the time of the *Didaché*,[41] for example, which proscribed them under the same title as it did infanticide, up until *Evangelium Vitae*,[42] which

---

38. Congregation for the Doctrine of the Faith, *Declaration on procured abortion* (18 November 1974), extract from *Evangelium Vitae*, § 60.
39. The penetration of an oocyte by a spermatozoon leads normally to the formation of two nuclei, one masculine and one feminine, and whose fusion gives birth to the genetic patrimony of the new cell. The non-formation of these nuclei or even the presence of one single type of nucleus leads to the formation of a cell which is not endowed with all of the genetic potentialities necessary for the development of a complete organism; hence, here we are not in the presence of a zygote which is the bearer of the characteristics specific to the human race.
40. Here we need to recall that our point of departure is theological and does not take note of the differences from the perspective of the eternal destiny of beings, between a person already constituted such as the newborn child or the imperfectly constituted embryo. In the same way, we do not consider here the discussions among biologists on the expressive inertia of the genome of the embryo with 4–8 blastomeres, which has led some people to question the individual character of the organism (cf. Colombo, Ibid.)
41. Cf. *Didaché Apostolorum* V, 2: "You must not kill the fruit of your womb; you must not cause to die the infant who has already been born."
42. John Paul II, *Evangelium Vitae*, § 58.

leaves no doubt, in this respect, about the definitive nature of the doctrine.[43]

It is interesting to see how, among the various arguments invoked, the one related to the concern of God for the embryo is the one which predominates, his benevolence carries the implication that this extends to their eternal destiny. Already in their mothers' wombs, children "are the object of the attention of divine Providence;"[44] the protection of human life from its beginning is grounded also on the fact that it requires, from the start, *the action of God the Creator.*[45] "Temporal human life, lived out in this world, does not exhaust everything that involves the person."[46] The human being, who has just begun to live, is *entirely entrusted* to the protection and to the care of the one who carries him or her in the womb.[47] All of this is expressed admirably in *Evangelium Vitae* (§ 61):

> From his mother's womb, the human being belongs to God, who scrutinizes and knows everything, who formed him and fashioned him with his hands, who looks upon him already when he is still a small, unformed embryo and who perceives in him the adult which he will be tomorrow, whose days he has already counted and whose vocation has already been consigned to the "book of life" (cf. Ps 138; 139 1:13–16): there, too, when he is still in his mother's

---

43. The term *definitive tenenda* is not explicitly formulated, but the text does refer to it, when it invokes the nature of the authority that is being exercised here: *conferred by Christ upon Peter and his successors* and when it affirms the unanimous communion expressed by all the bishops and the successor of Peter; and, finally, when it recalls its foundations, which are the natural law, the written Word of God, the Tradition and the ordinary and universal magisterium of the Church. For the sake of completeness, it is good to underline the reference to *Lumen Gentium* (§ 25) on the infallibility of the magisterium of the bishops, as well as to the judgment of Paul VI on the immutable character of the doctrine of the Church in this regard (Discourse of December 9, 1972 to the Catholic Jurists of Italy).
44. Congregation for the Doctrine of the Faith, *De abortu procurato*, § 6.
45. John XXIII, Encyclical Letter, *Mater et Magistra*, (AAS 53, [1961]. p. 447).
46. Congregation for the Doctrine of the Faith, *De abortu procurato*, § 9.
47. John Paul II, *Evangelium Vitae*, § 58.

womb—as is witnessed by numerous biblical texts— the human being is the most personal object of the loving and paternal Providence of God.

Consequently, to kill a child who has not yet been born is to kill someone who lies under the benevolent and paternal protection of God. It has to be expressed in these terms: as the object of the care of the Creator, the embryo enjoys the dignity of a son, which grounds his right to be protected from the beginning of his existence.

Baptism and Salvation

The doctrine of the Church grounds baptism for the sake of salvation upon the words of the Risen Christ himself. Christ entrusted to the Eleven, in the form of a will, this directive: "Go and make disciples of all the nations, baptising them in the name of the Father and of the Son and of the Holy Spirit" (Mt 28:19), a directive which makes explicit what is stated in Mark: "Whoever believes and is baptised will be saved, whoever does not believe will be condemned" (Mk 16:16). The question of salvation is posed clearly in these terms. The human being is conceived outside of the state of justice, by reason of original sin; it is baptism which makes him just and which enables him to pass from the state of being a son of Adam to that of a son of God. How should we judge the situation of the embryo who dies without baptism? To be sure, other factors need to be taken into account and in the first place the pleas for baptism which the Church has recognized, baptism by blood and baptism of desire. The first concerns the case of the martyr for the sake of Christ and who, for the love of Christ, endures the torments to which he is subjected, supporting them with patience. There is no difficulty here, in the face of such a unanimous Tradition. The second is more difficult to analyze, by reason of the explicit character of the desire that is generally required. In a strict sense, several different elements together constitute a baptism of desire: the existence of a sincere desire to be baptized, true repentance for the faults committed, and the firm intention to receive the sacraments, as soon as this becomes possible. All of this is true in the normal situation of an adult; the first illustration of this can be found in the Scriptures with the example of the good thief in St Luke's gospel or, yet again, in the case of Cornelius in the Acts of the Apostles.

More complicated in the case of children who have not been baptized and who die before they attain the age of reason. We are aware of this long theological tradition, which nowadays has fallen into oblivion, which envisaged a place of natural beatitude, in which these children would live, deprived of the beatific vision. Whatever may be the authority of those who, in their time, envisaged the existence this *limbus puerorum*,[48] it must be recognized that this theological opinion has fallen nowadays into desuetude,[49] as indeed is witnessed by the document published by the International Theological Commission (ITC) in 2007.[50]

Given the fact that the embryo lacks the exercise of conscience, it would seem to be unaffected by questions either of the baptism of blood or of the baptism of desire. The pleas of which we have spoken stem from the personal commitment of the subject prior to his decease. We recognise also the validity of the desire expressed by the parents on behalf of their child; thus, the Church allows a ritual of burial for children born without baptism, even if this is permitted with great pastoral prudence.[51] In particular, there should be no doubt as to the determination

---

48. Cf. Duns Scotus, St Bonaventure, St Thomas, St Robert.
49. The Catechism of the Catholic Church does not even make any allusion to it (CCC § 1261).
50. International Theological Commission, *The Hope of Salvation for Children who Die without Baptism*, January 19, 2007.
51. In fact, by making available this ritual, the Church does not make any explicit announcement; at the beginning she seems to limit this rite to children who have died without baptism, "when the parents wanted them to be baptized and when, normally, their intention to do this had been made clear by a request made to the parish;" subsequently, the text recommends that this practice "not obscure in the minds of the faithful the doctrine on the necessity of baptism" (cf. the *Roman Missal*, introduc-

of the parents to have their child baptized. At least, it should be possible to presuppose such an intention on their part.[52]

Quite logically, we could extend the doctrine which underlies this practice to the case of a child who dies *in utero*, at least to the extent that the intention of the parents to have the child baptized after birth cannot be put in doubt.

We take note of the fact that, in creating this ritual, the Church does not intend to take a position on the question of the destiny of children who die without baptism. She contents herself with entrusting them to the mercy which wills that all persons be saved. In this way, she manifests her hope.[53] On the other hand, during the Eucharistic sacrifice, she prays for *all people*, a formula which expresses the conviction that all human beings without exception are the object of her concern. In the last analysis, she places her confidence in the communion of the saints, as is shown by the unanimous prayer expressing her hope that her children may be saved. All are included in this intercession, which embraces also all those children who have died during the first days of their embryonic life, even when no-one, not even their mothers, has had any awareness of their existence.

The Universality of Redemption

We have remarked upon the prudence of the Magisterium on the question of the eternal destiny of children who have died without baptism and have shown that one of the reasons which lie behind this is the concern to remain faithful to the doctrine on the necessity of baptism for salvation.

The mystery of the destiny of the embryos may be cleared up, if we examine the universal character of Redemption. The two poles between which the pastoral prudence of the Church expresses itself are, on the one hand, the need for baptism and, on

---

tion to the ceremony of funerals of children who have died without baptism).
52. This would be the case with a child, whose older brothers and sisters had themselves been baptized.
53. Cf. *Catechism of the Catholic Church*, §1261.

the other, the universality of the Redemption. If the magisterium has not responded to this question in *Evangelium Vitae*, then it remains open to theological debate.

We may begin from this fact, namely, that salvation is offered to everyone in Christ. The plan of God has made of "Christ the principle of salvation for the whole world."[54]

> In [him] the whole revelation of God, the Most High, is brought to fulfillment ... having accomplished in himself and having proclaimed with his own mouth the Gospel, promised first of all by the prophets, [Christ, the Lord] ordered his Apostles to preach it to all people as the source of all saving truth and of all moral norms, bestowing upon them the divine gifts.[55]

This theme is developed continually by the texts of the Second Vatican Council.

God, who instituted the sacraments as the ordinary means of salvation, would not make himself a prisoner of these same means. Hence, the fact that the sacraments were instituted as the ordinary means of salvation certainly creates a serious obligation for human beings, but it does not create a constraint for God. He remains always all-powerful and can chose to pour out his grace through another channel. Nevertheless, this universal offer of salvation cannot be considered as if it were an automatic beatitude for children who have died without baptism. Otherwise, there would be a contradiction with the Church's practice of conferring baptism in some cases of emergency.

It is necessary, therefore, to examine this practice more deeply. If a child is baptized urgently if he is on the point of dying, this is because we think of that child as someone with the need to be saved, just like all those who share that child's human condition and that we judge that the child can only be saved, at least in terms of what it is possible for us human beings to know, by baptism. We could change our perspective; how would we judge the attitude of

---

54. Vatican Council II, *Lumen Gentium*, § 17.
55. Vatican Council II, *Dei Verbum*, § 7.

Christian parents who neglected to have recourse to baptism in such a case of emergency? Who would dare to suggest that taking such a step is pointless? Or that it is superfluous? Such questions demonstrate the devastating responsibility that Christian parents would be assuming, were they to choose not to give their child, through baptism, the grace of Christ who has died and has risen. Moreover, this aspect of the question shows the importance and the seriousness of the bond of solidarity of all those who live in the communion of the saints, but that does not answer the question of what will be the eternal destiny of those children who have not been baptized in case of emergency. Here there is a mystery, upon which, in the absence of a dogmatic definition, we cannot make a statement with any certitude.

Baptism in case of emergency shows that the Church has an understanding of the Redemption, which is that of a salvation that intervenes in the form of a personal event,[56] and not as something that operates as a global condition.[57] Baptism in case of

56. Often, we find expressions such as "the salvation of mankind," "universal salvation," "the salvation of humanity," and "the salvation of the world." They bring out the cosmic dimension of salvation, not in the sense of its being a universal phenomenon, but in the sense of its universality; if no person is excluded from the loving plan of God, who wishes that all people be saved, then we can speak of the salvation of humanity, that is to say of all persons: "The cosmic Christ as such does not exist in the strict sense of the term; it is the Risen Christ who exists, the new Adam. In him there begins a new humanity, which shines upon the world around him. The theme of the new Adam makes possible a rigorous analysis of the position of humanity in the world; this serves to express the cosmic dimension of salvation, while respecting the Tradition which recognizes in Jesus the perfect divinity of the Logos and humanity brought to its perfection at the moment of Easter." J.-L. Maldame, *Christ et le cosmos* (Paris: Desclée, 1983), p. 197.

57. In this regard, there is a very real ambiguity in the notion of a "supernatural existential" as a kind of salvation, which would apply to all persons, irrespective of their attitudes and behaviour."The fact that human persons are really determined by the grace continually offered to them is not only something of salutary importance, but it is the stable and inevitable situation in which they live. This state of affairs in order that it not to be left to itself and that it not be abandoned, can perhaps be called a super-

emergency is a practice that manifests the necessity, in the case of the threat of an imminent death, that even newborn children be baptized. Were they not to have recourse to baptism, that would be a sign that salvation is no longer perceived as an event and, besides it must be emphasized that, in the Tradition of the Church, there has always been the certitude of salvation for children who have died after having received baptism. It is this combination of factors, let us repeat, which explains the prudence of the Magisterium on this matter, a prudence present also in *Evangelium Vitae*, in which the delicate question of children who have died without baptism has not been resolved.[58]

Some Other Elements for Reflection

A certain number of observations must be made to specify this question further; we will formulate some hypotheses. The first refers to the personal event of salvation; salvation is not extrinsic to the will of the person. In the earthly state, the reception of baptism, for an adult, normally presupposes the profession of faith. When the person baptised is a child who has not yet reached the age of reason, this *confessio fidei* is pronounced by those who are the first guarantors for the child, the parents and the godparents.

In the heavenly state, the beatific vision fills the person in their spiritual nature, it satisfies their will completely, which is eternally directed towards God. This consideration is valid also for children who have died before they have had an opportunity to exercise their own consciences; they have received from their Creator a soul, they have an intellect and a will. In the same way that the blessed destiny of adults who are saved is expressed through a will directed towards God[59]—or which is separated from God in the case of the damned—in the same way, the

---

    natural existential." (Karl Rahner, "Esistenziale; Applicazione alla teologia" in *Sacramentum Mundi*, III, [Morcellana], p. 592).

58. John Paul II, *Evangelium Vitae*, § 89.
59. As far as adults are concerned, we can exclude the possibility of them being separated from God through the pain of hell; with regard to young children who have died before the age of reason and after having been

eternal destiny of young children must be expressed through their spiritual faculty that is directed towards God.

We should recall that the grace of baptism that has been received had already directed towards God, in a mysterious way, the will of the children who had been baptized and who had then died. This kind of orientation must be seen as a very real dynamism, certainly one which is not conscious insofar as it affects them, a dynamism that is nothing other than the sanctification received when the grace of baptism for the remission of original sin has removed all obstacles. Incorporated into Christ, the child has become a new creature, a child of God. All the supernatural fruits of this indelible character, which baptism has imprinted in the heart of the child, cannot be limited to his or her earthly existence.[60]

The beatific vision necessarily responds to the yearnings of his heart, filled with the Holy Spirit and which continues to cry out mysteriously "Abbà, Father."

For those who have not been baptized, original sin, in principle, renders their will incapable of turning towards God without grace. That is as true for young children as it is for adults. As far as adults are concerned, the Second Vatican Council expressed itself very clearly:

> Those who, without fault of their own, are ignorant of the Gospel of Christ and of his Church, but who nevertheless, with a sincere heart, search for God ... and who, under the influence of his grace, strive to act in such a way as to accomplish his will, to the extent that it is known to them through the dictates of their consciences, are also capable of attaining to eternal salvation.[61]

As far as young children are concerned, they find themselves

baptised, we have already noted the certitude of the Church about their salvation.

60. For example, if baptism provides the seeds of the theological life, it is impossible for this seed not to correspond to the supernatural fruit of eternity.
61. Vatican Council II, *Lumen Gentium*, § 16.

necessarily in an economy of grace, if it is true that God wills the salvation of all; it is impossible that, in one way or another, totally mysterious to our eyes, salvation would not be offered to them. Therefore, as we have already said, such an offer cannot be a matter of an automatic salvation; otherwise, contrary to a very long tradition, there would be no reason to baptise a child before he attained the age of reason.

And so, in these circumstances, on what does this salvation depend? We can only formulate two hypotheses:

The first hypothesis is that, for these children, by means of pure grace, physical death may be the occasion on which they could make a decisive and mysterious choice, which positively, would equate to the baptism of desire. They would be capable of such a choice[62] by grace because they have a fully constituted, spiritual soul. This choice could be orientated towards salvation through the supplication of the Church, of their parents and of all those who, in the communion of the saints, intercede for the dead.[63] Such a hypothesis is certainly unimaginable in the strict

---

62. If this capacity is a fruit of grace, it would be impossible to represent it; still, it is a question of a theological possibility. Theological possibilities exist, of which it is impossible for human beings to have a mental representation, for example all of those which are related to the fact of the resurrection of the flesh have continually been the object of reflection on the part of Christian theologians. In the case of infants, as also in the case of adults, it is the perspective of eschatology which is the point of departure for such a reflection. Rather, it is the certitude of the perfection of the body in eternal life which gave St Augustine the idea that bodies not formed in their earthly nature, would receive in some way, the perfection which they were lacking: "Who would dare to deny, even if he would not dare to make the claim, that the effect of the resurrection is to be added to an organism that is being formed, in such a way that he would no longer be deprived of the perfection of what he was lacking, but he would have acquired it in the course of time, even taking into account the defects which time would have inflicted upon him?" (Cf. St Augustine, cited by P. Caspar, "Elements of the eschatology of the zygote," *Revue Thomiste*, XCII, 1992, pp. 460–481).
63. Here we have in mind that attitude which St Paul had noted among his contemporaries, of having themselves baptized on behalf of the dead, and

sense and cannot be expressed in scientific terms; on the other hand, it does not clash with what is theologically appropriate because it is not absurd. It would have to be admitted that it is inexplicable outside of the context of Christian faith, as is the case with a certain number of other truths.[64]

It would be even harder to imagine, under this hypothesis, an eventual refusal of salvation expressed by a soul that, by definition, had not already sinned personally in advance. It seems to me that we could put forward the hypothesis that, if there were already a certain form of salvation, it would be rendered dynamic by the influence of the grace of God; in a way that would be analogous to the influencing action of the grace that we have indicated above upon those who act in a way which fulfills the will of God, without knowing the Gospel of Christ or his Church.[65]

The second hypothesis is that, for children killed in their mothers' wombs, could we not find some light in the theology of the Holy Innocents? These latter died because of Christ, without knowing him and without having the means of knowing him. Nevertheless, the Church has always considered them to be true martyrs and it venerates them as saints. If their death is considered like that of a martyr, it is because in them there was present the Christ whom others wished to suppress.[66] By virtue of this fact, all innocent victims would be identified with Christ.[67] The massacre of children in their mothers' womb configures them to Christ and makes them participants in the mystery of the Cross of Christ.[68]

---

   in which he saw a sign of the hope of Christians in the resurrection of the dead.
64. For example, the resurrection of the flesh is, humanly speaking, likewise inconceivable and unimaginable, if we think of the physical reality of the event of death and of the subsequent reduction of the body to dust.
65. Vatican Council II, *Lumen Gentium*, § 16.
66. Cf. C.-V. Heris, "Innocents (Saints)" in *Catholicisme*, V, 22, pp. 1674–1675.
67. By analogy, in Luke 16:25, the poor man, Lazarus, is directed to heaven, about whom we know nothing beyond the simple fact that he had been a victim during his earthly life.
68. "The moment in which the Son was designated a man *par excellence*—

We have done no more than express certain hypotheses; these enable us to maintain everything that the Church believes and teaches, in respect of original sin, of baptism being necessary for salvation, and on the universality of the Redemption. Furthermore, both of the hypotheses express this truth, so well expressed by St Augustine, and according to which, God has created us without our aid, but he does not wish to save us without our cooperation.

Ecce homo—is rightly the moment in which, like the Suffering Servant of Isaiah (52,14). 'He no longer had the appearance of a man': and it is this holy Face of Christ, disfigured in his Passion, which manifests to the fullest extent the face of God. For this reason, if he who 'no longer had the appearance of a man' is still even so someone with a face, can it not be said, by analogy and looking at him with the eyes of the Father, that those who seem to our eyes to be a collection of cells produced by fertilisation, but with whom the Son has already identified himself, are human persons?" (Cf. M.H. Congour-Deau, "L'embryon est-il une personne?" in *Communio*, IX, Nov- Dec., 1984.)

2 Evangelium Vitae[1]

In the course of the public presentation of the encyclical, *Evangelium Vitae*, the then Cardinal Ratzinger was concerned to stress the doctrinal purpose of chapter III:

> Chapter III of the encyclical, *Evangelium Vitae*, is an illustration of the commandment of God: "Do not kill" in the contemporary context. If the other chapters are more pastoral in nature, that chapter is a doctrinal text, in which the Pope presents the teaching of the faith, which indicates the path for all pastoral activity. In this chapter, it is possible to distinguish three great thematic focuses. In the first place, the concern is to specify the meaning of the fifth commandment, within the totality of the message of the faith. Subsequently, the concrete ethical imperatives which derive from it are pointed out, and, finally, the implications for ethics in the political sphere are put forward.[2]

These remarks are valuable both in furnishing an introduction to the text, as also in offering what amounts to a veritable method for understanding it.

The reactions which followed the publication of the text, the partial presentations of its message, and at times the caricatures of its content on the part of some of the media, have shown that it is impossible to take full account of its message if it is taken out of the context of the totality of the message of the faith. The Pope proclaimed the Gospel of Life as something that belongs to Revelation (§29); as the Gospel of salvation, the Good News about human life is addressed to all human beings.

---

1. "*Evangelium Vitae*" was published under the title "Evangelium vitae. Aspects théologiques et doctrinaux" in *Nouvelle Revue Théologique*, n. 117, 1995, pp. 821–842.
2. In *L'Osservatore Romano*, March 31, 1995, pp. 1–15.

The aim of this article is to expound the theological and the anthropological foundations of the encyclical. In this way, it will be possible to gather the doctrinal richness of a text, which appears to be destined to be considered a milestone in the magisterial teaching of the pontificate of John Paul II, alongside the encyclical *Veritatis Splendor*. It is within the unity and the internal coherence of the Christian mystery that the value of every human life can be appreciated. Respect for life is no less a precept of the natural law; the profound desire for truth inscribed with the heart of human beings makes them capable of understanding that life is a good. The doctrinal content of the text, in fact, elaborates an argumentation based upon reason, which will need to be brought out. Finally, in a pastoral style that is directly accessible, *Evangelium Vitae* repeats a number of concerns to political authorities, which had already been signalled in the encyclical *Centesimus Annus*, which marked the hundredth anniversary of the first great social encyclical, *Rerum Novarum*: notably on the need to maintain or to restore the link between the natural law and civil legislation (§ 90).

This last point would need to be elaborated at some length. Here, we shall limit ourselves to disclosing the theological aspects of the encyclical and to discerning its doctrinal nucleus.

Theological Aspects: The Meaning of the Encyclical Within the Totality of the Message of Faith

From *Veritatis Splendor* to *Evangelium Vitae*: Eternal Life as the First "Evangelium"

The very first sentence of the encyclical, *Evangelium Vitae*, presents the fuller meaning of the message of life: "The Gospel of life is to be found at the heart of the message of Jesus" (§ 1). The content of the redemptive mission of Christ is the proclamation and the transmission of the life which comes from God. Commenting upon the gospel of St John (10:10): "I have come so that they may have life and may have it to the full," the Pope sets forth symbolically the principle that guides the whole of the text of the encyclical:

> In truth, he (Jesus) is referring to that "new" and "eternal" life, which consists in communion with the Father, to which every person is freely called in the Son, by the power of the Sanctifying Spirit. It is precisely in this "life" that all of the aspects and stages of human life achieve their full significance (§ 1).

The eternal life offered in Jesus Christ illuminates every human life and reveals its deepest meaning. The text starts from the proclamation of the coming of the Saviour and of the joy that accompanies it (Lk 2:10–11). This messianic exultation marks the birth of Jesus, the long-awaited Messiah: "Today a Saviour has been born to you" (Lk 2:11). From the introduction of the encyclical, the mystery of human life is contemplated within the context of the joy which comes from God and which recognizes the long hoped-for Saviour. In the same way that this messianic joy is the foundation for and the fulfillment of every joy that accompanies the birth of a child, so is eternal life the foundation for and the fulfilment of the whole of human life. From the beginning, therefore, the quality of life is revealed; it is a gift; it is, already here on earth, good news, and, for that reason, it is the reason for our joy. It is in this sense that the value of earthly, bodily life, which for the believer is not an absolute, is properly perceived (§ 47).

A link can be established between *Evangelium Vitae* and the encyclical, *Veritatis Splendor*, which expounds the moral teaching of Jesus, starting from the question of the rich, young man: "Master, what must I do to inherit eternal life?" (Mt 19:16). There, eternal life appears as the crowning of an upright life that is devoted to respect for, and to the observance of, the commandments. This encyclical thus focused upon the path of the moral life as the way to salvation, open to all people (VS § 3). If eternity symbolically provides earthly life with value in *Evan-*

gelium Vitae, while in *Veritatis Splendor* it appears to be linked to fidelity on earth to the commandments, there is no contradiction between them. Bringing light to bear upon eternal life from the beginning in *Evangelium Vitae* was only for the purpose of taking a position, at the right moment, on specific moral attitudes in relation to life here below. As for the demands of the Master, these make sense, for *Veritatis Splendor,* only when rooted in the vocation to eternal life of the rich young man. Jesus Christ is the principle of eternal life, as he is of the Law. From the one side and from the other, the perspectives adopted are resolutely Christological.[3]

The relationship between earthly life and eternal life deserves to be examined here more deeply. The human person is called (*vocatio*) to a plenitude of life (*plenitudo vitae*), the characteristic of the divine life in which we become participants ("*participatio Dei ipsius vitae*"). The expression "plenitude of life" in *Evangelium Vitae* indicates our supernatural vocation (§ 2). Now, in *Veritatis Splendor*, it signals in the first place the deepest aspiration of the rich, young man: "All this (keeping the commandments) I have done; what else must I do?" (Mt 19:20). Offering to his interlocutor the way of perfection, Jesus seizes upon his yearning for a fulness that surpasses the legalistic interpretation of the commandments (VS § 16). Furthermore, still in *Veritatis Splendor*, the word "fulness" is itself used just a few lines before, in order to locate in Jesus the fulness of the Law, that is to say, its perfect fulfilment, according to the expression of St Ambrose: "*Plenitudo legis Christus est*" (VS § 15). Finally, in the text of both encyclicals, eternal life is defined in the same terms, as the "participation in the very life of God" (VS § 12; EV

---

3. The following two sentences, expressing the same methodological principle, can be compared with interest: "[The human person] must, so to speak, enter into Christ with the whole of his being; must 'make his own and "appropriate to himself and assimilate the whole of the reality of the Incarnation and of the Redemption in order to be able to find himself" (VS § 8); "This saving event (the Incarnation) reveals to humanity... *the incomparable value of every human person*" (EV § 2).

§ 2). Thus, in both encyclicals, the primary revelation is that of eternal life, even if, in *Veritatis Splendor*, the perspective consists first of all in demonstrating its link with the observance of the commandments, that is to say, its value in terms of promise and of recompense. In fact, both encyclicals develop the key idea that the gift of the Holy Spirit makes us, already in this life, participants in eternal life:

> Dead to sin, those who are baptised receive the new life (cf. Rom 6:3–11): living for God in Christ Jesus, they are called to walk in the Spirit and to manifest the fruits of the Spirit in their lives (cf. Gal. 5:16–25) (VS § 21).

> To know God and his Son, is to welcome the mystery of the loving communion of the Father, Son and Holy Spirit into one's own life, which even now is open to eternal life through participating in the life of God (EV § 37).

In both texts, eternal life is referred to the figure of Christ, the Redeemer. *Veritatis Splendor* implies this by stating that the desire for eternal life is joined to the aspiration to be with Christ, who is the fulfilment of the commandments. *Evangelium Vitae* does so by declaring that the incomparable value of every human person is linked to the eternal plan of God to unite to himself our human nature. The mystery of the Incarnation is evoked here in the light of Vatican II: "Through his Incarnation the Son of God has united himself in some way to every human being" (EV § 104, citing *Gaudium et Spes*, § 22). In addition, the reference in the notes to the encyclical, *Redemptor Hominis*, § 10 and 14, underlines the universality of the effects of the Redemption:

> For them (those who do not know Christ), access to salvation is possible by virtue of a grace, which, while being in a mysterious relationship with the Church, does not introduce such persons into the Church formally as such, but enlightens them in a way that is adapted to the state of their spirit and to their

situation in life. This grace comes from Christ; it is the fruit of his sacrifice and it is communicated by the Holy Spirit; it makes it possible for everyone to come to salvation through their free cooperation with that grace (Cf. EV, § 2).

The Truth of the Creation of the Human Being Opposed by Sin

If human life is inscribed in the eternal plan of God and if its final destination is that those who are alive should live for the whole of eternity, its incomparable meaning and value come prior to any deliberate and voluntary orientation that human beings might wish to give to it. Here, the encyclical refers to the creation of the first man in the image of God. The Yawhistic account is very evocative in this respect, because it associates the act of creation with the breath of life that makes man a living being (Gen 2:7). To clarify this point, the Pope then appeals to Gregory of Nyssa: "By virtue of its similarity to the universal King, human nature, created in order to subdue the face of the earth, was brought into being as a living image, which participates in its archetype, sharing the same dignity."[4] The breath of life is breathed into the human being; it is given to us. Every action taken against human life, therefore, contradicts the truth of the original act of creation. "Death ... casts its shadow of meaninglessness over man's entire existence" (EV § 7); it contradicts the original intention of the Creator, who "created man for incorruption" (EV § 7).[5]

---

4. Gregory of Nyssa, *De hominis opificio*, 4 PG, 136, cited in EV, § 52.
5. Commenting, in another context, upon the Pauline theme of incorruptibility (1 Cor.15), John Paul II writes that this cannot mean no more than a simple *restitutio in integrum*: "Such a return would not correspond to the internal logic of the whole of the economy of salvation, in terms of the deepest meaning of the mystery of the Redemption. Reconnected to the Resurrection and to the reality of the next world, a *restitutio in integrum* can be no more than an introduction to a new fulness." ("The spiritualisation of the body: source of its incorruptibility' in Catechesis

Evangelium Vitae

Their common destination establishes among human beings an equality of dignity. This personal dignity is denied by every attack upon life: "Every murder is the violation of a *'spiritual'* kinship" (EV § 8). To this, acts of abortion and of euthanasia add the sense of a violation of the *"kinship of 'flesh and blood'"* (EV § 8). If death entered human history in a violent manner with the murder of Abel, this is a result of original sin. Here the Pope refers to the *Catechism of the Catholic Church* (n. 2259), which he explains in the light of St John's gospel (Jn 3:11–12): Abel's murder is the absolute contradiction of the commandment of love of neighbor. The Pope is able to summarize in this way the expansion of evil, by way of a very succinct formula: "Man's revolt against God in the earthly paradise is followed by the deadly combat of man against man" (EV § 8). This formulation gives the impression of a remarkable shortcut, since the sin of our first parents and Cain's crime in this way come to synthesize the violation of the two great commandments, love of God and love of neighbour. The profound union between these commandments had been affirmed in *Veritatis Splendor*, starting from the person of Jesus. Here it is presented in history: the murder of Abel is the product of anger and of envy, the consequence of the original offence. This murder constitutes at the same time, in and of itself, an offense against God (EV § 9).

The choice made by the Pope here of the example of Cain and Abel is not a neutral choice. In the *City of God*, St Augustine had already made these two brothers the symbols of the two cities, the earthly city and the city of God, between which jealousy had inaugurated a relationship of hostility. The whole of the human race lives out the tension between these two cities; this is in the intermediate time, in which not only are good and evil divided one from the other, but also the good are divided between themselves and within themselves. Augustine puts it in these terms:

LXXII, *Uomo e donna lo creò: catechesi sull'amore umano* [Rome: Libreria Editrice Vaticana 1985), pp. 284–286]).

As far as those are concerned, who are making progress, who are not yet perfect, it is possible that they struggle against another, in the way that every good man is divided against himself, because, in each one of us, "the flesh is hostile to the spirit and the spirit to the flesh" (Gal 5:17). Thus, the spiritual desire of the one may fight against the fleshly desire of the other or the concupiscence of the flesh in one may struggle against the concupiscence of the spirit in another, just as the good and the wicked fight against one another.[6]

The figures of Cain and Abel, at the starting point of *Evangelium Vitae*, provide an illustration of a struggle, to which no human being, good or bad, can be a stranger.

Calvary: The Place of Revelation of the Value of Life

The plan of God, the Creator, is enough to confer upon human life its character as something intangible and sacred. The commandment: "You shall not kill" appears as one of the most fundamental divine prescriptions of the Covenant of God with his people Israel. However, the encyclical does not intend to limit itself to the value of life as belonging to the Creator. It seeks its meaning in the sacrifice which the Incarnate Word has made of his life. In fact, the purifying Blood of Christ on Calvary expresses the inestimable value of the gift made to us human beings, introducing us to the divine life by means of communion with his Passion. This Blood, by which the New Covenant is sealed, is the Blood "poured out for many, for the forgiveness of sins" (Mt 26:28). This outpouring of the blood of Christ reveals also to us human beings our most exalted vocation, that of being able to give our lives out of love. "No one can have a greater love than this, to lay down his life for his friends" (cf. Jn. 15:13). The sacrifice of Christ makes possible the sacrifice of his own life by the disciple. The latter draws the strength to make this commit-

---

6. St Augustine, *De civitate Dei*, XV, V, in P. Schaff (ed.), *The Nicene and Post-Nicene Fathers*, first series, vol. 2 (Peabody, MA: Hendrickson, 1995), pp. 286–287.

ment from this sacrifice and finds there, too, the confidence to do so in that life which is victorious over death. At the end both of the first and of the second chapters, the Pope alludes to the Blood poured out for us; in the first place, to bring out the incomparable value of the human being in the eyes of God (EV § 25–28) and, in the second, to contemplate in the Cross the source of life (EV § 50–51). The meditative character of the encyclical owes a great deal to these two passages.

Blood is the symbol of life, and thus, belongs to God. It is sacred. Offered in sacrifice in the Old Covenant, it sought to appease God. In fact, through the blood of the sacrifices, "God expressed his will to communicate his own life to men, purifying and consecrating them" (EV § 25). From a Johannine perspective, the encyclical invites us to contemplate the outpouring of blood and of water from the side of the crucified Jesus. The Pope brings out three elements in this. First of all, blood and water verify the complete fulfilment of the redemptive mission; they witness to the fact that the gift has been effected. They symbolize, too, the offering of the divine life, in which it is henceforth possible to participate through the sacraments. Finally, they reveal what is the greatest of all loves: "on the Cross the culmination of love" is revealed (EV § 51; cf. Jn. 15:13).

The Cross is simultaneously "the fulfilment and the complete revelation of the whole of the Gospel of life" (EV § 50). Forming the conclusion to the lengthy exposition of Chapter II, this affirmation invites us to read the following chapter of the encyclical, which forms its doctrinal nucleus. This fulfilment is that of the mission of the Son, who, on Calvary, brings to its completion the sacrifice of his life. At the same time, the Cross has also a cosmic dimension, which is emphasized; signs in the heavens accompany the death of Jesus, the veil of the Temple is torn in two (cf. Mt. 23:45). The encyclical sees in this "the symbol of a great cosmic upheaval and of a massive conflict between the forces of good and the forces of evil, between life and death" (EV § 50). The Cross is the place where these forces converge. It also marks their separation, one from the other. After connecting Calvary to the present-day struggles between "the culture of death" and "the culture of life," the Pope expresses very clearly the apocalyptic nature of the threats described in Chapter I: "The glory of the Cross is not concealed by this darkness (of the present-day situation); rather, the Cross...is revealed as the center, the meaning, and the goal of all history and of every human life" (EV § 50).

At the very worst moment of Christ being stripped naked, the identity of the Son is revealed to mankind; the Cross has manifested its glory. It is revealing to note that, meditating upon the Passion in Luke's account, the Pope focuses upon the last two instances of forgiveness expressed by Jesus: his intercession for those who were persecuting him (Lk 23:34) and his promise to the good thief (Lk 23:43). Even upon the wood of the Cross, mercy is offered to us all, including to those who have been in the front ranks as artisans of death.

The striking light of the Resurrection and the out-pouring of the Spirit of Pentecost will bring to its culmination the saving work of Christ, the source of eternal life for all persons. Still in our days, this hope, springing from the heart of the Redemption, must illuminate our thinking and our assessment of the new threats to life.

The Loss of the Sense of God and of the Sense of the Human Being

In the light of these truths of faith, the rereading by the Pope of the account of Abel's murder enables him to put forward a diagnosis of the many crimes and attacks upon human life.[7] Work-

---

7. Right from the start (§ 2 and 3), the encyclical cites *Gaudium et Spes* at length, and notably § 27, which delineates the various threats to human life: "Everything that is opposed to life itself, such as any form of homicide, genocide, abortion, euthanasia and even voluntary suicide; everything which constitutes a violation of the integrity of the human person, such as all mutilations, physical or moral torture, psychological constraints, ... arbitrary imprisonment, deportations, slavery, prostitu-

ing back from the effects to the causes, throughout Chapters I and II, the encyclical examines the roots of that evil in the human being (EV § 21) that is specific to our contemporaries, plunged into a culture that has been secularized. The Pope undertakes this analysis in minute detail, dismantling the vicious circle within which human beings are trapped, devoid of all sense of direction.

In this way, John Paul II translates into a form that is accessible to our contemporaries the link already established between original sin and the infamous crime of Cain: the loss of the sense of God (cf. Gen 4:5; Cain was very annoyed that God had not accepted his offering) brings with it the loss of the sense of the human being (Gen 4:9; "Am I my brother's keeper?"). This explains how it is that people offend against their own dignity through acts which violate the moral law, something that is not without its consequences for our capacity to welcome the lifegiving and salvific presence of God (Gen 4:14): "I will have to hide myself far from your face."[8] The circle is closed. Only the presence of God makes it possible for the human being, a sinner, to appreciate the true gravity of his or her offence. In fact, the

---

tion, trafficking in women and children; or, further, degrading conditions of work, which reduce workers to the level of mere instruments in the relationship, without regard for the fact that they are free and responsible persons; all of these practices and others of an analogous kind are truly infamous."

8. "When the relationship to the absolute comes under attack, it is the personal face of the absolute which fades away. Absolute transcendence becomes threatening, its holiness inspires fear and terror and people, following Adam and Cain, hide themselves away. In the flight far from the gaze of the absolute, there is the perception of a mystery which causes fear and which ceases to attract. The impersonal sacred (*Mysterium tremendum*) draws them into an alternative, in which the impure and the pure are opposed, one which replaces that which opposes the sinner to the saint. How can the sinner come to be brought into relationship with the source of all holiness? Almost without fail, the natural desire to be forgiven by God is obscured in the conscience of the person who is guilty and it no longer finds a way to express itself in truth" (J. Laffitte, *Le Pardon transfiguré* [Paris: Desclée Emmanuel, 1995], p. 142).

sense of God can become clear to us once more only if God himself takes the initiative to reveal himself as a personal being, ready to grant forgiveness. It is his salvific presence: "Yahweh put a mark on Cain, so that whoever encountered him first would not strike him" (Gen 4:15). God, in his Son, Jesus Christ, has taken the initiative in regard to a salvation that, at one and the same time, is both unexpected and yet for which we were waiting. The vicious circle is broken by the event of the Redemption.

From the loss of the sense of God and of the sense of the human being flow several consequences that are enumerated by the encyclical: the lack of recognition of the transcendent character of the human being (EV § 11), the loss of the sense of the specific place of the human being in the created world, the inability to integrate the meaning of creation into culture and into thought, the substitution of the values of having for those of being; the substitution of the values of having for those of being,[9] the loss of the Christian understanding of suffering. Consequences of this kind play a decisive role in the behaviour of persons, which is directed against the value of life. John Paul II classifies such kinds of behavior as individualism, utilitarianism, and hedonism. These constitute the three principal forms of practical materialism (EV § 23). Each one of them represents a general attitude towards the human body; it is no longer perceived in its personal dimension but is reduced to its material aspect, such that it is treated as an object of pleasure (hedonism) or of exploitation (utilitarianism). As a result, sexuality ceases to be seen as a language of love—it is depersonalised—and its "ontological truth"[10] is no longer recognized as such. Finally, indi-

---

9. "The possibility of loss (at the level of being) is like its opposite or the ruinous counter-part to every possession" (G. Marcel, *Être et Avoir*, Paris: Aubier, 1935, p. 131).
10. The "ontological truth" (of the conjugal act) is an expression used several times by John Paul II, to indicate the indissoluble character of the two dimensions of the unitive and the procreative in human sexuality; it coincides with what Paul VI, in the encyclical *Humanae Vitae* (§ 12), calls the intimate structure of the conjugal act. To speak of "ontological truth"

vidualism constitutes an obstacle to that inter-personal encounter, which presupposes respect, gratuity, and service.

All of these very real threats to human life demonstrate the danger which arises from the confusion between good and evil, which has spread to a very large part of contemporary society (EV § 24). Cain's crime is perpetuated in the human city.[11]

The Doctrinal Nucleus

Veritatis Splendor shows how the encounter between Jesus and the rich young man provides a motive for conduct that is in conformity with the will and with the call of God. The approach is similar in *Evangelium Vitae*. After Chapter II, devoted to the mystery of life which is stronger than death, the Pope asserts very logically in the following chapter that this victory implies human beings adopt moral decisions of a certain kind and a specific kind of behavior. People understand that respect for life is the main area in which these are to be applied and that, on this subject, John Paul II wanted to clarify the issues at stake in the most sensitive, contemporary discussions.

In this Chapter III, entitled "You Shall not Kill," the questions are confronted in an order, which reveals the desire not to expose the text to interpretations which might be confused or which simply lumped them all together. The chapter begins by

---

enables him to bring out the objective nature of this inseparability, to which the spouses bestow its subjective and psychological dimension, when they respect the norm which it lays down, which is a norm of the natural law (cf. John Paul II, *Uomo e donna lo creò*, pp. 453–458).

11. St Augustine sees a relationship between the murder of Abel by Cain on the one hand and, on the other, that of Remus by his brother, Romulus, at the time of the foundation of Rome, destined to preside over the human city. This second crime repeats the first: "We must not be surprised, then, much later on, at the time of the foundation of the city which was destined to become the head of this earthly city, of which we are speaking, and to reign over so many nations, to see reproduced a sort of image of this first example, this archetype, as the Greeks call it" (St Augustine, *The City of God, loc. cit.*, n. 5).

setting out the foundation for what follows, namely, with the sacred character of human life, which the Pope relates to the action of God and to his divine will (the commandments). This sacred character is the basis for the inviolability of human life: God alone is the master of life (§ 55). This life, then, has an intrinsic value, which determines in every human being a right to respect for his existence. From this, after a long, preliminary exposition on legitimate defence and on the death penalty, three declarations flow forth in the text:

- the act of directly and deliberately killing an innocent human being is *always gravely immoral* (§ 57);
- direct abortion, namely abortion undertaken as an end or as a means, always constitutes *a particularly grave moral disorder*, insofar as it is the deliberate killing (murder) of an innocent human being (§ 62); and
- finally, euthanasia is *a grave violation of the Law of God*, insofar as it is the morally unacceptable, deliberate killing (murder) of a human person (§ 65).

The encyclical establishes the sacred character of human life with reference, as has been said, to the commandments of God[12] and to his act of creation. However, there is a serious risk involved in not reading Chapter III in its entirety. We know that it concludes with a section addressed to the civil authorities, in order that human life be defended and respected. This appeal is grounded upon the natural law. Although the encyclical starts from Revelation, it relies here upon the normative character of

---

12. To examine, at the exegetical level, the difficulty of the absence of a precise object in the commandment which forbids homicide in Ex. 20:13 and in Dt. 5:17, H. Schüngel-Straumann affirms that the verb *rasah* is applied in the Old Testament to human beings alone. It is used neither for the action of killing animals, nor for punishment by God, nor for deaths caused by wars. It indicates in general a violent action that provokes the death of the victim, often with an emphasis upon this specific circumstance, namely that the action is not one of defence. Cf. H. Schungel-Straumann in *Decalogo e comandamenti di Dio*, translated from the German, (Brescia: Padeia, 1970), pp. 49–59.

the respect for the rights with which every human being is endowed.

The chapter begins by affirming that "You shall not kill" is the first commandment of the Decalogue, of which Jesus reminds the rich young man (Mt. 19:18). Now, in the same explanation, the lordship over life entrusted to the human being follows immediately upon the reminder of the command of the Creator: "Be fruitful, multiply, fill the face of the earth and subdue it" (Gen 1:28). This command, which here takes the form of a blessing of fruitfulness, is linked directly to the act of creation by God of man, as "male and female in his own image" (Gen 1:27). The link between this account of the beginning and the words of Jesus to the rich young man is, thus, a particularly a strong one; it draws attention to the fact that the first directive given by the Creator to his creature has to do with human life. Human life is the primordial good and, from the beginning, human beings have received the mission to extend it. It is together with this gift of life that the power of dominion over all other living creatures was given.

Thus, human beings enjoy a very real lordship over life. Nevertheless, it is not absolute, and they must exercise it, not by means of "an arbitrary will which no one may question," but as "ministers of the plan established by the Creator."[13] This mission of service to life is confirmed by the encyclical, which refers to the Covenant concluded by God with Noah in this sense. Here we find already a principle, which, though not formulated negatively, is yet expressed in the form of a threat of judgment: "Whoever sheds the blood of man will have his own blood shed by man, for the human being was made in the image of God" (Gen 9:6). This command is situated between two reminders of the original mission to "Be fruitful and multiply and fill the face of the earth" (Gen 9:1, 7).

In this way, a relationship is established between the abiding mission to spread life and the command always to respect it;

---

13. Paul VI, *Humanae Vitae*, § 13.

both express its character as sacred and as inviolable. The reference to the image and likeness of God indicates the origin and the foundation of that inviolability.[14]

The commandment "You shall not kill" is formulated in the form of a prohibition. In this way, the moral norm expresses the inalienable duty to defend the good of life. *Veritatis Splendor* had already explained at length the paradoxically positive function of prohibitions. Just like the other commandments, "You shall not kill" is a condition for eternal life and is an illustration of the commandment of love of neighbor:

In this commandment, we find a precise expression of the singular dignity of the human person, "the only creature whom God wanted for his own sake" (cf. GS, § 24). The different commandments of the Decalogue, are really only so many reflections of the one commandment about the good of the person, at the level of the many different goods which characterize that person's identity as a spiritual and corporal being in relation to God, to neighbour and to the material world (VS § 13).

The personal nature of the human being in the substantial unity of body and soul, then, is put forward to show the value of life. It makes it possible to recognize at one and the same time the intention of the Creator, in regard to the dignity of every human being wanted for themselves and directed towards their end, and, ultimately, of their unique and continual relationship to the Creator. In fact, God never ceases to be "Master of life, from its beginning until its end."[15]

Legitimate Defence

On this point, *Evangelium Vitae* refers us to the *Catechism of the Catholic Church* (nn. 2263–2265) and, like the *Catechism*, the encyclical refers to St Thomas: "The act of defending oneself

---

14. "God proclaims that he is the absolute Lord of the life of man, who is formed in his image and likeness" (cf. Gen. 1:26–28). Human life is thus given a sacred and inviolable character, which reflects the inviolability of the Creator himself" (EV § 53).
15. Congregation for the Doctrine of Faith, *Donum Vitae*, Introduction, § 5.

(against an unjust aggressor) can carry with it a double effect; one is the preservation of one's own life and the other is the death of the aggressor...the first is willed simply, the second is not."[16] The *Catechism* (n. 2264) derived from the fundamental principle of love towards self the legitimacy of insisting upon respect for one's own right to life. The formula used in the encyclical is notably stronger: "Certainly, the intrinsic value of life and the duty of love towards self..." (EV § 55). Furthermore, *Evangelium Vitae* reminds us of a distinction concerning this right, that of legitimately foregoing the exercise of this right, but "only by virtue of a heroic love, which deepens and transfigures the love of self into a radical self-offering, according to the spirit of the Gospel beatitudes" (EV § 55). In the end, the two texts use the same expression to state that, in the case of people with responsibilities for the lives of others (in the family, in the city, or in the state), legitimate defence is a "grave duty."

The Death Penalty

By contrast, as far as the death penalty is concerned, a clear difference between the *Catechism* and the encyclical can be noticed. The latter moves towards a greater restriction in the area of the application of the death penalty. The question is presented differently in the two documents: the *Catechism* recalls the traditional teaching that recognized as well-founded "the right and the duty (of the public authorities) to inflict punishments proportionate to the gravity of the crime" (§ 2266), without excluding, in case of grave necessity, recourse to the death penalty (§ 2267). It appeals then to the idea of punishment, indicating its three constitutive elements: its value in terms of expiation, its preserving of the public order and security, and finally, its medicinal value. Then, it proclaims the principle of the prefer-

---

16. St Thomas Aquinas, *Summa Theologiae*, IIa IIae, q. 64, a.7. Concerning the hypothesis of the suppression of the aggressor and that of his being in a fit of madness and hence of not being morally responsible, the encyclical adds to the justification of St Thomas a reflection by St Alphonsus Liguori, *Theologia moralis*, I, III, tr. 4, c. 1, dt. 3.

ence for bloodless means, insofar as these are sufficient, "because they correspond better to the concrete conditions of the common good and are more in conformity with the dignity of the human person" (§ 2267).

As far as the encyclical is concerned, it begins by noting the growing tendency to demand a very limited application, even a total abolition, of the death penalty. It situates this punishment within the context of penal justice, not in order to recognize its legitimacy without further ado, but in order to express the desire for a justice that would be in as great a conformity as possible with the dignity of the person and thus, in the last analysis, with the plan of God for human beings and for society. Taking up itself the question of the meaning of punishment, whose "primary purpose (is) to redress the disorder introduced by the offence" (§ 56), the encyclical refers to its two-fold objective, that, by way of a sufficient expiation of the offence, the guilty person be permitted "to regain the exercise of his or her freedom" and that they "may be rehabilitated" and "change his or her behavior." It is also in the light of these two purposes that "the nature and the extent of the punishment" must be established. These two criteria—and it is here that the encyclical differs from the *Catechism*—"ought not to go to the extreme of executing the offender, except in cases of absolute necessity, in other words, when it would not be possible otherwise to defend society" (§ 56). Cases of this kind nowadays are, if not non-existent, yet at least very rare, the encyclical states, as it reaffirms the preference for the use of bloodless means.

A new element is to be noted: it is no longer the principle of the just proportion between the offense and the punishment that determines matters, but the fact of there being an absolute necessity, explicitated by the encyclical as "when it would not be possible otherwise to defend society." No one would deny that there are practical difficulties laying down the limits involved. Since the only case of absolute necessity envisaged is that of the defence of society, it will be difficult to establish the cases in which the principle of legitimate defence, the concept employed up to now, above all in the context of the actions of individuals, would be applicable. Indeed, what are the circumstances in which a society finds itself in the absolute necessity of defending itself? The state of war is one. There, the principle of legitimate defence is applied, the Tradition having always recognized as licit a war that is defensive, under certain conditions that are to be applied. But, the struggle of a state against a powerful drug cartel, for example, or against an organization such as the Mafia, which paralyzes either a whole region or public administration itself, does that require that the death penalty be applied? In the last analysis, it is the legitimate authority, which will have to assess a situation of a threat to a society, for which it is responsible, to determine what the adequate responses may be and to put them into effect.

Treating in advance these two delicate questions, of legitimate defence and of the death penalty, means that they will not confound the discussion of what remains the principal purpose of the encyclical, namely, to engage the doctrinal authority of the Church in the matters of voluntary homicide, abortion, and euthanasia.

The Act of Killing, Directly and Deliberately, an Innocent Human Being

"The commandment 'You shall not kill' has an absolute value, when it refers to the innocent person. And, all the more so, when it is a question of a weak and defenceless human being" (EV § 57). The encyclical introduces in this way its first solemn declaration.[17] With great depth of insight, the text notes here that weak and defenceless innocent human beings "find their

---

17. "Therefore, by the authority which Christ conferred upon Peter and his successors, and in communion with (all) the Bishops of the Catholic Church, *I confirm that the direct and voluntary killing of an innocent human being is always gravely immoral.* This doctrine, based upon that unwritten law, which man, in the light of reason, finds in his own heart (cf. Rom 2:14–15), is reaffirmed by Sacred Scripture, transmitted by the

ultimate defence against the arrogance and caprice of others only in the absolute binding force of God's commandment" (§ 57). The unconditional respect for human life is founded upon the singular and unique value, not of the person in general, but of each and every human person in particular.[18] In their earthly existence, in fact, every human person is the bearer of a whole series of values, human and divine, which both make that person autonomous and sovereign with respect to other creatures, and also place them in continual dependence upon the Creator. In every person, there is present the image of him, from whom they have their life, as also there is present in them an eternal destiny, grounded in the vocation to eternal life which they have received from God. The dignity that flows from this is a dignity that each person has in common with that of each and every other human being. This is why the human being may never be treated as a mere means, but must always be treated as an end. Physical life is the place in which the person fulfils their vocation; to suppress that life, therefore, in others or in oneself, is always to violate in a serious way the Law of God.

This teaching is not new ("*I confirm,*" the Pope writes) and its object imposes itself in an absolute manner both by faith and by reason. In fact, the inviolability of the life of the innocent human being has always been "clearly taught by Sacred Scripture, constantly upheld in the Tradition of the Church and consistently proposed by her magisterium" (§ 57). The Pope refers this unanimity to the "supernatural sense of faith", thanks to which "the totality of the faithful," as *Lumen Gentium* had taught (§ 12), "cannot err in matters of faith ... when, 'from the bishops to the last of the lay faithful' (St Augustine), they bring a universal consent to truths of faith and of morals."

Besides, the law of the Church is united here to the natural law. The inviolable character of human life imposes itself also in

---

Tradition of the Church and taught by the ordinary and universal Magisterium (cf. *Lumen Gentium*, § 25)" EV § 57.

18. Cf. St Thomas Aquinas, *Summa Theologiae*, Ia, q. 30, a. 4.

virtue of our reason. The declaration made by the Pope recalls, moreover, the Letter to the Romans (2:14–15):

> When the gentiles, not having the Law, still by nature do what the Law commands ... they show in fact the reality of this Law inscribed in their hearts; it is proven by the witness of their consciences, namely, by their interior judgments accusing or excusing one another.

In contrast to the *Catechism of the Catholic Church* (nn 2268–2269), the encyclical does not use the generic term of "voluntary homicide," but the expression "to kill directly and deliberately an innocent human being." In this way, it brings strongly into focus the act of killing, insofar as it is a free and deliberate act. The encyclical is concerned in the first place with the object of an act of killing that is imputable to a free subject, who is responsible for his or her acts. Semantic disputes at various levels over terms such as death, murder, homicide, deprivation of life, are thereby avoided. This accent placed upon homicidal freedom is reinforced by the expression, a few lines earlier in the encyclical: "the deliberate decision to deprive an innocent human being of his life."

Finally, we need to specify more precisely the meaning of the expression "right to life," used at the end of the paragraph (§ 57). The "right to life" is the primordial right in the scale of all rights. Its fundamental nature stems from the fact that it expresses the incomparable value of human nature; it conditions the existence of all the other rights of the person. Therefore, it cannot be put into the balance with any other right whatever it may be, nor can it be brought into question either by individual freedom or by the requirements of (or by what is tolerated by) legislation. The "right to life" cannot be reduced to being one right among others. Besides, it grounds the equality of every person in the respect that is due to him or to her and, in this sense, it ensures a *de facto* solidarity among human beings.

Abortion

After having confirmed authoritatively the immoral nature of murder, the encyclical goes on to make statements about two particular instances of that act, abortion and euthanasia.

The encyclical is not unaware of the dramatic circumstances within which the decision for abortion is often taken, nor of the conditioning of public opinion on this question. It speaks, notably, of an obscuring of the sense of right and wrong in the consciences of many persons and takes note of the development of a terminology that is ambiguous (§ 58).

The condemnation of abortion is elaborated around two points. First of all, the act itself is defined as "the deliberate and direct killing (murder), by whatever means it is carried out, of a human being in the initial phase of his or her existence, extending from conception to birth" (§ 58).[19] Then, following from what has been said on the subject of the murder of an innocent person, the text insists on the complete innocence of the human being at the beginning of his or her life, "lacking that minimal form of defence, consisting in the poignant power of a new-born baby's cries and tears."

On two occasions subsequently, the Pope situates the problem on the strictly ethical plane, rejecting the competence of the sciences to decide upon the moment of the presence of a soul in the embryo.[20] Still, he relies upon the sciences to recall that,

---

19. In this definition, the incision concerning the means ("by whatever means it is carried out") is of great importance. It excludes any middle position, such as the legitimacy often claimed for this act based on its conditions of execution; when, for example, gynaecological doctors are recognised as able to perform it. According to A. Laun "such a decision protects the woman up to a certain point, but, for the child, it is a matter of indifference to know how it is killed, in a professional manner or in an amateur fashion", in *Fragen der Moraltheologie heute* (Wein: Herder, 1992), p. 34. Translator's note: The French text uses the word "*meurtre*," whereas the English uses the term "killing," but a deliberate, direct killing of an innocent human being is a murder.
20. "The presence of a spiritual soul cannot be established by any experimental methods....over and above scientific debates and even of

"from the first instant there is established the (genetic) programme what this living being will be" (§ 60). The identity of the subject who is in the process of being formed is already present: "Right from fertilisation, the adventure of a new human life begins and each of his or her great capacities requires time to find its place and to be in a position to act" (§ 60). Citing the *Declaration on Procured Abortion* of the Congregation for the Doctrine of the Faith, the text makes it understood that it is a matter of these "great capacities," specifically human capacities, such as the spiritual faculties of the intelligence and of the will. In fact, it concludes by asking: "How could a human individual not be a human person?[21]" Whatever the differing views may be, the ethical principle is expressed by means of a prudential judgment:

> What is at stake is so important that, from the standpoint of moral obligation, the mere probability that a person is involved would suffice to justify an absolutely clear prohibition of any intervention aimed at suppressing a human embryo (§ 60).

---

philosophical claims, in relation to which the Magisterium has not expressly committed itself" (§ 60).

21. On this important point, we take note of the very clear argument of Fr. Cottier. After having underlined the role of the soul as the principle of unity in the Aristotelian-Thomistic understanding, as also its specific character, compared with the vegetative soul and the sensitive soul, G. Cottier relies upon the rational recognition that the intellectual life transcends organic life. In this regard, he recalls the position of Christian philosophy: "The soul, not being intrinsically organic, cannot be transmitted by generation, but it requires a directly creative act on the part of the Creator". Cottier acknowledges that the sciences cannot recognise the simultaneity of the two interventions (those of the parents and of God), but he affirms, nevertheless, that, in every case, "starting from the moment of conception, human nature is really—virtually or actually—given." In this latter case, we have a person, already constituted ontologically, while, in the first case, we have a person in a virtual fashion, but "on the basis of a real virtuality, ontological, already constituted, because a certain degree of its natural development requires, as an ultimate disposition, the infusion of the spiritual soul, to whose reception it is intrinsically ordered." (*Scritti di etica* [Casale Montferrato: Piemme, 1994], p. 220).

The absence of a direct and specific condemnation of abortion in the Scriptures does not indicate, in any instance, any toleration of what Vatican II calls "an abominable crime" (*Gaudium et Spes* § 51). On the contrary, in the Scriptures is to be found a recognition of the embryo as "the most personal object of God's loving and fatherly providence" (EV § 61).

Once it has specified these various points, the encyclical refers to the unanimous Christian Tradition in its condemnation of procured abortion, before arriving at its second great declaration:

> By the authority which Christ conferred upon Peter and his successors, in communion with the bishops—who on various occasions have condemned abortion and who, in the aforementioned consultation, albeit dispersed throughout the world, have shown unanimous agreement concerning this doctrine—I declare that direct abortion, that is abortion willed as an end or as a means, always constitutes a grave moral disorder, insofar as it is the deliberate killing (murder) of an innocent human being. This doctrine is based upon the natural law and upon the written Word of God; is transmitted by the Church's Tradition and taught by the ordinary universal Magisterium (cf. *Lumen Gentium*, §25); (EV § 62).

This is a strong and solemn declaration. If the terms *definitive tenenda* are not explicitly employed, a certain number of elements leave no doubt about the intention to expound here a doctrine that is definitive. We find here a reminder of the nature of the authority engaged ("conferred by Christ to Peter and to his successors"), as also the affirmation of the bond of communion between the Pope and the bishops, whose judgment is unanimously expressed, even though they are dispersed throughout the world. We find here, too, that the text recalls the foundations of the natural law, the written Word of God, the Tradition, and that it refers to the ordinary and universal Magisterium.[22]

---

22. Beyond the reference to *Lumen Gentium*, § 25, we note that the recalling of the three elements, Scripture, Tradition and Magisterium, goes back to the conciliar doctrine on Revelation in the Constitution, *Dei Verbum*,

Evangelium Vitae

Very significant is the use here of the expression "intrinsically illicit," something not unconnected with the encyclical *Veritatis Splendor*, one of whose purposes was to pronounce upon the existence of such acts—often called into question.[23] In the end, it is in the light of this moral evaluation of abortion that different practices are analyzed: experimentation upon embryos, the exploitation of living embryos as biological material (including cases of the donation of organs and of the transplantation of tissues), the eugenic abuse of prenatal diagnosis. The whole of the argumentation of *Evangelium Vitae* is orientated towards the object of a particular act[24] unceasingly invoked: the murder of an innocent human being. The sole purpose of *Evangelium Vitae* is clearly to defend human life against all that threatens it.

Euthanasia

The encyclical examines the question of euthanasia in the context of the eclipse of the sense of God, which had been already the subject of a lengthy reflection in the first two chapters. The refusal of death, when it puts an end to a happy life, and, on the other hand, seeking death, when existence seems to be absurd,

---

§ 10. Not to be forgotten either is the reference to the judgment of Paul VI in his discourse to Italian Catholic jurists of December 9, 1972, on the unchangeable nature of the Church's teaching in this regard: cf. *AAS*, 64 (1972), p. 777.

23. "The thesis proposed by *teleological* and *proportionalist* theories must be rejected, according to which it would be impossible to qualify as morally wrong according to its genre—its object—the deliberate choice to engage in certain kinds of behaviour or to perform certain determined acts, in isolation from the intention within which the choice has been made or from the totality of the foreseeable consequences of that act, for all of the persons involved". (VS § 79). For a clear presentation of the issues at stake in this debate, reference should be made to Livio Melina *Morale: tra crisi e rinnovamento*, II, *Gli assoluti della morale in discussione* (Ares, Milano, 1994), pp. 41–61; cf. also Servais Pinckaers, *Ce qu'on ne peut jamais faire: les actes intrinsèquement mauvais: histoire et discussion* (Paris: Ed. Universitaires, 1986).

24. On the object of the act, the decisive criterion for moral evaluation, cf. John Paul II, *Veritatis Splendor*, § 75–78.

mark the attitude of people who reject or who have forgotten their fundamental relationship with God (EV, § 64). This is especially true, when the attempt is made to deprive a dying person of his self-consciousness.[25] In fact, only a perspective which incorporates eternal life makes it possible to accept that people should prepare themselves in a fully conscious manner for their definitive encounter with God (EV § 65).

In this way, the judgment about euthanasia raises the question of the meaning of death, as the passing from this earthly life to eternal life. Here the text cites five times the *Declaration on Euthanasia*, published by the Congregation for the Doctrine of the Faith.[26] Euthanasia is defined in the strict sense as "an action or an omission, which of itself or by intention, causes death, with the purpose of eliminating all suffering" (EV § 65).

The "omission" refers to the cessation of ordinary care: food, hydration, artificial or otherwise, the aspiration of pulmonary secretions, etc. The "action" indicates all those means directly aimed at ending the life of the sick person. The Pope recognizes, notably within the context of palliative care, the liceity of having recourse to different types of analgesics and of sedatives, to ease the suffering of the sick person, even where there is a certain risk of shortening life. He makes use also of the classical distinction between euthanasia and the refusal of aggressive therapy, that is to say of "extraordinary" or of "disproportionate means."[27] On

---

25. Cf. Pius XII, Allocution to an international group of doctors, February 24, 1957, *AAS* 49 (1957), p. 145.
26. In AAS 72 (1980), p. 546.
27. Elio Sgreccia observes that the term "extraordinary," as used at the time of Pius XII, referred then either to the increase of suffering linked to those means or to their cost. He notes, correctly, that some means considered in the past as extraordinary have nowadays become ordinary. Hence, the accent placed upon the therapeutic outcome rather than on the therapeutic means, which has led some people, according to the declaration *Iura et bona*, to speak of proportionate means and of disproportionate means, E. Sgreccia, *Personalist Bioethics: Foundations and Applications*, translated by J. A. Di Camillo and M. J. Miller (Philadelphia: National Catholic Bioethics Center, 2012), pp. 683–686.

the other hand, the administration of a certain dosage of products mixed so that they necessarily involve the death of the patient is to be proscribed as being an act of homicide of its very nature. It is then that we find the solemn declaration:

> In conformity with the Magisterium of my predecessors and in communion with the bishops of the Catholic Church, I confirm that euthanasia is a grave violation of the Law of God, since it is the deliberate and morally unacceptable killing (murder) of a human person. This doctrine is based upon the natural law and upon the written Word of God, is transmitted by the Church's Tradition, and taught by the ordinary and universal magisterium (cf. *Lumen Gentium*, 25); (EV § 65).

In this third solemn declaration, the accent is placed upon the underlying meaning of euthanasia, as the violation of the Law of God and as the deliberate murder of a human person. By provoking the death of the sick person in anticipation, human beings make themselves masters of death. Euthanasia can be committed in circumstances that aggravate the malice involved. If, at times, it has the meaning of an "assisted suicide," something which rests upon a "false compassion"[28]—the text takes up the moral qualification of suicide already present in the *Catechism of the Catholic Church* (nn. 2281–2283)—the act of euthanasia is defined as homicide pure and simple, but at times aggravated by the arbitrary decisions of those "who arrogate to themselves the power to decide who is to live and who is to die" (EV § 66).

---

28. We note that justifications for euthanasia are put forward (and, besides this, also for the justification of the "freedom to abort") on the basis of a terminology, which is deliberately ambiguous—an aspiration to fall into a definitive sleep, the request for someone's existence to be interrupted—as also on the basis of an erroneous conception of the dignity of the person, making that dignity depend upon the person's degree of consciousness. Cf. P. Gauer, J. Laffitte, "Una proposta di legge sull'eutanasia" in *L'assistenza al morente, Atti del Congresso Internazionale di Roma, 15–18 Marzo, 1992* (Milan: Vita e Pensiero, 1992), pp. 447–449.

Before inviting people to be at the service of a culture of life and following this declaration, the encyclical devotes a long section to the relationships between the civil law and the moral law. The threats to life, in effect, have taken on a planetary dimension, which brings into operation the political power of numerous States and the intervention of some of the most powerful of international organizations. These relationships between civil law and moral law would require a more profound analysis, which goes beyond the framework of this article. Guarantor of the respect for the rights of citizens, the civil law has a particular responsibility to defend the most fundamental of those rights, and most especially the first of them, the inviolable right to life of every innocent human being. The Church is doing no more than fulfilling the mission entrusted to her, when her defence of the weakest is united to her proclamation of the Gospel of life. She is not mistaken about the audience being addressed when she directs herself to the city of mankind, nor does she give offence to that audience, when she makes her own the words of St John: "All of this we have written to you, so that our joy may be complete" (1Jn 1:14).

3 Health as an Ethical Issue: The Donation of Organs[1]

There are not very many definitions of health.[2] Among the more common, but also among the more disputed, appears the proposition of July 22, 1946 of the World Health Organisation and that formulated more than half a century later by John Paul II on the occasion of the World Day for the Sick.

The first definition identified health with a state of complete physical and mental well-being and not only as the absence of a sickness or of an infirmity.

The second is more articulated:

> Health is not to be identified only by the absence of sickness, it presents itself as a tendency towards a greater harmony and a sound equilibrium at the physical, psychic, spiritual and social level. From this perspective the person is called to gather all of the forces available to them, in order to fulfil their own vocation and to bring about the good of others.[3]

These two definitions will enable us to structure our reflections: both underline the fact that health is not to be reduced to the

---

1. "Health as an Ethical Issue: The Donation of Organs" was published under the title «Humanité et santé: l'approche de la théologie catholique» in *Politique internationale*, n. 130 hiver 2010–2011, pp. 103–121. The text has been published also in English in the English-speaking edition of this journal.
2. A brief, historical summary of the relationship between sickness and health can be found in E. Sgreccia, *Personalist Bioethics: Foundations and Applications*, translated by J. A. Di Camillo, and M. J. Miller, (Philadelphia: National Catholic Bioethics Center, 2012), pp. 129–132, 178–179.
3. John Paul II, *Message for the Seventh World Day for the Sick* (August 6, 1999).

mere absence of an infirmity. Health must be thought of, then, in its own right, starting from the elements which make it what it is. This is an objective approach, to the extent that, paradoxically, even at the level of subjective experience, it is generally sickness that causes health to be valued as a good. If, on the phenomenological level, the objective content of health can be circumscribed clearly by physiological, medical, political, and social elements, from the perspective of the Christian faith, the concept of health, as such more complex, needs to be understood at a deeper level, in order to avoid two possible excesses. The first is that of minimizing the reality by reducing health to a gift of nature, and hence to a gift of God, a gift which, moreover, is not given to everyone—something which does not make sense, except in a spiritual approach (ideas of election or again of the theology of the Cross) and the second, opposing excess, which is that of a kind of idolatry of health. It is the Christian vision alone, which is a balanced one, a vision that can be understood only by starting from the figure of Christ as doctor, and of his mission, his words, and his actions. This will be the first point in our reflection.

If we reread attentively the two definitions of health just mentioned, we can perceive a fundamental difference between them: while, for the WHO, health is a good which has the value of an end in itself to be sought as an absolute (complete well-being), from a Christian perspective, on the other hand, health is a good which is ethically important[4] to the extent that it promotes a sense of responsibility in the personal subject in relation to other goods which are judged superior to it (the Kingdom of God, eternal goods); it is from these superior goods, then, that the responsibilities of authorities in society, and specifically of health authorities, derive. This in no way reduces the anthropological significance of health problems, but it does provide a vision of

---

4. Elio Sgreccia notes that, in Greek culture, in particular according to Plato, the measure of health is not something quantitative, but rather qualitative, axiological, and that this implies a relationship of value.

primordial importance for a large number of persons. This is not the only aspect that characterizes the specifically Christian aspect of this question. John Paul II's definition, in fact, situates health in the context of the realization of the personal vocation of the human person: in this way it becomes a good for, a good in view of, salvation. The theological and the spiritual dimension of health constitutes the second aspect of our reflection. In the end, from this perspective of the Christian faith, certain ethical implications can be brought out. We shall limit ourselves to the paradigmatic case of organ donations: a specific feature of this case is the need to integrate or to bring together at the same time the health of the sick recipient and the health of the donor, who, by the very fact of deciding to donate an organ, is voluntarily going to undergo a change in his health.

The Exemplary Figure of Christ, the Healer

Health and Sickness as a Revelation of the Relationship with God in the Old Testament

We would never be able to understand completely the central importance of the actions of Jesus towards the sick, during his public ministry, if we were to forget the value that the good of life had for the people of Israel. Every child of Israel aspired to be able to live to the *fulness of his days*; a long life was a blessing in itself. If we cannot find a precise term to specify what health is, yet we have the word "peace," or *shalom*, which goes beyond the purely material aspect of the mere absence of enemies; it extends to the immaterial, namely to a *healthy life*. This latter is often a kind of mediation, which makes it possible to understand the state of the relationship between the human being and the Creator: "It is I who cause to die and who give life; when I have struck someone, it is I who bring healing" (Dt 32:39). The one who bestows life is the one who is able to heal infirmities. Health, then, comes to signify the sign of the action of God and it is in this respect that it can be invested with a prophetic meaning. On the other hand, to be removed far from God creates a form of privation of health, a sense of being unwell, a spiritual infirmity. Health becomes the object of the incessant prayer of someone who wants to find peace once more. The Psalms abound with prayers directed to God who is far away, in order that he may deign to come close: "Do not abandon me, Yahweh, my God; do not depart far from me" (Ps 38:22). It must be said that, in the Psalms, the prayer for healing is often accompanied by the confession of the person's own faults.[5] The waiting for the Messiah was accompanied by the conviction that he would re-establish the health of the sick and of the infirm. The prophetic literature insists on the healing to be accomplished by him who must come to liberate the People of Israel:

> Then, the eyes of the blind will be unsealed and the ears of the deaf will be opened. Then, the lame will leap like the deer and the tongue of the mute will shout for joy (Is 35:5).

In the oracles of the prophets, God is presented as the one who gives once more healing to the sick; for example, through Jeremiah: "Here, it is I who will bring them remedy and healing, I am going to heal them and reveal to them an ordinance of peace and fidelity" (Jer 33:7); then, in Ezekiel: "I will seek out the one who is lost; I will lead back the one who has gone astray; I will dress the wounds of the one who has been injured; I will give strength to the one who is sick" (Ezek 34:16). Little by little, the traits of the Messiah who is awaited are prefigured, and he is presented as a pastor who will take care of his sheep.

Life is seen as a gift from God. From this arises the responsibility of human beings for their health. In the Old Testament, sickness could have several causes: natural (Tobias was blinded after being hit in the eyes by bird-droppings), medical errors (again Tobias became definitively blind through the treatment he received: "The more they applied the ointments, the more the spots blinded me, and, in the end, the blindness was complete"

---

5. Ps 38:2.6; Ps 39:9–12; Ps 107:17.

(Tob 2:10)). But, paradoxically, God could be seen as he who would strike someone to put him to the test, or, more simply, to punish him. This sense of putting him to the test will be taken up more fully by the sapiential tradition, especially in the books of Job and of Sirach. We cannot develop this aspect of the Old Testament here, but we can understand already that, in the Jewish tradition, sickness was an anomaly, a *hilloul*, a wound inflicted upon a creature.

In a certain sense, the responsibility for this is ambivalent; it was a question of being vigilant not only about the prudent care to be given to a gift which had been received (the person's own life), but also about his own relations with God. This is the explanation for the great esteem in which the doctor was held, as we find in the sapiential books, particularly in Sirach (38:6–14). These verses merit attention for the highly balanced picture they present of the relationship between God who cares (by creating not only medicines but also the doctor) and the practitioner, whose services are often needed:

> [God] has given knowledge to human beings so that they may glory in his mighty works. He uses them to heal and to relieve their pain; the pharmacist makes a mixture for them. Thus, there is no end to his activities and, through him, health extends across the world.
> My son, when you are ill, do not be depressed, but pray to the Lord and he will heal you. Renounce your faults, keep your hands clean, cleanse your heart of all sin. Offer incense and a memorial of fine flour and make as rich an offering as you can afford. Then, let the doctor take over— the Lord created him, too, and do not let him leave you, for you need him. Sometimes success is in their hands, since they in turn will beseech the Lord, to grant them the grace to relieve and to heal, that life may be saved.

In this extract, we find the distinction has been recovered between the one who is the author of health and the mediator (the doctor), the double duty to pray to God and not to reject scientific treatments; hence, the proper esteem for the latter. The text avoids opposing faith in the God who gives life (and health) and medical science, then in a phase of rapid development in Alexandria.

The New Testament: Christ and Health

The public activity of Jesus is centered around two kinds of action: healing the sick and pardoning sinners. Despite the importance of the presence in the Gospels of passages in which health is restored to the sick, the two acts of healing and of forgiveness, although they are almost always connected, are not to be placed on the same level. Healing is an act that makes the authority of Jesus, and thus his power over life and death, public and visible. Forgiveness, the perfect gift, offers the very substance itself of salvation. In order that the authority of the Master to remit sins be manifested to all, the action of forgiving is accompanied by a visible sign. Naturally, this pedagogical meaning of healing is not the only link between the two realities, between salvation and health; we find elsewhere in the Gospels different passages in which healing is not explicitly attached to forgiveness. Nevertheless, it is to be noted that the first sign by which Jesus makes himself known to the disciples of John the Baptist is the presence of signs of healing, signs connected to the proclamation of the Good News. Jesus uses the words of the prophet Isaiah: "Go back and tell John what you hear and see: the blind see again and the lame walk, lepers are cleansed and the deaf hear, and the dead are raised to life, and the Good News is proclaimed to the poor" (Mt 11:4–6). In this sense, in the Gospel, the restoration of health accomplished by Jesus evokes the salvific action of God and his will that all people may be saved through the work of salvation brought about by the person of Jesus.

In the synoptic gospels, no less than forty-seven episodes are to be found in which a thaumaturgical action of Jesus is present, often expressed by the word *thaumazein*. The healings often involve afflictions of the body, but there are also psychic and spiritual afflictions. In the latter case, the intervention may heal the lack of faith or may free the person's spirit from evil spirits. At times, we have all of these elements, to which is to be added the action of confounding those who murmur and who express doubts (and who, thus, act in a way which would impede the spread of the Kingdom). Let us take the example of the paralytic at Capernaum (Mk 2:1–12). The scene takes place in front of the crowd, gathered there as a result of the miracles performed by Jesus throughout Galilee. Jesus's first words are addressed to the paralytic, not to heal him to start with, but to proclaim to him that his sins have been forgiven. His healing, which comes about after Jesus has heard the interior murmurings of the Scribes who are present, becomes the paradoxical way that Jesus has chosen to insist upon the power that he has to remit sins. We take note of the fact that the Scribes participate neither in the joy at the healing which has come about nor in the question which all the people ask about the identity of someone who speaks and who acts in such a way as to forgive sins. Rather, they object to what has been stated, interpreting it as a blasphemy and they use their knowledge of the law to justify their conduct: "Who can forgive sins, but God alone?"

The words and the actions of Jesus towards sinners are often interpreted in this sense of blasphemy (or of the violation of the Sabbath) and are placed in contradiction to the letter of the Law.[6]

The interventions of Jesus seek not only to elicit a *conversio* among the witnesses and the subjects who are healed, but they bring out the compassionate nature of Jesus' being. The terms used in the sacred texts help us to deepen our knowledge of Jesus the *thaumaturge*. In him, we find the two attributes of mercy: compassion and mercy in the strict sense. Compassion is the behavior of someone who takes pity upon those who are in need, in a material sense (*oiktrimos*); mercy is directed towards sinners, it expresses the forgiveness of sins. Mercy translates the word *eleos,* what the Old Testament denotes by the term *hesed*. The person

---

6. J. Laffitte, *Le Pardon transfiguré* (Paris: Mame, 1995).

who is merciful is the one who exercises mercy in the broad sense. In Greek, the word is translated by the adjective *eleemon*. In the New Testament, this qualification is attributed to God alone, the only one who can treat the sickness of sin, often described as a leprosy. It is never applied to a man, with one single exception, in the Letter to the Hebrews, where it is attributed to the person of Christ, the only one capable of being at the same time compassionate and also merciful, revealing in this way the divine origin of his authority (*exousia*) and the power which emanates from him.

It must be observed that the mission of healing the sick was subsequently entrusted by Jesus to the disciples, a mission which the Apostles will not fail to perpetuate and to transmit.[7]

Human Life and Health in a Christian Vision

The point of departure for a Christian vision lies in the distinction between what characterizes the life of the human being from the life of all other living beings. Whereas the relationship of the latter with God is a generic and indirect relationship, every human being, by contrast, is in a relationship with him that is direct and personal. This relationship finds its foundation in that individual act of creation that is expressed in the book of Genesis (1:26): "Let us make man in our own image and likeness." In the second account of Creation (Gen 2:7), the life of the human being, even if it comes from the clay of the earth, also gives way to a direct intervention of the Creator: "He breathed into his nostrils a breath of life and the man became a living being." Every human being has been created *with a view to* personal communion with God, in knowledge and in love (created *in the image and likeness of God*). In a Christian vision, the gift that is made to human beings (their natural life) is seen as a gratuitous and supernatural gift of participation in the life of God itself as son or daughter, a participation restored by the Redeemer after the Fall. As can be seen in the light of this, the full value of human life,

---

7. Cf. The Acts of the Apostles and the Letter of James.

from its origins and from its most elementary biological beginnings, cannot be understood and accepted in a balanced way except from the perspective of the supernatural end to which the life of the human being is ordered. From this, it follows that only he who is life and the source of life can reveal the meaning as such of every human life.

Christian thought sees the sacred character of human life in the fact that it is a gift of the love of God. It is only from this foundational perspective that it is possible to understand the Christian vision of health. Health is a vital good, but human life is not reducible to this good. The link between health and salvation that we have illustrated in the actions of Jesus helps us to understand why the conditions of earthly life must be considered in the light of the Revelation about our ultimate destiny. It is not without interest to note that the encyclical, *Evangelium Vitae*, for example, expresses the relationship that unites earthly life to the life of the world to come in the following way:

> This supernatural calling highlights the *relative* character of each individual's earthly life. After all, life on earth is not an 'ultimate', but a 'penultimate' reality; even so, it remains sacred reality entrusted to us, to be preserved with a sense of responsibility and brought to perfection, in love and in the gift of ourselves to God and to our brothers and sisters (§ 2).

In this sense, we could attribute to health, so-to-say, a position of being *antepenultimate*; in the pyramid of Christian goods, health is to earthly life what the latter is to eternal life. However, to be more rigorous, it must be admitted that health must be considered rather as a *qualitas* of life. Every human being is the bearer of a "certain" quality of health. This state of health can be seen as a sort of capital, or patrimony, for which, within the context of certain limits, each one is personally responsible.

The Christian vision, then, includes a fundamental anthropological given: the awareness and the acceptance of our own limits. Health makes it possible for each person to experience in his own body, in his spirit, and in his own psychological experience, the finite character of his being. This is verified in particular when health undergoes a change. We cannot elaborate here on all the aspects of the human experience of sickness. Yet, we can say that the moral suffering which accompanies this experience is always linked to the discovery that this patrimony is not unlimited. Obviously, from the Christian perspective, the precarious nature of health exercises a pedagogical role, to the extent that it recalls to the mind of human beings their final end, which is not physical death perceived as a definitive state, but which, on the contrary, is that unimaginable condition of a life with neither suffering nor *diminutio*.

The Christian vision of health presupposes a conception of the human being that, at the anthropological level, avoids all dualism. The psychosomatic nature of the human person shows how much the factors that concern the body are important for the person as a whole. The impulse which everyone feels, even if at times this is implicit, to grow and to develop themselves, to mature, presupposes a certain harmony between these two dimensions of their nature. The need for an *adequate anthropology*, to take up an expression dear to John Paul II, is a requirement directed to us, independently of our adherence or otherwise to a given truth of revelation. The Christian vision undoubtedly has some features specific to itself, to the extent that it incorporates, theologically, every person in Christ. In this sense, health, for the Christian, is a notion that goes beyond the strictly medical understanding; it includes the totality of his being, including his psycho-spiritual dimensions.

Thus, the healthy person is not only someone who enjoys good physical or psychological health but someone who is in good spiritual health. The expression *sickness* is also used traditionally, in the context of spiritual accompaniment, to describe the recurrent causes of sin.[8]

---

8. Cf. J.-C. Larchet, *Thérapeutique des maladies spirituelles* (Paris: Ancre, 1983); B. Biju-Duval, *Le Psychique et le Spirituel*; Preface by J. Laffitte, (Paris: Émmanuel, 2001).

Health as an Ethical Issue: The Donation of Organs

That being so, attention to the spiritual dimension of the human being does not prevent Christian thought from developing a whole reflection on the strictly physical aspect of health; there, health defines the good or the optimal condition in that human beings may grow in those personal and social values which are theirs. It is a gift of nature but a gift that is not given to everyone, something which does not fail to provoke deep questions of a philosophical and theological kind. We cannot develop these questions here, but can only make mention of some of them: the meaning of infirmity, divine justice, the meaning of suffering, etc. The loss of health, otherwise called sickness, causes us to ask for the intervention of the doctor, to the extent that health is a true good of the person and a good of which the person is to take care. To this natural approach, an approach of good sense, Christian thought adds the conviction that sickness is not systematically foreign to the integral development of the person or at least that it is not *a priori* an obstacle to their development. In fact, there is a certain ambivalence in the experience of sickness; it can contribute to an over-all weakening of the person, but it can also offer the opportunity for the moral and spiritual growth of the subject, which furnishes him with a meaning of sickness, which is in harmony with the goods he is to enjoy in the future.

It must be noted that only a strictly utilitarian vision of society and of human relations can lead us to think that the sickness of a person is always and under all aspects a *deficit* at the social level.

The way Christ conducted himself towards the sick and towards sinners, which we have recalled briefly, is exemplary in terms of the attention directed to each of the persons involved in particular. We do not find generic declarations about health, pain, or cures (except for spiritual cures: almsgiving, fasting and prayer). Even when the crowds were present, the teachings were always expressed by way of the concrete experience of a personal encounter.

To conclude this second stage in our reflection, we can say that the attention of the Christian faith is concentrated upon the integral good of the human person, whether that person is in good health or is undergoing the trial of sickness. This attention to the person who is alive, who is suffering, and to the one who is doing well, is decisive for the understanding that the Church has of the art of medicine and of the ethical issues surrounding the question of health.

Health as an Ethical Issue: The Case of Organ Donation

From what has been said above, there arises a whole series of ethical implications: some concern the behaviour of the person in relation to his own health, others relate to actions undertaken with regard to the health of someone else. Here let us give a summary of the implications, from both perspectives, before moving on to illustrate our proposals for a given case, that of organ donation. The act of donating an organ, both medical and profoundly human at one and the same time, requires us, in fact, to examine the donation both from the point of view of the donor and from that of the recipient; thus, the question brings into play also a certain number of social dynamisms, such that the Church could not remain detached from the debate.

To the extent that it depends on them, all persons have the moral duty to do what is necessary to keep themselves in the best state of health possible. Yet, their concern over their health must remain within reasonable limits, thereby avoiding, on the one hand, that they turn their physical well-being into an absolute and, on the other, that they become negligent over the care that is necessary for the preservation of their health. In general terms, a precarious state of health places the sick person in a condition of dependence, not only with regard to the doctor, but also with regard to those close to them and with regard to society. If the sick person is conscious, he is sufficiently free to inform himself about the true state of his health and about the treatment that is necessary. This is his right and, in the majority of cases, it is also his duty. There are limits, though, to this freedom; the relationship between doctor and patient is grounded upon a relationship that is not merely contractual; it presupposes a disposition of trust, which often operates as a conditioning factor for the efficacy of the therapy.

Any one of us may find ourselves in a situation in which we are informed that we are suffering from an illness with an unfavorable prognosis; the concrete possibility of dying may lead us to reconsider our values, on the basis of a new hierarchy and of new criteria. Dying is a personal act, which cannot be reduced to the succession of physiological phenomena involved; in several traditions of spirituality, and in particular in Christianity, there is the sense of handing back one's existence to God. What is true in facing up to the foreseeable reality of the occurrence of one's own death, is true also of suffering, to which it is possible to give a meaning. In this respect, there has been no lack of effort by philosophy to offer an explanation, some approaches seeing a sense of individual or collective trial in suffering (Kierkegaard; Schopenhauer; Jewish philosophy in the last half-century), others a sense of punishment or of expiation (Dostoyevsky; Ricoeur).

Looked at as someone else's good, health is a political and a social issue; here the fundamental principle of the rejection of all discrimination towards the sick person prevails. This goes for access to medical care, of which no-one should be deliberately deprived, as also for treatments of which a sick person who is totally dependent may have need, for example, someone in a persistent or permanent vegetative state. This principle is grounded on the dignity inherent to every person, irrespective of their actual state of health. The respect due to the sick person requires that his freedom be respected within the reasonable limits of what he has a right to request. Corresponding to the right of the sick person to be informed about the treatments which are to be administered to him is the duty of the doctor to furnish him with this information, though in accordance with the criteria of prudence, which allow the doctor to judge whether, in the specific cases, communicating such a truth is really appropriate or not at the moment. The sick person's freedom, then, is not an absolute; he cannot ask the doctor, in a morally upright way, for something that the latter has no right to give: for example, in the case of a request for active euthanasia, whether this comes from society, from the family, or from the patient themselves. On its part, Christian medical ethics has recourse to two major principles, which are respect for the inviolable character of human life and respect of the dignity of the person of the sick individual.

These principles illuminate the problems involved in organ donation: although they take place concretely in the framework of medicine, the donation and the acquisition of an organ, constitutive parts of a medical act, are not reducible to that act alone. Rather, they represent a living reality that goes beyond the simple givens of a clinical and technical order, and involve questions of symbolic importance and of value, at the anthropological, ethical, social and theological levels.

The University of Osaka in Japan has recently presented a robot, endowed with incredible capacities, which are proper to human beings. With a feminine appearance, it can effect elementary gestures, such as moving the lips, the eyebrows, the arms, and the head and shoulders; it has a skin made of silicon, which hides a whole series of receptors, which ensure the coordination of the different parts of the body. Thanks to the expectations that it has aroused, the theme of robotics attracts ever more writers and filmmakers, who often produce representations of a world peopled by these humanoid beings, which can hardly be distinguished from human beings in flesh and bones. We can think of the famous film of Ridley Scott, *Blade Runner*, in which it seems that the "person" in the end is capable of feelings and sentiments that are typically human (remorse, sadness, pity). It would be easy to imagine such a "person" who could receive from another a spare part, to replace a defective part of his or her body, thus giving rise to a kind of organ donation between machines. Even were such a fiction to be possible, this attitude between two robots would be totally different from what is produced between two human beings through the experience of organ donation, especially if we think about the symbolic and anthropological values which surround this type of experience for human beings, bringing into play such different aspects as solidarity, altruism, suffering, and the eventual sensation of one's own death or of that of the other.

In order to understand organ donation in its complexity, as practised these days in almost all contemporary cultures, it is necessary first of all to understand that which concerns the anthropological structure of gift.

We must distinguish between organ donation coming from a living being and those coming *ex cadavere*. In organ donations between living persons, various elements of anthropology come into play: the perception that a person has of his own body, the feeling of physical diminution, and the desire to be really useful, are among the more important. When, however, it is a question of a donation coming from a cadaver, we are in the presence of other symbolic elements: the idea of our own death, the mourning of those close to us, the expression of our last wishes, to give a few examples.

Obviously, different systems of thought will refer to different criteria; from a purely *utilitarian* (and also from a *consequentialist*) perspective, the fundamental criterion of choice will be that of the outcome, independently of the intentions of the subject who undertakes these actions, of the means employed, and of the end of the action. The only criteria for practical action are those of efficiency and of effectiveness. Organ donation seems to be a positive act because it has as a consequence the important probability of saving a human life. *Opting-out* ("silence gives consent") is the most effective system for this, insofar as it is the system that ensures the greatest number of possible transplantations. This approach is nowadays very extensive, by virtue of the mentality that underlies it, which is inspired by the practical logic of the result.

As far as the *communitarian* approach is concerned, this gives priority to relations between persons and is very attentive to making the needs of the community the fundamental criterion of those choices that it would consider legitimate. In this model, the common good has priority over private interests; the *ethos* of public service is exalted. In relation to organ donation, communitarianism does not affirm an explicit duty for citizens to donate their organs, but it evokes kind of social responsibility, which would have every individual participate in the common good through the eventual donation of their organs, if this does not involve excessive risk or harm. Here, the *opting-in* system (not proceeding to transplantation except on the basis of the explicit agreement of the donor) would be favoured.

The more classical *deontological* approach of Kantian inspiration places the accent upon moral norms and on moral responsibilities demonstrated to be such through being universally valid. It emphasizes the sense of duty, understood as requiring adherence to objective moral norms, independently of circumstances or of other factors external to the act being undertaken. The *opting-in* system, applied to policies for seeking organs, is the one that most respects the principle of the non-manipulation of the donor.

The Christian vision of the world and of the person, without denying the value of other perspectives, attempts to unite a medical ethics, emerging from a long Hippocratic tradition, to an ethic of the virtues. This conception presumes a rediscovery of the natural law in the classical sense of the term (and not according to the physicalist caricature that is often presented). It places at the centre of attention the authentic good of the person and the person's complete fulfilment. The question that arises, then, is to know whether the donation represents a true good for the person. The finality involved in organ donation, undoubtedly, presupposes the necessary intention to do good, but it implies also the obligation to avoid doing what is wrong, which presupposes, for example, the prohibition of suppressing one life in order to help another or, indeed, of removing an organ from a non-consenting person. From such a perspective, it would not be possible to address the needs of a sick person by violating the true good of the person of the donor. The end does not justify the means. Thus, donating an organ is seen also as a good which is morally perfective of the person of the donor, made aware of the needs of the recipient, and disposed to provide this help, by making available the means required for this, to the extent that they are proportionate and are morally legitimate.

Let us look at the expression *donation of organs* and, in particular, at the meaning of the word *gift* or *donation*. An attitude of altruism is already present in Greek philosophy. As is indicated by the verb *khairein* (to rejoice), from which it comes, the word *kharis* points to a motive for joy and, by extension, to a favour or a gift. A gift is an action that brings it about that someone is enabled to benefit from a *kharis*, which is produced by a subject and is expressed by means of an object. Since, for the Greeks, everything that exists comes from a supreme source, which is represented by the gods, everything that causes the human heart to rejoice is thus a divine gift. For the poet, Homer, for the Greek dramatists, for Sophocles in particular, for Socrates, there is this conception of a supreme and original gift, a favour which the divinity makes to human beings and which expresses a divine *philia*. Insofar as this represents the life of all the members of the *polis*, the gift establishes bonds which are constitutive of *koinonia*; thus, it is connected to the common good and, in this sense, it is not foreign to the sphere of morality.

Later on, *kharis* becomes *gratia*, a term which carries a different meaning, depending upon whether it is used in a profane or in a sacred setting. For the Latins, and above all for Seneca, we find an understanding of gift in its most sacrificial sense, a gift which everyone can make to someone close to them or to someone unknown to them. In his *De Beneficiis*,[9] Seneca goes to the point of saying that the practice of bestowing gifts (*beneficia*) constitutes the most powerful bond in human society. For him, bestowing gifts represents what is essential in human relations; to the extent that, in his vision, a gift is a unilateral act, we have in

---

9. Seneca, *De Beneficiis*; I. IV, 2.

him the first rupture with the traditional concept of gift as something habitual or as ritual. It is for this reason that many have seen in Seneca the father of modern individualism.[10]

Nowadays, the debate over gift is marked by two opposing tendencies:

The first tendency in modern times is to deny the possibility of being able to make a donation of the kind understood in the Christian Tradition. In the gift, people would, no doubt, recognize a relationship of solidarity between the one making the donation and the one receiving it, but they would also recognize a relationship of superiority of the donor with regard to the beneficiary. In the famous study of Marcel Mauss (*Essai sur le don*, 1929), we find the most developed sociological and anthropological study on this subject. According to Mauss, a large number of societies were structured around an economy and a morality of gift, due to the fact that, in these societies, personal relations were predominant. Individuals and groups have an interest in showing themselves to be disinterested. People are pressed into making gifts because the action of giving places the beneficiary under an obligation.

The second tendency is represented above all by the Christian Tradition. Gift enters into what is constitutive of communion and can promote the development of an *ethos*. The person, created in the image and likeness of God, is bound to other human beings by the fact of their common origin. From the equality of this shared dignity derives the fact that relationships of a biological nature and familial relationships can be extended to a kind of relationship that is transfigured and spiritual, one which makes of the whole of the human species one family, within which the obligation of altruism is born. In the Protestant family, to take up the famous expression of Max Weber,[11] the concept of *a religious ethic of fraternity* makes out of every relationship with another

10. M. Henaff, *Le prix de la vérité. Le don, l'argent, la philosophie* (Paris: Seuil, 2002), pp. 337–339.
11. Max Weber, *The Protestant Ethic and the Spirit of Capitalism* (London: Allen and Unwin, 1931; London, New York: Routledge Classics, 2002).

human being a personal relationship. The communitarian experience of fraternity marks a necessary stage towards establishing a society, in which a universal goodness would be established in the future, which would make every person worthy of being considered the term of a self-giving love.

It will be helpful, now, to examine the two forms of organ transplantation on the basis of the source of these organs, from persons who are deceased and from persons who are alive.

Organs from Cadavers

In the case of taking organs *ex cadavere*, there are two ways of expressing consent; either from the person himself before his own death, or through a relative, if the person concerned has died before having given the slightest indication of his intention. To consent directly to the gift of one's own organs is what expresses to the fullest the meaning of gift in its most developed form, a decision which has matured within the intimacy of that person and which has been freely chosen. In such consent, there is present a certain idea that the person has of his own body and of his own death: full consciousness and recognition by the subject of the limits of his own existence.

In the case of consent expressed by a relative after the death of a dear one, account needs to be taken of the idea that they may have of the body of a person who is deceased, to whom they were particularly close; this body represents still, at the level of imagination, a bond with the deceased person. In the case of consent expressed by a dear one, the value present in the act of self-giving itself remains intact, to the extent that it is necessary that there be a deep acceptance of the death of the person who was loved, before being able to give consent for his organs to be removed. He consents, then, to a "physical diminuition" of the cadaver of the dear one, still perceived as a centre of presence of his or her being, a centre of life, of bonds of affection, of existential bonds, and as the bearer of meanings of great depth. To be able to overcome such feelings towards the lifeless body of a person who is loved, is only possible through a recognition in conscience of the need of another person and through the perception of a good which is recognized as a superior good.

A process of this kind, however, is a very arduous one; usually, we come up against the reticence of the family to giving consent to the removal of organs. The idea that it is possible to manipulate the body of the deceased person is sometimes resented as a lack of respect at a crucial moment, in which they are beginning to work through their mourning for their loved one. The cadaver is perceived in some way as still "belonging" to the family.

On May 14, 1956, Pope Pius XII, with a view to making relatives more sensitive on this point, addressed the Association of Cornea Donors and the Italian Union of the Blind in the following terms:

> It is necessary to educate the public and to explain, rationally and respectfully, the fact that giving consent, expressly or tacitly, to interventions which violate the integrity of the cadaver, in the interests of those who are suffering, does not constitute an offence against the duty which is to discharged towards a deceased person, if the reasons for this are particularly strong.[12]

Organs Removed from Living Persons

In medical practice, there exist these days numerous forms of organ donations from living persons, which involve a relatively reduced risk both for the donor and for the recipient. This is the case, clearly, with blood donation and with the donation of spinal marrow. In particular, the donation of blood is considered by now as a routine medical intervention, and it attracts large numbers of donors. As for the donation of bone marrow, by contrast, the procedure is more complex and the number of donations is much less significant, especially because of the difficulty of finding a donor compatible with the patient at the

---

12. Pius XII, *Allocution to the Association of Cornea Donors and to the Italian Union of the Blind* (May 14, 1956).

immunological level. There exists also a substantial difference between the two forms of obtaining the donation: to donate part of one's spinal marrow, in fact, requires hospitalization and an anaesthetic, general or local.

These forms of donation and other besides, such as the donation of a kidney, or part of the liver or part of a lung, make it possible to see with special clarity the value of the gift of self, of part of one's own body, for the good of another person and without any posing of conditions or requiring any benefit to oneself. Furthermore, in some cases, donations of this kind are sometimes carried out without there being any personal bond between the donor and the recipient; the one who decides to make a donation does so simply on the basis of the values present in the act itself, independently of any affective relationship with the person who, concretely, will benefit from this gift.

The donation of an organ aims at eliminating a deficiency in someone else; obviously, that is a good for the recipient, a good for his health, but the recipient becomes the beneficiary of an act that is altruistic and generous, through which he discovers and sees confirmed the fact that his healing and his health constitute an authentic good for society.

Through placing themselves at the service of the physical good of the sick person, donors discover a good that is their own moral good and, for this reason too, they wish to bring it to fulfilment. We have gone beyond simple justice here. The gift is an act of "doing good," an act of beneficence (a *beneficium*, Seneca would say).

In the gift there is a logic that presupposes the principle of asymmetry between the donor and the recipient; consequently, there is a disproportion between the gift that is made and the good that the recipient derives from it. The gift is prior. It cannot be derived.

Organ donation is located within the originary structure of the gift; at the beginning, we have a life, which we experience spontaneously as a gift that we have received. It is to be noted, first of all, that the expression *gift of self* is to be understood not in a literal sense but analogically. *Gift of self* can be understood in two ways; first of all, the expression denotes the offering of one's own life; in its second meaning, *gift of self* refers back to the object of the gift. The object of a gift can take on several forms. For example, someone may give up his own time, make himself available, give some of his most basic personal goods, he may place his own liberty at another's disposal, he may assume risks on someone else's behalf; in such a way, people may donate an organ.

In the case of the transplantation of organs, the object of the gift refers to a part of the body.[13] This part of the body, in a certain way, can be assimilated to an exterior good, in that the donor does not cease to be himself, after having donated his kidney or a part of his liver. The expression is ambiguous because here we find ourselves in a medical context, which specifies first of all the position of the recipient. We cannot examine more deeply here what basically it is that is the foundation of the medical act as such, but we recall that the doctor exercises his art by respecting the unity of the organism of the patient.

How, then, is the act of donating an organ to be defined; in what does it consist? The donor chooses to sacrifice his own physical integrity, to the *extent* that this act may save the life of another person. Hence, we are dealing with a good which is *proportionate*, simply because between the donor and the recipient we have one and the same human nature. Here the measure of the legitimacy of the *gift of self* is the health of the other; it is not a matter of an irrational act, of a romantic act, but of a concrete act that is also realistic. It is located within a finality that is strictly medical.

How can a transplant be the expression of a gift, in the sense that we have given to this word? It is not a question of adopting a religious or a philosophical position *a priori*, because it is in this

---

13. John Paul II: "As I have already had occasion to emphasize, in every transplantation of organs, there is generally, at its foundation, a decision of great ethical value; the decision to offer, without recompense, a part of one's own body, for the health and the well-being of another person" (August 29, 2000, (*Insegnamenti*, XXIII/ 2, 2000, p. 282).

way that people naturally perceive their own life; the life that we possess precedes all consciousness of self and hence precedes the taking of a personal position in regard to this original given. This life can give rise to various expressions of *self-gift*, the gift of organs is one of those. John Paul II wrote that the decision to offer a part of one's body, without recompense, has the characteristics of love:

> The nobility of this gesture resides in the fact that it is configured as an act of authentic love. We do not give simply something that belongs to us as our own, we give something of ourselves, insofar as, by virtue of its substantial unity with a spiritual soul, the human body cannot be considered solely as a totality of tissues, organs and functions ... but is a constitutive part of the human person, who manifests and who expresses himself or herself through that body.[14]

From this perspective, what is an organ? It is the instrument of the gift, not in itself, but in the service of the whole, of an organism.

No adequate counterpart to this gift is possible. In the world of interpersonal relations, which the philosopher, Levinas, liked to characterize by the expression *asymmetrical reciprocity*, the only gift that could be a response to the donation of an organ is that of gratitude. It is the gratuity of the gift, which elicits gratitude.

In the case of organ donations made by a living person, the perspective of the recipient must not be ignored. The latter necessarily assumes a sense of responsibility for the organ which has been received, usually being well aware that the donor will have had to accept a kind of diminution of his own state of health. This responsibility takes on particular importance in terms of his behaviour.

We have been able to show that the gift obeys a deep and fundamental tendency in the human heart. As with every moral value, it is possible that it may not be understood. It is certainly

---

14. *Ibid.*

not compatible with a certain utilitarian philosophical position, which sees in the human person a fundamentally egoistical being. Here, we hold that the true gift does exist and that it corresponds of its nature to a very deep aspiration in the human being. The donation of organs is morally justified when the subject has expressed his own consent to that donation, but, in the process which leads to the decision to donate an organ, there arises another level of reflection, which is that of its anthropological significance. If we wish to encourage this kind of gift, an effort must be made in terms of the formation and education of persons. The body of the human person can be considered neither as an object nor as an item to be bought and sold. It preserves its dignity, even after the person has died. Only the form of gift makes it possible to make use of the body, without denying the profound meanings of which it is the bearer. In this sense, the commercialization of human organs must be rejected.

The act in which the donation of organs consists is always the strong and natural symbolic expression of a form of love. Already, the apostle, St Paul spoke, by way of an image, of the love with which the faithful of Galatia had embraced him: "I bear witness to the fact that, if it had been possible, you would have gone to the point of tearing out your eyes, in order to give them to me" (Gal 4:15).

4 The Church's Concern for those Sick with Aids[1]

In the course of recent years, the epidemic of the immuno-deficiency virus, HIV, the cause of the acquired immuno-deficiency syndrome, AIDS, has continued to rage in various parts of the world, in particular in the continent of Africa. This has contributed to the fuelling of numerous debates about epidemiological measures, disputes that, unfortunately, have revealed a large number of ideological prejudices, fostered by what in truth is a very real ethical relativism.

The form of the epidemic and its various, specific social features have developed in the meantime, above all in sub-Saharan Africa. Up until the beginning of the 2000s, the population affected by the infection consisted mostly of celibate persons, generally young, who rapidly fell foul of the disease. Little by little, many of these young people became the object of treatments, more or less effective, which provided them with a survival time of some significance. Many of these then married, to the point where the number of couples who were HIV-discordant—namely, of whom one was HIV positive and the other negative—has increased notably. The possibility of children being born from these unions, who, in their turn, may be infected, explains why it is by now the case that it is HIV-discordant couples who are contributing the most to the diffusion of AIDS in sub-Saharan Africa, as the most recent statistics have

---

1. "The Church's Concern for those Sick with AIDS" is the version of a lecture delivered in English to the Bishops of Africa at Dar-es-Salam (Tanzania) on July 4, 2009 and published under the title «La solicitude de l'Église pour les maladies du sida. Sida, exercice de la sexualité, usage du préservatif dans et hors du mariage. La situation de l'Afrique subsaharienne» in *Studia Moralia*, n. 49/1, 2011, pp. 19–33.

shown;[2] today, one person in two with the infection lives in a couple.

It is understood that this situation poses challenges not only to the scientific community and to public authorities, but, beyond that, to pastors, catechists and all those who have the mission in the Church of teaching, educating, caring, and accompanying those affected. On many occasions, the bishops or even the episcopal conferences in Africa have intervened publicly, untiringly recalling the teaching of the Church in the areas of marriage, the family, and sexuality. The drama of AIDS raises two aspects of the problem, which cannot leave us indifferent. The first is the extreme poverty of the persons, of the couples, affected and of the families thrust into a situation of bearing great burdens, often including mourning; every Christian cannot but offer them the witness of the deepest compassion and express the very real proximity of the suffering Christ to those who are suffering, the sick, and also their dear ones. The second aspect consists in the ethical implications of interpersonal relations; the fact that the virus of this sickness is transmitted in the first place through sexual relations brings to the forefront the question of the exercise of the sexual faculty by persons who are part of an HIV-discordant couple; secondly, this fact poses the fundamental question of the ethics of conjugal and of family life. In fact, the means proposed by health authorities at various levels, of international organizations, and of NGOs, with a view to prevention, are often limited to the recommendation that a condom be used in relations between the couples, thus raising moral and spiritual questions which we will address further on. The Church makes heard another message. Her concern extends to all areas of the lives of the persons for whom she is responsible, the area of health, to be sure, but those of the moral and the spiritual domains as well. This she does in the name of

---

2. B. L. Guthrie et al., 2007, and D. De Walque, 2007. (Translator's note: the statistics quoted in this article were those valid at the time it was written in the original French.)

her conception of the dignity of the person and of the high esteem that she has for human love and for its expression in marriage. She does this also in the name of the mission that is hers, to teach in the name of Christ what is good for man (and for woman).

It is this perspective that is illustrated by the words spoken by our Holy Father, Benedict XVI, at the moment of his departure for his visit to Africa in March of 2009. In response to a question about the way we should combat AIDS, the Pope gave this very precise response:

> I would say that this problem of AIDS cannot be overcome on the basis of advertising slogans alone. If there is no soul, if Africans do not help themselves, this plague cannot be resolved through the distribution of condoms; on the contrary, the risk is that the problem will get worse. The solution can only be found in a two-fold commitment: the first is in the humanization of sexuality, that is to say, in a spiritual and human renewal, which entails a new way of behaving towards each other, and, secondly, a real friendship also and, above all, towards those persons who are suffering, the readiness, even at the cost of personal sacrifices and giving up other things, to be at the side of those who suffer.

A simple and honest reading of these lines shows the extent to which all the essential aspects of the question are to be found in this response: the humanization of sexuality (there are the expressions: *if there is no soul*, or again, *spiritual and human renewal*); active compassion towards the sick; finally, a consideration of the methods. Without soul, without the humanization of sexuality, technical means alone (slogans in advertising, the distribution of condoms) are not suitable means for the resolution of this plague; there is even a *risk* (the prudence of this term is to be noted) of making the problem worse. In summary, this response of the Holy Father offers us an ethical and a spiritual consideration of sexuality and a consideration of an epidemiological nature, formulated, it may be said in passing, in very moderate terms. It seems to me that it will be interesting now to enter into this double perspective in more detail, in order to examine in turn the epidemiological data, then HIV-discordant couples, in their anthropological and ethical dimensions. Finally, we shall address an aspect that is often forgotten, that of the action of pastors, prudential action which does not belong to the public debate, and that we shall examine, in particular, in the context of extra-conjugal relations.

Some Data

It will be helpful to recall here, very briefly, certain statistics which are well known: in November, 2007, the number of adults sick (15 years of age and over) with AIDS, living in sub-Saharan Africa, was 22.5 million out of 33.2 million in the world, namely 68%. The same percentage, 68%, in that same year was the figure for the number of adults, of 15 years and over, who had been newly infected (1.7 million out of 2.5 million in the world). The rate of its prevalence in adults from 15 to 49 years of age was of 5%, against 0.8% in the world. The number of those deceased, putting adults and children together, reached 1.6 million in sub-Saharan Africa, namely 78% of those deceased throughout the world (2.1 million).

Another point of note, 61% of the sick are women. In 2005, the rate of prevalence superseded 15% in eight southern African countries: Botswana, Lesotho, Mozambique, Namibia, South Africa, Swaziland, Zambia and Zimbabwe.

Since the 2000s, the creation of the PREFAR Programme the President's Emergency Plan for AIDS Relief, under the aegis of the United Nations (UNAIDS), has consisted in the distribution of generic medicines, to treat persons infected; in 2007, only 23% of the sick had had access to this programme of anti-retroviral therapy (ART), namely hardly a quarter of those affected. Yet, a programme like this did enjoy real success in certain countries:

Botswana, Kenya, Malawi, Namibia, Rwanda, South Africa, Uganda and Zambia. It would be important, then, both to extend the number of countries covered by this programme and also to ensure, in countries with existing coverage, that this is durable. The sums of money for programmes to combat AIDS reached 8.9 milliards (American: billions) of dollars in 2007, which is not negligible, but the discrepancy between the resources requested and those available has passed in three years (2005 to 2007, inclusive) from 2.8 milliards of dollars to 8.1 milliards. The figures which I have quoted come from UNAIDS.

Some remarks are in order. Seen at the global level, the epidemic has lost some of its vigour and has levelled out. In the last four years (translator's note: to 2009), the rate of infections has fallen. The reason for this is the wider availability of the ART treatments in rich countries, which, as I shall explain later on, has not been without its impact upon prevention. In Africa, as everyone knows, in countries where policies have been adopted which have relied almost exclusively upon the use of the condom, the results have been poor (South Africa, for example). By contrast, in countries where a more balanced preventative policy has been established (ABC), aimed first of all at changing behaviour (through the reduction of the number of partners, deferring the age when people engage in their first sexual relationships, encouraging exclusivity in loving relationships, being *faithful*), results have been much better (Uganda, Kenya, Tanzania). These claims are not based on data from specifically Christian contexts, but they are scientific data, recognized also by those entities that do not have *a priori* ethical objections to the use of condoms.[3]

Looking at matters schematically, there are three possible approaches to preventative measures which can be distinguished:

---

3. Cf., for example, the Report of Edward C. Green, Harvard Center for Population and Development Studies and the article he has published: *If Pope Benedict Were Right?*

- methods which go to the source of the infection and which concern themselves, as a consequence, with behaviour; changing habits, education in self-mastery;
- methods aiming to contain the epidemic: that is the use of prophylactics, masculine (condoms) or feminine, to which are to be added the use of various vaginal creams, called 'microbicides' (which kill spermatozoa); sometimes these means are combined, as with condoms coated in such a cream;
- and, finally, the third method; it would be a vaccine.

The unilateral manner in which prevention based mainly upon the use of the condom has been encouraged, at least by the media in rich countries, requires that, to conclude this first section, we examine now the question of the efficacy of such means, a question which has given rise to polemical debates.

To be able to respond to this question, it will be useful to keep in mind the distinction between *perfect* (or ideal) *use* of a method and its *typical* (or actual) *use*. The statistics published in the 1990s[4] speak of a rate of HIV-conversion of from 0 to 1.14%, but they relate to stable couples, who are faithful, who do not suffer from any genital infection and in which the infected spouse was faithful to his or her treatment, and who have had no further infection after the initial contagion. It is commonly agreed nowadays that, in the case of *perfect usage*, the condom prevents the transmission of HIV in 95% of cases (with 5% risk in the case of each act undertaken).[5] Out of a sample of a hundred persons, the number of those who will be infected after ten years of so-called 'protected' intercourse is estimated also at 5%. Very obviously, everything changes when we examine the statistics for *typical usage* of a condom, namely in those conditions which are normal and real. In the latest edition of the Cochrane Database Review,[6] the mean which was calculated, starting from 4709

---

4. De Vincenzi, 1994, Nicolasi, 1995.
5. N.S. Padian, 2008.
6. S. Weller, K. Davis, *Preventive Medicine* (Galveston, TX: University of

initial references, concluded that there was an *effectiveness* of 80% in the reduction in HIV-conversion in heterosexual relations (the study makes it clear, amongst other things, that it is not speaking of *efficacy*, because this does not enter into consideration when it is a question of knowing whether the use made in each sexual act was correct or not). To make things clearer, a woman who had relations with a man who was HIV-positive, according to this detailed study, would have a 20% chance of being contaminated at the end of one year. After ten years, this occurrence would become a probability of over 80%! According to a study by these same authors in 1999, the typical use of a condom, examined in HIV-discordant couples results in an incidence of sexual transmission of HIV of 6.8%. Common sense helps us to understand that it cannot be expected that typical use will be transformed into perfect use, in order to ensure the future of HIV-discordant couples. This is true everywhere, but it goes especially for those persons living in sub-Saharan Africa. From the epidemiological point of view alone, it is preferable to advise couples who are HIV-discordant to abstain from having sexual relationships rather than to invite them to have recourse to the use of a condom, which (statistically) will betray them in about 20% of cases.

Finally, for the record, we note that there is a lower risk of infection in the cases of men who have been circumcised. From this fact, it has sometimes been deduced that circumcision could enter into the methods of prevention.

HIV-Discordant Couples: An Anthropological and Ethical Dimension

The use of a condom does not leave the nature of the conjugal act intact, insofar as, of its very nature, it brings about a separation of the two dimensions, which are inseparably linked in that act, those of union and of procreation. Obviously, with two spouses, of whom one if infected by the virus and who decides to use the condom, a contraceptive intention does not always exist (it could

---

Texas Medical Branch).

exist, when there is present the will not to conceive a child, which would have a certain possibility of being contaminated). Let us take the hypothesis, on the other hand, of two spouses who have a real love for life, who have been able to demonstrate this through their readiness to accept children in the spirit in which the Church holds is morally correct. They could find themselves with a subjective disposition of wishing to exercise the conjugal good, to express sincerely their love by means of gestures which, normally, express their right and their duty to unite themselves to each other (*jus et debitum ad copulam*). The decision that they take to use a condom could be motivated, at the level of their intention, by the sole need to avoid contagion by the virus. Besides, they could have chosen to come together in the present circumstances in order to safeguard and to consolidate the goods of their conjugal love (fidelity, avoiding intemperance, etc.). The moral problem posed by undertaking the conjugal act in these specific circumstances does not concern their intention, which could be perfectly good. The question concerns the means chosen: a condom; the problem consists in asking ourselves whether that act is morally licit, independently of the correct intention of the spouses. In this choice, it is probable that spouses, acting in good faith, in their imperfectly formed conscience, do not see any moral difficulty. Hence, the need for them to be accompanied, to give them advice in a delicate way, with prudence, respect, and in an attentive manner.

At the theoretical level, the judgment about the means chosen cannot but be negative. It is true that the separation between the two meanings, unitive and procreative, of the conjugal act, of which *Humanae Vitae* (§ 12) speaks, had been formulated in the context of a magisterial teaching (it may be said, in passing, of the infallible ordinary magisterium) on contraception. In our hypothesis, it is not a matter of contraception. Nevertheless, the fundamental reason why *Humanae Vitae* had declared the use of any means which sought to render the conjugal act deliberately infecund (§ 11, and 14) was exactly the separation between the two indissoluble dimensions of union and of procreation, independently of any right intention on the part of the spouses. The incision in *Humanae Vitae* (§ v14) *whether as an end or as a means*, demonstrates that the intention of the spouses could be perfectly upright, but, nevertheless, the goodness of that intention could not make good an action which *per se* and *in se* was morally illicit. The inseparability of union and of procreation characterizes the true nature of the conjugal act; when the unitive and the procreative dimensions of that act are separated by a deliberate act, the conjugal act is in some way *de-natured*, however much the intention of the spouses may be an upright one.

At the level of the acting person, the two spouses who use the condom to avoid the contagion (and for other good reasons, already mentioned) in order to be able to unite themselves, perform an act which is not of itself a conjugal act, whose nature is being respected. Let us recall that, according to the definition given in *Humanae Vitae* (§ 12), a conjugal act is an act, which "by its own intimate character, while it associates the husband and the wife in the closest bond, also makes them suitable for generating new life, according to laws inscribed in the nature itself of man and of woman." John Paul II often used the expression the *ontological truth of the conjugal act*, for example, in his "Catechesis on Human Love," to characterize this structural openness to generation (which does not mean necessarily an actual disposition on the part of the organism on the physiological level). In the case with which we are concerned, we have an act of a sexual nature, perhaps invested with values of an individual and subjective kind of sincere tenderness, but which is an act which cannot be said to be *conjugal* in the sense that the Church gives to that expression.

The choice cannot be justified for the therapeutic reasons referred to in *Humanae Vitae* (§ 15), which concern the contraceptive pill, used medically at times to treat certain conditions (the regularization of the female cycle, for example), the reason being that the condom is not a therapeutic means. It neither cures any illness, nor offers anything other than a very imperfect protection, as we have already seen above, at the preventative level. The fact that it is claimed that this possible preventative function, even if imperfect, would fall under the intention of *Humanae Vitae* does not seem to be a claim that is rigorously grounded, nor does it constitute an acceptable reading of this section of Paul VI's encyclical. In fact, when Paul VI used the phrase *as an end or as a means*, he extended his negative judgment to acts which were not specifically motivated by a contraceptive intention, but which might be undertaken by spouses for good reasons, for serious motives (*justae causae*), to defer or even to avoid a possible pregnancy, with foreseeably damaging consequences. Among these *justae causae* could figure a serious reason of a medical nature. Such a reason, which would render legitimate deferring or avoiding a further pregnancy, and which could even make this a moral duty, would not thereby make legitimate performing an act which deliberately sought to separate the two dimensions, the unitive and the procreative, of the conjugal act.

Thus, a criterion exists which is decisive at the moral level; it is the objective intentionality of the choice of an act, which someone proposes to perform *hic et nunc*, something which is inscribed in the object of that act, as *Veritatis Splendor* put it (§ 78). Two spouses who wish to use a condom to avoid infection from a contagious virus (here AIDS) are prepared to perform an act, whose objective intentionality is the objective separation, by means of this barrier method, of the two inseparable dimensions normally present in the specific act which unites the two spouses, making them one flesh (*una caro*). In this sense, and certainly without judging the persons concerned, it can be said that such an act in itself does not belong to those conjugal acts, which express the virtue of conjugal chastity.

Pastors of souls, spiritual directors, and those who accompany people pastorally are concerned for those persons. Naturally, in the exercise of this service, they are called to enter into the distinction between moral alternatives that may be available, in cases of HIV-discordant spouses, to the spouse who is infected and to the one who is healthy. There can be no doubt that the HIV-positive spouse must certainly give up conjugal relations in order not to expose to the contagion the spouse who is healthy. Already, at the epidemiological level, we may note that such a duty of prudence and of respect for the life of another person exists, even before any attention is given to whether or not the use of a condom is involved. As far as the healthy spouse is concerned, without entering here into cases of the kind which would bring into question specific problems relating to the *bonum pacis* or to pressure from one of the spouses, or to any other serious constraint, which would raise issues in the prudential order, the classical principle remains valid, according to which no one may dispose of his own life, especially for the sake of a precarious peace, founded upon the acceptance of an act, which on the part of the infected spouse, would be gravely illicit by putting in danger the life of his or her healthy partner. We take note of the fact that, in general, it is estimated that the proportion of HIV-discordant couples who spontaneously choose to forego the exercise of the sexual faculty is up to 50%. This sacrifice is motivated by the natural love for the other spouse and for the children already born, in that they do not wish to take the slightest risk of making them orphans.

For the sake of completeness, it will be helpful to say a word about HIV-discordant couples who wish to have a child. The desire to have a child, within a properly married couple, is in itself legitimate, because the coming into existence of a child is always a good in itself. A married couple cannot be prohibited, *a priori*, from procreating; that would be an abuse and also a contradiction in respect of what is taught by Christian ethics. What would the situation be at the epidemiological level? It is known that, in an HIV-discordant couple, in which the wife is HIV-positive, the risk of the transmission to HIV to a future child is one in 25% if the woman has not been treated. If the wife is treated appropriately (if the viraemia has become negative), the risk is lower than 0.5%. The child who, despite everything, would be born HIV-positive, would be subjected immediately to a treatment, which, nowadays is held to be effective. It would be somewhat analogous to the situation of parents who know that they have a very low probability, but not one that is non-existent, of transmitting a hereditary disease to a future child. In general, they would be advised not to conceive, but a strict duty is not imposed upon them (if this were to be done, we would be in a situation of pure eugenics). Thus, it must be said that the decision belongs to the parents, who must be properly informed. It is clearly understood that, in such a situation, all the counsels of prudence, which have already been expressed for HIV-discordant couples in general, remain valid in a very special way with regard to the responsibilities of future parents, which the spouses intend to assume.

To bring this point to a conclusion, uniting sexually is the implementation of a choice, which always carries with it issues of a moral nature. When two spouses find themselves in the situation described (of being HIV-discordant), there is always an alternative available to them, that of not engaging in the conjugal act. If they abstain, they do so for the reason of a grave necessity, that of safeguarding the health of the healthy spouse and in order not to subject their love to an expression that would be unsuitable with regard to conjugal chastity. This is not a choice that they find naturally easy; in some cases, it may be a matter of a choice that is truly heroic, and which is inspired by a profound conjugal love. Nevertheless, the very fact that this alternative exists and that there exist, in fact, couples who make that choice, demonstrates that the use of a condom cannot be recommended as morally upright when one of the two spouses is infected by the AIDS virus.

The human values, affective and spiritual, which are present in the choice of the spouses to abstain in a situation of risk of the infection indicated presupposes an accompaniment, grounded in respect and in pastoral prudence. Such assistance, obviously, is very personal and can be expressed only with difficulty outside of a true journey of conjugal spirituality.

Here are a few possible ways forward:

- A hope can be transmitted to the spouses, which is rooted in the capacity of their love to be able to express itself also by means of such a choice of abstention. This capacity is inscribed within the perspective of a love that includes the singular gift of sacrificing the exercise of the sexual faculty. In a broader fashion, love can be put to the test in many ways in the common life of the spouses, in suffering, mourning, sickness, accidents, etc. There are various cases in which love finds the power to sacrifice the good of sexual union, for the good of the partner or for that of the children who have already been born.
- They can be told that their sacramental union includes a personal bond with the sufferings of Christ.
- It can be explained to them that illicit sexual acts would not offer them a morally good means to confront the specific trial they are facing of AIDS. In a discrete and delicate manner, they could be invited to prudence in their gestures and manifestations of affection, because the choice made presupposes the use of prudent means, in order for it to be carried out in a persevering way.
- Since the choice represents a true journey of sanctification, appropriate spiritual means (accompaniment, the Word of God, community life, and the sacramental life) should be proposed to them.

For the sake of real completeness, it will be useful to say a word about young people who would wish to marry and where one of the fiancés is HIV-positive. There is general agreement that these young people should be dissuaded from marrying, even when the healthy fiancé is insistent. The conditioning of the future life of the spouses by this sickness is such that the real difficulties that await them cannot be hidden from the two fiancés.

Extra-Conjugal Relations

Pastors are not only challenged by the sad situation of HIV-discordant couples. Even if more rarely, it can happen that they may also be asked about such issues at times by persons who are not married, but who have a sexual relationship with each other that, by definition, is morally illicit and who, in the context of the risk of a contagion, for one reason or another, seek some justification for them to use the condom in their situation. Even though, at the level of simple morality, they are aware of being in a situation that is immoral, they think that using a condom will serve to avoid an even greater evil. It can be understood that the Christian who accompanies them, whose opinion on this matter is requested, may be inclined to think that, in this case, the use of the condom might serve to avoid an even greater moral disorder (the risk of AIDS, or the conception of a child outside of marriage).

All the arguments from reason that have been used in the context of accompanying married persons (HIV-discordant couples) remain valid here too: personal responsibility with regard to one's own health, the absolute duty not to expose a partner to a grave risk of contagion, the persistence of a real risk, even if attenuated, in a so-called "protected" relationship. The only case that we could imagine would be that of a person with behaviour that is at risk, who knows that he or she is infected and who, not wishing (or not being able) to give up the exercise of the sexual faculty personally here and now, would not wish to infect his or her healthy partner, who, in their turn, fully informed of the risk they are running, wishes to have a sexual relationship with that person. As can be seen, we find ourselves here in a situation of the pure casuistry of evil. The Church has no duty to establish a system of casuistry for immoral actions, trying to imagine in advance all sorts of disordered situations. Faced with a person whose conduct would be at risk and who would not be led to decide to change his or her personal pattern of behaviour, despite all the reasonable arguments which might be put forward, she does not have the vocation to indicate in a systematic fashion to such a person the least dangerous way possible of acting. If someone accompanying such a person were to be asked, this would certainly be with the concern first of all to protect that person's partner.

It seems to me to be of primordial importance here to insist on this particular and delicate point, which raises the question of what constitutes a prudential action. In such a case, the Church can only act at the strictly individual and prudential level and can never do so publicly. She can act through the spiritual accompaniment of a person, for example, of a person with habitual difficulties, who might wish sincerely to be able to escape from this personal situation of slavery (of sexual promiscuity, for example), without having the psychic capacity to do so (whatever the pathology involved might be), but still being sufficiently determined in his intention to be accompanied and assisted also at the spiritual level (besides, obviously, a therapy of a psycho-medical nature).

It is the charity of Christ which impels the Church, in this way, to go in search of the lost sheep, however far away they may be, just as it is the same charity of Christ, which causes her to teach everything that is good for every single one of them, the beauty of their vocation to love and the greatness of the call to holiness.

Finally, it will be useful to distinguish different levels of responsibility involved, according to where people are from the point of view of the personal freedom of the individual and of the responsibilities of the political and health authorities. The perspective for assessing responsibilities in relation to political or to health authorities is that of the *common good*. It is impossible to elaborate on this aspect here, nor is it possible to give a complete list of the criteria of judgment, which should direct a possible participation of Christians in the public debate. For the questions which concern us, it seems to me possible to say that Christians and, in particular their pastors, quite apart from giving witness to their faith, are right to express the Christian approach to those issues, the relevance and the rational nature of which we have tried to explain. As for what specifically regards the struggle against AIDS, they are right to require of the public authorities that they act with justice, in terms of access for all (men and women) to the treatments they need and, finally, concerning prevention, that they give honest and serious attention to proposing abstinence to the sick, in which the good of the persons concerned and the common interest of the populations meet together.

5 Is There a Christian Way to Die?
Ars Pagana et Ars Christiani Moriendi[1]

> *Our life is short and dreary; nor is there any relief when man's end comes, nor is anyone known who has come back from Hades. By chance we came to birth and after this life, we shall be as if we had never been. The breath of our nostrils is a puff of smoke, reason a spark from the beating our hearts; put this out and the body returns to ashes, and the spirit melts away like idle air.*
>
> Wisdom 2:1–3

The Book of Wisdom attributes a conception of life such as this to the wicked, but to this it opposes the fate of the just, those whose hope is rich in immortality:

> The souls of the virtuous are in the hands of God, No torment shall ever touch them. In the eyes of the unwise, they did appear to die, their going looked like a disaster, their leaving us like annihilation, but they are in peace (Wis 3:1–4).

From these two irreconcilable positions, there follow two ways, also opposed one to the other, of confronting death. The martyr would appear to be the illustration of the extreme limit of what could be perhaps a legitimate way of dying. It designates the *ars christiana moriendi par excellence*, which has marked out two thousand years of Christianity with a mass of witnesses and which has enriched Christian thought, from the letters of St Paul to the most recent texts of the Magisterium. Thus, the encyclical, *Veritatis Splendor*, itself sees in the act of martyrdom the affirm-

---

1. "Is there a Christian Way to Die? *Ars Pagana et Ars Christiana Moriendi*" was published under the title «Ars pagana et ars christiana moriendi» in *Anthropotes*, n. 13/2, 1997, pp. 273–295.

ation of the inviolable nature of the moral order, in which is reflected at one and the same time the holiness of the Law of God and the inviolability of the personal dignity of the human being created in the image and likeness of God.[2] The text recognizes in this act that attitude which is coherent with the witness given to moral truth. There have been very many who have preferred the sacrifice of their lives to the violation of the moral Law. The text recalls the case of Susanna, who judged it preferable to fall into the hands of her accusers, rather than to sin in the sight of the Lord (Dn. 13:22–23); John the Baptist, who was himself the precursor of the Messiah, even to the point of martyrdom (Mk. 6:17–29); Stephen and James, who died as martyrs in order to confess the faith and to avoid denying the Master (Acts 6:8–7.60; 12:1–2). In this sense, the sacrifice of one's own life operates as the witness to the truth of a message. To die for the moral truth is the expression of a life that belongs already to the truth and which is handed back to God, Source of all truth and of all good.

In order to illustrate a choice of this kind, it is noteworthy that the first lines of the spiritual testament of Fr Christian-Marie de Chergé, written a short time before his kidnapping and assassination with six of his brother Cistercians from the monastery of Notre Dame de l'Atlas at Tibhérine, rightly insists upon the fact that his existence belonged already to God:

> If it happens to me, some day—and it could be today—that I fall a victim to the terrorism which seems at present to wish to encompass all the foreigners living in Algeria, I would wish my community, my Church, my family, to remember that my life had been *given*[3] to God and to this country. That they accept that the sole Master of my whole life would not have been able to remain extraneous to this brutal departure. That they pray for me: how could I be found worthy of such a sacrifice?[4]

---

2. Cf. John Paul II, *Veritatis Splendor*, § 92.
3. Emphasis in the original.
4. Cf. *Documentation Catholique*, 2140 of June 16, 1996, p. 588.

What follows here seeks to bring out the understanding of death that is the presupposition for the choice of every martyr; this will be done by way of contrast after having examined another approach, one which denies any intelligibility and hence any hope to this decisive event. The move from one approach to the other does not claim to satisfy all the demands of logic, legitimate as these are.[5] Between what is finite and what is eternal, between what is inescapable and what is predestined, between rebellion and obedience, there is indeed an absolute discontinuity and the distance of an insuperable abyss. The vision of faith, which is witnessed in the choice of martyrs, expresses the certitude that such an abyss has been broken by the historical event of the death of Christ and by the new specification that this has given to the death of every human being.

Ars Pagana Moriendi: The Common Condition and Fragments of Meaning

Since it is the inevitable expiration that everyone must confront, death is something both of universal and of deeply personal significance. From the outset, this first paradox should be noted: namely, that at the collective level of human societies, death has engendered attitudes—of fear of spirits, worship of ancestors, funeral rites—which already imply that a particular position has been taken. If it is right to honour those who have preceded us in

---

5. "And whether it is the one or the other, whether it be being made eternal acquired from the lofty struggle of a figure which is destined to disappear, or pure and simple failure, from these fragments of sense, at the level of what is finite, can we conclude to a fulfilment through a destiny that is eternal? The development of a reasoning, which would come to this conclusion, has been attempted unceasingly and with passion in religious and philosophical thought. But, more often than not, has this not been at the price of an abusive extension of logic, which makes the leap from the earthly plane, which cannot be recovered, to that of an eternity in which we hope or to that of a new avatar of reincarnated life?"; H.U. von Balthasar *La Dramatique divine (Theodramatik)*, vol. III, *L'Action* (Namur: Culture et Vérité, 1996), p. 456.

death and to keep their memory alive in a kind of cosmic continuity, if the relationship with those who have departed has been the object of an exclusive responsibility entrusted through initiation rites to castes of sorcerers and of priests, if, in the end, the habit of giving a burial to the deceased marks a decisive step in civilization, this is because there exists, at least in so-called primitive societies, a kind of consensus about the reality of a becoming after death, whatever may be the form that this may take. In the primitive cult of the dead, there is postulated the possibility of a relationship which may be pursued after death between the visible world and the world of the spirits. It is not important here to be able to know whether the permanence of this relationship between the two is orientated towards ritual actions of a beneficent or of a maleficent kind for those who are living; we need only to recognize that, at the collective level, the death of others marks a real rupture but not a total disappearance of the subjects. What is presupposed as the fate of the deceased within tribes, clans and families is the continuity, in another form, of an existence, which has only been transformed.

From Primitive Cults to Philosophical Questioning

Such a conception, common to the totality of primitive societies, precedes all personal questioning, essentially not only of a religious but also and predominantly of a philosophical kind,[6] by each one about their own death. To be sure, there is no linear continuity between these two relationships to death, the collective-religious and the personal-philosophical. Between the two, it would be helpful to give a summary of the different

---

6. When the relationship to death is limited to the duties of the community to honour its dead, we are still in the domain of the religious or at least of the *sacrum*; when it becomes a personal questioning about one's own future becoming, inevitably bound to this horizon, it is transformed into a philosophical problem. It would be interesting to show how each philosophical system, by reason of its choice for or its refusal of a metaphysics, has its own implicit or explicit presuppositions for the position it takes on death itself.

mythical models of the very first intervention of death in the destiny of human beings; the fall of the gods, violations of a taboo, vengeance on the part of the gods against the realms of hell. Myths are attempts to provide an explanation for the coming of death into the midst of the living. Thus, they act like a natural preparation for later developments in philosophical reflection upon death.

If we exclude, for the moment, the contribution of the Old Testament literature, in which the mortal destiny of human beings is clearly linked to original sin, we must await the reflections of the Greek philosophers for death to appear as the object of their questioning, a topic which is hardly raised in Aristotle, who barely seems to take a position on the matter, other than to retreat behind the commonly-held opinion, according to which an unworthy line of descendants and a dishonourable primogeniture are not unconnected to the deaths of ancestors. However, the author of the *Nichomachean Ethics* adds, also, that the good or bad conduct of the living cannot have any influence, not in any case, upon the happiness or unhappiness of the dead. Happiness is the fate, the end and the sanction of a virtuous life, but the question of knowing whether this happiness is durable beyond death seems to be hidden from us.[7]

---

7. "Thus, can we not call another person happy any longer, as long as he is still alive, and will we have to await his end, as Solon says, before doing so? And, if we have to accept this position, would it be necessary to say that a person is not happy until he or she is dead? Now, is such an affirmation not absurd, especially for us who say that happiness is an activity? And, if, on the other hand, we do not call happy the one who is dead, and if it is not that that Solon intends, but rather than we can hold a person happy only when they are out of reach of misfortune and of wrong-doers, well such a position can be a matter for discussion. In fact, it is a matter of common opinion that there is good and evil for the dead, as well as for the living person who is not aware of it; for example, honour or dishonor, success or lack of success of one's children or of one's descendants in general, but, even there, we come up against the following difficulty: someone who has always lived happily and who dies in the same way can have descendants who are subjected to all kinds of different fates, according to the life which they have deserved. It is clear that descendants, as their

Very different is the very fruitful, Platonic doctrine on this specific point, which has interpreted death as the separation of soul and body. The immortality of the former and the inevitable corruptibility of the latter lead to the idea of thinking of death in a purely spiritual sense of liberation. This becomes the great issue of life, the subject matter itself of philosophy[8] and even the heart of ethics, if it is held that living well is to prepare for death. Furthermore, whatever reading may be given to the conflict between Plato and Protagoras,[9] the problem of death becomes a question of the substance of religion to the author of the *Laws*: "For us, I think the divinity must be the measure of all things, to the highest degree, and much more so than man, as some people claim."[10]

From Socrates to Seneca

Obviously, it is with the person of Socrates that there appears an approach to death, which gives to this event a fulness of meaning. In the *Apology of Socrates*,[11] all the great topics are present, which

---

generations proceed, can be very different from their elders. Undoubtedly, it would be absurd if the fate of the dead person were to change on the basis of their descendants and if he or she were to become happy or unhappy in correspondence to their situation" (Aristotle, *Nichomachean Ethics*; 1,1 10,1100a, 13, 1100a, 29).

8. "All those who concern themselves with philosophy....in truth concern themselves with nothing other than dying and being dead [...] Those who philosophise occupy themselves directly with dying." Plato, *Phaedon*, 64 a and c. cf. G. Bof, art.' Morte' in *Diz. Teol. Interdisc.* (Marietti, 1977), p. 607.

9. Plato asks Protagoras, the sophist, who claims that the person is the measure of all things, "Why did he choose the human being as the measure of all things rather than piglets or cynocephali?" (*Theaetetus*, 2, 161c). As Boutroux observes, there are two ways of understanding the term "measure," in a relative sense and in an absolute sense; in this latter sense, it would have to be understood to mean that things exist only to the extent that they are perceived by human beings (E. Boutroux, E. Leçon XI bis in *Leçons sur Platon*, given in 1878–1879 at the Ecole Normale Supéieure (Paris: Ed. Universitaires, 1990), p. 93.

10. Id.*Laws*, IV, 716c.

11. Id.*Apologie de Socrate*, (Paris: Ed. Delaloin, 1829); the numbers in brackets in the text refer to this edition.

will not cease to inspire not only all subsequent thinkers, but even more the most influential among the ancient tragedies. We will highlight some of the more important features; some will be found again in the Christian attitude of the martyr:
- witness to the truth and witness of the truth:

    I have been condemned not for lack of words, but ... for not having been willing to say to you what you would have liked to have heard (170)

    I leave, condemned by you to death, and they are condemned by the truth in their vice and their injustice; I stand ready for the punishment which has fallen upon me, and they for theirs (171).

- the judgment of posterity

    I tell you then, Athenians, you who have brought my death warrant, that you will receive immediately a punishment more terrible than the one you have inflicted upon me ... The number of those who condemn you will increase ... If you think that, by putting a man to death, you will prevent others from telling you that your conduct is depraved, you are very sadly mistaken. (173)

- the judgment of the gods:

    If death is like an exit from this world to pass to another and if everything people say is true, that, after death we all live in the same place, what is preferable, o Judges? If someone, a descendant in the kingdom of Pluto, considers himself thereby delivered from these people who pride themselves in knowing how to render justice and if they find there their real judges, who, it is said, judge the souls in this other world, Minos, Radamanthys, Aeacus, Triptolemus and all the demi-gods who were just during their lives, would he lose anything by this change? As for me, I would die happily a thousand times, if it were thus ... The inhabitants of that world (the kingdom of Pluto) would certainly not condemn me to death after such an examination; for, among the other advantages which

> makes them happier than people here below, they enjoy a life which is immortal, always, if what is stated is true (181).
>
> For the rest, O Judges, we must be full of hope in our approach to death, we must not be concerned about anything but about this one truth, that nothing can be harmful for a person who is good, living or dead, and that the gods never forget that (189).

Here what must be underlined is the conviction of Socrates that there is a justice beyond death and that there is retribution for human actions. A connection is made between the immortal life of the demi-gods and the fact that they were just during their lives. In this way, justice unites together those who have been just in the kingdom of Pluto. Thus, the hope of happiness is present, and it reveals its formidable character at the very moment of death. The fate of the body is not apprehended for its own sake, since it is destined irremediably to corruption; it is of no concern to the one who is about to die and who is going to identify his future with that of his soul. Finally, there is indeed a witness of fidelity to the truth and courage in the face of condemnation; without any doubt, this witness is given to the world, as also to future generations, and in an exemplary fashion. Nevertheless, strictly speaking, the death of Socrates cannot be assimilated to the sacrifice of a life, in the personal sense of the term.

The same heroic example can be found in the personages of classical tragedy. The most striking remains Antigone's choice to die, to obey the eternal laws of the gods rather than the iniquitous decree of Creon. In the confrontation between the two adversaries, Antigone compares the physical sufferings and the moral sufferings that disobedience to the gods brings to the conscience. In the specific case, the sacred duty to give her brother a funeral has priority over every other consideration, even that of the threat to her own life.[12]

---

12. "I did not think that your defence of yourself was strong enough to allow a mortal person to pass beyond to other laws, to the unwritten laws, un-

Is There a Christian Way to Die?

In Stoic thought and ethics, death acquires an educative function for a person's own life. The idea, according to which death would not be something formidable to someone who, in his life, had already had experience of death is not new, but the fact of dying well, that is to say, with courage and with full acceptance[13] of what is happening, becomes a constitutive and virtuous element in what, for example, the Romans understand by *humanitas*. Death is not seen as a brutal rupture; it is as if it were immanent to the life, which is entirely orientated towards death itself.

> It is not only the out-flowing of the last drop which empties the water-dial, but it is everything which has been poured out previously, in such a way that it can be said that the last hour, that in which we cease to live, will not bring about death, but will only bring it to its fulfilment; at the moment then, we reach death, but for some time beforehand we have been journeying to meet it.[14]

The combination of these two elements, heroic virtue and life being lived towards death,[15] leads to the justification of the act of

---

breakable laws, of the gods! ... But, to die before your time, I proclaim this loudly, it is nothing but a benefit; when someone lives, as I do, in the midst of innumerable misfortunes, how would it be possible not to gain from dying? To submit myself to death, for me, is not a suffering. There would have been such suffering, though, namely, if I had permitted that the body of a son of my mother had not obtained a tomb after his death, That, yes, would have made me suffer; from this, I do not suffer; no doubt, I appear to you to be acting like someone who is mad. But the mad person could very well be the one, who is treating me as if I am mad" (Sophocles, *Antigone*, II, Sc. 3, 454–6; v. 462–470).

13. "A person who is over-anxious to prolong their life and who counts it among the greatest of blessings to be able to see numerous consuls succeed each other cannot have a life which is at peace. Every day, you must meditate upon how to depart from your life with a peaceful spirit." (*Hoc cotidie meditare, ut possis aequo animo vitam relinquere*)"(Seneca, *Ad Lucilium*, I, IV).
14. *Ibid.*, II, III (24: On Cato).
15. Some echoes of this preparation for death can be found in contemporary philosophy, in particular in Martin Heidegger's concept of an "authentic life": in human existence, death is one inevitable and constitutive pos-

suicide in the eyes of the Stoics. Thus, Seneca recognizes that the great Cato has the right to put an end to a life, in which there remains nothing but to lament the fate of the human race, and his right to bring this about then by an act of his own freedom.[16] However, we must not translate into the anachronistic terms of nihilism the acceptance of suicide by all the Stoics, beginning from Seneca himself, because the latter often went together with acute awareness of good and of evil and with the conviction of having to account, one day, for one's own actions.

> The gods are not content with understanding the conduct of human beings; they inspire in them the best of actions. No one can succeed in being a truly good person without god; in fact, no-one could succeed, without his help, in rising above their destiny. It is he who inspires ideas which are great and upright.[17]

Suicide Seen as Revelatory of the Meaning of Death in Philosophy

It is strange to note that all of the philosophical positions on the meaning of death, from Cicero down to our own days, are expressed around the particular question of suicide and of the

---

sibility among a mass of other possibilities. It is important to assume this death into full consciousness, in order to be able to live authentically all the other possibilities of human existence (cf. Martin Heidegger, *Sein und Zeit*).

16. "It is not for my freedom, but for the freedom of my county that I have fought this far and that I have worked with great perseverance not only to live in freedom, but rather to be able to live among free people; and, since now there is nothing left but to lament the destiny of the human race, it is necessary that Cato be led to a secure place. Subsequently, he will inflict upon himself a mortal blow." (*Nunc quoniam deploratae sunt res generis humani, Cato deducatur in tutum. Impressit deinde mortiferum corporis vulnus.*) (Seneca, *Id.*)

17. "*Sacer inter nos spiritus sedet, malorum bonorumque nostrorum observator et custos: hic prout a nobis tractatus est, ita nos ipse tractat. Bonus vero vir sine Deo nemo est; an potest aliquis supra fortunam, nisi ab illo adiutus exsurgere?*" (*Ibid.*, IV, XII, 41.)

morality of the act of suicide. In harmony with the line of argument developed in this article, suicide is interesting in the history of moral ideas if it is true that the act of killing oneself can be considered as the exact antithesis of the act that consists in sacrificing one's life in the martyr. It is impossible to provide here a review of the whole discussion, but it is possible to group together the moral judgments unfavourable to suicide into four different types of argumentation, independently of the period from which they come. By contrast, the positions in favour of suicide, clearly in a minority, will be indicated, though most attention will be directed to the one which is the most fully developed, that of David Hume.

- *The social argument* (Aristotle): suicide is an act of cowardice, contrary to the good of society.[18]
- *The argument from nature* (Kant): this consists in bringing into focus the duty of the human being to preserve their own life, by virtue of the very fact that he or she is a person.[19]
- *The argument from moral fulfilment* (the Neo-Platonists): to consent to suicide means to abandon the possibility of making moral progress.[20]
- *The religious argument* (Pythagoras, Plato, Cicero, Plotinus, etc.): suicide is seen as an act of disobedience to the divinity.[21]

It will not be without interest to keep before us this four-fold level of condemnation,[22] because, strangely enough, it will be

---

18. Aristotle, *Nichomachean Ethics*, V, XI, 10–14.
19. Kant, *Metaphysik der Sitten*,1,I.1, 6.
20. Plotinus, *Enneades*, I, 9.
21. Reference should be made to the article "Suicidio" of G. Masi, in *Encicl. Filos* (Sansoni), vol. VI, col. 262–264.
22. Here, we have in mind philosophical arguments that are not specifically Christian. In Christian ethics, other arguments are invoked, both concerning Revelation or the theological life and concerning the nature of human persons and of their life in society. For the record, in the first group, we will quote the opinion of St Augustine, according to whom suicide is *contra caritatem* (*De civ. Dei*, I, 17); in the second, we note on

seen that the Christian theology of martyrdom, in fact, takes up the responsibilities—natural, social, moral and religious—which underlie them.

On the other hand, it is clear that an effective argumentation in favour of suicide will have to confront these arguments. That is precisely the case with Hume, who, from this point of view, constitutes an exception in the history of philosophy.

The Case of David Hume

A hardened opponent of all metaphysics, paradoxically, Hume understood that it is only by destroying the religious foundation of certain positions which refuse suicide that he would then be able to respond naturally to the other arguments. Hence, in his preamble to his *Essay on Suicide*, there is a violent diatribe against superstition, from which it can be perceived that this is directed above all against Roman morality. Hume begins by noting, with regret, that many unhappy people do not dare to escape from the condition in which they find themselves, for fear of offending God.[23] The whole of his argumentation will consist in trying to deny the criminal nature of the act of killing oneself. If suicide were a crime, he affirms, it would have to consist in a transgression of our duty towards God, towards our neighbor, and towards ourselves.[24] Hume does not challenge the idea of a Creator, but he interprets him as a kind of great clockmaker, like Voltaire:

---

the one hand the revival of the classical argument, already cited in regard to Kant, (suicide contradicts the natural inclination of the human being to preserve himself or herself in existence and to perpetuate his or her life, in the *Catechism of the Catholic Church*, 2281) and, on the other hand, the nature of the scandal given to others (*Ibid.*, 2282).

23. "Although only death can put an end to his miseries, he (the person in misfortune) does not dare to take refuge in such an act; he prolongs his miserable existence, in the vain fear that he would offend the Creator, if he used the power with which this beneficent being has endowed him" (David Hume, "Essay on Suicide" in *Philosophical Works*, (Biblioteca Univ. Laterza), vol. III, pp. 585–594.

24. *Ibid.*

> He creates the universe, in which indeed we find human beings, but it is a universe with immutable laws, fixed once and for all, the laws of nature, in which he would not be able to intervene, Human beings are no more than one element in this universe and enjoy no special dignity among living creatures.

Hume is very explicit in this sense: "For the universe, the life of a human being has no more importance than that of an oyster."[25] Everything that exists in the world is submitted to these laws; nothing can be produced which can escape from the inexorable fatality of all those laws; biological phenomena, to be sure, but all of that affects the human being:

> The passions follow their course, the judgment which guides us, our members in their obedience, are all the works of God and it is on these principles of the animate, as well as of the inanimate world, that he has founded the government of the universe ... There is no event which occurs, however important it may be for us, that God has exempted from these general laws of the universe or that he has reserved specifically for his immediate intervention.

We can understand this: this vision offers no bond of cause and effect between the Creator and a human life, and so there is no good reason to preserve one's own life. In such a conception, human suffering is nonsense.[26] To put it better, the motivations themselves for suicide, the distress and the weariness, like the decision to proceed to the act itself, are themselves all subjected to the laws of matter and of movement.[27] We cannot go into detail

---

25. *Ibid.*
26. Cf. S. Grygiel, "Il senso della sofferenza in un mondo secolarizzato", *Nuovo Areopago* 1995/2, pp. 12–28.
27. "What sense, then, has the opinion, according to which, a man who is exhausted by life and who is tortured by pain and misery and who would conquer the natural fear of death with courage by departing from this cruel scene, would such a man, I ask, incur the indignation of the Creator for having violated the work of his Providence and for having disturbed the order of the universe? Are we to think that the All-power-

here about the distant origins of this position of Hume, which is to be found already in his theory of knowledge and in his rejection of any rational foundation (quite apart from metaphysics) for ethics. Beyond the immediate influence of various currents of Enlightenment thought, we are able to see in Hume the source of many modern and contemporary positions, which, without denying categorically the existence of a world beyond, yet reject the status that the Ancients recognized in it, as the ultimate measure of human actions and, in particular, of actions related to the life of human beings. A distant echo of the theses of Hume can be found also in the current proposition of a lay spirituality, which some call a spiritual humanism,[28] a kind of diffuse, syncretistic movement, which is expressed especially by a humanization of death in the accompaniment of the dying. The attention given to the sick who are in their last agony, in this humanist conception of palliative care, can go to the point, for example, of implicitly substituting the traditional sacramental means of salvation by an accompaniment that is specifically Christian.[29]

---

ful has reserved to himself particularly the power to dispose of the life of human beings and that he has not subjected this event, as he has with all others, to the general laws of the universe: To make such an affirmation would be to claim what is false" (Hume, *Ibid.*)

28. M. De Hennezel, J.-Y. Leloup, *L'Art de mourir. Traditions réligieuses et spiritualité humaniste face à la mort aujourd'hui* (Paris: Ed. Laffont, 1997).

29. "If this [Christian] inspiration is there, present in the values of a great number of carers and of voluntary helpers, that does not mean that it is being imposed. I think that it is even true to say that palliative care has succeeded in establishing itself on the basis of an ethics that is sufficiently open, that persons with roots in other traditions (Buddhists or even agnostics) can find a place for themselves there. Whatever their beliefs or philosophy may be, the women and men who are part of this movement of palliative care are serving an ethic that is the same; it is a question of respecting the person who is dying and of the quality of the time that is left for them to live, and of offering them the care and a listening ear, sufficiently open and respectful for them to enter in a living way into death." (M. de Hennezel, J.-Y. Leloup, *op. cit.*, pp. 49–50).

Bringing the Will into Question

We have seen that David Hume denied the meaning of an act of the will, itself given over to a kind of practical determinism. There is nothing of this in a Schopenhauer, who introduced the possibility of suicide as a means of freeing oneself from the will itself and of coming thereby to the peace of the *voluntas*. In the conception of the German philosopher, this involves three levels, that of justice, that of love, and that of ascesis. It is only in this last stage that the person can liberate himself from a hostile and atrocious world by means of various ethical attitudes, such as chastity and poverty. Suicide, at the extreme end of this stance of black pessimism, will be the way to reject the last obstacle, the will to live: "Suicide is the deed of someone who, instead of rejecting the will, suppresses the phenomenon of this will;"[30] thus, such a person rejects not the will to live but simply rejects living as such.

The whole universe resounds with the oracle of Zarathustra, who, in the choice to die freely, exalts his own will:[31] "Before you I pay homage to my death, a free death, the death which comes to me because *I* want it."[32] The exaltation of the impulse for life goes hand in hand, in Nietzsche, with an absolute nihilism, or at least with a nihilism that is asserted, which will find its most violent emphases in the *Genealogy of Morality*. Here, it is no longer just the idea of the intervention of God in the lives of human beings which is rejected, but the God of Christians, who, in the eyes of Nietzsche, incarnates all the counter-values to the Superman of the morality of the strong. Behind this Dionysian excess what comes to expression is the rejection of everything that seeks to deny that which is nothing.

Quite naturally, all these authors who seek to bring out the absurd nature of existence will give consideration to suicide and

---

30. Schopenhauer, *Die Welt als Wille und Vorstellung*, I, § 69, cited by Masi in *art. cit.*col.263.
31. Frederich Nietzsche, *So sprach Zarathustra*, I, 21.
32. Emphasis by the author.

will go the point of making it the only serious question for philosophy.³³ This is the case with Camus in the *Myth of Sisyphus*; he observes that no one has any desire to die for the sake of the ontological argument, but that, on the other hand, many people commit suicide because they judge that life has no meaning. Then, Camus defines what he calls "philosophical suicide," as that existential attitude which designates the movement by which a thought denies itself and tends to go beyond itself in what brings about its negation.³⁴ Philosophical suicide is illustrated, according to him, by Kierkegaard, who, starting from a philosophy of the nonsense of the world, ends up by finding a meaning and a depth in it himself. The step taken by the Danish philosopher, for Camus, is in its essence religious; it is all the more pathetic, according to him, because it expresses itself in a realm that is irrational.³⁵

For Camus, it is understood that the absurd is a metaphysical difficulty and that it defines an existential doubt. The conception of life and of death that emerges from this is devoid of the nihilistic meaning given by Nietzsche or the meaning attributed to them, in an analogously violent way, by Sartre. Sisyphus teaches the higher fidelity, which denies the gods and which lifts up the rocks.³⁶

To all of these philosophical positions as a whole, it is right to add the practical refusal of existence, which is dictated by the feeling of absurdity in the face of the reality of suffering (the justification of assisted suicide or of euthanasia): the illusion a per-

---

33. Albert Camus, *The Myth of Sisyphus and other Essays*, translated by J. O'Brien, 1953, on-line, pp. 4ff.
34. *Ibid.* pp. 20ff.
35. It is a very particular kind of death about which Kierkegaard theorized; it is the supreme death of despair, which he defined as the lack of final hope. Despair is the mortal sickness from which death itself provides no liberation: "For someone to die of despair as from a sickness, what is eternal in us, in the 'me', would have to be able to die, as does the body from sickness. It is a chimera! In despair, death continually changes itself into living" (Soren Kierkegaard, *The Sickness unto Death* (Princeton: Princeton University Press, 1941), online, p. 15.
36. Albert Camus, *The Myth of Sisyphus*, p. 78.

son has of bringing to its fulfilment his own liberty by disposing of his life, when he judges that the moment has come to depart from the scene of this world, the judgment about the dignity of the life of a person in terms of the degree of their state of consciousness. The increase in the number of those adopting this position, often stemming from a scientific milieu, from influential political parties, or from powerful international organizations, has led the Church to reaffirm the sacred value and the inviolable nature of every human life and to renew its condemnation of the murder of the innocent, of procured abortion, and of the act of euthanasia.[37]

This long survey of non-Christian ideas on life and death has enabled us to present an oscillation between two poles: on the one hand, the proud affirmation of the absolute sovereignty of the human being over his or her life—whatever is materially possible is morally licit—and, on the other hand, the temptation to despair—death is the sole way out of a life without hope. The two poles are inseparably linked, because the one inevitably refers back to the other. In the first case, death is an event which people wish to master; it has no sense and, therefore, it must fit into that which human beings already dominate in their existence, in such a way that, to this justification of a death with dignity, there will be added that of an unlimited power over life, with all of the genetic manipulation that this presupposes. In the second case, death has no other meaning than that of an inevitable annihilation, which projects its shadow across the whole of people's lives. In the end, death is the sole master and the human being becomes its slave. From this arises despair, which is the collapse of pride.

Finally, the conception of a life without any other way out and without hope often goes hand in hand with the Dionysian exaltation of the life of the senses. The relationship between despair and moral licence has always seemed sufficiently clear for it to be incorporated into literary fiction in figures of universal signific-

---

37. John Paul II, *Evangelium Vitae*, § 57, 62, 65.

ance, the most common of which is that of Don Juan.[38] Opposed to this, there is a kind of hope in the moral vitality of which Socrates, for the love of truth and of the fatherland recalled above, is the emblematic figure. People will insist upon the fact that the choice of the virtuous life finds its support in the fear of an immanent justice, whatever may be thought of the demi-gods who incarnate this, and awaiting a just recompense in the next world. These elements will be found once more in the Christian conception of life and of death.

Ars Christiana Moriendi

The Second Vatican Council reserves for the martyr a passage located, and not by accident, in Chapter Five of *Lumen Gentium*, itself dedicated to the universal call to holiness in the Church. The life of the martyr, then, is a path that is a possibility in the life in the Church; to be sure, it is a path of holiness and is not given except to a small number of people. Yet, it concerns every member of the Church, precisely because we all have to be ready to confess Christ before others and to follow him to the point of the way of the Cross. We have already said that the encyclical, *Veritatis Splendor*, sees in martyrdom the coherent attitude of

---

38. The figure of Don Juan is an example of despair, not only in relation to debauchery, but also because of the superficiality with which he treats his own death (and thus, as a corollary, the life of others: he is a murderer as well); even when the imminence of the judgment of the next world is manifested to him, incarnated in the Commander who appears to him, he has no other resource available to him other than to defy death and to treat the Commander with insolence (inviting him to dine with him) and to refuse conversion at the last moment. In some way death is camouflaged and is not treated seriously. We note also that in psychoanalysis this connection is to be found between an anarchic sensual life and death. The compulsion of repetition falls back upon pleasure and, beyond pleasure, upon an impulse towards death (cf. the couplet *eros-thanatos* in Sigmund Freud, *Beyond the pleasure principle* (Vienna, 1920). Finally, a connection is already to be found, explicitly stated, in the letter to the Hebrews between the existence which we live and the slavery to and the fear of death (Heb. 2:15).

the Christian when the latter intends to render witness to the moral truth. Thus, in the eyes of the Tradition and of the Magisterium of the Church, martyrdom is the very opposite of an action which is absurd.[39] Its coherence rests upon the teaching of the Master, on the example of his life, and on the power of his Spirit, who makes the Christian capable of giving witness even to the ultimate extreme; since Jesus, the Son of God has shown his charity by giving his life for us; no-one can show a greater love than in giving his life for him and for his friends (cf. 1Jn 3:16; Jn 15:13).

> To this supreme witness to love, given before all and especially before their persecutors, from the earliest times, some among the Christians have been called, and, without ceasing, others will be called to this witness. This is why the martyr, in whom the disciple is assimilated to his Master, accepting death freely for the salvation of the world, and made like him in the shedding of his blood, is considered by the Church as an eminent grace and as the supreme proof of charity. And, if this is not given except to a small number, nevertheless, all must be ready to confess Christ before other people and to follow him along the path of the Cross, in the midst of persecutions which will never be lacking in the Church.[40]

Death as a Free and Loving Sacrifice

From the very first lines of this article, an element which is fundamental to what is specific to the Christian martyr has been presented; martyrdom is an act of love for Christ and for his brethren, and it relates to the love which first of all is that of him who made known his charity by giving his life for us. This is the reason why the martyr freely accepts death for the salvation of the world. This formula describes the sole way possible between, on the one hand, the revolt against the fact of having to die and

---

39. The martyr had no meaning in the eyes of pagans, if not that, according to Tacitus, of a hatred for the human race (Tacitus, *Annals*, XV, 44, 6).
40. Vatican Council II, *Lumen Gentium*, § 42b.

the against the despair to which this is connected, and, on the other hand, the act which consists in seizing the moment of death for a final exaltation of liberty. However, let us evaluate the path we have undertaken in the study of suicide; this study revealed an extraordinary power which has been left to human beings to make of their death an opportunity for a violent act of refusal of life or indeed the opposite, to abstain from such an act (pointing to the experience of death through their example). This capacity to dispose freely of this last moment did not fail to attract the attention of Kant, who saw in it, the indisputable proof that the person has escaped from nature and belongs to liberty.[41] It is in love that the martyr, on his part, assumes all of the values of freedom which are proper to the human condition and which are partially inscribed in the non-Christian approaches to the mystery of death.

What is fundamental to the act of the Christian martyr is that the love of Christ, which inspires it, transforms the very being of the person who himself sacrifices his life; the disciple is assimilated to their Master ("*Discipulus Magistro assimilatur*"); he becomes like him through the out-pouring of his blood ("*Eique in effusione sanguinis conformatur*"). The conformation of the disciple is brought about not only by the imitation of Christ, but, on

---

41. This remark has been made by J. Lacroix, who himself observes: "Here, we touch what is deepest in the notion of courage in the human being. The sense itself and the essential meaning of the struggle consist in this, that the eminent dignity of the human person finds, certainly I will not say its origin and its source, but at least its most obvious and its most characteristic expression in this; the human being is a being who is capable of exposing himself or herself voluntarily to death." The author adds that it is in the courage that is at times involved in the decision to attempt to put an end to his days that Kant grounds his argument: "If I do not have the right to kill myself, following him, it is precisely because I could take my life, which means that the human person infinitely surpasses the human person, and that, in killing myself, I am attempting to annihilate, insofar as this depends upon me, the subject of morality" (J. Lacroix, *Personne et Amour* (Paris: Seuil, 1955), pp. 13–14).

the contrary, it is this eminent grace,[42] of which *Lumen Gentium* speaks and which is obtained by the Blood of Christ, which renders the disciple capable in the faith of imitating the Master.[43] There is a strict relationship between the Blood of Christ and the new life of the disciple. Ignatius of Antioch addressed himself thus to the people of Smyrna: "I have become aware, in fact, that you have perfected yourselves in an unbreakable faith, as if you were nailed flesh and spirit to the Cross of Jesus Christ and solidly established in charity by the Blood of Christ."[44] A religious conformation is necessarily connected to a moral conformation:[45]

> Conformation to Christ derives ... from participation in the paschal mystery. The two moments of the death and resurrection always exist together. At times the self-abasement of the kenosis of the Servant predominates; at other times, his glorification and his life-giving presence predominate. In this ambivalence, the authenticity of the

---

42. Without the grace of Christ, the act of the martyr would be a heroic act, which would reproduce the actions of the Master, reduced to the level of a simple moral example; attempts to conceive of martyrdom as such an imitation have not been lacking: "Whoever takes on a model tends to resemble or to be become similar to that model and, in doing so, engages in the lived experience of the obligation of what they ought to be," Max Scheler, *Formalism in Ethics and Non-formal Ethics of Values: A New Attempt toward the Foundation of an Ethical Personalism* (Evanston: Northwestern University Press, 1973), pp. 572–583.
43. "Love must be conformed to Christ, the perfect Image of infinite love, the first-born brother, on whom we have all modelled ourselves in advance. But the conformity of acts and of efforts is not sufficient for love; there needs to be a participation in the life, a communion which makes of the human being one sole spirit with God" (J. Mouroux, *Sens chrétien de l'homme* (Paris: Aubier, 1953, p. 221).
44. St Ignatius of Antioch, *Letter to the Smyrneans*, I, 1 SC, 10, 133.
45. "As sensitive as we may be to the ethical meaning of the mystery of Christ, nevertheless, it should not be forgotten that this needs to be put into relationship with another dimension of this mystery, the properly religious dimension, thanks to which this imitation goes beyond the reference to the master of morals and becomes a participation in the very condition of the Incarnate Word." C. Bernard, *Vie morale et croissance dans le Christ* (Rome: PUG, 1973), p. 263

conformation to Christ can be recognized: "To know him, in the power of his resurrection and in communion with his sufferings, to become conformed to him in death, in order, if possible, to come to rise from among the dead" (Phil 3:10–11).[46]

The Christian martyr dies by the death which Christ has chosen, a choice which is also the choice made by God in his redemptive act: "The suffering of Christ was not necessary with the necessity of a constraint neither on the part of God who decided on this suffering, nor on the part of Christ who underwent this suffering voluntarily."[47] The sacrifice which the martyr makes of his or her own life finds no sense except in that of the Sacrifice of Christ: the *pro mundi salute* of the disciple[48] goes back to the *propter nostram salutem* of the death of Christ, which is proclaimed in the Credo. From this latter to the former, there is nothing else but the continuity of the work of salvation, a continuity which allowed St Paul to live out his trials joyfully and to offer them up for the Church: "I find my joy in the suffering I endure for you and, in my flesh, I make up what is still lacking in the sufferings of Christ, for the sake of his Body, which is the Church" (Col. 1:24). Through their deeds and by virtue of their will not to deny the Christ, the first martyrs were led to an act of explicit proclamation of their faith, something that irremediably entailed their death. In fact, a simple retraction could have saved their lives. It is possible to see a providential intention in this resounding act of moral freedom.[49] The historian, Allard, has

---

46. *Ibid.*, p. 266.
47. St Thomas Aquinas, *Summa Theologiae*, IIIa Pars, q. 46, a.1.
48. Vatican Council II, *Lumen Gentium*, § 42b.
49. "We may be allowed to see a providential will in this exceptional legislation, which made condemnation to death depend upon the will alone of those who were thereby exposed by their fidelity to the Christian faith. By destiny, the martyr will become the most beautiful and the most meritorious triumph of moral freedom. Up to the last moment, Christians could escape from their agony. Their crown was completely glorious just because they accepted their death voluntarily." (R. Hedde, art.

observed that, among all those accused by the Romans, the Christians alone were deprived of the service of a defender. The sole possibility they had of escaping from death, then, was denial:

> All the factors involved in the judgment were summarised in establishing the refusal of the accused person to deny their faith. Could they give their consent to apostasy? On the basis of their word alone, they are released. Will they persist in saying they are Christians? They are condemned. Thus, it is indeed of their own free will that they endured a violent death and their condemnation, voluntarily accepted, thereby becomes the most resounding triumph of moral freedom which Christianity has brought to the world.[50]

The Witnesses and Their Witness

Etymologically, the martyr is a witness. In the world's understanding, a witness is not only someone who attests to the reality of a fact, but is also someone who gives witness to a truth of which they are convinced. In ancient times, to attest to the truth of a fact, people called upon the gods, to the point where someone who produced false witness exposed himself *ipso facto* to a divine punishment. As for witness rendered to an opinion, the person considered most suitable to offer such witness was the philosopher: "he gave honour to the truth of his doctrine when, in all serenity, he could face banishment, defamation or exile."[51] In the Septuagint, the truthful witness (*martus pistos*) is God himself; he witnesses to the reality of a pact between protector and the protégé, of a covenant between two houses or between two friends. God is the witness to the friendship established

---

"Martyre" in *Dictionnaire de Théologie Catholique*, T X I, (Paris: Letouzay et Ane, 1928), col. 235.
50. Cf. Penchenard, preface to ALLARD, *Dix leçons sur le martyre* (Paris, 1906), XVIII.
51. H. Strathmann, art. "Martus", in *Theologisches Wörterbuch* (ThW), IV, pp. 477–520.

between David and Jonathan.⁵² Already in the Old Testament, the witness offered by someone could lead to death. In this sense, the first figure of a martyr is the eschatological figure of the Servant of Yahweh. Invested with a prophetic vocation, he must at the same time preach the true religion, renew and extend the *Covenant*, and make intercession. In the exercise of his mission, he is necessarily faced with contestation. The logic of his vocation leads him to give himself over to death.⁵³ It has been rightly observed that this death, interpreted as a voluntary sacrifice of expiation, is undertaken precisely in order for the plan of God, the restoration of Israel, to succeed.⁵⁴ In the New Testament, we find once more this double object of witness. The first witnesses, on the one hand, attest to the historical fact of the Resurrection of Christ and, on the other, to the truth of Christian doctrine. In reality, these two understandings coincide with each other: the witness takes on a new and exalted value; the Apostles are essentially witnesses to the Risen Christ.⁵⁵

Now, to give witness to the Risen Christ, is to give witness to eternal life; in other words, it is to proclaim the reality of the victory over death. The martyrs proclaim that Christ has been victorious over death and, simultaneously, this victory gives them complete assurance that, in their turn, they will overcome the final trial triumphant. This witness is, at one and the same time, a heroic act of courage and of fortitude, and also the manifestation of an indefectible hope in the power of the Risen One. We take note of the fact that, in the gospel of St Luke, all the essential elements of this concept are reunited in the sending out on mission of the disciples by the Master: Jesus refers to everything that is written about himself in the Law of Moses and in the Psalms (thus, it is written that the Christ would suffer and would rise from the dead on the third day, and that, in his Name, repentance

---

52. 1Sam 20:23.42.
53. Is 53:12.
54. A. Gelin, "Les origines bibliques de l'idée du martyr" in L. et V, 36 (1956), pp. 123–129.
55. P. T. Camelot, art. "Martyr, Martyre" in *Catholicisme*, 36, col. 770–776.

for the forgiveness of sins would be preached to all the nations, beginning from Jerusalem—Lk.24:46–47). The mission that Jesus gives to the Apostles is to transmit this message: "To this, you are witnesses" (Lk. 24:48). It is worth noting that the Apostles are not capable by themselves of fulfilling such a mission. Their witness will not be possible except through the assistance of the divine power itself. It is exactly this that is the object of the last promise that the Master makes to them.[56] The help of the power from on high is not immediately orientated to martyrdom. It is simply the power to give witness. Nevertheless, there is the requirement to remain faithful to this witness, which carries with it the possibility that the disciple, in the end, may have to confront a violent death. From the second generation, the disciples become witnesses to the point of the outpouring of their blood, out of pure fidelity to the content of the faith. It was of little significance that they had not been contemporaries[57] of Jesus and, hence, that they had not been able to relate a personal experience of the content

---

56. "And now I am sending down to you what the Father has promised. Stay in the city, then, until you are clothed with power from on high." (Lk 24:49).

57. The passage from the direct knowledge of Jesus by his contemporaries to the knowledge of Christ by faith inspired Kierkegaard, who wanted to compare the two conditions. The Danish philosopher finds the knowledge by faith infinitely superior to that which the friends of Christ were able to have of him when he was alive on earth. With regard to the sinful woman (Lk 7:37ff.), he writes: "We learn from the sinful woman (finally)—to be sure, not directly, but by the comparison of our condition with hers—that we have the benefit of a consolation that she did not have. We enjoy a consolation impossible at the time of the life of Christ; he could not offer himself to someone. Thus, the consolation of his death did not exist as the gauge for reconciliation and for the forgiveness of sins. During his life, the Christ was for his contemporaries above all a model... But, he dies. And his death changes everything and infinitely. Not that it abolishes the meaning of the fact that, at the same time he is a model, no, but this death becomes the infinite consolation, the infinite gauge; whoever struggles can base their struggle upon the assurance that the infinite satisfaction has been accomplished; whoever is in doubt, whoever is discouraged, can see that they are offered the highest guarantee, and with a certainty that is unsurpassable; Christ has died to save them; the death of Christ is reconciliation, it is satisfaction. This consolation, the sinful

of the life of the Master. The knowledge that they had through the faith and through fidelity to its transmission, made of them authentic witnesses. Hence, Stephen is called a witness (*martus*) by Paul, in his harangue to the Jews in Jerusalem.[58] We know that, little by little, the term of *witness* will come to mean, in a derived sense, the one whose fidelity to the message transmitted has been at the cost of his or her life.

Fidelity carries with it the price of heroic courage. Having noted that the martyr is orientated towards this action by charity, as the first and essential mover, St Thomas attributes its being carried to completion to the virtue of fortitude. In fact, it belongs to fortitude to confirm the person in the good of the virtue against danger, in particular the danger of death. Now, it is clear that, in the martyr, the person is solidly confirmed in the good of the virtue, when he does not abandon the faith and justice in the face of the mortal perils which confront them, especially on the part of their persecutors, in a kind of special combat.[59] At the same time, martyrdom is an act of patience, which allows the witness to overcome the obstacles he faces.[60]

Among these obstacles, there figure fear and pain. Fear has the particular effect, that it makes it possible to avoid all presumption. It is remarkable that the Christian tradition has never given the title of martyr to those who have sought death. In the Fathers, this distinction can be found, namely, between the legitimate desire for martyrdom and seeking it irresponsibly. For example, in the *Martyrdom of Polycarp*, at the decisive moment the weakness

---

woman did not have." (Kierkegaard, 'La pécheresse' in *Discours Édifiants*, Trad. J. Colette (DDB, Bruges, 1962), 78–79; 81–82.
58. "When the blood of your witness, Stephen, was being shed, I was standing by in full agreement with his murderers and minding their clothes" (Acts 22:20).
59. St Thomas Aquinas, *Summa Theologiae*, IIa IIae, q. 124, a. 2.
60. Patience holds the last place among all the virtues (after the theological and the cardinal virtues), but it is "the root and the custodian of all the virtues, not because it brings them about and preserves them directly, but solely because it eliminates the obstacles to their development" (*Ibid.* q. 136, a. 3).

of a certain Quintus is related, who had brought with him several brothers, to accompany him spontaneously to the tribunal. "By his prayers at that time, the proconsul succeeded in persuading him to take the oath and to offer sacrifice. That is why, brothers, we do not praise those who offer themselves of their own will, because that is not the teaching of the Gospel."[61] All authentic martyrs, by contrast, present themselves for execution in the humble attitude of those who know that they can rely upon nothing other than the strength of God. St Ignatius of Antioch, with his desire to find God by becoming fodder for the beasts, does not cease to beg his brethren to intercede, so that, at the appointed time, he may be lacking in neither the interior nor the exterior fortitude needed.[62] The very fear of presumption inspires in him the greatest wisdom, when he addresses the Trallians: "I have great thoughts of God, but I must restrain myself, so that I may not be lost through my vanity. For now above all, must I have fear and not pay attention to those who would tempt me to be swollen with pride."[63]

It is to be noted that Christ, the model of all martyrs, experienced not only pain, but also fear. According to St Thomas More, this fear of Christ had as its object as much to give courage to our puny soul as to preserve it from all presumption. The fear experienced by Christ teaches humility to his disciples:

> Above all, our captain, Christ, teaches his soldier by his example that we must begin with humility, the foundation in some way of all the virtues, from which we may rise up more surely to the higher levels. Although he was God, equal and similar to God, the Father, nevertheless, be-

---

61. *The Martyrdom of Polycarp*, IV, S.C, 10, 215. An illustration of someone seeking martyrdom, a request that was not heard, can be found in the figure of the sub-prior in the *Dialogue of the Carmelites* by Bernanos. Without the authority of her prioress, she had asked to make a vow of martyrdom before all her sisters. She would be the only one to whom the grace of the supreme witness was not granted.
62. St Ignatius of Antioch, *Ad Rom*. III and IV, SC, 10, 111.
63. Id. *Ad Trall.*, IV, 1–2, SC, 10, 99.

cause he was also man, he prostrated himself as man before God, his Father, with his face to the ground, in an attitude of supplication.[64]

It can be said, then, that the agony of Christ was the human means by which Christ in his Passion kept those who were his own from all risk of pride, by giving them the means to conquer every temptation to presumption.

In the same way that Christ, in agony, was comforted by divine strength, so also his disciples will themselves be comforted by the strength of Christ. The very fact that the martyr could pass through the trial of death with hope and joy attests the reality of this help that comes from Christ. The perspective, then, is reversed; every martyrdom is the personal witness rendered by Christ himself to this member of his faithful. The union of the disciple to his Master takes the form of a double witness in the Blood of the Lamb, that of the disciple to his Master and that of the Master to his disciple.

The Passage of Death

The trial of the martyrs was not limited to the duration of the persecution and other sufferings inflicted. It knows its highest degree in the death that is imposed. The fortitude of the disciple in these circumstances comes from the fact that he knows that this ultimate enemy has been defeated definitively. Alone the Resurrection of Christ can ground the hope in the resurrection of a human being; here, we are at the heart of the Gospel message. The disciple does not have to search for motives to hope in the resurrection in the future anywhere else but in the message that has been entrusted to him to transmit.

Death is the trial through which Christ has already passed. It is essential for his witnesses to rely upon the reality of the Risen Body of Christ. To affirm that Christ has risen is to proclaim at the same time that this flesh of ours, even though it be the flesh of sin, which had clothed the Word in his Incarnation, is not only

---
64. St Thomas More, *De tristitia Christi* (Paris: Tequi, 1990), p. 43.

fully associated with his victory but is itself victorious. When he invokes the redemptive efficacy of the death of Christ, St Thomas takes care to distinguish the two meanings that can be attributed to this term. First of all, when it has occurred, death designates the state of separation of the soul and of the body, but it can also be considered in its becoming, as the process which inevitably leads to this. In this latter sense, the effects of death are identified with those of the Passion. In the former sense, however, death is the cause of salvation, but, according to the Angelic Doctor, this is uniquely by way of efficiency; the Body of Christ acts in virtue of its divinity, which has been united to it. In order to be able to grasp the significance of this affirmation properly, we must remember that St Thomas attributes to the humanity of Christ the function of being an efficient, instrumental cause.[65] The same truth is expressed in this way in the *Catechism of the Catholic Church* (n. 626). "Since the 'Prince of Life,' whom they put to death (Acts 3:15) is indeed the same as the Living One who has risen (cf. Lk 24:5–6), it is necessary that the divine person of the Son of God had continued to assume his soul and Body, separated one from the other by death."

Very many martyrs have had a very acute awareness of the fact that the fidelity of the disciple involves being united to the flesh of Christ. Thus, Ignatius of Antioch, making his farewell to the Magnesians,[66] wished for them a union in the flesh and in the spirit of Jesus Christ. Writing to the Trallians, he even goes to the point of making the flesh of Christ the object of the faith: "Arm yourselves, then, with a sweet patience and be recreated in the faith, which is the flesh of the Lord and in that charity which is the Blood of Christ."[67] What is particularly remarkable here is that the martyr unites himself to the humanity of Christ, anticipating in some way, through the sacrifice of his life, the union of every Christian with the Body and Blood of the Lord in the

---

65. St Thomas Aquinas, *Summa Theologiae*, IIIa Pars, q. 48, a. 4 and 6.
66. St Ignatius of Antioch, *Ad Magn.*, 1,2, SC, 10, 81.
67. Id. *Ad Trall.*,8, 1, SC 10, 101.

Eucharistic mystery. Nothing astonishing, then, in the fact that the Church has always considered that the Eucharist offered every Christian all the means necessary to be able to make a complete sacrifice of themselves; the encyclical, *Veritatis Splendor* (§ 21), speaks of the Eucharist as "the culmination of our assimilation to Christ, the source of 'eternal life', the source and power of that total gift of self." Conversely, every improper power violently assumed over one's own life or over the lives of others appears to be a direct contradiction of the truth of the Eucharist.[68]

Contemporary theological thinking has reconsidered the death of Christ to include in it all of the elements which constitute the state of the Saviour between the moment of his death on the Cross and that of the resurrection. Some people have insisted on the redemptive character of the extreme dereliction of Jesus and of his absolute solitude and see in this the summit of his filial obedience. The most famous example is, undoubtedly, Balthasar's theology of Holy Saturday. Others have underlined, in Jesus's descent into hell, the trait which is common between his death and the death of every human being.[69] Karl Rahner affirms not only how eminently appropriate it is that the salvation of human beings has been brought about by the death of Jesus but also that only his death could have had this efficacy.[70]

68. "By virtue of his Passion suffered for us and of the Eucharistic sacrifice of his life offered for us and under the form of communion with him, Christ, as the concrete norm, renders us interiorly capable of accomplishing with him the will of the Father". (Balthasar, "First Thesis for a Christian Ethic," in ITC, *Texts and Documents: The Christian World and its Norms* (Paris: Le Cerf, 1988), pp. 85–92. The counter-position between the Eucharist and the act of euthanasia, proposed by L. Melina is interesting (Melina, "Eutanasia o Eucaristia? Dalla retorica della 'buona morte' al morire con Cristo," *Communio* (Ed. Ital., 145, 1996), pp. 57–67.

69. "This establishes the essential similarity of Christ's death with our own; for that descent into hell is considered not simply as a redemptive activity performed after Christ's death (Acts 2:24.31), but as an essential factor in his death, and this accords with Old and New Testament ..." (Karl Rahner, "The Death of the Christian as Dying with Christ," in *On the Theology of Death*, (New York" Herder and Herder, 1961) p. 57.

70. "Man's death, insofar as it is his own personal act, extends through his

Thus, the passage of death is a journey that we make with Christ. The union with Christ that is that of the martyr conformed to his Lord, as has been shown, is in the end the eternal reality of Christian destiny, of which the martyrs are the first witnesses. It is not death itself that the martyr seeks in death, but it is Christ: "Close to the sword, close to Christ, with the beasts, with God; as long as it is in the name of Jesus Christ."[71] The beatific eternity which we desire and which we welcome could not be expressed in other terms than those of an eternal life with Christ. "Heaven's existence depends upon the fact that Jesus Christ, as God, is man and makes space for human existence in the existence of God himself."[72]

The Desire for Martyrdom: Theresa of Lisieux

If it is true that martyrdom, in the strict sense, is a grace that *"is not given except to a small number of people,"*[73] the desire to make of our death a sacrifice for Christ or the salvation of the world is something inscribed in the life of every coherent Christian. The writings of St Theresa of Lisieux, recently proclaimed Doctor of the Church, which remain to us demonstrate the daily nature of this tension towards death as an offering. In the commemoration card of her profession, she makes explicitly the vow of martyrdom.[74] She had already asked

---

whole life [...] And, insofar as any moral act of man is to be considered as a disposing of his entire person with regard to his interior destiny, and insofar as such a disposition receives its final form only in death, it is clear (on the supposition that Christ received the flesh of sin and death) that we cannot really say that Christ could have redeemed us through any other moral act than his death, even had God been disposed to accept some, other act. Therefore, it is just as correct to say that his obedience is redemptive because it is death, as it is to say that his death effects our redemption because it is obedience." *Ibid.*, pp. 62–63.

71. St Ignatius of Antioch, *Ad Smyrn*, 5, 2, SC, 1, 137.
72. Joseph Ratzinger, *Eschatology: Death and Eternal Life*, 2nd edition (Washington, DC: Catholic University Press, 1988), p. 234.
73. Vatican Council II, *Lumen Gentium*, § 42b.
74. "Jesus, that I may die for you as a martyr; martyrdom of the heart or of the

for this special grace in the course of her visit to the Colosseum. Theresa will always call the offering of her life "martyrdom for Jesus." She makes her sister party to her desire on several occasions: "Perhaps, Jesus would really like that, after having asked us for love in return for love, to ask further blood for blood and life for life."[75] The long trial of the last years leads her to discover the oblative dimension of extreme poverty, that which has neither merits to propose nor wishes to make heard.[76] In this sense, martyrdom is present in the cloister of Carmel; she wishes to convince her sister, Céline, of this.[77] She encourages Fr Belière towards the martyrdom of the heart, which, according to her, is *no less fecund than the shedding of blood.*[78]

Never will the desire for martyrdom become less for Theresa. She expresses it always in a manner that opens up into infinity of a primary desire, that of being joined to the Master. This is the

---

body or rather of both" (St Thérèse of Lisieux, "Prayer 2" in *The 21 Prayers of Thérèse*, numbering from the Centenaire edition, 1988).

75. *Letter to Céline*, 132, October 20, 1891. We note the expression *love in return for love*, which is found frequently in the contemplative literature and very especially in the devotion to the Heart of Jesus, in whose sufferings in the agony in the garden of Olives we share, for the conversion of sinners (*redamatio*). She had already told her sister, "Jesus is asking us both to take away his thirst, by giving him souls" (*Letter* 96, October 15, 1889).

76. "My desires for martyrdom are nothing; it is not they which give me the unlimited confidence that I feel in my heart....Understand that to love Jesus, to be his victim in love, the more someone is weak, with neither desires nor virtues, the more they are part of these operations of this Love, which consumes and transforms" (*Letter to Sister Marie of the Sacred Heart*, 197, September 17, 1896).

77. "The more I go on, the greater the intimate certitude I have that one day you will come here. Mother Mary of Gonzaga has urged me to tell you.. ...Do not be afraid of anything; here you will find the Cross and martyrdom to a greater degree than everywhere else" (*Letter to Céline*, 167, July 18, 1894).

78. "I know that you aspire to the happiness of being able to sacrifice your life for the divine Master, but the martyrdom of the heart is no less fecund than the shedding of blood, and from now on this martyrdom is yours" (*Letter to the Abbé Bellière*, December 26, 1896).

Is There a Christian Way to Die?

desire that is so great that the desire even for martyrdom itself will not be enough to translate it. Hence, her wish to be called to live all the vocations all at once, even if her preference is for that of the shedding her blood.

> These three privileges are indeed my vocation, Carmelite, spouse and mother (of souls); however, I feel within me other vocations; I feel in myself the vocation of the Warrior, of the Priest, of the Apostle, of the Doctor, of the Martyr, in the end, I feel the need and the desire to accomplish for you, Jesus, all the most heroic works ... I would like above all, O my Beloved Saviour, I would like to pour out my blood for you, down to the last drop [...] Martyrdom, that is the dream of my youth, but I believe that my dream is a madness, because I would not know how to limit myself to desire one particular type of martyrdom [...] To satisfy me, I would have to have them all[79].

And in the same spirit, she dedicates this verse to the martyr, Théophane Vénbard:[80]

> Happy Martyr, at the hour of sacrifice
> You savoured the happiness of suffering,
> Suffering for God seemed to you a delight,
> And, smiling, you knew how to live and how to die ...

---

79. "Autobiographie" in Manuscript B, *Œuvres Complètes*, pp. 225–227.
80. *Poésie* 47.

The Family

6 The Irreplaceable Role of Marriage and the Family[1]

Among the innumerable texts in which the Church proclaims her understanding of marriage (conciliar texts, the Code of Canon Law, encyclical letters, apostolic exhortations, Papal discourses, liturgical rites), it will be helpful to reread a document which is not often mentioned generally, either in civil society at large or in the various points of reference within the Church, for reasons which, obviously, are different, but which is of interest because it established the basis for a possible dialogue between the Holy See and the governments to whom the letter was directed; it concerns the *Charter of the Rights of the Family*, published on October 22, 1983. In Part B of its preamble, the text provides, indirectly, a definition of marriage:

> The family is founded on marriage, that intimate and complementary union of one man and one woman, which is established by the indissoluble bond of marriage, freely contracted and publicly affirmed, and which is open to the transmission of life.

As can be seen, here we are not dealing, properly speaking, with a definition *stricto sensu* of Christian marriage, in the sense that what qualifies the latter in the eyes of the Christian faith is not mentioned; its divine origin on the one hand and its sacramental dignity on the other. These two elements, which can be found in numerous texts of a theological or canonical nature, are connected to each other and must be explained, however briefly. As far as the sacramental aspect is concerned, we may cite, for

---

1. "The Irreplaceable Role of Marriage and of the Family" was published in Italian under the title "Il ruolo insostituibile del matrimonio e della famiglia" in *L'Osservatore Romano*, April 16, 2004, p. 4.

example, canon 1055 §1, quoted by the *Catechism of the Catholic Church*:

> The sacramental covenant, by which a man and a woman establish between themselves a community of the whole of their lives, ordered of its very nature to the good of the spouses, as also to the generation and education of children, has been raised between the baptised by Christ the Lord to the dignity of a sacrament.[2]

As with every other sacrament, as the efficacious sign of the presence and action of Christ, Christian marriage makes present a covenant which is broader and more original, that which unites Christ and the Church, to which he has made a gift of himself and which becomes the covenant between Christ himself and the spouses.[3] It goes without saying that here we find ourselves within a specifically Christian perspective, which is not understandable except from the standpoint of the faith. However, what the Church calls a sacrament, that is to say an event of grace, has also an anthropological content, requirements which build up its structure, which are not different, humanly speaking, from those which have characterized civil marriage, such as it has been transmitted to us by our law; these requirements bind Christians, just as they do other people. Before examining them and before then seeing in what way, in the institution of marriage, they remain necessary for society, it seems to me that it will be useful to recall briefly how Christian reflection upon marriage and the family constituted itself

---

2. *Catechism of the Catholic Church* § 1601.
3. "For, just as in earlier times God bestowed upon his people a covenant of love and of fidelity with his people, so in the same way now the Saviour of mankind, the Spouse of the Church, comes to encounter Christian spouses in the sacrament of marriage. He continues to dwell with them, so that the spouses, through their mutual self-gift, may be able to love each other in perpetual fidelity, as he himself loved the Church and gave himself up for her. Authentic conjugal love is taken up into divine love," Vatican Council II, Pastoral Constitution, *Gaudium et Spes* (December 7, 1965), § 48, 2.

historically as a factor in both the development and in the stability of society.

A Brief Historical Summary of Christian Reflection upon Marriage and the Family

One of the consequences of the Christianization of the Greco-Roman world for social life consists, undoubtedly, in its being rooted in a new conception of the relationship between man and woman. In the communities of the apostolic writings and in particular of the conjugal morality which inspired many of these (the *Shepherd of Hermas*, the *Letter of Diognetus*, etc.) contributed to the establishment of a new status for women, founded upon their equality of dignity. The two spouses are bound by the irrevocable nature of their commitment, the sacrament binds the one and the other, the violation of the unity of marriage through an adulterous relationship possesses the same grave character for the one and for the other. If such a dignity seems to be countered by certain of the letters of St Paul, in terms of the precedence of the man, in conformity with the ideas of his time, its repeated affirmation undeniably represents a novelty of the Gospel, which could seem to endanger the equilibrium of some areas of the Greek world, and of the town of Corinth in particular. In a way that is agreement with this development, although historically independent of it, we find analogous currents of thought in philosophy, especially in neo-Stoicism and in its points of contact with Etruscan culture.[4] The master of

---

4. In the history of philosophy, Neo-Stoicism is the first doctrine in which marriage comes to be praised. Thus, in Caius Musonius Rufus (d. 100), called the Etruscan, who was the Master of Epictetus, we find this Stoic idea that the whole of nature, having been marked by the presence of the logos, enjoys a certain normativity, which grounds the equality of dignity between man and woman, and also this very Etruscan trait of the great importance given to the woman ("Women, too, should engage in philosophy"), to the great scandal of the Romans (cf. L. Gallinari, [Rome: Catholic Book Agency, 1959]).

Epictetus, called the Etruscan, Musonius Rufus, for example devotes a whole diatribe to the essence of marriage. It is known that the reputation for immorality in Etruscan culture comes in large part and quite rightly, in Roman eyes, from the excessive importance which it gave to the woman, both in terms of social functions and of artistic representations. Whatever the truth of this may be, Christian thought in the patristic period did not hesitate to emphasize these points of convergence with its own doctrine, as is borne out for example by the long extracts from the work of Musonius quoted by Clement of Alexandria in his celebrated *Pedagogue*.[5]

Nevertheless, the Fathers of the first centuries were going to have to confront two types of difficulty: on the one hand, they were witnesses to the implosion of a world, which they attributed to the collapse of morals; on the other hand, formed by neo-Platonic thought, they had to struggle against sectarian currents of thought which regarded marriage and the whole carnal dimension which it contained with suspicion. Thus, at the doctrinal level, there was, paradoxically, a double task: to exalt purity and to ground virginity as a state of life on the one side, and to reaffirm the goodness of the state of marriage on the other. So, there would be an emphasis on one aspect or on the other, according to the different authors, both in the East and in the West. At times, the two themes were treated by the same author, as was the case with St Augustine of Hippo,[6] from whom Christian thought would take up the famous doctrine of the three goods of marriage (*proles, fides, sacramentum*). It is noteworthy that, at the social level, influential groups inspired by the Gnostics, who condemned the institution of marriage and who surrounded it with derision for rigoristic reasons of a theoretical nature, were renowned at the level of their conduct, for their extreme liberalism in sexual matters.[7] The Fathers, then, had to re-

---

5. Clement of Alexandria, *Le Pédagogue*, SC, 70 and 108.
6. St Augustine, *De sancta virginitate* and *De bono coniugali*.
7. ID. *Contra Faustum Man.*, PL 42, 494; *De haer.* 47, 494; cf. also St Irenaeus, *Adv. haer,* 1, 6 and 1, 13.

affirm continually the goodness of marriage, while at the same time defending that of consecrated virginity. The intention to underline the moral demands in the sacrament of matrimony can be understood: monogamy, indissolubility and fidelity, at a time when this was being more and more inserted into the perspective of a theology of creation: marriage is naturally good because it has been created by the Author of nature. The theological debate over the full sacramentality of marriage would occupy the essence of medieval reflection and then also the Council of Trent, faced with currents of the Reformation which, by denying it, called into question once more the indissolubility of the conjugal union. Over and above this essential dimension, it is known that the canonical requirements, which there were in that period, made a decisive contribution to the debate over the Church-State relationship. It was a matter of being able to ensure the public nature of the conjugal covenant. In fact, in the Middle Ages, the idea had become accepted that marriage was in itself a contract established by consent. The practice of entering clandestine marriages had become so diffuse[8] that it had become a real plague, requiring a reform that was desired by everyone. Nothing could prevent a husband or a wife, clandestinely married, from abandoning the husband or the wife in order to contract another marriage in another place, possibly publicly, and leaving the abandoned spouse without any recourse and without the possibility of being able to prove that they were already united in marriage. While the decree *Tametsi* recognised as valid clandestine marriages contracted in the past (*vera et rata matrimonia*),[9] it decided, henceforth, the conditions for the public nature of marriage, guaranteed by the presence of a legitimate priest and two or three witnesses, would be required from then on, not only for the liceity of the marriage but also for its validity. Anyone who did not satisfy these requirements would be con-

---

8. We may recall Manzoni's great novel, *I promessi sposi* (1827).
9. Council of Trent, Sessio XXIV, Decretum *Tametsi* (November 11, 1563); *Canones supra reformatione matrimonii*, in Denzinger-Schönmetzer, § 1813–1816.

sidered as incapable of marriage (*inhabilis*) and their union would be declared null. Over and above the need to provide a remedy for a grave aberration, the decree *Tametsi* had the effect of limiting the number of forced marriages—if it may be put like that—and of ensuring in numerous cases the full consent of the contracting parties. The requirement of the public nature of the contract, without any doubt, went socially in the direction of providing a defence of individual liberty that was essential.

The modern period which followed and which led to the threshold of the Second Vatican Council has certainly been marked—in respect of the increasing secularization of European societies—by the Church-State relationship—by the necessity for the Church, on the one hand, to develop a deeper understanding of the relationship between contract and sacrament, and, on the other, to reaffirm the moral demands of marriage. It is to be noted that the slow maturation of Christian thought in this area across the centuries has been concentrated above all on the theological and juridical essentials of marriage, notably on the question of sacramental grace and on that of the minister, and that aspects more specifically pertaining to the family remained on the margin of this development. On the anthropological plane, the question of children, for example, was treated only as one of the *goods* or as one of the *ends* of marriage, the *proles* encompassing both their procreation and their education, including both their moral and religious education.

Deeper Understanding in the Reflection of the Contemporary Magisterium

The least that can be said is that the general situation of western societies has experienced a radical alteration—secularization, a hardening of lay thought, changes in traditional behaviours—such that it has led Christian thought to a true renewal in its approach, orientating it towards the anthropological issues at stake in human love. The person, conjugal union, sexuality, and procreation are topics that have given rise to considerable research and to the production of numerous writings. We need, at least in general terms, to trace the essential stages involved, in order to be able to concentrate then upon the more important themes in the cultural context which is ours today.

The General Context of Christian Thought at Present

As a matter of fact, the mid-twentieth century saw the development in several European countries of very lively forms of conjugal spirituality, something completely unheard of and which had been favoured by two sets of factors. The first was the extraordinary repercussion in the Churches in Europe of the encyclical, *Casti Connubii* of Pius XI (1930). Indeed, the text was revolutionary, presenting traditional doctrine in a perspective centred upon the subjects in the act that unites them together. Thus, consent was presented as an act of conjugal love. The conjugal life itself brought with it a genuine perfecting of the spouses. Here, mutual aid was emphasized. To sum it up, marriage brought about a real sanctification of the spouses. For half a century, this text would inspire in this field a fully committed laity; we may think, for example, of the Italian or the French Catholic Action, of the reputation which the review, *L'Anneau D'or*, came to have in France under Fr Caffarrel, the founder of the Equipes de Notre Dame, of the movement launched in Germany by Rupert Mayer. The second set of factors was the contribution to this reflection by philosophers of great renown: J. Maritain, G. Marcel, J. Lacroix, M. Nédoncelle, J. Guitton, D. von Hildebrand, M. Scheler, E. Mounier and R. Guardini. It could be said that personalist philosophy gave a very great stimulation to Christian thought; we may think, for example, of the debate between Catholic and Protestant theologians, signalled by the diffusion throughout the world of Anders Nygren's book, *Eros and Agape*. In summary, we could say that this effervescence prepared the way for the great texts of the Second Vatican Council, and in particular for the question which interests us here, that fundamental contribution that is represented today by those passages from the constitution, *Gaudium et Spes*, dedicated to marriage and the family. These few pages (nos. 47–52) are to be counted among the most widely diffuse of conciliar texts; they prepared the way for a whole series of subsequent magisterial texts on specific themes: on human procreation with *Humanae Vitae* in 1968 and the instruction, *Donum Vitae*, of 1987, on the family in society with the apostolic exhortation, *Familiaris Consortio* in 1981, the dignity of women with *Mulieris Dignitatem* in 1988, the sacred value of human life with *Evangelium Vitae* in 1995, without counting the astonishing body of doctrine represented by the collection of the *Catecheses on Human Love* of John Paul II, delivered between 1979 and 1984, and without forgetting the *Letter to Families* of 1994. To conclude this summary presentation of different texts of the contemporary Magisterium, we note that the contribution of the current Magisterium to the reflection upon marriage and the family is, without any doubt, the most important there has been in history. To explain this, it will be helpful to make two observations: the reasons for this are as much to do with the urgency and seriousness of the problems which have arisen in our days as they are to do with the very specific attention which the Holy Father, John Paul II, gave to these questions, which he judged to be fundamental for society. This profound analysis has brought about the creation and the mobilization of a large number of structures: a Council for the Family, an international university Institute for studies on marriage and the family which consists of ten sessions in the five continents, a Pontifical Academy for Life, which relies upon the collaboration of numerous specialists from all perspectives and also upon an active political presence in inter-governmental structures and of conferences of international organisations (Copenhagen, Cairo, Peking).

Fundamental Aspects of the Contribution of the Church to Current Debates on Marriage and the Family

The True Nature of Marriage

The Church speaks of marriage from a perspective whose logic it is important properly to understand, to avoid erroneous interpretations of its position. This perspective, which is that of the Christian faith, affirms that "the intimate community of life and love which the couple establishes has been founded by the Creator, who has endowed it with its own proper laws."[10] In what sense? The aspiration of a man and a woman to give themselves to each other, to form a community of the whole of their lives, corresponds to the deepest needs inscribed into the being of man and woman. It corresponds to what they are, to their nature. The institution of marriage is called to express these requirements, in such a way that the form with which it is vested cannot be subjected to upheavals of such a kind that would contradict them. We shall return to these requirements, which are called *natural*—in the sense that we have explained—but let us note that this perspective leads us, very logically, to refer those natural traits back to him who is the Author of nature. On this point, it can be understood that expressions such as "the plan of God for marriage and the family" in *Familiaris Consortio* or "the integral truth of conjugal love," far from constituting affirmations of a fundamentalistic kind, are located within the natural logic of a theology and of a philosophy of Creation, one which is accessible to reason.

The first natural requirement is founded upon the natural aspiration—which the Church, within the logic just indicated calls a *vocation*—of every human being to love. Hence, we speak of a *communion of persons.*

The particular communion of persons between one man and one woman united by marriage is ordered to the good of the spouses, and to the generation and education of children. It rests upon their mutual consent, which is a reciprocal gift that the

---
10. Vatican Council II, *Gaudium et Spes*, § 48.

spouses freely make of their own person. This gift is affirmed publicly and forms the bond of marriage, a bond which has the feature, in the eyes of the Church, of being indissoluble. These different aspects must now be explained in more detail.

The condition of freedom, in which consent must be given, does not create any great difficulty. It is accepted by everyone. The public nature of the exchange of consent, as we have seen, provides a certain guarantee—even if, of course, it is not absolute—that the marriage has been entered into with free consent. A defect of consent would be a ground for the nullity of a marriage, both for civil law and for canon law. The public nature of the consent has another function: society is a witness to this choice and to the consequences which it entails; the new state contracted by the spouses is imposed upon society, society guarantees in some way the objective existence of this bond, which transcends the persons of the spouses, and society cannot ignore it. As far as its juridical aspects are concerned, these are a manifestation of the fact that the bond that has been created is considered by society as a good that is to be protected.

The question of the irrevocable character of the consent and of the indissoluble bond which it creates in the eyes of the Church is a more delicate one. It is often imagined, quite wrongly, that indissolubility, for the Church, is a requirement that arises from sacramentality alone. In fact, it is not sacramentality that creates indissolubility, even if this contributes to increasing its solidity. Indissolubility is born of the interior requirement of the covenant of love between the spouses. It could not be constituted as an external adjunct to some kind of institution. It is a permanent quality which is proper to a marriage that has been validly established and it is an intrinsic requirement of the essence of marriage. This is because marriage is a personal gift, in which the whole of the person commits himself in an exclusive way—something which, besides, is expressed by the acts which are proper to this union between husband and wife—, the temporal dimension being assumed through a commitment which, in principle, is definitive. If the person were to reserve to himself the possibility of deciding otherwise in the future, how would it possible to speak any longer of fidelity? The public commitment to fidelity, at the anthropological level, cannot place a limit upon itself in terms of time; this is here an essential characteristic of the loving relationship, in which the dignity of the person of the spouse to whom the other makes this commitment is recognized and is honoured. A difficulty arises, undoubtedly, from seeing marriage in terms of the category of a contract, a category that is perfectly legitimate from other perspectives, since this is a specifically juridical notion. A contract specifies all of the conditions as to its actualization and it is thus subjected to clauses; it does not aim in the first place at expressing indissolubility. The texts of the Church, in the personalist perspective that we have evoked, quite deliberately employ the term *covenant*, which has the advantage of being able to express a reality that is at one and the same time both natural and sacramental. The natural aspect comes from this conviction that the human being has been created by God and has been endowed by him with the capacity to commit himself or herself in an indissoluble union; the sacramental aspect goes back to the biblical idea of *Covenant*, which expresses the definitive gift of God to his people, as an offering of which marriage is the image and which Christ has brought to its complete fulfilment. On this point, we take up this formulation, which is entirely new in the Second Vatican Council, when it says that, in the sacrament of marriage, Christ "comes to meet Christian spouses" and that he "continues to dwell with them."[11]

Marriage as the Place in which Life is Transmitted

The Church considers that marriage is the natural place in which life is to be transmitted and that the family is the place in which that service to life that consists in the education of children is to be fulfilled. There is nothing original in this, to the extent that

---

11. *Ibid.* § 48.

this conviction has been shared practically unanimously by human society across all the latitudes until very recent times. The breakdown of the cell of the family in the West, with consequences for the lives of children, and the development of techniques which make it scientifically possible for procreation to occur independently of the relationship between a man and a woman, have made necessary an anthropological reflection at a profound level on questions pertaining to human life and its transmission. It is impossible to address here aspects concerning sexual ethics within the context of the family cell. In very general terms, it will be helpful to explain why, from the Church's perspective, the transmission of life is necessarily linked to the reality of the family. If marriage is ordered to procreation, it is so by reason of this natural disposition of the Creator, according to which, in the order of nature—and obviously not in the order of what can be manipulated—the union of a man and a woman can be fruitful and can have the consequence that a new human being can come into existence. In marriage, by definition, this union is not anonymous; it is the expression of an act of love, such that it has given rise in the spouses to a gift of self that is total, exclusive, and definitive. It is indeed love, in its most complete expression, which is fecund. On the theological plane, it is known that the Church refers to the start (to the *beginning*) such as it is presented in the symbolic account of Genesis. The words: "Be fruitful and multiply" (Gen. 1: 28) is a formula for blessing, addressed to man and woman. For this reason, the spouses are said to be "co-operators with the love of God, the Creator, and its interpreters."[12]

As for the question of the openness of marriage to procreation, a question that is central to the teaching of the Church, it shows first of all a deep wisdom; we can understand this better nowadays if we think of the contemporary demographic collapse in western countries. The decision not to have children is the expression of an interior lack of hope; it rests upon the implicit

---

12. *Ibid.* § 50.

conviction that there is no value in transmitting life and, in the end, that in itself it does not represent a value worthy of being transmitted. Anyone who excludes having any posterity does not grow himself. In this sense, the decline in population rests upon a truly pessimistic anthropology at the heart of our societies. Hope is not only the Christian virtue that is dear to Peguy; it is also the natural motive force of human activity.[13]

The Family and its Place in Society: Anthropological Requirements

Conjugal communion is not an end in itself; it is the foundation upon which the family is built, which the Church considers to be an enlarged communion of persons, according to various interpersonal relations of paternity, maternity, filiation, and fraternity. It is the natural place of contact between members of different generations, it assumes the role of mediation between the individual and society, and it constitutes the first school for the socialization of persons. There exists, in fact, a great number of functions of the family, which make the defence of the family a necessity for society: education, help for the sick, assistance to the elderly. Functions such as these will never be assumed by the state in a way that will be as satisfactory as when they are discharged within the family context. In the context of the crisis within the institutional family, society inherits those functions which were those of the family, something which can be understood easily enough. These values then become public functions. Here it is not a matter of being scandalized by society's efforts to alleviate deficiencies in the family. The question is much broader, and it amounts to what is truly a major, cultural upheaval. We are in the presence of a symbolic dispossession of the family. The institutional family is becoming the locus of a tension between its concrete and material functions, for ex-

---

13. Cf. John Henry Newman, *The Grammar of Assent*. In the study that he makes of natural religion, which he distinguishes from revealed religion, Newman draws out three distinctive traits, one of which is precisely hope.

ample, paying for the studies of children, and its spiritual functions: education, consensual moral values. This rapidly increasing evolution is leading to an ideological marginalization of the family; family values are regarded as being conservative and traditional. When the Church defends strongly a model of the family which is often qualified as being "classical," she is not laying claim to a model from the past; her reasons are grounded in the conviction that the family cell cannot be lost without there disappearing from society a certain way for the different generations to live together in solidarity and of preparing individuals to occupy a place in society in the future that will not be something which they find alienates them.

The wisdom of peoples seems always to have recognized—it is a commonplace to say this—that societies could exist in the past without any organization of the State, but a society could not exist without norms for regulating the covenant between man and woman. From this point of view, family law is even older than State law. If human beings have always institutionalized the relationship between man and woman, this is because they could see in the cell that it generated the place that made possible the transmission of values from one generation to another. Solidarity was not a value that was taught there at the level of theory, but it was transmitted and learnt in the concrete from infancy onwards. Therefore, it had a strength of experience which was acquired.

In the culturally dominant model, the family is becoming an option for individuals, people emphasize its private nature, and its dimension of being at the service of the common good has become almost entirely blurred. Very readily people contrast such a model to the patriarchal family, in which the bonds between the spouses are inserted into a complex network of relationships with other members. The personal, alternative family options, which juridical dispositions of an *ad hoc* nature make possible these days, remove from the classical model of family its status as a point of reference as the basic cell of society.

The Irreplaceable Role of Marriage and the Family

This is the case with legislation in various countries that, for example, grants juridical recognition to unions between homosexual persons. In this way, society forbids the juridical consolidation and promotion of the institution which has constituted its foundation, and which has been its anchor and its point of equilibrium across the centuries. Marriage is no longer recognized in its function of guaranteeing to the couple, entrusted to itself, anything more than a *primacy of affectivity*,[14] which, according to the predominant opinion, as D'Agostino has rightly observed, specifies the essence of what the family is. In the end, attributing juridical recognition to unions which present themselves as alternatives to the conjugal union means, just in terms of the legal measures which are introduced, pretending to grant claims for concrete solutions to be provided in a way which is totally disconnected from what properly is the foundation of law, namely the safeguarding of the common good. It is then no longer possible to judge objectively the social role of an alternative to the conjugal union on the basis of the criteria of sharing in the common good of society. It is within this perspective of the common good that an intervention of the Congregation for the Doctrine of the Faith on this subject is to be situated.[15]

An analysis such as this is not pessimistic. In reality, it seeks on the contrary to bring out the central value, still very much relevant, of the family, which remains a fundamental good for society today, as it was for all of the cultures that preceded it. The reality of the family models and structures the personality. Among the constitutive and structuring principles of the family, we cannot conclude without recalling at least briefly the most essential of them, namely the relationship of paternity and filiation. This ought to be examined more deeply, not only from a

---

14. These observations are in harmony with the penetrating analysis of F. D'Agostino in "Verità, moralità, diritto: Profili giuridici su matrimonio e famiglia,"*Anthropotes* XV/2 (1999), pp. 375–392.
15. Congregation for the Doctrine of the Faith, *Considerations relating to projects for the juridical recognition of unions between homosexual persons* (June 3, 2003), § 8.

psychological perspective, but also in terms of its morally and spiritually structuring function. For every person, it is important to be able to know that he or she is the fruit of a love, which in the natural order, is a faithful love between a father and a mother. It is within the context of such an experience that the child perceives the existence of a love that is even more radical, towards which he or she will turn with confidence, as towards its divine source.

While the Church exalts the family and defends family values, she does so, undoubtedly, on the basis of ethical, philosophical, and theological convictions that she does not seek to impose upon others, but she does so also in consideration of the good of society, which she has a vocation to serve. She devotes all her attention and reflection to this because, being a question of the common good, she knows that this good is also the good of the Church itself.

7 Created in order to Love[1]

> One in body and in spirit, the human being in his condition as a corporeal being, gathers into his or being the elements of the material world, in such a way that, through the human being, he attains his full development and with a free voice may extol the praises of the Creator. Therefore, it is forbidden for human persons to despise their bodily life. On the contrary, they must consider their body as good and as worthy of respect, since it has been created by God and is to rise on the last day.[2]

In the form of a particularly effective synthesis, the constitution, *Gaudium et Spes*, in this prophetic text, has studied and examined in a profound manner all of the values inscribed in the bodily nature of the human being, as also their ethical implications. This profound analysis has been continued in the Magisterium of the Church for more than forty years since then. Confronted by a revolution in moral standards without precedent and by the need to rethink the relationships which exist between faith and anthropology, the Church found itself in the situation of needing to intervene in numerous, new problematic areas, provoked, among other factors, by biotechnological developments never before imagined. Contraception (*Humanae Vitae*, 1968), abortion (the Declaration of the Congregation for the Doctrine of the Faith on procured abortion, 1974), the procedures of artificial fertilization (*Donum Vitae*, 1987), the foundations of Christian ethics (*Veritatis Splendor*, 1993), the situation of the institutional family (*Gra-

---

1. "Created in Order to Love" was published in Italian under the title "Creati per amare: la sessualità umana secondo Giovanni Paolo II" in *Medicina e Morale*, September-October, 2007, pp. 939–973.
2. Vatican Council II, *Gaudium et Spes*, § 14.

tissimam Sane, 1994), the threats to human life (*Evangelium Vitae*, 1995), are some of the problems linked to a certain destructured conception of human beings and of their dignity. In the common mentality, the human body has become a good of which we may dispose as we wish; acts which are specifically bodily acts, and in particular, those which involve the sexual faculty, in a way which can be understood, have been relegated to the private sphere of family life and have been exalted in a culture which has become ever more eroticized. In such a context, the need for a deeper reflection upon the human body and upon human sexuality can be understood, a reflection which would be attentive to all of levels of the dynamism of anthropology, the sensitive, the psychic, and the affective, and also the moral and the spiritual. It is thus that a rereading of this *adequate anthropology*,[3] so dear to John Paul II, has become necessary, a rereading in the light of Revelation and of the vocation of the human being to holiness, and of the essential keys to the interpretation of the teachings of the Council on human nature and on the essence of the Church, both in *Gaudium et Spes* and in *Lumen Gentium*. John Paul undertook such a reflection in a work of grandiose breadth, the *Catechesis on Human Love*, delivered between 1979 and 1984 and which has been the source of innumerable studies, as well as of several critical editions of great quality.[4]

The pages that follow are intended to offer a synthesis of the contribution of John Paul II, essentially on the basis of the catecheses but also on the basis of other magisterial texts of his pontificate. Obviously, we find ourselves faced with a certain difficulty of a methodological kind; on the one hand, we must

---

3. Cf. J. Laffitte, "Storia dell'Istituto Giovanni Paolo II" in *Anthropotes* XV/2 (1999), pp. 467–471.
4. The following critical editions may be mentioned: Spanish, English, Brazilian and Czech. The original edition is that which was published in the Italian language under the title *Uomo e donna lo creò. Catechesi sull'amore umano* (Città Nuova, Roma: Libreria Editrice Vaticana, 1985). This text is in its 17th edition.

consider what was strictly the object of the magisterial output of the Pope, but, on the other hand, we cannot remain silent about certain sources that, prior to his becoming the successor of Peter, had inspired the philosophy of Karol Wojtyla. Therefore, we shall not fail, whenever it may be useful to do so, to refer to a work that we can hardly begin to grasp in its totality. We shall examine in order:

- the interpretation of John Paul II of the first three chapters of the book of Genesis;
- the experience of love and the ethos of gift;
- the profound meaning of love and the ethical experience of sexuality; and
- the mystery of the nuptial love between Christ and the Church.

The Interpretation of John Paul II of the First Three Chapters of the Book of Genesis

The Book of Genesis: 1:28 and 2:25

For John Paul II, the double account of Creation lays out the particular features of the personal being, called into existence by his Creator. The expression: "Let us make man in our own image and likeness" (Gen 1:26) takes the form of a kind of deliberation, revealing a particular intention that was not present in the act of creation of all the other living species. In other words, from the beginning, the human being was placed in relationship with the One who created him. According to the first account, man began to exist "in the image of God" (verse 26). The following verse shows that, in her turn, woman also received her existence from a direct act of creation: "Male and female he created them." The theme of the *image of God* was treated by John Paul II on many occasions in the course of his pontificate;[5] here, in the catecheses, this theme offers the Pope an opportunity to analyze

---

5. Cf. John Paul II, *Familiaris Consortio, Mulieris Dignitatem, Gratissimam Sane*.

more deeply the condition of original communion, linking this verse to the second account of Creation. The perspective of this latter account is quite different. The second account offers the definition of the human being under the aspect of his subjectivity. The first relationship which the person experiences unites him to God; it is from him that he received the commandment not to eat of the fruit of the tree of the knowledge of good and evil. Here we have a bond of dependence, which also has the meaning of a fundamental gift, that of freedom. For the first time, the person finds himself faced with a choice; this is the first moral experience. Moral experience has a very great importance in the thinking of John Paul II. And, in the moral life of the human being, the experience of love is central in his eyes.

The usage which the deceased Pope makes of the Scriptures is a very liberal one. He does not hesitate to interpret what the biblical text expresses from a philosophical and from an existential perspective, in this way illustrating the inexhaustible richness of the meaning of the sacred text.[6]

From Original Solitude to the Communion of Persons

In order to introduce the theme of original solitude, without any doubt one of the most original in the thought of John Paul II, the Pope intends to insist upon the historical continuity of the human condition, uniting the human being after the Fall with the human being in his and her original condition. Original sin is an event in history, which helps us to understand the wounded

---

6. "What, it seems to me, is important to emphasize is that John Paul II cites the opinion of biblical scholars of his time, without, however, making his own argument depend upon them in any way. His reflections upon man as the image of God or upon the meaning of the original solitude of the human person are not influenced at all either by the fact that a text belongs to one literary tradition or another or by the fact that one may be more or less ancient compared to the other." (B. Ognibei, "Giovanni Paolo II davanti alla Sacra Scrittura" in: Livio Melina and Stanislaw Grigyiel (ed.), *Amare l'amore umano. L'eredità di Giovanni Paolo II sul matrimonio e la famiglia* (Siena: Cantagalli, 2007), p. 118.

nature of the human being. It is part of the history of every human being, who, with his or her own weaknesses, may yet have some intuition of what they have lost: their innocence. The originality of the thinking of John Paul II lies in this connection, which he wishes to bring out, between the present condition of the sinner, in which every human being finds himself and his previous condition. He writes in very strong terms:

> The human being, historically then, is so to speak rooted in his or her revealed, theological pre-history. And for this reason, every element of their historical 'sinfulness' is to be explained (as much for the soul as for the body) by reference to original innocence.[7]

This opening to the innocence of our origins allows the Pope, then, to develop two essential points which characterize the whole of the first cycle of the catecheses: the first is the objective reference which, in his dialogue with the Pharisees, Jesus refers back to *the beginning*, a point to which we shall return later; it involves a reference to every human being, touched by the words of the Master, who reveals to them the obscure mystery of sin, of their sin, but opening up to them the way of the truth of their being, a truth which is accessible in the discernment of the will of the Creator. The second essential point is the manifestation, after the Fall of the redemptive will of God. By relying upon the first promise of redemption in the book of Genesis (3:15), a passage known under the title of the *Proto-Gospel*,[8] the Pope sees in the words of Jesus the presence of the mystery of the redemption. In his dialogue with the Pharisees, Jesus opens his interlocutors to his mystery, when he refers to the beginning:

> If this beginning ... did not open up at the same time the perspective of a "redemption of the body," the response of Christ would not in fact have been understood in a way

---

7. John Paul II, Catechesis IV, *Uomo e donna lo creò*, pp. 40–43.
8. "I will place envy between you and the woman, between your descendants and hers. He will crush you head and you will tread him underfoot" (Gen 3:15).

which was adequate. It is precisely this perspective of the redemption of the body which guarantees the continuity and the unity between the hereditary condition of sinner of human beings and their original innocence, although, historically, they had lost this innocence in an irreparable manner.[9]

The Pope then studies the profound meaning of the solitude according to the Book of Genesis (2:18), the verse in which the following words are attributed to the Creator: *"It is not good that man should be alone. I shall make for him a helpmate from his own being."* According to the sacred author, the account of the creation of the first man precedes that of the creation of the first woman. John Paul II notes the significant change of terminology: *Adam*, created from the dust of the earth becomes *ish* after the creation of the woman. The Pope sees two essential meanings in the solitude of the man.

On the one hand, the text reflects the solitude of the nature of the human being in general. From this perspective, created at the end of the Creation of all other living beings, man gives names to all the species ("all the wild beasts and all the birds of the air"); he experiences in this way his superiority over the created world, but, at the same time, he does not find the "helpmate" similar to himself (Gen 2:19–20). This first meaning makes it possible to discover in the human being a process of knowledge of self, which is mediated through the knowledge of the visible world around him. This self-knowledge is produced in him when he stands before the Creator.

On the other hand, solitude is referred to the relationship of man-woman. The discovery of the other as different from oneself introduces the person into the experience of his or her own body and delimits the latter. This second aspect is central for the stages of our analysis; we shall develop this later on.

Thus, from the beginning of the *Catecheses*, it is possible to identify certain themes, which have already been analyzed in

---

9. John Paul II, Catechesis IV, *loc. cit.*

depth by the philosopher Wojtyla: the experience the human being has of himself—through his acts of knowledge, through his expectation of communion and, as we shall see, through his interpersonal relations and through his free acts (of *self-determination*)—forms the structure of *The Acting Person*; on the other hand, the aspiration of the person to establish bonds of a conjugal nature had already been the object of the study in the last part of *Love and Responsibility*. The work of personalization accomplished through love figures already in his philosophical work, where he recognizes it as a gift from God.

The Beginning (Arche)

It is in the fifth cycle of the *Catecheses* that we find the part of John Paul II's thinking which is the most developed, the heart of his teaching. These pages are based upon the Letter to the Ephesians, in order to define the foundations of the sacramentality of marriage; nevertheless, and here we have the novelty and the difficulty of the enterprise, they are based upon what the preceding catecheses have developed on the language of the body, and which, it is supposed, therefore, is known. Still, some elements need to be recalled, even if only briefly. The whole is a reflection upon the mystery of Creation, viewed as the expression of the original loving regard of God. This is articulated by a word in the Gospel employed by Jesus in his dialogue with the Pharisees: *"archè"* which we could translate as *beginning, formal principle, original form*; here we shall make use of the term used in the English translation of the Catecheses: *beginning*.

In the *beginning*, it was according to a particular plan that God created the world and fashioned man as male and female: "Male and female he created them." John Paul II uses a simple method; he undertakes a philosophical and theological reading of the first three chapters of Genesis, examining the human being first of all in the condition of original solitude, then in terms of the sexual differentiation, after the creation of Eve. However, everything is expounded, let it be repeated, in contemplation of the divine plan. From the beginning of the *Catecheses*, therefore, we have a hermeneutical unity, between the reflection upon what God willed and enacted, to the extent that it is possible to know this (theological approach) and on what the human being is by nature (an anthropological approach). Theology illuminates our reading and interpretation of the observable, anthropological givens and these, in their turn, help us to understand the nature of what God reveals of himself, when he creates man and woman, associating them with his work of creation.

An Adequate Anthropology

The purpose of the Pope's efforts is first of all anthropological; in fact, he considers it to be a matter of urgency to offer the world a vision of human love and life which is not the caricature presented by a hedonistic culture, but which expresses and reveals the reality of a greater love. This kind of anthropology has often been expressed by John Paul II by means of different terms, according to whether he is focusing his attention upon the divine mystery (*consilium Dei, veritas matrimonii et familiae*) or indeed upon the conduct of the spouses (*the ethos of gift, the language of the body*). The expression *theology of the body* takes account of both aspects.

The Experience of Love and the Ethos of Gift
The Fundamental Experience of Love

Concept and Reality

The term *experience*, taken from the context of Western thought, needs to be specified more fully. People have often opposed experience and conceptual intelligence in a dialectical manner. At times, experience has gone to the point of substituting itself for discourse; in the opposite sense, a certain kind of hard rationalism has sought to purify the conceptual operations of the human spirit of all the sensitive aspects of experience. Here, we find the signs of a confusion that has often occurred between the two points of comparison: the relationship of experience-reflection on the one hand and the relationship of the sensitive-intelligible on the other. On the contrary, both realities ought to be affirmed; the fact that experience includes both the sensitive and the intelligible, and the fact that the category of the intelligible represents something more than merely conceptual knowledge.

Concepts are produced from simple knowledge; they are not known as such. First of all, we know the human being in the concrete, and, in this knowledge, there is the production and the conservation of the concept *man*, human being. We can understand the implications of this on the Christian level; a healthy philosophy of knowledge enables us to avoid false dualism between Christian experience and doctrine, between charisms and institution. Jean Mouroux defined experience like this: "Experience is the act by which persons become aware of themselves in relation to the world, together with themselves and together with God."[10]

From Christian Experience to the Experience of Love

In the light of these distinctions that we have made, we can link Christian experience to two realities: to a precise event and to acquired wisdom. As *event*, the experience of the Christian implies or, rather includes, a theologal act; in effect, it embraces everything that is joined to the faith, it is the life of the faith; thus, for example, praying, offering a sacrifice, going to receive a sacrament, taking care of the sick in the name of Christ, etc. Experience brings out the cognitive dimension, which exists in this life of faith and in all the other acts which are constitutive of it.[11] In terms of wisdom, experience refers to the growth in virtues

---

10. J. Mouroux, *L'Expérience chrétienne*, (Montaigne: Aubier, Paris, 1956), p. 21.
11. We may take the example of conversion in the Christian meaning of the

and in the gifts. The Christian with experience is the one who, thanks to a long journey undertaken and to the theological virtues that have been infused, has acquired a kind of spontaneous understanding of their life, and of its importance at the Christian level. Christian experience, then, is an elaboration of all the Christian experiences that have been lived out and unified.

Christian experience possesses several features that are characteristic of it. It does not necessarily imply that the intellectual and psychological awareness on the part of the subject is perfectly clear. We must admit that spiritual experience can exist without the subject being aware of it. To give a simple example, if we consider the verse where the Apostle Paul evokes the Spirit who cries in our hearts "*Abba, Father,*" the fact that no-one has ever heard the Spirit cry out "*Abba, Father*" does not prevent the Christian from recognizing himself or herself as a son or daughter through the gift of the Holy Spirit. And, on the basis of this verse, the Church does not err when she recognizes in this interior presence of the Spirit in our hearts who it is who structures our filial being in a very deep way.

Another example, this time negative: to become aware of one's own sin—a condition necessary for authentic contrition—

---

term: the act of conversion is an act of the will brought about by grace, but the experience of conversion is the cognitive aspect of this act of conversion (in the sense of the knowledge of the thing, in this instance the knowledge of the personal and transcendent love of God, who offers himself, for example, in the image of the Risen Lord, in the person who is suffering, etc.), but it is a matter of an experience which can be conceptualised. And very often, such and such an experience has a very real need to be conceptualised, in order to be better understood, evaluated and eventually purified, explained and transmitted or taught (we may think of Augustinian conversion, which was a conceptualisation of the personal conversion of St Augustine); this kind of elaboration can then later be compared to Christian doctrine (an intellectual elaboration). There are many other examples that could illustrate this process, such as that of the discernment of the charisms of founders or again such as the doctrinal judgment about the writings of a person in the course the process of their beatification or canonization.

does not mean that, prior to this moment of recognition, there had not been a real experience of sin.

These examples illustrate the danger that there is these days of reducing experience to that of which we are explicitly conscious. Christian experience has other characteristics:

- It includes an awareness of the transcendent and, for this reason, it requires an elevation of our faculties of knowledge through the grace of faith;
- It is specific by reason of its object, whereas there exists a disproportion between God and every other object of knowledge;
- The initiative does not come from the subject, but from God himself; the day when someone is converted, it is God who converts that person to himself. The human being, then, has the experience of encountering God, either through an outpouring of the Holy Spirit or through the reception of a sacrament.

The point which must be underlined and which is essential for our reflection is that an authentic Christian experience cannot be detached from an experience of love, an affective experience of the divine, which can sometimes be expressed by analogies of the senses (the taste for God and for things divine) or even by symbolic expressions proper to the mystical life (mystical wedding, illumination, etc.). Let us add that this experience does not occur without the discovery and acceptance out of love of moral responsibilities.

It should not surprise us to find some of the following characteristics in the experience of love.

The first human experience of love, filial love, is the place in which an original love is revealed.[12] It is only over time that the child acquires an awareness of himself and of his duties. He is built up morally little by little over time; what is good and true in the reality of behaving correctly is revealed to him within the experience of a trusting love. To behave properly, then, means to behave within a reality of a submission which is completely filial.

---

12. On this point, see below, J. Laffitte, "What is a filial anthropology?," pp. 290–308.

John Paul II makes this comment about the discovery of the Absolute and of the demands that this brings with it:

> This man, of whom the first chapter (of the book of Genesis) says that he has been created in the image of God is revealed in the second account as the subject of the Covenant, that is to say as the subject who is constituted as a person, constituted to the point of being the partner of the Absolute, insofar as that person must discern in their conscience and must choose between good and evil, between life and death. The words of the first commandment of God-Yahweh (Gen 2:16–17), which speak directly of submission and of dependence on the part of the man-creature vis-à-vis his Creator, reveal indirectly just such a level of humanity: subject of the Covenant and partner of the Absolute. The human being is alone, which means that, by virtue of his humanity as such, because he is, he is at the same time constituted in a relationship which is unique, exclusive and non-repeatable with God himself.[13]

The Experience of Conjugal Love

For John Paul II, conjugal love reveals itself also as the place of a love which is final. The fundamental experience of love builds itself up around the experience of one's own body. Consequently, it is necessary to go back to this original experience, in the sense that the Pope gives to it in Catechesis XI, an experience that lies at the root of every subsequent human experience. The male (or the female) who is different from oneself presents himself (or herself) so that he or she may be contemplated precisely in that which reveals them to be specifically different. Subsequently, the Pope comments upon two verses of the book of Genesis: "Now, they were both naked, but they felt no shame" (2:25) and "The eyes of both of them were opened and they saw that they were naked" (3:7).The primordial exper-

---

13. John Paul II, Catechesis VI, *Uomo e donna lo creò*, pp. 48–50.

ience of nakedness reveals the human being insofar as that being is man and woman:

> What we called at the beginning the "revelation of the body" helps us to discover in some way what there is that is extraordinary in the ordinary. This is possible because Revelation takes into consideration precisely those primordial experiences in which there appears, in a way that is almost complete, the absolute originality of who the human being is as male and female; as man therefore equally through the body. The human experience of the body, such as we discover it from the biblical texts, can certainly be placed on the threshold of every subsequent 'historical' experience. However, it seems to rest equally upon an ontological foundation, which is so profound that we do not perceive it in our daily lives, even if, at the same time, it is presupposed and postulated as part of the process of the formation of the image we have of ourselves ... The passage which teaches us that the first human beings, male and female, "were naked", but "felt no shame", undoubtedly describes their state of awareness, better their reciprocal experience of the body, that is to say the experience by the man of femininity which is revealed by the nakedness of the body, and, reciprocally, an analogous experience of masculinity on the part of the woman.... This kind of precision (that of verse 25) reflects a fundamental experience of the human being, in the 'common' and pre-scientific sense, and responds also to the demands of anthropology and notably of contemporary anthropology, which deliberately returns to experiences which are called "basic," such as that of the experience of modesty (cf. Scheler on *Scham und Schamgefühl*).[14]

The Wounding of Love and Negative Religious Experience

The reading in parallel of verses 2:25 and 3:7 of the Book of Genesis, according to the words of the Pope, shows:

---

14. John Paul II, *Ibid.*, pp. 65–67.

> a radical change in the meaning of original nakedness of the woman before the man and of the man before the woman. This arises from their consciences, as the fruit of the tree of the knowledge of good and evil ... Such a change concerns directly the experience of the meaning of one's own body before the Creator and before creatures ... But, in particular, it refers directly to the relationship of man-woman, of femininity-masculinity.[15]

What, then, is the nature of this change of meaning? What is the content of this experience? The fear of the other, whose gaze is perceived as a potential threat. Innocence is lost, in every sense of the word, one's own innocence and the innocence of the other. Fear is the loss of confidence before the gaze of someone else. It is interesting to see in this respect an inversion of the structure which is present in the love between parents and children, in which rightly the trust which is manifested enables the subject to grow. In the change present in the book of Genesis (3:7), as interpreted by the Pope, it is precisely the otherness expressed in the immediate experience of the body that poses a problem: femininity for the man and masculinity for the woman.

With respect to the Creator, we are in the presence of the first negative religious experience. The human being distances himself from his Creator; his experience ceases to be personal. As J. Mouroux had observed already, there is religious experience when a person experiences contact with God. According to him, St Paul had formulated a principle that is universal; human beings have been created "so that they may search for the divinity in order to reach it, if possible, by groping towards it until they find it" (Acts 17:27).

The Values That Are Always Present in Love

Despite the obscuring of the meaning of the body and of the perception of the value of love (the *perfect* ethos *of gift*), after the Fall, this meaning did not cease to provide human love with its

---

15. *Ibid.*

moral standards. The passage from one condition to the other did not extirpate from the heart of the human being the sacrificial dimension of love, but, rather, this perception was now experienced within the difficulty each one had of being able to commit himself or herself. The fall into sin marks the beginning of a new experience, in which giving oneself becomes arduous. To rediscover the original value of love encounters a difficulty now in being able to consider the other always as a subject and of being able to preserve the awareness of the nuptial meaning of one's own body. The *ethos of gift*, according to John Paul II, indicates an essential feature of the subjectivity of the person.

> After original sin, man and woman will lose the grace of the innocence of their origins. The discovery of the nuptial meaning of the body will cease to be for them a simple reality of revelation and of grace. However, this meaning will remain as a commitment given to the human being through the ethos of gift, written in the depths of the human heart, like a distant echo of original innocence. It is through this nuptial meaning that human love will form itself in its interior victory and in its subjective authenticity. And human beings—even through the veil of shame—will continually rediscover themselves there as guardians of the mystery of the subject, that is to say of the freedom of the gift, to the point of defending it against any attempt to reduce it to the level of a pure object.[16]

Authentic love of the other is the source of knowledge. On the one hand, the other is revealed in the totality of his personal being and not in an act of knowledge that is partial and reductive; he responds with love to the gift which is received and thus discloses all of his potentialities. On the other hand, the one who loves reveals himself to himself, to the extent that he discovers that he is capable of a full knowledge of the whole reality of the being whom he loves. It is in conjugal love that such a love is

---

16. John Paul II, *Ibid. loc. cit.*, pp. 90–92.

brought about, because the specific reciprocal gift of the husband to the wife and of the wife to the husband requires that there be a commitment forever, for the whole of life, a guarantee for that form of love which is conjugal love. Authentic conjugal love never obscures the mystery of the other. Dietrich von Hildebrand, an author familiar to the philosopher, Wojtyla, remarks:

> The features of tenderness, of mystery, of ineffable union, of sweet intimacy, are only capable of penetrating into the sphere of sexuality when the latter is an expression of the deepest conjugal love. When sexuality is isolated and when it is sought for its own sake, it undergoes a violent alteration in all of its values. The depth, seriousness and mystery disappear to give way to a maleficent force, which does nothing but attract, excite and throw away in sadness.[17]

Love personalizes all the dynamism of the human being and unites them. Far from being an obstacle to the preservation of the mastery of the person, the dimension of *eros* is integrated into the process of personalization:

> Eros, says C.S. Lewis, makes a man really want not a woman, but one particular woman. In some mysterious, but quite indisputable fashion, the lover desires the Beloved herself and not the pleasure she can give ... Eros thus wonderfully transforms what is par excellence a "Need-pleasure" into the most Appreciative of all pleasures.[18]

When it is lived at such a level, the experience of love is also the mediation of a knowledge which goes well beyond the person of the loved one, not only because the latter opens up a horizon towards which the one who loves can always grow in love, but also because the self-giving love between the two spouses is the sign of a divine gift:

> The human being appears in the visible world as the highest expression of the divine gift because he retains in

---

17. Dietrich von Hildebrand, *Pureté et Virginité* (Paris: Desclée de Brouwer, 1947), pp. 108–123.
18. C.S. Lewis *The Four Loves*, (Harvest Books, 1960), pp. 135–136.

himself the interior dimension of that gift. And, with it, he brings into the world his particular resemblance to God and, thanks to that, he transcends and rules over in equal measure his 'visibility' in the world, his bodiliness, his masculinity or femininity, his nakedness. What reflects this resemblance also is the primordial awareness of the conjugal meaning of the body, an awareness impregnated with the mystery of original innocence.[19]

At every level of the experience of human love, there is revealed the presence of an aspect of truth and of goodness. It is within the totality of their nature that human beings carry within themselves this resemblance, which renders them capable of fulfilling the divine plan:

> The natural loves are not self-sufficient. Something else, at first described as 'decency and common sense', but later revealed as goodness and finally as the whole Christian life in one particular relation, must come to the help of this mere feeling, if the feeling is to be kept sweet.[20]

Hence, there is a fundamental question that concerns human love, lived out within a Christian perspective. It seems to me that this question was formulated by Lewis himself when he asked himself, on the hypothesis that natural affections could appear as rivals of the love which is due to God, which of the two loves—love of God or love of the beloved—would occupy the first place. He responds to this question like this: "We may love him (another human being) too much in proportion to our own love for God, but it is the smallness of our love for God, and not the greatness of our love for the man, that constitutes the disproportion."[21]

In the plan of the Creator, the perfect resemblance of the image is thus brought about in love through the unifying and integrating of all of its dynamism. The experience of love and of reli-

---

19. John Paul II, Catechesis XIX, *loc. cit.*, pp. 90–92.
20. Lewis, *The Four Loves*, p. 163.
21. *Ibid.*, p. 170

gious experience in this way are united and are not confounded one with the other.

The Ethos of Love and the Ethos of Redemption

The event of Calvary and of the Resurrection of Christ mark out the whole of a sacramental economy, whose novelty is present and is transmitted in all of the sacraments. According to the vision of the Apostle Paul, it is on the basis of a very unique title that marriage is united to the mystery of the Redemption, something that makes of marriage, to take up the expression of John Paul II, a kind of prototype of all the other sacramental signs. As primordial sacrament, marriage is the model according to which salvation unfolds, that is to say, the nuptial gift received through the Church-Spouse. According to Balthasar, "original unity consists in the fact that the Church is born of Christ, as Eve was born of Adam; arising from the side of the Lord pierced on the Cross ... she is his body, as Eve was flesh of the flesh of Adam."[22]

The new sacramental reality is not directed to man and woman before the Fall but to those who are bowed down under the burden of original sin and in whom "the flesh fights against the spirit and the spirit against the flesh; there is an antagonism between them, such that [they do] not do what [they] would wish to do" (Gal. 5.17). The drama of sin impedes the realization of the gift, according to the grandeur and the strength present in the initial plan of God. The gift that characterizes the covenant between the spouses needs to be continually purified: the *ethos of gift* is an *ethos of the Redemption*, to take up once more the expression of the *Catecheses*. Here the term *ethos* indicates the free acceptance on the part of the spouses of the truth inscribed in their being, a truth that we articulated at the beginning with the formula *adequate anthropology*. In the concrete, the Redemption implies a consolidation of all the aspects present in

---

22. Hans Urs von Balthasar *Gli stati della vita cristiana* (Milano: Jaca, 1985), pp. 202–203.

this natural truth; for example, it reinforces the indissoluble character of the covenant between the spouses present at the beginning of Creation (the *beginning* to which Jesus returns, but which the hardness of their hearts prevents the Pharisees from recognizing). The body of each of the spouses is inscribed sacramentally within the horizon of the Redemption and this takes up all the values inscribed in its nature. That excludes, for example, adultery, which contradicts the nature of the conjugal covenant and deprives the body of its deepest meaning. Adultery will never be a gift. In the light of this, we can understand better that adultery is not compatible with the reception of the Body and Blood of Christ. The Redemption is at work within the interiority of the human being, purifying our hearts, since it is in the heart that evil desires arise. *"You have heard how it was said*: 'You shall not commit adultery'. *But I say this to you*: 'Whoever looks at a woman with lust has already committed adultery with her in his heart' " (Mt. 5:27–28).

It is in fact within an indirect interpretation of this passage that John Paul II uses words which are very strong: "Jesus entrusts the dignity of every woman to every man and (even if this is indirectly) of every man to every woman."[23]

The redemption of the body roots the spouses in the hope of the Revelation of the sons and daughters of God, in which that love of charity abides, which will have inspired the lives of the husband and the wife in the transitory condition of this world. John Paul II observes that, in the form itself of the sacrament of marriage, the words of consent exchanged by the spouses—"I take you as my wife, as my husband"—there is present "this eternal language of the body, unique on each occasion and impossible to reiterate."[24]

The expression, the *"language of the body"* points out the reading which man and woman make of the profound meanings inscribed in their nature (as a sexed nature) and which renders

---

23. John Paul II, Catechesis XV, *Uomo e donna lo creò*, pp. 77–80.
24. *Ibid.*, pp. 87–89.

them capable of expressing in their bodies the reciprocal gift of themselves, which they make one to the other, through the exercise of their sexual faculty. This language must not be denatured. John Paul II said that the human body speaks a language of which it is not the author. The redemption of the body anticipates the time of the resurrection, because it is only when they are risen that man and woman will live the truth of their being in its integrity, a truth which embraces also their corporeal nature.

The Deep Meaning of Love and the Ethical Experience of Sexuality

Masculinity and Femininity: The Communion Between Man and Wife

For John Paul II the completeness of the created human being is manifested in the communion of persons, expressing sexual complementarity. The book of Genesis speaks of the deep desire of Adam for "a helpmate similar to himself." The event of Eve's coming to be at his side fills him with joy and admiration: "At last, this is bone of my bone and flesh of my flesh! She was to be called 'woman', for she was taken from man" (Gen 2:23). Thus can be seen, inscribed from the beginning in the Creation of the human being, the bodiliness of man and of woman as a call to communion.[25] John Paul II rightly saw in this dimension of communion the regal sign of the Creation of the human being in the image of God.[26] On the one hand, there is present the idea of

---

25. "Sexual difference is constitutive of the human being and taking that into consideration is the *sine qua non* of being able to realise our vocation; to be the image of God", J.-B. Edart, "L'Androgyne ou la communion de personnes?" *Communio*, XXXI (2006), p. 94.
26. We note the continuity of the thought of John Paul II with that of his successor on the Chair of Peter. In the first encyclical of his pontificate, Benedict XVI writes: "There are two aspects here which are important: eros is as if rooted in the very nature of the human being: Adam was seeking this and he 'left his father and mother' to find himself a wife; it is only together that they represent the totality of humanity, that they

a similarity to God, which human beings, through their visible (and so bodily) aspect bring into the world;[27] on the other hand, this resemblance refers the communion between man and wife back to the communion which there is in God.

> The human being becomes the image of God, not so much in the moment of solitude, as in the moment of communion; from the beginning, in fact, it was not only the image in which there is reflected the solitude of one Person who governs the world, but also and essentially, the image of a divine and impenetrable communion of Persons."

Nor has this analysis, which illuminates human love with a great theological vision, failed to open up broad perspectives for anthropology; we may think of the opening numbers of *Mulieris Dignitatem*.[28]

---

become 'one flesh'. The second aspect is no less important: according to an orientation which has its origins in Creation, eros draws people to marriage, to a bond characterized by unicity and by its being definitive; in this way, and only in this way, can the human person fulfil their deepest destiny. To the image of the God of monotheism corresponds monogamous marriage. Marriage, founded upon a love which is exclusive and definitive, becomes the icon of the relationship of God with his people and vice versa; the way in which God loves becomes the measure of human love. The bond between eros and marriage in the Bible finds practically no parallel outside of biblical literature" (Benedict XVI, *Deus Caritas Est*), § 11.

27. John Paul II, Catechesis XIX, *Uomo e donna lo creò*, pp. 90–92.
28. John Paul II, Apostolic Letter, *Mulieris Dignitatem*, § 7: "The fact that the human being, created as male and female, is the image of God does not mean only that each one of them individually is similar to God, insofar as they are rational and free beings. It means also that man and woman, created as a 'unity of the two' in their common humanity, are called to live a communion of love and to reflect in this way in the world the communion of love which is in God, by which the Three Persons love each other in the intimate mystery of the unique life of God. The Father, the Son and the Holy Spirit, one sole God through the unity of the divinity, exist as Persons by reason of their unfathomable, divine relations. It is in this way alone that the truth becomes understandable, according to which God in himself is love (cf. 1Jn 1:4)."

The Specifically Moral Significance of Corporeal Experience

We shall have to return to the concept of *experience*, which we have already studied, in order to see how the corporeal experience of sexuality, far from constituting a limit for the domain of anthropology, extends also to the moral sphere. Common opinion often perceives in moral experience the free re-elaboration by moral conscience of events of an existential nature. How could a judgment of conscience be in a position to judge *a posteriori* and in a correct manner the morality of act which is perceived only as an experience? How could the deep meanings present at the heart of corporeal nature be identified in a deductive way through an abstract operation? The philosopher, Karol Wojtyla, was conscious of this difficulty when he wrote:

> The point of departure for ethics is the experience of morality. It is only a question of being able to find immediately in this point of departure such a specific element of experience and not another ... The method in ethics will be that of a reduction and no longer of a deduction.[29]

Like all of the different sectors of morality, that of human sexuality needs to rethink moral experience and its status. The deep orientation of the body to incarnate and express the gift of self in love, discovered at the most intimate level of the person,[30] is recognized as the origin of a natural moral aspiration, an interior law, which brings the subject to make a gift of himself, independently of the state of life which he takes on. We may see an illustration of this, for example, in the choice of consecrated virginity.[31] In the reciprocal love of spouses, the freedom of the

---

29. Karol Wojtyla, "Il problema dell'esperienza in etica" in *I fondamenti dell'ordine etico*, (Bologna: CSEO, 1980), p. 13.
30. Such an approach is typical of personalist philosophy, which, according to Perez-Soba, is marked by "fidelity to personal experience", J-J Perez Soba, "La pregunta por la persona," in ID. *La respuesta de la interpersonalidad*, Studia teologica Matritensia, (Madrid, 2004), pp. 234–242.
31. "In virginity and in celibacy, chastity preserves its original meaning, that

gift will always make this gift an object in need of protection, in which the human being does not cease to recognize himself or herself as the custodian of a mystery. Human sexuality manifests this intentionality at all levels, disclosing the spouses and their expectations:

> In the same way that the natural tendency to maintain our own existence rests upon a natural instinct for self-preservation, it is upon the sexual instinct in its turn that the tendency to abide with the other rests, upon the foundation both of a deep resemblance between them and a difference linked to the diversity of the sexes.[32]

Karol Wojtyla had written this already in *The Acting Person*.

In other words, the aspiration to make a gift of oneself is inscribed in the whole person, in his sexuality as in the deepest aspirations of his heart.

The future Pope devoted a part of his philosophical research to the critical analysis of an ethic of values, which has not always been attentive to identifying the specific moral moment in personal choice. It is without any doubt because of the merit of Max Scheler that he underlined the link between experience and values. The whole question, for Wojtyla, rests upon the way in which we come to know values. In *The Acting Person*, this problem, already discussed in a number of his articles, considers the need to integrate sensitivity with truth, the condition for the morality of an action. The philosopher is attentive at this point to distinguish emotionalists, like Scheler, who, according to him,

---

of human sexuality lived as an authentic expression and as a service necessary to the communion of love and of the gift between persons. This meaning remains fully present in the virginity which, by renouncing marriage, realises the 'nuptial meaning' of the body through a communion with and a personal gift to the Church." L. Vives Soto; "La renovación teológica y su incidencia sobre la relación matrimonio-virginidad", *Anthropotes* XIX (2003), 2, p. 343.

32. Karol Wojtyla, "Persona e Atto" in G. Reale and T. Styczen, *Karol Wojtyla. Metafisica della persona. Tutte le opere filosofiche e saggi integrativi* (Milan: Bompiani, 2003), p. 1109.

"claim that sensations or perceptions are the sole source of contact that the human being establishes with values and that, outside of these perceptions, there exists no other authentic knowledge of values."[33] It would be an error to think that Wojtyla underestimates the emotive and sensitive power of experiences of love. His concern is to show how, from the level of perception, we should integrate the ethical aspect, in a process which he calls one of *integration*. Moreover, he adds:

> The lived experience of values, founded upon the integration of sensations in conscience, alone is not enough. In fact, a further integration is made necessary by reason of the transcendence of the person through his or her action; it is a question of integration in the truth, if it may be expressed in that way. The transcendence of the person in the act consists in that person's reference to the truth, which conditions the freedom of their self-determination.[34]

Following Max Scheler, there have been numerous philosophers who have employed the term *value* to express what, in the sphere of morals, attracts the human person. The most well-known of all, and whose thought was very familiar to Karol Wojtyla, was Dietrich von Hildebrand, who defined love as a *"super-response to value."*[35] Despite the profound and most inspiring richness of the treatise, *Das Wesen der Liebe*, published after Hildebrand's death, a real difficulty for the author can be noted in thinking through the relationship between love and will, demonstrating *a posteriori* how well-founded were the concerns of the moralist, Wojtyla.

In *Veritatis Splendor*, John Paul II emphasized quite rightly the link between reason and free will, as also their relationship with all the other psychological and sensitive faculties: "The person, understanding his or her body, is entirely entrusted to

---

33. *Ibid.*, p. 1129.
34. *Ibid.*, p. 1130.
35. Dietrich von Hildebrand, *The Nature of Love* (2009).

themselves, and it is in the unity of the soul and body that they are the subject of moral acts."[36] The freedom of the subject cannot be isolated from his corporeal dimension. From this, it follows that the natural law can be understood as the proper articulation of the spiritual and corporeal dynamisms of the person. The desire to give oneself totally sets in motion all of the spiritual faculties, but these rest naturally upon everything that the body is, both in terms of its physiological originality and of the symbolic richness of its own dynamisms, and, in the same way, the will to make a gift of oneself is not determined by physical and sexual needs, but it is the content of an act of the person, who chooses freely to do this.

Conjugal Chastity and the "Ontological Truth" of the Union of the Spouses

He who, at the time was no more than the Archbishop of Cracow, had understood that the whole of the argumentation which Paul VI had employed in *Humanae Vitae* rested upon the affirmation of the inseparable character of the two dimensions of the conjugal act, the unitive and the procreative, an affirmation already present in *Gaudium et Spes*. The Council had not treated directly of the problems connected to contraception because Paul VI had referred their discussion to the study of an *ad hoc* commission. *Gaudium et Spes* intended to situate itself within the perspective of the virtue of chastity, the only one capable of protecting the integral meaning of the mutual gift of the spouses and of human procreation. At this point, we note that this point of view of a renewal of the formulation of the virtue of chastity was that of Karol Wojtyla, in 1960 in his phenomenology of love, *Love and Responsibility*. Far from confusing this with abstinence, chastity involves an integration[37] of true love,[38] it is a quality of love and not a flight from love: "Sexual relations," wrote Wojtyla, "do not teach love, but, if love is a virtue, then it will be so also in the sexual relations of the spouses."[39]

In *Humanae Vitae*, we find very strong formulae, such as "the intimate structure of the conjugal act" or again "intrinsically immoral," to designate an action by which it would "rendered deliberately infecund."[40]

In the same way, the inseparable character of union and procreation would be the centre of the argumentation of the Instruction, *Donum Vitae*, of the Congregation for the Doctrine of the Faith, in the context of its moral analysis of recourse to the

---

37. "The integration of the sexual faculty into the will, and as a consequence, into the person, is the work of the moral virtue of chastity: the person is orientated to the intelligible good of sexuality by becoming chaste." (C. Caffara *Etica generale della sessualita* (Milan: Ares, 1992), p. 55; Cf. also J. Noriega, who speaks of the intentionality "which the virtue of chastity introduces into the whole dynamism of love: giving oneself up totally and making of oneself a gift capable of engendering a communion of persons", *El destino del eros* (Palabra, Madrid, 2005), p. 176; J. Laffitte, "La castità come forma dell'amore vero" in J. Laffitte - L. Melina (ed.), *Amore coniugale e vocazione alla castità* (Turin: Cantalupa, 2006), pp. 75–93.
38. The heart is the seat of the chaste life. The pure heart is not the privilege of consecrated virginity; the whole originality of John Paul II consisted in his showing how chastity penetrates all the states of life and how the two states of life, marriage and consecrated virginity, illuminate each other mutually. Fourteen catecheses are devoted to Christian virginity (from LXXIII to LXXXVI). This inter-dependence between the two states has been synthesised in the following way by Stanislaw Grygiel: "We cannot understand consecrated virginity as a state of perfection in time except with reference to the full gift of self of the human being which will be accomplished in the resurrection. But, since the resurrection constitutes an organic unity with creation, it is only together that virginity and marriage can be understood and, I would dare to say, that they are good only when they are understood in their mutual relationship", S. Grygiel, "Introduzione al Quarto Ciclo" in *Uomo e donna lo creò*, p. 289.
39. Karol Wojtyla, *Amore e responsabilità: morale sessuale e vita interpersonale* (Turin: Marietti, 1980).
40. Paul VI, Encyclical Letter, *Humanae Vitae* (July 25, 1968), § 14.

procedure of artificial fertilization. We shall find this affirmation in all of the texts of the ordinary magisterium on moral matters. In his *Catecheses*,[41] John Paul II takes up the expression *"intimate structure,"* giving it the name of *"ontological dimension,"* and recalling that *Humanae Vitae* had referred to *laws written in the very being of man and of woman*: such an ontological dimension needs to be expressed in the acts of the spouses.[42] Here it is then a question of the *subjective and psychological dimension* of the truth of the conjugal act. This formulation of the Pope sought to bring out the fact of the presence in the conjugal act of objective and subjective aspects of sexuality, these intrinsic values and their assumption by the spouses. Here we rediscover the approach already present in *Love and Responsibility* and in *The Acting Person*. The person in his or her acts or, in the case of sexuality, the spouses who act, appropriate to themselves, the good inscribed in the act which they are preparing to accomplish.

If the transmission of life does not depend always upon the will of the spouses, their readiness to engage in acts that are open to that transmission involves an interior attitude that is always possible. This is not some act of violence against the will of the spouses; it is a mission, that is to say, in biblical language, a blessing: *"Be fruitful and multiply"* cannot be a categorical imperative, but it is rather a blessing, which, when it is welcomed, opens the hearts of the spouses to the joy of a gift—the gift of life—and to the joy of participating in an act of the Creator (pro-creation).

The fact that this act of procreation, in its authentic form, may be an act of love assists Christian thought in associating, analogically, in God, Creation and Love. God creates out of love.

---

41. John Paul II, Catecheses CXVIIIff, *Uomo e donna lo creò*, pp. 453ff.
42. We indicate here the pertinent observation of Olivier Bonnewijn, who remarked that, for the Christian, respecting the two deep meanings of the conjugal union is not only a "natural imperative," but it is also a "sacramental imperative," to the extent that the conjugal act, in its double meaning, expresses in a special way the reality of the covenant, O. Bonnewijn. *Ethique sexuelle et familiale* (Paris: Emmanuel, 2006), p. 132. We shall see this aspect of the sacramentality of love later on.

The divine act of creation is the super-abundant expression of a Love that is infinite, transcendent and personal.

The Mystery of Nuptial Love Between Christ and the Church

The Nuptial Love Between the Church and Christ

As the preceding pages have shown, John Paul II's vision of sexuality is extremely broad. It is rooted in the contemplation of the principle, according to which the Creator gave to man and to woman their vocation. The Pope explored all of the anthropological and ethical aspects of their union and of their love. Nevertheless, it would be an error to think that this attention devoted to the nature of the human being, as also to the moral concerns of the pastor, could have neglected the ecclesiological and the sacramental significance of human love.

As both theologian and pastor, John Paul II's reflections were always developed within a Christological perspective. For him, Christ is the source and model for the relationship between the spouses. The mystery of Christian marriage is an insertion into the nuptial Mystery of the love between Christ, the Bridegroom, and his Church-Bride. The communion of life and love between husband and wife has the specific mission to express and to make present the union between Christ and the Church. This latter is also a communion of love, a communication of eternal life and of eternal love. The life and the love thus communicated, by virtue of their divine origin and nature, are the seal of a union that necessarily is indissoluble.

People have often connected the birth of the Church from the side of Christ with the birth of Eve from the side of Adam; the New Eve is born from the side of the New Adam. The bond between the two events is not necessarily merely symbolic. Both of these births, the one and the other, are two mysteries of life. Sacrifice becomes victory over death and over sin: the Son of God has ransomed us human beings, assuming our nature and conquering our death by his death and resurrection and he has transformed us into new creatures (cf. Gal. 6:15; 2Cor. 5:17). "By communicating his Spirit to his brothers, whom he has gathered from all the nations, he has constituted them mystically as his body."[43] The fidelity of Christ is certainly a divine fidelity, but it was lived out in our human nature; hence, it was also fully human. All of the sacred authors and the Tradition of the Fathers have described the union between Christ and the Church in terms inspired by the mystery of spousal love. The vision of the heavenly Church that St John describes in the Apocalypse refers to the image of the Spouse (Apoc. 19:7). In the context of an instruction on marriage, St Paul is not afraid to refer to the model of Christ, who takes care of his Church (Eph 5:29–30). The Church nourishes herself in the expectation of being eternally united to her Lord. This definitive union thus appears as the celebration of an eternal wedding with his Spouse.

For the world, the Church, made fruitful by the gift of the Holy Spirit, is the place where Christ abides and gives himself so that people may encounter him and be loved by him. The marriage which the Church has the mission to administer is an act of Christ who "comes to meet the couple … dwells with them, so that the spouses, by means of the mutual gift of themselves, may love each other in perpetual fidelity, as he himself loved the Church and gave himself up for her."[44] Hence, the spouses have a prophetic mission: saying this prevents us from imagining a conjugal spirituality removed from its situation in real life, which is the Church. This is the reason why John Paul II devoted the whole of the fifth cycle of the *Catecheses on Human Love* to Christian marriage, and why he does not hesitate to say that the sign of marriage as a sacrament is built upon the language of the body, reread in the truth of love.[45]

---

43. Vatican Council II, *Lumen Gentium*, § 7.
44. Vatican Council II, *Gaudium et Spes*, § 48.
45. Cf. John Paul II, Catechesis CXVII, *Uomo e donna lo creò*, pp. 443–445.

The Bond Between the Gift and the Body According to John Paul II

In order to understand the originality of the thought of John Paul II on the sacramentality of marriage, it will be useful to specify what it is that unites body and sacrament. Every sacrament presupposes a bodily reality; it is sign of something and it refers to some other reality. In order for a sign to be able to signify some reality, it must be visible; this is a requirement linked to the conditions of the Incarnation. From the perspective of the letter to the Ephesians, on which John Paul II meditates at length, the reality being signified is the charity-love of Christ. The visible sign of the love of Christ is his body, dead and resurrected. The fact that this Body was resurrected indicates that it is also the sacrament of the love of the Father, since it is to the Father that the Son offered himself in sacrifice. It is he who had the power to liberate him from death.

The letter to the Ephesians (5:28–32) offers to the spouses the example of Christ:

> In the same way, husbands must love their wives as they love their own bodies. To love his wife is to love his own self, since no one ever hates his own flesh (body); on the contrary, he nourishes it and takes care of it. This is what Christ does for the Church because it is his Body. This then is why a man leaves father and mother and cleaves to his wife and the two become one flesh. This mystery is great, and I am applying it to Christ and the Church.

The word *body* is used in two different senses; in the strict sense, it refers to the body of the husband and of the wife, which makes it possible for them to unite themselves and to form *one flesh*; in a metaphorical sense, the Church is called the *Body of Christ*, which suggests the depth of the bond which unites the Son of God to all human beings. Two implications follow from this:

- The sexual union between man and woman consists of a reciprocal gift, which each one of the two makes to the other.

The human body is being considered in its sexual dimension, masculinity and femininity (the letter to the Ephesians takes up the book of Genesis 2:24).

- The phrase "no-one ever hates his own flesh (body); on the contrary, he nourishes it and takes care of it" contains an implicit reference to the Eucharist; it is by means of his own Body that Christ nourishes the Church.

The analogy that St Paul draws between the relationship of husband-wife and the relationship of Christ-Church, according to the Pope, makes a contribution to clarifying the meaning of the divine mystery. In other words, it teaches us something about the reciprocal love which unites Christ to the Church, and, at the same time, it transmits to us the essential truth about marriage, whose vocation it is to reflect the gift of Christ to the Church and the love of the Church for Christ. In order to understand this mystery well, we have need of both of St Paul's analogies. The first is that of the head and the body. To what does this correspond in the conjugal life? To the extent that it underlines the organic link between Christ and the Church, it has an ecclesiological significance. The Church is this Body that lives in Christ. The metaphor refers back to the somatic unity of the human organism. Applied to husband and wife, the image signifies the organic union which they form together, the *una caro* (the one flesh) which they constitute. The second analogy is that of the relationship of husband-wife. The marriage of Christ and the Church is brought about on the Cross, the place from which the fruitfulness of the Holy Spirit is bestowed. If the sacrament has as its aim to express this mystery, it must be admitted that it will never be in a position to do so perfectly. The mystery always exceeds the sacrament by reason of the human limits involved, but it presupposes the adhesion of faith. John Paul II underlies the fact that the sacrament goes beyond the meaning or the simple proclamation of the mystery. In effect, it is destined to make this mystery effective in the human being.

By virtue of the irrevocable entry of husband and wife into the nuptial covenant of Christ and the Church, and by virtue of their baptism, their intimate communion of life and love founded by the Creator, is raised up and is assumed into the nuptial charity of Christ and it is sustained by his redemptive power. In conclusion, it will be helpful to consider, as John Paul II does, the presence of the mystery of Christ-Spouse in the gift of the Eucharist, the gift which Christ makes of himself to his Church.

The Sacramental and the Nuptial Dimension of the Gift of the Eucharist

The institution of the Eucharist corresponds to the desire of Jesus to celebrate the Passover with his disciples. Over and above the rite—a festive meal, the blessing of the cup of wine, thanksgiving, breaking of bread—the disciples participate in a moment of intense communion made very special by the words of Jesus: "This is my Body, offered up for you; this is the chalice of the New Covenant in my Blood poured out for you." These words anticipate the free sacrifice that Jesus made of himself. The divine love which he inspires takes the form of a sacrifice; Jesus has affirmed not only that what he was giving to them to eat and to drink was his Body and his Blood, but it expresses also the value of sacrifice by making present, in a sacramental form, his own sacrifice which he was to accomplish on the Cross a few hours later for the salvation of all. The life that is sacrificed is also signified by the gesture of offering separately the bread and the wine; the Body is handed over so that the Blood poured out may express the actual or effective gift of his own life.

The Body handed over and the Blood poured out do not have the meaning only of being a symbol; they are also offered as food and as drink to the disciples, who, united to Jesus through their intentions and united between themselves, are at that precise moment united bodily to him. John Paul II develops this theme in the encyclical, *Ecclesia de Eucharistia*; it is theme formulated in the following way by Marc Ouellet:

The paschal gift of Jesus on the Cross is thus entrusted to his Church, established at that very moment and forming with him one flesh: the Eucharistic *una caro*, sealed in the Blood of the Cross and offered to all the generations in the celebration of the Eucharist, in this way brings to its fulfilment the nuptial mystery of Christ and his Church.[46]

This affirmation is very concrete: to be united bodily to Christ implies being associated with his redemptive sacrifice. The disciples who receive the Body and Blood of Christ become, so to speak, "co-corporal" and, if we may be pardoned for the expression, "con-sanguine" (or 'blood brothers') with him. We can understand why unity in charity is required in order to receive the Body and Blood of Christ worthily and efficaciously. It is to the whole Church, the Spouse of Christ, that this gift is made, a gift that continually regenerates the Church. In this way, it can be seen how the Eucharist is of its essence a nuptial reality; it is the gift which the Bridegroom makes to his Bride and which his Bride welcomes in faith.

In the Eucharist, marriage finds once more the power on which it is founded. The mystery of the Covenant between God and humankind is re-proposed every time they share in it. The Eucharist reinforces and regenerates the communion between the spouses. The Eucharistic mystery of the sacramental presence of the Son of God makes present once more the gift of his Body and continues to be the sign and the reality of the communion between God and the human race.[47]

---

46. Marc Ouellet, "Il sacramento del matrimonio e il mistero nuziale di Cristo" in R. Bonnet, *Eucaristia e matrimonio, unico mistero nuziale* (Sienna: Cantagalli, 2001). Cf. Id., "Il mistero nuziale di Cristo è eucaristico" in Id., *Divina somiglianza. Antropologia trinitaria della famiglia* (Rome: Lateran University Press, 2004), pp. 205–216.
47. The Christian Tradition and the liturgy of the Church have had the intuition of this bond between the sacraments, emphasizing their permanent character; as long as the spouses are alive, their union is always a sacrament, in the same way that the Eucharist persists through time, in its sacramental form, in the consecrated bread.

The Mass reveals to Christian spouses the truly Eucharistic identity of Christian marriage; in some way, it becomes a memory of the gift which the spouses promised to each other and which they are called to bring about throughout the whole of their existence. It teaches them that their love, a source of joy, has the capacity also to pass through suffering and death, leading them together with all those who are chosen, to the encounter with the Lamb in the eternal Passover.

The light of the Eucharist makes it possible to situate human sexuality once more in its proper dimension, that of a total gift, open to a fruitfulness that transcends it.[48]

The communion of the Body and Blood of Christ must not be seen just as a simple union of the soul with God. In our earthly state, by reason of the way each one of us is constituted as one in body and spirit (*corpore et anima unus*), it concerns the whole person, including our corporeal dimension. This opens up immense perspectives for conjugal spirituality and, practically, for the sanctification of the spouses.

> The Eucharist brings about contact between our flesh and him who healed the sick ... it causes us to grow and expands the affinity of our bodies with Christ, the Head, risen from the dead and the first fruits of those who have fallen asleep in death. When the union between body and soul is destroyed, the soul remains, made to love its body, the glorified soul awaits the glorification of its body; and it is the Eucharist which has placed within it a requirement, a principle, a radical power of resurrection.[49]

---

48. This has been developed several times by John Paul II in the apostolic exhortation, *Familiaris Consortio*, as also in the *Letter to Families*.
49. J. Mouroux, *Sens chrétien de l'homme* (Montaigne: Aubier, Paris, 1945), pp. 88–89.

8 The Body and Natural Law[1]

> *Since there can be no movement of the body without an interior movement of the soul, our external, visible acts amplify, how I do not know, the interior and invisible acts, which unleash them. And it is in this way that the feeling of the heart, which precedes them in order for them to be accomplished, is increased through their performance.*
>
> Tertullian, *De cura gerenda pro mortuis*, 5, 7

In a few words, Tertullian articulated in this way the strict interdependence between acts of the body and the invisible acts of the soul. The *motus corporis* refers back to the *affectus cordis*, which precedes it, without, however, leaving it intact as it was, but modifying it in some way. In the first place, concerned about the dignity of the body which one day is destined to rise again, he affirmed in this way the moral significance of the flesh which envelopes us, which participates in every human activity, something which was to lead it to share in the eternal destiny of the soul.

> Is there some good on which the soul can feed itself without passing through the body? And what would it be? Through the body, the soul is furnished with the instrument of all the senses: sight, hearing, smell, taste and touch. Through the flesh, the divine power is infused into the soul; she can accomplish nothing without the word, at least being tacitly preconceived; now the word comes

---

1. "The Body and Natural Law" is the text of a lecture delivered at Buenos Aires on September 14, 2004, and published in Spanish under the title «Libertad y naturalezza humana. El cuerpo humano en su relación con la ley natural» in *La Verdad los harà libres*, Congreso internacional sobre la Enciclica "Veritatis Splendor" (23–25 septiembre, 2004), Buenos Aires, Ediciones Paulinas—Pontificia Universidad Católica, Argentina, 2005, pp. 147–164.

from the organ of the flesh ...Thus, the flesh, insofar as it is taken to be there to help and to serve the soul, finds itself sharing the fate and the heritage of the soul. If it shares in things temporal, why not equally in things eternal? ... The soul does nothing without the flesh because, without her, she does not exist.[2]

"The works that you do in the flesh are spiritual because it is in Jesus Christ that you do everything,"[3] St Ignatius of Antioch, for his part, confided to the Ephesians. The first Christian thinkers were concerned to promote the dignity of the human body and, even if their conceptual apparatus was still metaphysically inadequate, we cannot but take note of the fact that, in this way, they allowed Christian thought to overcome the conceptual dualisms of human nature which were proper to Hellenistic culture.

The encyclical, *Veritatis Splendor*, devoted several paragraphs to reaffirming the need to recognize a proper relationship between human freedom and the nature of the human being. It took note of how much ignorance and an *a priori* rejection of any reference to the natural law in ethics was rooted precisely in an inadequate articulation of the relationship between the two terms. In reality, to affirm that there is a human nature implies that we enter into precisely what constitutes that nature and, in the end, this comes down to drawing attention to the place of the human body. This is what sections 48ff. of the encyclical address; this elaboration is necessary.[4] In effect, it would be possible to

---

2. Tertullian, *De carne resurrectionis*, VII, 36, 7–21; XV, 44, 26–27.
3. St Ignatius of Antioch, Eph. VIII, 2.
4. John Paul II, *Veritatis Splendor*: "It will be useful to consider attentively the precise relationship which exists between liberty and human nature and, in particular, *the place of the human body from the point of view of the natural law*" (§ 48); such a doctrine (*which dissociates the moral act from the bodily dimensions in which it is exercised*) revives in new forms certain ancient errors which the Church has always contested because they reduce the human person to a "spiritual" freedom which is purely formal. This reduction misunderstands the moral significance of the body and of the kinds of behavior attached to it." (§ 49); "Thus, we can understand the true meaning of the natural law: it refers to the nature

think of human nature in terms of a freedom that decides what should be and which creates the conditions for its own choices. Absolutist conceptions of liberty have not been lacking in these recent decades.[5] They underlie attempts to justify the goodness of erroneous moral conduct, including those which would deny existence to others, as for example to justify the act of voluntary abortion, or the affirmation of a supposed right of the woman to do as she pleases with her own body. Within such an understanding of freedom, it can be seen that, in the end, it is the rhetorical affirmation of personal liberty, against which there is no appeal, which makes it possible to obscure completely the existence of another body and implicitly that of another human being. Let us observe also that, strictly speaking, it is not the right of a woman to dispose of herself which is being affirmed, but the right to dispose of her body, that is to say of a good which would belong to her, about which there is nothing to indicate that it would be in fact something quite other than a good of which we may dispose at will, or to indicate that there would be there already at stake in that choice another reality, precisely as subject. The body is reduced totally to the level of a thing; it loses all possibility of being able to recover its dignity as a subject.

This kind of example shows that, in moral matters, the natural law must not be thought of without explicit reference to the human body. The body must be constantly affirmed, as much in its ontological dignity, as also in its effective participation in the moral choices that it makes possible through acts which are effective, visible, and concrete. This is the reason why it will be necessary to draw attention to the body in the concrete and, more specifically, to the experience of the body. The body is invested

---

    which is proper and original to the human being, to the nature of the human person", who is *the person themselves, in the unity of soul and body*, in the unity of their inclinations of a spiritual or of a biological order and of all the other specific features necessary for the pursuit of their end (§ 50).

5. This is the case, notably, with the existentialism of Sartre (cf. *L'Existentialisme est un humanisme* [Paris: Gallimard, 1946]).

with a large number of meanings, which refer, beyond physical appearances, to those that are unspoken and invisible. The body is expressive, it is the bearer of numerous functions which are not homogenous, nor are they all of equal importance. Finally, in the body there appears the ambivalence of the person in his capacity to appropriate external goods or to offer himself in an act of sacrifice. Among all of these, we need to explain the place of freedom, the natural law, and the corporal sphere of the person.

The subsequent sections examine in turn: the separation between freedom and nature, the root of the impossibility of thinking in terms of the natural law, the place of the human body from the point of view of the natural law, and the body as the place of the revelation of what is human.

In conclusion, we shall show briefly how, from the perspective of the Christian faith, the human body has become the place in which the freedom of God is revealed.

Freedom and Nature

In the course of the last few centuries, the concept of the natural law has become the object of various debates and disputes; that is due essentially to an erroneous use of the word *nature*, which has brought with it a misunderstanding of what traditional teaching understood by natural law and, more particularly, the reasons why the Magisterium of the Church refers to it in regard to questions of morality. No doubt, it would be interesting to offer a survey of the history of the concept of natural law in philosophy and in moral theology.[6] We could appreciate that the contestation of a certain understanding of nature is a given which, in the history of ideas, is relatively recent. Until the time of Ockham and the end of the Middle Ages, the observation of natural phenomena led more to the discovery of analogies which could be revealing about certain human qualities and behaviour

---

6. Cf. for example, J. De Finance, *Ethique générale* (Rome: Gregorian University Press, 1967).

than to that of an antagonism between strange, neutral, at times hostile and threatening dynamisms, and the sovereign control of the learned expert. The order of nature was perceived as the source of rationality, of providential origin, and the laws inherent in the behaviour of living species were studied and contemplated in their countless finalities. Since this perspective did not disturb the tranquillity of this order, the human person did not pose a great problem; his liberty was exercised within the intellectually harmonious context of social relations, clearly structured in a hierarchy and recognized by all. Natural law regulated the way in which the human being participated in nature taken as a whole. The manner of this participation was presented to him through the precepts of natural law, which communicated to him an objective knowledge of the moral rules of behavior. To be sure, we must take care not to give an idyllic interpretation of the social order that might derive from this. The concept of human nature did not provoke any great upset, if we may dare to put it like that, so much so that it did not concern itself unduly with the interiority of its human subjects. The latter might have been of interest to confessors, to poets of courtly love, and to the great Christian theologians; in the realm of philosophy, it was not addressed in and of itself, as we shall see until after Descartes.

Two factors seem to have been decisive in the revolutionary change which was to come about in the course of the following centuries; the affirmation, with Ockham, of a liberty which was absolute, elaborated as such and abstracted from its psycho-physical conditioning and from its social demands, and the separation of the concept of nature from its transcendental origin, involving the loss of the notion of Providence.

Freedom rendered absolute: medieval thought had not failed to concern itself with the status of human freedom, but it had done so within a Christian perspective, concerned at the moral level with being able to show that the implementation of the moral good was eminently suitable for the spiritual nature of the human being. The distinction between *libertas ut natura* and *libertas ut ratio*, around which the whole of *Treatise on Human Acts* in the *Summa Theologiae* of St Thomas was structured,[7] both rooted freedom in human nature and, by virtue of the rationality which characterizes this nature, determined which expressions of that freedom were appropriate in human action; to behave well meant to respect the order, the *ratio*, which is the structure of the spiritual creature. Laws existed which applied naturally of themselves because they possessed an intelligibility and because they fitted in with the rational nature of the human being, who could perceive that intelligibility. We take note of this kind of affinity, presupposed in this approach, between the human being and natural law. This would never be understood fully if it were to be detached from its Christian context. Nature, considered in this way, possesses an intrinsic goodness, communicated to it by its Creator. The act of creation is not morally neutral; it is good in itself, and it is the fruit of God's goodness. The precepts which flow from the natural law are not seen as a limit imposed upon the acts of human beings, but, on the contrary, as the salutary rule for the rectitude of such acts. The precepts of themselves are both a stimulus and a source of protection for their actions. It was when natural law came to be considered outside of its benevolent origin that it would become a constraint and that its precepts would appear as a limit imposed by another upon personal liberty. Then, it would lose its capacity to attract those persons whose freedoms would be violated by it. Within a vision such as this, adhesion to the laws can still exist, but it will be to laws which emerge from a consensus or which are accepted on the basis of their practical utility.

We can recognize how much these two factors, the claim of a liberty that is absolute and the loss of the sense of the world as created, are closely linked to one another. The idea of a divine Providence bestowed upon the natural law and upon the precepts that flow from it the dimension of a real good, willed by God and in him finding their objective good. The loss of these

---

7. St Thomas Aquinas, *Summa Theologiae*, Ia IIae, q. 7–21.

The Body and Natural Law

two structuring elements brought in its train the inability to grasp and to accept the moral relevance of the natural law and its reduction to a simple law of biology, when it concerned the nature of the person and his bodily condition.

The consequences of the disassociation between nature and freedom brought about by modern thought are numerous. On the ethical level, it is important to stress the loss of the conviction that good and bad specify two radically different ways of behaving and that they concern specifically human action. Separating human freedom from its bedrock in nature leads to people placing the accent upon two possible aspects; thinking of human nature without integrating into it the free exercise of the spiritual faculties, as occurs in all forms of naturalism and of determinism, or quite simply making free will an absolute.

Each one of these positions ends up in some form of aberration. As far as the naturalist vision of the world is concerned, it is not unusual to see authentically human feelings and forms of behaviour being attributed very seriously to animals. By way of illustration, there is the way in which the theory of evolution is explained in a textbook used for teaching in high schools. After pointing out resemblances between the genomes of human beings and those of chimpanzees, the author writes:

> If chimpanzees and human beings share so many characteristics in common, it is because the former have been linked to us through a common ancestor, living somewhere in Africa seven million years ago...At the level of mental capacities, the common ancestor has the ability to imitate, is self-conscious, has the tendency to lie and to manipulate others, the capacity for display or presentation (for transmitting a culture), the capacity to divulge or to conceal his intentions, and the aptitude for reconciliation.[8]

---

8. P. Picq, *Les origines de l'homme. L'odysée de l'espèce*, (Paris: Tailandier, 1999). It is known that the analyses of ninety-seven functional genes between man and the chimpanzee (common chimpanzee and baboon) by researchers at the Wayne State University in Detroit show a coincid-

It can be seen how the reconstitution of behaviours that appear similar between the human being and the monkey is expressed by employing uncritically categories that are univocal, which take no account of the analogical nature of these resemblances. What is the actual meaning of expressions like *self-consciousness, tendency to lie, transmit a culture,* and *capacity for reconciliation*, when they are applied to the behaviour of a humanoid that is not a man? Conversely, as applied to the human being, they have a very precise meaning: the behaviours to which they relate presuppose judgments and choices which are proper to the human being. It can be understood that, in the deterministic state of confusion that we have illustrated, the originality of what is human freedom is reduced to the level of animal conduct. Hence, it has simply disappeared.

The other consequence, that of making free will into an absolute, nowadays has a significance which goes well beyond the anarchic claim to a freedom without constraint. It involves much more an insidious dependence upon a power that is very real, that of a science without any horizon. This dependence is expressed by the axiom: *everything that is scientifically possible may be attempted and must be attempted.* Any reservation that is expressed with reference to the possible application of a new discovery is considered to be the manifestation of an obscurantist mistrust in the face of science. In the end, then, it is science that has the last word and which, without any pre-defined criteria, establishes what is good. Yet, such an *a priori* confidence in what is technically possible is accompanied in the subject by the illusion of a freedom without limits, because, apparently, the limits of what is possible are in fact always receding. In reality, however, it is no longer the subject who decides, but it is alternative models of society that are imposed upon the subject, as

---

ence of 98.4% between the two genomes. From this, comes the proposal of Morris Goodman and his colleagues to classify common chimpanzees and baboons within the genus Homo. In this way, Homo sapiens would be dethroned: cf. H. Morin, "Génétiquement, l'homme est très proche du chimpanzé", *Le Monde* (November 29, 1983), p. 24.

new stages in the process are imposed gradually through the media upon moral choices through pressure groups which do not always identify themselves. Therefore, we have passed from scientific freedom that is claimed as absolute to a reification of the human body and to a manipulation of the body of society.

It is noteworthy that the majority of these alternatives, imposed without any debate, concern for the most part the human body and its status. The way in which we have passed in less than twenty years in western countries from the debate on heterologous or homologous artificial fertilization to the establishment of a homosexual "marriage," with the possible homosexual adoption of children, is very revealing in this respect. Once recourse to artificial procreation has been justified, the status of the embryo, already poorly respected by permissive laws on procured abortion, is reduced to being purely a material reserve for possible transfer and then an agglomeration of cells at people's disposal in view of a possible cloning. In any case, it was to lead to permission for any project for the manipulation of the embryo to be put into effect and for any individual choice for an alternative "family" to be implemented. The sterile couple, for whom, in theory, IVF-ET had initially been thought out is no longer of any interest to a large number of people, in that a single woman on her own can have access now to such techniques. In this way, without being aware of it, we have passed from a plan that was in principle designed for the family to what is now the satisfaction of the desire of individuals. Obviously, such a desire can become that of a woman or of a man engaged in a relationship that is not necessarily heterosexual. Who cannot see that the claim of certain homosexual couples to adopt children is one which fits very logically into the path which the manipulations effected upon the human body and which have become so widespread, have opened up at the material level? Now, twenty years ago, no one would have offered a moral justification for such a claim and no one would have dared to formulate such a claim in public. How is it, then, that, on the scale of whole societies we have passed, from one situation to the other? Through the knowing manipulation of public opinion, always one step behind with regard to a scientific discovery and of the possibilities that this opens up for changing society. At no point, however, have citizens been in a position to make a free choice about what was being proposed to them, about something that was offering them the illusion of an additional degree of freedom. It can be seen that absolute freedom, separated from its natural moral demands, generates situations in which human beings find themselves less and less free to choose the framework of their lives and to share in protecting the values which they judge to be just for the society in which they live.

> Ideology is a voracious god. It is seductive, in that in it the human being and peoples at large see in it an instrument of knowledge and of power which is in their hands. But, the moment comes when they become aware that they will have to submit themselves to it, allowing themselves to be reduced to accepting the explanations that it offers them, allowing themselves to be re-formed on the basis of its demands. The scientific researcher who proceeds to undertake the genetic manipulation of the human being may believe that he has dethroned God from his role as Creator, but what will become of the human being in his hands, reduced to the level of being a biological object?[9]

The Body and Its Relationship to Natural Law

Veritatis Splendor drew attention to objections to a physicalist and materialistic approach that had been raised against the traditional conception of natural law. Moral laws inspiring moral behaviour, in reality, would have been merely biological laws. In a particular way, the whole of conjugal and family morality taught by the Magisterium of the Church would illustrate this. The encyclical cites contraception, direct sterilization, auto-eroticism, pre-marital relations, homosexual relations and arti-

---

9. D. Biju-Duval, *Le psychique et le spirituel* (Paris: Emmanuel, 2001), p. 121.

ficial fertilization. As can be seen, the question underlying all of these examples is that of the exercise of sexuality. It is true that the Magisterium has constantly referred to the natural law to qualify as morally illicit an auto-erotic act or homosexual behaviour. It does so on the basis of a certain conception of natural law, which it will be useful to specify more precisely. One example will suffice because it was the first occasion on which this accusation of biologism had been formulated contrary to the Magisterium; it concerns the encyclical, *Humanae Vitae*, on the transmission of life. Paul VI's text refers at several points to the natural law; first of all, to recall to the faithful that the interpretation of natural moral law is also part of the competence of the Magisterium (§ 4), then to teach that *"every matrimonial act must remain open to the transmission of life"* (§ 11), and finally to underline the profoundly rational and human character of the fundamental principle of safeguarding the two essential aspects of that act, of union and of procreation, which constitute its intimate structure (§ 12). Among the different *Catecheses on Human Love*, which John Paul II devoted to the commentary on *Humanae Vitae* in 1984, that which was proclaimed on July 18th to explain why the norms of the encyclical—not to separate the two dimensions of the conjugal act—appeal to the natural law: "The norm concerns all people, in that it is a norm of the natural law and in that it is based upon what is in conformity with human reason (when, it is understood, the latter is seeking the truth)."[10] John Paul II comments then upon the reference to natural law in number § 14:

> This reasonable character concerns not only the truth in its ontological dimension, as to what corresponds to the real structure of the conjugal act. It concerns this truth equally in its subjective and psychological dimension, that is to say, in the correct understanding of the intimate structure of the conjugal act, the adequate re-reading of

---

10. John Paul II, "*Humanae Vitae*: Moral Norms grounded in the Natural Law and the Tradition," Catechesis CXIX, pp. 456–458.

the meanings which correspond to this structure and the consideration of their inseparable connection, in view of conduct which is morally right. It is precisely in this that the moral norm consists and, as a consequence, the uprightness of human acts in the area of sexuality. In this sense, we can say that the moral norm is identified with the taking into consideration the rereading of the language of the body in the truth.

The moral act is a choice, and it presupposes that the relevant values are recognized. The inseparable connection between the two dimensions, unitive and procreative, of the conjugal act inspires the norm, but not only insofar as it is a biological law, but insofar as it is clothed with a "meaning which is born in conscience when taking into consideration the (ontological) truth of the object."[11]

In this commentary we find an illustration of the classical conception of the natural law. In the questions that he dedicates to this problem of the natural law,[12] St Thomas shows that all beings, by the very fact that they are subjected to divine Providence, share in the eternal law. In what way? By receiving in themselves an imprint of that law; all beings have within them inclinations that impel them towards acts that are proper to them. Among all of these beings, it is the human being, as far as he is concerned, who is distinguished by reason, and it is this that allows him to participate in a certain way in Providence. We know that a being endowed with reason has the capacity to decide for himself and for others; the person is in himself *"ipsi et aliis providens."* In the human being, then, in the eyes of St Thomas, there is a participation in the eternal law that consists in the fact of being able to act naturally in a suitable fashion, in accordance with the ends that reasonably impose themselves upon him (*"ad debitum finem et actum"*). Beyond the existence of inclinations towards goods that are common to creatures which are animals,

---

11. *Ibid.*, p. 456.
12. St Thomas Aquinas, *Summa Theologiae*, Ia, IIae, q. 91–94.

there exists in every rational creature a natural inclination towards everything which accords with the eternal law, especially towards the good which conforms that creature to its specifically rational nature. The desire to know the truth about God, to know, to avoid ignorance, belongs to these natural inclinations. We take note of the fact that in this classical vision a genuine equilibrium in the human person is honoured between the physical dimension (what is in common with inferior natures) and the rational dimension. The natural law, without neglecting what belongs to the former, is interested in the first place in the latter, through the rational choice of the good. The physicalist accusation levelled against the Christian conception of natural law in its magisterial sources and in its theological tradition thus has no serious foundation to support it.

In the specific field of sexuality, the moral choice is expressed through the body. This explains, no doubt, why conduct in this area is not spontaneously understood as the result of a totally free choice, in that these attitudes contain and require a real intelligibility. At the root of this difficulty, we find a representation of moral experience that has been falsified. This would consist in the free re-elaboration by our moral conscience of the brute events of existential nature. How could the judgment of conscience judge in an adequate manner *a posteriori* the morality of an act perceived as an experience and how could meanings inscribed in the bodily being, to remain with the example of sexuality, be rendered capable of being understood through an operation of abstract thought? As with every other field of morality, human sexuality demands that thought be given to moral experience and to its status. To take an example, the homosexual tendency would be a brute fact of experience; it would then fall to personal conscience to assume this in its acts, according to the moral meanings that it would attribute to it. We can find an illustration of this precise case in the exclusive glorification of homosexual love, which is expressed by a certain gay culture.

Natural Law and the Freedom of the Gift

Natural law cannot be understood and received except through a proper understanding of the spiritual and corporeal dynamisms of the person. The aspiration to give oneself totally is not an operation only of the spirit; it engages all of the spiritual faculties, but it rests naturally upon everything that the human body is, in its physiological singularity, as also in the symbolic richness of the dynamisms that are proper to it. And, in the same way, the will to give oneself is not determined by corporeal and sexual needs, but it is the content of the act of the person who chooses to do this.

The natural law which impels us towards the gift and which makes known naturally to human beings the goodness inscribed in sacrificial love, is revealed, if it may be put like this, in each of the portions of its nature. In this sense, it allows itself to be discerned in the finalities of the organism, at the same time that it attracts the subject in his freedom and in his fundamental choices. The accusation of biologism made against the Magisterium points to a basic incapacity to perceive that the organic nature of the human being can be the bearer of values and of meanings. Curiously, it implies a difficulty in thinking about the human body from a moral perspective. This is brought out and is manifested, as identified above, in the use of the body as an instrument for reasons of pure pleasure or as material simply to be disposed of. Conversely,

> the natural moral law expresses and prescribes finalities, rights and duties, which are grounded in the corporeal and spiritual nature of the human person. Nor can it be conceived of as a normativity that is simply biological; rather, it must be defined as the rational order according to which human beings are called by the Creator to direct and to regulate their lives and their acts and, in particular, in the way they are to use and to dispose of their own bodies.[13]

---

13. Congregation for the Doctrine of the Faith, "Instruction on Respect for Human Life in its Transmission and the Dignity of Procreation," *Donum*

If the natural law possesses a power, grounded on its conformity with the demands of reason, it is susceptible to being able to speak to the intelligence and to the heart of every human being. It is in this sense that the passage of *Gaudium et Spes* must be understood, which emphasizes the normativity of the precepts which it decrees, with the purpose of underlining the dignity of moral conscience. The Conciliar text refers the natural law to the Creator; he has inscribed it in the heart of the human being, and it is through that conscience that the person is placed in the presence of God. It establishes a continuity between this interior revelation and the observance of the commandments: "In a remarkable way, conscience discovers that law which is fulfilled in the love of God and of neighbour."[14] Thus, in the human being of good will, there is an intimate preparation for the acceptance of the revealed commandments, a preparation brought about by the operation of the natural law. This takes away nothing, in a perspective of faith, of the absolute gratuity with which God reveals himself to us human beings, but it does prevent us from seeing in the gift of revelation some kind of violence done to our human nature. The dignity of the human body, the ethical meanings which are found inscribed in it, and, particularly, the dynamisms of the gift of self have their exemplary figure in the mystery of the Body of Christ, given up out of love for all people, dead and resurrected.

In the sacrifice of his life, which Jesus accomplished on the Cross for the salvation of the world, there is to be found in his body a sacrifice made visible and brought to its fulfilment before our eyes, the full meaning of oblation inscribed in the bodily nature which he assumed. In the glory of his resurrection on Easter morning, his victory over death and sin, the redemption of the human body was accomplished, the manifestation of the Father's plan. The loving and humble welcome of the natural law inscribed in the body of the human being can only be lived out

---

Vitae (February 22, 1987), Intr. 3.
14. Vatican Council II, *Gaudium et Spes*, § 16.

fully in the grace of Christ, dead and risen again, and made accessible in the Eucharist. There the baptised person can find the strength to fulfil the instruction of the Apostle: "[Offer yourselves] as a living sacrifice, holy and acceptable to God" (Rom 12:1).

In this way, it is made manifest that the liberation of his own freedom is brought about in the human being. "The openness to the fulness of truth imposes itself upon the conscience of the human being; the person must search for it and must be ready to welcome it when it presents itself to them."[15] It is not without interest that the encyclical, *Veritatis Splendor*, in Chapter III, goes to the point of inserting martyrdom into the line of the logic of the moral demand, with which in certain cases the Christian may be faced:

> Even in the most difficult of situations, the human being must observe the norms of morality through obedience to the holy commandments of God and in conformity with their own personal dignity. Assuredly, the harmony between freedom and truth at times requires personal sacrifices which are out of the ordinary and it is achieved at a high cost, which can go to the point of martyrdom.[16]

While having its own inner consistency, which these pages have tried to draw out, the natural law finds its ultimate significance only in the humanity of Christ, in which it is brought to its full completion.

---

15. Congregation for the Doctrine of the Faith, "Instruction on Christian Liberty and Liberation," *Libertatis Conscientiae* (March 22, 1986), § 4.
16. John Paul II, Encyclical Letter, *Veritatis Splendor*, § 102.

9 The Eucharistic Body and the Body of the Church[1]

> *No one ever hates his own flesh, on the contrary, he nourishes it and takes care of it. This is what Christ did for the Church; are we not members of Christ? This, then, is why a man leaves his father and mother and cleaves to his wife and the two become one flesh: This mystery is great, and I say that it applies to Christ and the Church.*
>
> Ephesians 5:29–32

These verses from the letter to the Ephesians sum up perfectly the mystery of communion that we have sought to analyze so far. They offer three essential dimensions of that mystery: the relationship of Christ to the Church, the union of each human being to the Person of Christ, and finally, viewed in this light, the *una caro*, the union of husband and wife; the two will be but one flesh. By taking up the verse from the book of Genesis (2:24), St Paul unites the principle of the creation of man and woman to the divine act of their redemption, accomplished in the union of Christ to his Church. Here, we have the human body, its symbolic richness and its capacity to unite, situated brilliantly in the light of salvation. In the context of a correct theology of the body, the two plans of Creation-

---

1. "The Eucharistic Body and the Body of the Church" was written on the basis of the two following interventions: "Vocation à la communion et théologie du corps", a lecture delivered in the context of the sixth international Colloquium of the Guilé Foundation (October 24–25, 2003) and published in the Acts of the Colloquium; *Jean Paul II face à la question de l'homme* (Guilé Foundation Press, Zurich, 2004), pp. 215–232, and the lecture delivered on July 24, 2006 at Paray-le-Monial in the course of the international, Session for Families, the text having been made available through digital support systems.

Redemption, are unified together without being confused. It is the merit of John Paul II, in his Wednesday *Catecheses*, to have given us the keys with which to interpret this unity. He does this, beginning from the category of *mysterion (sacramentum)*; the word, used by St Paul, which we express in English, not without risk of misunderstanding by the word "mystery." "Mystery" is not, as may sometimes be feared, a vague concept, which would do no more than bring out what we do not understand; on the contrary, the word designates what we know belongs to the eternal thinking of God, to his plan, even if we cannot exhaust the depth of its meaning. This meaning is the object of revelation; therefore, it can be examined in depth unceasingly and it can also be manifested in its reality through a sign, a sacrament. The love which unites a husband and a wife is thus inscribed, theologically, in a salvific reality which goes beyond us, but which, nevertheless, is revealed to us little by little and, through the sacramental sign of marriage, it becomes a sign which is suitable not only as a pointer to salvation, but also as one which produces the effects of its grace. The intention of what follows here is to show how the sacramentality of marriage, considered both as a specifically ecclesial reality and also as the integral union of the spouses, is illuminated by the mystery of the Eucharist, which is *par excellence* the reality of the gift which Christ makes of himself to the Church. In order to understand the context, it must be explained that, since the Second Vatican Council and most especially following the constitution *Gaudium et Spes*, theological debates have centred upon the themes of the sacramentality of Christian marriage and upon the spouses as ministers. For the traditional understanding of a natural reality raised up to the dignity of a sacrament, little by little, and in particular in relation to the *Catecheses*, a perspective that resituates marriage at the heart of the sacramentality of the Church has been substituted for this. What goes for the sacraments as a whole, all of which are understood in terms of the mystery that unites Christ to his Church, goes in a particular way for the sacrament of marriage. The community of life and of love formed by the Christian couple, expresses, represents, and incarnates the nuptial union of Christ and the Church. Thus, we have an ecclesial reality of marriage, which is primordial. *Familiaris Consortio* did not fail to bring out the value of this.

> Through baptism, the husband and the wife are definitively inserted into the new and eternal Covenant, the nuptial Covenant of Christ with the Church. It is by virtue of this indestructible insertion into that mystery that the intimate community of conjugal life and love, founded by the Creator, has been elevated and assumed into the nuptial charity of Christ, sustained and enriched by his redemptive power (§ 13).

On this basis, the text observes that the first and immediate effect of marriage is not the sacramental grace itself, but the Christian conjugal bond, a communion of the two, typically Christian, because it represents the mystery of the Incarnation of Christ and the mystery of his Covenant. Christian spouses who are nourished by the Body and Blood of Christ are nourished from the source of grace and of charity. The Eucharist, as the most complete gift which Jesus makes of himself, is inscribed within the logic of the Incarnation of the Word, a logic of total self-giving which goes to the point of the most radical self-emptying of the person. There is a participation of the spouses in the life of Christ and it has a very specific content, as John Paul II emphasizes:

> Conjugal love involves a totality, in which all the components of the person are involved—the call of the body and of instinct, the power of feeling and of affectivity, the aspiration of the spirit and of the will; it envisages a profoundly personal unity, one which, beyond that of the union in one flesh, leads the spouses to become but one heart and one soul. (§ 13)

The Intention of Christ in the Eucharist

In the Scriptures, the institution of the Eucharist is recounted on the one hand by each of the three synoptic gospels: the gospel of Luke (22:14–20), of Mark (14:20–25) and of Matthew (26:26–29), and on the other by St Paul in the first letter to the Corinthians (11:23–33), a text, which in fact is the most ancient testimony of the practice of Christians of celebrating the Eucharist. On the occasion on which he supplies instructions as to the discipline to be followed for the regulation of assemblies and as to the way people are to participate in them in a dignified manner, the Apostle gives witness to a tradition which goes back to the Lord: "I received from the Lord what, in my turn, I have handed on to you, namely, that the night before He died, the Lord Jesus, took bread." Finally, there is another text of fundamental importance, in St John, in Chapter 6 of his gospel on the bread of life, accompanied by Chapters 12 and 13 on the Last Supper. In what follows, we shall content ourselves with relying upon the account of St Luke, then very briefly that of St Paul and then at greater length that of St John on the bread of life. Other texts, too, to be sure, should be read again, such as the Letter to the Hebrews, of which we shall read just a few essential verses.

In a second stage, we shall try to bring out some doctrinal and ecclesiological aspects which concern the sacrament of the Eucharist; this doctrine is the fruit of the deeper understanding by the Church over the course of the centuries of the content of revelation and it is part of our Catholic faith (what I mean is that is not just a theological opinion). Finally, in a third stage, with the assistance of some special examples, we shall try to understand what is going on in the Eucharistic communion, at the communitarian level and at the personal level, allowing the attitude of the Virgin Mary, a figure of the Eucharist *par excellence*, to inspire us to make real progress in communion with the divine mystery.

The Gospel of St Luke

And he said to them: "I have longed to eat this Passover with you before going to suffer, because I say to you that never again shall I eat of this before the Kingdom of God comes to its fulfilment (Lk 22:15).

In these two verses, we note the ardent desire of Jesus to celebrate this Passover, the last, with his own disciples. It takes on the value of a will, if we may say so (a manifestation of his last will, and also the heritage which He passed on because the disciples are called to renew this action, just as Jesus accomplished it: "Do this in memory of me.") An essential point must be noted; this Passover, in fact, is not like the others, it was necessary that it be "accomplished in its fulness in the kingdom of God" (cf. Lk 22:16). Between this last Passover and the kingdom, a whole series of events would intervene, which were to complete it: the sufferings of the Passion, the death on the Cross, the descent into hell, the Resurrection on the third day, the seating of Jesus at the right hand of the Father, the pouring out of the Holy Spirit. This Passover here is not just a ritual, a memorial; its final point of completion, its fulfilment, is to be found in Heaven; it is a divine action also in this sense.

The actions of Jesus are located within the tradition of the festive meal of the Jews; we note that, very quickly, Christians would cease to celebrate the Eucharist within the context of a meal; the blessing of the cup to offer thanks to God for the gift of the fruit of the vine, the breaking of bread by the father of the family who would distribute portions of it to those sharing the meal. All of that was familiar to the disciples, but one thing was radically new, and it filled them with amazement; the words of Jesus: "This is my Body, given up for you; this cup is the new covenant in my Blood, poured out for you." We are so used to hearing these words that sometimes we forget their full meaning. The Body given up and the Blood poured out anticipate the sacrifice that Jesus made of himself for his disciples. It is an offering of love ("A man can have no greater love than to lay down his life for those whom he loves" (Jn 15:13), but also an offering of sacrifice.

As John Paul II says: "Jesus affirms not only that what He was giving them to eat and to drink was his Body and his Blood, but He expressed also its sacrificial meaning, making present in a sacramental fashion the sacrifice of himself, which He would accomplish a few hours later on the Cross for the salvation of all."[2]

We note also that Jesus's sacrifice is expressed here not only in words but also through his actions. The bread and the wine are offered separately; it was necessary that the Body be handed over first, so that the Blood, which would be separated from it, the Blood poured out, could complete its role as the sign of the gift of his life actually carried out ("He loved them to the end" (Jn 13:1). The sacrifice of Christ would be a bloody sacrifice. The wisdom of the Church does not cease to inspire us to meditate upon the dreadful sufferings of the Passion, considered at one and the same time from the point of view of us human beings as an atrocious action of uncontrolled evil and of the sin of mankind, and, considered from the point of view of God, as an action of God, as the adorable offering of a God, who did not shun any means in order that He might reach all human beings, actually handing himself over to them out of love, and indeed through that very act by which they rejected him by putting him to death. It is always necessary to keep this before us, in our spirit, in order to avoid de-naturing what each Eucharist is in it essence; the rendering present of the sacrifice of Christ. To put it briefly, the Mass is not some anodyne or banal event; it is marked by a certain gravity, even if its celebration, for reasons to which we shall come, is a joyful one. It is no secret to point out that one of the reasons for the recent publication of the encyclical *Ecclesia de Eucharistia* was precisely that people often forget what the Mass in truth really is; the celebration of the sacrifice of Christ for the salvation of the world. To conclude, the last aspect of this passage from St Luke but not the least: the Blood seals a new coven-

---

2. John Paul II, Encyclical Letter, *Ecclesia de Eucharistia*, § 12.

ant between God and mankind; in other words, a covenant which reconciles us human beings with God. Its significance, then, is infinite and its efficacy is truly universal (the Pope speaks of a cosmic dimension).

The First Letter to the Corinthians (Chapter 11)

As we have said, this passage is an instruction or rather an admonition to the Corinthians on the subject of their assemblies of prayer. The Lord's Supper, in the course of which the Eucharistic action was brought about, had become the occasion of divisions: "I have learned that, when you assemble for prayer, divisions have arisen among you" (11:18). "Your meetings do not do you any good, but rather do you harm" (11:17). For Paul, divisions among brothers could not render the meeting beneficial to the participants. True communion is a fundamental requirement for the Eucharist, in order that it be truly fruitful in grace. Besides, the responsibility for the division was something which exposed those concerned to condemnation and to punishment. In reality, there are some divisions that we do not seek, but to which we are subjected and for which we are not responsible. When St Paul says: "Whoever eats the bread or drinks the cup of the Lord unworthily will have to answer for it to the Body and Blood of the Lord" (11:27), the word "Body" must be understood first of all in its literal sense as the Body of Christ really and personally present in the consecrated bread and which must be recognized as such, but the Body indicates also the totality of the believers united to Christ, the Head of the Church; it demands unity absolutely because it is not thinkable, is not acceptable, that the members of the Body of Christ should be divided or separated. Division between brothers and sisters necessarily implies that some of them are interiorly separated from Christ; their participation in the sacramental Body of Christ (the consecrated bread) could not be of any benefit to them and it would become a reason for their condemnation.

In this text of St Paul, another cause of contradiction appears also; that of not taking care oft the poor: "shaming those who have nothing" (11:22), according to the expression of St Paul. The lack of care of the poor, in fact, is objectively a contradiction of what the Eucharist is, the bread of life offered for the multitude. God gives himself to everyone; the poor, just like the others, have the capacity and the legitimate title personally to receive the infinite richness of the Presence of Christ, which is offered to them by God and offered to them with a special love on the part of Christ.

The Gospel of St John

The fourth gospel does not represent directly the account of the institution of the Eucharist by Jesus, but, in this gospel, Jesus announces it prophetically and he unveils its meaning. It concerns Chapter 6 on the bread of life. The passage announces in advance that Jesus, before entering into his Passion, would make his sacrifice sacramentally present under the appearances of bread and of wine. Jesus insists on the need for his disciples to eat his Body and drink his Blood. Here we are surely at the heart of the very real scandal, of the real stumbling block of our Catholic faith. How can a man give his Body to be eaten and his Blood to be drunk? A glance at the context of this message: after the multiplication of the loaves, the crowds followed Jesus and looked for him everywhere, according to the very words of Jesus, "because you have eaten the bread and have had your fill" (6:26). They were not looking for what was beyond the signs he had accomplished and did not believe in the One whom God had sent; they referred to Moses who had given their fathers bread from heaven (Ps 78:24); at that moment, Jesus made this revelation to them, the terms of which we re-read in the gospel of St John (6:32–30). Those listening to him understand that the bread from heaven is a gift which comes from the Father and that he would give his life for the world; up to this point, all well and good: "Lord, give us that bread always" (6:34). Then, Jesus identified himself with this bread of life and it was this which provoked the murmurings among the Jews: "You can see me and yet you do not believe [...] I am the bread which has come down from heaven...If anyone eats of this bread, he will live for ever. And the bread which I shall give is my flesh for the life of the world" (6:36, 50–51). We know that this revelation was to lead to people deserting Jesus: "Then, many of his disciples deserted Jesus and no longer went around with him" (6:66). It is clear that faith in the bread of life goes hand in hand with faith in the Son of man. Whoever rejects the Son of man cannot receive the bread of life. The discourse on the bread of life raises an important question: why did Jesus offer himself in the form of food? What meaning does that have? Here we find once more the reality of sacrifice. When the Jews offered sacrifices to God, they united themselves to them by assimilating them by consuming them; sacrifices of libation included eating. An act of this kind, which united the person making it to the victim being offered, then, presupposes a personal sacrifice of oneself to God, something that cannot have any legitimate standing without an act of love. Moreover, what the prophets reproach in those hearts which are hardened is precisely making an offering without personal commitment: "What I want is love, not sacrifice, knowledge of God, not holocausts" (Hos 6:6). When Jesus gives himself as food, he associates those who are his own intimately with his own sacrifice, with his offering of himself to the Father. The same love which impelled the Son of God to become bodily present among us ("The Word became flesh and dwelt amongst us") impelled him to remain in bodily form, to prolong his presence among us, and not only among us, but within us, in each one of us, in each one of his disciples.

St John introduces us into this mystery of communion by placing it after two very significant events; six days before the Passover, Mary anointed the feet of Jesus with a perfume of great value and wiped them with her hair, in this way and in anticipation, through what was a funeral rite, showing homage to his

Body given up for us. In *Ecclesia de Eucharistia*, the Pope makes this comment:

> Jesus is thinking of the imminent event of his death and of his burial and he sees in the anointing which has just been given to him an anticipation of the honour of which his Body will continue to be worthy even after his death, because it is indissolubly bound to the mystery of his Person. (§ 47).

The second episode is the washing of the feet, revealing an attitude which he left as an example to those who were his own: "If I, the Lord and Master, have washed your feet, you also must wash the feet of one another" (Jn 13:14). The communion between the disciples of Jesus involves a service that is mutual and humble. This gesture was made by Jesus in the course of a meal, the symbol of communion, the moment in which Jesus announced to his disciples that he was going to be handed over and in which the very one who would hand him over effectively departed from the common table. In St John and also in the other evangelists, the meal of communion between Jesus and his disciples becomes also the meal in which the greatest offence to that communion is given.

As has already been indicated for St Paul, the disposition of the heart towards communion is in this way originally a requirement necessary for participation in the meal to be taken with Jesus. This was already true for the participation specifically in this last meal, in which Jesus revealed the secrets of his love. Judas was not capable of remaining to the very end because another work, the work of darkness, drove him outside. It is to be noted all the same that he had right to the same signs of communion as the others; Jesus had washed his feet, as he had those of the other disciples, and he had also offered to him a mouthful to eat which would have honoured him in the eyes of the other eleven. We know that in Palestine, as in many other Eastern cultures, the mouthful of food offered by the master of the house always has the meaning of an invitation to communion. Up to the last minute, Judas had benefited from the same signs of communion as the others. If taking part in this meal demanded being united to Jesus through true feelings of communion and of love, the same requirement accompanies our sharing in the Body and Blood of Jesus in the sacrament of the Eucharist. The encyclical, *Ecclesia de Eucharistia*, elaborates on this point: "The celebration of the Eucharist cannot be the point of departure for the communion, which it presupposes to be already in existence, in order for it subsequently to be consolidated and brought to its perfection" (§ 35). It cites St John Chrysostom:

> I, too, raise my voice, I make supplication, I pray, and I beg you not to approach this holy table with a conscience that is sullied and corrupted. An attitude such as this, in fact, could never be called communion, even if we were to receive the Body of the Lord a thousand times, but rather it means condemnation, torment and the accumulation of punishments (§ 36).

The Eucharist: The Place of Union with Christ

What happens objectively in each Eucharist that is celebrated? We say "objectively" because the subjective aspect, that is to say, relative to the believer who receives communion will be addressed later on. It will be helpful to start from above, from the intention or the plan of God. God wills that the whole world be saved. Jesus, who, in full conformity with the will of his Father, willed to save the world through the unique offering of his life on the wood of the Cross, makes this sacrifice, effected once and for all, immediately and miraculously present to his Church. In this way, we are made miraculously present at this sacrifice that took place once and only on Calvary. Why? In order that this Church, at every point in time and in space, might enter in its turn into this offering of its Saviour, through him, to be sure, but also in him. 'Through him'; this part is obvious because this sacrifice was brought about by Christ, it is Christ who acts and the Church enters into this sacrifice because of the action of Christ. But "in him;" this means that the Church enters spiritually into this sacrifice, she associates herself with this same sacrifice, and it is in Christ that she is able to make her own offering acceptable to the Father. The Eucharist is indeed a real sacrifice. The Apostles were united at the Supper to this sacrifice, taking part in the bread and in the wine, which had become in anticipation, by virtue of the words of Jesus, his Body and his Blood, which were on the point of being handed over and poured out. The question is then: is it possible nowadays to be united to this sacrifice, to this offering, exactly as the Apostles were on Holy Thursday? It was in order to make such a participation possible that Jesus left the Apostles this instruction: *"Do this in memory of me,"* but he left them also that power which is bound to him. It can be understood that, if this sacrifice is a divine sacrifice, and if the Apostles had the mission to represent it, it is necessary that the power to do so was transmitted to them by Christ. Hence, they received both this instruction and that power.

Participation in the sacrifice of Christ is, at the same time, a participation in his Resurrection. It is indeed necessary to keep the spirit of this reality present; the offering of Jesus to his Father did not end with his death; it came to a head, it burst forth, it spread, and it took on its full extension through the Resurrection. For this reason, we speak of an eternal sacrifice or better of the *unchangeable priesthood*, according to what we read in the letter to the Hebrews, whose Chapters 7 and 8 we must reread. Here are just a few verses to illustrate what I cannot develop any further here:

> Jesus did not become a priest] according the rule of a prescription of the flesh, but rather through the power of an imperishable life (7:16).
> It is a greater covenant, the one of which Jesus is the guarantor. Moreover, whereas they became priests in large numbers because death prevented them from continuing, he, by the fact that he remains forever, has a priesthood

which does not pass away. Thus, it follows that he is capable of saving, in a way that is definitive, those who come to God through him, living for ever to intercede on their behalf (7:22–25).

Christ does not cease to offer himself. Until the consummation of the ages, he continues to offer his sacrifice to the Father. He is, then, priest of a liturgy that is eternal. In order to understand everything which follows, we must start from the Resurrection. It is because Jesus is living that we can keep the memory of the death of Jesus and, it is also because Jesus is living that he can make his offering present, his death and his Resurrection. Here we have the very heart of our faith. Every time, then, that I speak of sacrifice, remember what has just been said about the Resurrection. We have started from this light of the Risen One, and it is this that sheds light upon what has taken place.

Let is return to the Mass: the words of the consecration pronounced by the priest, according to the power of the sacrament of Order conferred by the bishop, successor of the Apostles, are the words of Jesus himself. In pronouncing them, the priest acts in the Person of Christ, *in persona Christi*; according to this traditional formula, it is Christ who acts. Such is the faith of the Church; such is the content of the faith, handed on without interruption from the Apostles until our days. When we say, handed on from the Apostles until our days, we do so with reference to the most ancient testimony that is available to us, that of the First Letter to the Corinthians (11).

It seems to me that the text that expresses this truth with the greatest force and simplicity is that of St Ambrose:

> This bread is bread before the words of the sacrament; once the consecration occurs, the bread becomes the flesh of Christ ... How can what is bread become the Body of Christ? By which words then is the consecration brought about and whose are these words? They are those of the Lord Jesus. In fact, everything else which is said before is said by the priest: we offer praises to God, we pray for the

> people, for kings, for all the others. Once we come to bringing about the venerable sacrament (*ut conficiatur*), the priest no longer uses words which are his own, but he uses the very words of Christ. It is then the word of Christ which brings about this sacrament. What is this word of Christ? It is that very word by which he made all things ... If, then, there is in the word of the Lord Jesus such a great power that what there had not been started to be, how much more efficacious is it to bring it about that things which do exist already [...] be changed into something else...Thus, before the consecration, the Body of Christ was not there, but after the consecration, I tell you, as soon as it occurs, (*iam*), there is the Body of Christ.[3]

This faith has been studied deeply and elaborated throughout the centuries and it has been settled in this way by the Magisterium of the Church:

> Since Christ our Redeemer has said that what he offered under the species of bread was truly his Body, the Church has always believed and the Council of Trent declared anew that, through the consecration of the bread and of the wine, a conversion of the whole of the substance of bread into the substance of the Body of Christ our Lord and of all of the substance of the wine into the substance of his Blood, is effected ... a change which the Catholic Church calls, and it is the right word to use, transsubstantiation.[4]

In reality, what happens? The unique sacrifice of Christ, offered once and for all in Jerusalem, is made present to us. The words pronounced by the priest are as if penetrated by the power of the Most High God and enable us, by the double consecration of the bread and of the wine, a sign of the sacrifice, to participate, as did the Apostles in Jerusalem, in one and the same sacrifice of Christ. There is no second sacrifice, there are not thousands of

---

3. St Ambrose, *De sacramentis*, ch. 4, 13–20.
4. Council of Trent, Session XXII, *Doctrine on the Holy sacrifice of the Mass*, DS 877 and 884.

sacrifices made in the thousands of Masses which are celebrated every day throughout the world. What is multiplied every time a Mass is celebrated is the rite of sacrifice, through which the unique sacrifice of Calvary is rendered present to us on each occasion through the words of consecration. "The Mass makes present the sacrifice of the Cross; it adds nothing to it, and it does not multiply it."[5] In order to distinguish well the sacramental action of the priest from the sacrifice of Christ on Calvary, it is sometimes said that this latter alone was a *bloody* sacrifice. This is true in one sense, but it is necessary to pay careful attention to the words that are used; there are not two distinct sacrifices, of which one, that of the Passion, is bloody and the other, that celebrated in the course of the Eucharist, is not. There is but one single sacrifice of redemption, in which the Blood of Christ was poured out for the salvation of the world and of which we are made contemporaries at each Mass through a sacrificial rite, the double consecration of the bread and of the wine. When we speak of bloody offering (on Calvary) and of a non-bloody offering (in the Mass), we understand very well that it is the rite of the offering which is not bloody in each Mass, but the reality of the offering, that is always bloody. As for the expression *sacrificial rite*, this is what Pius XII called the "manifestation in the memorial" (*memorialis demonstratio*, cf. the encyclical, *Mediator Dei*, of November 20, 1947, the expression being adopted by the Pope in number 12). Thus, at each Mass, this miracle is produced, which transcends the limits of time and of space. Of time: we are in the presence today of an action which unfolded two thousand years ago; of space, we are not in Jerusalem today, but it is here that we celebrate the sacrifice of the Mass. Every time that the Eucharist is celebrated, it is the work of our redemption which is accomplished. Another text of the Council of Trent brings out very well this unity between the sacrifice of Jesus and the sacramental action of the Church in the Eucharist:

---

5. *Ibid.* DS 1743.

> Although he had to offer himself only once on the altar of the Cross by his death, during the Last Supper, the Christ offered to God, his Father, his Body and his Blood under the species of bread and of wine, with the purpose of leaving to the Church, his Spouse, a visible sacrifice, precisely to re-present the bloody sacrifice which he was about to accomplish once and for all on the Cross and to perpetuate its memory until the end of the ages, as also in order to apply its saving virtue to the remission of those sins which we commit every day.[6]

The sacrificial memorial of Christ is a central, essential dimension of the Eucharist, one that is often forgotten and passed over in silence in our days. The Pope has insisted very much on this (*Ecclesia de Eucharistia*, § 11, 12, 13), for example in the following terms: "This sacrifice is so decisive for the salvation of the human race that Jesus Christ did not bring it to fulfilment and return to the Father until after he had left us the means of participating in it, as if we had been present there" (§ 11). You see: this is another formulation of what Trent had stated; the same intention of Christ at the Supper and the same reality.

We could ask in what sense the sacrificial nature of the Eucharist could concern spouses in the mutual gift that unites them. When we speak of the sacrifice of Christ, we must not forget that that this is an offering made to the Father, not the satisfaction of a cruel divinity thirsty for blood, and what is more for the blood of his son, as occurred in pagan mythologies, but it is a sacrifice of love, with a sweet fragrance, through which the salvation of the world was accomplished. God wants the world to be saved; the eternal Son, by his Incarnation and by his sacrifice on Calvary, has accomplished this divine work of salvation. The fact that this offering was an effusion of blood reveals simply that it was fulfilled to the very end and that it was the total gift of the life of Jesus, the Incarnate Word, which had been made. And, since this man was truly the Son of God, his free offering,

---

6. *Ibid.*

we may say, has had a divine efficacy; it has fulfilled the divine plan for every person to be saved and, in this very precise sense, it has brought about satisfaction, as they used to say in the Middle Ages (*satisfactoria*). It corresponded in some way to the divine plan of the Father for all people to be saved. The sacrifice of Christ was the instrument of the salvation of God.

The sacrifice of the Mass is offered to the Father; it is a thanksgiving (the meaning of the word *Eucharist*) and praise. We speak sometimes of the sacrifice of praise. Why thanksgiving? As a result of the gifts which God has given us, of all the gifts of the Creation—among which there are bread and wine—but also of all the gifts of the Redemption: the presence among us of Christ dead and risen again. Besides, before the priest consecrates the gifts, he beseeches the Father to act through the power of his Holy Spirit. To sum it up, in every Eucharist, God acts with power; the Father accepts the sacrifice which we offer him, we know this with certitude because it is precisely the sacrifice of this Son; he acts through the power of his Holy Spirit and it is also by the power of the Holy Spirit that the Son, dead and risen again, is rendered present to us. God himself is present.

As for the love of Christian spouses, this enters into the same dynamism of a gift without repayment, brought about in the concrete humanity of their persons. It has the capacity to signify the offering of Christ through the strong symbolism which characterizes it; it expresses in a singular fashion the nuptial mystery of Christ and the Church and hence it is on the basis of a very particular title that the sacrament of marriage, like the other sacraments, makes present the baptismal immersion in the life, the passion, the death, and the resurrection of Christ. It possesses all the richness and all the fecundity of the grace of a sacrament of salvation.

The importance of the Eucharist for the spouses can be understood; it is appropriate, as Marc Ouellet has written, that the spouses seal their consent to give themselves one to the other through the offering of their own lives, "uniting themselves to the offering of Christ for his Church, made present in the

Eucharistic sacrifice, in order that, entering into communion with the very Body and with the very Blood of Christ, they may form but one body in Christ" (1 Cor 10:17).

The Body of the Church

Everything we have just recalled provides us with illumination about the mystery of the Church; the Church lives from the Eucharist; the Eucharist builds up the Church. It transforms her into one Body, of which Christ is the Head. It is true that historically, the Eucharist has had a determining role in the building up of the Church, since, according to the most ancient testimonies, the first Christians used to unite themselves certainly to give praise to the Lord, to plead with him and to seek his intercession but above all in order to perpetuate this memorial, according to the instruction which the Apostles had received from Jesus. The Church and the Eucharist are bound together very closely; the one cannot be understood without the other.

Another aspect of the Church that is illuminated on basis of the Eucharist is its plenitude. At the moment of the institution of the Eucharistic rite, during the Last Supper, the Apostles were twelve, truly twelve; the number twelve is pointed out with great precision. Let us take the case of Judas; he could have left the group before this last encounter, but no; there were twelve at that moment; Judas was there; he also participated in a certain way in this foundation by his physical presence. Why twelve? Because that number represented the twelve tribes of Israel, that is to say, the totality of those who made up the chosen People. Twelve, that is the totality of those chosen. Let us note that this number would be reconstituted from the time of the first meeting of the Apostles after the Resurrection, through Matthias, chosen from among those who had been witnesses to the actions of Jesus during his public life. It is in this way, as integrally constituted as the Body, that the Church from the start was to bear all of her fruitfulness.

Another dimension that interests us in a very special way is that of ecclesial communion; to participate in the Eucharist presupposes that we are in communion. There is an invisible communion, and it is this communion that counts because the Eucharistic communion, the visible communion, does no more than lead this spiritual communion to its perfection. This invisible communion is not something abstract; it presupposes at one and the same time a life of grace which is united to the action of the conscience of the person, the practice of the moral virtues and the fulfilment by the person of the divine commandments, and, through the theological virtues of faith, of hope and of charity, it makes the person capable of reaching God. This goes for spouses invited to persevere also in this sanctifying grace and in love. It is possible indeed to participate in the Eucharist and to believe that Christ makes himself really present, but without uniting ourselves to him through love with the whole of our person. Faith may well be present, but this would be a dead faith. To persevere in faith and in charity makes it possible for us to remain in the Church, according to the formula which John Paul II used in the encyclical, *Ecclesia de Eucharistia*: "to persevere…remaining within the Church 'bodily', and also 'with the heart'" (§ 36). In the Eucharist, as he notes in the Apostolic Exhortation, *Familiaris Consortio*, there is the transmission of divine charity which is the source of conjugal charity; in the Eucharistic gift of charity, the Christian family finds the foundation and the soul of its own communion and of its mission; the Eucharistic bread makes the different members of the family community into one single body (cf. § 57).

The assembly that celebrates is constituted truly as the Body of Christ. Why? Because it presents to the Father the offering of his Son, who reconciles us with him. In doing that, it is situated in communion with the whole Church, that of heaven and that on earth. The Church in heaven, we can understand, is present because it gathers together all of the elect, all of those who are reconciled with God. As for the Church on earth, she is the

Church only because she is united to the Church in heaven, and because she preserves faithfully the deposit, the words of eternal life which are those of Christ, as the faithful and legitimate guardian of the keys of the Kingdom. She is holy, even though each day she must be purified in her members, which we are. Sharing in the Eucharist, then, implies a union of all the pastors, united between themselves and to the successor of Peter. Such a union, which is called *communion*, is a work that is divine and not human; it is the Holy Spirit who brings this about, and He does not do this without communicating himself, such that at every Eucharist we receive the Spirit. He is present here and he is fully present. To express this with the words of the great German theologian, Matthias Scheeben:

> The Holy Spirit, the Spirit of the Son, is united in the most real way to the Body of the Son, in whom he reposes and dwells. In the same way, he comes to us in this Body, to unite himself to us and to establish communion with us. In the Body of the Word, which he fills we receive the Holy Spirit, so to speak, at the very source from which he springs up. Like the Blood, the Holy Spirit spreads out from the heart into all the other members, of the real Body of the Word in the members of his Mystical Body, who are substantially united to him.[7]

Why do we speak of the real presence and in what sense? To gain the measure of this mystery, it is good to refer to the Incarnation. The Word became flesh because of the need to have someone with a body which we form and which we are destined to form eternally as the Spouse of Christ. This is due to the need for each member, the bearer of a nature which is wounded and falsified through sin and its consequences, and who has become incapable of remaining faithful in communion with God, to be completely healed and purified by the glorious flesh of the Lord. It is the healing of like by like. On the hypothesis that the human being had not sinned, this communion would have been effected

---

7.   Mathias Scheeben, *Les mystères du christianisme*, 1865.

quite naturally because then our flesh would not have needed to be healed and sanated by this contact with the Body of Christ.

When we take part in the Mass, we unite ourselves to the offering of Christ; as we know this and as we try to live this here, in communion and in fraternity, we share in it, to the extent that is possible, together. The communitarian aspect of every celebration of the Eucharist corresponds to, responds to, the plan of God to give the members of his Body to his Son. It is an act which symbolizes the Body of Christ and which builds up that Body. It is a participation in a common good, in a meal, we say also, in a Eucharistic banquet in which are co-hosts at the table. And, when we are able to do so, we receive the Body of Christ in communion. In his Eucharist, Christ unites himself to his Body.

At the personal level, there are consequences that flow from this very naturally. The Eucharist purifies our heart, and it effects in the members of the assembly healing and the remission of sins committed, insofar to be sure that they are sins which have not separated us from the Body, that is to say, through deliberate acts in a grave matter contrary to the commandments of God and of the natural law, such as the Church teaches, acts whose remission requires, as we know, the remedy of the specific sacrament of reconciliation. You see, the purpose of the Eucharist, from the point of view of the baptised person, is to bring about effective communion, which is above all a spiritual communion with the redemptive sacrifice of the Saviour, a communion which is totally fulfilled, brought to such fulfilment through the real and effective communion with the Body of Christ under the species of bread and of wine.

Thus, in the Eucharist, each one receives Christ, dead and risen again, not only as risen, but also as dead, that is to say sacrificed. Let us take note of the fact that, in communion, there is a movement that is the reverse of that which occurs when we eat ordinary food. When we eat bread, it nourishes our body, and it becomes, in a way, part of ourselves. When we receive communion, to be sure, we receive the Body of Christ, who, in giving hHimself to us, extends in some way his Incarnation, but also, by a movement which is the inverse of the metabolism which we observe in nature, we become Christ a little more, sharing in his eternal life. In the Eucharist, Christ receives us. We become what we have received; it is truly a work of God.

The Redemption of the Body

If the Eucharistic bread confers upon those who receive it under the required dispositions the first-fruits of eternal life, saves them from sin and death, it transmits, especially to spouses, the reality of salvation. Since it has been subjected to the consequences of original sin, human love finds itself in need of being assumed into divine love. In this way, there is a redemption of conjugal and of family love which the *Catecheses* often call the "redemption of the body." For what reason? The Pope relies upon the Letter to the Ephesians (Chapter 5), on the words of Jesus in his dialogue with the Pharisees (Mt 19), when he refers his interlocutors to the beginning, to creation: "Have you not read that the Creator, from the beginning, made them male and female?" It is the human being, as a bodily being who is at issue, the human being as sexually differentiated. In the act of creation, man and woman had received in their being the capacity to unite themselves to each other, in conformity with the plan of God, that is to say, in giving to their union the most perfect personal expression. They are reciprocally aware of the conjugal meaning of their bodies, which expresses the freedom of the gift and which manifests all the interior richness of the person as subject.[8] Thus, we may speak of an original chastity. The Pope speaks of original holiness. With reference to the debate over the created world (the beginning), he uses also the expression, of central importance, "primordial sacrament." To avoid a major misunderstanding, it will be helpful to keep in

---

8. John Paul II, Catechesis XIX, *Uomo e donna lo creò; catechesi sull'amore umano* (Rome: Libreria Editrice Vaticana, 1985), pp. 90–92.

mind the fact that primordial sacrament does not at all mean natural sacrament, for the reason that the order originally chosen by God, theologically, is an order in Jesus Christ; thus, concretely it is a supernatural order. "Primordial" means to say an order already in act at the moment of Creation, as a sign of the mystery that is manifested in Creation. The primordial sacrament is situated within the logic of the eternal choice, which is at issue in the Letter to the Ephesians. "The sacrament, as a visible sign, is constituted with the human being insofar as the latter is a body, through the visible character of his or her masculinity and femininity. In effect, the body and only the body is capable of rendering visible what is invisible, the spiritual and the divine. It has been created to transfer into the visible reality of the world the mystery hidden from all eternity in God and to be its sign."[9]

Eucharist: Church and Marriage

The sacrifice of the Cross, accomplished once and for all the covenant between God and the human being. The supreme paschal gift of Christ does not remain an event isolated in time, but it is, as it were, remitted to the Church and rendered present in her, when she celebrates the Eucharist. The Eucharistic *una caro*, sealed by the Blood of Christ, brings to its fulfilment the nuptial mystery of Christ and the Church. The Body and the Blood of the Spouse are entrusted to the Church, which emerges as a new Eve from the side of the new Adam, sleeping on the Cross. The Eucharist truly is the place of the *una caro* between Christ and humanity. Communion with the Body and Blood of the Risen Christ unites baptised humanity to its Redeemer and, through him, to the Trinity. In the Eucharist, God and the human being become one, maintaining their difference in what is not a fusion, but a common union, a communion. Those who receive communion become, in some way, blood-brothers of Jesus. They are his. The Church-Spouse, born from the side of

---

9. Id., Catechesis XCVI, October 6, 1982, *Ibid.*, pp. 440–442.

Christ dead on the Cross, is thus continually generated by divine love, which blossoms in the Eucharist. It is then a question of a love given by God and welcomed by the Church, of its essence nuptial, because it is a matter of the gift that the Spouse makes continually of himself to his Bride, who welcomes him in faith.

The human being is born open to communion. We have heard this several times. There is a quality of communion imprinted by God in the couple. It is the image of God expressed in the unity-duality of husband and wife. The body that has been redeemed is our human body touched by the grace of Christ and made capable by the power of the Holy Spirit of expressing and of fulfilling its original spousal vocation, in a way that is in conformity with the specific vocation of each person to marriage or to virginity. The Eucharist, then, renders the Christian a participant in the spousal love of Christ for the Church and makes him capable also of making a gift of themselves.

The Eucharist, which gives the Church her nature as Spouse, is the source of marriage. What characterizes these two unions, Christ-Church and husband-wife, is the permanence of the bond. The Eucharist, as the permanent rendering present of the covenant of Christ with the Church, is in strict interdependence with marriage as a sacrament of the covenant. The movement goes from the Eucharist to marriage. In that the Eucharist is the principal sacrament, it determines in effect the meaning of the other sacraments, but marriage is one particular determination of it. Spouses who celebrate the Eucharist enter into communion with the foundation of their nuptial union; insofar as they are baptized, they have given themselves one to the other *in Christo*.

The Eucharist vivifies and fortifies the communion between the spouses. The unity which they live in the flesh, is it not a sign of that profound and sincere unity which Christ binds with every person in the mystery of his Body and of his Blood? This is the work of the Holy Spirit. In the same way, as he acts upon the bread and the wine, He thus transforms the gift of the spouses, such that they are made capable of loving each other with a new heart. As long as the spouses are alive, their union is always a sacrament, just as the Eucharist perdures in time as a sacrament under the species of bread.

The Eucharist reveals the Eucharistic identity of Christian marriage, which has become a memorial of the gift that the spouses promised one to the other, and they are called to fulfil this all through their life. It is in this sense that the meaning of the ordinary celebration of marriage must be understood within the celebration of the Eucharist. Obviously, this permanence is of great existential significance for the spouses; it enters into conjugal charity, into their reciprocal self-giving, and into their openness to life. The divine charity in the Eucharist feeds the charity of marriage. The choice of definitive and faithful conjugal love is reinforced by the event of the Eucharist. Christian life tends towards the Eucharist as towards its summit because it is there that divinization is brought about in the act of nuptial love, which consists in eating the flesh of the Son of Man and of drinking his Blood.

This we can see: human nuptial love tends towards divine nuptial love, as towards its archetype and towards its fulfilment. Christian initiation has prepared Christian spouses, insofar as they are baptized and confirmed, to receive the Eucharistic Body and in this way to live out the divine wedding with the Lord Jesus.

A difficulty can arise: as possible opposition between marriage and the absolute claim of the Kingdom which Jesus put forward to those who were his own and in which marriage, insofar as it was an institution of the first Creation, would not fit (Mt 22:29–30). A better understanding of the sacramental grace of marriage leads us to recognize not only that total love for one's spouse is not incompatible with the Kingdom, but also that sacramental marriage is made capable of building up this Kingdom. The Holy Spirit transfigures the love of the spouses into a permanent love, offered for the sanctification of a conjugal life.

The sacrament of marriage commits the spouses to a path on which they will be able to encounter the Cross. In the Eucharist, the spouses receive the gift of the Spirit, in order to be able to relive fully the sacrificial love of Jesus Christ for his Church. In this way, the spouses live a sacrificial love, whose model, celebrated and made present in the Eucharist, is the gift of Jesus even unto death. The "yes" which the spouses say in the Eucharist is a "yes" to the Cross, to their confrontation with weakness and with sin, to the acceptance of suffering in the heart of conjugal and family life. It is above all a question of a "yes" to the call to love even unto death.

Finally, it needs to be said that the Eucharist proclaims and prepares us for the return of the Lord and for the definitive fulfilment of the Covenant. The husband knows that his love for his wife is nothing other than the sign of a greater love, the love for God lived in Christ. There is no opposition between these two loves, but there is the fulfilment of the first in the second. It is to this eschatological tension that the Eucharist calls people in marriage. It is there also that consecrated virginity plays an essential role. This latter reminds everyone that the gift of God *par excellence* is not a creature, however worthy of love he or she may be, but it is the Lord himself: "Your spouse is your Creator," says Isaiah (54:5). Celibacy for the Kingdom, in renouncing what is involved in conjugal joy, does not despise conjugal love nor the practice of sexuality, but is rightly a reminder of the definitive wedding between the Church and the Lamb, something which will come to fulfilment in the world to come.

10 Conjugal Holiness[1]

The subject of conjugal holiness poses all of us with the question, which is the same for every baptized person, whatever his or her state of life may be: on the one hand they are called to holiness in the sense that the human dimension only makes sense in an intimate encounter with God. On the other hand, everyone is conscious of the difficulty there is in becoming holy, to the point where it may be asked whether such an enterprise is not meant for just a very few people, only an élite, or quite simply whether it is in fact possible. Conjugal holiness is not the characteristic feature of the couple living an unusually successful or exceptional life. On the contrary, it designates the normal state of the Christian couple, which is already a holy reality. All their lives, these spouses strive to live by specific human and spiritual values, which are the expression of a holiness which they have received. In order to understand this better, from this moment on, we must stop identifying holiness with the moral effort of the will; holiness is never to be reduced to the level of some human merit, however heroic it may be. It is a gift of the grace of God and, on the part of the spouses, it is a docility towards the dynamism of that grace. Those spouses who are docile correspond with the totality of their lives to that which they receive personally through baptism and to that which they receive together in the sacrament of marriage.

Marriage as the Gift of Grace

---

1. "Conjugal Holiness" is the text of a lecture delivered on December 11, 2010, at Bordeaux in the context of the first Colloquium of the Course for Families organised by the Commission for Family and Society of the French Episcopal Conference.

Conjugal holiness can be understood in two different ways. These may never be separated. Marriage is holy by reason of its origin; it is the holy law of the Creator, who founded it, establishing the rules which are proper to it, and who gave it the form of a personal covenant between one man and one woman. This covenant has been raised by Christ to the dignity of a sacrament. The love of the spouses is configured to the love of Christ for his Spouse by virtue of a gift of the Holy Spirit, who inspired this love, who consolidates it and transforms it. The whole of their common life, their love itself, their activities, their paternal and maternal care, become the expression of what we call conjugal love (*caritas coniugalis*). The spouses wish to sanctify themselves in the holiness of their state, which is a permanent one. Their state is that of a permanence which is that of Christ in their midst. The Second Vatican Council speaks of the sacrament of marriage as a sacrament of encounter, not only the encounter between the spouses themselves, which is obvious, but of the encounter with Christ himself.

> Christ comes to meet the spouses in order to dwell with them…and he dwells with them so that, in the same way that he himself loved the Church and gave himself for her, the spouses in their turn may love each other faithfully, for ever in a mutual gift of self.[2]

Let us come down to practicalities; when the spouses marry each other, Christ establishes a covenant with them, he assumes the commitment to be faithful towards them, that is, however, only if they wish this. Since this involves Christ, we know that his commitment is inscribed in that of God himself. The spouses are not alone. It seems to me that, if it is possible to keep this certitude of the presence of Christ always present in their memory, very many difficulties may be overcome more easily. If Christ is present, this means that they may call upon him, ask him to help them, to inspire in them acts of kindness, attention and even of pardon.

---

2. Vatican Council II, *Gaudium et Spes*, § 48.

Conjugal Holiness

The person of Christ is the source and the model of the relationship between the spouses. The Church has always approached Christian marriage from the standpoint of the mystery of love which unites Christ, the Spouses par excellence, with the Church, his Bride. We recall the verses of St Paul's letter to the Ephesians:

> Husbands, love your wives as Christ loves the Church, when he gave himself up for her, purifying her with water with a form of words, in order to make her holy, because he wanted to present her to himself completely resplendent, without any spot or stain, but holy and spotless. In the same way, husbands must love their wives, as they love their own bodies. To love his wife is to love himself. No-one ever hates his own body; on the contrary, he nourishes it, and takes care of it. This is exactly what Christ does for the Church; are we not the members of his Body? This, then, is why "a man leaves his father and mother an cleaves to his wife and the two become one flesh". This mystery is great, and I wish to apply it to Christ and the Church (Eph 5:25–32).

As can be seen, St Paul refers to baptism. The gift of baptism, which every Christian has received, unites him or her to this total gift which Jesus made of his own person. All those who have a share in this gift form the body of the Church. We can understand that holiness cannot be anything other than the ordinary way for the Church to be united to Christ.

Thus, there is a universal vocation to holiness. Holiness is not a kind of first place to be gained by means of a race in a large school; it is the simplicity of a gift which has been received. The saint is someone who loves God and who lives in union with his Lord, with all the sentiments of his heart and through all the actions which he performs throughout his existence. The spouses love each other all the more when they are united to Christ; the love by which they live, they recognize its origin in Christ, and the family which they wish to establish is inscribed naturally in the great family of the Church. There is not, on the one hand, the love of the spouse, as if it were a kind of territory under protection, like some private property which the spouses could keep out of the sight and of the light of God. The first time that spouses wished to live out of the sight of God, they wished to conduct themselves without taking account of the loving instructions which he gave, they hid themselves away from him and ended up by being divided, unloading the responsibility for their fault upon each other. We are conscious of the damaging consequences of this initial transgression in our own hearts, in terms of the difficulty we experience in being able to love in the truth. The Christian couple cannot pretend to leave God outside their love for each other.

The sacrament of the spouses is not just some kind of highly symbolic richness; in reality, it is an event in which God acts, by giving himself to each of the spouses, in blessing them and in sanctifying the covenant which they have contracted with each other, in giving them, through his grace, all of the spiritual and moral strength which they need in order to be able to live out this new state of life as husband and wife. When a man and a woman marry in the sight of God, a communion is created, which is a source of richness for all those who know them and, in particular, for the Church herself. Christian spouses are holy because they share in the development of the communion of the Church and, thus, they contribute to extending the boundaries of the kingdom of God among mankind.

The Holiness of Spousal Love

The love of the spouses is expressed in everything which will constitute their common life, in particular, in all of those actions which express the love which unites them. The expression of love between a husband and a wife united in the sacrament of marriage sets in motion all of the dynamisms of their persons, bodily, affective, moral and spiritual. The union of their bodies in the exercise of the sexual faculty expresses in a particular way the total gift which each of them makes to the other of his or her person. In fact, in this sexual expression, there is a dimension which is unique to each of them and which, to the extent that it is a gift, presupposes exclusivity; each of the spouses is in turn the sole recipient of this gift. It is this human mystery that expresses the characteristics of marriage: its unity and its indissolubility. Christians often think that the indissoluble nature of marriage is a requirement of the Church. In fact, it is not the sacrament which creates the indissolubility of conjugal love, but indissolubility is a requirement of that love itself. The sacrament consolidates and reinforces this feature of indissolubility and imparts to it the perspective of its completeness, by referring it to the indissoluble love that unites Christ to his Church. But, when the Church says that marriage is indissoluble, it does no more than affirm a property of human love, understood obviously in its full human breadth and beyond any superficial approach. There is a reason for this, that Christ himself offers us, by referring the mystery of the love between husband and wife to the intention of the Creator. This is the whole meaning of the conversation he held with the Pharisees in Matthew's gospel. To put him to the test, his interlocutors had asked him why Moses had authorized husbands to give their wives a writ of dismissal. With great delicacy, Jesus does not challenge Moses, but he explains that, if Moses had had to act in this way, this was by reason of their hardness of heart. And he adds that, in the beginning, it was not thus:

> Have you not read that, in the beginning, the Creator "made them male and female and that he said: 'This is why a man must leave father and mother and cleave to his wife and the two will become one flesh.' Thus, they are no longer two, but one single flesh. Now, what God has united, man must not divide (Mt 19.4–6).

The acts which express this unique gift form what John Paul II readily called the *language of the body*. In this way he expressed the idea that the sexual union of the spouses enjoys a human dignity, which requires that it be surrounded by great respect. He took up a passage from the Second Vatican Council which says, "the acts which are proper to the conjugal life, conducted in accordance with authentic human dignity, must themselves be surrounded by great respect."[3] In fact, there is something specific to human sexuality, if this is compared to simple animal life. This union does not have the effect simply of engendering a new life, but it also has the capacity to express true love. In the couple and *a fortiori* in the Christian couple, this love takes the form of a gift because it entails a commitment which is definitive. These two dimensions, of loving union and of openness to life, together define the conjugal act, for example. These two dimensions are inseparable, not in the physiological sense (not all such acts are fecund), but in the deep sense of the union of the spouses; it is when they are deeply united that their love receives the capacity to become fecund and that their union can have the consequence of the coming into being of a new life. According to the Creator's intention, it is indeed an act of love which is fecund. It seems to me that here is a mystery upon which everyone could meditate; in the domain of nature, there is no mediation, no possible means for the new life of a human being to come to be outside of a deep act of love, which unites the two spouses between themselves. Here two mysteries come together, that of love and that of life. There is a holiness of life because in every human life, there exists a divine love, which creates every human being, in an individual and unique fashion, by way of this human mediation, which is the gift of love. The love of the Creator comes to meet the love of the spouses. It is this divine love which creates immediately the soul of the one who will be called to become a son or daughter in his image and likeness. When they engage in acts which render them open to welcoming a possible new life, the spouses become, as it were, collaborators with the Creator. This is the reason why they are called *procreators*. The contemplation of such a mystery as that of our origin and of the

---

3. *Ibid.*§ 50.

origin of every child who is born in this way from a relationship of authentic love helps us to understand why sexuality could not avoid being involved in the work of the sanctification of the spouses; on the contrary, through acts which as *noble and honourable,* as the Second Vatican Council describes them,[4] human sexuality is associated with the work of the Creator. Let us be realistic, for over half a century we have been part of a culture which considers separately these two dimensions of sexuality and of the transmission of life, whether people consider only the aspect of gratification which a harmonious sexual relationship can bring and exalt sexuality only as a source of immediate pleasure, or whether people do not recognize any longer in human life the love which generates it. In the first case, there develops a culture which is purely contraceptive: life is no longer a matter of good news, a pregnancy is seen as a threat. In the second case, human life can become the fruit of an artificial manipulation; it is not the immediate fruit of a loving relationship. The sexual and affective life of the spouses is truly one of the loci of their sanctification, on the condition that they preserve, in a context of true love, the total meaning of a giving which is reciprocal and of a procreation brought about in accordance with the dignity of the human being.

Holiness in Work

> Be fruitful and multiply and fill the face of the earth and subjugate it (Gen 1:28).

In the verse from the book of Genesis, we can see that the conjugal life has a fecundity which operates in two directions. In fact, these two terms imply each other mutually. The instruction "multiply" includes the choice to establish a family, to have children within the perspective of the subjugation of the earth by the human being, created in the image of God. "Subjugate it" evokes that work which is specific to the dignity of the human being,

---

4. *Ibid.* § 49.

but, at the same time, work makes it possible to promote the cell of conjugal and familial life. Most of the time, it is the material condition necessary for the existence of the family. From this fact, work has an immediate finality: that of making possible the realization and the expansion of this community of love. For this reason,we cannot ignore the dimension of human work, when we are trying to understand the holiness of marriage and of the family. That would be to forget human dignity and the way in which it contributes to enriching the common life. It would be to forget also that it is by this means that the spouses are sanctified in their daily lives. In what sense, though, may we speak of work as holy? Work is holy in itself. Insofar as it constitutes a kind of prolongation of Creation, it perfects it, it brings out its value, and it orientates it towards its fulfilment in the kingdom of God. To extend the work of Creation, in a certain way, is to make one's own what is a divine action and to cooperate with it. In the activity of the human being, we can see a personal participation in the fulfilment of the plan of providence in history, to take up an expression of John XXIII (in *Pacem in Terris,* which was employed in *Gaudium et Spes,* § 34). The human being participates in the work of his salvation through the whole of his readiness to act for the good, something which begins from his habitual activity.

We note also that there is no work in the strict sense that is not directly or indirectly undertaken for others, orientated towards others. It is the responsibility of each individual to work towards communion. To work for justice, for peace, introduces the person into holiness, or at least prepares him for this.

Since it is also the object of an instruction from the Creator, work is a holy duty. The sanctity of human work is analogous to the sanctity of the work of the Creation of the world by God. It was in view of the human being that everything was created, and it is in view of God that work will reflect his original holiness. In view of God and in the sight of God. In the hidden life of Jesus, we have the simple image which best evokes the sanctity of work: that of a child, of an adolescent, of an adult, who works under the eye of his father. Work is holy when it is done confidently in the sight of the Father.

The human being works for those who are his own, but he works also for others. His labour contributes to the building up of society as a whole. It is in this that the Church recognizes the exercise of what is "charity in action" (in imitation of Christ).[5]

The work which is undertaken by the spouses is marked by the state of life of marriage, which is theirs. It can be said that it has a particular conjugal quality, a family quality, about it. The state of life of the husband or of the wife transforms work; at the level of personal experience, the person becomes aware that he works no longer in the same way as husband or as father as he had done when he was working just for himself. To work out of love for those who are their own and, by extension, to work for others is to make of their work a sacrifice acceptable to God: "No matter what your work may be, do it from your heart, as if you were working for the Lord and not for men, knowing that he will repay you by making you his heirs" (Col 3:23–24). This liturgical dimension culminates in the Eucharistic sacrifice, in which the work of human beings is offered up: "Blessed are you, Lord, God of all creation, for through your goodness, we have received the bread to offer, fruit of the earth and work of human hands; it will become for us the bread of life."

Human work, its difficulties and its burdens, are united to the sufferings of the Crucified Lord and so they acquire a redemptive dimension. Already, through the gift of themselves, which they make one to the other, spouses give witness to the Eucharistic dimension of conjugal love. As this gift is permanent, and as it embraces the totality of their existence, it tends to develop itself into an expanded communion, and it encompasses all of their activities, which receive in this way from God who accepts them, their highest degree of holiness.

We know very well that work is often marked by ambiguities. It can become an idol, all the more dangerous in that at times it

---

5. ID., *Lumen Gentium*, n. 41.

hides another idol, the unrestrained desire for money, for power, for domination, when natural ambition is falsified by pride. It can become also the place of oppression, of slavery, or of humiliation. Work, which, as has been seen, is a good in this way reveals its vulnerable aspects. An imbalance in professional activity can be perhaps the source of difficulties for the couple, depriving the family of the presence of the father, at times also of the mother, and giving the children the impression that the only value which is esteemed in their house is such activity. By contrast, when work occupies its proper place, it becomes easier for the parents to communicate to their children a healthy assessment of its value. It is to be noted that, for children, as for adolescents, work is identified with secondary or with higher studies. There again, possible imbalances can arise, when work is not located within a general scheme, favouring development of the person and of the family. From this perspective, studies which are properly understood can become a focus for harmonious development at the human and spiritual level and, as a result, an occasion for growth in holiness.

From the Holiness of the Couples to the Holiness of the Family

The holiness of the spouses is something that is communicated to the children by force of example and not through teachings of a moralizing nature. Children or young people are never wrong when they discern in their parents a faith and a hope which are resolute. This is true about their whole way of being, on the human and on the moral level. When parents are thoroughly sincere and honest, there is every possibility that these personal virtues may be transmitted to their children. Over and above the human values which are valid for all cells of family life, Christian parents are called to transmit to their children all the elements of a genuine spirituality. It is through education that conjugal holiness becomes a holiness of the family. Here, several elements need to be recalled.

In conformity with the great Christian tradition, parents must not deprive their children of the fundamental grace of baptism. It is their responsibility to have their children baptized as soon as possible, because there exists a life of grace in the soul of every human being even before they attain the age of reason. If they are convinced that their children have been entrusted to them by divine Providence, their first care should be to facilitate, for each of their children, personal and family contact with God. Family contact through family prayer, the sanctification of the Lord's day through participation in the Sunday Eucharist; at the personal level, with full regard for the respect and discretion which are required in this area, it is always possible to foster moments of personal prayer, for example during the course of a visit to a church or by entrusting intentions of prayers to one another, prayers at the family grave, decades of the rosary recited during a long journey in a car, etc. As far as Sunday is concerned, children who have never seen their parents give up their participation in the Mass under any pretext whatsoever will never forget this example throughout their lives. If they happen to spend some time far from the Church, even if it is prolonged, sooner or later they will return to the practice of their faith. In this sense, there is a credibility of the Christian faith which stems from the example we give, something that we need to relearn. On this point, some other cultural traditions could be instructive for us (like India or the Philippines). We may add that a Christian family is nourished regularly by sacramental grace, by the Eucharist, as has been said, but also by regular access to the sacrament of reconciliation; a family which is united is also a family which is reconciled.

It belongs to parents to foster the growth of the virtues of generosity, of altruism and of gratuity; in this realm, they could give preference to places where these qualities would be able to grow, movements of young people, commitments, pilgrimages, visits to the sick.

There are also habits that may be adopted that may foster the harmonious spiritual development of their children; for example, the practice of not criticizing third parties in their presence, of patiently correcting them when they express unjust judgments, or again taking care over their appearance and of their feelings. To be practical, they would not install a television in the child's bedroom. They can also promote relationships of trust, such that the children may open up naturally to express what is of interest to them or what is of concern to them. Special attention must be given to contacts that they may have with the world through the Internet. Nowadays, it is appropriate to exercise a certain vigilance with regard to the social fora, in which inevitably they will be invited to participate.

The conjugal and family dimension of the holiness of couples has been discovered these days in people who have become authentic examples for Christians: couples such as the Martins, the Beltrame Quattrocchis, the Maritains, and in some of these a particular kind of fecundity can be discerned. For example, Louis and Zélie Martin have offered to the world not only St Thérèse of the Child Jesus, but they have also created an extraordinary communion between each of their daughters, which lasted until death. The same could be said for the children of the Beltrame Quattrocchi family. When we read the correspondence of some of them, we are struck by the simplicity of their holiness; no indiscreet devotion, no encroachment upon the conscience of others, but a delicacy and a constant solicitude towards one another, with absolute respect for the freedom of each one.

A Christian family which is united makes the presence of Christ in its midst something which is felt. It becomes something which is attractive, and which begins to shine forth to those around. Human virtues of welcome, hospitality, compassion in visiting the sick and in care for the poor then come into particular focus. They become true Christian virtues and become capable of bearing fruit in holiness beyond the visible limits of the family. It is helpful to recall the words of the nuptial blessing, proclaimed during the celebration of marriage, when the celebrant implores the Lord on behalf of the new spouses:

> Send down on them the grace of the Holy Spirit and pour your love into their hearts, they may remain faithful to the covenant of marriage.

John Paul II comments upon this prayer in the Letter to Families: "It is from the 'out-pouring of the Holy Spirit' that the interior strength of families is born, as also the power of being able to unite them in love and in the truth."

SOCIETY

11 The Family and Society[1]

> *Through its close bond with the truth, love can be recognized as an authentic expression of humanity and as an element of fundamental importance in human relationships, even those of a public nature ... Truth frees love from the narrowness of an emotivism which deprives it of relational and social content, and of a fideism which deprives it of its human and universal breadth. In the truth, love at the same time reflects the personal and the public dimension of faith in the God of the Bible, who is at one and the same time Agape and Logos: Charity and Truth, Love and Word.*
>
> Pope Benedict XVI, *Caritas in Veritate*, 3

These words from the introduction to the encyclical *Caritas in Veritate*, extrapolated from the realm of human and of family love, seem to me to be a perfect key to sum up and to understand the perspective of the conception that the Church has of human love and of the relationship with the family and with society.

The Family Is a Concrete Experience

In this chapter, with the aid of some examples taken from the recent Magisterium to illustrate what I am proposing, I would like simply to begin from what, for the last two Popes and especially for John Paul II, is fundamental in human love and in its

---

1. "The Family and Society" is the text of a lecture delivered to the European Parliament in Brussels on September 14, 2010 in the context of a Colloquium on *Caritas in Veritate*, organised by the European Popular Party (PPE); it was also delivered in English at the Sophia University of Tokyo in the context of the Faculty of Philosophy and was published in Japanese in the revue *Katei no Tomo* in December, 2010.

relationship to the institutional family. The family is first of all a concrete experience before becoming the matter of a philosophical choice or of public opinion.

The experience of the family teaches us something of the love between a husband and a wife, but it also gives rise to the most profound questions present in the heart of every human being. John Paul II had the habit of speaking about the fundamental experiences of the person, which at times he called also *basic experiences*. Among these, he cited the most profound aspiration of the human heart, the desire to love and the desire to be loved, to which other experiences, such as suffering, the fear of death, mourning, the desire for offspring, the desire to leave something of oneself to those who are loved, the desire to be useful and still other desires, are attached.

The term *experience* needs to be defined more precisely. It is a question of a *lived experience*, an *Erlebnis*. Put briefly, it could be said that human experience includes as much the sensitive dimension of the person whom it stimulates, as it does also the intelligibility of that experience. We may note in passing that the intelligibility of experience cannot be verified except through the word, which allows personal experience to be transmitted to others. Here we have the transcendent and the social dimension of experience, which indicate in different terms the two phrases of the encyclical that have been cited already. Every authentic human experience (that is to say, one not deprived of intelligibility) brings about the growth of the person by means of the objective relationship that it encompasses with someone other than that person.

The Fundamental Experience of Love

What is true of every human experience applies in particular to the fundamental experience of love. Someone other than oneself is offered for contemplation in what in fact reveals that person to be specifically *other*: that person's body. It will be remembered that it was from this given that John Paul II began in order to develop his reflection on the originary experience of the human body, in the first part of his *Catechesis on Human Love*. According to him, love is accompanied by the discovery of the *nuptial* dimension (Italian: *sponsale* or spousal) dimension of the body, which is perceptible in what he calls the *ethos of the gift*.

Love personalizes all of the dimensions of the person and unifies them. *Eros*, far from being an obstacle to the protection of the mystery of the person, actually integrates it into this process of personalization.

We take note of the fact that, at all levels of the experience of love, there is revealed the presence of what is true and of what is good. We are aware of the theological aspect of this truth about love. John Paul II saw its origin in the plan of God (*consilium Dei*) for human love, taking his inspiration from the dialogue in the gospel of St Matthew (Mt. 19) between Jesus and the Pharisees, on the question of the indissolubility of marriage. To those who put forward the writ granted by Moses to repudiate their wives, Jesus objected that, in the beginning (*apo archè*), that is to say when God created man and woman, this was not so. The *archè* here is the principle of love.

It is interesting to see how the successor of John Paul II expresses this intrinsic bond between love and truth: in the encyclical *Deus Caritas Est*, after having affirmed with a certain audacity the existence of a divine *eros*, Benedict XVI sees the truth of love in an equilibrium between *eros* and *agapè*, and not in a separation of these two dimensions:

> *Eros* and *agapè*—ascending love and descending love—never allows the one to be separated completely from the other. The more these two forms of love, even in their different dimensions, find their proper unity within the unique reality of love, the more the true nature of love in general is established ...
> Even if, initially, *eros* is above all sensual, ascendant—a fascination for the great promise of happiness—, when it

is approached together with the other, it will always pose fewer questions about itself; it will always seek more the good of the other, it will be more and more concerned about the other, it will give itself and it will desire 'to be for' the other. It is thus that the moment of *agape* inserts itself into it; otherwise, *eros* decays and also it loses its own very nature. On the other hand, neither can the human person live exclusively in a love which is oblative, descendant. He or she cannot always and only give themselves; they must also receive. The one who wants to give love must himself or herself also receive love as a gift (§ 7).

Caritas in Veritate insists upon the oblative dimension of love, which finds its true character in the gift, but not in a way that is amputated from its ascendant significance:

> Love in the truth places the person before the astonishing experience of gift. Gratuitousness is present in the life of the person in multiple ways, which often are not recognized by reason of an existence that is purely productive and utilitarian. The human being is made for gift; it is the gift which both expresses and actualizes their transcendental dimension (§ 34).

From Love to Marriage, from Marriage to the Family

In order to understand the bond between family and society, it is not enough to examine further the nature of love; in reality, there are two further steps that must be taken, the passage from love to marriage and the passage from marriage to the family.

Without spending inordinate time of the first of these steps, let us simply recall the fact that getting married provides the experience of love with its social dimension. It causes that experience to emerge from the individual limits of inter-personal intimacy and makes it possible for it to be enriched by investing it with a new meaning. The very existence of the conjugal covenant (civil or religious) means that society is not uninterested in what occurs between the spouses, but that, on the contrary, it considers their relationship as a good; then it proceeds, by the authority which belongs to it (the authority of civil society or the authority of the society of the Church), to provide it with the means to ensure its stability. Society incorporates into itself what is a new given, the fact that in its midst this specific man and this specific woman are united in a unique way, not only through a commitment on their part as to the future, but even more as something which imposes upon it, upon society itself, the duty to take this union into consideration, to give witness to the fact that it is interested in it, values it, helps it to establish itself or to consolidate itself, and to consider as an enrichment the possibility that it might expand by becoming a family. From the point of view of the persons directly involved, it would be necessary to show how the fact of taking such a public step, which entails a commitment to the future, bestows upon their union its maturity and its objectivity. Far from diminishing the intensity of their love, as those who are attached to what Maritain, in his book, *Amour et Amitié*, calls *romantic love*, as opposed to the *love of cherishing* the other, the *love of benevolence* of the ancients, this public act, on the contrary, confers upon it its integration in truth. The expression *"integration in truth"* is employed by the philosopher—not yet Pope—Karol Woityla, in his famous book, *Love and Responsibility*. In the concrete, is there a better proof of love than to give to the person who is loved not only one's availability in the present time but also for the future? And is there a better gauge of this will than to call as a witness upon God (in the religious framework) and, in any case, upon the society of human beings?

The second passage is that which connects marriage to the family. The experience of the family can be appreciated from three different points of view: the point of the view of the child, that of the spouses themselves at the moment when they become parents, and, finally, that of society itself.

Let us examine briefly the experience of someone who discovers little by little that they are part of a family. This is a question of an experience that was that of the vast majority of people until a few decades ago, an experience that becomes a conscious experience from early childhood. How can we avoid thinking here of John Paul II's famous *Letter to Families* (*Gratissimam Sane*) in which, in relation to the conception and the birth of a child, he had evoked the genealogy of the person: "*The genealogy of every human being—the genealogy of the person—is linked to the family.*" The personal aspect of this event finds its full meaning, in his eyes, in the nature of every human being, created in the image and likeness of God:

> Every generation finds its original model in the paternity of God. However, in the case of the human being, this "cosmic" dimension of similarity to God is not sufficient to be able to define in an adequate manner the relationship between paternity and maternity. When, from the conjugal union of the two, there is born a new human being, that person brings with them into the world a specific image and likeness to God himself; in the biology of generation there is inscribed the genealogy of the person.[2]

The *genealogy of the person* makes it possible to reconnect the natural aspiration of every human being to found a family to the more secret and originary experience of the human being; every human being perceives themselves as the fruit of a mysterious love. We may remember the extraordinary lines written by Gabriel Marcel on the mystery of the family in *Homo Viator*. He writes:

> Behind the abstract words of paternity and of filiation, I am led imperceptibly to glimpse hidden and prohibited realities which make me dizzy ... I shall come to understand, at least, that, far from being endowed with an existence which is absolute, without initially having willed or suspected it, I am the incarnation of a response to a double calling, that of other beings who have cast themselves into the unknown and who, without having any doubts about what they were doing, launched beyond

---

2. John Paul II, Letter to Families, *Gratissimam Sane*, § 9.

themselves, to an incomprehensible power which does not express itself except by giving life. I am this response, at first in an unformed way, but then little by little, to the extent that this comes to be articulated, someone who will know themselves as response and as judgment. Yes, I am led irresistibly to make this discovery, that, by means of the very fact that I am who I am, I myself am the bearer of a judgment over those who have introduced me into being, and at the same instant an infinity of new relationships is created between them and me.[3]

The second point of view is that of the spouses; the coming into existence of one or more children changes the nature of what they have lived up to this point; the child not only introduces the one into the new experience of paternity and the other into that of maternity, but also they discover themselves as father and mother, the one through the other. This occurs in such a way that it is indeed their love which acquires a new dimension, one which is infinitely broader, one which brings them well beyond their limits as a couple into this family cell, and which transcends their relationship. The passage from marriage to the family is thus a transformation of the love of the spouses, and not something that is a substitute for love, which, in the first place, would be the bearer of burdens and of limits to the liberty which they had enjoyed hitherto. Here we may observe that such an experience does no violence to the subjectivity of the spouses. It is entirely correct to say that, before being parents, they had been children in an earlier time, when they discovered themselves as members of a family, objects of a love which was unconditional and reassuring; the essence of paternity and of maternity can only be perceived within the context of a filial anthropology. Joseph Ratzinger, at the time when he was directing the Congregation for the Doctrine of the Faith, organized a seminar of several days' duration in 2003 precisely on this theme: *What is a filial anthropology?*[4] The context for this was that of the

3. Gabriel Marcel, *Homo Viator* (Paris: Aubier-Montaigne, 1945), pp. 98–99.
4. See below, *What is a Filial Anthropology?*, pp. 349–371.

common divine filiation of the baptized in a Christian vision, but several of the interventions dwelt upon the substance of the human experience of being sons (or daughters). Here, we can do no more than refer readers to other chapters in this volume.

Finally, the point of view of society leads us towards the term of this relationship. Up until these most recent decades, the fact had been commonly recognized in the laws which had been enacted in various countries that the family was founded upon a public commitment between one man and one woman: the recent extension of the term *family* and of the term *marriage* to other forms of social realities: restructured families, free unions (with no other founding act other than that of the sole will of the partners) and, in the legislation of different countries to unions between persons of the same sex, without any doubt has weakened the perception of the structural and foundational bond between marriage and the family. Hence, recognizing the rights of a family founded upon the conjugal covenant has always had the sense of a recognition that the family cell is a good for society, that such a cell fosters the progressive socialization of future adult citizens through the tasks of education, that this accompaniment by their parents of children and of adolescents is something which contributes to the stability of the bond of society. Here we may think of Article 16 of the *Universal Declaration of Human Rights*, approved by the Assembly of the United Nations on December 10, 1948, which affirmed: "The family is the fundamental cell of society and of the state and, as such, it must be recognized and protected." Such an affirmation, in a text which was not inspired on the basis of religious confession, clearly expressed the idea that, if the family has such a great importance, it is because it corresponds to the general interest and that it had an obvious connection with the common good in the eyes of the legislators of that time.

To relativize the institution of the family amounts to rendering fragile an essential foundation of life in society. This arises through a complete privatization of the family, which becomes the place of *privacy*, the space in which the person finds an immediate gratification for his affective desires. Here the juridical question is displaced elsewhere: the right (or rather the duty) is recognized for civil authority to guarantee the private freedom of choice of individuals and no longer to sustain the union that gives it its natural basis and its cohesion.

To be sure, at the beginning of this new millennium, the family institution is still present in numerous societies, which it cements and unifies. Nevertheless, it is dangerously badly placed in many western societies, which do not cease to wish to impose and to export their social and cultural models. Over and above any specifically ethical consideration of the question, it is indeed a model of anthropology with which we have been confronted for some time. It is one which consists in thinking about the person in an exclusively individualistic manner, like an isolated monad and as entitled to a liberty which is absolute, ignoring its original social dimension and hence no longer seeing in marriage and the family a natural society, which stems precisely from this natural social character of man and woman. The social risk is that of a lack of political interest in safeguarding the institution of marriage and of the family, which, in the eyes of governments, would no longer be substantially linked to the common good and thus worthy of being defended and promoted. Here, too, it would be necessary to develop further what impact the disappearance of this stable bond might have in terms of demography and of the replacement of the generations.

The encyclical, *Caritas in Veritate*, having in view the very future of human society, calls upon legislatures to honour and to encourage the family for reasons which are not only ethical, but which concern in the first place the very substance of the bond of society:

> To continue to propose to new generations the beauty of the family and of marriage, the correspondence of these institutions to deepest demands of the heart and of the dignity of the person becomes

also a social and even an economic necessity. From this perspective, States are called *to adopt policies to promote the central nature and the integrity of the family*, founded upon the marriage between one man and one woman, the first and the vital cell of society (§ 44).

It is indeed with the culture of the family that society finds the means for this cohesion, for the development of fundamental structures of solidarity, at the same time as reasons to hope in the future.

12 The Effects of the Sexual Revolution[1]

Before expounding the key points as to what would allow us to explain what we understand by the effects of the sexual revolution, I would like to set out the context in which the observations that follow are made.[2] These are situated within the framework of a round table discussion, entitled: *The excesses of sexuality today* (*Les dérives de la sexualité aujourd'hui*). We need to adopt a premise; a title such as this would seem to orientate our reflection in a negative direction, if we have understood the teachings and the witnesses expressed in the preceding contributions on the beauty of human love, on the exercise of sexuality within the context of a conjugal relationship, that is to say of a definitive and reciprocal gift which one man and one woman make of their person in the service of communion and in the service of life. It will be helpful, from the start, to keep in mind the spirit of everything that has been transmitted to us on the vocation of love, the call to grow in communion and the vocation of every man and of every woman to holiness. In fact, it is only within this positive light shed upon the person, his or her aspirations, his or her body as sexually differentiated, and the acts which express in the most intimate

---

1. "The Effects of the Sexual Revolution" is the text of a lecture delivered on March 26, 2010, at Rocca di Papa in the course of an international gathering of youth, organised by the Pontifical Council for the Laity, and made available through the internet site of that dicastery.
2. This text is the transcription of an intervention made amidst a thousand of adolescents and young people gathered together at Rocca di Papa, near Rome, in the context of a gathering organized by the Pontifical Council for the Laity. The oral style, of a more directly pedagogical nature, has been preserved. This text has been published at the request of many young people.

manner the love of one man for one woman who have truly given themselves one to the other, that we can understand what has been happening in the last half-century in the history of human thought and of morals and which people designate by the term *sexual revolution*.

Recalling History

We call the *sexual revolution* the totality of the changes that have arisen in the vision of sexuality on the part of western societies, both with regard to the exercise of sexuality and with regard to the emancipation of morals. At the theoretical level of thought, this revolution is first of all of a philosophical, moral, and social nature. At the level of morals, it involves above all a complete reversal of the sexual ethics, of the habitual ways of life and of the legal structures of different countries. From a juridical standpoint, it is also possible to speak of a real revolution. The expression *sexual revolution* itself was invented in the 1920s by Wilhelm Reich and Otto Gross, who wanted to elaborate from a sociological perspective the results of the work of Freud. The latter was involved in the beginning of a new science, psychoanalysis, one of whose findings was the link between every kind of human behaviour and the libido. But what Freud developed within the context of what was a personal therapy, some of his disciples would take forward, driven by feelings of anarchy, within a social setting. Talk of sex, which up until then, had always been surrounded by reservation and modesty, and which had been limited to the sphere of accompanying someone undergoing therapy, little by little would become a subject of public debate, giving rise to a whole series of studies, and to writings and to political claims of all sorts. The revolution consists in this, namely, that a discussion about sexuality, limited until then to its connection to procreation, would concentrate upon human sexuality insofar as it entails simply a dynamism which is physically gratifying, and it would be conducted in a manner which has become totally autonomous with reference to a possible transmission of life. Such a discussion would not remain restricted for very long to the description of psycho-affective and genital phenomena. In fact, the research that would be developed subsequently would concern the practice of sexuality as such, or more precisely sexual practices such as they are to be found concretely in human society. Once sexuality had become disconnected socially from its essential finality of the transmission of life within the context of a stable relationship between one man and one woman, it can be understood that any consideration of the sexual attitudes of men and women would cease to be a taboo, however marginal in character they might be. Topics never raised in public before would become objects of popular discussion: the practice of male or of female homosexuality, the search for maximal pleasure in the relationship, the claim to a sexuality which would be separated from all commitment and from all responsibility.

A second key for understanding this sexual revolution lies in the fact that these public discussions led to the private, modest, and strictly personal dimension of the exercise of sexuality being rendered banal. In fact, the move from "immodest" discussion to the claim to a complete freedom in sexual behaviour occurred naturally. The *cultural revolution* became a *political revolution*. It was not a matter of mere chance that its great theoreticians, Reich and Marcuse, based themselves explicitly upon references to the dialectical materialism of Karl Marx.

The third key point, then, is that, since the *sexual revolution* could not be limited to inter-personal behaviour, it became a veritable *social revolution*, whose purpose, ever more openly declared, was to call into question in a radical way all of the foundations of civil and of religious society. This can be understood very easily because the character of the publicity given to these themes, reserved until then to the strictly intimate sphere of the person, brought with it the seed of the radical calling into question of the institution of the family, the only civil context in which the exercise of the sexual faculty had been universally recognized, and the calling into question of the Churches, as moral reference points and bearers of an ethical and spiritual position on the dignity which, according to them, is necessary for those acts which involve the profound union between man and woman. This key helps us to understand that a position which is adopted which trivializes the exercise of sexuality, in the most diverse and contradictory forms, contributes to a radical reversal of all the values which have cemented the society of human beings across the centuries: the exclusivity of the loving relationships between spouses, reverence for human life, whose transmission always appeared as a blessing, love for children, the positive vision of future generations, respect for previous generations, the sense of personal and family history, the religious nature of the commitment of the spouses, always giving rise to a liturgical celebration in all religions, and finally protection for the intimate sphere of persons, especially of the young.

The fourth key, bringing into question the morality of the Church and the morality of families being presented in caricature as the morality of the "petite bourgeoisie," according to the Marxist expression of the theoreticians of the time, was presented necessarily as a liberation from the yoke of a Judaeo-Christian ethic and of a patriarchally dominant family tradition.

The fifth key: in a way which is coherent with this, the claim for complete sexual freedom, as also the emergence of a permissive morality completely unthinkable only a few decades before, would be accompanied by the rejection of all norms of authority, in whatever domain it might be: family, politics, education, religion. In this way, then, the following would be systematically and violently contested: the figure of the father within the family, the figure of those who govern within the nation, the figure of the teacher and of the professor within the educational system, the figure of the moral and spiritual authority of priests, of bishops and of the Magisterium of the Church in general. This list destroys all of the supporting columns of society, character-

The Effects of the Sexual Revolution

ized by the movement described by the expression "May, 1968", which points at one and the same time to the specific short-term, but very violent events, and also to a current of libertarian thought, of which the very delicate questions which agitate our societies today are the heritage.

Historically, the period between 1930 and 1990 has produced political and social reforms that have also been stages of a powerfully symbolic kind. In 1948 the *Kinsey Report* was published, giving way subsequently to studies of the sexual behaviour of men and then, some years later, to the sexual behaviour of women. These studies, effected in the context of the University of Indiana, undoubtedly provoked some backlash, but they ended up by becoming established. In fact, they were followed by the *Masters and Johnson Report* of 1966. At the end of the 1950s, the female contraceptive pill was put on the market in 1960 in the United States and then in Europe in the course of the following years.

The 1960s as a whole were the scene of animated debates about contraception. As we know, the position of the Church was expressed through the encyclical, *Humanae Vitae*, published on July 25, 1968. In 1975, for the first time the depenalization of abortion was voted into law in France with the Veil law. At the beginning of the 1980s, we saw the beginnings of the procedures of *in vitro* fertilization; from that time on, it became possible to bring about the existence of a human being outside of any sexual relationship between a man and a woman.

In the 1980s, we also saw the suppression of the difference between children born legitimately and natural offspring, in regard to rights of succession in various European countries.

In the same years, in many countries, there was a public debate over euthanasia and juridical measures were adopted aimed at legalizing it.

In 1998, for the first time, there was the institution of the juridical status of *de facto* unions.

Finally, in the 1990s and 2000s, we have witnessed the application of genetic techniques within a context that is no longer exclusively therapeutic, but which has a eugenic purpose.

In the course of the 1950s and 1960s, it is worth noting the progressive disappearance, at the cultural level, of any criterion of censure in the area of art and in particular in cinematography. This development in the cinema was no more than the most spectacular manifestation of the abolition of any filter in artistic culture as a whole: literature, painting, and currents of musical variety.

We are aware today that there has been a systematic deconstruction of all of the criteria that in the past led to the establishment of filters of an ethical kind in the representation of scenes in the cinema; in 1966 the Hays' Code was abolished, and thereafter there was an extension of the pornographic industry.

From this brief survey of reforms of a symbolic nature, which have marked our western societies and which tend to be extended to legislation adopted throughout the world, it is possible to identify some other keys for understanding.

The sixth key: given the separation in sexuality of the procreative dimension from the unitive dimension, the result has been, necessarily, the development of a purely hedonistic sexuality, totally deprived of any responsible commitment. The effects of this have become obvious; the generalization of sex outside of marriage (that is to say, without any responsibility within the framework of a stable relationship), the disappearance of the need to think of sexuality in connection with the gift of life, which brings with it the growth in recourse to contraception, and the progressive loss of the sense of the beauty of the transmission of life; a pregnancy becomes a threat, a sexual relationship requires protection or is at risk. Finally, the possibility of a procreation, completely foreign to any sexual relationship has brought about the possible disappearance of the context of love, within which the transmission of life was conducted in the history of mankind until now. Besides, this has opened the way to all manner of possible manipulations of human life, reducing the child in this way to being seen as the satisfaction of someone else's personal desire.

The seventh key: with reference to all of the reforms, at no time was the interest of the child or the child's right to be born of a stable and loving relationship between his or her parents, taken into account as an essential element in the process. The same comment could be made in regard to legislation allowing divorce. Moreover, in this specific case, it is the right place to point out the disappearance of the sacred character of marriage, something that naturally had been respected in civil legislation prior to the appearance of legal divorce.

The eighth key: in the area of education, human sexuality is presented in biology text books for secondary schools in a way which adopts a strictly physiological position on the sexual relationship, without any mention of its psychological or affective dimensions or of that of any moral commitment. In recent years, we have witnessed the presentation of minority behaviours in ways which have trivialized and legitimated them. Forms of behaviour judged in other times unanimously as deviant have been presented as if perfectly normal. In a large number of educational systems in Europe, a new form of morality has been taught, which is marked by the emergence of values inspired by relativism, such as toleration, in its ideological form. New forms of what is considered as civilly transgressive, such as homophobia, sexual discrimination, intolerance, have arisen.

The ninth key: the chronological study of these reforms reveals a very real intention of imposing a new morality. We are in the presence of very active political pressure by international organizations, exerted upon the legislation of different nations, in order to impose new ethical criteria. This is done through the creation of new concepts, such as, for example, that of *reproductive health*. The case of abortion is typical in this respect. In the 1970s, people spoke about the *depenalization of abortion*; a few years later, the expression the *liberalization of abortion* was imposed. It is to be noted that the motivations invoked at the beginning of the debate—that of avoiding clandestine abortions—in reality was only a pretext, used with a view to committing people to the path of this revolutionary reform, which consisted in making legal the right of adults to kill the children in their mothers' wombs. Furthermore, we note that the generalized practice of recourse to contraception over the last forty years has done nothing to diminish the number of abortions.

The tenth key: at the beginning of the 1980s, the HIV virus was spreading. At the beginning, this infection was transmitted in situations of risk, in homosexual settings or among those using drugs. For any other sexually transmitted disease (STD), abstention from such behaviour at risk has always been recommended medically (tuberculosis, hepatitis C), but, for AIDS, such a measure would have appeared politically to have been a condemnation of the behaviours at risk and, as a consequence, to have brought into question the "gains" of the *sexual revolution*. It was in this way that there developed a prophylactic action that was exclusively centred upon contraception, with the results which we all know. Let us mention that the three countries which sought another strategy, one founded upon the education of adolescents and young people in abstinence or upon the strict limitation to one sole partner, obtained spectacular results within the space of barely two or three years (Uganda, Zimbabwe, and Tanzania); when a return to a policy of the systematic diffusion of contraceptives was imposed upon them, new cases of infection regrettably started once more to increase.

The eleventh key: we may be permitted to read, in the will of states to impose a new culture and a new ethic, the desire to reach perfect mastery over human life, in particular over its transmission. One of the motives often put forward for this is the so-called overpopulation of the world, which, people say, would be the cause of poverty, misery, and sickness. It must be noted that the fear of overpopulation is invoked in general mostly in western countries. Now, with a few exceptions, these are precisely those countries which are suffering from the opposite evil, namely that of demographic collapse, something accompanied by a notable ageing of their population. On the economic level, this has caused several of them to adopt policies favouring waves of migration, to compensate for the lack of manual labour. It is beyond doubt that the loss of the sense of the beauty of life, which we have already mentioned, has led some people to pose the question of whether, within the lapse of two or three generations, there would be the disappearance of the populations of some countries. The statistical demonstration of this state of affairs would require too long an analysis.[3]

This brief panorama will have seemed to you, certainly, very alarming. In fact, it is so, at the social, political, and moral levels. However, I would like to conclude this chapter on a note marked by hope. I think, on the contrary, that the present circumstances, for all people of good will and for all Christians in particular, are an invitation of Providence to assess more deeply the meaning of everything that is at stake within a conception of human life and of its transmission through the exercise of the sexual faculty, that is balanced, healthy, and holy. The richness of sexuality within the plan of God is something always to be reflected upon in greater depth. The vocation of every man and of every woman is a vocation to communion and, through that, to holiness. When someone finds himself at a young age in the cultural context that we have described, there remains always a personal dimension that no ethical relativism and no cultural ideology can touch. The personal freedom of those who wish to respond to this call is something that is written in their bodies, in their desires, in their aspirations, in their will to transmit life in union with that person with whom they wish to share their existence. In this sense, there is no reason to be pessimistic, if we consider what has been given to us within a vision of faith. Knowledge of the cultural context in which we find ourselves will help us simply to be lucid, to expand the scope of our freedom in the face of the concerns, explicit or implicit, of the media-conscious

---

3. Cf. "The Demographic Situation in Europe," pp. 269–284 below.

society which is ours. Besides, this knowledge impels us to prudence, to discernment, and to the search for friendships that are reliable. In our days more than ever, with a courage that is both human and spiritual and with all the strength of their souls that young people will find what is necessary for their own personal liberty to expand into the gift of self and in love. Love is always a victory. How could it be possible to forget the words that Pope John Paul II addressed to young people at the dawn of the third millennium in the course of their gathering at Tor Vergata during the World Youth Day in Rome in 2000:

> Dear young people, in the face of this noble task, you are not alone: With you, there are your families, your communities, your priests and those responsible for your education; there are also all of those, and they are very many, who, in some hidden way, never tire of loving Christ and of believing in Him. In this struggle against sin, you are not alone; there are many who struggle, as you do, and who in the grace of the Lord, are victorious.

13 THE DEMOGRAPHIC SITUATION IN EUROPE[1]

Let us recall some recent statistical data, so that then we may examine not only the social implications of the demographic collapse but also offer some key criteria for interpreting it.

An important premise is the following: the problem of demography, from hence forward, must be considered as a political question. Paradoxically, demography brings into focus the limits of political action, but, at the same time, political action will never be able to get to the roots of the problem of demography without the assistance of the world of politics. Thirty years ago, when speaking about demography, people assessed the totality of the social and human aspects of the problem, in some cases referring to specific local situations and problematic issues. For example, I remember that, in the 1960s, demographic problems were always addressed in the light of the question of hunger in the world and of the redistribution of wealth. The distress of certain countries was attributed, often with too much haste, to their overpopulation. Fortunately, several experts have demonstrated the methodological danger of reasoning on the basis of globalized data. We may observe that this very questionable approach, which consists in saying that the world's resources would not be sufficient for a population of ten or twelves billions of persons is still to be found in many ideological positions. I will give one single example: in my country where, despite certain difficulties, the situation is much less worrying than in others, a politician,

---

1. "The Demographic Situation in Europe" is the text of a lecture delivered on December 1, 2010, at the Pontifical University of the Lateran in the context of the Colloquium *La Sfida Imminente della Cura Etica degli Anziani*, organized by the Acton Institute Foundation.

whose name I shall not give, proposed that the state should suppress family allowances for every family after the first child. Behind such a proposal, there is an absurd vision of the wealth of the nation or of the world, as if it were a question of sharing out a cake; it would be necessary to reduce the number of those sharing the different parts. Clearly, the problems involved do not present themselves in such simplistic terms.

The Demographic Situation in Europe

I would like to limit our reflection to the continent of Europe, in the heart of which we are in the presence of a veritable demographic collapse. There are several instruments that exist for examining the situation of the evolution of a population in a given area. As we know, the basic means is the level of fecundity, which corresponds to the number of children who are born of women who are in the age-range in which they are able to procreate. Another instrument is the age pyramid, which allows us to measure this evolution in the long-term.

The level of fecundity has passed below the threshold of 2.0 children per woman of procreative age in almost all of these countries. The European country which runs the greatest risk of ageing is Slovenia; the rate of fecundity there is of 1.2; by contrast, the country which is experiencing the least risk of ageing is Ireland, the country having attained a level of fecundity of 2.0 in these recent years. Together with Ireland, there is also France, whose rate of fecundity in 2007 was 1.97. The other countries have levels consisting of between 1.9 and 1.25.

In the countries of Western Europe, there exists a contrast between the countries of the North, among which some have experienced a notable increase (Sweden), and the Mediterranean countries, where the situation is more than worrying: Spain, Italy, and Greece. In these countries, we can see a significant change in the situation from one region to another. Some provinces show a birth rate which is such as to run the risk of their population disappearing: five years ago, the province of Asturias had a rate of 0.70, which was almost the lowest rate in the world, but the same concerns could arise in Italy for the regions of Liguria (1.0), of Lombardy, or of Venetia (about 1.05).

In order for the renewal of generations to be effective, it is known that the rate of fecundity must be at least 2.1. Now, none of the countries of Europe is reaching that threshold. By contrast, if a level of 1.3 is maintained through two generations, all demographic experts agree in estimating that this population, at the end of a hundred years, will diminish by a quarter with respect to its present level. At the moment in Europe, the mean does not exceed 1.5.

We must note that, if the larger part of these rates is abnormally low, they would be even more so, had European countries not experienced the waves of immigration that we have seen in the last thirty years or so.

It is known that families arising from recent immigration have more children. This is notably the case in France, Germany, Italy, Spain, and the Netherlands.

Europe is not limited to the western countries. Among the countries that have joined the European Union, we do not see better birth rates; Slovenia and the Czech Republic have respectively a rate of 1.22 and 1.23. Countries which were fecund in the past are undergoing the same tendency: for example, Poland (1.23). I have no intention here of dramatizing a situation which is already in itself very worrying. Besides, there is always a risk in offering perspectives within fifty or a hundred years, to the extent that circumstances could arise which might overturn all of the estimates. However, I would like to draw your attention to two factors: normally, new circumstances which appear in the history of a country or on the scale of a continent, do not go in the direction of an improvement (except at times of strong and endurable economic growth); on the other hand, the unforeseeable events which alter the normal course of the life of a people are wars, revolutions, or natural disasters. In the past, these examples were frequently verified and traces of them can be detected in the graphs of the population in the age pyramid. In relation to the continent of Europe, it is possible to observe the impact of the Napoleonic Wars, of the First World War, which, up to the present, is the one that has had the most damaging consequences for the populations of France and of Germany. In the other continents, we could make the same affirmation, with the effects on the populations of those countries of the genocide in Cambodia and of the war in Rwanda.

The second observation is connected to these accidents of history; in the past, the tendencies towards demographic decline were limited in time. The First World War lasted for four years and, in the years that followed, a kind of baby boom could be observed. The same thing was repeated after the Second World War, in particular in the Federal Republic of Germany of that time, in Italy and in France.

The new reality that, in my opinion, demonstrates even more the importance of the topic which we are addressing today, arises from the fact that the present demographic decline has been affecting European countries now for more than thirty years.

Those responsible for politics and for civil society were not interested in the question until recently, up until only ten years ago; we can state that, as of now, the demographic situation has entered into the realm of politics. For example, the European Parliament has dedicated several sessions to work on this topic and also has organized studies on the challenge represented by the absence of new generations. The Committee for employment, social affairs, and inclusion has issued a Draft Report *"On the Demographic Challenge and Solidarity between the Generations."*[2]

I would like to conclude this first point on the positive givens of the problem by taking two examples, which, at the world level, are very worrying and which will not fail to have effects also in Europe. The first of these concerns Russia. Russia not only has a

---

2.   2010/2027, INI.

very low rate of fecundity, estimated at 1.1, but the ageing of its population and the precarious state of the health of a large number of persons, added to an elevated death rate and to a life-expectancy lower than that observed elsewhere, is leading that country to a decline at the rate of 900,000 persons per year! Such a situation, in the medium-term, will have consequences for the socio-political stability of Europe more broadly. The other example, further away, is China. As we know, China has a little less than 1,000,400,000 inhabitants. This number seems to all of us to be enormous and few people give much thought to another aspect of the demographic equilibrium of this country; for more than half a century now, a very strict policy has been conducted of limiting the number of children per family to one unit. Now, in China, as in many other countries in the world, life-expectancy is increasing and, in twenty years, we shall have the following configuration: a third of the population will be more than sixty years old, which in terms of the number of inhabitants, will represent 450,000,000 persons. The question which will arise then will be the following: how will the active population, which is much reduced today by reason of the drastic measures to reduce the number of children, be able to maintain and to care for this very large number of persons in the third and fourth age? It seems that the rulers have understood the situation and that they are preparing to legislate in the opposite direction, by extending to two the number of children to be tolerated for each family. By reason of the size of this country, which is really that of a continent, the measures that will be adopted will not fail to have extraordinary consequences for international relations and on the socio-economic equilibrium at a planetary level.

If we focus now upon the evolution of this question, starting from the 1960s up to the 2050s, according to groupings of age ranges, we can see that the proportion of persons younger than 14 years of age, which in 1960 was 27.1%, had declined to 16.3% in 2004 and that it will decline probably to 15.2% in 2010. In 2050, it is foreseen that the percentage will be 11.9%. During this time, the percentage of persons above 65 years of age (the average age in Europe for going into retirement) has passed from 13.5% in 1960 to 23.8% in 2004 and to 25.5% in 2010; it will increase to 34% in 2050. To be precise, a third of this 34% will be above 85 years of age, if the probable evolution of the increase in life-expectancy should be confirmed. Thus, we shall have a continual increase of those in the third and fourth ages. Moreover, we wish to point out that people are beginning to speak these days of the fifth age, to indicate those who attain the age of being 100 years old (150,000 persons in 2050 for France).

Year	Under 14 years	Working age	Above 65 years
1960	27.1%	59.4%	13.5%
2004	16.3%	59.9%	23.8%
2010	15.2%	59.3%	25.5%
2050	11.9%	54.1%	34.04%

(of whom a third will be 85)

We may observe that, during these 90 years (from 1960 to 2050), the proportion of persons of working age does not alter. It is the only sector of real interest to politicians, to the extent that it represents productive human capital and thus that sector which mostly pays the quotas for old age pensions. We shall see later on what gives the appearance of this numerical stability in the social group of working age.

Another measure is concerned with the distribution of families according to the number of children. If the rate of fecundity of 1.5 children per woman remains unchanged on the continental scale, we shall have the following situation:

Families without children 41%
Families with one child only 27%
Families with two children 24%
Families with three children 6%
Families with more than three children 2%
(of whom more than 35% will be single-parent families).

The only remark which can be made is that only 8% of families then will have a sufficient number of children to make possible a renewal of the generations.

The Anthropological Reasons, Effects, and the Anthropological Significance of the Demographic Collapse

Without analyzing in depth all of the reasons for this collapse, three series of reasons are nevertheless to be highlighted.

The first concerns the total change in the redistribution of the population within the three sectors, primary, secondary and tertiary. In 1945, after the war, Europe was still for the most part rural and the mechanization of agriculture then provoked an exodus from the countryside towards the great urban centres. The possibility of being able to welcome a significant number of children then diminished considerably.

This affirmation is not limited to the material element. It is not only the conditions necessary for being able to feed a large family which have changed, the exodus from the countryside has also had the effect of changing the habits of life and the perspectives for families: the length of studies has become ever longer, the lack of a desire on the part of the children to take on the family's property, the appearance of new fashions, of new styles of life, of new desires with regard to the world of work or towards a possible professional career. In this area, the only question which remains without a response is: why is it that the disappearance of the rural world became a reality in the post-industrial age, when this phenomenon had not occurred during the Industrial Revolution? If the situation is such that an increasing number of Europeans have lost contact with nature in the area of their own professional activity, this means that other qualifying factors have entered into the picture.

Among the causes of a qualitative nature, beyond the reduced number of children, mention must be made of the banal consequence of the increase in life expectancy, namely the ageing of the population. It is not only that children are missing; there is also a lack of youthfulness of spirit, with a will to undertake things, a desire to found a new family, a desire on people's part to project themselves into the future; to sum it up, the lack of all the energies which contribute to the normal development of a nation in directing it towards the future.

A country in which the majority of people are old will always be less creative and hence less well-prepared to confront the vicissitudes which inevitably arise in the course of the generations.

I will give just two examples, which illustrate this anthropological change. The first is the interest, which has become almost obsessive that people, including young people, show in problems of health. This is established, on the one hand, by the extraordinary use of medicaments of all kinds in the countries of Europe as a whole and, on the other hand, by the fact that ethical questions to do with the end of life and with the care to be provided to old people, for example, provoke an ever-increasing interest on the part of the young. At the anthropological level, there is a globalization of anxieties, insofar as every person's problems concern all of us, even when there is no immediate reason in the concrete for us to be interested in them.

There is another, recent example, drawn from the political situation in France at present, upon which it will be interesting to reflect. There has been a reform of the pensions system, which has given rise to reactions in society and on the part of trade unions. All of that is extremely banal. What is less banal, however, is that tens of thousands of students and of young people have taken part in this movement against the reform. Beyond the classic phenomena of social contagion, the question which arises is: how is it possible that young persons who have not yet begun to work, who normally would have forty years of professional life before them and who, in addition, are not even certain of being able to find employment, can come to involve themselves in demonstrations over retirement? In my opinion, there is unfortunately only one explanation; these young people have become old in their spirit and in their perception of life. Retirement has become a kind of *eldorado* and, in order to be able to benefit from it, it is necessary to put up with the whole of a professional life. This latter has not been integrated psychologically into the development of the person as such. I believe that, at the anthropological level, this phenomenon is a factor hitherto unheard of, very relevant to the loss of enthusiasm about people's circumstances and to the psychological ageing of a society.

The third cause is politically incorrect. In fact, it has never been expressed in the terms in which I would like to express it now: it relates to the millions of people in Europe who cannot who simply do not exist by reason of the laws which have made abortion into a "right." This has happened in a short space of time; when I was a student of political sciences, I followed with close attention and with great interest the debates which at that time animated society, as also the mass media. At the time when the Parliament was debating the Loi Veil, I remember that the issue raised then by the deputies in favour of abortion was that of depenalizing the act of abortion for the reason—they said—of the injustice of the previous law which hit the poorest of women. At the time, it was said that women who had the means would encounter no problem in going to have an abortion abroad. It was said also that, with the new law, clandestine abortions would be reduced; it was estimated to 175,000 per year. The law depenalizing abortion was approved. Some years later, people no longer speak about depenalization to describe the Loi Veil, but they use the term liberalization of abortion. A few years later again and they were speaking of a right to abortion, a right which had become a right of women, thereby putting the responsibility of the man into the shade. Yet another few years later and they were speaking about the right of women to decide what to do with their own bodies, this time putting the body of the embryo into the shade. Recalling this historical process on the abortion law makes it possible to see an important effect on the evolution of the population. If I quote now the data on the situation in France, it is because the reasoning involved there could be extrapolated for those countries in Europe which have liberalized abortion. The reasoning is as follows: the law has not caused the number of abortions to decline; two years ago, the number of legal abortions had risen to 210,000 a year. A large number of specialists point out that clandestine abortions, difficult to assess in terms of the numbers that have been conducted, in spite of everything, have not disappeared and that they are more and more in evidence every day among young people. If we remain with the total number of 210,000 abortions per year, then in ten years we reach two million citizens, in twenty years to more than four million, in thirty years to more than six million and in thirty-five years, the time that separates us from that law, to more than seven million, who are now missing. Nevertheless, this calculation does not take account of the fact that, for fifteen years, the vast majority of them having become adults, would have had one or perhaps two children. Without running the risk of making a mistake or of exaggerating, it is estimated that the number of persons who are missing in France lies today between 9 and 9.5 million. Each one can extrapolate, for the different countries, that part of the population which is missing and, in this way, can form an idea of what Europe would be today, if there had not been, in the majority of countries, this deadly and suicidal law.

Thus, at the strictly political level, independently of any moral consideration, if people wish to confront the current population problem in a coherent way, people cannot avoid posing the question of whether it would not be opportune to go back and bring once more into question a law which has become a taboo in the countries of Europe. It is pointless to say that any responsible politician who might make such a proposal tomorrow would be immediately marginalized. Besides, no one has ever inscribed such a proposal into his political programme.

The consequences of the practice of abortion in a society are not reducible to the absence of millions of births. They have an influence upon the behaviour and upon the vision that new generations have of human life and, more specifically, of the exercise of the sexual faculty. A possible pregnancy is not wanted except at certain times in the life of spouses or of persons who are cohabiting. For the rest of the time, there are always circumstances which make it undesirable, such that the paradigmatic use of the sexual faculty these days is that of a contraceptive sexuality; their relationship must be protected, when a pregnancy is envisaged, which might be a risk or even a threat. Those who are used to living their sexuality in this kind of climate are no longer in a position to perceive the beauty of the coming into existence of a new human being, of wishing for that child above anything else, of marvelling at the fact that the love that they are in the process of living could become fruitful. At the anthropological level, the relationship of love is often reduced to a couple of partners who lose sight of the transcendent dimension of a child. One aspect of this reality can be seen in those couples who live together and who decide not to get married, who thus do not prepare the setting which is the ideal one in which they could welcome children. The number of children born outside of marriage is constantly increasing and, in some countries, has surpassed these days 50% of births. New priorities arise, where the wife studies and goes to work, the age of marriage or the first birth is often long deferred. The average age of marriage today is twenty-nine for those women living in western Europe.

All of these factors, which have changed the conception of the conjugal life and of the family, contribute to emphasizing the current demographic tendency. Motherhood and fatherhood still benefit certainly from a certain esteem at the cultural level, but they are perceived by the young generations as one choice of life among others and no longer as the normal path for them to fulfil themselves as man and as woman.

False and Good Responses to the Problem

This evolving society is much less used to children: family policies are not very effective, insofar as they place on the same level concubinage and the family. In this way, family allowances and assistance to the family do not favour the stable cell of marriage and the family, thereby participating directly in maintaining the common good. As we know, the family fulfils different functions that, in fact, do not weigh directly on society as a collective entity. In the early years, families provide on their own for the needs of the child; they educate the child, and naturally and progressively they prepare the child to take their place in society, first of all, through the course of studies, and then through their professional work. Furthermore, the family fosters the exchange between the generations, it takes care of and surrounds older people who need its intensive care and, finally, it offers children the best conditions in which they may be able to develop. The growing number of families who make the choice to have only one child do not offer that one child the fundamental experience of fraternity. Fraternity is something precious because it brings to young people their first experience of socialization on the basis of an equality of right. In the home, young persons must take account of the others and of their freedom. They do this naturally because, in the stable family, all are in theory subject to the natural authority of the two parents. When the couple separate and when they are recomposed, only with difficulty is it possible for the child grow with the desire and with the affective capacity to found some day a stable family themselves, and to have a number of children.

The question of demography is rarely analyzed in its various different dimensions. The way that those responsible for life in society respond to this challenge at present is through bringing in other populations, thanks to an increase in immigration. Certain countries claim that it is necessary to foster immigration in order to face up to the decline in the population. They see in this a natural solution to be able to respond to the economic demands connected to labour. Immigrants into Europe come from Morocco (France, Spain, Belgium), black Africa (France), Turkey (Germany), the Balkans (Italy), Pakistan and India (the United Kingdom). Many agree to work in positions that the European do not wish to fill. In order to justify this option, we are often reminded that European civilizations are the historical fruit of ethnic mixing of different cultures. This argument is true in part. In reality, what was produced in the past was the outcome of a slow evolution of what nowadays is present at an accelerated pace and on a massive scale. Few persons would dare to formulate the question of how to know whether a culture can absorb in such a short space of time (thirty years for France, twenty years for Italy) such a migratory influx. The question carries with it a number of risks, to the extent that every possible ideological deviation of the problem must be avoided, but the question deserves to be posed. I shall quote only the case of Italy, referring to the statistics in the annual directory of Caritas for 2009 (the Nineteenth Annual Report). On p. 89, it is reported:

> On December 31, 2007, the total residential population reached 59,619,290 persons, of whom 3,432,651 are of a foreign nationality (5.8% of the total population). With the knowledge that on December 31, 2002 (the first official data from Istat) the foreign population was 1,549,373 persons (2.7% of the total population), it can be stated quite simply that, in five years, that population has more than doubled, both in absolute terms and in relative terms.

The report provides details of the differences within each region of Italy. I shall not enter into detail. This evolution is spectacular; it is a legitimate question to ask whether, at such a rhythm and in such proportions, a harmonious integration is possible. In fact, no culture is capable of integrating changes of such significance at the human, economic, and social level. As far as the example just cited is concerned, it must be noted that, by definition, these figures do not take account of clandestine immigrants. It is to be remembered that, when ten years or so ago it had been decided to offer the possibility for clandestine immigrants to be regularized, the estimates which had been made were revealed to be wrong in the proportion of one to twelve! It is thought that between 12,000 and 15,000 of those without papers would present themselves within the ten days foreseen to allow their situation to be regularized; in fact, there were no less than 180,000 persons who arrived.

To conclude, we cannot limit the response to the question of demography in Europe to an appeal to immigration, with a view to maintaining a certain level of gross national product and so by avoiding calling into question our way of life. Until now, immigration has been the sole proposal on the part of those responsible for civic life. Faced with this situation, it would require a revolution of morals, and more specifically, a profound cultural and moral change in the area of respect for life and of assistance to large families, a greater appreciation of the role of the mother in the family, when she is bringing up her children, the development of health structures in the local area marked out for older persons. It would be necessary to find a way for persons who choose to found a family not to be penalized at the economic, social or professional level.

Those reforms of society, such as have been offered up to now, do not go in this direction. There can be no doubt that numerous laws are in the process of fashioning a new way of life and of conditioning the future of society (concubinage, legal recognition for unions between persons of the same sex, the promotion of the gender ideology, contraceptive sexuality as the ordinary way for living out male-female relationships, the promotion of all forms of artificial fertilization, the abandonment of older persons who are less and less present in the cell of the family to the point that they represent a world that is totally foreign to young people) and, in the end, towards the development of and the establishment of laws in favour of euthanasia.

The Demographic Situation in Europe

As can be understood, we are confronted by a question that is no longer only social or political, but one that has become a question of the moral and of the spiritual order. We would add that, in the area of births, every change that is decisive and of great import manifests its concrete effects at the distance of a generation later (between twenty and thirty years are needed for a newborn child to be able to contribute effectively to the economic stability of their country). Without hiding away any of the questions that have been raised, it is then necessary that people as a whole be made aware of this subject and that it be addressed to everyone: to politicians with responsibility at the national and the international level, to associations, young people, entrepreneurs (it is known that a declining birth-rate constitutes a brake upon economic growth[3]), to intellectuals, jurists, and those who form public opinion.

The Church reminds us that economic growth is not incompatible with ordered development,[4] something which besides is necessary. Already, in *Populorum Progressio* (1967), Paul VI wrote, in regard to the problem of population, that the rights of families must be respected. Of what rights was he speaking? Of the right to live with dignity, the right to procreate and to educate, of the right to be respected as a person, and to decide in conscience to procreate or not, to decide upon the number of children, to receive effective help and support from society. When these elementary rights are not observed, a logic of violence, of greed, of thirst for power and conflict is established and hence a recoiling from human life. In his social encyclicals (*Sollicitudo Rei Socialis* and *Centesimus Annus*), John Paul II was very attentive to the theme of population: he always highlighted the close link between *personal ethics* and *social ethics* (*Familiaris Consortio* and then later the *Letter to Families*, *Evangelium Vitae*, and the *Charter of the Rights of the Family*).

---

3. Cf. E. Gotti Tedeschi, *Meeting Rimini*, 2010.
4. Cf. John Paul II, Encyclical Letter, *Sollicitudo Rei Socialis*, § 25.

If contemporary societies decide to address the problem of the question of demography, they will need to do so, taking into account the institution of the family. Benedict XVI made explicit reference to this in his encyclical, *Caritas in Veritate*, in which he expressed the hope that there would be authentic social progress that would respect human laws, would be led by divine love, and would foster the transmission of life.[5]

---

5. Benedict XVI, Encyclical Letter, *Caritas in Veritate*, § 28: "Openness to life is at the centre of true development."

14 Conscience as Inviolable[1]

The most ancient writings of Greek literature, philosophy, and drama, the philosophical writings of the Roman Stoics, and the books of the Old Testament provide us with the witness of men and women who, having come to a decisive moment in their existence in which a personal choice of a religious or moral nature was inevitable, found themselves in the position of having to disobey the law of their country. Even if the concept of conscientious objection did not exist at that time—as is known, properly speaking the theory of conscientious objection came to be analyzed only recently a little more than a hundred years ago, in regard to bearing and using arms in a military context—the reality itself of such an act of *refusing to obey a civil law, judged in conscience to be seriously unjust*, seems always to have existed.

Nowadays, recourse to conscientious objection has passed beyond the context of a pacifist struggle, to which it had been limited, to impose itself in the areas of medicine and political action. The testimony of previous centuries shows a general agreement existed on the *values* considered to be essential as a foundation for political authority and social equilibrium; acceptance of duties towards one's own country and towards God, personal rules of behaviour, the dignity of work, care for the cell of the family, filial piety, paternal authority, and many other aspects of life in society.

It would be excessive to say that all of these values today have disappeared, but realism requires us to recognize that they are no longer the object of an undisputed agreement. Quite clearly,

---

1. "The Demographic Situation in Europe" is the text of a lecture delivered on December 1, 2010, at the Pontifical University of the Lateran in the context of the Colloquium *La Sfida Imminente della Cura Etica degli Anziani*, organized by the Acton Institute Foundation.

the attenuation and, in some cases, the disappearance of certain values has given rise necessarily to new social norms of behavior. We find ourselves in the presence of social and political reference points which have emerged from philosophical alternatives and from currents of thought which have become more and more cross-cultural in a globalized world. These ideas have generated unusual judgments and behaviours, to the extent that these rely upon conceptions of human nature which are truly revolutionary, marked by a cultural and ethical relativism.

Ideological Toleration and Conscientious Objection

One of these new concepts, without any doubt, is the current concept of *toleration*, which seems to prosper because of a very real ambiguity, which will emerge further on. Let us note straight away that the idea of tolerating patiently some temporary evil that could not be avoided in the immediate situation without causing greater harms or indeed of confronting peacefully contrary opinions has always signified a classical expression of the *virtue of prudence* and of its expression in a reasonable form. Today, *toleration* has ceased to be a *practical virtue*; it makes a claim to the rank of a *theoretical virtue*. This claim is *essentially political*, even if innumerable consequences in the order of *ethos* have emerged from it. The concept of *toleration*, as also that of *conscientious objection*, has a relatively brief recent history; we could take it back to the time of the Protestant Reformation. From Erasmus[2] to Locke[3] and from Spinoza

---

2. Erasmus, despite his rupture with Luther, whose friend he had been, but whose seditious conduct he deplored, committed himself publicly to arguing that violent methods should be avoided in the struggle against the Reformation. He recommended a kind of political compromise, which would allow different regions to practise their faith while awaiting an agreement between the various parties. This is what led him to become the best friend of Thomas More, earning a reputation for tolerance. For Erasmus, tolerance was more a question of a religious attitude than the fruit of relativism, something which has often been attributed to him, quite wrongly.
3. Locke's *Essay on Toleration* (1667) constitutes the first philosophical work

and de Bayle[4] to Voltaire, in the century of the Enlightenment, it was the object of several successive studies and was vested with various nuances. It would not be honest not to attempt to provide a precise inventory of the latter, but the semantic evolution of the term after Locke's *Essay on Toleration* in 1667 illustrates the fact that the term nowadays has become a veritable instrument of politics, which, paradoxically, contains within itself some frightening forces in the direction of totalitarianism and of exclusion.

If the nature of the subject requires us to think simultaneously of two quite distinct questions, that of *conscientious objection* and that of *toleration*, it must be understood that the act of refusing in conscience to obey an unjust law is something which today is carried out in a context of ideological toleration, which, of its nature, is not disposed to accept such an act of refusal. It is our thesis that a society which is ideologically intoler-

---

on the subject of toleration. In a period marked by the crisis of the Reformation, Locke's position consists essentially in placing back-to-back the parties which had been in conflict with each other for more than a century, for the purposes of assuring peace in society, which, for him, were inspired by the teaching of the Gospel (John Locke, *Lettre sur la tolérance*, translation into French by Jean Le Clerc, 1710, in the edition numbered by J-M. Tremblay, Chicoutimi Université de Québec, 2002, 7). A further step is taken, with reference to Erasmus: orthodoxy is not conceded to any religion. Like every ideologically tolerant person, Locke places himself above the parties and puts forward criteria, which for him are the authentic criteria of the true orthodoxy: the person who is truly Christian is the one who is tolerant. Together with Spinoza, for Locke, the criterion of the social order will find its limits in respect for individual freedoms.

4. Pierre Bayle (1647–1706), a French Calvinist, is considered as one of the theoreticians of toleration. His work, entitled *A Philosophical Commentary on the Words of Jesus Christ: Let Them Enter In*, unleashes a polemic around the idea of toleration. If Bayle has remained famous, this is by reason of his *Historical and Critical Dictionary*, which defended a thesis of total scepticism, according to which human beings are incapable of coming to absolute certitude. From this, there arises an appeal to toleration, founded upon the primacy of personal conscience.

ant cannot accept conscientious objection, since the latter in some way would escape from its dominion.

Such an opening affirmation is somewhat surprising; that toleration may be intolerant, that is a paradox and expressing it like this could seem to be provocative or simplistic. Nevertheless, the ideologically intolerant person is a little Epimenides; this thinker's fame has spread across the centuries under the form of a paradox, known as Epimenides' paradox:

> Epimenides, the Cretan, said:
> All Cretans are liars.
> Epimenides is a Cretan
> Therefore, Epimenides is a liar.
> Therefore, the Cretans are telling the truth
> Therefore, Epimenides is telling the truth because he is a Cretan and,
> Since he was telling the truth, all Cretans are not liars ...

As we can see, we swing unceasingly from one affirmation to the other. The reason is that Epimenides, by uttering this sentence, through its content, destroys the validity of the act of making the affirmation. By saying, "All Cretans are liars," he calls himself a liar and thereby destroys the validity of his own affirmations.

The *ideologically intolerant person* is a little Epimenides. Why? By saying: "All opinions are valid," he affirms as a general rule what has never been any more than one opinion among others, according to his own affirmation. How is it possible to emerge from this impasse? Only by violence, which would amount to saying: "If you contradict me, when I say that all opinions are valid, then you are a dangerous, intolerant person, who is to be resisted by all means available." In fact, the alternative, which would consist of saying: "But toleration is only one opinion among others" is not sustainable for that person. *Ideological toleration* wishes to impose itself upon everyone. This is the reason why we said that it is of *an essentially political, not of a moral* nature, even if it is the manifestation of an abusive moral claim. Since this intolerance in reality remains unconscious, it exerts even greater violence.

What Toleration cannot Tolerate

The paradox of the *ideologically intolerant person* is not an exercise in rhetoric. It enables us to understand that a society that asserts loudly and forcefully that it is a tolerant society is not in a position to put up with what endangers its unstable and contradictory equilibrium. In particular:

- it does not tolerate the idea that there is a truth to be sought
- it does not tolerate the idea that such a truth can have a universal character
- it imposes the exclusion of any debate on the question of fundamentals. In fact, in any debate on fundamentals, the interlocutors could end up by not being in agreement, but they have in common the desire for a truth that is valid between all the parties to the debate. In a society of *ideologically intolerant persons*, the question of the search for truth is abandoned and, by this move, the debate on fundamentals is transformed into an exchange of ideas that are relative. Each of the interlocutors *informs* the others of his or her own ideas and they must forbid themselves from considering their own ideas in the end as valid for others. They cease to be ideas of a fundamental nature. The debate can have no outcome:
- such a society does not accept the ethical implications of ideas of a fundamental nature;
- it places itself always above debates on fundamentals and claims the right, legitimately to judge the parties who are present; moreover, in so doing, it does not exercise any true arbitration—as would be expected from an authentic political power— because its position of toleration in practice places it always alongside the positions of those interlocutors who in theory are the most tolerant, positions to

be sure which would be the least disturbing for the balance of the consensus which it claims to maintain.

To sum it up, a *tolerant society* imposes one sole way of thinking. It is, in this sense, that it is totalitarian and, without knowing it, that it establishes the bases for systems of totalitarianism, at times within a short space of time. For example, the proclamation of the revolutionary ideas of toleration by the theoreticians of 1789 gave way, in the space of three short years, to the establishment of a very real reign of terror.[5] It was in vain, a little later, that some priests sought to make heard an objection of their conscience, which forbade them to swear an oath to the *Civil Constitution of the Clergy*. The refusal of this oath by those who were called, very eloquently, the *refractory* clergy earned for them death or, in the best case, exile, with the loss of their civil rights and of all of their goods.

The ideology of toleration is not exempt from philosophical prejudices. It has been emphasised quite rightly that the great theoreticians of toleration at the time of the Protestant Reformation were, for the most part, sceptics. This is particularly true of Bayle. This philosopher did not content himself with claiming the same rights for those who were in error as for those who were not. He went to the point of seeking recognition of the same status for doctrines which were erroneous as for expressions of the truth: "A conscience which is in error must be able to be assured of the same privileges for its erroneous convictions as those which an orthodox mind obtains for the truth," he wrote in his *Dictionary*. To the objection that, in that case, people would be exposed to clashes with those who consciences would oblige them to persecute others, Bayle could only reply by referring to the rational character of moral conscience.[6] He did so in

---

5. Reference may be made to the brief, synthetic critique: "La Révolution ou la mort," which forms Chapter 9 of J. Sevilla, *Le terrorisme intellectuel*, 2nd edition (Paris: Perrin, 2004), pp. 156–167.
6. Cf. H. Kamen, *L'éveil de la tolérance*, trad. J. Carlander, (Paris: Hachette, 1967), pp. 236–241.

a way that was almost a reflex, without being aware of the *contradictio terminorum* present in his theses; if conscience must obey reason, it is because the latter offers it criteria of truth. It would be for this reason that Bayle would meet the greatest opposition from among the very ranks of those who initially had been his supporters, for example Jurieu.

We must be fair. Pierre Bayle was perfectly sincere in his wish to struggle against the very real intolerance of his time. He proved this by devoting several chapters of his work to the abuses committed by his own Huguenot brothers against minorities, Anabaptist, Catholic and also Jewish (the murder of Nicolas Antoine, strangled and burnt to death in Geneva in 1632).

The position of Locke, the father of modern toleration, is much more problematic than that of Bayle. His conception was quite broad; indeed, he intended "to open civil society not only to Jews, but also to the Mohammedans and even to pagans. However, he associated this with two reservations; excluded from toleration were Catholics and atheists."[7] Leaving aside the exclusion of Catholics, no doubt very much conditioned by the prejudices on which English society under James II was based, we note with interest that the exclusion of the atheists was grounded on that idea of Locke according to which "an atheist, even if virtuous, could not commit himself to remain so, either in relation to himself or in relation to others; it would be a virtue without consequences, since the atheist denies the need for penalties or for rewards in the next world."[8] Thus, toleration, in Locke, sensitive to the role of the social bond exercised by religious beliefs, is not grounded upon a nihilistic or even upon a merely neutral conception of the society of human beings; in this it is to be distinguished from the ideological toleration of contemporary secularist societies.

---

7. Cf. P. Thierry, *La tolérance. Société démocratique, opinions, vices et vertus* (Paris: PUF, 1997), pp. 35–57.
8. *Ibid.*, p. 38.

If, now, we wish to seek a response to the legitimate concern of Bayle, Locke and many others about the danger of totalitarianism, let us observe that this cannot be found in a theoretical demand for toleration. *Ideological toleration* is a false response.[9] To say that, in order to escape from totalitarian control, all opinions are valid would be to make legitimate what it is we are trying to avoid. The only truly realistic response at the philosophical level is the positive affirmation of the dignity of the human person as a truth which is valid for everyone, on condition that this is grounded in the natural law. It establishes the possibility of a real debate, because the interlocutor is considered worthy in all cases, that is to say as someone entitled to be respected for that fundamental liberty which, it is understood, is to be recognized in that person. Such an attitude is authentically tolerant, if it may be put like that, in a sense that is classical, respectful and patient, but it is not located in *ideological toleration*, insofar as that authentically tolerant attitude presupposes and affirms a truth which is universal.

In reality, *ideological toleration* suppresses the only point of view which respects the dignity of the human being. How can we be surprised, then, that it is in the name of this toleration that people attack the life of infants in their mothers' wombs or that they manipulate human embryos? Everything becomes possible, other than affording unconditional respect for the human person. Since what is involved is a short-circuit of human reason,

---

9. "We are living under the sway of a kind of moral terrorism...a morality of comfort. The only kind of thought and the sole form of morality allowed, moreover, are very often reactions of comfort. Once upon a time, this was called conformism ... Under a despotic régime, conformism can tend in the direction of violence. In a democracy, it always goes in the direction of moderation. The problem is that moderation can become despotic. Tocqueville has explained this very well... There is something of the totalitarian in the weak kind of thinking which governs us these days." (P. Tesson, "Un terrorisme intellectuel assez bienveillant," incorporated by D. Lensen into J.-M. Chardon and D. Lensel (ed.), *La pensée unique. Le vrai procès* (Paris: Economica, 1998), pp. 34–35.

invective takes the place of a debate which is well-argued and honest.

The dignity of the human being is situated in the realm of philosophy; it is a fundamental given which is able to contribute socially to bringing several different philosophical conceptions closer together. This, however, is on one condition, that of avoiding indifferentism, which reduces choices of a fundamental nature to mere expressions of differing opinions. The dignity of the human being would require, above all in what concerns respect for human life, a political prudence which cannot legislate in a morally upright way to permit that which many citizens consider to be an action unworthy of the human person.

On the religious level, the concept of dignity includes also a vision of the human being as a created being. Hence, in the Christian perspective, human beings find their ultimate foundation in their being in the image of God. This takes into consideration, then, a certain plan of the Creator which can be read in the givens of nature (in relation to human life, for example, part of those givens includes the growth of the human being, and the purposes of the biological phenomena involved in the formation of their bodies). Believers cannot impose upon others a particular understanding of some living phenomenon, which incorporates explicitly what stems from a perspective of faith. Nevertheless, Christian faith and culture have certainly contributed to our thinking about the coming into being of a new human being, in terms of the event (or better of the advent) itself. The *a priori* rejection on the part of an ideologically tolerant society of the expression of such a sensibility cannot but lead to the impoverishment of the social awareness of the fact that human life, including its very first moments, is a good which is to be respected unconditionally, to be protected and to be served. It is understandable, in the context of such a rejection, that human life is trivialized and is more and more reduced to being treated as a mere biological given.

In reality, ideological toleration deprives society of the specific contribution of philosophical and religious approaches which it refuses to incorporate into its perspective, preventing them from adding their own contributions to the common good.

The Loss of the Objectivity of the Judgment of Conscience

Ideological toleration is always linked to an individualistic conception of moral conscience, according to which the individual who decides to act and to adopt a particular kind of behaviour is viewed as a sort of monad who is totally autonomous in its choices. The moral norm becomes a threat to freedom. In the best case, the norms received from moral authority, from social tradition, from the magisterial instructions of religious authority, would be received as indications, no doubt interesting, or opinions which might stimulate reflection, but in any case, they would not be binding upon the subject. From such a perspective, the idea that there is a law, written or unwritten,[10] that might be binding upon the subject, by reason of the certain truth of which this law could be the expression, is an empty one. The unwritten laws, to which, after Socrates and after Sophocles, Christian thought would refer with St Paul, make possible the harmonious integration of rational demand and divine teaching. By contrast, once the idea of unwritten laws present in the heart of the human being is rejected *a priori*, any connection between God and conscience is irremediably excluded. In other words, God is put to flight from the moral sphere and any possibility that he might intervene in human action is no longer recognized. Well beyond the question of ethics, it can be seen, for Christians it is the whole conception of divine grace, of its efficacy, and of its power to justify the spiritual being which is brought into question. Individualistic conceptions, which are also by definition necessarily relativistic, cannot leave the foundations of the faith intact.

---

10. Vatican Council II, *Gaudium et Spes*, § 16.

The relationship between freedom and moral truth is not the only one to pose problems in the tolerant vision of conscience. The whole problematic of the erroneous conscience is also evaded. Either the error of conscience is an opportunity which allows someone to act normally without moral fault[11] or indeed the reality of moral error is itself denied, through the very fact that people grant to moral conscience the status of being infallible, thereby producing a confusion between two levels of conscience classically designated by the terms *synderesis* and *conscientia*. The fact that there exists a kind of sovereignty of the moral subject, who, by his acts, decides about himself and about his becoming a virtuous person or otherwise, was always at the heart of classical thought. It is the character of the judgment of conscience as reasonable,[12] following the truth inscribed in the moral good, which alone gives this freedom the means to attain its true autonomy (in this sense, we speak usually about the freedom of the saints). Reasonable persons, submitting themselves to divine Providence, participate in this Providence in some way. Such persons have the capacity to govern themselves and to govern others. However, autonomy is often seen as a capacity of conscience to decide for itself about the good. In this sense it affirms a kind of primacy for the moral opinions of the subject, who can never make a mistake morally, if he is being sincere. At the very most, someone might admit the possibility of making mistakes, but these would be considered to be errors of knowledge, in the end understandable, and the moral conduct which follows from such errors would no longer be in itself a motive for blame. It would be qualified as inadequate or as inappropriate.

> The change in the meaning of the concept of autonomy of conscience is expressed in this way in the semantic shifts in the language of ethics, which often prevents us from making judgments of value about human behaviour. By

---

11. Cf. Joseph Ratzinger, "Coscienza e Verità" in Id. *La Chiesa. Una comunità sempre in cammino* (Cinisello Balsamo Paoline, 1991), pp. 113–137.
12. St Thomas Aquinas, *Summa contra Gentiles*, III, 114.

way of illustration and remaining within the area of autonomy, Carlo Caffarra has shown very well how the fact that people speak about the decision of conscience rather than using the traditional term of the judgment of conscience has contributed to removing the possibility of referring to criteria of truth in the realm of human action.[13]

The Double Issue at Stake in Conscientious Objection

The interior debate which precedes any moral decision and then the visible and public manifestation of that decision is a *deliberatio* or practical judgment which refers to what we propose to do (or, in the case of conscientious objection, of what we propose not to do). To choose not to do something is also a moral act, with a clearly defined object; to object is to accomplish an action of refusal, by reason of convictions which are important enough for them to be referred to our personal conscience.[14] We do not object to fulfilling a positive law for the simple reason that we do not like this law or that we have a different opinion from that of the legislator. Positive laws bind us, when they are produced by a legitimate authority, to which we are subject. They form the legislative structure which must ensure justice between citizens, regulate their relations and the good ordering of their roles and functions, in all the areas of social life: economy, education, health, culture, information. These laws bind us because they are assumed to protect goods and rights in a perspective, which, in principle, is that of the preservation and promotion of the common good.

The motives for disobeying a law must be capable of being referred to the instance of conscience, where other laws enter into play besides positive law. These are distinguished from this latter

---

13. C. Caffarra, "L'autonomia della coscienza e la sottomissione alla verità" in AA.VV, *La coscienza, Conferenza internazionale patrocinata dallo Wethersfield Institute di New York, Orvieto, 27–28 maggio, 1994,* (Vatican City: Libreria Editrice Vaticana, 1996), pp. 142–162.
14. Ratzinger, *art. cit.*

in that they are not subject to change as is human legislation; they are immutable laws and they engage the person in his or her totality. Here are some examples which posterity has left to us.

Socrates's Condemnation to Death

We could ask ourselves the question of how the putting to death of the philosopher could indeed have been the work of the first democratic government in history. It is interesting to look at the political and cultural context of this trial because there is no lack of resemblances to the context in the western world at the beginning of the twenty-first century. Athens had emerged battered from a war which had cost the lives of almost a quarter of its population (the Peloponnesian War): if two attempts to overthrow the democratic power had failed, the intellectual debates were still animated by the paradoxes of the Sophists. Their art, the heritage of Ioanian rationalism, consisted in bringing into question all the foundations of the city-state, in particular the gods and the laws. Insinuating doubt about everything that had contributed to the glory of Athens in the century of Pericles, they were considered as a threat. It was by playing on the original character of Socrates and on the impact of his teachings that his accusers managed to formulate against him two charges, the corruption of youth and belief in gods who were not those of their city, and in having him condemned to death at the end of a trial, of which the admirable pleadings of the one condemned have passed on to posterity.

His death was approved by a majority of 280 against 221; here already we have a democratic consensus for a work of death! In his defence, the philosopher put forward the uprightness of his own conscience and affirmed that, in death, he had a fate more enviable than that of those who condemned him unjustly:

> You should realize that, if you put me to death, since I am everything that I have just affirmed, you will do more harm to yourselves than you will to me. In fact, neither

Anytos nor Melitos will do me any harm; they cannot do so because I do not believe that it is in the power of an evil person to harm a man of the good.[15]

We could ask what, in the eyes of Socrates, makes death a more enviable fate than the injustice which consists in condemning an innocent person. Here religious sentiment is united to moral conviction and confers upon it the whole of its perspective. It is a matter of the judgment of the gods and of all the just who have gone before us into Hades.[16]

The Confrontation between Creon and Antigone

A similar unity between moral requirements and religious duties is to be found once more in the person of Sophocles' Antigone. The drama sees two wills opposed to each other, that of Antigone who intends to give a burial to her brother, Polynice, and that of Creon, the king of Thebes, who is the incarnation of positive law. The context is that of a fratricidal war which opposes his two sons, Eteocles, who is destined to reign and Polynice who, exiled by his brother, attacks the city. The two brothers are killed; the king decides to honour the younger son as a hero and refuses to give a burial to the older son. The order becomes law; the body is abandoned to the dogs and whoever attempts to bury it will be condemned to death. Antigone is surprised by the guards when trying to recover the body of her brother and is led before Creon, who in fact has her imprisoned, to await being put to death. It is only by the intercession of his soothsayer that Creon recovers himself, gives a burial to Polynice and wishes to liberate Antigone. His remorse comes too late; Antigone has been hanged in the prison. Creon's son and fiancé of Antigone puts an end to his days. Eurydice, Creon's wife, commits suicide also, when she learns of the death of her child. Thus, Creon has lost everything. There is nothing left for

---

15. Plato, *Apology of Socrates*, 30c and 30d.
16. *Ibid.* 41a.

him but to desire a death which will liberate him. The dialogue between Creon and his daughter merits attention. In the face of the blind power and injustice of the law, she makes herself the advocate of the rights of *phusis*, of the demands of nature, which expresses the will of the gods.

The dialogue presents with great clarity the opposition between the two concepts of duty; in this sense it has a gripping relevance to our time. Creon expresses the point of view which is that of all positivists:

> Obey, obey, in small things and as in great, in the just as in the unjust, always and everywhere, obey the man who is in the governance of the State. It is anarchy which is the worst of all evils; it destroys cities and overthrows houses, puts to flight and destroys armies in battle. But, it is obedience, obedience to the leaders, which is the source of salvation and of victory. We must be obedient to the laws, to the laws which have been put into writing.

Antigone expounds his views before the king, in the following way:

> I do not think that your decrees have such force that you, who are a man, would be capable of overthrowing the laws of the gods, those laws which are unwritten and indestructible. They do not date only from today or from yesterday, but they exist always and always did exist. No-one knows when they appeared.

The antagonism is complete; divine laws against human laws, temporal decrees and unwritten, eternal laws. We note that Antigone, when referring to the gods, evokes also the precept of a law of nature. We may not, under any pretext, leave the body of a man without burial. The nature referred to here is the will of those to whom nature is subject, the gods. Conscientious objection is naturally united to religious duty, since the latter imposes itself rightly upon conscience; it is good, it is right, it is just to obey the gods. Antigone draws a comparison between physical and moral sufferings which the fact of disobeying the gods brings to conscience: "To undergo death for me is not a suffering. It would have been a suffering, on the contrary, if I had allowed it to happen that the body of the son of my mother, after his death, had not obtained a tomb."[17]

Seneca and the Sacred Character of the Duty of Conscience

Despite the justification for suicide which was to be found in Rome among the Stoics, an action condemned by minds as diverse as Pythagoras, Plato, Cicero and Plotinus, the conviction existed there that, one day, people are destined to have to respond to their gods for their own behaviour. For Seneca, it was not possible for a person to rise above his destiny without god and to become truly good without god. The claim of conscience that we conduct ourselves well enters into the perspective of our having to give an account of ourselves one day to the divinity.[18] Here once more, we have the unity of the two dimensions, religious and moral, required to lead a virtuous life, whatever it may cost.

The witness given to the One God as Motivation for Conscientious Objection: the Seven Brothers of the Book of Maccabees

From the perspective of its religious significance, since it was situated within an act of cult *par excellence*, the examples of the seven brothers of the Book of the Maccabees offers the perfect example of conscientious objection. Although essentially religious, their action was also profoundly moral. Their refusal to eat sacrilegious meats offered them the possibility to give the witness of martyrdom. Each one of the seven brothers, before dying, expressed his submission to the laws of his country and his certitude that he would receive his recompense from God.

---

17. Sophocles, *Antigone*, II, Sc. 3, v. 462–470.
18. Seneca, *Ad Lucilius*, IV, XII, 41.

Conscience as Inviolable

God would fulfil the demands of justice completely by punishing their impious persecutors. We may observe that, in their case, as in the case of Eleazar who had preceded them in death, we find also witness to the one God, as the youngest of the brothers expressed it in accepting his ordeal: "I sacrifice my body and my life for the laws of our land, as my brothers have done already, imploring God soon to reveal to our people that he has been appeased" (2Macc 7:37). Giving witness to the One who is God, is an obligation of their conscience. It is interesting to see that, in the case of the aged Eleazar, there was also present the concern not to give a bad example to the young, who could have been disturbed if he had appeared to have eaten the sacrilegious foods, as they had tried to make him do. In this example, conscientious objection clearly includes a *responsibility for others*. This adds to the perfection of wishing to save oneself from all compromise.

The Structure of the Freedom of Believers

From the beginning, Christians found themselves hanging in an uneasy position in their relationship to the law, first the Jewish law and then the Roman law. Their witness is clearly in the first place essentially religious, which explains the unleashing of the persecutions. It was thanks to the intervention of Gamaliel that the Apostles who were together with Peter escaped the anger of the Sanhedrin, which had wanted to put them to death. Their crime was to have disobeyed the order no longer to teach in the name of Jesus. Peter's response began by giving an absolute rule of discernment: We must be obedient to God before being obedient to men (Acts 4:19), a principle which would accompany all of the baptized after him. Then, that response expressed the kerygma to which, the Apostle added, he and his companions were witnesses, together with the Holy Spirit, whom God had given to those who had submitted themselves to him. These words, related by the Acts of the Apostles, provide the structure of what became for

Christians the specific conscientious objection which could lead to martyrdom. It expresses the freedom of the believer.[19]

The elements constitutive of its structure are the following:

- Divine laws have predominance;
- It is only when human law formally contradicts divine law that the Christian may be in a position of having to disobey it;
- Their witness is a transmission of a precise truth about God, teaching *in the Name of Jesus;*
- Their witness was made possible by the power and the assistance of the Holy Spirit;
- The believer could not escape; objection is a duty of conscience because the gift of the Holy Spirit has been made to that person.

Do Not Sacrifice to Idols; Do Not Worship False Gods; St. Phileas and St. Cyprian

Henceforth, the witness given by the Christians prepared for martyrdom would comprise all of the same elements. Examples abound: under the persecutions of Diocletian, in the year 304, St Phileas was interrogated by the president of the tribunal of Culcien. The latter ordered him to sacrifice to the gods.

> "I will not offer sacrifice, replied Phileas.
> "Are you behaving like this through a scruple of conscience?
> "Exactly for that reason."
> "Why then do you not observe, with the same scruples of conscience, your duties towards your children and towards your wife?"
> "Because my duties towards God are more important than other duties."[20]

---

19. M. Schooyans, *"Le terrorisme à visage humain* (Paris: F.X. de Guibert, 2006), p. 112.
20. The martyrdom of Sts. Phileas and Philorome in *Atti dei martiri,* (Milano: Paoline, 1985), p. 753.

Conscience as Inviolable

For Phileas, giving witness to the true God, by abstaining from the worship of false gods was indeed a duty of conscience.

The martyrdom of St Cyprian is well-known; what is less well-known is the exile which the bishop of Carthage had had to suffer first of all, after his earlier appearance before a tribunal. In the course of his first interrogation, the future martyr associated to the fulfilment of the will of God the uprightness of the one to whom God had revealed himself. To the proconsul, Paternus, who asked him: "Will you persist in this will [of not sacrificing to the gods]?" Cyprian replied: "The upright will, which knows God, cannot change."

At times, people say, as did Voltaire in his time, that these persecutions stemmed in reality from the necessity for the Empire to prevent the diffusion of Christian doctrine from weakening the unity of the Empire. The philosopher even added that this was not a sign of intolerance. Here we find once more an illustration of what we said at the beginning of our analysis about avoiding the real questions. If the Christians had not claimed a doctrine of salvation that is universal, their cult would have taken its place alongside the other religions tolerated in the Empire. This is the reason why it would have sufficed for them to have recognized the Roman rites, while still practising their own religion.

This was exactly what was unacceptable to true Christians and so this is what Cyprian and the others clearly refused. In the interrogation which preceded his exile, Cyprian formulated what was being asked of him in the following way:

> The most holy emperors, Valerian and Gallius, have deigned to address a letter to me, in which they have ordered that all those who do not practise the Roman religion nevertheless recognize the rites of that religion. What do you say in reply?

> "I am a Christian and a bishop, said Cyprian, and I recognize no other god, except the one true God, who created heaven and earth, the sea and all it contains."[21]

We may observe that the witness of the martyrs, on which the Church of the first centuries was founded, made it possible to recognize the opposing act of counter-witness represented by apostasy and by the idolatrous cult to the Roman gods. We take note of the fact that, among the *lapsi*, in the eyes of the Christians, there figured not only those who had abandoned the one God, but also those who had seemed to have done this by offering sacrifice to the gods of the Empire.

The attitude of Cyprian poses a question of great contemporary relevance and one which merits being posed in an ideologically tolerant society. This is precisely the object of the famous controversy which saw Ambrose and Symmachus opposed to each other: why would Christians not recognize the Roman gods, given that Rome accepted that they might practise their religion?[22] Voltaire could not prevent himself from saying in his *Treatise on Toleration* that, in his eyes, the Roman Empire had shown itself to be tolerant towards everyone and even from adding that it was the Christians who had shown themselves to have been intolerant, by not accepting the gods of the city.[23] On

---

21. *Ibid.*, p. 467.
22. The controversy turned on the question of knowing whether, over and above the restoration of the Altar of Victory, it was be right to reestablish the pagan cults. Symmachus preached tolerance on this point, while Ambrose showed himself to be intractable, on the basis that a Christian could not recognize false gods. (St Ambrose, *Letters* XVII and XVIII; Symmachus, *Relatio* III, in *La maschera della tolleranza*; (Milan: Bur, 2006).
23. "What? The Romans would have put up with the infamous Antinous be placed in the rank of the secondary gods and they would have tortured and thrown to the wild beasts all those who could justly have been accused of peacefully adoring one who was just! What! They would have recognized a God who was supreme, who was sovereign, the master of all secondary gods, as witnessed by this formula: *Deus optimus maximus*, and they would have searched for those who adored the one God! It is unthinkable that there would ever have been an inquisition against the Christians

the basis of what he wrote, which has never been the object of a critical examination by historians and by philosophers, the accusation made against Christianity of being intolerant has been continually repeated up to our own days. According to the thought of this Enlightenment philosopher, Christians could have and should have tolerated the Roman gods. We could extrapolate from this, without forcing the text, and say that, then, they would not have disturbed the tolerant structure of the society of the Empire.

Whatever may be said about the specious character of the reasoning, such an accusation demonstrates at least that, from the time of the rise and the diffusion of its ideas, *ideological toleration* has seen symbolically in Christianity an adversary to be combatted. As we shall see later on, this affirmation does not involve prejudging other more positive aspects to be found in reflections on the theme of toleration. Nevertheless, it remains true that, in its most forceful form, it is indeed in regard to Christian thinking that *ideological toleration* would reserve its most violent attacks.

The Letter to Diognetus or the Moral Coherence of the Christian Faith

In any case, the faithful preservation of doctrine and the clear witness of the martyrs would enable Christians to give an example that was coherent and credible of a rule of life, which excludes a certain number of practices. Moral rectitude and uprightness of will are indissolubly linked in a witness rendered

---

under the emperors, that is to say that these would have come to them to interrogate them about their beliefs. Under that title, they never troubled either Jew or Syrian or Egyptian, or poet or druid or philosopher. The martyrs, then, were those who rose up against the false gods. It is something just, pious, not to believe in these; but, in the end, if they (Christians) are not happy with adoring a God in spirit and in truth, if they burst forth violently against the received cult, however absurd it might be, we are forced to admit that it is they themselves who are intolerant" (Voltaire, *Traité sur la tolérance*, [Paris: Garnier-Flammarion, 1989] pp. 70–71).

to the true God. Some among them put forward objections to performing certain activities (for example, carrying arms, as would be the case with the Christian apologist, Lactantius, and for Tertullian), but everyone showed respect for the laws of the city, to the extent that they did not contradict the demands of morals. This is the description of the disciples of Christ, which is made in the *Letter to Diognetus*:

> Christians discharge all their duties as citizens and put up with all their burdens as if foreigners. They get married and they have children, like everyone else, but they do not abandon their new-born children to death. They share the same table with other people. They obey the laws which have been enacted and their manner of life brings them to a perfection beyond the laws.[24]

Fidelity to the Church as the Content of Conscientious Objection: the Case of St Thomas More

Christians knew already that, in the end, they could be put under pressure by events to choose the narrow path that would lead them not to deny their faith. Without any doubt, St Thomas More, at the beginning of modern times, constitutes the most striking example of conscientious objection, made for religious reasons and more specifically reasons of belonging to the Church. As is known, having abandoned his wife in order to be able to marry Anne Boleyn, King Henry VIII found himself needing to have his marriage declared null, under pain not only of being excommunicated, but also of having to confront insoluble problems of his succession. Once Catherine of Aragon had referred her case to Rome, and Rome rejected the request for the marriage to be declared null (March 23, 1534), the legitimacy of the royal succession of the children who would be born of the marriage of the king with Anne Boleyn was immediately brought once more into question. The king reacted by causing his Parliament to adopt a new law of succession for the

---

24. *Letter to Diognetus*, 6–10.

English crown. Anyone who refused to accept its content would be declared a *criminal*. All high functionaries had to swear an oath, the members of the Commons as well as those of the House of Lords. In the Lords, only Bishop Fisher refused the oath.

In reality, there were two different oaths; the one concerned the royal succession and was addressed to the laity, the other was addressed to the clergy, upon whom the suppression of all authority on the part of the Pope in England was imposed. When More came to judgment, he would put forward the invalidity of the law of the succession on the basis of the natural law. But the question of the succession was not the only one posed to More. In fact, when the text of the oath was presented to him, he discovered that they were putting him in the position of having to approve not only the royal succession, but also the authority of the king over the Church of England. We know from his son-in-law, Roper, how stark was the interior struggle he endured. In fact, Thomas had to resist the pressure of the affection of those close to him, up to the time when he was summoned to Lambeth to take the oath. He had the courage to contest the illegal nature of the double oath which was being required of him. He was asked explicitly to put his duty towards the sovereign before his own doubts and his conscience. He replied that he was in the position of having to obey his conscience rather than his king, but that he did not wish to condemn anyone. With the exception of Fisher, the episcopate, in fact, had already denied its bond with Rome.

Thomas More was then imprisoned for *contumacy*. The firmness which he would demonstrate up to the end was accompanied by a very acute awareness of his own weakness, such that the example he gives of conscientious objection, profoundly Christian in its motivation, is, in the first place, an expression of a gift of God:

> I cannot but hope that they will not have recourse to violent means of coercion and, further, that, if they do, then God, with the help of his grace, as well as through the

> many prayers of faithful people, will give me the strength to remain firm ... because, of this I am sure, if ever I were to swear the oath, I would be acting completely against my personal conscience.[25]

More shows that the right to object to an unjust law is not the fruit of a haughty human decision of someone who puts himself above the law. Besides, the difficulty, as in his specific case, of exercising it by stages proves that martyrdom is never chosen *a priori*; it represents the point of arrival after a careful attempt at every stage to find a solution which would safeguard the rights of conscience at the same time, if possible, as respecting authority.

Thomas More was not a revolutionary. The course he took was not in the first place of a political nature. Thomas More did not divest himself of any of the duties which were placed upon him; he went to Lambeth, when he was summoned, he gave the witness of respect and deference towards his sovereign, and he did not reject any of the formal obligations which were imposed upon him, with the exception of that which quite rightly was the object of his objection; the rejection entailed by the oath of the authority of the Pope. At no point did he challenge the legitimacy of the legislator as such, *his objection related only to the object of a law which he judged to be unjust*. As with any authentic conscientious objector, "his passivity, his docility in regard to the sanctions he incurred, prevent us from considering him to be a traitor or a rebel. Even the impotence which he accepted gave witness to his attachment to the State, whose sovereign authority and whose power to legislate he recognized."[26]

The refusal to act against our own conscience was developed naturally in the course of the centuries within a fertile Christian terrain; as we have seen, it involved such diverse matters as bearing arms, denying the faith, laws against the Church on the part

---

25. Quoted by E.-M. Ganne, *Thomas More. L'homme complet de la Renaissance* (Cité 'Historique: Nouvelle coll. 2002), p. 216.
26. Cf. M. Broc, R. Pietra, "L'objection de conscience," *Esprit*, 10 (October, 1963), p. 375.

of the temporal power. Behind the rejection of a law or disobedience to an immoral order, there is always present a power, which, beyond the firmness of personal witness, is something endured and interpreted by the civil authority as a potential threat. For example, the refusal of the adolescent martyrs of Uganda to bow before the immoral caprices of the king, was interpreted and judged as a crime of *lèse-majesté*.

The Secularization of Conscientious Objection: Modern Times

Conscientious objection of its nature is exposed to retaliation and to sanctions, unless it is contained in the law itself. In modern times, conscientious objection has been secularized and has become crystallised around two themes in particular.

The first is that of *military service,* a civil duty required by the majority of legal systems, imposing on all young adults a certain period of time of service in the army; such service implies learning how to handle arms, in case the country were to be exposed to armed conflict. The refusal of this duty on the part of those who invoke "conscientious objection" has given place to legislation which was the fruit of a long process of development of more than a century. The status of conscientious objection, the current political and cultural context in the West in which this action has been legitimized by law, as well as the object of what has often become a claim of a political character, demand that we compare it with the tradition of classical conscientious objection.

The second field of application is more recent and for less than half a century has concerned the question of the practice of abortion, depenalized and then legitimized. The fact that procured abortion is not only tolerated, but that it is even claimed as a right and as an individual freedom has created a situation totally unheard of in the history of public expressions of personal conscience. It is the very object of a positive right, which has become the object of conscientious objection.

Let us examine these two more recent forms of conscientious objection.

Military Service

Christian conscientious objectors draw the foundations of their position from the Scriptures: the expression of the fifth commandment, the teaching of love of enemies, the command to Jesus to Peter to replace the sword in its sheath (Jn 18:11); the prospect of performing an act, shedding blood, against their conscience convinced them to incur the rigours of divine justice on the day of judgment.[27]

However, taking the step of refusing to bear arms has never been an attitude shared by all Christians. With the reign of Constantine, the legitimate nature of the State's demand to employ all means—and hence including the arms of soldiers—to safeguard the common good seemed to have been affirmed. The authority of the sovereign came from God and there was no opposition in principle between the precepts of the Gospel and the duties of the citizen. The protection of the common good was the responsibility of every citizen, and the Christian himself is also a citizen. For example, nowhere in the Gospel, it seemed, did Christ reproach the Roman centurions (even though occupiers) as to the nature of their service. It is known that only a contemporary, ideological re-reading of the period of Constantine interprets as a compromise towards the Empire the Christian thinking on the temporal power, which, following St Ambrose and St Augustine, had begun to develop.

Medieval reflection would be attached to the idea of showing that circumstances exist in which a war conducted by a sovereign state could be held to be just.[28]

---

27. P. P. Gelasius, *Epistula* VIII, *Ad Anastasium imperatorem*; PL, LIX, co.l. 42.
28. Extrapolating the Roman notion of a just war (*justum bellum*), a purely formal notion, to the extent that a war was considered just if it was declared according to the rites which had been envisaged, undertaken by the magistrates who had the capacity to do this, Christian thought, with

Conscience as Inviolable

The protection of subjects and the integrity of the territorial limits, in the case of an unjust aggression, are two examples of this.

In reality, the refusal to bear arms by Christians has involved much more those currents which emerged from the Reformation, including Anabaptists, Mennonites, and Quakers in Anglo-Saxon countries.

Dispensation from military service, granted for religious reasons, existed in the sixteenth century under some European governments: for example, the Dutch Mennonites and then, much later, those in Russia, benefitted from a freedom of cult which was accompanied by a dispensation from the duty to serve in the armed forces. Moreover, this concession was not, strictly speaking, dictated by philosophical motives; people registered themselves under the exemptions which were habitually granted, on the basis of privileges in various juridical fora, civil and religious. These communities operated their own rites, law courts and educational establishments. Hence, it was in favour of the Mennonites that for the first time a service of a civilian nature, substituting for military service, was granted and created in Russia in 1875; they had to participate in works in the forests. Their number never went beyond a thousand. It was only at the beginning of the twentieth century that measures in favour of conscientious objectors were established in different countries, but that was on condition that the request was made on an individual basis. We may cite Sweden (1902), Australia (1903), South Africa (1912), Great Britain (1916), Canada, the United States and Denmark (1917), Norway (1922), and the Netherlands (1923). The persons involved had the choice of entering a non-armed military service or a branch of the civil service. Very

---

St Augustine and then with St Thomas, would specify the conditions of a just war. Such a war could be declared only by the competent authority; a just cause (a requirement of punitive justice) and, finally, an upright intention were needed. The war could not have any other purpose than the reestablishment of peace and of justice.

quickly and in a proportion which was not negligible, some objectors rejected all pretence and chose the absolutist option.²⁹

The same phenomenon could be observed everywhere. In some countries, legislators were very much behind in providing a law. This was the case in France, which had to wait until December 21, 1963, before voting for a first law in favour of objectors. The law of 1963 was ambiguous; on the one hand, it recognized the right to conscientious objection claimed by a part of the population (in fact, a small minority at the time) and thus resolved the issue of those objectors who were still in prison. On the other hand, it surrounded this right with administrative conditions which were so restrictive that they made this a *right of which to be ashamed*, if we may say so, by means of measures intended to dissuade people from exercising it (double the length of civil compared to military service, forbidding people from publicizing the fact; and, moreover, the request was only accepted if it was presented several months before the date envisaged for starting the service). The suppression of compulsory military service, as a consequence of the professionalization of the army, has made the question less acute in several countries. Military service has been displaced in the direction of service in other areas of social life, making them more and more politicized. Conscientious objection has become a purely *political objection*; it is no longer a matter of refusing personal participation in military activities, which would require bearing arms, but of fighting—and moreover at times not without violence—against the whole of a political or economic system in force in western countries. In the most extreme cases, the mere fact that the constituted bodies (army, public function, Church) are structured hierarchically has been a sufficient motive for them to be con-

---

29. According to J.-P. Cattelain, the absolutist choice, by way of example, affected 6,261 objectors out of a total of 15,925 in Great Britain for the period 1916–1918. The statistics which we have given are taken from the historic work on this question: J.-P. Cattelain, *L'objection de conscience* (Paris: Emmanuael, 1973), coll. 'Que sais-je?', pp. 50ff.

sidered as enemies to be destroyed. Political opinion then becomes a *libertarian option*, according to Cattelain's expression.[30]

The ambiguity of the concepts employed explains the difficulties encountered by the legislators in establishing objective criteria for the *status of being a conscientious objector*. Could the refusal to do military service be based upon adherence to very imprecise principles (non-violence, for example) or indeed upon philosophical opinions? Where would the limit be? It is known, that, in many countries, the legislator has cut things down, in order to recognize only objections dictated by religious demands. This would constitute a paradox, insofar as, in the last analysis, it is precisely personal conscience which should dictate the attitude of the one making the objection. Obeying religious prescriptions is also a moral duty, but to limit the right to what is religiously motivated would amount to excluding those who could be very sincerely motivated by moral factors. Having said that, the development of ideologies, as illustrated above, and the gallery afforded to them in the numerous media outlets, show how necessary it was to make a distinction between moral demands and simple political opinions, a distinction expressed in the beginning by the rigours of the law.

This allows us to understand the liveliness of the debates surrounding the taking into account of the second modern form of conscientious objection, that relating to questions immediately bound, in biomedical ethics, to problems of respect for human life and to various actions of healing.

The Recent Development of Conscientious Objection in Matters of Health

The current debates over conscientious objection in the medical field were crystallized around the question of the *depenalization* and of the *legalization* of abortion, for it to be extended then to a great number of questions raised nowadays in very different

---

30. *Ibid.*, p. 76.

circumstances. The issues which have arisen are numerous. Among the problems which give rise to such objection, apart from abortion, is to be found the question of the refusal by certain patients of subjecting themselves to certain treatments (for example, the case of the refusal of a blood transfusion by Jehovah's Witnesses), the refusal to provide help to acts of euthanasia, the refusal of sterilization, the refusal to participate in acts of capital punishment, in research entailing the death of the embryo, in techniques of assisted procreation, and in numerous other questions addressed here, from the particular standpoint of what characterizes this type of conscientious objection.

From the point of view, of the authority of the State, it is a concession made to the citizen, exactly like the licence granted to someone objecting to bearing arms. We may note that this right to abstain from participating in "medical" acts (or in pseudo-medical acts, since it concerns abortion and everything which is a threat to human life) or in acts of research which imply manipulations judged by the person as morally unacceptable, is founded either on ethical requirements (the Hippocratic tradition) or on religious motives; besides, often the two coincide, for reasons already explained in relation to the witness of martyrs.

From the point of view of the subject who makes the conscientious objection, these new fields of application, compared with the field of military engagement, give to the objection of conscience, at least every time the life of human being is at issue, an even greater moral significance. To refuse to serve in the context of the armed forces of one's own country is a recognized object of conscientious objection; nevertheless, the genuine right of a country to take proportionate means in defence of its own territory and for the protection of its own citizens cannot morally be called into question. By contrast, putting the existence of an innocent human being into certain danger through a deliberate act not only justifies an act of conscientious objection, but it imposes such an objection absolutely as a matter of duty.

Let us observe that international law did not recognize the existence of such a duty, because, in certain cases, it could have reproached subordinates, in the context of a conflict, with having carried out orders which they ought to have disobeyed (participating in war crimes), including when those acts had been falsely covered up under the pretext of scientific research; this was the case in the course of the second of the Nuremberg trials in 1946–1947, undertaken against Nazi doctors.

In the light of these remarks, let us keep in mind the fact of the chain of responsibility involved in the evil which is perpetrated. This is to be found once more in a particularly elaborate way in the question of abortion: the preparation of the law, lobbying the mass media, the work of legislation, with the various contributions of jurists, the participation of parliamentarians who vote for the laws, the setting up of the material conditions which encourage and orientate people to have or to facilitate an abortion (hospital establishments, social services, "medical" prescriptions), and finally the implementation of the act, with all the aspects of cooperation, immediate and mediate, in the act of abortion. The laws which depenalized abortion had been a particularly subtle means of presenting to public opinion what had already been dictated by the will to legislate, pure and simple; in this sense the Loi Veil (1975) in France had been but the first in a long series of acts in western Europe. In order to negotiate its passage, it had been convenient to present it by employing the technically neutral term, morally aseptic, if we may dare to put it like that, of the *voluntary termination of a pregnancy* or, even better, through its initials alone (VTP). For some years now, the term *medical termination of pregnancy* (MTP) has been used to designate a procured abortion, effected in the context of the medical care of the mother. The recent history of the last thirty years has only broadened a movement which has presented it not only as an individual right (the right of a woman to do as she pleases with herself), but which has established the conditions of a very real eugenics, inserting so-called *therapeutic* abortion among the habitual procedures of selection of healthy embryos through the elimination of embryos who are bearers of infirmities (for example, in the context of pre-natal diagnosis).

In this context, conscientious objection is an issue at different levels, that of the health personnel and that of the political community. Let us take as an illustration the example of the legislation in France.

The law in this country does indeed foresee a right to conscientious objection for health-care professionals, but the possibility of its exercise is so restricted that it has established in effect a real *right to abortion*. Everything revolves around the distinction between public establishments and private establishments, since the right (of conscientious objection) is not recognized in respect of establishments, but only of persons, a problem which has been seen in other countries, moreover, such as in Argentina for example, where all public establishments must allow services under which abortion can be practised. Obstetrics doctors who work in these establishments may not refuse to allow abortions to be practised in their services. If, by chance, they do so, they would be asked to leave the public structure. In the private sector to be sure, doctors are not compelled to practise abortions, nor to accept them, if they are the ones responsible for the structure. However, they must indicate to patients who wish an abortion an alternative structure, where they will be able to undergo the interruption of the pregnancy. To refuse to direct them to such a place would lead to them incurring serious sanctions, if the patient decided to make a complaint (for example, invoking medical factors, such as infections or something else).

For nurses who may be working in a service in which abortions are practised, they certainly have the freedom to ask for a transfer to another area, something which at times, however, is granted only with difficulty.

Conscience as Inviolable

This system has implications which require several comments. The first is that, with conscientious objection, we have indeed a *theoretical right* but not a practical right. It does not have anything like the same status as the right to abortion; it is accompanied by restrictions and by conditions for its application, such that its public exercise effectively marginalizes anyone who makes use of it and at times exposes them to sanctions. What is true for obstetricians in the public sector is true *a fortiori* for pharmacists, who may not refuse to sell products considered to be and catalogued as contraceptives, even when they can be in fact abortifacients. Thus, in the area of conscientious objection raised against abortion, we find once more the same limitations as the restrictive arrangements already indicated in the area of the objection raised against military service.

The second observation is an implication of what has just been said; the higher values which, in principle, alone justify someone making a conscientious objection to participating in an action which is judged morally unacceptable are not considered by state authority to be truly superior, nor even of equal standing to those values judged to be politically consensual (such as freedom of the individual or toleration).

The third observation: doctors who are obstetricians and gynaecologists are no longer in a position to exercise their art in conditions of serenity. They are exposed to possible sanctions if, in the context of a pre-natal diagnosis, they commit an error of assessment, which might underestimate the infirmity of a fetus, influencing thereby the decision of the mother to allow the child to be born. But, here we note the lack of balance; when, on the other hand, the error of the doctor leads to the death of the fetus when the mother wishes for the chid to be born, the doctor is not prosecuted.[31]

The course of the recent history of abortion in France allows us to understand a state of decline which, as is happening in an ever greater number of countries, leads more and more to the

---

31. Cf. *Génétique*, 72, December, 2005.

person making a conscientious objection being marginalized. The fact that, since 1982 (Loi Roudy), abortions have been reimbursed through social security shows that the act of abortion is no longer considered to be a negative action, which the law of 1975, despite its long-term intentions, claimed to wish to dissuade mothers from committing. Practically, the act of abortion has become the alternative in an iniquitous choice, since it no longer encounters any greater disapproval than the decision to bring a child into the world. The State itself has facilitated the conditions for its implementation and the fact that it reimburses people for this act is symbolically the spectacular and sad expression of this fact.

Conscientious objection is also limited in terms of the choice of its action. In an analogous way to what happened before 1963 concerning actions to do with military service, the law imposes sanctions for certain actions involved in campaigning, which are interpreted as not being respectful of the law and as being intolerant. Since 1993, a new crime has even been created: that of *obstructing the voluntary termination of pregnancy*. The parallel with the crime of *insubordination*, in the military context in earlier times, is instructive. *Obstructing VTP* incurs comparable penalties (of imprisonment of two to three years), but the charge of the crime seems to indicate VTP as a designation of an objective social good and not as some evil that the State would abstain from punishing by depenalizing it. By contrast, *insubordination* pointed only to a subjective attitude (the action of not submitting oneself to the duty of military service). We have understood in our contemporary culture that VTP has become a good, not only for the person free to practise it, but for the society itself which allows it, encourages it, promotes it, and finances it. Historically, such an approach cannot but develop ever further the practice of abortion by trivializing it. In July, 2001, the conditions of access to this procedure were the object of new measures, some of which could be qualified, without injustice, as inciting people to commit abortion. The legal time limit was reduced to twelve weeks, parental permission for minors was suppressed, and even the dialogue which had been obligatory up to then for adult women disappeared. The crime of obstructing abortion has been extended even to moral and psychological pressure. As for the conscience clause for doctors, it has been greatly obstructed and has even been suppressed for the heads of hospital services. In November, 2004, a decree authorizing medical abortion in the home was signed by the Minister of Health.

The case of abortion is paradigmatic. The ideology which established it and which encouraged it, by presenting it as a personal right of pregnant women, has deprived society of any possibility of reflecting calmly on the fundamental question of the status of the human embryo, precisely for fear that it would call into question this legislative choice. By doing this, society no longer has the capacity to confront ethically the challenges represented by a number of medico-surgical practices and by manipulations linked to biomedical research. How, and on what basis, could it manifest some reservation of principle towards procedures which involve the destruction of several embryos, if it has not accepted up to now confronting objectively the problem relating to the act of abortion? In regard to any future reflection on these themes, it has wiped out the essential criteria which would have allowed it to address them calmly.

Such a political action has the immediate effect upon the possibilities which citizens will have in the future of exercising a right of conscientious objection in relation to scientific procedures which threaten human life. This political action sets the conditions for a limitation in the immediate future and then for a suppression sooner or later of the right to conscientious objection in the area of respect for human life. Already, there has been a manifestation of the juridical will, seeking to move towards the abolition of this human right, linked still to the most fundamental requirements of the moral conscience of the human being. The reason invoked is the classical one: the objection would be an expression of a means of evading the law and it would violate the principle of the equality of all before the law.

Thus, it is that what has been our thesis from the outset would be brought about: a society which is tolerant cannot tolerate the fact that, within its midst, people may exercise a right of conscientious objection, because it is no longer in a position to accept the higher values which it would be honouring by their being exercised in its midst. Hence, it chooses consensual values, some of which infallibly lead to death.

15 THE SOCIAL DIMENSION OF HUMAN EXISTENCE: THE STATUS OF THE SOCIAL DOCTRINE OF THE CHURCH[1]

> *Discovering that he or she is loved by God, the human being understands their own transcendent dignity, learns not to be satisfied with themselves as individuals and to meet others within the framework of relationships which are ever more fully authentically human. Renewed by the love of God, they are in a position to change rules, the quality of relationships and also of social structures; they become persons who are capable of bringing peace where there are conflicts, of constructing and of cultivating fraternal relationships where there is hatred, of searching for justice where there is the exploitation of one human being by another.*
>
> Compendium of the Social Doctrine of the Church 4.

This paragraph, taken from the introductory part of the *Compendium to the Social Doctrine of the Church*, published in 2005 by the Pontifical Council for Justice and Peace, has the double advantage, on the one hand, of situating the reflection of the Church on the life of human beings in society within an anthropological vision that is complete and, on the other hand, of suggesting that the establishment of relationships which are pacific, fraternal, and just requires the transformation of human subjectivity on the part of God, a renewal of human

---

1. "The Social Dimension of Human Existence: The Status of the Social Doctrine of the Church" is the text of a *Lectio Magistralis*, delivered on December 1, 2006 at Madrid in Spanish under the title *La dimension social de la existencia humana: El estatudo de la Doctrina Social de la Iglesia* on the occasion of the erection of the Chair Ángel Herrera Oria of the Social Doctrine of the Church at the CEU University of San Pablo de Madrid.

beings through divine love. In this way, the synthesis expresses theologically the vision that the Church has of human relationships and of social organization. The action of God is not something foreign or extrinsic to the social conduct of human beings. Furthermore, at the anthropological level, the text unites our relational life to human dignity, qualified as transcendent.

The fundamental elements brought into focus in this way can offer a structure for our reflection. In the first place, we shall attempt to trace the contours of a Christian anthropology, elaborated on the basis of the originary insertion of man and woman in a human setting. This approach should allow us then to address the epistemological question: the social doctrine of the Church has a status that links it to different disciplines, but in a specific manner, always taking them from a practical perspective. This will be the second stage of our analysis. Finally, we shall try to illustrate our proposal with two particular examples: peace, through the concrete problematic involved in reconciliation in civil society, and the question of the family, which locates us at the natural meeting point between the individual and the adult, actively inserted into society. We shall limit ourselves to these two areas; to be sure, other questions could be studied, for example the question of human life, which in recent decades has become a major political and social issue. These areas are certainly not the only ones we could examine, but without any doubt they are to be counted among the principal factors capable of transforming societies and cultures in a durable fashion, something that can be appreciated over a number of decades in the West. We note that, on these key themes, the social doctrine of the Church has a specific teaching to transmit and a *praxis* to propose.

The Social Dimension of the Human Being at the Heart of Christian Anthropology

The title given to this first stage of our reflection is not a neutral one. It seeks from the start to avoid two dangers.

The first consists in thinking of the human being first of all as an individual, in his psychosomatic nature and then of his personal capacity for recognizing, discerning, willing, and putting into action the good, and finally, of his virtuous commitments in the service of others. The social dimension of the person is seen then only as a secondary quality and his action in this domain comes to mean bringing to fulfilment some personal moral perfection. Within such an optic, commitment is like some external radiance, something that is externally fruitful, as if other people were the theatre or the almost accidental occasion for the expression of personal generosity. From our point of view, this vision is reductive in a double sense, insofar as it does not succeed in thinking about the requirements of social life in themselves, but only through the prism of the individual, who situates himself or herself face to face with the society to which they belong. Furthermore, and this aspect is linked to the first, the implications in the order of action will be more often a transposition of individual issues into the social order and such a transposition will often be characterized by a misunderstanding of the rules of society. This aspect will emerge more clearly when we speak of the question of reconciliation as a path to social peace.

The second danger is that of an excessive theorizing of the principles of the social doctrine of the Church, which tends to reduce the latter to a corpus of principles, often losing sight of their capacity for application and integration. We know that the very concept of *social doctrine* has been criticized very strongly by certain authors who have perceived it as a teaching, an assemblage of texts more or less forming an ideology, according to the expression of Marie-Dominique Chenu, in a work that has remained famous.² This great theologian made the criticism that the period 1890–1960 had produced abstract texts, dictated according to him by the desire of the Church to play a role of an ideological nature (social Catholicism) and to exercise power over the organization of society. By contrast, he saw in the encyclicals of John XXIII and of Paul VI the beginnings of a promising change of perspective.

The harshness of the analysis is to be explained in part by the lack of perspective. René Coste rightly remarks that today we can measure the precise contribution of the Magisterium of that time, on the one hand, by the way Christians were made aware of social questions and, on the other, by the condemnation of totalitarian régimes.³ Despite the passionate nature of the social debates that developed at the time of the Second Vatican Council, we note that certain criticisms touched upon some technical points of interest. For example, with Chenu, the comment, according to which Christian thought had been deployed around the concept of the natural law, did not develop a real theology of the Incarnation and of the assumption of earthly realities.

Thus, it is by being fully aware of the difficulties that have been raised, that we must rethink the social status of the human being, something that is constitutive of our nature. There are a number of theological and anthropological elements that are characteristic of a Christian vision that is non-reductive.

The Notion of Communion

At a first and fundamental level, the eternal divine communion revealed in God is that of a society in which each Person exists insofar as he is in relationship with the others; this is not by means of playing with a static mirror, but through an unceasing gift of love, which is eternally fecund. Human beings are invited

---

2. Marie-Dominique Chenu, *La 'Doctrine sociale' de l'Eglise comme idéologie* (Paris: Cerf, 1979).
3. R. Coste, *Les dimensions sociales de la foi. Pour une théologie sociale* (Paris: Cerf, 2000), pp. 159–162.

to participate in a personal way in this gift: "The eternal Father, by means of a thoroughly free and mysterious plan of wisdom and of goodness, created the universe; he decided to raise human beings to a participation in his divine life."[4] The vocation of the human being to holiness corresponds to the eternal plan of the Father to introduce him into this intra-trinitarian communion and this *predestination*, if we may put it like this, grounds the communitarian nature of the human being. The reformulation of the themes of the image and likeness of God in the Magisterium of John Paul II, in terms of the interpretative key of communion, has undoubtedly helped to clarify the nature of the bond that unites the Three divine Persons and the communion which unites the children of human beings between themselves:

> If ... we wish to draw from the Yahwistic text the concept of the image of God, we can then deduce that the person has become the image and likeness of God not only through his or her own humanity, but also by means of the communion of persons.[5]

In fact, from the beginning, it is not only an image in which there is reflected the solitude of one Person who rules the world, but it is also and essentially the image of the unfathomable and divine communion of Persons. More systematically still, we find the same idea once more in the apostolic letter, *Mulieris Dignitatem*. What is affirmed there about the specific communion between man and woman was in fact seen as a paradigm of the human condition:

> Being human involves a call to inter-personal communion. The text of Genesis 2:18–25 shows that marriage is the first dimension, and, in a sense, the fundamental dimension of this call. But it is not the only one. The whole history of the human being on earth develops

---

4. Vatican Council II, *Lumen Gentium*, § 2.
5. John Paul II, Catechesis IX, November 14, 1979, *Uomo e donna lo creò: catechesi sull'amore umano* (Città Nuova, Roma, Libreria Editrice Vaticana, 1985), pp. 58–61.

within the framework of this call. In terms of the principle, according to which everyone lives 'for' the other in inter-personal 'communion', at the heart of this history and in harmony with the will of God, we see that man and woman can grow in humanity itself, integrating what is 'masculine' and what is 'feminine'. The biblical texts, starting from Genesis, allow us constantly to rediscover the ground in which the truth about the human being is rooted, a ground which is solid and inviolable in the midst of the multiple mutations of human existence.[6]

Here it could be objected: is this notion of communion not an improper Christianization of the social dimension of the human being? Is it not going too far? Social life, we hear sometimes, requires justice and respect; with the term "communion" we would be entering into a vision that is that of a specific religious confession and is no longer universalizable. This criticism does not hold: Christian thought, in fact, sees in God the origin of all human communion. By doing this, it does not distort reality; it provides clarity, thus furnishing it with its intelligibility. As for the term "communion," which indicates both a particular quality of inter-personal relationship and its concrete extension, its origin, and its anthropological meaning are already found in Aristotle, who speaks of friendship as a sort of benevolence, which goes beyond justice and which completes it.[7] Since it is reciprocal, it establishes between its terms a communication, a common reality, a common good (*koinonia*). What is generated then is the common good of each one, a reality which Christians would adopt the habit of designating under the term of communion.

The Aspiration to live with Others and for Others is Profoundly rooted in Human Nature

This dimension is a constitutive dimension of the human being. Balthasar saw in the binomial *individual-community* one of the

---

6. John Paul II, Apostolic Letter, *Mulieris Dignitatem*, § 7.
7. Aristotle, *Nicomachean Ethics*, VIII-IX.

three tensions that are constitutive of the human being (together with those of *spirit-body* and *man-woman*). An individual human nature that does not contain within itself, from the beginning of the existence of the individual, this fundamental orientation towards the other does not exist. The vision of Rousseau of a good person who subsequently becomes social (and who subsequently becomes corrupted through the contacts which arise) belongs to a romantic, naturalistic vision, which later would become, as we know, the vector for various analyses of an anarchic character. The matter is explained quite clearly: society is viewed as a threat to personal happiness and to personal fulfilment, to such a point that all recognition of its authority is denied.

The recent study by anthropology of the originary and structural bonds of filiation and of its corollaries of paternity and maternity is very useful for understanding how deeply the social experience of the human being is rooted. Here, it seems to me of decisive importance to say that the best means for social doctrine (and for other disciplines besides) to escape from abstraction is to allow experience to play its full part. At the anthropological level, the first experience of the human being of their social dimension is the discovery that they are filial. Every human being is naturally led to recognize their origins and their identity. In the natural order of things, he or she is always *"son or daughter of."* They do not choose their name, which they receive from their parents or from those who take their place. It is by the name which they receive, conferred upon them by others, that they begin to be recognized in society, both in terms of their origins (parents) and in terms of their personality (the forename designates them among those close to them, parents and friends). Thus, the experience of self is inscribed for the child within a human anteriority, which cannot be completely listed in an inventory (at best a few generations would be accessible to the person).[8]

---

8. Cf. D. Biju-Duval, *Le psychique et le spirituel*, Preface by J. Laffitte (Paris: Emmanuel, 2001).

If the very first social experience is provided for the child in a relationship of total dependence through the relationship with their mother, the time will come when the figure of their father will intervene in a more conscious way in their life. The father is the figure of authority who begins to bring the very young child to realize that their rights are not unlimited, in particular in their relationship with their mother. In this sense, this stage, fundamental for the psychic development of the child, is the first call upon the child's freedom, to give their consent to this authority and to accept its legitimacy, to recognize themselves as the child of this father, in the way that, up until now, they have experienced themselves as the child of their mother.

The issue is important; through this there begins that experience of the autonomous existence of others; the exterior world is offered there, but it is at the price of conquests which are won painfully and of freedoms which pose resistance.[9] It is in this way, step by step, that the human being is inserted concretely into society; the principles of social life are learnt little by little as a lesson of life (reality is first of all lived) and never as abstract principles. When the Church teaches universal principles, such as subsidiarity or the universal destination of goods, she does not put forward theories which are to be applied, she formulates what persons who have attained maturity and who are reasonable have discovered already naturally, as a standard of conduct in their relationship with their fellow human beings.

The Social Dimension, Constitutive of the Human Being, can be studied also at the Ontological Level

So far, we have considered the social dimension of the human being in a purely descriptive manner through the psychic development of the individual. However, this dimension of the person

---

9. On this point, we refer to our text, Jean Laffitte *What is a Filial Anthropology?* in a colloquium organized by the Congregation for the Doctrine of the Faith, under the presidency of Cardinal J. Ratzinger September, 2003; cf. below, pp. 349–371.

is an originary reality, which has an ontological depth. The human being is incapable of being self-sufficient and has the structural need to receive help and assistance from others. In this sense, each one finds himself in a situation characterised by finitude. Moreover, they have a constitution which several authors, particularly the German writers, Ferdinand Ebner, Martin Buber and Edith Stein, have qualified at times as *a dialogical structure*. Others, such as Bruaire, have gone even further, to speak of the human being as an *être-de-don* (a *being-gift*). At the existential level, persons fulfil themselves through the gift of themselves, finding in love the means to reach their perfection. This reality of experience specifies what is involved in belonging to a family cell, a group, a culture, a nation. Human nature is in essence communitarian; we note with interest that this fundamental given is fully assumed in the ideal of the Christian life (in liturgical assemblies, families, religious congregations, spiritual associations and finally in the communion of the saints). This reality arises simply from the nature itself of the Church. The human being participates in the life and in the *ethos* of groups and communities in whose destiny he or she shares. The community of destiny generates, at the ontological level, what can be called a *perfect society* (here we are not situated at the level of its realization in history).

Familiarity (Family Proximity) as Basic Sociality

Basic sociality needs the recognition that comes from the law. In a text which was designed to bring out the juridical character that is constitutive of *familiarity* (in contrast to the antithesis which is commonly asserted between *familiarity* and law), F. D'Agostino distinguishes several levels of recognition: the *taboo of incest* is a norm which guarantees the constitution of the subjectivity of the *I*; the acceptance of one's own sexual identity on the basis of the illusory character of every claim to bisexuality;[10] the dimensions

---

10. "Bi-sexuality is illusory because it is the symbol of auto-genesis and of immortality, in short of omnipotence; it is the divine attribute par ex-

of parenthood-filiation, the asymmetric binomial in which the archetype of the principle of responsibility dear to Hans Jonas is rooted; the fraternal principle, to which is linked to the principle of equality, and finally, the last level, conjugality in its monogamic expression; in fact, only marriage allows *familiarity* to experience durability. The author sees in commitment and fidelity *the opposite of lying and of deception*. The juridical organization of society must necessarily take into account the fundamental relationships of solidarity that ground it, the penalty for not doing so being levels of instability that would be perilous for society itself. In contrast to this, the "de-institutionalizing" of family proximity and confining it to the private domain (the primacy of affectivity) in Western countries are the illustration of this truth.

We could multiply the examples of the elements that illustrate the sociality of the human being. It would be possible also to show how, in Christian experience, all of these aspects have been taken into account (baptism as entry into the community of believers, charity towards our neighbor as the expression of a bond of fraternity, sacramental marriage as commitment before God and before other people, and many other dimensions of belonging to the Church).

The aspiration of human beings to live in society is manifested by the assumption throughout the whole of human existence of new relationships of solidarity, in associations, trade unions, economic, and ecclesial bodies.

The social doctrine of the Church begins, therefore, from a given of nature, from a concrete reality; it thinks it through, regulates it and provides it with the means for its harmony. Since its

---

cellence ... being born of a man and a woman, in the bosom of a family structure, the subject is established in their monosexual determination and learns that their *I* does not represent a totality, but a polarity, which constrains the person in terms of the desire of the other and through having to recognize the other, as a living sign of their own ontological poverty and of their structural incapacity to transcend it," F. D'Agostino, "Verità, moralità, diritto: profili giuridici su matrimonio e famiglia," *Anthropotes*, XV/2 (1999), pp. 375–392.

field of activity is unlimited, so that it attaches itself to everything that manifests the expression by human beings of their sociality, it will be helpful now to consider it in terms of its status and of its methodology.

The Status of the Social Doctrine of the Church

It is customary to see in the encyclical *Rerum Novarum* the first of the great texts that continue to enrich a body of doctrine dedicated to social questions. If we think of the context in which Leo XIII wrote this fundamental text, we can recognize that two new conceptions of social existence and organization confronted each other, the one, that of the Marxist analysis, being rigorously theoretical, the other being implicit in the choice of the free development of the economy.

The radical nature of the opposition between the two visions and the ethical implications that were generated by the one and by the other, although in totally different ways, could not allow the Church to remain silent.

We may observe that it was with a view to responding to a grave necessity of a practical order that the text was proposed to the faithful throughout the world. *Social doctrine* began to be formalized in a process of evangelization which had to come to terms with an urgent social need. The word *doctrine* is ambiguous: in current language, it evokes a body of principles and of rules, which gives the impression of a specialized teaching, something theoretical, which subsequently it would be proposed should be applied in the context of social life. Some people wanted to circumvent this semantic difficulty by speaking of *social theology* or of *social ethics* or of *practical theology*. Whatever choice of terminology may be the most pleasing, it can still give the impression of being a specialization, contributing in this way to the compartmentalization of theological knowledge. The debate on the status of social doctrine is undoubtedly destined to remain an open question for a long time and, without any desire to seek to close that debate today, it seems to me that the question of epistemology must be articulated around the following points.

Social Doctrine Exists Fundamentally Because the Gospel is Fruitful

From the beginning of apostolic times, the life of Christians and ecclesial organization have been directly confronted by life in society. The teaching of Christ was never a stranger to a whole series of issues which not only marked out his times, but which have remained present throughout the whole of history: the relationship with civil society (God and Caesar), poverty as opposed to extreme wealth, the application of the law, marriage and family. The fact that some areas have given rise to more interventions than others, in different periods and in different Churches, could certainly be the object of a specific study, but in the end that remains a matter of historical contingency. The questions remain the same; however, some became a matter of urgency, such that, at times, Christian reflection has been led to concentrate predominantly upon them.

Christians in Solidarity and Individual Christians

Some Christians have allowed themselves to be tempted by a religion of intimacy, centred exclusively on interiority; others by contrast have been able to work towards operating an absolute separation between the spiritual and the temporal; others again, more recently, have been able to devote themselves exclusively to a commitment to bringing about a change in iniquitous social structures. This does not alter the fact that from the beginning Christians have been conscious at one and the same time of being in solidarity with all people (in this respect, it would be interesting to look at the social structure, altruistic also on the basis of prayer itself) and of being individuals. To make ourselves aware of this, it is enough to reread the *Letter to*

The Social Dimension of Human Existence

Diognetus. When the Fathers of the Church adopted positions on education (Clement of Alexandria), pagan games (St Augustine in his *Sermons*), worship rendered by imperial authority to the gods (St Ambrose in controversy with Symmachus), injustice in the distribution of wealth (St John Chrysostom in his preaching), to be sure they offer a moral teaching to the baptized and they offer moral criteria to all people of good will, but they express themselves also publicly on what there is in society which, in their eyes, is opposed to the true good of the human being. Whatever the form it might take (homilies, writings, letters, treatises), their teaching is a contribution to the common building up of the city of mankind.

The underlying logic that presides over all of these successive commitments is charity, seen as a service to the human being in the concrete reality of life.

What has been said so far enables us to understand that the social teaching of the Church is not a theory to be applied but a charity practised through our acts, whose field of operation is the human being as a social being and the society of human beings. It follows that everything which is related to the understanding of the human being from this angle enriches and inspires the social doctrine of the Church. In a very special way, beyond the totality of what has been revealed and its conceptualization in the Tradition, we may refer to Christian anthropology as it was presented in the beginning (social anthropology, personal and social ethics). In regard to practical necessities, it enters also into a very large variety of fields: economic sciences (many of its principles relate to the economy, such as the universal destination of goods and the right to property) and political sciences (the notions of the common good and of subsidiarity); we note further that the Church could not avoid becoming involved in making pronouncements at the right time on democratic values; finally, in these most recent years, biology and biomedical research have taken on considerable importance.

In the midst of all these disciplines, the epistemological question has concerned most especially the relationship between social doctrine and moral theology. In an important interview given by Karol Wojtyla in 1978 and published in the review *Nuovo Areopago*, the future Pope, who was a moralist, made social doctrine practically a branch of moral theology:

> We recognize that social ethics and moral theology have a formal object in common, whereas in relation to their material object, there are some differences because Catholic social ethics interests itself, at the normative level, only in human activity of a social character.[11]

The Archbishop of Krakow, whose contribution, as successor of Peter, to the teaching of the Church on social matters was to be so decisive (we may think of the encyclicals *Centesimus Annus* and *Sollicitudo Rei Socialis*, as also of various *Messages for Peace*) looked at social questions then from the angle of the action (the morally good action) of the Christian. Quite naturally, social doctrine thus fits in with moral theology. Karol Wojtyla added that it was also an integral part of evangelization.

This epistemological question has been examined more deeply in the course of recent years.[12] In his commentary on the interview with Wojtyla, Sergio Lanza put forward a whole outline of the discipline, in which he identified the material object of social doctrine with social action; this latter is viewed from the theological perspective of ecclesial action, in its programming and in its fulfilment. Thus, according to Lanza, the methodology can be neither deductive nor inductive, but must be identified eventually with evangelical discernment. On the delicate question of its relationship to moral theology, the author comments on the conclusion to the encyclical *Sollicitudo Rei Socialis*: "Doc-

---

11. Karol Wojtyla, *La dottrina sociale della Chiesa*, intervista con Vittorio Possenti, Commento di Sergio Lanza (Rome: Lateran University Press, 2003), p. 19.
12. Cf. G. Colombo, "Per l'idea della dottrina sociale della Chiesa" in *La dottrina sociale della Chiesa* (Milano, 1989).

trina igitur illa non ideologiae sed theologiae ac quidem theologiae moralis accensetur" in a simple way. According to him, we are indeed in the realm of theology, but here the term "moral" refers to the whole field opened up by the expression *"de moribus,"* which "is not limited to those treatises generally assigned to moral theology, but it includes certainly spiritual theology, law and, with a very significant claim, pastoral theology."[13]

We see that the disciplines that may be involved are numerous. Two areas of particular importance may serve to illustrate what has been said: the first concerns peace and the second, the institution of the family.

Two Examples of Social Action: Social Peace and the Family as a Good of Society

Civic Reconciliation and the Conditions for Peace

I would like to approach the question of peace from the perspective of civic reconciliation. This is a delicate topic, which requires at one and the same time an understanding both of justice and of prudence. It will be helpful to remind ourselves of the words expressed by John Paul II on January 1, 2002, on the occasion of the World Day of Peace: "There is no peace without justice. There is no justice without pardon."

Justice

In order that forgiveness may be effective in the area of social peace, it needs to satisfy an initial requirement: justice. In reality, it would be possible to show philosophically that an unjust pardon has never been a true pardon. It remains no less difficult, from the standpoint of positive law, to assess what it is that makes pardon just. Objectively, law is the measure of what is due to each one, without conditions and without consideration of

---

13. S. Lanza, "Magistero sociale e teologia sociale. Profilo ecclesiale culturale disciplinare" in Karol Wojtyla, *La dottrina sociale della Chiesa*, pp. 91–133.

intentions. Usually, the legislative and the judicial apparatus of a State provides for this duty in the government of persons; in serious clashes between nations, on the other hand, the delicate question of arbitration arises and that of the judicial authority which presides over it. Under this political and judicial model (within a State), could a civil authority which is recognized exercise its functions perhaps by imposing itself on both parties?

At the international level, in what way is reconciliation between nations an act of justice? It seems to me to be useful to start from a simple example: the reconciliation between Germany and France, two countries which opposed each other in three murderous wars within less than a century, but which have become allies to the point where no citizen in either country can consider their neighbours today as hereditary enemies. It must be admitted that the present peace between the two peoples is of a very different kind from the precarious and burdensome peace of threats, which existed between the two wars and which historians are agreed in qualifying as an unjust peace, founded upon unjust rules, the bearers of future divisions. A just peace is rarely a peace imposed by the victors and when it is such by force of circumstances, it cannot be one which is humiliating for the party which has been vanquished.

Concord

It is known that the present peace between Germany and France was founded on the common will of certain people, whose philosophical motivation was of Christian inspiration, to establish a new web of relationships between the two countries. Instead of remaining a simple question of regulating the consequences of the last conflict, they committed themselves to creating an interlocking structure of various kinds of solidarity, economic, political, and cultural, creating, at all levels, habits of action in common in all the areas of social life. A peace such as this was not founded through a mere armistice, a conclusion to the hostilities, but on a veritable *concord*, in the deepest sense of the term. There is no doubt that the precursors of what later became the Europe of the Six (notably, Adenauer, Schumann, and De Gasperi) were animated by a very real *determination* to achieve *concord*.[14] *Concord* involves a unity of intention, which does not allow serious injustices to develop, precisely because it is situated at the deep level of the interiority of the persons thus united. In this sense, the best assurance of justice between nations is to be found when the persons who represent them are suited to do so.

What is interesting in this process is the way in which the mentalities of people have changed; at the beginning we had the determination of certain persons, expressed by the establishment of new treaties; these treaties then created a new and habitual way of living out the relations between the two countries, and, in the end, the process of peace extended itself to the individual consciences of the citizens of the two nations.

A second aspect of the reconciliation between nations, just noted, concerns the *representative character* of those who implement the process of peace. The capacity of those who are responsible for representing their own country with an authority which is recognized varies according to the nature of what it was that had been able to bring their peoples to oppose each other. Three types of circumstances can be distinguished: war in the classical sense, crimes against humanity committed in the context of clashes between peoples, and civil wars.

War in the Classical Sense

In the classical context of two countries going to war over serious differences between them, such as, for example regulating matters following an earlier conflict or over annexations of territory, citizens who, in obedience to the mobilization ordered by their governments, have confronted one another on the field of

---

14. H.-A. Schwartz-Liebermann, *La réconciliation franco-allemande in Actes du colloque* (1985); Laffitte, *Le pardon transfiguré* (Paris: Mame, 1995), pp. 301–309.

battle may not necessarily have developed political attitudes of a kind which might feed mutual hatred (for example, when the German soldier, Schmidt, kills the French soldier, Dupont, at Verdun, this does not unleash in the family of the latter a personal and eternal hatred, which would be transmitted from one generation to the next). In classical wars the equitable measures of political settlement of themselves made it possible to return to a durable peace.

Crimes Against Humanity

A second set of circumstances involves the presence in the clashes that occur of *crimes against humanity*: the murder of civilians, the extermination of villages and of populations. Precisely because such acts enter into the category of acts that are *unpardonable*, the question that poses itself is to know how to address these politically.

In these cases, by definition, the requirement of justice cannot be totally satisfied. Bringing heads of state before an international tribunal is a real novelty. Justice aims to sanction what is punishable, by the punishment of those who were responsible directly and in a determining way for those crimes. However, it can well be seen that there are very many who escape justice. Besides, the investigations to establish the facts come up against the lack of historical proof and only with difficulty can political pressure and, these days, pressure from the media be avoided. It must be admitted quite simply that we have here an expression of a justice that is incomplete and necessarily imperfect; nonetheless, this justice is indispensable for the consciences of peoples and of those responsible for the nations. It is the bearer of that rationality which Hannah Arendt, for example, saw in forgiveness, when she observed that anger and resentment are as much a threat to peace as is violence. There, then, is a realignment of purpose, if we want to put it like that; this imperfect justice is not based upon the reality of the crime and of its necessary punishment alone, but is based also upon the need to pursue peace. To create in this way the conditions for peace through a public act of judgment for crimes and at times of the inculpation of their authors, is that not already a work of justice?

We can see that, in the case of crimes against humanity, we do not have a form of forgiveness that can be immediately expressed. That is the reason why action is limited to promoting the conditions for reconciliation. Several factors are involved:

- To say, state, and qualify what the facts are with the greatest precision possible;
- To honour the memory of the victims and to ensure the perpetuation of that memory;
- Resolutely to put a limit to actions of violence; and
- To make the repetition of these crimes impossible by dismantling the structures which have produced or fostered them.

Civil War

The third circumstance is that of *a civil war*. Here, we have a dimension that is particularly difficult to analyze. By definition, the dynamism of a civil war can lead to the destruction even of a nation and of a State. How can the criminal acts committed by each of the parties be taken into account?

At times, for obvious reasons, there is an exterior mediation that helps such a process of peace, but normally it is the political authority of the country in question that enters into the process of reconciliation. There was the case of the Truth and Reconciliation Commission created by Nelson Mandela under the presidency of Desmond Tutu to establish the roots of post-apartheid social peace in South Africa. We note the fact that there exist today about twenty Truth and Reconciliation commissions in the world (Sierra Leone, Salvador, Argentina, Chile, Burkina Faso, etc.). There, too, faced with the practical impossibility of forgiveness in the strict sense, the only action possible on the part of authority was the negotiation of a procedure for an amnesty. We note further that the Anglican archbishop, Tutu, was accused of having introduced into his speeches terms such as "repent" and "pardon," terms which were judged to be too Christian. Is this not itself an indication of specifically Christian values having entered into the juridical patrimony of the nations?

The principles under which these commissions worked are known: to bring out the truth before the eyes of all, to stigmatize those who were culpable, given the inability to impose upon them a just punishment, to listen to the accounts of the victims or of their dear ones, to foster in this way the process of grieving, to broadcast the debates through the media, to establish a day of remembrance, and eventually to build a monument. In spite of the indisputable advantage of wishing to effect a clear rupture with the past, certain defects in the system have appeared: effecting reconciliation and producing the relevant texts little by little became the work of experts; above all, in certain cases, the organization of demonstrations was exposed as entailing political or ideological manipulation under the guise of the promotion of a new democratic spirit.

This third case, that of a civil war in particular, poses a problem which is often insoluble; the memory of the victims generally cannot be undertaken within the context of a clear presentation of the responsibilities of the guilty for obvious reasons: the guilty come from both sides and there is a lack of historical distance.

There exists a third condition which is necessary for there to be forgiveness, namely preserving the memory; in fact, there is a very close relationship between the healing of the wounds of the offences committed and the active celebration of the memory. Already at the individual level, it is necessary to be able to commemorate what has been suffered in order to be delivered from it. On the collective plane, memory plays a special role, in the sense that the memory that is evoked is that of a nation. The victim is not alone in their trial. When a nation commemorates what was murderous and divisive, the suffering of the victims is in some way inherited through that memory. It is necessary that this national commemoration be accompanied by coherence, expressed by fidelity to that memory and to its perpetuation. In this way we find a sort of anamnesis, whose practice is familiar to Christians, since it lies at the heart of their liturgical assemblies.

The Family

The Church considers the family under three aspects, interconnected with each other: as the natural place where the child is born and grows and where he receives the first determining notions about the truth and the good, as the place in which human life is naturally transmitted (conjugal and family ethics), and finally, as a "natural community, at the heart of which that human sociality is experienced which contributes in a unique and irreplaceable way to the good of society."[15] It is this latter perspective which holds our attention now. In fact, the affirmation that has just been made, and very many others in the same sense,[16] is not situated in the first place at the ethical level, but it considers the cell of the family in its relationship with society. The communion between the spouses, dear to the Magisterium of the Church, is not an end in itself; it is the foundation upon which the family is built up, viewed as an expanded communion of persons, according to various interpersonal relations (paternity, maternity, filiation, fraternity) already recalled above. It is the natural place of contact between members of different generations, and it assumes the role of mediation between the individual and society. The existence of the institution of a healthy family is an effective factor in making society more human and personalized. There are very many activities that make it necessary for society to defend the institution of the family: education, assistance to the sick, help for the elderly. Such functions will never be assumed by the State in way that is as satisfactory as it is within the framework of the family. The

---

15. Pontifical Council for Justice and Peace, *Compendium of the Social Doctrine of the Church*, § 213.
16. Cf. Vatican Council II, *Gaudium et Spes*; John Paul II, *Familiaris Consortio, Centesimus Annus, Letter to Families*, among other documents.

fact that all of these tasks are being assumed more and more by society is a pointer to a crisis in the family. When the family breaks down or disappears, it becomes necessary to effect a transfer of responsibilities. These values, then, become public functions. We are faced with what some people have called a symbolic "delegitimization" of the family. It is being marginalized. Family values are considered to be conservative and traditional.

For this reason, when the Church, its pastors and its pastoral theologians, defend strongly a model of the family which is often characterized in a pejorative way as a classical model, they are not proposing a return to a model of the past. Their reasons are grounded on the conviction that the cell of the family cannot be lost without losing a certain way of living the reality of solidarity between the generations and of preparing individuals, so that one day they may occupy a place in society, which would not be something they would experience as alienating. In this sense, the family is the primary and the most fundamental element to be incorporated into what *Centesimus Annus* called a *human ecology*.[17] Protecting the family offers "the best guarantee against any deviation of an individualistic or of a collectivist kind, because in it the person is always at the centre of attention, insofar as the person is always to be treated as an end and never as a means."[18]

---

17. John Paul II, Encyclical Letter, *Centesimus Annus*, § 39. M. Spieker explains the expression in this way: "By the expression 'human ecology', Pope John Paul II intends those anthropological and ethical principles of a human society, which do not arise from agreements based upon consensus, but which reside in the personal nature of the human being…A policy of this kind must strive for the healthy advance of the life of mankind and the well-being of society must be bound in the first place to the prospering of marriage and of the cell of the family" (cf. *Gaudium et Spes*, § 47) in *Centesims Annus und die Familie, Vortrag im Rahmen der Vorlesungsreihe* "15 Jahre Centesimus Annus" des Acton Instituts (Grand Rapids, Michigan) im Päpstlichen Kolleg der USA in Rom am 21. January, 2006.
18. Pontifical Council for Justice and Peace, *Compendium of the Social Doctrine of the Church*, § 213.

In a very positive way, Carl Anderson sees in the family a cultural expression of the virtue of hope. He notes that, where hope is lacking, families are destined to disappear, and he proposes as the first criterion of authentically family policies the restoration of hope as a cultural value.[19] Such a vision coheres with the *leitmotif* of John Paul II, according to whom the future of humanity passes by way of the family. Let us observe in this regard that this virtue of hope underlies also every decision to bring children into the world. If the teaching of the moral Magisterium of the Church insists upon openness to procreation in marriage and if it makes this a matter of fundamental importance, this is in the first place because it expresses a wisdom that is profound. This can be appreciated all the more these days, when we consider the contemporary demographic collapse in western countries.

The decision not to have a child is also the sign of a profound interior despair; in effect, it rests upon the implicit conviction that there is no value to be transmitted and, in the end, that it does not represent in itself a value that is worthy of being transmitted. Hope is not only a Christian value; it is also the natural engine of human action in history.

As we can see, the reflection on the centrality of the social role of the family can be addressed at various levels: anthropological, ethical, sociological, political, philosophical, and theological. Each one of these concerns social doctrine in its task of analyzing reality in order to understand it and to interpret it, in order for it to become matter of practical action. As we have seen, its first purpose is not to lay out a doctrine on morals, even if it may never abandon its connection to ethics. What it is interested in is in establishing the conditions for practical action. In order to be able to do this, it does not hesitate to draw upon multiple sources and to bring the light of Revelation to bear upon them.

In all these fields of action, Christians, by their witness and by their commitment, offer to society, of which they are members

---

19. Carl Anderson, "Criteria for Policies on Marriage, Family and Life" in *Anthropotes* 15/2 (1999), pp. 459–509.

in the full sense, what they consider to be their most precious good and which they know they cannot keep to themselves, since it is a question of a good which is destined for all by him who is its source.

II

CHRISTIAN ACTION

FORGIVENESS

THE HEART OF CHRIST

CHRISTIAN ACTION

16 WHAT IS A FILIAL ANTHROPOLOGY?[1]

Prior to any ethical reflection, the encyclical, *Veritatis Splendor*, unveils a whole conception of the filial condition of the human being, by suggesting from the start a link between the Christological title of the Son of God and the adoptive filiation of the human being. Those persons who are animated by love, who allow themselves to be led by the Spirit (Gal 5:16), and who wish to serve others, find in the law of God that path which is fundamental and necessary for putting into practice that love which has been chosen and which is lived out in freedom. Still further, they grasp the interior urgency—something that is a true necessity, not something constrains them—not to limit themselves to the minimal requirements of that law but to live out those demands in their fulness. This is a path which is as yet uncertain and fragile, as long as we are on earth, but it is made possible by the grace which enables us to possess the full freedom of the children of God (cf. Rom 8:21) and so to be able to respond to our sublime vocation, that of being children of God by living the moral life. The filial vocation of the human being presupposes foundations which are not only of the order of the Redemption but which are also of the order of Creation. It is this latter aspect that will occupy our attention in the present reflection. As a first step, we shall examine the human experience of filiation, since, in our eyes, this is the place where the human person acquires a certain intuition of another filiation, which is even more original. Then, we propose to con-

---

1. "What is a Filial Anthropology?" is the text of a lecture proclaimed in Italian titled *Un'antropologia filiale: cosa signifca?*, in the context of a Symposium organised by the Congregation for the Doctrine of the Faith (CDF), from September 23–26, 2003, on the theme of *L'antropologia della teologia morale secondo l'enciclica Veritatis Splendor*, and published by the CDF, Libreria Editrice Vaticana, 2006, pp. 73–88.

sider the mystery of the Incarnation from the perspective of one particular meaning, namely the revelation of a complete filial life. This radically new given introduces not only a new understanding of the natural experience of being someone's child but beyond that it involves a new specification. In the end, it is in the light of this latter that the characteristics of a new experience of filiation, that which belongs to the Christian, can be drawn up. The Christian is a child who recognizes his or her ultimate origin, welcomes his or her identity as a son or daughter, and lives in accordance with his or her filiation.

The Human Experience of Filiation

Personal Fatherhood and Motherhood in the Service of what Precedes them

Human filiation is discovered and is lived out on the basis of a double relationship, the relationship to father and to mother. The father and mother help the child to discover who he is, but neither is the primary source of the child's personal identity. They do not choose the subject whom they are preparing to bring into the world; in the order of nature, they do not have the capacity to determine his distinctive features (of course, we are not talking about genetic manipulation), his sex, the profound tendencies of his temperament, his physiological complexion, or the power of his intellectual qualities, of his artistic dispositions or of his sociability. Through the totality of those points by which someone lets himself be known within his milieu, parents can act by means of the education and the example which animate their own existence, but this action is never *a priori*; it is entirely subject to the respect for what the child is and which unfolds itself in the course of the months and the years. Education is a form of accompaniment and not an act of violence. Parents who bring up their child make themselves in some way the servants of something that precedes them. It is certainly true that a good education will help the child to discover his own identity but such an education will never be the sole key to this. Responsible fatherhood and motherhood presuppose that there is an object for their responsibility which is prior to them as parents and which is recognized by them. It is the recognition of this object, the acceptance of its proper nature, and the undertaking of acts that make manifest both of those attitudes which help to define such a responsibility. We may remark that the current reference to a project of parenthood, to promote new legislation in the field of assisted procreation or again, for example, in the area of the destination of frozen embryos, connotes quite literally an inversion of this order of precedence. The child, in relation to a project, ceases to be the first point of reference and becomes the object of the fulfilment of his parents' wishes.

Filiation and Human "Anteriority"

If we consider filial experience, we can affirm that every human being is led naturally to seek out his identity on the basis of his origins; in this, he is located by his name in numerous cultures, from Israel to the Scandinavian peoples, from Spanish-speaking cultures to very many African civilizations. He indicates his particular filiation by taking on the father's name (or sometimes the mother's). In the natural order, the human being is always the *son or daughter of* ... Another characteristic feature is that the child does not choose his name, which he receives from his parents or from the one who substitutes for them. In the majority of cases, it is a name that he keeps, by which he begins to become known in society, both in terms of his origin (member of the family, clan or tribe whose name he bears) and in his personality (the first name which designates him among his intimate relatives and friends). The fact that, in a number of Asiatic cultures, this first name may be the bearer of a meaning which expresses perhaps a particular characteristic of the person (the texture of the skin, the length of the eyelid, the color of the hair) or a wish to emphasize a virtue which is wished for the new-born child (courage, competence, affability) changes nothing about this fundamental given; the child receives what expresses his origin and personality. Despite everything, what is received here and that is already something quite significant, is not enough to get to the bottom of the central question which every being poses about himself, which is that of the distant source of his being. Human origins are not enough to furnish a satisfactory response to this question and every being who is in search of that which constituted his first beginning can well refer naturally to the love of his parents as a decisive event. That person is no less prone to preserve the intuition that this love cannot say everything, even if this is only because that love would not have the capacity to provide him or her, consciously and deliberately, with those specific traits which are their distinguishing features.

The Search for an Original "Anteriority"

The human being who is searching for their origins is necessarily directed back to an origin that is more radical. That person is orientated towards the research for a paternity that is absolute. It is not without interest to observe that, in the Book of the Apocalypse, there is nothing to prevent us from seeing the prerogative of such an absolute paternity in the reference to each chosen person not only to a family identity, if we may express it like that (belonging to the great family of the elect), but even that of their true personal identity, expressed symbolically, by the "white stone, the stone which bears *a new name* which no one knows except the one who receives it" (Apoc 2:17). The stone symbolizes the introduction into the heavenly kingdom, but, in biblical symbolism, the proper name defines the one who bears it and it settles their personal destiny.

The fact that the human experience of filiation at the same time in the relationship to the mother and in the relationship to the father expresses the incomplete nature of such an experience. Here we do not have a pointer to a negative aspect of nature, but, viewed from the perspective of faith that can discover there the pedagogical intention of Providence, this powerlessness is a sign that orientates us towards a revelation that is more complete. We could even say that it assures us of the dynamism by means of the aspiration, the desire, the need to accede to this. If it is true that the paternal and the maternal origin of the person enables us to obtain a glimpse of an origin which is more radical, it is appropriate to examine the dual nature of that origin, a sign of its anthropological richness.

Human paternity and maternity complete each other, to the point that their proper role is exercised in turn in a way which is decisive. If certain functions and certain roles are in fact fulfilled in a joint way (for example, the moral education, on the hypothesis, to be sure, that there are two parents who are united and in agreement between themselves about the values to be transmitted), it is not the same for the major stages in the development of the personality of the child, which is marked successively by the greater presence of the mother or of the father. Before indicating certain features which indicate the influence of the one and of the other, it must be admitted that, if the father or the mother together refer the child back to his human origin and if, as we have said, that human origin orientates us back to an origin which is more radical, then it is right to place not only paternity, but also maternity, in the perspective of that origin. It may be recalled in this context that the *Letter to Families* does not hesitate to re-read the verse where St Paul says "bend the knee in the presence of the Father, from whom all paternity in heaven and on earth takes its name," adding "and all maternity."[2] Motherhood, too, must be referred back to the radical paternity of God. A filial anthropology must not be afraid to examine the human experience of filiation in its particular bond with the mother, as also in its particular bond with the father.

---

2. John Paul II, *Letter to Families*, § 9.

Filial Experience in Relation to the Mother

If it is true that the parents are two at the mysterious moment of conception, very quickly afterwards there appears the very special role of the mother, who is going to be not only the instrument, but also the place, of a communion of life and of love upon which the child whose existence is beginning is completely dependent. It can be said that the organism which is beginning to form itself very slowly is the fruit of this communion; this exercises a very real structuring role: cells, tissues, organs appear according to a mysterious order, which is made possible physiologically by the cells, the tissues and the organs of the mother. Their growth, invisible to human eyes, is brought about by an irrigation and by channels whose source is the mother and which, little by little, preparing the child for life, form this little body which will owe its subsistence to her; thus, it is a communion of a very particular kind which is unfolding, uniting them literally together. Quite rightly, since this takes the form of a fusion, this relationship is not constructed in one direction alone, as if the dependence of the embryo had no function at all. The fact is that the child who is to be born transforms his mother, prepares her for the event through which she will give life in a way that is visible, that is to say, in which she will deliver him to the world at the cost of a wrenching, of a pain and of a very real violence, symbolized by the cutting of the umbilical cord. So it is that the experience of filiation begins in a phase which is one not of pure inertia or passivity, but of interaction, in which the embryo, apparently reposing in its mother's womb, to take up the expression of Gustav Siewerth, is not "an unconscious, vegetative process, but a process—in the sense of a reality which is proceeding—which has a soul—a soul which makes itself felt from one side and the other and which arises from roots which are very deep."[3]

---

3. G. Siewerth, *Aux sources de l'amour. Métaphysique de l'enfant (Metaphysik der Kindheit,* Einsiedeln, 1957, translation into French by T. Aville (Paris: Parole et Silence, 2001), pp. 45–46. The author continues

What is a filial anthropology?

This same idea of an action that is humanizing and of the reciprocity of the mother-child relationship in this first stage during pregnancy can be found also in *Letter to Families*.[4] From the point of view of the child, this first experience will lead him later to seek in his mother the security and the refuge which he will have experienced in this way. This kind of search, of course, is made obvious to everyone in the early years. This natural dependence of the child is extended by lactation for some time more, such that the proximity which continues in this way to the body of the mother prepares the child for the discovery of the exterior world. The day will come when the child will have to accept that this body will be withdrawn from him. This process of being distanced from a world in which everything is given unconditionally will have to be undertaken by means of an apprenticeship in the autonomous existence of others, who are always escaping from the gaze or from the grasp of the child. The exterior world presents itself, but it is at the price of conquests that are painful and of freedoms which offer resistance. It will surrender itself only after a long and difficult exploration, something which is demonstrated by the uncertain groping of the first few steps and by the precarious nature of the first few words.

---

thus: "His being at repose (the child) is a gift and it is a witness to the virtuous power of the love, in which the spouses repose, trusting in each other, and providing the family with peace. The power of that love not only allows the child to make progress in its maturation, but it allows it also to have a real experience of that hopeful expectation, in the context of an interior agreement about the foundations of life. So it is that mother and child form between themselves bonds not only of a physical kind, but even more going to the very depths of their souls, making manifest the bonds which are being woven in a communion of life and of love."

4. John Paul II, *Letter to Families*, § 16: "In the pre-natal period, the mother provides the structure not only of the child's organism, but indirectly of that of the whole of his humanity. Even if this is a process which is orientated by the mother towards her child, the specific influence that the child to be born exercises upon his mother must not be forgotten. The father does not play a direct role in this mutual influence, which will be revealed to the light of day after the birth of the baby."

Filial Experience in Relation to the Father

It is at this moment that the figure of the father enters more consciously into the life of the child. Experienced first of all as a rival, this provokes a resistance in the child, who grows up under this threat to his security and to that bond with his mother which affords him that security in such a tangible way. The father is the authority figure, who begins to make the small child aware that their rights are not unlimited, in particular towards their mother. He is the incarnation of the first great demand which is made upon the conscious freedom of the child, that of consenting to this authority, by accepting its recently discovered legitimacy, and of thinking of themselves as *the child of this father*, in the same way that the child has thought of himself up to now, without any effort, as the child of his mother. The discovery of the two parents through the recognition of the bond which unites them is an obligatory stage in the first elements of the structuring of the child's personality. Therefore, filiation will never be the fruit of two actions divisible one from the other and even less so if they are not symmetrical; the mother refers back to origins of a natural kind, the father to origins which are personal.

> Since the child has lived first of all in symbiosis with their mother, she will always represent for them the origin, in terms of dependence and place of protection, in which everything is given unconditionally, in which they can abandon or forget every worry. Since the child has emerged from this symbiosis and has become aware of themselves as a distinct subject, from the time of the presence of their father, their father will be for them the one who has taught them to say 'I' and to confront reality as something differentiated, with its laws…The mother brings a person back to their natural origins and dependencies…the father brings them back to their personal origins because he is the one who confronts them with difference.[5]

---

5. Cf. D. Biju-Duval, *Le psychique et le spirituel* (Paris: Emmanuel, 2001), p. 235; preface by Jean Laffitte.

Clearly, parental roles do not exhaust themselves in the early years of a child's life, even if it is at this moment that they acquire their main symbolic force. They are the first people to call the child by the name that they have given him, they initiate him into this completely new existence by educating him in a sense of responsibility. Under this aspect, they represent the parental function conjointly, in theory, in a way which is benevolent, before which the child learns, little by little, that he will receive retribution for his free acts. Introduced progressively to his own responsibility, he will form himself morally, accepting rules of conduct which he has not given to himself, but which he can receive with docility and with trust.

The Trust Which Leads to Trust (*Zutrauendes Vertrauen*)

This last feature, that of an attitude of trust, is certainly the most fundamental in the experience of filiation as it is lived out in the early years of childhood and of adolescence. Trust is only offered spontaneously to parents because the child perceives that he deserves it and because the demands which they may present later on in terms of personal conduct are legitimate; they are rooted in the good and more precisely in the good that they will for the child. Thus, it is that the child is led into the exercise of the virtues, but more fundamentally still, he is brought up in such a way that he assents to this. There is nothing abstract in this process, but rather we have here a perception that is intuitive; the child knows that his parents are worthy of his trust and, consequently, what they require of him necessarily involves something that is for his benefit, even if he does not understand its implications. Moral experience is accepted in its demands, when it is the fruit of a concern for the child that is recognized as such. It can be seen that the human being learns, from a very young age, to refer to moral authority, provided that it is credible and provided that it expresses without ambiguity some good in which it is rooted. Once again, it is important not to see in this primordial experience anything more than the reception of knowledge about the good which is to be accomplished and the evil to be avoided; in the first place, for the child, it is the perception of a trust which is offered to him, which respects him, and which takes care of him in a way which affirms his own freedom. In reality, a trust such as this does not remain without a response; it stimulates a burst of emotion and gratitude, and it creates *de facto* the conditions for a trust that will be offered in its turn by the child. Day by day, the child becomes more and more himself, his personality is elaborated not by affirming a will for autonomy, but by means of an inventive assent. "From this trust of approval, in the persistent conception of life, there arises an act of continual giving, involving response and what is required by duty," says Siewerth on his part, giving to that phenomenon of benevolent reciprocity the name of *zutrauendes Vertrauen*, literally, *a trust which leads to trust*. The awakening of the child to other qualities, such as gratitude or loving fear of authority, are indissolubly linked to the trust which is the first word of a love which learns how to give itself because it recognizes what it has received.

We can see that this experience is something that humanizes us as persons. It makes it possible for the child to acquire a genuine development of his potentialities, and in the first place, of a capacity to love and to situate himself within the framework of benevolent personal relationships. It teaches him the discernment of good and evil. The painful experience of evil is identified as a wound inflicted upon an object of love.[6] The moral genesis of the person begins in this way through an education in the good that the person receives from his parents and from which he acquires a personality, tuned by discernment and constant in a life of virtue. The issues at stake can be assessed in the following way. In this sense, the experience of filiation is rooted in the recognition of an antecedent moral good. The child remains ex-

---

6. It is precisely in the offence done to an object of love that J.-C. Sagne sees what characterizes culpability in the true sense: "Il n'y a de culpabilité qu'en référence au tort causé à un objet d'amour;" J.-C. Sagne, *Péché, culpabilité et pénitence* (Paris: Cerf, 1971), p. 78.

posed naturally to actions which contradict this good, such as moral wrongs which are committed, but the fact that the good has been known previously and has also been identified concretely with the person of the parents who are worthy of trust, implies that these acts will be perceived as a disorder, an incoherence, and an offence directed towards an object of love. It would be helpful to deepen our understanding of the role which each of the two figures is called to play in the ethical upbringing of the child; in synthesis, in the mother we may detect an interiorization of the good that is wished towards others, and thus a capacity to be able to receive the good in return; in the father there will appear the figure of the one who will formulate in a more explicit way the moral norm in the family context and who will require that it be respected. Such a distinction only makes sense, however, within the perspective of a loving unity; the roles are perceived then as different modes in relation to a single truth, which is put forward naturally to elicit the personal assent of the child.

This concrete knowledge of the good, in the duality of its expression, is itself a mediation that makes it possible to detect also another source of the good, a source which is more radical. One of the ways which it is possible to explore would consist in asking ourselves whether the paternal and the maternal mode of incarnating the good and of transmitting moral values may not be a real symbol, which could enable the human being to glimpse, respectively, something of divine justice and of divine mercy.

In this way, throughout the whole of their existence, their childhood and their growth, human beings have the means to perceive intuitively an origin that is more distant than the immediate presence of their earthly parents.[7] However, an intuition is never a revelation. In this sense, the possibility of coming to

---

7. To illustrate the bond that exists between the creation of the world before that of the first human being and the Creator considered as Father, J.-P. Batut writes that God is not Father of his Creation, but that he creates in a way that is paternal. The creation of the human being in his image and likeness expresses a relationship that the author calls

know and of living a more radically filial existence is not something that is given in and of itself. The desire to be a son presupposes the revelation as something totally new, and the gratuitous and unexpected communication of a paternity which is absolute.

The Mystery of the Incarnate Word and the Revelation of a Paternity which is Absolute

The mystery of the Incarnation of the eternal Word alone could bring a light appropriate to the aspiration to a filial life that is complete, and that, for human beings, is impossible to grasp and to attain. On this point, it will be worth referring to the reflections of Réal Tremblay, who rightly brings out on the one hand the relationship between filiation and the paschal mystery and on the other hand this *predisposition*, this *inclination*, of the person towards filiation, for so long obscured by a static conception of personal being. Such an inclination, to become children, cannot be fulfilled except by means of an action of divinization. Here, in this connection, it will be appropriate to re-read how Irenaeus of Lyons or indeed Maximus the Confessor handed on this mystery of filial predestination. For example, with reference to the Letter to the Ephesians, J-M. Garrigues summarizes the thought of St Maximus like this:

> It is in the definitive fulfilment of this likeness in the Spirit, which unites him by grace to the Son like an elder brother (Rom 8:29), that the human being, recapitulating in himself the cosmos, is immersed forever with the Son in the bosom of the Father, the original source of uncreated unity and the final end of the unification of the created universe in him...This is what St Maximus calls the "mystery according to Christ," in the loving plan of God, the Son is the Christ par excellence, since he possesses that natural filiation, from which, like an anointing in the grace of the Spirit, our adoptive filiation flows. This ad-

---

originating; J.-P. Batut, *Dieu le Père Tout-Puissant* (Saint-Maur: Parole et Silence, 1998), p. 47.

What is a filial anthropology?

optive anointing in his Son, which the Father has predestined for us, was lost through Adam and had to be restored to us through the redemptive Incarnation of his Son in our nature.[8]

We shall not develop this essential element any further, in order to be able to point out another aspect which is complementary to it: the human experience of Jesus as Son. Like every human being, to whom he is united through his Incarnation, Jesus lived in his humanity a double filiation, in his relationship to the Virgin Mary and also to Joseph. The Son of God, according to the flesh, was *son of Mary*. It can be understood that this aspect could be studied usefully in greater depth, on the condition that it is recognized that it is situated within a perspective of a disposition of divine Providence, which must be formulated in the following terms: the Father gave Mary to Jesus as Mother. Jesus's filiation in relation to Mary does not add anything to his filial identity (his nature as eternal Son), but it manifests this in the flesh, in conformity with the Father's plan. This implies already that it is not devoid of teaching for us, but there is more: it amounts to saying that the maternity of Mary, also, draws its name from the paternity of God. The filiation of Jesus incorporates fully this disposition of the paternal Providence of God.

There are certain features that specify this human experience of Jesus:

Like every child, Jesus was absolutely dependent upon Mary in his flesh. Like every mother, Mary bore Jesus within herself, nourished him, took care of him, and, together with St Joseph, she exercised a parental authority over him: "He was subject to them" (Lk 2:51). At no time was the figure of Mary ever an obstacle for Jesus in the fulfilment of his mission as the *One Sent* by the Father. In the same way, the role of Joseph cannot be ig-

---

8. J.-M. Garrigues, "Le dessein d'adoption du créateur dans son rapport au Fils d'après saint Maxime le Confesseur," in *Maximus Confessor: Actes du symposium sur Maxime le Confesseur, 2–5 septembre, 1980* (Fribourg: Ed. Universitaires, 1982), p. 191.

nored—it was a key role; through the attention and the care which it was his to show, Joseph was an authentically paternal figure for Jesus. He saved him from Herod, he educated him, he prepared him for a simple existence, transmitting to him the fundamental values of life in Nazareth, the dignity and sanctity of human work, respect for civil laws (the census). He led an exemplary life and he contributed as head of the family to offering Jesus that environment which was favourable to him, in which he could *grow in grace and in holiness*. But Joseph was also for Jesus the one who gave way before the Father. Of course, there was there was that unique act of faith, which consisted in giving credence to the words he had heard in a dream: *"Do not be afraid to take Mary as your spouse"* (Mt 1:20), but, in this ceding of position before the Father, how can we not see also a special quality, which made him suitable to exercise a fatherhood that was very real, to point out the Father to his Son, to lead him to his real and proper origin. In his original and unique identity, Jesus is the Son of the eternal Father, but in his humanity, he had also the experience of a human filiation, in his relationship with Joseph, as well as in that with his mother.[9]

A filial anthropology must necessarily integrate both of these relationships, on the condition of structuring them according to that of which they are the vectors, namely, leading them back to that filiation, which is radical and original, orientating them towards the Father, from whom all paternity takes its name. In this perspective and on these conditions, we cannot remain silent about the relationship with the mother. In regard to what touches this experience, lived out in his humanity by Jesus, it is clear that Mary did not cease to exercise her maternity, at the time when her son's public ministry was unfolding. Luke mentions her presence among the group of women who followed Jesus and who assumed the responsibility for looking after him (cf.

---

9. We may note, in St Luke, the ascending genealogy of Jesus, which goes back from the paternal figure of Joseph to the very first paternity in the order of nature, Son of Adam, and which from there is referred to its absolute and radical source, Son of God (Lk 3:23–38).

What is a filial anthropology?

Lk. 8:1–3). In a much more significant way, she was present at Calvary and at that moment when the salvation of the world was accomplished upon the Cross. This episode, humanly speaking, involves a violent rupture, against nature, in the relationship between a mother and her son, but here it acquires a radically new meaning: a second offering of this son to the world, a painful, but real union with the mysterious and divine mission of Jesus, the whole significance of which, nevertheless, was not yet accessible to her. At this moment, in which Mary gives her last human witness of the fidelity of a mother, she receives the capacity to extend her maternity to all human beings, such that the filiation of Jesus begins to extend itself to the whole of humanity. Jesus' own words give legitimacy to this unheard of fecundity—"*Son, behold your mother*" (Jn 19:27)—of what becomes now a spiritual maternity, a new generating in faith. John is the first witness to this and its first depository. He receives Mary as mother, in the sacred expression of a will, of Jesus' last will. It is at the very moment in which Jesus makes of us the sons of the Father, that he entrusts us to the maternal solicitude of Mary. This maternity which is now being sacrificed would be deployed at the moment of the Resurrection and of the out-pouring of the Holy Spirit at Pentecost. The Virgin Mary is once more indicated by Luke among the group of the Apostles. The gift of the Holy Spirit makes perfect the form of this maternity, since it extends the gift of faith to all those for whom Mary is the figure, the exemplary fulfilment (the *typos*) of she who believed.

The Tradition and the Magisterium have given to Mary the title of *Mother of believers* or *Mother of the Church*,[10] recognizing in her the figure of humanity that has been saved. This indicates the totality of those who adhere by faith to the reality of the salvation effected by Christ, and it indicates also the totality of those who have been introduced by Christ, in the Holy Spirit, into the relationship of being adoptive sons and daughters of the Father. It is right, therefore, to maintain in the Person of Jesus a

---

10. Cf. Vatican Council II, *Lumen Gentium*, § 58–59.

unity between the mission of making us sons and daughters of the Father and that of making of us the children of Mary (*"Mother, behold your son"* (Jn 19:27). The first of these relationships and the second are not situated at the same level, but if, in the faith, the second is naturally subordinate to the first, nevertheless, it remains true that, each one according to its rank, they point towards a Christian anthropology of filiation. In the same way that we have shown that the human experience of filiation of Jesus includes his relationship with his mother, it is also appropriate to affirm that the Christian's experience of filiation must include his or her relationship with Mary.

The Christian is a Child who welcomes his Filiation

Christians are rendered capable of exercising their identity as adoptive sons or daughters. They are conformed to the Son; we may add that, by means of this, they are introduced into a relationship with Mary and with the Church.

It is in the Church that every person discovers his or her true origin in the radical and absolute paternity of God. We should not be afraid to say that the bond between every baptized person and the Church takes on immediately the depth of a filial relationship. Baptism confers upon the person who receives it the dignity of son or daughter of the Church. Here, we have the expression of a concrete relationship, which has nothing of the rhetorical or of the abstract about it. The Church welcomes the gift of a newly baptized person as a mother welcomes the gift of a new life; she never ceases to provide her child with the means of subsistence, she teaches that child and confers upon him the capacity to become an adult in the faith, she accompanies him throughout his existence, making each stage of this journey the occasion for deepening the bond which unites him to her. She is present also at the end of his earthly existence, in this way reproducing the act of the maternal presence of Mary at the moment of the death of Jesus upon the Cross. The Church unites her children to Christ sacramentally; in this way, she prolongs this bond of Christ with each one beyond death, in the economy of the Resurrection. The bond between each member of the baptized and the Church involves the perspective of eternal life, in which all of them, that is to say all of her children, will be *in Christ*. An adequate anthropology cannot obscure the relationship of the Christian to the Church, since it is the Church that is the true and the unique place in which the radical and absolute filiation of every person with the Father can be lived out to the full.

It would not be without interest to elaborate upon the specific way in which each sacrament that is conferred strengthens in the Christian his or her nature as son or daughter. Baptism confers filial identity, it marks out a person's entry into the relationship which unifies Christ with all the members of the Body, marked as he is from that moment by an indelible seal, renewing that act by which Jesus immersed himself in the waters of the Jordan and received that solemn witness, startling to human eyes, of his filiation: "This is my Son, the Beloved, who enjoys my favour" (Mt 3:17). Through confirmation, the one who is baptized enters spiritually into adulthood; the gift of the Holy Spirit makes the grace of baptism more perfect and, as the faith of the Church teaches, the sacrament of confirmation "roots us more deeply in divine filiation."[11] Through the Eucharist, instituted in order that the Church "could enter in its turn into the sacrifice of its Saviour at every point of time and of space," as the encyclical, *Ecclesia de Eucharistia*, recalls insistently, Christians are really united to the sacrifice which Jesus offered to his Father. The liturgical assembly is constituted truly as the Body of Christ; she presents to the Father the sacrifice of his Son, which reconciled us to him. In some way, this becomes a filial sacrifice, a sweet-smelling sacrifice, for the Father. As for the Christian who is separated from the grace of Christ through his own grave, personal, and deliberate fault, on the basis of the authority of the Church alone, that person receives the capacity to exercise his filiation fully and efficaciously. The sacrament of penance or of

---

11. Cf. *Catechism of the Catholic Church*, § 1316.

reconciliation expresses this unique encounter between the divine action that purifies and absolves the sinner and the disposition of the baptized person, through repentance and conversion, to enter anew into effective filiation. In this sense, sacramental reconciliation is the experience that a child of God has of the merciful love of his Father. In sacramental marriage, the spouses are closely united between themselves, as Christ is to his Church. Through the sacramental grace and through the holiness of their lives, they give witness to a radical source of life; in the community of life and love which they establish, they show themselves to be open to the transmission of life and they experience, the one through the other, a human paternity and maternity which points them towards a more radical paternity still; through the education which they give to their children, they prepare their children to make welcome the gift of filial life and to exercise that gift in all its fulness. For their part, sick persons who are baptized are associated in a particular way with the sufferings of the Passion of Christ; they live out in a more intense way their closeness to him who made the filial sacrifice of his life to the Father. Through the sacramental forgiveness of their sins and through the sacramental bread received as viaticum, they are prepared to undertake their passing to the Father. Finally, the ministerial priesthood, which renders visible in the midst of believers, the presence of Christ as the head of the Church, is orientated to the service of this communion. In this way, the unfolding of the filial identity of the Christian is put into operation in the Church. The priest himself is orientated towards the Father. The identity of the son is also made present in the relationship of spiritual and sacramental filiation of the baptized person with the minister, the dispenser of the mysteries of Christ. How could this not call to mind here the paternal condition of the ministerial priesthood of the Apostle Paul, who considered himself to be father and mother of those whom he had engendered?[12]

---

12. "Just as a mother nourishes and cares for her children, such was our

What is a filial anthropology?

All of these dimensions which we have evoked, the motherhood of Mary, the motherhood of the Church, the sacramental life which configures the baptized person to the Son, the fatherhood of ministers, all of this draws its name from the fatherhood of the Father. In this sense, what has been developed here adds nothing to what we have understood from the preceding paper,[13] but it expounds some elements contained virtually within it.

The filiation of the Christian, throughout the whole extension of his life, is not to be seen in a linear fashion, as if it were a question of a process of adoption which is pacific and which would continue of itself, a process by which someone, having become a Christian through baptism, would live his or her filial reality henceforth in complete peace, in the existence of a child of the Church, which would lead necessarily to the gates of the kingdom of eternal life. The whole of this process of filial configuration is structurally redemptive; Jesus does not lead children to their Father by any other road than that of Golgotha and of the Cross. Christ does not make sons and daughters of those persons who would simply remain in a state of aspiration, of expectation, and of desire. The real condition in which the future adoptive children of the Father find themselves includes, from the time of original sin onwards, a history of the refusal of such filiation. The nature of the human being is wounded precisely in its capacity to be, quite naturally, a son or daughter of the Father.

From this point of view, the history of salvation could be expressed in terms of a rupture in the filial bond and of its reestab-

---

affection towards you, who have become so dear to us, that we wished to hand over to you at the same time not only the Gospel of God, but our own life as well…Just as a father to his children, as you know, we have exhorted, encouraged and abjured each one of you to lead a life that is worthy of God, who has called you into the glory of his Kingdom" (1Thess 2:7; 11–12).

13. Cf. R. Tremblay, "Un'antropologia filiale: cosa significa?" in Congregazione per la Dottrina della Fede (a cura di) *L'antropologia della teologia morale secondo l'enciclica Veritatis splendor. Atti del simposio promosso dalla Congregazione per la dottrina della fede, Roma, settembre, 2003* (Rome: Libreria Editrice Vaticana, 2006), pp. 57–72.

lishment through the sacrifice of Christ. Here, we can only trace a few ways in which this point could be explored more deeply. The instruction not to eat of the tree of the knowledge of good and evil, an illuminating symbol of every divine disposition, has the meaning of a paternal gift of the Creator to Adam and to Eve. The insinuation of the tempter throws suspicion upon this paternal love, which lies behind this prohibition. The transgression of the Law takes on then the meaning of a refusal of the Father, present in the demands made by his authority. This authority ceases to appear as benevolent. In this new pretention to be autonomous, detached from divine protection, the human being engenders himself. In some way, becomes his own father and refuses to receive his humanity from a Father. In this transgression and in the consequences which it entails for human nature, this refusal of filial dependence is always present; the latter is no longer perceived as a dependence of love, but it becomes a dependence that thwarts the human being, and which generates the insatiable, Promethean desire for self-sufficiency.[14]

In the light of this, it will be helpful to see in the Christian sinner a son or daughter, but one who is incapable of exercising their filiation and so incapable of recovering this of themselves. Sin sets up a situation that is objectively one of contradiction; the human being who cannot find himself or herself, who cannot reach their origin except insofar as they are a son or daughter, denies this dimension through sin. They render themselves incapable of finding themselves, of realizing themselves, of discov-

---

14. On the contrary, the prayer of the Our Father, taught by the Son, fills the distance between an inaccessible God (in heaven) and his creatures, who do his will here below and who receive their bread each day; it may be observed that the distancing suggested by the words "in heaven" is corrected, to a certain extent, by the content of the prayer, in which the first three requests terminate with the formula "on earth as it is in heaven." It is on earth that the Name of the Father must be sanctified, that his Kingdom must come and that his will must be fulfilled. J. Galot, *Notre Père qui est Amour* (Saint Maur: Parole et Science, 1998), 147.

ering who they are; this is a situation which, once it is rendered perennial, is hell.

The Church alone has the capacity to heal this wound to filiation. Sin that is pardoned becomes an extension of filial experience. The son or daughter who is forgiven sees a new space open up before them, in which, in an experience of mercy received, they are able to live their being as son or daughter. This refound communion in the Church is the way by which human beings rediscover themselves as children of the Father. In this way, sin can be seen as a wound in the relationship to the Father and so also in the relationship to the Church. It is possible to assimilate sin to a situation that is anti-filial, since, in its essence, it consists in refusing the will of the Father.

The Good Conduct of the Christian is always Filial Conduct

To welcome our filiation, in the light of what has been said above, is to give a response to the promptings of the Spirit of the Father. As a response to the gift received, filiation encompasses the whole of conduct of a Christian, who becomes incapable of thinking of a good action that is not, at the same time, an act of love, orientated towards the Father. The hymn of jubilation in St Luke's gospel speaks of a revelation made to those who are least, namely, their personal knowledge of the Father, a knowledge which is transmitted, not acquired: "No one knows the Son except the Father and no one knows the Father except the Son and those to whom the Son has chosen to reveal him" (Mt 10:22; Lk 11:27). This knowledge is only possible in the Son, which means through participation in the personal identity of the Son. By participating in Christ, the human being discovers who he is as man or who she is as woman, and also that he or she is a child of the Father. Knowing the Father, here, is expressed by a term that emphasizes rather a *recognition*. To *recognize* the Father brings out what is a natural state of dependence. To act in a morally upright way is to act in a way that is in conformity with our filial nature. The first issue for a filial anthropology for moral behaviour, then, lies in the acceptance of something that precedes the identification of the good to be accomplished. The good is something that goes before us. It consists also in the acceptance of a transcendent and welcoming reality, which recognizes us and which knows everything about us as his children. Here the words of Cardinal Journet are illuminating: "The fact that God can read in the depths of our hearts our acts of shame and of betrayal is something which naturally terrorises us. What shall we do? There is only one way out; to acquiesce in this completely."[15]

Another aspect would underline the interior freedom of the one who is fulfilled through love: "interior necessity and not constraint," as *Veritatis Splendor* expresses it (§ 18). In regard to the Eucharist, we have recalled how the sacrifice of the Son expressed and fulfilled a total and free submission to the salvific will of the Father. Filial behaviour goes to meet the desire of the Father and so it incorporates into itself those expressions of this will, which are the commandments and divine teachings. A filial anthropology places at the heart of morality an attitude that is fundamentally one of assent and of trust. It implies an existence which is inspired by that of Christ, a life of the Son within us, witnessed "from within by the conformity of our thoughts, of our feelings, of our wills with those of Jesus."[16]

A filial anthropology cannot be conceived outside of the context of the Church, the family of God, and the totality of its children. A morality founded upon a filial anthropology necessarily includes a filial relationship with the Church, the place in which

---

15. C. Journet, *Entretiens sur Dieu le Père* (Saint-Maur, Parole et Silence, 1998), p. 87.
16. E. Guerry, *Vers le Père: 89 méditations* (Desclée de Brouwer, 1947; Saint-Maur: Parole et Silence, 1999), pp. 92ff. In order to underline the mediation of the humanity of the Son, the author adds: "If, by pure hypothesis, it had pleased God to send us his grace directly, without passing through Jesus, this would not have impressed upon our hearts the condition of being his sons and daughters"; *Ibid.*, p. 94.

the Son revealed himself as Son and in which he reveals to believers *who* the Father is. The filial conduct of the Christian, then, cannot be understood without the dynamism of the sacramental life, of which the Church is the source. The relationship between freedom and grace could be formulated in categories which bring out even more the relationship which unites the children to their Father. The words of M-J. Guillou take on here the meaning of a formidable warning to theologians: "It is when the theologian no longer gives witness to the Father in a convincing manner that Christian conscience becomes afraid before the formidable figure of an arbitrary Omnipotence."[17]

A fourth elements lies in the characteristic that, in the sources of revelation, qualifies the action of the Father. The terms here are too weak, when they do no more than evoke the goodness of the Father, his generosity, his mercy; the moral conduct of the Christian is filial when it is animated by the same unconditional attitude. The love of enemies and mercy are thus described as conduct which resembles that of our Father in heaven, he who "makes the sun rise upon evil and good alike and who makes the rain fall on the just and on the unjust" (Mt 5:41–48), or again a conduct which makes them become "sons and daughters of the Most-High, he who is good to the ungrateful and to the wicked" (Lk 6:35).

---

17. M-J. Guillou, *Le mystère du Père* (Paris: Fayard, 1973), p. 265.

17 Christ: The Contemporary of all People of all Times[1]

In Chapter 19 St Matthew' Gospel, Pope John Paul II chose for the encyclical *Veritatis Splendor*, in his own words, "*a connecting thread, useful to enable us* to hear once more, *in a living and direct way*, the moral teaching of Jesus" (§ 6). A few lines earlier, he announced the aim of the encyclical: "It seems necessary to re-read the whole of the moral teaching of the Church, with the precise aim of recalling some of the fundamental truths of Catholic doctrine..." (§ 4). The moral teaching of Jesus, the moral teaching of the Church, the quasi-juxtaposition of these two expressions is already evocative of the faithful preservation and transmission by the Church of "the Gospel, as the source of all saving truth and of moral discipline," according to the expression of the Second Vatican Council.[2]

In the first chapter of *Veritatis Splendor*, the connecting thread is Jesus's dialogue with the rich young man. This is not the only time that the Pope has used a biblical account in this way; rather, the parable of the prodigal son had formed the thread of *Dives in Misericordia*, as the account of the murder of Abel by his brother, Cain, was later to furnish that of *Evangelium Vitae*. In the same way that every human being was invited to recognize himself in the figure of the prodigal son, so he is invited to see himself in the rich young man: "here we can recognize every person who, consciously or otherwise, approaches Christ, the Redeemer of man-

---

1. "Christ: The Contemporary of All People of All Times" is the text of a lecture delivered on June 16, 1995, at Lugano, in the context of the ninth international Colloquium of Theology on the topic *Primo capitolo dell'enciclica «Veritatis Splendor»* published in the Acts of the Colloquium, *Gesù Cristo, legge vivente e personale della Santa Chiesa* (Piemme, Lugano, 1996), pp. 211–223.
2. Vatican Council II, *Dei Verbum*, § 7.

kind, and poses to him the question about morality" (§ 7). If the didactic interest here is obvious, it is not enough to note that the exchange between the young man and Jesus concerns every human being to the extent that everyone poses the same questions as he does, about the good to be done and the means for attaining eternal life. It does not suffice either that the responses of his interlocutor are so wise, so deep, and so pertinent that they could be adapted, so to speak, to the preoccupations of all those who ask themselves about these matters. The purpose of this relationship is to show how, throughout the whole of the first chapter of the encyclical, Jesus is the contemporary of every human being of every age and to bring out how this theological perspective alone makes possible a theologically correct interpretation of the Master's responses.

We shall address the following points in order:

- The historical and the eternal uniqueness of Christ, the Redeemer;
- From the moral life to eternal life; the vocation of the Christian;
- Discipleship (*sequela*) as the beginning of our participation in the divine life; and
- Christ present to human beings of all times.

The Historical and Eternal Uniqueness of Christ the Redeemer

Paradoxically, it is by beginning from the young man that, beyond the responses of Jesus, the Pope concentrates upon the identity of the Master. The question: "Master, what must I do to inherit eternal life?" (Mt 19:16) opens up that area, which is properly moral or, rather, it encompasses it, by placing attention in the first place on the ultimate perspective of all action, eternal life. It is a very good question to ask, one which reveals our concern about the next world and also about the whole of our existence. In this sense, it is a question which goes beyond the one who posed it; it "expresses an aspiration to the absolute Good, which attracts us and which calls us to himself; it is the echo of a vocation which comes from God, the origin and the destiny of human life", the Pope writes (§ 7). From the beginning, even before analyzing the responses of Jesus, the text places itself resolutely within the perspective of the mystery of Christ, referring to the "very high vocation which the faithful have received in Christ." It is not anodyne to emphasize that this expression has been chosen from *Optatam totius*, precisely from §16, devoted to the teaching of moral theology. Furthermore, *VS* § 7 operates as an interpretative key for the Gospel account; Jesus, who is approached by the young man, is the *Christ, the Redeemer of man*, whom every person approaches, and the place of this extended encounter is the Church, which "wishes to place herself at the service of this unique objective."[3] The Pope returns to the account to recall *Jesus of Nazareth*, who, it seems, exercises a form of attraction upon his interlocutor. The parallel is significant; previously, he had evoked an "aspiration to the absolute Good, which attracts us;" here, it is said that "the attraction of the person of Jesus causes to be born in him (the young man) new questions about the moral good" (*VS* § 8).

The transposition of Matthew's account continues: the mystery of salvation and the presence of Christ in every moment of the history of human kind are recalled, "Christ, the Alpha and the Omega of human history" (§ 8). The affirmation of Christ as the contemporary of every human person is followed by the explanation of what must be involved in the movement of approaching Christ in our days. "To appropriate" Christ to oneself is to assimilate the whole of the reality of the Incarnation and of the Redemption" (§ 8). Here we are provided with the key, and we are invited to search for "the meaning of Jesus's response, allowing ourselves to be guided by him." Thus, the whole of the reality of the Incarnation and of the Redemption gives access to the meaning of Jesus's response. From this point onwards, the text can develop the dialogue and can proceed step by step.

---

3. John Paul II, *Redemptor Hominis*, § 13.

Here we have an example of what Balthasar called a *Christological ellipse*,[4] which makes it possible, within a vision of the faith, to adhere to and to give witness to the Incarnate Word, to him who is the source and origin of this vision of faith (here the Pope describes this vision as an assimilation of *the whole of the Incarnation and of the Redemption*). Far from relativizing the unique character of Jesus Christ, the uniqueness of the historical event, such an integration of the whole content of Revelation makes it possible for us, on the contrary, to grasp how this unique event is decisive for the salvation of all people. The salvation of the world through the Cross, Death, and Resurrection of Jesus is communicated, made present, to all, but it allows all of us to recognize, within a vision of the faith, what it is that is going on there, in this unique moment. To recognize the universality of the effects of the Redemption, in the end, is to be able to avoid making of the life of Christ and of his humanity what Kierkegaard, very much preoccupied by the question, called the moment of opportunity; he wrote: "As long as eternity and history remain exterior one to the other, history is nothing more than an opportunity.[5] The reciprocity of the content and of the form, proper to the Christological ellipse, is brought into focus throughout Chapter 1; for example, the commentary on the Gospel of St Matthew (19:17): "there is one alone who is good" enables the Pope, after having placed the accent upon the religious nature of the young man's question, to speak of the "goodness which attracts and which, at the same time, engages the human person, which has its source in God and which, even more, is God himself" (§ 9). We could multiply these examples: "To recognize the Lord as God is the fundamental nucleus, the heart of the Law" (§ 11); a little later there follows the reminder of the Revelation of God: "I am the Lord, your God", linked to the transmission of the Decalogue (§ 13). Thus, all through Chapter 1, we have a reading of the (historical) encounter of Jesus and the

---

4. Hans Urs von Balthasar, *La dramatique divine*, II/ 2 (Namur: Culture et Vérité, 1998), pp. 45ff.
5. Soren Kierkegaard, *Miettes philosophiques* (Paris: Gallimond, 1990), p. 100.

young man, in the light of the eternal mystery of Christ, and the access to this mystery by faith refers back to the account. It appears indeed that the Christ is the contemporary of every human being, as he has been the contemporary of the young man who had come to meet him.

From the Moral Life to Eternal Life

The second aspect which draws our attention is the link between the historical dimension of human action, inscribed in time, and the eternity which is promised. While it is religious, the young man's question is no less a moral question. Jesus reveals to the young man that eternal life is strictly linked to the observance of the commandments. These latter are a gift of God and are now a gift of Jesus; through the mouth of Jesus, the commandments of the Decalogue are given once more to us human beings. Thus, there is a divine origin to the commandments, whose observance makes it possible to enter eternal life. The commandment are not only the key to eternity ("If you want to enter into life, keep the commandments"), but they are also an eternal presence in history; the Decalogue is entrusted by God on Sinai; it is the expression of the will of God, but, above all, it relies upon the Revelation of God by himself: "I am the Lord, your God." It is also a gift of him who is the sole Good.

Reformulated by Jesus, the commandments retain their authority, and their relationship with the new law of the Sermon on the Mount is affirmed by the encyclical as *obvious* (cf. § 12). Thus, it is possible to glimpse a kind of *continuity* between the commandments and eternal life; in effect, there is no eternal life that is not referred henceforth explicitly to God. Even more, eternal life is a "participation in the very life of God;" (cf. § 12), it is identified with the Kingdom of God. The purpose of the observance of the commandments (the moral life and the historical vocation of the Christian) is thus a participation in the eternity of God.[6]

---

6. "By virtue of his Passion, which he suffered for us and of the sacrifice of his

Purpose, end, destination, meaning: none of these make it possible still to establish *hic et nunc* a contemporary relationship with Christ, if that participation remains simply the object of a promise. The encyclical clarifies this point at § 12: "This (participation in very life of God) is brought about perfectly only after death, but, in the faith, it is already from the present moment a light of truth, a source of meaning of life and the beginning of participation in the plenitude by following Christ." The principle is established by this phrase that seems to us to be a veritable synthesis of Chapter 1; it will be helpful to disclose the two following elements that are of particular interest from our perspective:

Faith is the sole mode of access, in this life, to divine eternity. It makes *possible a beginning of our participation in that plenitude*.

How? By following Christ. This *following* of Christ is already proclaimed by the quotation of the gospel of St Matthew: "Whoever leaves house ... in my name, will receive a hundred times more and will inherit eternal life" (Mt 19:29). "To receive a hundred times more", in the logic of § 12, includes this *beginning to participate in this plenitude*, which has been treated above. Access to Christ through the faith is already this entry into eternal life, but that is only valid in virtue of everything that has been said above about *assimilation of the Incarnation and of the Redemption*. In this line of thinking, we may consider the thinking of the Danish philosopher who has been quoted already: "the relationship of the disciple with the Master is that of a believer, that is to say, that the latter is concerned eternally with the historical existence of this Master."[7]

It remains to establish the relationship of Jesus with the commandments. For that, let us go back to the historical perspective, to the words of Jesus: "If you wish to enter into life, keep the com-

---

life in the Eucharist, effected on our behalf and under the form of communion with him, Christ, as the concrete norm, renders us interiorly capable of accomplishing with him the will of the Father," in Balthasar, "The First Thesis of Christian Ethics" (International Theological Commission, *Texts and Documents: Christian Morality and its Norms*, 1988).

7. Kierkegaard, *Miettes philosophiques*, p. 101.

mandments." The precepts which are quoted belong to the second tablet and explicitate the commandment of the love of neighbour, which is inseparable—the Pope recalls, as he relates Chapter 19 of St Matthew's Gospel to Chapter 10, verses 25–27 (*VS*, § 14)—from the commandment of the love of God. This unity between the two commandments that sum up the whole of the Law and the Prophets is not something exterior to Jesus; he has pointed this out elsewhere in his dialogue with the doctor of the Law (in Luke's account). It is necessary, therefore, to bring out this unity in Jesus. This is what the encyclical does, in a formula that establishes the intrinsic link between Jesus and the commandments: "The two commandments…are united profoundly between themselves and penetrate each other mutually. Jesus renders witness to their indivisible unity by his words and by his life; his mission culminates in the redemptive act of the Cross…the sign of his inseparable love for the Father and for humanity (cf. Jn 13:1). "The formula of St Ambrose provides a good summary of this link: "*Plenitudo legis in Christo est.*" Above all, if Jesus is the living fulfilment of the Law, if he is the living Law in person, this is through the gift of his life in his redemptive sacrifice (§ 15). Only the mystery of the Redemption, called to mind once more, makes it possible to understand the significance and the meaning of the response of Jesus to the rich young man about the commandments that are to be observed.

Following Christ (the Sequela) as the Beginning of Participation in Divine Life

In Matthew's account, we can observe that the dialogue goes back to the question of the young man: "All of these I have kept; what else must I do?" How can we explain the fact that the response of Jesus did not please him? If it is true that the young man has observed all of the commandments, he would obtain eternal life one day. The very words used by Jesus should have reassured him. The young man is not able to express the deepest desire that lies within him. Also, he expresses himself in terms of having it, which, let us note, is a temporal category. No one can obtain salvation except by having the desire for it.[8] It is this dissatisfaction, whatever may be the way it is expressed in the end, which impels Jesus to offer him the way of perfection. The encyclical underlines the fact that Jesus has taken hold of the "nostalgia for a fulness which surpasses the legalistic interpretation of the commandments." The term *nostalgia* is already a word that is more evocative than the term *desire*; the nostalgia for a plenitude certainly describes the desire for the supernatural which is inscribed in the human being, but with that nuance of rediscovering some good from the past. We have nostalgia for some good that has been lost; and here the good which has been lost concerns the depths of our identity,[9] the depths of our being.[10] Nevertheless, there is actually much more implied in this expression. It is very significant that the text makes use of the term *plenitude*. This is what, a few lines above, served to explain, according to the words used by St Ambrose, the perfect fulfilment of the commandments in Jesus. Thus,

> Without doing any violence to the letter or to the intention of the text, we could say that, before that which is the plenitude of the Law (of the commandments), the rich young man experienced a nostalgia for plenitude. This is a nostalgia for a different way, of keeping the commandments, one which is not legalistic, but, beyond that, it is the nostalgia for him, who observes the Law in this way, who is the fulfilment of the Law, the nostalgia for Jesus himself.

---

8. F. X. Durwell, *Dans le Christ, Rédempteur* (Le Puy: X. Mappus, 1960), p. 232.
9. Von Balthasar, "*Homo creatus est*" in Id. *Creaturalità* (Brescia: Morcellana, 1991), pp. 9ff.
10. "If the soul is filled according to its capacity, God always remains beyond everything that the soul is capable of grasping. But, in communicating himself to the soul, he expands its capacity and he makes it capable of a new communication. In this way, the soul is at one and the same time filled and yet always thirsting." J. Daniélou, *Dieu et nous* (Paris: Grasset, 1956), p. 143.

Jesus' response: "Come, follow me," then, is, at one and the same time, both the precise answer to the question posed, one which in this sense does not entail an evasion of time and of its constraints, and also it is the only response which is adequate to the inexpressible desire, to the nostalgia for plenitude, to that desire which is eternal.

That which precedes this "Come, follow me" in the order of the means to be employed: "Go, sell everything you own and give it to the poor" has the meaning of removing the obstacles to welcoming the eternal. Besides, when they are given to the poor, temporal goods are transformed into eternal goods, into a treasure that is in heaven. Following Christ (the *sequela*) is the path of perfection, fulfilment, plenitude, and eternity.

The analysis developed on the Beatitudes (§ 16) is a complete corroboration of this perspective. On the one hand, like the commandments, these refer to the eternal good (and, in this way, cannot be foreign to the concerns of the young man). On the other hand, as a *self-portrait of Christ*, they are an invitation to follow him. The beatitudes are just as much ways of responding to the call: "Follow me."

If the content of this perfection is to follow Christ ("If you wish to be perfect, follow me"), the path to be followed requires first of all the fulfilment of certain human conditions (§ 17, 18 and 19).

The first of these conditions is keeping the commandments (the imperfect freedom of St Augustine), a condition *sine qua non* of eternal life, the "first and imprescriptible," writes the Pope. The second is "maturity in the gift of self, that to which the freedom of man is called." There, too, the fulfilment of freedom is brought into focus by means of the relationship time-eternity. For this, the Pope makes use of the distinction of St Augustine between partial freedom and total freedom. "The first is marked by this other law, which rises up against the law of my spirit ... it is not yet total freedom, pure freedom, full freedom, because it is not yet eternity."[11]

---

11. St Augustine, *In Johannis Evangelium tractatus*, 41, 10, CCL, 36, 363, cited in John Paul II, *Veritatis Splendor*, § 17.

Apart from the human demands, following Christ introduces the disciple into an imitation of the Master; the total gift of Jesus, his precepts and his life, his sufferings, and his Passion, constitute a new moral rule (*new commandment*), accessible by faith. The believer is introduced into the time of God by the Holy Spirit: "Following, by the response of faith, him who is Wisdom made flesh, the disciple of Jesus becomes truly the disciple of God" (VS § 19).

> Thus, the imitation of Christ, impossible on the basis of the efforts of the disciple alone, brings with it, in faith, a transformation; life in Christ is a conformation to him. The God of the divine life is, here below in temporal Christian existence, the gift of the condition of the disciple; as a corollary, life in Christ, since it signifies the presence of Christ, dead and risen again, is a reality (to be sure, one which is given) which makes of the believer a contemporary of the Son of God (cf. VS § 21).

Christ Present to All People of All Times: The Church

Finally, and this will be our last point, the gift of the presence of Christ to each person cannot be made outside of the mediation of the Church. Conformation to Christ is first of all an objective reality for the baptized person, immersed in the Paschal mystery of the death and Resurrection. Baptism clothes the believer with Christ and introduces him to the new life, that is to say, into the very condition of being a disciple. This is the life of grace, the place in which the new law is fulfilled. Here we shall limit ourselves to four observations.

All of Jesus' acts which are going to inspire the life of the disciple could not be grasped in their real depth unless they were referred to the very form of the gift of Jesus in his redemptive sacrifice. These acts are made present (in the efficacy of the sacraments), but their character of being a unique event will be identified.

Angelo Scola pointed out the importance of recognizing

that the Church as sacrament represents these days the efficacious sign, by means of which Christ himself has chosen to pass in order to be able to make it possible for us to encounter him (literally to make himself en-counterable—*rendersi incontrabile*) by human beings. The sacramental function of Jesus is different in his humanity, at least by reason of the fact that it is present to us today only in correlation to the Church-sacrament and in a particular way in the sacrament of the Eucharist.[12]

Let us take the example of the Last Supper, which was the beginning of the Sacrifice of Christ, which is made present in the Eucharist. At this moment of the deepest communion between Jesus and those who are his own, faith will see that unique episode in which Jesus' gift of his Body as the bread of life has been historically brought about for the salvation of the world. There are very many who have examined this theme in depth (Mouroux, Balthasar, Tremblay, Schürmann. Garrigues, and so forth, as well as Scola who has already been cited). The encyclical itself speaks of participation in the Eucharist as "the highest degree of assimilation to Christ, the source of 'eternal life', the principle and the power of the complete gift of self" (§ 21). Mouroux had written already: "At the root of this memorial and of this intercession, there is the Holy Spirit who communicates the 'power of sanctification' contained in the saving sacrifice."[13]

Veritatis Splendor recalls the request of Jesus that we celebrate this memorial, according to the witness of St Paul (1Cor. 11:26). What has been said above would make it possible to show the presence of salvation in every liturgical action. The human being recalls a unique event in the anamnesis, the *occasion*, if we may put it like that, on which God *remembers his Covenant* and when he acts through his grace.

---

12. A. Scola "L'essenza della Chiesa nella *Lumen Gentium*" in ID. *Avvenimento e Tradizione: questioni di ecclesiologia* (Milan: Jaca Book, 1987), p. 32.
13. Mouroux, *Faites ceci en mémoire de moi* (Paris: Aubier-Montaigne1970), p. 83.

If Christ makes himself the contemporary of every human being in the new Life, it would be necessary to show in what sense it can be said that, still through the mediation of the Church, he is made the contemporary of all those who preceded him in death, those who had been kept in view of Christ,[14] and whom he went to meet in the course of his descent into hell. Through the Incarnation and the Redemption, these antecedent graces are bestowed.[15]

Finally, the times after the Christ event would have to be considered in their unity. The category of suffering seems to us to be the most suitable for showing how Jesus is the contemporary of human beings of all times. By adhering to the Cross of the redemption "human beings discover there their own sufferings, they rediscover them, thanks to the faith, enriched by a new content and a new meaning."[16] By uniting these freely to the sacrifice of Christ, each person is associated with the Redemption of the world. "I am happy to suffer for you and to make up in my own flesh what is lacking in the sufferings of Christ, for the sake of his Body, which is the Church" (Col 1:24).

On the Cross, in fact, history and eternity have ceased to be realities which are exterior one to the other.

---

14. "The descent into hell ... is the last place of Jesus's messianic mission, a phase condensed in time, but immensely vast in its real meaning, extending the work of redemption to all people of all times and of all places, since all of those who have been saved for, have been made participants in, the Redemption." *Catechism of the Catholic Church*, § 634.
15. St Thomas Aqunias, *Summa contra gentiles*, IV, q. LVII: *On the difference that there is between the sacraments of the old Covenant and those of the new Law.*
16. John Paul II, Apostolic Exhortation, *Salvifici Doloris*, § 20.

18 Knowledge of God, Knowledge of the Truth[1]

At first sight, the convergence of the two most basic questions in the heart of the human person, the question about God and the question about good and evil, seems something obvious, at least for whoever accepts the competence of the Magisterium of the Church in the realm of morals. Christian morality finds in Christ its "essential and original foundation,"[2] and it is conveyed in concrete terms by the fact of someone sets out to follow him.[3] Christ is not only the end of the Law (*finis legis*), but he is also its fulness (*plenitudo legis*).[4] To say that Christ is the end of the Law and its fulness means already to have passed beyond the observance of its precepts and the law of Moses, which were at the heart of its teaching. It will be useful to recall here, as Ignace de la Potterie has remarked, that essential verse of St John's Gospel (1:17);[5] if the grace of truth has been brought to realization in the Person of Christ, then to adhere to him means to attain the fulness of truth and, in particular, the fulness of truth about the moral good. Now, adherence to Christ poses the moral question in terms of

---
1. "Knowledge of God, Knowledge of the Truth" is the text of a lecture delivered in Italian in Rome on November 14, 1998, in the context of the international Colloquium *Domanda su Dio e domande sul bene*, November 1314, 1998, organized by the Pontifical Institute John Paul II and published with the title *Cognitio Dei et cognitio veritatis* in the Acts of the Colloquium (Mursia, Rome, 1999), pp. 215–221.
2. John Paul II, *Veritatis Splendor*, § 19.
3. *Ibid.* § 15.
4. Cf. *Ibid.*, § 119.
5. "The Law has been given to us by Moses, but grace and truth have been given to us by Jesus Christ"; cf. Ignacio de la Potterie; I "Non sono venuto per abolire ma per dare compimento" in *Veritatis splendor. Testo e commenti* (Vatican City: Libreria Editrice Vaticana, 1993), p. 163.

a personal relationship with God; we shall speak of the encounter of conversion, of personal identification in Christ, of vocation, of following him (*sequela*). Morality acquires a personal character and the character of dialogue, which is born, in human terms, of the encounter with the other,[6] once the image of God has been recognized in the other. It is certain that to recognize in Christ the splendour of the truth, without any trace of reductionism, amounts to affirming that this truth has been revealed; in other words, that the truth implies action on the part of the free individual who has rightly accepted that such a truth has been revealed. In this acceptance, there is a criterion of authenticity of personal freedom,[7] a criterion which is essential and which, nevertheless, does not exhaust the legitimate question about moral action and which even demands it. The encyclical, *Veritatis Splendor*, in its introduction, speaks of the "nostalgia for absolute truth" and of the "thirst to attain the fulness of this knowledge;" such is the search for the meaning of life, that, it is in this way, that the fundamental question about the moral good becomes indispensable. The mystery of the good and the mystery of God illuminate each other reciprocally. Two questions express this double illumination:

- How is God concerned in human moral action?
- In what way are human moral acts an integral part of the plan of God?

---

6. Livio Melina, Tesi e questioni circa lo statuto della teologia morale fondamentale in ID. *Lo statuto della teologia morale fondamentale: tesi e questioni* (Roma: Pontificio Istituto Giovanni Paolo II per studi su matrimonio e famiglia, 1997), p. 14.
7. "Christ has revealed to us above all that the condition for authentic freedom is to recognize the truth honestly and with an open spirit: 'You will learn the truth and the truth will set you free' (Jn 8:32)"; John Paul II, *Veritatis Splendor*, § 87.

The Question of God, Beginning from Human Acts

The merit goes back to St Augustine for having shown how, at the basis of the motivations for acting well, is to be found the search for a happiness which is only accessible through the possession of a good which surpasses all other goods, a supreme good, which—at the end of a rigorous reasoning which brings out the whole value of his *De moribus Ecclesiae Catholicae*—the Bishop of Hippo identifies with God. He begins by affirming that we all wish to be happy, an affirmation, moreover, to which allusions are to be found several times in his writings,[8] but which, in this work, is formulated in a particularly clear way: "There is no doubt that we all wish to live happily and that there is no person existing in the human race who does not give his or her assent to this proposition, even before the proposition has been formulated."[9] Happiness is attained when that which constitutes the supreme good of the human person is loved and comes into his possession. The whole of the difficulty lies in being able to determine in what this good consists. It is a case of bringing into relationship the good with the person who desires that good. As a consequence, Augustine excludes the idea that this good which is possessed could be something inferior to the subject. Someone who would make a good which was inferior to his own being into the supreme good would become himself an inferior being.

On a more concrete level, the problem is complicated when we consider the hypothesis of a good that certainly could not be a good which was inferior to the human person, but which would be a good equal to the person. This would be the case of placing our happiness in the enjoyment of merely human goods.

---

8. St Augustine *Confessions*, 10, 20, 29; *Enarr. in Ps* 32:2, d. 2.15. We note, in the *Confessions*, the distinction between the happiness which makes people happy when it has been obtained and the happiness which makes people joyful when, deprived of it, they hope for it: "*Et est aliud quidam modus, quo quisque cum habet eam, tunc beatus est, et sunt qui spe beati sunt*".
9. ID. *De moribus Ecclesiae Catholicae*, 1, 3, 4.

At the highest level, the moral goods would enter into this category. Augustine does not examine this question in this passage, but, later on in his treatise, it will appear clearly that it is of the Stoics that he is thinking, those who identify the supreme good with virtue. He makes an allusion to suicide, an action which was admitted by them, and underlines, ironically, the incoherence of someone who would wish to put an end to an existence which he claims is a happy one: "O, what a happy life it is that, finally, ends up by demanding the help of death!"[10]

The only possibility which remains, then, is that of a supreme good which is superior to the human being; if this exists, according to Augustine, such a good would have to possess a number of characteristics; as a good superior to the person, it would have to be able to be a good which he could possess; furthermore, "it would have to be of such a nature that someone would not be able to lose it against their own will."[11] We find the argument employed on several occasions by the bishop of Hippo, according to which a good that could be taken away could not make happy the person who possessed it. There follows then a whole development of what the good of the person could be. After a long anthropological examination of the body and the soul, St Augustine concludes that such a good would have to be sought in "that which makes the soul excellent,"[12] that is to say, in virtue. Everyone admits, in fact, that it is virtue alone that makes the soul perfect. Now, the soul pursues virtue through the desire to acquire it; hence, it is necessary that we set out to follow something in order that virtue may be born in it.[13] The soul must follow either the wise man or God; since the person who is wise

---

10. ID. *De civitate Dei*, XIX.
11. ID. *De mor. Eccl. Cath.*, 1, 3, 5: "*Tale esse debet quod non admittat invitus*".
12. *Ibid.* 1, 6, 8: We note the fact that Augustine does not indicate here whether the person's good is a good both of the body and of the soul, or whether it is only a good of the soul.
13. *Ibid.* 1, 6, 9: "*Opportet ut aliquid aliud sequatur anima, ut ei virtus ei innasci.*"

could be taken from us without our consent, there remains then no other good than God.

It is interesting to observe that Augustine, with an argumentation such as this, does not claim that he is offering an ascending proof of the existence of God, a proof which would begin from the consideration of the moral good to ascend to the sole possible source of this good. He judges that a soul that is sincere cannot deny the existence of God. He intends to show that, if it is true that our reason can attain to God, it is, on the contrary, the work of faith to penetrate into his wisdom: "Up until now, it has been possible to lead reason, to the extent that this operates in human affairs more by the sureness of habit than by the certainty of truth."[14] In his treatise, there is an obvious apologetic intention, aimed at the Manichaeans, who claimed to be able to accede to a virtuous ideal, higher than that of the Catholic Church.[15]

Another way to reach God by starting from good moral conduct is to be found in the fundamental distinction that St Thomas made between the *intentio finis* and the *voluntas eius quod est ad finem*.[16] The choice of the means to be employed, according to the Angelic Doctor, follows the judgment that is like the conclusion to an operative syllogism, while the end, insofar as it presents itself as a principle (and not as a conclusion), cannot be the object of choice. However, different ends can be subordinated one to the other in such a way that the end of an action may be the means chosen to attain the end of another, further act. In this chain of actions that follow on from each other, each

---

14. *Ibid.* 1, 7, 11.
15. The apologetic case, to which the treatise seeks to respond, is obvious. St Augustine wished to provide clarification about the ascetic ideal, of which the Manichaeans were proud, and he wished, therefore to demonstrate in this way the unfounded nature of their claimed superiority, with reference to what was proposed and put into practice by the Catholic Church; A. Pierreti, Introduzione a *I costumi della Chiesa Cattolica e i costumi dei Manichei*, Opere di sant'Agostino (Roma: Città Nuova, 1997), XIII/I, 6.
16. St Thomas Aquinas, *Summa Theologiae*, IIa IIae, q. 12, a 4; q. 13, a 3; *De ver.*, q. 22, a. 4.

end is chosen as a means of attaining a more important end. However, this process cannot proceed *ad infinitum*; it must necessarily have a term, and the ultimate end cannot in any case be the object of a choice.

It is in this way that St Thomas would establish later that the ultimate end (which is God) is implied in every human act. This kind of relationship[17] between the acts which human beings accomplish makes it possible for us to understand the whole interior dynamism of human freedom; each time that the will orientates itself towards a moral good which is to be done, the subject is, as it were, led to go beyond the act in the direction of a further good. In this way, the subject "orders himself or herself according to their nature."[18] All of our acts, good or bad, carry implications in regard to God, immoral acts insofar as the good which is chosen in the bad choice remains a good, a partial good, *apparens*, but a real good. From this perspective, God is not the object of our choice, because we do not choose that God be the end of our acts. Charity does not intervene at this level, since even acts which are contrary to it express a desire for the ultimate end.[19]

Paradoxically, without the aid of grace, human actions cannot effectively attain their ultimate end. In fact, without grace, the desire for the ultimate end is blocked in its dynamism. Hence, it then concentrates upon the search for an end that is creaturely, which becomes an idol. In this sense, our moral acts do not allow us to adopt a neutral position; the end that we obtain, necessarily, is either God or an idol. This is the way Augustine underlined this truth: it is proper to the image of God, after our conversion, not to fall into slavery to idols:

> It is true that I was above created things, but beneath You, who were my true joy, when I submitted myself to you, as you had submitted to me those creatures which you had

---

17. Cf. Etienne Gilson, *Saint Thomas moraliste* (Paris: Vrin, 1974), pp. 75ff.
18. St Augustine, *De Trinitate*. X, 5, 7.
19. St Thomas Aquinas, *Summa Theologiae*, Ia IIae, q. 1, a. 7, ad 1: "*Illi qui peccant, avertuntur ab eo in quo vere invenitur ratio ultimi finis: non autem ab ipsa ultimi finis intentio, quae quaerunt falso in aliis rebus.*"

made which are beneath me. That would have been the perfect equilibrium and the centre of my salvation, I would have remained in your image and, at the same time, in serving you, I would have been in command over my own body.[20]

We have already said that God is involved in every human act, in a positive or in a negative sense. To complete this, it would be necessary to consider also venial sins, which, even if they bear upon choices and never upon the ultimate end, do not have the power to destroy charity. Despite this, venial sins are not neutral;[21] they imply the involvement of God, insofar as they constitute an offence against God. The moral disorder that they express reveals in human beings the incoherence which exists between the search for God and the choice of goods which distance them from the final end through their acts.

Human Acts in the Plan of God

In the great architecture of the *Summa Theologiae*, human acts can be approached from the double movement of the *exitus-reditus*, the expression of the economy of intra-trinitarian relations.[22] From this angle, human acts have a double meaning.

---

20. St Augustine, *Confessions*, VII, 7, 11: "*Superior enim eram istis, te vero inferiore, et tu gaudium verum mihi subdito tibi et tu mihi subieceras quae infra me creasti. Et hoc erat rectum temperamentum et media regio salutis meae, ut manerem ad imaginem tuam et tibi serviens dominarer corpori.*"
21. Cf. St Thomas Aquinas, *Summa Theologiae*, IIa IIae, q. 24, a. 6, a. 7, a. 8, a. 9. As for mortal sins, they bring with them the loss of charity in the moral subject by reason of the fact that they are necessarily orientated against charity. St Thomas remarks that we can never lose charity without the involvement of our own will. The human being, in a state of mortal sin, remains naturally capable of accomplishing acts which are morally good (for example, an assassin can still remain faithful to his marriage), but his acts are without any meritorious value. They have no efficacy in the order of charity.
22. A. Patfroort, *Thomas d'Aquin. Les clés d'une théologie* (Paris, 1983), pp. 62–70.

First of all, in their dynamism, they express the power that the human being has of fulfilling himself. The person truly is the master of his own acts,[23] and these acts are a manifestation of his personal responsibility, quite apart from any good and also, with regard to intermediate ends, in relation to the ultimate end.

Moreover, they express the creative power of God and the omnipotence of God, of which they are authentic signs. They are a participation in this power.

In the light of this, we can understand that, if it is orientated to the ultimate end, the moral act of the human being participates in the restoration of everything to God. Thus, we can measure to what extent personal responsibility goes beyond the personal destiny of the person who acts.

At the concrete level, this double movement is possible only by means of the choice of every person in Jesus Christ, in view of his salvation,[24] in the mystery of his predestination in Christ. This divine project with regard to the person is expressed through an adoptive sonship, which in its turn demands a filial response. It is through the good actions which one accomplishes in the order of charity that each person gives a response as son or daughter. The good acts are a kind of created participation in the eternal gift of the Son to his Father. Now, quite rightly, this gift was effected by the Son in his humanity; his acts (truly human acts) undertaken in full submission to the will of the Father in the most perfect obedience, were operative and made present,

---

23. St Gregory of Nyssa: *De vita Moysis*, II, 2–3, PG, 44, pp. 372–328, quoted in John Paul II, VS § 71: "All beings which are subjected to becoming never remain identical to what they are, but they pass continually from one state to another by means of a change which is always in operation, for better or for worse...Now, to be subject to change is to be born again continually....But here birth does not come about by virtue of some exterior intervention, as is the case with bodily beings...It is the result of a free choice and so, in a certain sense, we are own parents, creating ourselves as we wish to be and, through our choices, giving ourselves the form that we wish."

24. Patrfoort, *Thomas d'Aquin*, pp. 101–102.

and they expressed in the human condition his communion with the Father.

For a creature, such a response of obedience is possible only through divine grace, but, quite rightly, the function of grace is to render the person capable of this response. The human being acts in Christ, or better, when he undertakes an act of authentically human charity, there is in him an interior reciprocity between his act and the action of Christ. The mystical authors expressed this reality in a symbolic way by means of the notion of the "exchange of hearts."[25] The theologal acts that we accomplish have a nature that is truly both divine and human; such a dimension is given through the elevation of spiritual faculties by means of the infused virtue of charity. Thus, in the theologal life, we have the exact coincidence between God (received and encountered) and the good (exercised and obtained). We should not be surprised by the fact that such a penetration in the theologal act of the divine life and of human life is so difficult to welcome in Christian conscience. In history, there has often been the great temptation to keep hold only of the human aspect. It suffices to call to mind the various forms of Pelagianism which forget the promise of the Kingdom: "There will no longer be any evil or violence on all my holy mountain because the country will be filled with the knowledge of the Lord, as the waters cover the sea" (Is 11:69). We find, too, the extreme opposite, for example, in the pessimism of Luther or of Jansen,[26] who judged hu-

---

25. St John Eudes, *Le coeur admirable de Jésus* in *Œuvres complètes*, VI (Vannes, 1905–1991), pp. 107; 113–115 : "I beg you to consider that Jesus Christ, our Lord, is your true head and that you are one of his members...He is yours as the Head is to his members. Everything that is his is yours, his spirit, his Heart, his body, his soul and all of his faculties, and you must make use of them as you make use of things that are your own, in order to serve, to praise, to love and to glorify God."
26. «*Aliqua Dei praecepta hominibus iustis violentibus et conantibus, secundum praesentes quas habent vires, sunt impossiblilia ; deest quoque illis gratia, qua possibilia fiant*», C. Jansen, *Augustinus*, II, *De gratia Christi*, III, 13 ; Cf. INNOCENT X, const. *Cum occasione ad univ. fideles* (May 31, 1653).

man nature to be incapable of accomplishing the commandments of God, in this way denying any possibility of an authentic participation of human action in the divine action of grace.

If it is true that eternal life (the place of the *cognitio Dei* in St John's Gospel, Jn 17:3) is the very knowledge of truth itself, *cognitio veritatis*,[27] the knowledge of the truth in love, the total commitment of the human faculties remains no less necessary to seek and to attain the moral good. The severity of St Augustine towards those who neglect the moral depth of the human act, dissolving it into a merely spiritual vision is well known: "See how perverse and completely out of order are those who think that they can transmit to us the knowledge of God in order to make us perfect, when this knowledge of God is the reward for those who are perfect."[28]

God has made us come back to him in such a way that we ourselves may be also truly the authors of this return to him.

---

27. St Augustine, *De moribus Eccl. Cath.* I, 25, 47.
28. *Ibid.*

19 The Rational Conduct of the Believer[1]

> It is a matter of urgency, then, that Christians rediscover the novelty of their faith and the strength which it gives to their judgment in the face of a culture which is dominant and invasive ... We must find once more and represent anew the true face of the Christian faith, which is not just an assemblage of propositions to be welcomed and to be ratified by our intelligence. On the contrary, it is a knowledge and an experience of Christ, a living memory of his commandments, a truth to be put into action.

These words are quoted not from the encyclical *Fides et Ratio*, but from the encyclical *Veritatis Splendor*, § 88.

> The Gospel and the writings of the Apostles propose...both general principles for Christian conduct and teachings of specific precepts. To apply these to the particular circumstances of individual and of social life, the Christian must be in a position to engage his or her conscience and power of reasoning at a deep level. In other words, this means that moral theology must have reference to a concept of philosophy which is correct, both in regard to human nature and to society and to the general principles for making ethical decisions.

These words are quoted not from the encyclical *Veritatis Splendor*, but from the encyclical *Fides et Ratio*, § 68.

It would be easily possible to find much convergence between these two major texts and hence to show how the way in which

---

1. "The Rational Conduct of the Believer" is the text of the Inaugural Lecture, delivered on the occasion of the opening of the academic year of the Accademia Alfonsiana, Rome, and published with the title «L'agir rationnel du croyant: L'apport de l'encyclique, *Fides et Ratio*, à la théologie morale» in *Studia Moralia*, n. 38, 2000, pp. 523–539.

faith and reason are articulated in *Fides et Ratio* has been used and applied already with reference to the relationship between faith and morality in *Veritatis Splendor*. Among the main lines of convergence, we must stress: a dynamic which is essentially theological, an analogous centrality of the person of Christ, the same structuring of faith and reason, avoiding any kind of extrinsicism, bringing out the dangers connected to the claim to separate any form of rationality from the light of Revelation, a resumption in *Fides et Ratio* of the concept of truth applied to the moral good, elaborated at length in *Veritatis Splendor*, and finally an insistence upon the possibility of transforming reason. The aim of this reflection is not to develop a systematic comparison between the two texts, but to show that the teaching of *Fides et Ratio* is pertinent to human conduct. In other words, it is to try to respond to the fundamental question of knowing whether there exists a moral dimension to the exercise of our intelligence. Since the exercise of this reason is decisive for our relationship to Christ, it will be helpful first of all to demonstrate how the perspective of this latter encyclical is above all of a theological nature and to illustrate the central place of the figure of Christ in the text.

Fides Et Ratio: *Its Theological Perspective and the Centrality of the Figure of Christ*

The first sentence of the introduction to the encyclical could cause us to suppose that there are two ways of knowing the truth—by faith and by reason—and that the two ways would be, therefore, of equal importance: "Faith and reason are like the two wings which allow the human spirit to raise itself up to the contemplation of the truth." However, it is not a matter of a symmetrical double movement (of faith towards reason and of reason towards faith), a movement in which the two poles would be interchangeable. The intention of the text is theologically orientated (*Faith and Reason* and not *Reason and Faith*), as can be established from the order of the chapters: the *credo ut in-*

tellegam precedes the *intellego ut credam*. The entire relationship of the human being to the truth is considered in the light of God, who desires to communicate himself to us in Jesus Christ. It is this divine light that illuminates also the mystery of the reason which seeks God, without having found him; and the plan of God himself includes a natural dimension. God is to be found at the origin of the search for truth, and that is a theological given. We find the same approach in the two texts: in *Veritatis Splendor* there is reference to a "nostalgia for absolute truth,"[2] while in *Fides et Ratio* the divine origin of such a search is expounded with greater force.[3] Nostalgia is certainly a desire, but it is a desire with reference to a good that has been lost. If it is formulated in an abstract way in the first encyclical (the expression absolute truth is a concept), in the second the good is identified in this way: the supreme good, God himself.

It would appear that this nostalgia for the past contains already a moral dimension, as long as it is not confused with some mere sentimental yearning. It is a question of a nostalgia which is active, a kind of nostalgic research, if you like, something like what the philosopher, Simone Weil, sought to express, when she said: "only the highest part of our attention enters into contact with God, when prayer is intense and pure enough for

---

2. "The darkness of error and of sin could not suppress totally the light of God, the Creator, in the human being; from this fact, the nostalgia for absolute truth and the thirst to reach the knowledge of its plenitude remains always deep within our heart"; John Paul II, *Veritatis Splendor*, § 1. (Translator's note: The word 'nostalgia' is used in the Italian and in the French texts, rendered in English at times as "yearning:" the original 'nostalgia' is maintained here in the translation of *Veritatis Splendor* and in the equivalent translation of the word in *Fides et Ratio*, as well as in the translation of the main text of Mgr Laffitte, whose analysis depends upon the nuance of a contrast with the idea of an absolute in the past, captured by the English word "nostalgia", but not necessarily covered by the concept of "'yearning.'")
3. "The Apostle brings into the light a truth of which the Church has always made use; in the depths of the human heart are to be found the seeds of the desire and of the nostalgia for God"; ID. *Fides et Ratio*, § 24).

such contact to be established, but then the whole of our attention is turned towards God."[4] The whole of Christian Tradition has examined this attention, from the *"cor inquietum"* of St Augustine to the recent explorations of the personalists,[5] including the theme of the search for God present in the mediaeval current of Cistercian spirituality.[6]

Why does this attentive waiting for God create restlessness in the human heart? The passing from original innocence to sin and to its consequences, which characterized the beginning of the *historia salutis*, has as its principal effect, at least as far as interiority is concerned, the birth of guilt. Guilt can be seen as a moral sanction, acting in the heart of the person. The very broad perspective of Ricoeur's work, *Finitude et Culpabilité*, shows this very well. Nostalgia is the desire for a return to fulness, or to the integrity of love. It is above all this latter aspect that marks out its moral dimension. Love is a moral act, which implies the search for the one who is loved. God is experienced as absent, at times for reasons of awe or fear. Nédoncelle has attempted to express the reality of this expectation like this:

> This kind of restlessness is the foreboding in us and around us of the divine order; it rests upon humility and love...; through it, we are...very close to recognizing the gift of God, for it is God who has placed in the human being this aspiration for the infinite and this sudden

---

4. Simone Weil, *Attente de Dieu* (Paris: La Colombe, 1950), p. 114 ; cf. on this point J.-F. Thomas, J.-F. Thomas, *Simone Weil et Edith Stein: malheur et souffrance* in part III, ch. 1, "La mystique de l'attention" (Namur: Culture et Vérité, 1992), pp. 89–100.
5. Martin Buber, *Gottesfinsternis, Betrachtungen zur Beziehung zwischen Religion und Philosophie* (Zürich, 1953); M. Nédoncelle, *Les leçons spirituelles du XIX siècle* (Paris, 1936) ; Max Scheler, *Nature et forme de la sympathie. Contribution à l'étude des lois de la vie émotionnelle* (German : *Natur und Wesen der Sympathie*); Edith Stein, *Zum Problem der Erfüllung* (Halle, 1917).
6. We are thinking especially of the theme of spiritual friendship, understood as a means for desiring perfect Love: William of St Thierry, Baudouin de Ford, Aelred of Rievaulx.

terror which perturbs our souls when they discover their fragility or their malice.[7]

Fides et Ratio inserts itself into this long Tradition, which we have recalled, when it affirms at the outset that it is God who has placed in the heart of the human being the desire to know the truth and, in the end, to know himself, in order that, knowing him and loving him, man may attain the full truth about himself.

Now we move from the personal dimension of the search for God to the figure of Christ; in the very beautiful expression of Nédoncelle, which we have just quoted, it is important to underline the personal nature of this attentive expectation. The author speaks of a "foreboding of the divine order" within us and surrounding us. The person who searches for the truth of things involves himself ultimately in his own question. In some way, he knows that, if it is provided to him, the answer to the questions he is posing will not leave him intact as he is; he will have to adopt a particular position, quite literally so, in the sense that he will have to adjust his position in the light of the truth which he has discovered. This truth will affect him, it will change him, and it will transform the world around him. The fact that so few persons succeed in going to the foundations of the questions relating to the truth of things is a paradox for Christian understanding and for the sensitivities of the baptized. Perhaps, they do not really wish to know the answer, and the questions that affect their own existence (those questions recalled by the encyclical: Who am I? Where am I going? Why does evil exist?) are not considered to be the real issues of life.

We have the right to ask whether it may not be precisely in this that the authentically moral nature of the philosophical question of truth is to be found, namely in leaving aside serious questions out of fear of the possible consequences to which they may give rise. Prior to knowing the truth itself, we know one of its fundamental characteristics—that it is demanding. The moral

---

7. M. Nedoncelle, «La découverte de notre misère» in ID., *Les leçons spirituelles du XIX siècle*, p. 17.

choice is, as it were, buried in the heart of the question about truth. Now, if it is true that this infinite aspiration for the truth, and specifically together with nostalgia, is the desire to return to a love which has been under threat or lost, in the way that we have described, it follows that the discovery of the truth, if it is found, necessarily will take on the features of an experience of love, and such an experience cannot occur without some form of personal and benevolent causality. The truth, necessarily, must be revealed, because it is a requirement of love that it be revealed in order for it to be diffused. This kind of revelation can be expressed adequately through the category of *encounter*. Thus, we reach the Christocentric nature of the text. The Truth, which is Love, makes itself known and reveals itself in the person of Jesus Christ, according to the eternal plan of the Father. *Fides et Ratio* uses the term *encounter* to designate the discovery of this truth which is Christ: "At the origin of our being as believers, there is to be found an encounter, unique of its kind, which has brought about the opening up of a mystery hidden for centuries (cf. 1Cor 2:7; Rom 16: 25–26), but which now has been revealed."[8] Later on, the personal identity of this revelation is expressed like this: "The truth which God has entrusted to human beings about themselves and about their life is something, then, which is situated in time and in history…it has been proclaimed once and for all in Jesus of Nazareth." The encounter with Jesus is the heart of the answer not only to the question that the human being poses about God, but also to every question about the truth of things which have a significant effect upon his or her existence. "Insofar as he is the source of love, God wishes to make himself known and the knowledge that human beings have of him brings to its completion every other element of truth about the meaning of their existence which their spirit is in a position to attain."[9]

We take note of the fact that God does not give a metaphysical answer to the question of his existence. He wishes to make

---

8. John Paul II, *Fides et Ratio*, § 7.
9. *Ibid.*

himself known through the person of the Incarnate Word. It is a matter of the revelation of the personal love of God and this love is capable of fulfilling all of the expectations of the human being and of answering all of his questions, metaphysical or otherwise. At the same time, however, it is right to affirm the providential nature of God as a reality that is fully coherent. The human spirit contemplates in the figure of Christ both the fulness of Creation ("through him all things were made") as also the fulfilment of the divine plan of salvation. This unity of truth, natural and revealed, finds its living and personal identification in Christ.[10] It is to Christology that it returns, in order to establish a theoretical foundation for the requirements for such a unity in the truth that is in Christ.

The centrality of the figure of Christ is a common given in the two encyclicals. In *Veritatis Splendor*, the meeting with Christ is the fundamental encounter for the rich young man, his unique opportunity to find an answer to the question about morality. The text recognizes in this anonymous rich young man the figure of "every human being who, consciously or otherwise, approaches Christ, the Redeemer of man and who poses the question about morality." Christ is the answer to the moral question; he reveals where true moral goodness is to be found (*"Unus est bonus"*, Mt 19:17),[11] and his reply has universal significance: "The dialogue between Jesus and the rich young man continues, in a certain way, in all the periods of history, even to our days…and it is always Christ, in him alone, that the complete and final answer is to be found."[12]

Here, we have a personalization of action, presented in the history of an encounter with God in his humanity and in his divinity, in accordance with the norm of the human person;[13] this

---

10. *Ibid.* § 34.
11. Id. *Veritatis Splendor*, § 9.
12. *Ibid.* § 25.
13. J. Castellano Cervera, «Spiritualità e nuova evangelizzazione» in R. Lucas, (a cura di), *Veritatis Splendor: Testo integrale e commento filosofico-teologico* (San Paolo: Torino, 1994), p. 385.

historic encounter transcends the limits of time and of space. In *Fides et Ratio*, the revelation of God in the event of the Incarnation of Jesus Christ expresses a truth which "is no longer enclosed within a particular territorial or cultural context, but ...which is open anyone whomsoever, man or woman, who wishes to welcome him as the word with definitive value for giving a meaning to our existence."[14]

Does a Moral Use of Reason Exist?

The question that introduces the second stage of our reflection on some aspects of the relationship between faith and reason—does a moral use of reason exist? (if we may dare to put it this way)—is not politically correct. A theoretical and a practical separation between the two ways of knowing has entered so deeply into our habits of thought that, at times, exercising our reason may appear to be superfluous, an addendum to the faith, an unnecessary luxury, for someone who in any case believes, whereas, approaching the matter from the opposite angle, it happens that the adherence of reason to revealed faith is judged by some as an abandoning by reason of its own methodological and epistemological criteria. It is certainly true that, in these two extreme tendencies, we have a real betrayal of the faith in the first tendency (since such an attitude amounts to saying that there is no intelligibility in the faith) and a betrayal of reason in the second tendency (because it is the irrational attitude of a function which refuses to accept the possibility which is offered of overcoming its own proper limits). It would be impossible here to survey the philosophical history of such a separation between reason and faith. It would be possible to study the concept of reason expressed in *Fides et Ratio*.

Without pretending to be exhaustive, the following observations are brought out in the text: reason, whose presence in the human person is signalled by the questions about fundamentals

---

14. John Paul II, *Fides et Ratio*, § 12.

which arise, such as the question about the meaning of and the desire for the truth, belongs to the nature itself of the human being. Among the various applications of reason, there appears the capacity for speculation, which makes it possible to build up a body of systematic knowledge; then there are some attitudes which it mentions which are appropriate to reason, when it sets itself to acquire knowledge of some matters of a fundamental nature, for example, "the sense of wonder which arises in the human being through the contemplation of Creation, struck with admiration when discovering that we are located in a world, in relation to those who are like us, and that we share the same destiny as them."[15] We shall see further on that other attitudes are to be found which constitute an obstacle to the personal search for the truth. Reason has been able to bring out a certain number of elements of philosophical knowledge, whose presence has been constant in the history of thought.[16] The examples quoted are interesting: apart from the classical principles of non-contradiction, of finality, of causality, the encyclical mentions the concept of the human person as a free and intelligent subject and his capacity for knowing God, the truth, and the good; in effect what it describes later on as a capacity for metaphysics,[17] and which is made explicit in Chapter III, the heart of the encyclical, as a "capacity (of reason) to rise above what is contingent and to launch itself towards the infinite."[18] Let us leave aside the remarks made about the reinforcing of reason which is effected by the knowledge of the faith, in order to underline this remark, very fine and enormously powerful: "in the life of a human person, truths which are simply believed remain far more numerous than those which he or she acquires through verifying them personally."[19] The act of belief (which is anything but submitting to some proof) is not foreign to reason, causes no offence to reason, if it is

---

15. *Ibid.* § 4.
16. Cf. *Ibid.*
17. *Ibid.* § 22.
18. *Ibid.* § 24.
19. *Ibid.* § 31.

true that reason itself specifically uses many of these elements of knowledge that have been received and yet which have not been verified personally. We find ourselves in a situation that is analogous to that of the philosopher, Gadamer,[20] who has given a perfect illustration of the limits of the Enlightenment in its claim to consider as valid only those aspects of knowledge that are scientifically verifiable. If reason were to require the verification of all of the givens of which it makes use, and which it supposes to be true, in those propositions that form a coherent unity, practically it would lose all certitude beyond arithmetical truths and some of their practical applications. By recovering the Aristotelian concept of *phronesis* (prudence), Gadamer showed the need to safeguard our spiritual ends, with the assistance of tradition and of culture. For the German thinker, truth is also an opportunity for the human being to engage in authentic concrete experience.

How is it possible, theoretically, to take into consideration the validity of human experience? How can teaching which emerges from a human experience be held to be universally valid? Here, we are at the heart of a problem that is above all of a methodological nature. Two kinds of experience can illustrate the problematic involved here: the experience of the beautiful and spiritual experience. The first of these is marked by the strong emotion experienced before the work of art, an emotion, moreover, translated at times in terms of encounter, of interpersonal relationship—we may think of the description by the poet, Rilke, of a statue of Rodin: "Every point of the statue is looking at you," he remarks. Nevertheless, what seems to be a unique and personal event, lived out by the one who admires the work, prevents neither sharing the experience with others, nor seeking out the reasons for the admiration that is experienced (aesthetic criteria). The second is spiritual experience, which naturally must not be confused with mystical experience. Both of these have been studied by spiritual theology and by numerous authors of

---

20. Cf. Hans-Georg Gadamer, *Wahrheit und Methode* (Tübingen, 1960).

philosophy.[21] The spiritual experience of a person is his unique way of living certain truths about God. This experience reveals an infinite number of degrees of spiritual commitment, as C. Bernard has observed.[22] In the strict sense, authentic spiritual experience leads the subject to seek for an ever deeper relationship with the Three Divine Persons. Entry into a more developed theologal life functions like an internal verification of the authenticity of a loving experience, whose dynamism brings to its fulfilment this relationship with God. Viewed from the outside, spiritual experiences are to be found which are objectively foundational, not only for the person concerned, but for the whole community of believers. Among others, we may cite the transcendent experience that Saul had of Jesus Christ on the road to Damascus or again the intellectual and moral conversion of the future St Augustine.[23] These experiences, followed by a radical change of personal life, have offered to the Church the fundamental contribution of their specific richness. The whole of the teaching of St Paul was marked by this primordial event; as for the ineffable

---

21. Kierkegaard, R. Otto, M. Scheler, N. Hartmann, etc.
22. C. Bernard, S.J., *Vie morale et croissance dans le Christ* (Rome: PUG, 1973), p. 49: "In relation to the moral life, then, the precise question which the spiritual life poses is this: to what extent does the human being take on his or her condition as a Christian in order to live life *to the full*? [...] We cannot separate our consideration of the spiritual journey from the quality of the decision which makes it possible to make and to sustain that journey. Necessarily, at every moment, moral rectitude must go together with this qualitative aspect, so difficult to discern, which we may call generosity, magnanimity, gift of self, but also desire for God and spiritual trust."
23. In both instances, these two singular experiences have implications not only for the life of a large number of believers, for example, for the apostolic activity of each one of them, but they make it possible to examine in depth the profound meaning of what is meant by true conversion to Christ, which is both an objective source of richness for the totality of believers and also part of the universal patrimony of the Church. In a broader sense, the same thing goes for the spiritual experiences which preceded those works of foundation which the Church has acknowledged as her own.

moment lived out by St Augustine in the company of Alypius, it would form the basis for the whole of his metaphysical anthropology (the *conversio Augustiniana*). Aesthetic experience, as well as spiritual experience, can provide access to truths that are valid for everyone.[24] If we have said that the problem is in the first place a metaphysical one, this is because a critical assessment of these two types of experience is undertaken by means of instrument and of criteria proper to each one of them. In fact, it is only the unity of the faith which makes it possible to verify the relevance and the Christian coherence of the teaching which arises from a spiritual experience; in the same way, every work of art is located within a tradition, an area of knowledge or a science of the beautiful, if we may say so, which makes it possible to verify the specific contribution at a given moment or indeed in an absolute sense. Even in the case of a work which is revolutionary, it is relative to a certain body of knowledge, to an artistic patrimony, that an evaluation is made of what it is in the work which effects a rupture with what has preceded it and which thereby establishes what is new in its way of being. In any event, we observe that the existence in the history of thought of a metaphysics of the beautiful, claiming to see in this category one of the constitutive elements of being, illustrates the extent to which the two approaches are analogous. To sum it up, we find once more here what the encyclical stated about the capacity of reason to experience admiration and wonder.

It remains for us to examine how reason can be used in an inappropriate way, according to *Fides et Ratio*. From a theological perspective, the text shows the original capacity of human reason to rise naturally above beings which can be observed to the origin of all being, the Creator. Original disobedience, in the sense of a choice for an autonomy that is complete and absolute

---

24. Here, we do not intend to deny that the need at times for the minimal conditions to be met for the reception of these truths which have been transmitted to us: culture, education and formation in relation to aesthetic values, and interior disposition and the moral requirements needed to reach spiritual truths.

with regard to the Creator, has led to the obscuring of this capacity. *Fides et Ratio* speaks in this way of reason being wounded. One of the first wounds to be found in reason is the indifference to truth. Without any doubt, this is the most serious of the wounds; does not being indifferent mean, for the intelligence, to deny its own reason for being? No one can be sincerely indifferent to the truth of his knowledge. The word *sincerely* brings us back to the field of morality. Lying, as a deliberate choice for non-truth, is an offence inflicted upon the one to whom we are lying; in this sense, that person's right to the truth is violated. In one of his Wednesday Catecheses on the Holy Year of the Redemption, John Paul II described indifference to the truth as a "mortal wound to the intelligence."[25] The search for the truth is not expressed only on the theoretical level, but it applies also to the practical level. *Fides et Ratio* comes back to this point of *Veritatis Splendor*. There exists a right which is to be respected in each person's own search for the truth (and this, therefore, requires, let it be noted, that that truth be welcomed through a choice which is free). As a corollary, even prior to this, there exists the grave moral duty for everyone to seek for the truth and, once it is recognized, to adhere to it.[26]

One of the most important aspects of Chapter III of *Fides et Ratio* is the just equilibrium between the two sides of practical truth, the objective dimension and the subjective dimension.

The *objective dimension*: the question is formulated very clearly. Is it possible or not to obtain access to a truth which is universal and absolute?[27] In some sectors and areas of know-

---

25. John Paul II, *Catechesis at General Audience*, August 24, 1983.
26. Id. *Fides et Ratio*, § 24. *Veritatis Splendor,* § 34, refers back in a footnote to the Declaration, *Dignitatis Humanae*: "By virtue of their human dignity, all people, because they are persons, that is to say, that they endowed with reason and with free will and hence with personal responsibility, are impelled by their own nature and are also morally obliged to seek the truth, and in the first place religious truth. They are also obliged, once they know it, to adhere to the truth and to order their entire lives according to the requirements of that truth" (Vatican Council II, *Dignitatis Humanae*, § 2).
27. John Paul II, *Fides et Ratio*, § 27.

ledge, certain truths are accepted by everyone. Such a certitude does nothing to appease the thirst for truth which drives the human being to seek a truth which is absolute. Here, the text reconnects the character of the absolute with the final truth, which provides the foundation for all other truths, those we wish to discover and those that are already known. It is a matter of an existential truth because it concerns the totality of human existence; thus, it includes all of the questions which touch upon the origin of the person and upon the death he or she cannot avoid. The reference made here to the death of Socrates is very significant.[28] The response to the universal question is given by the faith; it is the truth that God reveals in Jesus Christ.[29]

The *subjective dimension*: *Fides et Ratio* shows how the whole problematic of absolute truth unfolds itself within the interiority of the subject. The originality of this perspective lies in this: we have a question which is objective, but it is a question which the subject appropriates to himself by way of the sincere search which he undertakes about the ultimate meaning of his own life. The subject cannot remain on the outside, adopting an attitude of neutrality. Access to the truth about the final end is made possible through a personal commitment on the part of the subject. Among the obstacles to this search for the truth which the encyclical recognizes is that of the inconstancy of the heart. The heart is seen as the intimate place where the most fundamental decisions of the human being are taken.

It will be useful to pay attention to another inappropriate usage of reason, that of doubt, and, on this topic, to clear up a veritable paradox. *Fides et Ratio* affirms that: "a person could never

---

28. "All of us wish to know and need to know the truth about our end. We wish to know whether death will be the definitive term to our existence or whether there is something which goes beyond death, whether it is permitted for us to hope for another life or not. It is not without significance that philosophical thought received a decisive orientation from the death of Socrates and that it remains so marked after more than two millennia," *Ibid.* § 26.
29. Cf. *Ibid.* § 34.

ground his or her existence upon, doubt, uncertainty or a lie,"[30] whereas doubt is seen from a broader angle as an opportunity to grow in maturity and for personal growth.[31] Thus, in itself, doubt is ambivalent; there does exist a doubt that is useful and good, but there exists also a doubt which is sinful, whose consequences are fear and anguish. How can we distinguish between these two attitudes, and how can we evaluate them morally? Doubt is legitimate when it describes the critical attitude of reason, in the search for the conditions of validity of an assertion that is founded upon a belief, or again, when it designates the initial moment of a process of verification of an affirmation whose truth has not yet been demonstrated. The critical examination of reason, then, is a natural experience of the human spirit, at the same time as it is a service rendered to truth. Doubt ceases to be a healthy attitude when it becomes an end in itself and when it is organized into a globalized system of thought. Then, we speak of scepticism, a form of thought which brings into question the personal relationship of the subject to reality and when, elaborated as a doctrine, scepticism makes impossible the discovery of absolute truth and of any universal truth. Then, it leaves wide open a space, in which false absolutes are developed, demonstrating in this way its incoherence. Analyzing the birth of philosophical systems such as this, which he calls "fundamentally sinful metaphysics" (*erbsündige Metaphysike*), Erich Przywara says that Adam and Eve, in partaking of the forbidden fruit in order to become like gods, in reality "did not allow the Absolute to be truly the Absolute for them, and for this reason they could not but fail to attain it."[32] Among the various reasons offered for such metaphysics, the author mentions the divinization of interiority. It can be understood that the endeavour to reverse the tendency and to substitute for these systems a metaphysics of ransom, to employ another of the author's

30. *Ibid.* § 28.
31. Cf. *Ibid.* § 31.
32. Cf. D. Biju-Duval, "La pensée d'Erich Przywara," *Nouvelle Revue Théologique*, April-June, 1999, p. 249.

expressions, consists in "restoring to human subjectivity its genuine status of creature before God and in relation to reality."[33]

The opening of reason to truths which surprise it and which, in the end, surpass it, is the condition for the full exercise of reason, since reason is also the guarantee of the validity of the method employed. Besides, this requires an attitude of confidence towards other people as well as towards oneself. Basically, scepticism is nothing more than the distrust of reason as to its own capacity to attain truth.

The Articulation of Faith-Reason or the Parable of Prodigal Reason

Before examining more deeply, if only briefly, some features relating to these two binomials, faith-reason and theology-philosophy, honesty seems to require that we make a simple observation. To think about these two orders of knowledge together, as we are doing in this chapter in the light of *Fides et Ratio*, is the fruit of long research conducted across the centuries by Christian and philosophical thought. It would not be an exaggeration to recognize here an obvious sign of the maturity of Christian thinking, a maturity that, moreover, has been favourably greeted outside of Christian circles, on the occasion of the publication of this encyclical. We have shown the two possible poles of separation between faith and reason; we note that there exists a widespread tendency no longer to trust reason in terms of what, by grace, it has been able to discover in the act of faith.[34] It is true that the wonder experienced before the splendour of the truth, when it takes on the face of Christ, brings out the limits of all areas of human wisdom. How could people adhere to the great philosophy of the Greeks, if the Cross of Christ appears to them as folly? The correct attitude, which con-

---

33. *Ibid.* p. 250.
34. We may think of the almost complete disappearance of apologetics, or again of the increasingly rare use of arguments of convergence in theological reflection.

sists in seeking out and in exploring the *semina Verbi* in the various systems of thought, is the fruit of an intellectual freedom, which is a conquest of the intelligence. Time is a necessary help in this. For this reason, a free reading of the parable of the prodigal Son may assist us by suggesting the real import of such a separation between faith and reason.

When reason distances itself from faith, it makes a move that is analogous to that of the prodigal son, who goes away from his father, who leaves to go to a deserted place. Reason no longer has at its disposal the food of wisdom that it possessed previously in the paternal dwelling of the faith. It would indeed be content with the seeds of a knowledge that is partial and sparkling, but it would no longer have access to knowledge as such. It loses the sense of its own identity, of its originary dependence upon the light of the faith, for which it experiences a great nostalgia. At the point of distancing itself from the faith, it formulated its requirements like this: "Give me immediately the part of my inheritance which is due to me." It had no awareness of the fact that part of that heritage, at that moment, had ceased to live, and had become independent of any living tradition. Very quickly, the parental home disappeared from view. Reason had dispensed everything that it had, forgetting that a liberty such as this, by now denatured in its new and sterile autonomy, had been itself a gift of the Father. It set out to search for various motives as to why it should exist and formulated the idea that existence was nothing more than an opportunity to enjoy sensations and experiences. It put itself at the service of one of the inhabitants of this distant country, who also proposed the primacy of the ephemeral. This person sent it to the fields to look after the pigs, because that was the concern at that time. No one gave to reason the seeds that it desired. Reason allowed itself to be at the disposal of the pigs and to desire what they had to eat. It came to its senses, began to reason and said: "I shall return to my father". It prepared a fairly brief speech of three sentences. The first two were intelligent: "Father, I have sinned against heaven and against you; I am no longer worthy to be called your son." The third was less intelligent: "Treat me like one of your paid servants." By chance, when reason returned to its father, it saw him coming towards it, to meet it and to take it in his arms. Reason began to proclaim its speech, at least its first two sentences, those that were the more intelligent. We do not know, in fact, whether it forgot the third or whether instead it did not have to the time to proclaim it, because it was filled with amazement, upon hearing the few words spoken by its father: "Hurry, bring the best clothes, prepare the fatted calf and get it ready. Let us rejoice and hold a feast." Now, while these things were taking place, the elder brother of reason arrived; he was very put out to see his father welcome prodigal reason in this way. He had always remained faithful to his father, he said to himself, and at the time and justifiably he had criticized reason's distancing itself, very severely. To tell the truth, he had judged it unreasonable, just as now he judged the attitude of their joint father itself as unreasonable. He could not come to understand the latter, refused vehemently to enter the house, and history does not tell us whether or not he chose, in the midst of his indignation, himself to go away in his turn.

This very free reading of the parable enables us to illustrate this: when reason claims for itself an absolute autonomy in regard to the faith, it believes that it is able to dispense with what comes from faith, since it does not dispense with any other thing apart from the inheritance of the faith. It is a fact that it was necessary to have the metaphysics of Creation for the human being to be able to acquire a stable understanding of the universe and real confidence in the value of reason itself, both of which laid the indispensable foundations for the birth and the development of the sciences. Autonomous reason would never have existed, if faith had not given it the means to operate. Guardini speaks of the "disloyalty of modern autonomous thought;" it opposes faith only to the extent that it squanders the heritage which has derived from faith. This heritage is taken apart, where there remains nothing other than nihilism, an attitude, whose immoral character is brought out in the encyclical. If it is true, as appears ever more clearly in the various currents of post-modern thought, that nihilism preaches the determined rejection of any commitment by the person, then, to nothing there must follow necessarily also a rejection of the nature of its norms, something that implies an ethics of despair:

> Before nature, Guardini adds, the human person of our times has ceased, to an equal degree, to experience the religious sentiments which had manifested themselves in a clear and serene fashion in Goethe, in the form of enthusiasm in the Romantics, or as sheer ecstasy in someone like Hölderin. It has passed through a crisis of disenchantment.[35]

Disenchantment is nothing other than the absence of wonder and of admiration. In its lack of hope, prodigal reason could imagine itself being treated by its father in no other way than as one of his paid servants. The father's welcome surpassed its own limits of understanding. As for the elder brother, his refusal to enter into the perspective of his father could very well prefigure the pusillanimous attitude of a reason which has become sad, which does not open itself up to the joys available to it. The fatted calf has always remained available: "Everything that is mine is yours." The elder brother made no move towards what, in our reading, could symbolize all the riches of the universe which come always from the Father. In what at times is a narrow attitude of reason, there is something that is similar to the elder brother of the parable, who cannot or who will not allow himself to be surprised by the gifts of the goodness of the father.

---

35. Romano Guardini, *Les fins des temps modernes* (Paris: Seuil, 1952) p. 66; German: *Das Ende der Neuzeit*.

20 The *Sequela Christi*[1]

> *The Christian who lives by faith has the duty to base his or her moral conduct upon that faith. And since the content of faith, Jesus Christ, the one who has revealed the divine love of the Trinity, took on the figure of the first Adam and assumed his sin at the same time as his anxieties, his perplexities and the decisions of his existence, the Christian is sure of being able to find in the second Adam the reality of the first human being, together with all of the moral problems which are proper to him.*
>
> H. U. von Balthasar, "On Christian Ethics and its Norms"

The introductory note which introduced the Nine Theses proposed by Hans Urs von Balthasar twenty-five years ago, in the context of the reflection of the International Theological Commission on Christian morality and on its norms provides, from the outset, the methodological principle of a Christocentric *ethos*; we do not need to search outside of the person of Jesus Christ for the foundation of upright moral conduct by reason of the Incarnation and of its implications. In the humanity of Jesus Christ, the moral question has been posed in all of its breadth, not only existential (the anxiety, the perplexities lived in the fragile condition of the human person and of which the Swiss theologian speaks), but it is also decisive for the Kingdom (in the sense in which the existential decisions of our existence are orientated towards the fulfilment of the Father's will). "It is the end alone which determines and which illuminates the way," the note adds.[2]

---

1. "The Sequela Christi" is the French version of an article published in Italian under the title «Ethos cristocentrico e virtù morali» in G. Russo (ed.), *La verità vi farà liberi*, with a presentation by Cardinal Joseph Ratzinger, *Itinerarium*, n. 12, 2004, pp. 125–135.
2. Commissio Theological Internationalis *"De ethica christiana et eius*

It was exactly in this same direction that the moral perspective of the encyclical, *Veritatis Splendor*, was directed. Starting from the dialogue in Matthew between Jesus and the rich young man, the text described the essential features of the moral problem, linking the question of moral norms to be observed to the call to the absolute good, which this question implied. This point of departure remains relevant for establishing a proper inter-relationship between Christ and the exercise of the moral virtues. We may centre moral action upon the Person of Christ, starting from several points of view, which the analysis which follows intends to summarize: the Christian acts like Christ by allowing himself to be inspired by the perfect model of conduct, he acts like this through the grace of Christ; he acts in Christ (*in Christo*) by participating in his action; he acts also for Christ, in view of Christ. This approach enables us to give content to the expression "following Christ" *(sequela Christi)*, seen as the synthetic principle for the virtuous conduct of the Christian. In order to illustrate the specifically virtuous character of conduct in imitation of Christ, in Christ and for Christ, we must show how, in reality, in each of its aspects, it is a matter of dispositions of conduct which are really stable and not just a succession of acts accomplished on the basis of the example of Jesus, in him and for him.

A First Approach: To Be Perfect

First of all, it will be appropriate to deepen our understanding of the concept of perfection, to which St Matthew refers, when rereading the dialogue between Jesus and the rich young man (Mt 19:16–21). In the question: "Master, what good must I do to inherit eternal life?" it is possible to detect a two-fold concern of the young man: the rightness of the act he is to accomplish and its

---

normis" (1974), "Novem theses qui a H.U. von Balthasar conscriptae et a CTI 'in forma generica' approbatae in Animadversio praevia". *Enchiridion Vaticanum*, 5, 29, p. 613. (International Theological Commission, "On Christian Ethics and its Norms," written by H.U. von Balthasar and approved *"in forma generica"* by the ITC).

purpose, obtaining eternal life. The acts to be undertaken, keeping the commandments recalled by Jesus, are not enough to satisfy his ultimate desire: "What else must I do?" This latter question expresses once more the perception of this man that his morally upright conduct is not sufficient to enable him to obtain what his heart desires and which the encyclical, *Veritatis Splendor*, subsequently calls "the fulfilment of his personal destiny," his "integral vocation,"[3] or again, "his participation in divine happiness."[4] The good that he has done up until now leaves the question of eternal life totally open. In this dialogue, we have a sort of paradox; on the one hand, respect for the commandments suffices and Jesus himself confirms this in his response to the first question of the rich young man. There is no trickery in the promise of eternal life, which is made to those who observe the Law and the commandments; on the other hand, it is the young man himself, who, although encouraged in his morally good life, expresses his concern in terms of what is missing. But, then, if he has done all that is necessary, what is it that he is lacking?

This Jesus reveals to him in two ways: through his presence and through his word.

Through his presence: before the Person of Jesus, the young man becomes aware that something within him is still lacking.[5] He has the intuition that, in Jesus, what he still seeks and desires is to be found; in his eyes, Jesus, in some way, must be linked to eternal life and, to some extent, must provide access to that life, which he desires so much.

Through his words: these confirm explicitly the young man's impression: "If you wish to be perfect, go, sell what you own, and give the money to the poor and you will have treasure in heaven; then, come, follow me" (Mt 19:21). The term "perfect" goes beyond the question that has been posed and opens up to the young man a perspective of becoming; it is no longer a question of doing

---

3. John Paul II, *Veritatis Splendor*, § 8.
4. *Ibid.* § 11.
5. Cf. *Ibid.* § 16.

something, but of becoming perfect. This perfection, which is no longer just something of a moral character, is expressed in the text by the qualification in Greek of *teleios*, which, in the evangelist Matthew, means the fulfilment of the Scriptures. The behaviour of the young man has been totally conformed to the demands contained in the old covenant, but it has not been achieved in the sense of a complete realization in the fulfilment of the plan of God. This kind of fulfilment of the Law and of the Prophets, in fact, is not to be found except in Jesus; it is precisely this which pushes the young man, leading him to ask Jesus for a response which would be capable of responding at the deepest level to his preoccupations. From this perspective, Jesus' reply means: "If you want everything which you have done to attain its greatest perfection, in regard to the Sacred Scriptures, whose demands you have out into practice, then, sell what you own..." Jesus' invitation includes two novel items: the good to be done knows no upper limit. To sell all one owns, in order to distribute it to the poor, is not only the surest way to be able to enter eternal life, but it will enable one to have a treasure in heaven. However, a gesture of this kind, which clearly carries with it a recompense (treasure), in Jesus' words, is linked immediately to the act of following him.

In truth, these two revelations constitute one single revelation; the purpose of giving everything to the poor is certainly the perspective needed to be able to obtain eternal life, but, at the same time, it is that of being united forever to the Person of Jesus. It is the Christ, who, in eternal life, will be the good in which he will rejoice eternally. In the words which they exchange, union with Christ *forever* is not mentioned explicitly, but it is suggested by the situation which is created by the sale of all his possessions; separating himself for all of them, is to reach the point of no return and of absolute novelty in the conduct of his own life. The life of this rich young man would only find its meaning in the fact of being with Jesus.

To Act like Christ: From Good Master to Interior Master

We could place ourselves at three different levels in order to understand what is meant by acting together with Christ. The first refers to the application of Christ's teachings to our own conduct; the relationship which the Christian holds with Christ is that of the disciple, who finds in the words of the Master the source of inspiration for our own good conduct. Jesus is at one and the same time the teacher and the master of doctrine.

The second is the level of a conduct which is inspired by the example of Christ, and which the disciple tries to imitate.

Finally, the third level refers to the interiority of the person, the place where Christ operates by transmitting to him his wisdom: "Christ himself is the source of all right knowledge" ("*Ipse Christus est autem fons omnis cognitionis rectae*").[6] It is not possible, methodologically, to separate these three levels of understanding; the words of Jesus take on the whole of their meaning in the light of his existence, his death, and his Resurrection, just as these events make it possible to understand retroactively his personal attitudes, the choices which he made, as also his relationships with the Apostles, his disciples, his own family, the fishermen, the sick, the publicans, the scribes and the pharisees.

To separate these different degrees of understanding would lead us to seeking in Jesus' moral teaching only that which could be found in continuity with the precepts of the Law. Then, there would be a danger, that of no longer seeing in Jesus the true fulfilment of the Law, and his most exalted teachings would seem to be reserved for only the very best of his disciples. Servais Pinckaers has shown how this defective methodology allowed the idea to gain ground,[7] according to which the Sermon on the Mount, for example, would be a moral doctrine incapable of application, an ideal beyond our reach. It is only when taken to-

---

6. St Bonaventure *Christus unus omnium magister, Sermo* IV, n. 1.
7. Cf. Steven Pinckaers, *The Sources of Christian Ethics* (Edinburgh: T. & T. Clark, 1995), pp. 134–140.

gether that the words of Jesus and his life constitute the ultimate criterion of judgment in moral matters.[8]

Thus, the disciple is called to imitate Jesus, who becomes the model for his or her behaviour. How is it possible to show the virtuous nature of a life modelled upon Christ? Two examples may prove useful. They concern two specific features of his teaching, the accent placed upon the human heart as the source of action and the love of enemies.

Jesus refers constantly to interiority as the source of human actions: all actions are born in the heart. We find him recalling this in various and different contexts: in teachings, according to which adulterous thoughts arise in the heart (cf. Mt 5:28), in associating murder with hatred for our brother (cf. Mt 5:22), in the appeal made to the disciples to learn from him ("I am meek and humble of heart," Mt 11:29), in the teaching of the Beatitudes ("Blessed are the pure in heart, for they shall see God", Mt 5:8). The idea common to all of these examples is that the heart is the centre of all human thoughts, good or bad, and that, consequently, it is the source of all human acts. It follows, in the first place, that it is in the stable attitude of the heart that we find the way to behave constantly in a just fashion, and also that the imitation of the model consists above all in having a heart similar to the heart of the Master. If intentions arise in the heart, then the question of virtuous action is focused upon the transformation of our own heart and of configuring it to the pure Heart of Christ. What is it that, over the course of time, is susceptible to modelling a human heart? It is the personal history of the subject, the actions he has performed, his stable relationships with other persons, and, in particular, his relationship with Christ, the relationship that structures his conduct as a whole.

The interiority of the heart of the disciple is not the place for an ethic of sentiment; the disciple is preserved from this danger by the fact that the Heart of Christ made itself known through

---

8. Cf. theses 1 and 2 of H. Schurmann, in *"Quattuor theses a H. Schürmann conscriptae"* in *Enchiridion Vaticanum*, 5, n.29, p. 649.

all of the actions which he accomplished throughout his earthly existence and which culminated in the gift of his own life.

The second example is the invitation that Jesus made for us to love our enemies. In order to understand the absolute novelty of this teaching, it would be good to reread what is said about this in the light of the Beatitudes, both in Matthew and in Luke. In Matthew, the series of the Beatitudes closes with the proclamation that those are truly blessed who are insulted, persecuted and subjected to calumny for the sake of Jesus; in Luke: "Blessed are you," says Jesus, "when people hate you, when they expel you, when they insult you and when they proscribe your name as infamous, for the sake of the Son of Man" (Lk. 6:22). In this way, those are proclaimed blessed who have enemies for the sake of Jesus. Jesus demands that his disciples love their enemies and pray for them (Mt 5:44, 6:28), and his requirement is valid for all time throughout their existence. Loving enemies does not admit of any limit (up to seventy times seven). This is a matter of behaviour which is stable, of a virtue, destined to be a merciful way of living. Let us observe that Jesus committed himself to the promise of a recompense in heaven.

The reason that Jesus gives for this love is unique; it is a matter of imitating the love of God himself ("In this way you will become children of your Father in heaven for he makes the sun shine on bad and good alike, and the rain to fall on the just and the unjust," Mt 6: 45). We take note of the fact that Jesus inserts the virtue of mercy into the perspective of being (you *will be*, you *will become*), and not in that of an action, pure and simple. The attention is directed both to the end that is desired (the recompense in heaven) and towards perfection (becoming children of the heavenly Father). In this example, we have an illustration of the fundamental connection in the Christian between the exercise of moral virtue and his filial condition and vocation. The divine filiation, to which every person is called, encompasses the whole of the conduct of the Christian and each one of those actions assumes the meaning of an act of love towards the Father.

Acting in Christ

The knowledge of the Father and the capacity of the Christian to fulfil his vocation to the full are only possible in the Son; the baptized person is introduced into the Paschal Mystery and cannot exercise the virtues except by the operation of the Holy Spirit, not by means of his own strength alone. He acquires knowledge in the faith, by adhering interiorly to divine love and to the form it has taken on in the gift which the Son has made of his life for the salvation of the world. Many people have asked themselves about the nature of such knowledge and about the place of the human being within such an activity of faith. St Augustine saw very well that to know God requires thinking about him *with attention and with desire*; thus, it is a matter of the spirit, but one that tends to become an activity of the heart. The Augustinian *cogitatio* does not imply in itself the use of concepts, because the language of the heart is proper to the interior person.[9] An analogous approach is to be found in St Bonaventure, with the notion of *intelligentia per cor*;[10] the knowledge of God becomes a journey of the spirit (seen as the highest or as the deepest part of the heart), which, at the end of various successive stages, discovers, and recognizes the presence of God. Here we have an act of love, in which the rational process is neither eliminated nor reduced, but in which it is integrated into an attitude of the heart that is searching. The work of the Holy Spirit is affirmed, who renders the soul capable of the theological virtues, restoring form to the divine image, and making it

---

9. It is important for the Doctor of grace that the *cogitatio* distance itself from any form of earthly desire, obliquely through some purification of the heart (*cor mundum*): «*Spiritus enim rectus est, credo, quo fit ut anima in veritate quaerenda deviare atque errare non possit. Qui profecto in ea non instauratur, nisi prius cor mundum sese cohibuerit et eliquaverit*», St Augustine, *De quant. An.*, XXXIII, 75, PL 32, p. 1076.
10. Knowledge is an ascesis and begins with purification; the spirit must return to itself by means of the memory; this exercise is impossible to the spirit that remains distracted by too many worries and by the imagination. (cf. St Bonaventure, *Journey of the Spirit to God*, IV, n. 1).

suitable for the heavenly Jerusalem, making it possible here below for it to exercise a capacity for spiritual hearing, sight, smell, taste, and touch; besides, the Seraphic Doctor reaffirms the need to allow oneself continually to be guided by Christ. Even though a person may be illuminated by the light of nature or by knowledge which has been acquired, no one is able to enter into themselves to rejoice in the Lord, unless this is through the intermediary who is Christ, who says: "I am the gateway. Anyone who enters through me will be saved; they enter in and go out, and they will find eternal pastures" (Jn 10:9).[11]

The image of the spiritual sense (hearing, smell, etc.) used by St Bonaventure, illustrates the fact that, in the present state of our knowledge, we do not yet have access to the joy and to the contemplation of the beautiful things of God, in a definitive quietude. The search for God remains a commitment of the whole of our being, appropriately symbolized by the spiritual senses. It is a union of the intention to the redemptive act of Christ. The knowledge of Christ in his work of salvation (words, acts, and offerings of sacrifice at the moment of the Passion) give to the believer the capacity to discern what is in conformity with this intention of the Lord, what is pleasing to him: thus, knowledge of Christ becomes knowledge of the good and of virtuous action. Spiritual experience is the occasion for a moral knowledge that is orientated towards the transformation of the heart of the believer in the Holy Spirit, rendering him capable of acting well in a stable manner and of practising the virtues.

The behaviour of the Christian is the fruit of the activity of the Spirit in him, without this conduct thereby ceasing to be proper to him as such. The process of the action of the Holy Spirit is that of an interiorization of the action of Christ in the very act of sacrificing himself. The Spirit stimulates the believer to act in a similar dynamic of sacrifice. The good conduct of the believer is rooted in the gift of the Holy Spirit and it displays itself in the various fruits that correspond to the different virtues. The moral

---

11. *Ibid.* IV, n. 5.

virtues thus become stable dispositions in the heart of the person, transformed by the Holy Spirit. They do not allow the person to respond to norms extrinsic to his liberty, but on the contrary, they express a demand that is interior to that freedom itself, namely, to follow the inspirations of the Spirit in their different moral choices. The works of someone who acts in Christ are of a spiritual nature: "The works that you do in the flesh are spiritual, because it is in Jesus Christ that you accomplish everything," St Ignatius of Antioch told the Ephesians.[12]

Affirming the pre-eminence of the action of the Spirit requires that we recognize the necessity for the believer to be united in a stable manner to the Person of Christ. The moral life can express itself here in terms of friendship; the continual presence of Christ in the heart of the disciple is a witness to the stability of his life of virtue. United to Christ, the believer fulfils his filial vocation; his virtuous acts are bearers of the same filial dynamism as are the acts of Christ and they orientate the disciple's love towards the Father. The exercise of a person's filiation is not open to human freedom on its own; in the same way, in order for a child of God to persevere in his good conduct, they need the dynamism of the Holy Spirit, who alone is capable of giving his stable character to our disposition to act for the good.

The virtuous life of the believer also offers to Christ himself a mediation, so that *hic et nunc*, he may continue to act; in the acts of the Christian, it is Christ who acts ("It is Christ who lives in me" says St Paul, Gal 2:20). The idea of an action of Christ that continues in the heart of believers shows that the sacrifice of the Son of Man, a perfect sacrifice, bears efficacious fruits until the end of the world. The virtuous action of the disciple, in a certain way, brings to fulfilment in the course of history the sacrifice by Jesus of his own life for the salvation of the world;[13] "I find my joy in the suffering I endure for you and I make up in my own body

12. St Ignatius of Antioch, *Ad Eph*. VIII, 2.
13. A. Feuillet, *Le mystère de l'Amour divin dans la théologie johannique* (Paris: Gabalda, 1972), p. 80. "It is Christ dying on the Cross who bears fruit, by attracting people to himself; in Jn 15:4,5,8, it is human beings

what is lacking in the sufferings of Christ, for the sake of his Body, which is the Church" (Col 1:24). It is interesting to see that the Resurrection of the Redeemer has not consigned to the past the historical significance of the salvation effected by him; in fact, all those who live and who act in him, immersed within his merits, participate in this work of salvation. Historically, the salvation of Christ continues to be offered by people in our days through the acts of those who are his true disciples. Here, we may associate the action of Christ with that of those Christians who live in him, expressing the sacramental life in terms of the actual presence of the salvation of the Redeemer. The salvation effected by Christ is rendered present sacramentally to the human person in all periods of time.[14]

Docility to the promptings of the Holy Spirit can be expressed in terms of a state of grace. The person united to Christ does not develop within himself all of the virtues to an equal degree; the free offering of his own gifts which the Holy Spirit makes to Christians can manifest itself through the exercise of this virtue or of that. Every saint is a manifestation of some aspect of the holiness of Christ. It remains true that the holiness of Christ requires that no virtue be neglected, since all of the virtues are linked to one another,[15] but it is only in Christ that we find the perfection of virtue in each one of its dimensions.

Furthermore, we may note that the presence of authentic charisms in the heart of a believer may be accompanied at the human level by entirely original features rooted in the subjectivity

---

    united in a living way to Christ...who bear fruit, which means that they attract people to Christ in their turn."

14. Here, we may refer to our contribution to the international Congress in Lugano in 1995; Jean Laffitte, "Contemporanéité du Christ à l'homme de tous les temps dans le premier chapitre de l'encyclique, *Veritatis Splendor*, in G. Borgonovo (a cura di), *Gesù Cristo, legge vivente e personale della santa Chiesa, Atti del IX Colloquio Internazionale di teologia in Lugano, 15–17 giugno, 1995*, (Casale Monferrato: Piemme, 1996), pp. 211–223.

15. D. Biju-Duval, «À travers l'équilibre singulier des vertus qu'élabore sa liberté, l'homme épanouit positivement sa personnalité morale unique» in Id. *Le psychique et le spirituel* (Paris: Emmanuel, 2001), p. 90.

of the person who acts. The saints always surprise us, when we compare them to the norm of human behaviour; besides, the Holy Spirit may allow this or that defect of personality to remain in a human person.[16] We can understand that the criterion of a just life cannot be found in a perfection that is human, but only in the permanence of a living friendship with Christ, expressed in the gifts conferred by the Holy Spirit. Moreover, although it is not able of itself to obtain the gifts necessary to live a faithful life with Christ, human freedom, nevertheless, does have the power to refuse such gifts, breaking in this way this divine friendship; the consequence of this rupture is the cessation of the presence of the Spirit in the heart of the believer. The person loses his capacity to accomplish meritorious acts at the theologal level and no longer has access to this source which makes his own spiritual faculties dynamic. The abandonment of the virtues marks the condition of the person in a state of serious sin.

It is in this dramatic aspect of the spiritual existence of the Christian that the limits of the identification with the life of virtue in the filial condition inaugurated by the Spirit appear. In fact, the identity of the believer who sins gravely does not cease to be filial at the ontological level, even if that person has become incapable of receiving spiritual goods. In the transgression and in the consequences that derive from it, there is always present a refusal of filial dependence; here, we situate ourselves at the level of a subject fixed in the deadly choice of sin. However, considered from the point of view of the call of God, the offer of filiation continues to be proposed to the sinner, even if in the unique form of those demands which are linked to conversion. The possibility of the sinner returning to God is one of the most important aspects of his filial condition, as is illustrated, for example, by the fact that in the Gospels, the figure which best expresses the divine action of mercy is that of a father

---

16. We may think of the imperfections present in the character of certain saints, a source of mortification, and then of maintaining a conduct which is both humble and yet full of filial trust.

towards his son. Although the prodigal child has indeed deprived himself of all the rights and privileges connected to the condition of son, yet he finds himself once more introduced into communion with the father, not however by reason of the merit of a virtuous life, but by reason of an initiative of the father, which is absolute and gratuitous.

Acting for Christ

The third and last aspect of action centred upon Christ would have to consider not only the presence of the Master as the end of the life of virtue (being united to him) but also the presence of the heavenly Father, who makes himself known only in the Son. This revelation is at the heart of the confidences that Jesus made to his friends in St John's Gospel. Like every disciple, Philip wishes to learn something from Jesus about God. He has already heard that God is Father. His exclamation: "Show us the Father" (Jn 14:8) is a coherent request for someone who is striving to live as a disciple of Jesus. It remains for him to discover in the person of his master the divine face of the Father. In truth, the whole of Jesus's teaching is nothing other than the manifestation of the love of the Father. "As the Father has loved me, so also I have loved you" (Jn 15:9). How can we not see in this truth, which Jesus revealed to those who followed him and who loved him, the definitive extension of Jesus's response in his dialogue with the rich young man in St Matthew's Gospel, in the passage with which we began? The "Come, follow me!" of Matthew finds its full and definitive intelligibility in the verse from John; beyond the fascination for Jesus, in all the features of his person, we meet God as Father. Even the gift of eternal life finds its concrete expression in this unheard of teaching, which reveals in the Son the face of the Father: "Do you not believe that the Father is in me and that I am in the Father?" (Jn 14:10). This reciprocal inclusion generates another, one which is decisive for the disciples: "Remain in me, as I remain in you" (Jn 15:5).

Virtuous action, then, is a condition for being united to Jesus; it is a requirement of the *sequela*: "If you keep my commandments, you will remain in my love" (Jn 15:10). The disciple acts well through the love of Christ; it is by love that the commandments are observed. This kind of conduct assures the disciple of being in union with the Father, not by reason of his own merits, but by reason of the presence of the Father in the Person of Jesus. The revelation of Jesus continues in the same verse 10: "If you keep my commandments, you will remain in my love, just as I keep my Father's commandments and remain in his love." The sign that Jesus remains in a permanent way in the love of the Father, according to this passage, is the fact that he has observed his commandments. It is interesting to note that, in this same verse, Jesus speaks of two types of commandments: his own and those of the Father. The disciple is invited to observe the commandments of Jesus, which are summarised in the single commandment of love, as the text of John explains further on: "that you love one another, just as I have loved you" (Jn 15:12), but it is in a singular and unique way that Jesus observed the commandments of the Father; he did this in such a way as to fulfil the ineffable plan of salvation.[17] His mission was unique, for the sole reason that he is our one and only Savior, but the disciples have been made participants in this mission: "Christ, dead and risen again, offers himself as source and as model," writes Biju-Duval.[18]

In these two chapters, John 14 and 15, we find all of the elements of a Christocentric ethos: the unique action of Jesus in favour of us human beings, fulfilling the will of the Father, our action as human beings invited, in imitation of the Master, to love one another, thus keeping the commandments of Jesus himself, the disciple remains in his love and, in him, each one remains in

---

17. Jesus's filiation is unique, as Durwell has explained: F.-X. Durwell, *Le Père, Dieu et son mystère* (Paris: Cerf, 1980), p. 30: "Jesus's filiation is absolute; there is no-one on earth who is the son or daughter of someone else so truly and to the same extent; it is the Son, who is essentially thus, who is permanently and who lives permanently in such a generation of fulness."
18. D. Biju-Duval *Op.cit.*, p. 53.

the love of the Father. The disciple seeks friendship with Christ and finds in him union with the Father.[19] This connection is expressed by John by means of the image of the vine and the branches, in such a way as to suggest at one and the same time, both the union of the disciple with Christ ("I am the vine; you are the branches," Jn 15:5) and also the fruitfulness to which the life of virtue of the disciple is called and of which he or she has to give an account to the Father; the Father is the vinedresser. "Every branch in me that bears no fruit, he roots out and every branch which does bear fruit, he prunes, so that it may bear more fruit" (Jn 15:1–2). Louis Bouyer identified the fruit of the union of the vine and the branches with the loving union between Christ and those who are his own, expressing in this way the circular nature of the loving life of the believer.[20] Thus, it is only by being united to Christ that he or she is able to act well, and it is only in acting well that the disciple can be fruitful, remaining in Christ in love.

Union with God is a loving union. It implies that all of the spiritual dynamisms of the disciple are unified in a life of virtue, animated by charity; charity operates in the heart of the Christian like a principle of action, which is perfect and free. "Charity is said to be the form of virtuous acts," writes St Thomas,[21] because it produces of itself specific acts of the love of God; it transforms every act of virtue into an act of love of God. In the end, the moral conduct of the Christian is action *propter Deum*.

Friendship with Christ implies necessarily love for the Father by means of the exercise of all of the virtues.

---

19. Livio Melina, "Amore, desiderio e azione in Cristo," in ID. *Cristo e il dinamismo dell'agire: linee di rinnovamento della teologia morale fondamentale*, (Rome: Mursia, PUL, 2001), p. 29.
20. Louis Bouyer, *Le quatrième Évangile : introduction à l'évangile de Jean: traduction et commentaire* (Tournai: Casterman, 1955), p. 205: "The branches of Christ must bear fruit ; otherwise, they are condemned to the fire, but the fruit which they bear comes completely from their belonging to Christ and are his fruit. And what is this fruit? The fruit of the organic unity of Christ and those who are his own; it is their union in love."
21. St Thomas Aquinas, *Summa Theologiae*, IIa IIae, q. 23, a.8.

Forgiveness

21 LOVE AND FORGIVENESS[1]

The delay of some weeks in the publication of the encyclical, *Deus Caritas Est*, in some way has been an advantage; in fact, 2006 marks the fiftieth anniversary of the publication of another encyclical, *Haurietis Aquas in Gaudio*, which Pope Pius XII offered to the Church and to the world on May 15, 1956. This text, the last encyclical which was truly Christological, sought to put forward the fundamental principles, inspired by Scripture and the Tradition, for the authentic worship of the Sacred Heart and to explain its symbolism. From a Trinitarian perspective, Pius XII saw in the Heart of Christ the symbol and the résumé of all of the fundamental mysteries of Christianity, from that of the eternal Trinity to that of the Church; putting it more precisely, he saw in it the place in which the gift of divine love (*caritas*) and of the Holy Spirit was made:

> The Spirit, the Paraclete, is the reciprocal love of the Father and of the Son, sent by both Father and Son ...This charity is a gift both of the Heart of Jesus and of his Spirit; and this Spirit is himself the Spirit of the Father and of the Son; from him the Church came to birth, in order to spread in a marvellous way throughout the whole universe ... It is this divine charity, the very precious gift of the Heart of Christ and of his Spirit, which inspired in the Apostles and in the martyrs the heroic strength to preach

---

1. "Love and Forgiveness" is the text of an article published in Italian under the title "Amore e perdono", in English under the title "Love and Forgiveness", in Spanish "Amor y Perdón", in the context of a volume offered by the professors of the Pontifical Institute. John Paul II, to his Holiness, Benedict XVI, entitled *La Via dell'Amore. Riflessioni sull'enciclica Deus Caritas Est di Benedetto XVI* in L. Melina and C. Anderson (ed.), Rai Eri/ Pont. Istituto Giovanni Paolo II, Città del Vaticano, 2006), pp. 135–146.

and to give witness to the truth of the Gospel, even to the shedding of their blood.[2]

At a distance of fifty years, *Deus Caritas Est* develops the dimensions of love (*eros* and *agapè*), whose presence in God it illustrates, not in a Trinitarian interpretation—that was not the object of the text—but in terms of the gift made to human beings, a gift which fosters a response of love. A strictly dogmatic approach, undoubtedly, would have developed further the study of the relationships between the Father and the Son, as also the pneumatological dimension of Love in God. In truth, these features are very much present in *Deus Caritas Est*, but it is as if they are hinted at when the attention is directed to the gift of God, which he makes to humanity. By offering himself, it is his Love that God offers. The intention of the encyclical is fundamentally one of evangelization; it seems to be preoccupied by the urgency of the need to proclaim the love which God bears towards us human beings, to each person in particular, making that person in their turn capable of loving not just God, in response to the gift which has been received, but also his neighbour. Basically, the text reformulates the content and the exercise of the faith in the following way: to believe in God is to believe in his love in action (the content of the faith). The act of faith is a loving adhesion to the Love that God has shown first (the exercise of faith). From this angle, the Church is not reduced to being an assembly of believers adhering to the articles of faith in themselves, but she is a "community of love" in action.

The directly evangelizing character of the encyclical spares nothing in regard to a rigorous, double methodological principle:

- Understanding the love of God presupposes a contemplation of the open side of Christ (DCE, § 7 and 12); and
- The Eucharistic nature of divine Love offers the Christological and sacramental foundation (on the basis of which) we can understand correctly the teaching of Jesus about love" (§ 14).

---

2. Pius XII, *Haurietis Aquas in Gaudio*, § 41.

Love and Forgiveness

The presence of numerous passages in which reference is made explicitly to the pierced Heart of Christ, in a certain way, makes of *Deus Caritas Est* an extension of *Haurietis Aquas*. More fundamentally, the encyclical joins forgiveness to divine Love, which is one of the essential themes of this text. We would not be able to understand the nature of this Love that God bears towards human beings, if we were to forget that it is a Love that forgives. We shall see it later on: the references in the encyclical to the Heart of Jesus, the place of love and of divine forgiveness; how the logic of forgiveness fits in with that of love; the logic of the Eucharist, a unity of gift and of response.

The Heart of Jesus in the Encyclical Deus Caritas Est

Looking upon Christ and the Witness of the Disciple

The first passage in which the Heart of Christ is mentioned unites the two texts of the fourth Gospel: Jn 19:34 and Jn 7:37–38 in a way which is classic (DCE, § 7). The event of Jesus' death and of the shedding of his blood and water from his side is the source which enables the disciple in his turn to become a *fount of living water*, according to the prophetic words of the Lord. The perspective of the encyclical is specifically Johannine.

The verses which relate the death of Jesus are among those which have most been commented upon in the Tradition, in particular in the medieval period. De la Potterie remarks somewhat pointedly that this abundance was in contrast to a certain contemporary exegesis.[3] According to the text of the gospel:

> One of the soldiers pierced his side with his lance and immediately there came forth both blood and water. This the witness of one who saw this, and that witness is truthful, and he knows that he speaks the truth—so that you too may believe. Because this happened so that the Scriptures would be fulfilled: Not one bone of his shall you hurt. And

---

3. Cf. De la Potterie, *Le coté transpercé de Jésus*; lecture delivered at Paray-le-Monial in October, 1990.

in another passage, it says further: they looked upon the one they had pierced (Jn 19: 34–37).

The encyclical does not go into the debate which the traditional interpretation of the pierced Heart provoked; in the text of St John the wound is designated as the side which was pierced: in § 7, Benedict XVI make the traditional interpretation his own, while in § 12, taking up verse 37, he speaks of "the gaze which is directed towards the open side." Here the broad interpretation of Pius XII is confirmed, who at this point indicated that what is written in the Gospel of St John (Jn. 19: 34) "about the side of Christ opened up by the soldier must be said equally about his Heart, which had been reached by the blow of the lance given by him, to be assured that Jesus Christ crucified had died."[4]

A second point of interpretation characterizes the encyclical: it speaks of the side opened, whereas the verb *nusso* (from the aorist *enuxen*) used by the evangelist is translated by *strike* or *pierce*. There again, the choice of the Tradition, inspired by the translation of the Vulgate, is a particularly felicitous one: "*it opened*" is what *enoixen* means. By "opening" the side of Jesus, the lance traces the path that goes to his Heart. To contemplate the open side, according to Benedict XVI, is to understand that God is love: "It is there that this truth can be contemplated" (DCE, § 12). Through the opened side, the gateway to life is opened up (the *vitae ostium*, so dear to St Augustine).

This kind of contemplation is not passive, but it is transforming; by means of this act, the disciple, that is to say, the one who believes in Christ according to the very words of Jesus, satisfies his thirst, drinking at the fount of the Holy Spirit.

> If anyone is thirsty, let him come to me and he who believes in me, let him drink. As the Scripture says, "From his breast flowed streams of living water." In this way, he pointed to the Holy Spirit, whom those who would believe in him would have to receive; in fact, there was no Spirit as yet because Jesus had not yet been glorified (Jn 7:37–39).

---

4. Pius XII, *Haurietis Aquas in Gaudio*, §3.

The juxtaposition of the two texts is in the context of the dialectic illustrated by the encyclical between ascending and descending love (the love which searches for God and the love which transmits). The priority of the gift received is affirmed, the precedence of divine love; let us note this observation, that the love of God never ceases to have priority; it is then a constant source of solicitation for a response to be given and it is also the content of what the encyclical, *Deus Caritas Est*, calls, several times, an experience. "The human being, living in fidelity to the one and only God, himself has the experience of one who is loved by God" (DCE, § 9). With regard to the relationship between God and the human being expressed by the Song of Songs, it is said that this latter "has become in Christian literature, as in Jewish literature, a source of mystical knowledge and experience" (§ 10). In §17, the Pope speaks of the liturgy of the Church, of its prayer and of the living community of believers, in whom we have experience of the love of God. Further on, the union of the will of the human being to the will of God is referred to the experience "that, in fact, God is more intimate to me than I am to myself" (§ 17).

The Unique Experience of the Love of God

The experience that is described in these different passages specifies a primordial event, an encounter (an intimate encounter, § 18) with a personal and loving God. This experience is foundational, because it establishes the human being in a relationship with God which banishes fear, in order to allow nothing but loving fear to subsist, made up at once of feelings of reverence (the God who is near does not cease to be God) and of the anxiety of being able to respond to this love which is offered (the love, which beyond feelings, really does establish the disciple in love).

The experience of the love of God constitutes an unexpected upheaval in human existence, causing it to refocus upon what is essential, extending itself to all dimensions of our life in the world, and thus to all of our neighbours, and leading ultimately to the Heart which has been pierced. The loving disciple makes the action of the Lord his own and integrates it by grace into his life. In this sense, the Cross is at once the place in which the sacrificial love of God offers itself for contemplation and also the place in which the disciple is reunited to the Master.

The experience that is at issue here has established the human being in a relationship of love with God. In Benedict XVI's encyclical, the love of God is specified in terms of its function of reconciliation. The dimension of forgiveness is introduced from § 10 onwards:

> The eros of God for the human being, as we have said, is at the same time totally agape. This is not only because it is given in a completely gratuitous way, without any preceding merit, but also because it is a love which forgives."

Further on, it is said that this love greatly surpasses the aspect of gratuity.

As we shall see below, gratuity is a feature that specifies every act of love and every act of forgiveness. The gratuity of love, like that of forgiveness, expresses the fact that these are not manipulated in the interests of something else. Observing that it is not enough on its own to characterize forgiveness, the encyclical introduces a notion which is not spelt out explicitly, but which we could call the excellence of forgiveness, in order to underline its unique and unlimited nature.

At its deepest level, Christian experience is accompanied by signs of the transcendence found in human existence (the forgiving love, of which the encyclical speaks, refers first of all to the transcendent love of God) and it is expressed in the life of the human being through the integration into his existence of a new way of life (conversion). The response of the person who is converted forms part of the experience of the love of God because it confirms the authentic nature of the latter. We note, quite simply, that such an experience is utterly unique and is distinguished by circumstances and by a personal history that are equally unique. Nevertheless, it possesses an intelligibility of such a kind that it can perhaps be transmitted through witness, in two senses of that term: in relation to the facts (the event) and as the witness of life (the coherence of the response). Furthermore, it becomes an objective source of richness for the whole Body. The basic experiences of those who have offered themselves up to the divine love has been revealed to them has been able not only to enrich the community of believers with new members but has also given birth at times to a teaching structured by the foundational event of the primordial encounter, thereby authenticated as an objective enrichment for all believers.[5]

The Human Heart in Tune with the Heart of Christ

The sacrifice which Christ made of himself on the Cross acts upon the hearts of human beings, making them capable of sacrificing themselves in their turn. It will be useful here to take up once more what the Pope pointed out about the need not to reduce the life of Christ to a mere example of morality and, for this reason, instead, to start from a basis which is Christological and sacramental (a Eucharistic logic, to which we shall return).

> The move which he makes from the Law and the Prophets to the double commandment of love of God and of neighbour, as well as the fact that the whole existence of faith unfolds the central character of this precept, are not simply matters of a morality which could exist autonomously alongside faith in Christ; faith, worship and ethos inter-penetrate one another mutually, as one single reality, which finds its form in the encounter with the agape of God (DCE § 14).

---

5. For example, the experience of Saul of Tarsus on the road to Damascus has been a source of fecundity for the whole Church in that it has given to the whole teaching of the Apostle its own specific characteristics; in the same way, the discovery by St Augustine of the love of God and of the demands that it makes for a change of life gave to the future doctor of the Church his deepest sensitivity for the primacy of grace and the dramatic nature of salvation (the Augustinian *conversio*). In truth, the same remark could be made about all of the saints; the form in which their holiness has been clothed has become a universal source of teaching for the whole Church.

We need to avoid a double danger; on the one side that of moral reductionism, in which the Christian life is presented as a pure imitation of the action of Christ; on the other side, that of conceiving this conformation as a kind of indistinct union with the divine, as a grace without the real commitment of personal responsibility. Neither Pelagianism nor spiritualism: conformation to Christ arises from a gift of the Holy Spirit, who comes to inhabit the interiority of the person, in other words, to dwell in that intimate place in which that gift is welcomed and honored: the heart. Human action, renewed in this way, arises from the contemplation of the Heart of Christ, where the most supreme act of love is accomplished and from where the gift of the Spirit of God flows forth. In this way, the Heart of Christ makes the person capable of acting in a supernaturally fruitful manner. The presence of the Holy Spirit in that person's heart becomes the condition for behaviour that is susceptible of resembling the action of Christ and so of being pleasing to the Father. In the light of this Johannine understanding, two particular actions of Jesus become paradigmatic: the washing of the feet, which is *par excellence* the act of a servant, and the sacrifice of his own life, which is the greatest act of love.

Finally, we find two references to the Heart of Christ at the end of the second part of the encyclical: the first puts forward the example, in Mary, of the most intimate union with God. In her, the condition has been fulfilled for that transformation of the human heart, which enables it, in its turn, and as promised by her Son, according to the text cited at the beginning (Jn. 7:38), to become a source, from which "streams of living water will flow." The second reference, in the final prayer addressed to Mary, expresses the intention that we should become, in our turn, "sources of living water, in a world that is thirsty" (§ 42).

The Logic of Love and the Logic of Forgiveness

It is from the dynamism of human love, in the first place, that the encyclical draws its unifying force; it unites the two terms of the relationship, in turn the point of departure and the point of arrival, in a double movement. It does this by means of a process of maturation, which the philosopher, Karol Wojtyla, happily designates by means of the term *integration*, meaning by that, from a moral perspective, the capacity of human beings to submit their physical and affective dynamisms to direction by their spiritual faculties. In the text of the encyclical, Benedict XVI employs the term purification, which brings out more the permanence of *eros*, completely assumed (purified) by *agapè*. In fact, it is the first purpose of the text to offer a realistic vision of love, avoiding the well-known forms of opposition between those two dimensions. Starting from human love, explained in this way, it would then be possible to speak of the Love of God.

At the beginning, the encyclical also brings out another constitutive element of love, without developing it, the presence of the two movements of giving and of receiving. The act of receiving, of welcoming, the love of another person is something which structures the person as such. It could even be said that this act is an originary structuring feature in the psychological and affective genesis of the human being,[6] an experience offered to every person who discovers that they have been preceded by the unconditional love of their parents (at least in a normal experience of the family). Starting from human love, made it possible to introduce the theme of divine Love, considering it first of all from the position of the one who receives it and who then becomes capable of transmitting it in their turn. Where will the disciple be able to find this Love? In its source, in the Heart of Jesus, which has been pierced, which is the place where this love of God is offered, inexhaustibly, to human beings.

---

6. Cf. two texts where we have had the opportunity to develop this point: "Esperienza dell'amore e Rivelazione", *Anthropotes* XX/1 (2005), pp. 23–34 and "Qu'est-ce qu'une anthropologie filiale?" in *L'antropologia della teologia morale secondo l'enciclica, Veritatis Splendor*: Symposium organised by the Congregation for the Doctrine of the Faith, September, 2003 (Vatican City: Libreria Editrice Vaticana, 2006), pp. 73–88. (Translator's note: for the second of these, cf. above, pp. xxx–xxx.)

> The one who wishes to bestow love must also receive love as a gift. To be sure, as the Lord tells us, the person can become the source from which streams of living water flow (cf. Jn 7:37–38). But, in order to become such a source, that person himself or herself must drink always anew from that primary and originary source, who is Jesus Christ, from that Heart which has been pierced and from which the love of God flows forth (cf. Jn 19:34, DCE § 7).

Here we think of the affirmation of *Dives in Misericordia*: "To manifest the Father as love and as mercy, in the consciousness of Christ himself, is to express the fundamental truth of his mission as the Messiah."[7] And, further on:

> To approach Christ in the mystery of his Heart enables us to stop at this point—in a certain sense at the central point and yet, at the human level, at the most accessible point—of the revelation of the merciful love of the Father, which constitutes the key content of the Messianic mission of the Son of man.[8]

The experience of the Love of God begins in this way through a gift that is received and welcomed. The encyclical illustrates the contours of a Christian existence that is informed by divine charity. The Love that God offers to every person is always an act of forgiveness, because in every case (except that of Mary), it is people who are sinners who are united to him in this way. Everything that can be said about divine Love *ad extra* can certainly be said about divine forgiveness; the forgiveness of God is always first and never ceases to be first ("I was a sinner from my mother's womb" (Ps 50:7). It expresses a divine fidelity, which never denies itself and which remains infinitely available. The encyclical develops this idea first of all in its expression through the manifestation of divine holiness in relation to people who are unfaithful and adulterous. The cardinal sin, if we may put it like this, is always expressed by the term that desig-

---

7. John Paul II, *Dives in Misericordia*, § 3.
8. *Ibid.* § 13.

nates a betrayal of love. Every offence against God is a betrayal of love, since it is committed against him who loves us unconditionally (gratuity) and who never ceases to love us. The forgiveness offered is the glory of God and it is this which specifies God's conduct towards the people of Israel: "I shall not give free rein to the course of my anger, I shall not destroy Ephraim again, because I am God and not man; I am the Holy One in your midst" (Hos. 11:9). The text sees in these words something like an unveiling of the mystery of the Cross, which is to come. The fulfilment of divine forgiveness on Calvary is expressed here through the original image of God who follows the human person (DCE § 10). The demand involved in the Incarnation includes the assumption of the mortal nature of the human being. Thus, the crucifixion of Jesus is, in this sense, the way by which God made man *follows* man, even unto death. This image is illuminating because it enables us to understand clearly that, in this act, the Word takes on everything that belongs to the nature of the human being and in particular death, the consequence of their sin.

For the human being, the move from the gratuity of love to what lies beyond it in the gratuity of forgiveness is born of contemplation. The attitude of the true pastor, according to Gregory the Great, quoted by Benedict XVI, consists in bearing the infirmities and the needs of others, but in a way which is profoundly interior (*per pietatis viscera*); this requires that transformation of the heart, of which we spoke above. Here it is a matter of an active compassion (*transferat*), which is not transposed into a mere feeling of superficial compassion. The *viscera pietatis* evoke the entrails of mercy (*splagchna*) of the father of the prodigal son, of whom St, Luke says that his "*entrails shivered*" between the moment he perceived his son and the moment in which the latter began to run to meet him (Lk 15:20). According to Gregory, thanks to his contemplation, the pastor reproduces the sentiments of the father. Compassion is a time of forgiveness, just as it is a time of love. It is the desire for, and the will towards, the good of the other that, in this way, makes us consider the sufferings which that person bears as a burden to take off their shoulders and to carry ourselves; in the first place, in themselves they constitute an obstacle to the good of the person who is loved.[9] In the figure of the merciful father of the parable, who incarnates the figure of the Father of all mercy, love, and forgiveness constitute but one single reality. His forgiveness expresses the quality of his love to the highest degree.

The experience that every person has of the Love of God is inseparable from the experience of his forgiveness, by reason of what God is and because of the holiness of his name. The human being discovers not only that he is loved, but that he is loved with such a love that it transforms that person and renders him just. God does not excuse. He is not complicit in the acts of abandonment and of treachery of his children, but he makes them just by penetrating to the depths of their subjectivity through his Spirit. He makes them better, that is to say, fully themselves, capable of loving and of forgiving. It is their hearts that are changed.

The human experience of forgiveness is, itself too, structured by a double movement, that of forgiving and that of being forgiven. The experience of forgiveness, which is desired, asked for and received, requires also a level of maturation; it introduces the offender into a work of truth, which is brought about in him and which demands time. The requirement to recognize their fault and the consequences of that fault upon its victim (admission and confession of sins) both reveals the person to himself as unjust and places him before the necessity of being freed from the debt he owes. This latter element implies that, by means of the act that he has committed, he has wounded the nature of a relationship. Humanly speaking, the offence is always an injustice, because it violates the natural order of the relationship

---

9. It is only later on that the sufferings of those we love can be seen as a stage on the way to their true good. The first reaction of love leads us to consider them first of all with compassion.

between human beings. Peace at the social level can only be restored if this initial order of justice is restored. No doubt, human justice will require that there be a penalty and punishment. At the personal level, however, the person who is culpable becomes aware that, apart from his victim, he has touched a dimension which is absolute. The experience of remorse and of culpability, which perdures at times after the fulfilment of the penalty, shows that a full reconciliation of the guilty person with himself is rendered possible only by him becoming the recipient of a forgiveness which is *other*, one which is indeed capable of justifying the offender to the very depths of his interiority, to where no human justice is capable of penetrating. The experience of forgiveness which is awaited for a serious injustice calls for the action of God, the gift of a Love which is always available. The divine mercy which forgives human beings takes on all the demands of justice in that efficacy which is its distinguishing feature, that of rendering the unjust person just:

> Human beings exercise mercy as human beings, but God will be merciful towards them as God. There is an enormous difference between the compassion of a human being and that of God, and they are as distant one from the other as evil is from the good.[10]

The second movement of human reconciliation is forgiveness that is given. The decision to forgive demands is also a process of maturation, for it is only when it has taken on the form of a decision that forgiveness can operate effectively. The stages which precede this make the human journey of forgiveness a complex one; the desire for vengeance, which is a perversion of the natural requirement of justice (the *vindicta* of the Romans); the rancour which identifies the guilty person with the offence they have committed and which inevitably engenders hatred for the aggressor; finally, the false motives for forgiveness which render forgiveness impure: the desire to establish a personal superiority, seeking the glory of clemency, or political calculation.

---

10. St John Chrysostom, *In Mattheum Homil.* XV, PG, vol. 57, col. 227.

When the aspiration to forgiveness has overcome such obstacles as these that may arise, forgiveness becomes an act of love and it is not disinterested in its beneficiaries; on the contrary, it is to that person that forgiveness is offered, it is the guilty person whom forgiveness intends to re-establish in their dignity and in their freedom. Forgiveness is fundamentally altruistic, and, in this sense, it is gratuitous, like any act of disinterested love. However, it goes beyond gratuity to the extent that, humanly speaking, the person who forgives gives up the exercise of his personal right that justice be done to him. Thus, forgiveness is essentially of a sacrificial nature. Sacrifice goes beyond a free gift, since it re-establishes an equilibrium in the order of relationships, without necessarily passing by way of the detour of distributive justice, which, moreover, is often powerless. The person who forgives assumes in some way the debt of the one who had committed the offence. We have seen that love is a gift, the bearer of a final purpose to unite. Forgiveness is a perfect gift (*per-donum*), the bearer of a redemptive purpose. It aims to bestow once more upon the culpable person their dignity and their justice, as it was before the offence.

Thus, it is that the two logics, that of love and that of forgiveness, come together, for every act of true forgiveness is also an act of love, one which recognizes and which honours the dignity of the other person.

Here there are two commonly expressed objections that arise. The first objection considers that forgiveness should not be understood as a duty, since, in some way, that would not respect the demands of justice in human society. There would be a kind of irrationality in forgiveness, which would disturb the rules of social life, would render its laws a failure, and would represent a danger to the balanced ordering among citizens. It would not respect the character of moral obligation, which is inscribed in justice, since it is said that there exist some acts that are *unpardonable*.[11] At the juridical level, these acts are described as *im-*

---

11. The two terms 'unpardonable' and 'imprescriptible' have been the object

prescriptible. The second objection is that forgiveness would only be acceptable insofar as it were to remain exceptional.[12] To sum it up, it would be like a privilege in an aristocratic ethic.

The first difficulty that has been raised is a real one; first of all, by the term *unpardonable*, people refer to the fact that, at times, an act is juridically or morally irreparable, even at the symbolic level. However, the term includes also another nuance, that of being *incapable of being expiated*, which implies a definitive judgment as to the impossibility that the person who is culpable may be some day transformed; in fact, expiation undoubtedly has the meaning of making reparation, but it also means changing the guilty person through the suffering of the punishment which they endure. We can see that such a judgment is one of a religious nature, even if it is a kind of secularization of hell. In actual fact, the question of what is unpardonable cannot remain very long in the philosophical domain. Very quickly, it will become theological and then it takes on the form of a refusal, in theory, that a pardon may be granted, even if it is divine. The question could be summed up like this: Does God have the right to pardon a crime which, humanly speaking, is unpardonable?

---

of considerable analysis in the philosophical literature for more than half a century. In the French-speaking world, these studies have been diffused by several authors, among whom are: W. Jankélévitch, *La mauvaise conscience* (1966), *Le pardon* (1967), *L'impréscriptible* (1986), *Pardonner?* (1970); W. Wiesel, *Le procès de Shamgorod tel qu'il se déroula le 25 février, 1649* (1979); S. Wiesenthal, *Les fleurs du soleil* (1969); Jacques Derrida, « Le siècle et le pardon » in *Le monde des débats* (December, 1999). For the Christian contribution to this debate, see Jean Laffitte, *Le pardon transfiguré* (Paris: Mame, 1995).

12. "I shall take the risk of making this proposition: every time that forgiveness stands in the service of some other purpose, be it noble and spiritual (ransom or redemption, reconciliation, salvation); every time that it tends towards re-establishing some normal situation (social, national, political, psychological for working through a bereavement, for some therapy or for some ecology of the memory), then forgiveness is not pure – nor is its concept pure. Forgiveness is not, nor should it be, either normal or normative or normalizing. It should remain exceptional and extra-ordinary," Derrida, art. cit., p. 2.

Does his power extend to the point where it covers the unexpiated slice of the fault, to take up the wonderful definition of forgiveness given by W. Jankélévitch? There is no easy response to this dramatic question. Only a loving adhesion to the words which the prophet, Hosea, put on the lips of God, "I am God and not man," makes it possible, in the terms of the encyclical, *Deus Caritas Est*, "to see, in a veiled manner, the dawning of the mystery of the Cross: God loves the human person so much that, in making himself man, he follows him even to the point of death and in this way he reconciles justice and love" (§ 10).

The second difficulty misunderstands the very essence of the act of forgiving, which always presupposes, over and above the person who proclaims such forgiveness, a person to whom that forgiveness is directed; why should this remain something exceptional and why should it be offered only in exceptional circumstances? If such is the case, forgiveness would lose all of its exemplary value; it would no longer be in a position to represent a source of richness and a virtuous moral norm for the society of human beings. A culture of forgiveness would become impossible. The very foundations of peace in society would be brought irremediably into peril.

The Logic of the Eucharist: The Unity of the Gift of the Response

The encyclical re-establishes the link between the mystery of the opened side and the institution of the Eucharist (DCE, § 12 and 13). On the doctrinal level, there is nothing new in this; the Church has always maintained that, every time that the Eucharist is celebrated, it is the work of our redemption that is accomplished. The Council of Trent expressed this reality in the following way:

> Although he had to offer himself only once upon the altar of the Cross by his death, Christ, during the Last Supper, offered to God, the Father, his Body and his Blood under the species of bread and of wine, in view of leaving to the

Church, his Spouse, a visible sacrifice, precisely to represent the bloody sacrifice which he was going to accomplish once and for all on the Cross and to perpetuate its memory until the end of the ages, as also to applying its salvific power in the remission of those sins which we commit every day.[13]

More recently, the encyclical, *Ecclesia de Eucharistia*, expressed in the following way the intention of Christ to leave this salvific heritage to those who were his own: "This sacrifice is so decisive for the salvation of the human race that Jesus Christ accomplished it and returned to the Father only after having left us the means of participating in it, as if we had been present there."[14] The novelty is not doctrinal, but, from the perspective of evangelization which we pointed out at the beginning, it lies in the double insistence upon the nature of the participation of the disciples of Christ in this mystery.

The first element unites the subjective dimension of the Eucharistic communion to its objective dimension. By the daring observation that that of which the ancient world had dreamed (nourishing itself on eternal wisdom, the *logos*) has become a reality for us, Benedict XVI insisted upon what connotes an assimilation of this kind, its loving character, which is understood at the same time as a gift of love: "This *Logos* has truly become food for us, *as love*.[15] The Eucharist draws us into the act of sacrifice of Jesus ... (and) we are drawn into the dynamic of his sacrifice" (DCE § 13).

Only the contemplation of the sacrifice of Christ on Calvary makes it possible to be drawn into his sacrifice. The wisdom of the Church, over the course of the ages, has not ceased to foster meditation upon the sufferings of the Passion; in fact, on the Cross, there is accomplished at one and the same time a horrible

---

13. Council of Trent, Session XXII, *Doctrine on the Sacrifice of the Holy Mass*, ch. 2, DS 1743.
14. John Paul II, *Ecclesia de Eucharistia*, § 11, 12 and 13; the citation is from § 11.
15. The emphasis is ours.

unleashing of the evil and the sin of human beings, and also the adorable sacrifice of a God who did not scorn any means of saving human beings, by giving himself to them, through the very act by which they rejected him, by putting him to death. That which was perpetrated against him was humanly irreparable. The massacre of the Innocent One *par excellence* was a crime that no human legislation could prescribe. The act of sacrifice annihilated the act of abomination. Unlimited forgiveness was offered to human beings.

The second point on which the encyclical insists concerns the social dimension of the Eucharist. The Eucharist builds up the Church, in the sense that it provides her with her form and with her stability. It is possible to participate in the Eucharist without being united to Christ through love. The faith that would inspire such a gesture would be a dead faith; in fact, it would not even be any more a question of an act of faith. A participation of this kind would not make it possible for someone to remain in the Church with the body and with the heart, according to the expression of *Ecclesia de Eucharistia*.[16] Christ comes in his Body and in his Blood and unites himself to the person who receives him, but, as he unites himself to each one of those who receive him, he brings about this unity, humanly impossible to effect, between the members of his Body. The love that is transmitted to each one is not a human love; it really is divine charity, the *caritas* of God, which is communicated to all of his members and which constitutes them truly as his Body, as the Family of God. The incarnate God draws us all to himself: the Eucharistic communion necessarily unites us then to all the other members. The purpose of the Eucharist, from the point of view of the baptized, is that of effective communion in the redemptive sacrifice of the Saviour and, for this reason, it is simultaneously communion with all those who are saved. In it is fulfilled the double commandment of love of God and of neighbor, because this love here is received from God and, in the Eucharistic communion, it

---

16. Cf. John Paul II, *Ecclesia de Eucharistia*, § 36.

possesses the most accomplished form that it is possible to have here below. When we receive communion, to be sure, we receive the Body of Christ, who, in giving himself to us, in some way prolongs his Incarnation, but also, by a movement that is exactly the reverse of all of the metabolisms that are observed in nature, in some way, we become Christ, participating in his eternal life. In the Eucharist, Christ receives us. We become what we receive; that really is a work of God.

The Eucharist is presented, as we observed above, as the Christological and sacramental foundation of a true understanding of the teaching of Jesus about love (DCE § 14). In it, there is present the double movement of love between God and human beings; in the sacrifice which it renders truly present, there is offered the source of all forgiveness; in it, there is given to each one the means to respond to the invitation of the Lord: "If anyone is thirsty let him come to me and if anyone believes in me, let him drink" According to the words of Scripture, "From his side have flowed streams of living water" (Jn 7:37–38).

22 The Structure of Sacramental Confession[1]

The new Ritual for Confession established the present form of the sacrament of penance. However, its basic structure goes back to apostolic times and rests upon the teachings and the deeds of Christ himself.

In the Nicene-Constantinopolitan Symbol, the Christian is invited to proclaim his or her faith in the power of that baptism, which made them a member of the Church: "I profess one baptism for the forgiveness of sins." Baptism is *par excellence* the sacrament of forgiveness. What a paradox it is that, among the number of the seven sacraments of the Church, there is present a particular sacrament of Christian reconciliation! However, there is nothing lacking in baptism, which needs to be completed, neither in terms of its efficacy to forgive sins, nor in its power of regeneration. Baptism is conferred once only; for every Christian it is a historic event, one that is not repeatable, which incorporates the person into Christ in his Paschal mystery and makes them a child of God. No one can receive this gift of divine filiation without receiving at the same time the gift of a justification which is complete. This term designates the passage from one state to another, from the condition in which they were born of the first Adam to the state of grace and of adoption as a child of God (Rom. 8:15), to take up the definition of the Council of Trent. The human being is justified, that is to say is rendered just; through baptism he is transformed, is made capable henceforth of acting in a way that pleases God. Thus, in baptism, there is a work of God (it is God alone who can regenerate) and, at the same time, there is a participation of the baptized person, who

---

1. "The Structure of Sacramental Confession" is the text of an article published in *Cahiers d'Edifa* (Paris, 1999), pp. 38–47.

proclaims their faith and who commits themselves to living in accordance with the gift which they have received. Through baptism all of their sins, original sin, and all of their actual sins committed up to the moment of baptism, are removed (and not merely covered over or non imputed); besides, all the punishments for sin are remitted. This is the reason why the Church has never imposed penance upon catechumens.

Why, then, another sacrament? Quite simply, because the purification effected by the water of baptism takes nothing away from the spiritual faculties of the believer.

The believer remains free and his capacity to choose is exposed to the misuse of his freedom, through the consequences of original sin. Thus, the baptized person is a sinner, who does not act always according to the holiness of his baptism. It happens that he sins, and, sometimes, sins seriously.

Sin After Baptism

From the beginning, the Apostles were aware of the particular gravity of sin committed after baptism. It was incumbent upon Christian communities to keep themselves holy and pure from what could threaten them from within.

We see the apostle, Paul, exhorting his brethren in Corinth to exclude from the community a man guilty of notorious misconduct (1Cor. 5). In the second letter to the Corinthians, this person is made the case of a veritable ministry of the Apostles, exercised through the word of reconciliation (cf. 2Cor 2:5–11).

To the baptized, penance seemed to be an anomaly. The disciplinary practices of penance, at times extremely severe, were aimed at preserving sinners from falling and not at discouraging them. They brought out the objective gravity of falling after baptism. One aspect of this was the stain inflicted upon the Church by the sin of its members, which undoubtedly explains the practice in the early centuries of a double penance, the one private and the other public. The latter was the seal of the reconciliation and of the communion with the Church that had been completely restored. The penitent, then, could accede once more to the sacraments.

The insistence with which the liturgy in our days places the accent upon the ecclesial character of reconciliation (which is a celebration) reflects a return to this conviction of the period of its origins that the forgiveness of a sinner has an effect upon the entire body of the Church. ("There will be more joy in heaven over one single sinner who repents than over ninety-nine just persons who have no need of repentance," (Lk 15:7).

Throughout its history, the Church has considered that the power that belonged to it to forgive sins knew no limits by reason of its divine origin. As far as the faults were concerned, some of them were capable of being considered at times as incapable of being remitted (Origen, Tertullian, at the time of the latter's becoming a Montanist), such as idolatry, adultery, fornication, murder or apostasy; from this arose the practice of imposing penances which endured for the whole of a person's life. However, the Church very quickly distanced itself from these positions, proceeding for its part to the reintegration of apostates. The refusal to recognize an unlimited power of ministers of the Church over these matters had lain at the basis of various heresies, which the pastors had had to confront. St Pacian of Barcelona, for example, replied to the Novatians: "You say that God alone can forgive sins. That is true, but what God does through his priests, it is still he who does it."[2]

The Contribution of the Council of Florence

We have to wait until the fifteenth century before the contributions of medieval theological reflection were incorporated into the sacramental discipline of the Church. Thus, it was the Fathers of the Council of Florence in 1439 took up the doctrine of St Thomas Aquinas, to apply it to the sacrament of penance. All of the elements necessary for a sacrament were identified

---

2. St Pacian of Barcelona, *Epistula 1, Ad Sempronianum*, 6.

there: the institution by Christ himself of the power to remit sins, the matter of the human acts of penance, the form of the forgiveness proclaimed by ecclesiastical authority, the effects of the reconciliation of the sinner with God and with the Church. The Council of Florence's Decree on the Armenians, then, attributes to the fourth sacrament a form constituted by the words of absolution: "I absolve you..."), proclaimed by the minister of the sacrament, that is to say by the priest, who has the faculty, through his office or delegation by grant or concession, and the power to absolve. The matter of the sacrament, so to speak (the text speaks of *quasi-matter*), are the acts of the penitent, which the Council designates as: "contrition of heart, oral confession, the penance established by the priest").[3]

The Contribution of the Council of Trent: From the Council of Trent to Vatican Ii

In different terms, this basic structure would remain up to our own days. Elaborated in the fourteenth session of the Council of Trent, it is to be found once more in later texts, particularly in recent Magisterium, in the new *Ritual of Penance* (*Ordo Paenitentiae*) of 1973, in the apostolic exhortation, *Reconciliatio et Paenitentia* of 1984, and in the *Catechism of the Catholic Church*.

To understand the importance of each of these elements that comprise the sacrament of penance in the form in which we have it today, it will be useful to start from the new Ritual of Confession. The Constitution on the Sacred Liturgy (*Sacrosanctum Concilium*) of the Second Vatican Council (1963) had wanted to underline the teaching role of the sacramental signs: these presuppose the faith, but further, through words and through things, they "nourish the faith, strengthen it and express it. That is why they are called 'sacraments of faith.'"[4] From this, there arose the recommendation of the Council to undertake a revision of the rituals of the different sacraments. For that of pen-

---

3. Council of Florence, *Decree on the Armenians*, DS, § 1323.
4. Vatican Council II, *Sacrosanctum Concilium*, § 59.

ance, one single phrase expresses the underlying intention: "The rite and the formulae of penance will be revised in such a way as to bring out more clearly the nature and the effect of the sacrament."[5] It was ten years later, on December 2, 1973, that the *Ordo Paenitentiae* was published in Rome by the Congregation for the Sacraments and for Divine Worship. The French version of this new ritual was submitted for approval to the bishops of the International Commission for French-speaking territories and was confirmed by the Congregation on June 14, 1978. Whatever the norms and the specific discipline that episcopal conferences and diocesan bishops are able to propose for the pastoral well-being of the faithful in different regions, it is required of ministers of the sacrament that they preserve the essential structure and, at the same time, the entire formula of absolution (*servatis structura essentiali et formula integra absolutionis*).[6] Before entering into the detail of its essential elements, it will be useful to recall very briefly, limiting ourselves here to individual reconciliation, the celebration of a sacramental confession. After preparing himself by an examination of conscience, the penitent is invited by the priest, after making the sign of the Cross, to turn with confidence towards God, to recognize his sins and the mercy of God. The reading of a passage of Scripture may be used to exhort him to this. Then, he confesses all the sins of which he is aware, assisted and advised, if need be, by the priest. The latter proposes a penance to the penitent. The member of the faithful manifests his sorrow for his failings by reciting an act of contrition. At the end the priest proclaims the words of absolution. The penitent thanks God for his mercy.

What may we observe in this peculiar dialogue? The priest proclaims the forgiveness of God, after having heard the confession of sins, having assured himself of the penitent's sincerity and having proposed a penance. Here, we have the four elements of the sacrament: absolution by the priest, the contrition of the

---

5. *Ibid.* § 72.
6. Congregation for Divine Worship, *Ordo Paenitentiae*, § 40a.

penitent (sorrow for his sins and repentance), confession of his sins and finally satisfaction (which is the penance freely accepted and fulfilled by the penitent). We note that three of the elements are those of the penitent and only one is undertaken by the priest. The *Catechism of the Catholic Church* groups these into two essentially equal parts: the acts of the person who is converted under the action of the Holy Spirit and the action of God through the intervention of the Church.[7] Now we must examine each of these more deeply.

Absolution: The Action of God

Absolution is the sacramental act *par excellence*, the effective sign of the forgiveness of God (that is to say, which makes that forgiveness effective). The divine work of salvation is applied to the sinner. The priest pronounces a formula of absolution, upon which it is worth reflecting. In fact, before saying the words themselves of forgiveness, it refers quite precisely to the event of salvation: it is the Father who effects this work of mercy and who, "through the death and resurrection of his Son, has reconciled the world to himself and has sent the Holy Spirit among us for the forgiveness of sins." The Holy Spirit continues the reconciliation that has been effected by the Son, but he does this in and through the Church.

It is from the Church of Christ, through the sacrament of Order in the presbyteral degree, that the priest holds his power to absolve, but it is from the Church that he has the juridical power to exercise it, that he proclaims in the following words: "Through the ministry of the Church, may (God) grant you pardon and peace," before granting absolution in this way: "I absolve you from your sins in the name of the Father and of the Son and of the Holy Spirit" (and not, for example, "May God forgive you ..."); but he does not do this except by virtue of the ministry which has been conferred upon him. In this regard, let us note that, even if the power of absolution is linked to the sacrament

---

7. *Catechism of the Catholic Church*, § 1448–1460.

of Order, the responsibility for exercising it is submitted to a requirement of jurisdiction: the priest received the mandate by faculty from his bishop or, failing that, from his religious superior (all priests having the faculty in danger of death). He does not dispose arbitrarily of a faculty by the fact that he is a priest, but, being a priest of the Church by virtue of the sacrament of Order which has been conferred upon him by a bishop, it is from the Church that he receives the responsibility for exercising this very faculty. Thus, we speak of a minister of confession.

Very often, it is forgotten that sacramental absolution does not have as its sole effect the remission of sins. It reconciles the sinner to the Church. In the *Code of Canon Law* of 1983, this dimension is recalled in the following way:

> The faithful who confess their sins…through the absolution given by the minister, obtain from God the pardon of the sins they have committed after baptism, and at the same time they are reconciled with the Church, which, by sinning, they have wounded (c. 959).

Here we find once more that which touches the communion of the saints and which will be elaborated upon in the chapter "The Church and Forgiveness."[8] Every sin wounds the Church and denatures its visage, without spot or stain.

The Three Acts of the Penitent

If these belong to the very essence of the sacrament, it is appropriate to consider the acts of the penitent first of all as a whole. Let us recall that they are:

- contrition
- confession
- satisfaction

In fact, all three of these acts involve the validity of the sacrament, even as they describe the free interior acts (contrition) or exterior acts (confession and satisfaction) of the penitent. We

---

8. Translator's note; see below, pp. 469–486.

must not be afraid to say that, in this sense, the human being participates freely in his own forgiveness by God and even that it is necessary for him to accept this forgiveness freely, together with the demands that it involves, in order for that forgiveness to be efficacious in its effects. God does not wish to save people against their will and his forgiveness would not be able to do violence to human nature. The freedom of the Christian is truly an efficacious freedom.

Of course, there would be some degree of naivety, if we were to imagine that freedom could derive a penitential action of this kind from its own depths alone; there is prevenient divine grace which prepares our freedom to amend itself, to turn itself towards God (conversion), in order to recognize our own sins and to confess them, so as to allow reparation for them to be made.

The very act of seeking to go to confession and to do so, however grave the sins we have committed may be, is already a beginning of justice, which fosters what the Tradition calls prevenient grace.

Contrition

This is the first act of the penitent and, to some extent, it is the most important one; contrition precedes and conditions the validity and the further stages in the sacrament. It is an interior act, through which the penitent regrets his faults and repents of having committed them. Contrition is not a subjective feeling; it is the principle and the soul of conversion;[9] it engages the whole interior reality of the Christian, who is called constantly to conversion.

Contrition is so important that the Magisterium of the Church has gone even to the point of specifying what it is in a dogmatic definition: a sorrow in the soul and a detestation of the sin committed, together with a resolution not to sin any more in the future.[10]

---

9. Cf. John Paul II, *Reconciliatio et paenitentia*, § 31.
10. Cf. Council of Trent, Session XIV, *Decree on Penance*, DS § 1676.

The Structure of Sacramental Confession

The sorrow in the soul comes from the sinner being conscious of having offended God. Thus, this gives witness to the reality of a love that is grateful towards God. When this sorrow is dictated solely by this fact, then it is the case of perfect contrition, that is to say of a contrition of charity.[11] Such an interior disposition remits faults, even serious ones, provided the resolution has been made to have recourse as soon as possible to the sacrament. Other motives, naturally, can be present, such as the fear of judgment. We speak of attrition, to indicate a contrition that is imperfect, that is to say, not capable by itself of obtaining the forgiveness of sins. However, it marks the beginning of a process, which can lead to taking the step of receiving the sacrament; then, in this sense, attrition also is a gift of God.

The classical distinction between contrition and attrition goes back to the Middle Ages, precisely to William of Auvergne. It formed the basis, subsequently, of a whole development in theological reflection, which made possible the doctrinal definitions of Trent, which have been taken up unceasingly by the Magisterium (for example, reference may be made to the *Catechism of the Catholic Church*).[12]

Detestation for the sin committed is a personal distancing of oneself from the offence, adopting the position, with one's whole being, of being against its nature as an offence to God.

The resolution not to sin any more in the future is a decision that commits the person as such. Often included in the prayer which the penitent recites before the absolution, as in the act of contrition proposed by the ritual,[13] it is a good thing that this resolution be manifested, whatever the actual prayer that is chosen. We note that the decision not to sin any more goes beyond momentary regret for the specific sins that a person is preparing to confess. It is a question of a real decision of conversion. Quite

---

11. *Catechism of the Catholic Church*, § 1452.
12. *Ibid.* § 1452–1453.
13. *Ordo Paenitentiae*, § 45.

rightly, many of the prayers available to the penitent place the accent upon the need for God's help in this conversion.

The Confession of Sins

The penitent confesses all the sins of which he is aware and which he recalls. In particular, it is incumbent upon him to confess all mortal sins which come to his memory, not forgetting those which are more hidden and which constitute violations of the last two commandments (the concupiscence of the eyes and avarice).

It is interesting to note this point, which was specified at the Council of Trent and which has been taken up by the Catechism.[14] The reason for this is that such faults wound the soul even more than sins that are manifested externally. Here we have a new illustration of the concern that the Church shows for the interiority of the Christian. Conversion is indeed a transformation of his interior being.

The integrity of the admission is necessary; the penitent who voluntarily conceals a grave sin, for whatever reason it may be, addresses himself in vain to divine mercy. The sacrament excludes lying or duplicity. We can understand also the need for a serious examination of conscience. Confession is not a conversation in a drawing room or a polite recitation. Above all, it is a personal accusation, which expresses a work of truth: towards the sin which has been confessed, towards oneself (the penitent recognizes himself as a sinner), and finally towards God, before whom the repentant sinner finds his proper place. The person who accuses himself espouses in some way the judgment of God, which loves the sinner, while hating his sin. On his side, the priest exercises the function, at one and the same time, of judge, as doctor and as pastor of souls, and restores the order of Creation, which has been compromised by sin.[15]

---

14. *Catechism of the Catholic Church*, § 1456.
15. Cf. International Theological Commission in John Paul II, *Reconciliatio et Paenitentia*, § 4.

The confession of grave sins at least once a year, the Church recalls, is a prescription from which the Christian cannot derogate.

The sacrament of penance is not only the place where mortal sins are raised. It is also the regular occasion for meeting the God of mercy, who helps, guides, and illuminates his children in their efforts to lead a holier and more perfect life. The sacramental confession of venial sins (called also devotional confession) is recommended by the Church,[16] which sees in it the means for making spiritual progress.

We must not conceal the painful character which is sometimes involved in taking the step of exposing one's conscience to a priest, who, if he makes present the merciful Person of Christ in sacramental form, does not remain any the less, in numerous cases, a person unknown to the penitent.

There is merit in making a confession, which involves at ties a victory over feelings of shame or of human respect. In the eighteenth century, Pope Benedict XIV saw in the shame that accompanies the admission of certain sins an important part of penance.[17]

Satisfaction or Penance, Properly so-Called

In the celebration of the sacrament, the priest proposes to the sinner a penance, which is to be carried out. Very often, the juridical or the penal dimension of the confessor's judgment has been emphasized, when he decides upon an appropriate penance. This aspect of retributive justice is present, but it is not the essential point. At times, it is possible to adapt a reparation which is proportionate to certain sins, as would be the case, for example, with the restitution of some good which has been stolen or with the compensation for a wrong which has been inflicted upon a neighbour, but every sin carries with it in the first place an attack upon the integrity of the sinner himself. The

---

16. Cf. *The Code of Canon Law*, c. 988 § 2.
17. Cf. Benedict XIV, Constitution, *Inter cunctas sollicitudines* (1304), DS, § 880.

sinner creates a disorder in himself, an attachment to the offence. A just penance, which has been adapted to the individual, will help that person to recover his spiritual integrity and will render them more just.

The ritual speaks of the remedy for emerging from sin.[18] In the concrete, the priest can recommend to the penitent certain particular perspectives for conversion; he can ask for the recitation of a prayer or again the reading of a passage of the Scripture. The penance is to be adapted to the gravity of the sins committed. In the case of serious sins, a significant penance is sometimes the means that enables a penitent sinner to cast their sin far behind them. In this regard, the sole recommendation of ecclesiastical discipline is that of salutary and appropriate satisfaction that the confessor is to impose according to the nature and the number of the sins, taking into account the condition of the penitent.[19] Here, then, we are in the area of prudential assessment.

In order to understand well the meaning of the penance, it must be held, in effect, that no reparation could be perfectly adapted to a sin, if it is true that sin is an offence against God. Hence, the sinner who has been forgiven and who has accepted freely to make satisfaction, gives witness to a new life, which has been recovered; the penance made with a good heart—an offering, a service to neighbour, voluntary sacrifices, patient acceptance of one's own Cross—is also the work of Christ in that person.[20] The penitent knows that this penance makes satisfaction, because it unites him to the Redeemer. Thus, it makes it possible to enter into truth, within the depth of the Paschal mystery.

The Three Rites of the Sacrament of Reconciliation

The ritual for sacramental confession (*Ordo Paenitentiae* of December 2, 1999), specifies three ways of celebrating the sacrament, according to three distinct rites:

---

18. *Ordo Paenitentiae*, § 6.
19. Cf. *The Code of Canon Law*, c. 981.
20. *Catechism of the Catholic Church*, § 1460.

- Rite A refers to the reconciliation of a single penitent: it specifies the structure of ordinary individual confession, which every Christian is called to practise regularly. In case of danger of death, this rite may perhaps be reduced to the sole formula: "I absolve you from your sins, in the name of the Father and of the Son and of the Holy Spirit."
- Rite B presents the same process of an individual confession and an individual absolution but within a communal penitential celebration. Organized often on the occasion of the preparation for certain feasts and solemnities or indeed for the purpose of bringing out the value and particular importance of a liturgical season (Advent or Lent), this communitarian celebration, with individual confession and absolution, makes it possible to bring out more clearly the ecclesial character of the sacrament, which, to be sure, is already present in Rite A.[21]

These two rites, A and B, are the sole ordinary rites for celebration of this sacrament. The Church's law is clear in this regard:

> Individual and integral confession and absolution constitutes the sole ordinary means by which a member of the faithful is reconciled with God and with the Church; physical or moral impossibility alone excuses from this confession, in which case reconciliation can be obtained also in other ways.[22]

There exists a Rite C, which serves for the reconciliation of several penitents in a certain number of exceptional cases:

- If danger of death threatens and there is insufficient time for the priest or priests to be able to hear the confessions of each of the penitents.
- If there is a grave necessity, that is to say, taking account of the number of penitents, there are not enough confessors available to hear the confession of each one within a reasonable time in a dignified manner, such that the penitents,

---

21. Cf. below *The Church and Forgiveness*, pp. 469–486.
22. *The Code of Canon Law*, c. 960.

without fault on their part, would be forced to remain deprived for a long time of sacramental grace or of holy communion, but the necessity is not considered to be sufficient, when confessors cannot be available by reason solely of the large number of penitents, such as could occur on the occasion of a major feast or of a large pilgrimage[23]. General absolution must not become the ordinary form.[24]

The diocesan bishop is the judge of whether these conditions are fulfilled; in accordance with other members of the episcopal conference, he can determine the cases in which this necessity is met. The member of the faithful who benefits from a general absolution must have the "intention to make an individual confession of the grave sins which he cannot confess as such at present."[25] This is the necessary condition, for the sacrament that he receives to be valid. Thus, it can be seen that, even in the prescriptions of its penitential discipline, the Church respects the right of its children to make an individual confession.

On the Precise Detail of the Confession

Some words of St Francis de Sales are appropriate, to conclude this short exposé. He treats of the question of the precision necessary in the admission of sins and offers, as a consequence, the means for making a confession that is spiritually fruitful:

> Many people have the custom of confessing venial sins and as a way of arranging them, without thinking at all of correcting themselves, they remain for the whole of their lives burdened by this, and in this way they lose very many spiritual benefits and gains ... Do not make only these kinds of superficial accusations, which many make out of routine: I have not loved God as much as I should, I have not love my neighbour as much as I should; I have not received the sacraments with the reverence which I

---

23. *Ibid.* c. 961.
24. Cf. John Paul II, *Reconciliatio et Paenitentia*, § 33.
25. *The Code of Canon Law*, c. 962.

ought to have shown, and many such similar statements. The reason is that, in saying this, you will not be saying anything in particular, which could enable the confessor to know the state of your conscience, so much so that all the saints in paradise and all the people on earth could say the same things, if they went to confession...Look, then, at what the specific issue it is, about which you have to make these accusation against yourself... For example, you accuse yourself of not having loved your neighbour as you should have done; perhaps, it is because, having seen some poor person in real need, whom you could have helped and consoled, you did not bother to do so.

Very well, accuse yourself of this particular thing and say: having seen a poor person in need, I did not help him, as I should have done, through negligence or through hardness of heart or through contempt, according to what you know to have been the occasion of this sin.

In the same way, do not accuse yourself of not having prayed to God with such devotion as you ought to have done; but, if you have had voluntary distractions or if you neglected to find the time, the place or the attitude required to be able to give attention in prayer, quite simply accuse yourself of that, according to what it was that you find you were lacking, without adding in the confession generalities which are neither hot nor cold.[26]

The Memory of the Saints

In the same way that there are two ways of knowing what is evil, the one by the power of the spirit which grasps them and the other through the experience of the senses which are subjected to them (thus it is one thing for all of the vices to be known through the teaching of Wisdom and another for them to be known through the corruption of the person who is foolish), so there are two ways of forgetting evils. The person who knows evils only through teaching and observation forgets them in a

---

26. St Francis de Sales, *Introduction to the Devout Life*, II.

different way from the one who knows them through having had experience of them and through having been subjected to them; the first neglecting what he has learnt, the other by being delivered from all suffering from them. It is in this latter manner that the saints will no longer have any recollection of their evil past; they will forget them all, to the point where they will no longer retain any, even the slightest, feeling for them. But, by virtue of the speculative faculty, which will be great in them, they will know not only their own evil past, but even the eternal misery of the damned. If it were otherwise, would it be possible for them, ignorant of the fact that they were evil, as the psalmist says, to sing eternally the praises of the Lord? Assuredly, nothing will be sweet any longer in this city, apart from singing this song of gratitude, to the glory of the grace of Christ, who has delivered us by his Blood.[27]

---

27. St Augustine, *The City of God*, XXII, 30, 4.

23 The Church and Forgiveness[1]

The Christian faith encounters a number of paradoxes, which reveal apparently divergent, though not contradictory, truths; they seek to elevate the faith, to ripen it by bringing it beyond the certitudes which human reason alone is able to attain. It is in this way that the act of faith has to confront, for example, the existence of God, at one and the same time all-powerful, and yet silent, before the suffering of the innocents or before the triumph of those who are violent (the victory of the wicked in Ps 10), or indeed that of a God who is merciful and yet who makes moral demands without measuring these by common standards against the reality of human weakness, or again the existence of the Son of God in the person of Jesus Christ, simultaneously with his true humanity which the faith asserts.

In the same way, associating the Church and forgiveness seems to lead to apparently insurmountable difficulties. All of those questions without answer with regard to forgiveness seem to be added to already insoluble questions relating to the identity of the Church and its role in the history of human kind:

- How is it that the Gospel and the teaching of the Church always appeal to reconciliation and to mutual forgiveness for offences, when it seems to be admitted today by everyone that some offences are unpardonable?
- How can it be that she claims to be able to reconcile human beings and yet, it seems, that she increases the instances of her public recognition of her errors and faults in the past?

---

1. "The Church and Forgiveness" is the French version of an article published in Italian under the title «Dono e Perdono nelle relazioni familiari e sociali», in E. Scabini e G. Rossi (ed.), *Università del Sacro Cuore, Università Cattolica del Sacro Cuore Centro Studi e Ricerche sulla Famiglia* (Vita e Pensiero, Milano, 2000), pp. 15–54.

- And would there be something to forgive in that which is affirmed by the sacraments, beyond the habitual mediation of the mercy of God, when he reconciles sinners?
- What the significance, then, if the Church has been wrong in the past, of her claim to teach immutable truths, to make hers the words of St Paul, who described her as the pillar and as the foundation of the truth (1 Tim 3:15)?
- What is the significance, also, if she has so much for which she needs to be forgiven, of this other claim, affirming herself to be the Church of Christ, of calling herself *holy and immaculate*? The Church is indeed poorly placed, people would say, to issue judgment and to forgive people their sins.

We can see that the questions can be multiplied infinitely. Let us say, straight away that they would be destined to remain without an answer, if we did not agree to submit them to a certain order. That order is that of the mystery of the faith, that is to say, to the interior logic that inspires and animates the Church. The nature of the Church, its role in the service of the salvation offered by God in the Person of his Son, Jesus Christ, her teaching cannot be understood completely, except in the light of the faith. It is also in the light of faith that all of the events of history can be read that involve the Church, which obviously includes a reading of her past which is courageous and honest, and at the same time daring and yet balanced. Let us observe that even a glance from the outside of the Church could not simply overlook a logic of this kind; historians know very well that a balanced judgment always presupposes research into the motivations, the social or political representations, which animated people whose behaviour they intend to study.

What follows here will examine in succession: the true nature of the Church, the mission in which she recognizes herself to be the instrument of the salvation of God (a mission which includes the exercise of forgiveness in all of its dimensions, moral and sacramental), the particular question of the public steps of asking forgiveness expressed by the Pope and by episcopal conferences. This last point must not be passed over in silence, by reason notably both of its theological and pastoral importance and of the passionate positions which it has aroused.

The Two Dimensions of the Church

"In Christ, the Church is in some way the sacrament, that is to say, the sign and the means of intimate union with God and of the human race."[2] With these words, which introduce the dogmatic Constitution of the Second Vatican Council, the conciliar Fathers wished solemnly to affirm the true nature of the Church. This has a double dimension, human and divine. Human, that seems to be true of itself: it is a clearly visible institution, with its own organization, its hierarchy, its discipline, and has places where it is visible. It has traversed the centuries and has reflected the changes and the traumas that have affected human society. Moreover, it is because she is perfectly situated in time that the Church has also experienced the judgment of history, as we shall see. When we speak of the divine dimension, we wish to indicate several realities: her origin tied to the redemptive action of Jesus Christ, true God and true man, and consequently, divine intention, her *raison d'être*: to make manifest (*sign*) the intimate union of God with all people and her being the means to that union (*instrument*).

It is clear that the Church does not give her own proper identity to herself, as any human institution whatsoever would do, defining its statutes and its rules, its aims and its activities. She is aware that her mission precedes her (every mission presupposes a vocation) and surpasses her. In this sense, she assumes the presence in herself of everything that is not visible: the ultimate destination of her children, together with the Father who is heaven, the reality of the communion of the saints which unites all her children in Christ, those who take part still in this life and those who already are asleep in death, and above all the presence of the Holy Spirit of God, who leads her invisibly, and through whom life is given once

---

2. Vatican Council II, *Lumen Gentium*, § 1.

more to human beings, whom sin had caused to die (Rom. 8:10). When she speaks of herself and of her mission, the Church is not engaged in some act of imagination, if we may put it like that; she does no more than give witness to the fact that she has received her life from God and has the responsibility of transmitting that life to others. Thus, she is rendered perfectly capable of requiring of her children an act of faith, which incorporates her own proper holiness: "I believe in the one, holy, Catholic and apostolic Church".

The Image of the Body Suggests One Single Life

The holiness of the Church comes in the first place from her origins: founded by Christ to announce to all peoples the Kingdom, which he himself had come to inaugurate, it is from him that she receives all of the gifts necessary for the accomplishment of her mission: The out-pouring of the Holy Spirit on each of the Apostles at the moment of Pentecost is at the same time the moment of the foundation of the Church, in Christ, Risen and ascended to heaven, and also that of the constitution of each of its members in his Body. The image of the body suggests that, from this point onwards, it is one and the same life that animates Christ and all of those who have been made like him through the gift of his Spirit. The Church knows her origins and, even if she wished to do so, she could not deny the holiness that the fact of being united to him has given her, whom Christian tradition since the time of St Paul has designated as her Spouse (cf. Eph 5:25–32).

We must be careful to represent the two dimensions of the Church, human and divine, as two strata that are super-imposed one upon the other. There is the temptation in every Christian of wishing to set in opposition to each other a true Church, invisible and inspired by God, acting under the empire of grace and exercising its supernatural powers and charisms and a human church, institutional, immersed in social life and political action, with its representatives, its canon law, and its discipline; or again, who would set in opposition to each other a Church of love and mercy to a Church of precepts and of commandments. The Church is at one and the same time visible and invisible; the theological faith which adheres to the invisible mystery that she encloses within herself embraces in the same way her visibility, insofar as it recognizes in it the unfolding of this mystery in time and in space. Historical time will come to an end in the return of Christ, when he comes in glory to judge the living and the dead (the Parousia); in space, it is the totality of the human race; the catholicity of the Church expresses the universality of salvation: "God, our Saviour wishes that all people be saved" (1Tim 2:4).

This presence of the Church in history explains why there is in her a path of purification that is to be pursued. She is at the same time both holy and in need of being purified. These two elements, far from excluding each other, are present simultaneously in her. We have said something about the first aspect, about her sanctity. The second element, her need for purification, operates not by way of a progress that is linear in all the aspects of her life and of her apostolate, but first of all by way of a consciousness which is ever more fully attuned to the reality of her mission.

The Church deepens, without ceasing, her understanding of what has been revealed to her; she does so often through prophetic words. All of the enrichments of dogma which have taken place in the course of the centuries are like visible manifestations of these instances of deeper understanding. The affirmation of the union of the two natures in Christ at Ephesus and at Chalcedon, the clarifications as to the nature and as to the necessity of baptism through the great medieval Councils, the justification of the sinner at the Council of Trent, are some examples of this. More recently, we may think of the insistent reminder of the Second Vatican Council of the universal call to holiness and to the dynamic of evangelization that that recall has encouraged, or again of the innumerable declarations in favor of the service of human life and of the unconditional respect which is due to it.

The work of purification is not limited just to the concerns of the Magisterium or of the apostolate. It affects also the incessant invitation to sinners within its midst to conversion. With the passage of time, the Church has not escaped from examining her conscience and, as a logical consequence, of recognizing errors or faults which it is possible she may have committed, not, to be sure, in the realm of her teaching which does not belong to her, as we have said, or on the exercise of the authentic gifts of the Spirit of God in her, but in the measures which she might or might not have taken "in the area of government, in her relations with temporal powers, in her internal divisions, to sum it up, in the sins and failures of her members, who bear their share of responsibility for the evils of our times."[3] We can understand that there is not on one side a true, edifying and ideal Church (moreover, from what perspective would that have been?) and, on the other, a Church that is unworthy and sinful. The Church forms one whole, real and concrete good, an assembly of people at once holy and yet formed of sinners.

We could ask why the Church takes into its heart the presence of sinners; it is that she never ceases to consider the latter as her children, unceasingly inviting them to turn away from sin and towards God. She knows that her purification passes by way of the conversion of each one of her members. Thus, there is a serious misconception to be avoided. The Church never rejects the sinners whom she teaches, exhorts, and reconciles with God. Only those sinners who are hardened remain outside such a purification, not in fact through the will of the Church, but through their own will. This means that the Church has no fear of accepting the need in which she finds herself, in this sense of purifying herself unceasingly. A small example will enable us better to grasp this aspect. When the priest presides at the Eucharist, he does not make a confession of the sins of the congregation that is present; he begins by confessing his own sins, as does each member of the faithful, saying: "*I confess to Almighty God.*" It is only after this act that he makes supplication to God and calls down upon the assembly of penitents, including upon himself, the divine benevolence: "May

---

3. John Paul II, *Tertio Millennio Adveniente*, § 36.

Almighty God have mercy upon us!" We should not be astounded if the history of the Church is marked on the one hand by the sublime witness of the saints and of the martyrs and, on the other, by the innumerable failures of the baptised.

The Reconciling Mission of the Church

From the beginning, forgiveness has been at the heart of the mission entrusted to the Apostles by the Risen Jesus. We could even say that, in the perspective of the Fourth Gospel, the first act of the Risen Christ was precisely to send forth the Holy Spirit upon the disciples, giving them together the mission and the power to forgive: "He breathed on them and said to them: 'Receive the Holy Spirit. Those who sins you forgiven are forgiven; those whose sins you retain are retained'" (Jn 20:22–23). The capacity to forgive sins is a power specifically given only to the Apostles, and this power is divine. At the last moment of his Passion, the Christ pleaded with the Father, begging him to remit this sin from people: "Forgive them, for they do not know what they are doing" (Lk 23:34). Only God can forgive the iniquitous sin of putting to death his beloved Son. This is the reason why Jesus, in his last agony, addresses himself to him. Raised up, he in his turn could transmit to those who were his own this divine prerogative. There is a striking symmetry between this last act of Jesus on the Cross and his first act as the Risen Lord; each one of these acts is related to divine forgiveness. This continuity naturally has a profound theological meaning; between the two acts the sacrifice of Christ is fulfilled, through which God reconciled the world to himself, no longer taking heed of people's sins, and placing within us the word of reconciliation (2Cor. 5:19). It is impossible, then, to understand the fuller meaning which forgiveness carries within the Christian mystery, if we do not contemplate this on the Cross, without ever dissociating the two levels of forgiveness, brought to their perfect fulfilment by Christ.

At the moral level, Calvary is the greatest example of forgiveness for sins effected by Jesus, who offered his life for those very people who put him to death; in this, he crowned the whole of his existence in the midst of us human beings, dedicated to the teaching of forgiveness and to its practical implementation in daily life.

At the theological level: the act by which Jesus sacrificed his life was a free offering made to the Father by the eternal Son for the remission of sins. Thus, it was the means of salvation that was chosen by God.

The Holy Spirit poured out upon the Apostles would make permanent in their midst the presence of the Risen Christ, with the whole efficacy of his redemptive action. More concretely, as every Christian who receives the gift of the Spirit through baptism, he or she becomes personally capable of living in Christ and of conforming their lives to his, in particular through the forgiveness of sins. Insofar as they are Apostles, they are clothed with the divine power to forgive sins. It is easy to appreciate this, by reading in the Acts of the Apostles, for example, how these Apostles proclaimed the reality of salvation and began to exercise the power it encompasses. It is this power, subsequently transmitted by the Apostles to their successors, which has continued to be exercised up to our days in the sacramental life of the Church.

Three Prerogatives

Tradition relies upon three texts of Scripture in order to ground the prerogatives of the Church in the remission of sins; apart from the passage from St John quoted above (Jn. 20:21–23), this concerns two texts of St Matthew. The first of these (Mt. 16:19) concerns only Peter, who received from Jesus a triple promise:

- To be the rock on which the Church will be built;
- To receive the authority to govern (the keys of the Kingdom of heaven); and
- To receive the power to bind and to loose.

This latter prerogative had been extended by Jesus to all of the Apostles, and this is the object of the second of St Matthew's texts: "In truth, I say to you: everything that you bind on earth shall be considered bound in heaven and everything that you loose on earth shall be considered loosed in heaven" (Mt 18:18).

What does binding and loosing mean? Essentially, it means to have authority to absolve sins, but also, in a broader sense, it means to exercise doctrinal and disciplinary authority. The use of these terms was frequent in the time of Jesus, in the synagogues, and it consisted also of the power to declare this or that action of human beings to be licit or to be prohibited. What is very interesting for us is to notice that, in this passage, Jesus addressed himself to those who were his own in the context of a teaching on fraternal correction, in which are to be found the features of an ecclesial discipline which was to come later. In fact, we recognize that the Church always reconciles sinners, except when the latter refuse this. The text indicates that it was only, through three successive refusals that the sinner excluded himself from the assembly, the refusal to listen to his brother, then of hearing him in the presence of one or two witnesses, and finally of listening to the community (Mt 18:17).

Continuity

The two levels of forgiveness, moral and theological, let us notice, have never been absent from the Church. She teaches always the same Gospel, with its demands for forgiveness, even of our own enemies, and her history, also from this standpoint, the history of its martyrs. She always exercises her prerogatives of reconciling human beings with God. She does this in different ways:

- First of all, through baptism, the first sacrament for the remission of sins;
- Then, naturally, through the sacrament of reconciliation, in which she offers help to her children: sacramental confession is the habitual way in which the Church gives to repentant

sinners the forgiveness of God (the structure of this sacrament has been examined earlier);
- Through the Eucharist, which associates this reconciliation with the sacrifice of Christ, which she makes present; every time that the sacrifice of Christ is celebrated on the altar, that sacrifice by which Christ, our Passover, was immolated (1 Cor 5:7), the work of our Redemption is effected;[4] and
- Through the strength and the comfort which she provides to those who are sick in the sacrament of Christian sickness, death, and resurrection.

Outside of these specifically sacramental actions, the Church remains free to establish the conditions for the readmission of her separated brethren into the fulness of her communion. In the same way, she is sovereign in the choice of the penitential discipline which she has always adapted to the spiritual needs of sinner, not unaware in this regard of the traditions and the customs of different cultures. By neglecting the particular sensibilities of a given epoch, we are exposed today to the danger of interpreting anachronistically certain disciplinary measures, considered at the time as perfectly suitable. This is the case, for example, with the development of public penances for serious offences, which clash so much with our contemporary sensitivities; they were aimed at protecting the radical nature of the public commitment to conversion, which the penitent had taken on at the moment of his baptism. The teaching of a Tertullian on penance is very revealing in this respect,[5] of the seriousness with which entering into the communion of the Church through baptism was considered in the early centuries.

In the context of its mission, the Church can establish solemn occasions for reconciliation, linked for example to the penitential practices in certain sanctuaries and places of pilgrimage or indeed at celebrations in privileged places of worship. It is in this context that the long tradition of jubilees finds itself, from the very first of

---

4. Vatican Counci II, *Lumen Gentium*, § 3.
5. Tertullian, *De Paenitentia*, SC, vol. 316.

these established in the year 1300, by the Bull, *Antiquorum Habet*, of Pope Boniface VIII until the Great Jubilee of 2000.

The Graces and the Demands of a Jubilee

Jubilees constitute a tradition by now very well-established. At their beginning, it was the practice, at the turn of each century, for the Church to grant pilgrims who came to Rome a great indulgence; in order to receive this, they had to visit the two great basilicas of St Peter and of St Paul. At the request of pilgrims, this custom became institutionalized; 1300 then marked the beginning of the jubilees, such as we know them today.

We find dispositions relating to jubilees already in the old Covenant. There is evidence of a Sabbatical Year from the time of the Code of the Covenant (cf. Ex. 23:10–11). To rules pertaining the lordship of Yahweh over the soil and over lands, were added very quickly recommendations for the remission of debts:

> You shall declare this fiftieth year holy and you shall proclaim the emancipation of all the inhabitants of the country. This shall be for you a jubilee; each one of you shall return to his own patrimony, each one of you shall return to his own clan" (Lev 25:10).

The jubilee is an anticipation of the liberation that the Messiah was to inaugurate. Jesus will apply to himself the passage of the prophet, Isaiah:

> The Spirit of the Lord is upon me, because he has anointed me with oil, to bring the good news to the poor. He has sent me to proclaim liberty to captives, to the blind their sight, the setting free of the oppressed, and to proclaim a year of favour from the Lord (Is 4:18–19).

The joy of a jubilee (a year of grace) is thus linked to the remission of debts and to a reestablishment of people to their integrity (they were released from slavery). Here, there is the work of Christ. Now, by reason of his sins, every person stands before

God in the situation of a debtor. The Church offers to the baptized the joy of being reconciled with God through the remission of their sins and through the remission of temporal punishment due to sin. What are the latter? We know that serious sin can have, as a consequence, the privation of communion with God for the whole of eternity; this is eternal punishment. There exist also temporal penalties, whose aim is patiently to purify the sinner who suffers them from the attachment to sin and to make that person a new man or woman. This temporal penitence (which, besides, helps us to understand the meaning of purgatory) explains why it is that, all through the holy year, the Church may proceed to the concession of indulgences. We cannot grasp the meaning of this term very well, except in the light of what has been said above about the nature of the Church: "We call an indulgence the remission before God of temporal punishment due to sins which have already been forgiven as to the offence, which the well-disposed member of the faithful, under specified conditions may receive through the intervention of the Church."[6]

The Meaning of Indulgences

How can we understand the existence of such a remission of penalties? We know that certain abuses, in particular, the anarchic development between the fourteenth and fifteenth centuries of numerous collections connected to indulgences, had been one of the reasons for the tearing apart of Christians at the time of the Protestant Reformation. The Council of Trent put an end to these abuses, decreeing the abolition of all unworthy trafficking in money for indulgences,[7] while still continuing to ground the concession by Christ to the Church of the power to establish indulgences on the Gospel of St Matthew (Mt. 16:19; 18:18). At the origin of the first sacramental dispositions, such a gravity was attributed to serious sin committed after baptism as

---

6. Paul VI, *Indulgentiarum Doctrina*, 1967.
7. Cf. Council of Trent, *Decree on indulgences*, December 4, 1563, DS § 1835.

to require a long and difficult penance. The idea of conceding an indulgence expressed first of all an aspect of the communion of the saints; when she remits temporal punishment, the Church plays her part in the penitence of her children. The deep meaning of these indulgences devolves from the power given to Peter and to the Apostles to bind and to loose; furthermore, they manifest the solidarity of the Church with the sinners who are in her midst. This dimension is found once more today in the dispositions of the Catholic ritual for sacramental reconciliation, which foresees a certain satisfaction by the repentant sinner who has been forgiven.[8] Pope Leo XIII rightly saw in this aspect of sharing penalties one of the specific objects of the communion of the saints, which, he said, is nothing other than:

> A mutual communion of help, of expiation, of prayer, of good deeds among the faithful, both those who are already in possession of their heavenly fatherland, as those who are condemned to the flames of expiation, as well as those, in the end, who are still on their journey on this earth, but all of whom form but one single city, which has Christ for its head and which has charity as its form.[9]

We can see here how this perspective could give rise to abuse, namely the multiplication of penitential tariffs, so much so that the Church, while undertaking a work of mercy in this field, has always been conscious that she was drawing upon the inexhaustible treasure of the merits of Christ. In the text which we have already cited, Paul VI did not hesitate, moreover, to take up once more in this regard the expression consecrated by long usage by a large number of his predecessors: *the treasure of the Church*.[10]

Obviously, the concession of an indulgence only bears its fruits if the penitent who seeks the indulgence fulfils the conditions of sincere repentance for their sins. Paul VI sums it up like this: "that the member of the faithful loves God, detests their

---

8. Cf. . 'The Structure of Sacramental Confession', pp. 453–468 above.
9. Leo XIII, Encyclical Letter, *Mirae Caritatis* (1902), DS § 3363.
10. Paul VI, *Indulgentiarum doctrina*, § 5.

sins, places their trust in the merits of Christ and believes firmly that the communion of saints is of great value to them."[11] Here we find once more, expressed in different words, the essential dispositions that are required for the valid reception of the sacrament of reconciliation, which we have analyzed elsewhere.

When the Church Asks for Forgiveness

For a number of years now, through the words of its supreme Pastor or through those of different episcopal conferences, the Church has asked publicly for forgiveness. We must not hide away from the fact that a step such as this has encountered scepticism, indifference or, at times, annoyance among our contemporaries. In any case, it is not always understood; at times, it can provide a pretext for hostile criticisms and for re-readings of history that are incomplete and one-sided.

Basically, by exhorting the faithful to penance, the Church wishes to play her part also in that penance. Why is this? Because, before God, and before human beings, she assumes the continuity of her history, which is not just a divine and consequently a holy history, but which is also a human history, subjected to all of the historical conditioning factors affecting the sinful freedom of her members, whoever they may be.

From the very fact that she has a personality of a supernatural order, insofar as she is one with Christ, she necessarily assumes the totality of her history, which implies also the faults of her sinful members. For her, it is an absolute requirement that she purify herself without ceasing, by virtue of the holiness of the One who is united to her.

> Christ loved the Church; he gave himself up for her, in order to make her holy, cleansing her with water with a form of words; for he wanted to present her to himself, resplendent, without spot or stain or anything of the kind, but holy and immaculate" (Eph 5:25–27).

---

11. *Ibid.* § 8.

The Church and Forgiveness

When St Paul speaks of spot or stain, it is obviously sin that he is evoking. When she prepares for a jubilee, then, the Church like each of the baptized whom she exhorts, enters into a process that is penitential.

Among the failures of her sinful children, some have had repercussions of a public nature or indeed have given rise to an awareness on her part, often a long time after the events themselves. In this sense, there is a refinement over time of the awareness that the Church has of her mission and of the demands that the latter makes upon those who constitute her members.

She has not hesitated, on various occasions, herself to identify these faults, to call them by name, and even to make a list of them, as in *Tertio Millennio Adveniente*, in which she distinguishes the following sins:

- those that have wrought damage to the unity willed by Christ for his people (TMA, § 34); hence, her encouragement of ecumenical prayer;
- those that consist in her having consented in certain periods to employing methods which are intolerant and even of violence in the service of truth (§ 35); and
- those that involve the responsibility of the baptized for the evils of our times: religious indifference, lack of theological rectitude in the faith, maintaining serious forms of injustice and of social marginalization, the (imperfect) reception of that great gift of the Holy Spirit to the Church which is the Second Vatican Council (§ 36).

Like every penitent, it is first of all from God that the Church asks forgiveness. When she recognizes the wrongs she has committed publicly, she wishes herself to honour the evangelical requirement of reconciliation: "When, then, you present your offering at the altar and you remember that your brother has something against you, leave your offering there before the altar, go an first be reconciled with your brother, and then present your offering" (Mt 5:23–24).

Besides, apart from texts devoted to a specific question of history (the Inquisition, slavery, disunity among Christians, etc.), it is remarkable that the majority of the declarations have been proclaimed in the context of homilies, precisely before the priest offers on the altar the sacrifice of the Eucharist. From this same perspective, when she has been able to do it, the Church in her turn has proclaimed publicly forgiveness for the offences to which she has been subjected, as, for example, during the canonization by Pope John Paul II of the Czech, Jan Sarkander, from Olomouc on May 21, 1995.

- Requests for forgiveness take into account events of faith, both past and present. How can the Christian evaluate both of these?
- As for historical facts, without any doubt, by uniting themselves with humility to the examination of conscience proclaimed by her pastors (as a Christian, the baptized person is necessarily concerned in the whole history of the Church), but also with extreme circumspection by avoiding anachronisms and false interpretations arising from prejudices of every kind. Not every Christian is necessarily a historian! In a commentary on *Tertio Millennio Adveniente*, Fr Cottier, O.P., remarks quite rightly, with reference to the Galileo case, that "about the errors and faults which have been elucidated and recognized by ecclesiastics who are responsible ... a myth of a scientist inspiration has come to attach itself; before the hero of the freedom of thought, there is opposed the obscurantism of the Church."[12]
- As far as the present is concerned, with an even greater vigilance yet. It is the sin of its members alone that disfigures the Church. The sin of a Christian is always a denial of the grace of baptism and hence it is a blot, a stain on the face of the Church. On her part, the latter will never cease to assume her own

---

12. Presidential Council for the Great Jubilee of the Year 2000 (ed.), *Tertio Millennio Adveniente: Commentaire théologique et pastorale* (Paris: Mame, 1996), p. 121.

The Church and Forgiveness

history; then history which will be made tomorrow by the Church will pass necessarily through an examination of what will be the truth and the quality of her witness over the course of time, in other words, through the holiness of her children.

With reference to the indefectible hope that dwells in the Church, the Second Vatican Council expressed itself in these words:

> The virtue of the Risen Lord is her strength, which enables her, with patience and charity, to conquer the afflictions and the difficulties which come to from outside and from within and to reveal faithfully in the midst of the world the mystery of the Lord, still enveloped in shadows, until the day when, finally, he bursts forth in the fulness of light.[13]

In its acts of memorial, the Church does not forget to pay honour to those who, throughout its long history, have been worthy witnesses to this victory of the Risen Lord and, in the front row, there are the martyrs. In this respect, it observes that the blood of the martyrs is already a common patrimony of Catholics, Orthodox, Anglicans and Protestants.[14] Pope John Paul II remarked that, at the end of the second millennium, the Church had become once more a Church of martyrs. In the martyrs there is the figure of the Church belonging to God. Before he was to be assassinated, Fr Christian-Marie de Chergé wrote in his spiritual testament:

> If some day, it happens to me—and so that could be today—that I become a victim of the terrorism, which now seems to wish to encompass all the foreigners who are living in Algeria, I would like my community, my Church, my family, to remember that my life had been given to God and to this country. That they may accept that the sole Master of every life could not be absent from that brutal parting. That they pray for me; how could I be worthy of making such a sacrifice?

---

13. Vatican Council II, *Lumen Gentium*, § 8.
14. Cf. John Paul II, *Tertio Millennio Adveniente*, § 37.

24 The Forgiveness of Sins According to St Augustine[1]

The homiletic activity of St Augustine extended over almost forty years, of which the key part (thirty-four years) constituted the heart of his ministry as a bishop. It would be saying very little to state that a very large number of texts have come down to us, that their transmission, the establishment of their authenticity, and the critical study of which have required centuries of research, a research which has been particularly fruitful over the last century, and which in our days still offers many wonderful discoveries.[2] Augustine's preaching

---

1. "The Forgiveness of Sins in St Augustine" was published under the title «Le pardon des offenses et amour des ennemis dans les *Sermones* de St Augustin», *Anthropotes*, n. 16/1 (2000), pp. 69–102.
2. After taking from volumes 38 and 39 of Migne's *Patrologia Latina*, from the great Benedictine edition of St Maur (363 sermons reputed at the time to be authentic and 21 doubtful, to which were added 27 fragments), Dom Germain Morin added 138 units to the number that he judged authentic; his most resounding discovery was that of the famous manuscript 4096 of Wolfenbüttel, a collection of which 29 sermons (*Sermones Guelferbytani*) are today recognized as authentic, but there are 12 other pieces to be added to this, which have been discovered on other occasions by Morin out of the 17 that he estimated should be kept (these are the *Sermons Morin*). To this contribution are to be added the sermons found by Dom André Wilmart (21, of which 15 are admitted as being authentic) and by Dom Cyrille Lambot, to the number of 29. More recently (1990), the unedited *Sermones* of the Sermonnaire of Mainz have been discovered by François Dolbeau; published between 1990 and 1995, they have been gathered together in a single volume under the title of *Augustine of Hippo: 26 sermons to the people of Africa* (Paris: Études augustiniennes 147, 1996). For the problems connected to the history of the transmission and of the redaction of Augustine's sermons before the discovery of Dolbeau as a whole, reference can very profitably be made to the very useful work of P.P. Verbraken, *Étude critique sur les sermons authentiques de saint Augustin* (Steenbrugge: Nijhoff, 1976).

was not limited just to his *Sermones*. It extended to anthologies and to treatises published under other headings, such as the *Enarrationes in Psalmos*, the *Tractatus in Epistulam Johannis*, or again the *De sermone Domini in monte*. What follows here is devoted exclusively to the *Sermones*, a term which, from the beginning, designated teaching proclaimed orally in the course of a Eucharistic liturgy. A sermon, then, always refers to specific questions of a pastoral nature. The topics treated in the course of sermons cover, quite naturally, the totality of the different aspects of the Christian mystery; they go from a deep doctrinal analysis of the liturgical texts of the day to a simple commentary upon them, passing by way of moral exhortations and meditations on the example of the lives of the saints and of the martyrs. At the hinge of all of these areas in which the pastor intervened, the forgiveness of sins and the love of enemies that grounds it, recur unceasingly. At times, they give place to very long metaphors, which go back to the great biblical figures, like those of Jacob and Isaiah; often, we find theological elaborations on the just and merciful action of God towards sinners, on retribution for impenitence, and of divine benevolence towards those who forgive their neighbours their offences.

The topic of forgiveness for injuries received is examined in so many ways in the preaching of Augustine that a systematic study of the *Sermones* seemed to us to be necessary in order to assess its major significance.[3] The question arises of the choice of the *Sermones* alone, if it is true that the love of enemies is treated by the bishop of Hippo in other works of preaching or of catechesis. Thus, the penitential Psalms give rise to numerous developments on this subject, and, in the same way, the com-

---

3. "The preaching of the forgiveness of sins in its relationship to the Sunday Prayer played a considerable role in the pastoral activity of St Augustine. This is surely the most important point in his moral teaching as a whole. At one stroke, he gave to his community of Hippo the purest essence of Christianity" (A.-M. La Bonnardière, "Pénitence et réconciliation des Pénitents d'après saint Augustin," I, in *Revue des études augustiniennes* (REA, 13, 1967), pp. 31–53.

mentary on the Sermon on the Mount provides the occasion for a grandiose construction around the Beatitudes of Matthew (Mt 5–7). Limiting ourselves, however, to the *Sermones* is a choice that is justified in our eyes by the period which the *Sermones* which have come to us actually cover, and no less by the totality of Augustine's apostolate. The collection of the *Sermones ad populum* thus offers a panorama of the whole of Augustine's thought on the forgiveness of sins. Furthermore, the daily exercise of forgiveness is an eminently pastoral aspect of the concern of the Church and the genre of the *Sermones* provides this with a perfect expression, since it is true that all of the *Sermones* had actually been preached. This is not necessarily the case with the treatises on Scripture, which are broader and more systematic, and which could have been composed in the course of a shorter lapse of time.[4] Finally, there is that which a pastor such as Augustine considered that it was essential to say to an assembly of the faithful, at times to a very large number of them, as on the occasion of the major feasts, for example that of the martyr, St Cyprian or, again, the celebration of the feast of St Stephen, after the passage through Africa of the relics of this protomartyr.[5]

Some sermons were dedicated basically to the love of enemies or to the forgiveness of sins; others do not touch this topic, except by way of its connection in the context of addressing other themes; then, they often constituted a digression or indeed they may offered the possibility of an association of ideas, which always had a very precise aim of teaching.

The sermons dedicated essentially to the forgiveness of sins or to the love of enemies are the following: XVI/A, XLII, LXVI, LXXXII, LXXXIII, CXIV, CXIV/A, CLXXIX/A, CCVI to CCXI, CCLIX, CCCXIV, CCCXV, CCCXVI, CCCXVII, CCCXIX, CCCLII, CCCLXXXVI. The different topics linked to this subject (fraternal correction, the number of times forgiveness of

---

4. Numbers 55 to 124 of the *Tractatus in Johannem*, just to take a single example, would have been composed within just one year (419–420).
5. It is estimated that these relics of St Stephen had reached the continent of Africa at the very latest round about 417–418.

sins must be given, divine retribution of human mercy) are the object of developments of thought which are mixed from one sermon to another, by reason of improvizations on the part of the preacher, who, facing different audiences, would repeat himself. Besides, the aim of his preaching was not *a priori* to be complete, even if one of the characteristics of his sermons was that they ended up giving the impression on certain points of being a unified construction. It remains difficult to discover the totality of his thinking in a single homily. By chance, in this list, two sermons together form a single whole, certainly not exhaustive, but still very complete. We refer to the two sermons LXXXIII and LXXXIV, the authenticity of which has never been brought in doubt. The bishop of Hippo seems to have proclaimed them in the course of a journey to Mileve, in about 408–409, one day after the other and before the same congregation.

Thus, the topics raised are complementary to each other. Whereas the first sermon comments upon St Matthew's gospel: "If your brother commits a sin, go and speak to him and correct him yourselves alone …" (Mt 18:15–18), and the second addresses Peter's question to Jesus: "Lord, how many times may my brother sin against me and I must forgive him? As many as seven times?" (Mt 18:21–22), which introduces the parable of the unforgiving servant. It is necessary, then to read these two homilies together as a unified whole.

We shall proceed first of all with an analysis of the thread connecting the whole, with a very precise purpose, that of examining what the act of preaching about the forgiveness of injuries that had been suffered meant to Augustine. Over and above the *ars praedicandi* of the pastor, it will be useful to structure the topics that emerge, to complete them with any contributions that may occur from other sermons and to interpret them in the light of the Augustinian theology of the Redemption. This second stage of the thematic analysis will incorporate, naturally, elements elaborated on the love of enemies and on the forgiveness of sins, present in the other sermons which were dedicated

The Act of Preaching on the Forgiveness of Sins: The Thread Connecting Sermons 82 & 83
The Unfolding of the Preaching

The Liturgical Service of the Readings for the Day

Augustine undertook the practice of commenting upon the readings of the liturgy, consisting on that day of the passage of St Matthew's gospel (Mt. 18:15–35) and that of the Book of Proverbs (Prov. 10:10), which had just been proclaimed. In fact, from the evangelist, he took the first three verses (vv. 15–18), the object of the homily on the first day,[6] reserving until the day after a long analysis on Peter's question and on Jesus's response (vv. 21–22). He illustrated the totality of the points arising from the parable of the unforgiving servant, which, at the beginning of his second intervention, he took care to relate in a free manner, according to his custom. If the text from Proverbs appears in the *Sermones* only here, we find a commentary on the verses from St Matthew's Gospel (Mt. 18:15–18) in another homily; in sermon 295 for the feast of the Apostles Peter and Paul, Augustine spoke of the power of the keys entrusted to Peter, who incarnates the Church as a whole. The preacher intended to insist, then, upon this unique role of the Apostle and he used the passage from St Matthew's Gospel in this sense, since they are words addressed to all of the disciples and not only to Peter, as in Chapter 16, verse 19. By contrast, the other great sermon on fraternal correction was attached to a parallel passage from St Matthew's Gospel (Mt. 7:3–4).

---

6. Thus, Augustine was not concerned with commenting upon the intermediate verses, which St Matthew had dedicated to prayer in common (vv. 19–20).

Augustine relied upon the Scriptures, which he did not use to serve as a pretext to illustrate a question that he wished to expound and to resolve. This manifests his desire to understand what the texts (here liturgical texts) say, exploiting all of the richness of meaning and the nuances which one verse can bring to our understanding of another verse. What is striking is that he drew out from the texts themselves the paradox that he would use in order to pose a question, whose resolution would only appear much further on in the homily. This was the case with the two sermons, 82 and 83. In sermon 82, for example, the question arises of a comparison between the Gospel and the first reading; according to the latter, which contained the verse from the Book of the Proverbs (Prov. 10:10), the person who corrects someone in public (*palam*) obtains peace; how can this judgment of King Solomon be expressed in relation to what Matthew says: "If your brother sins against you, go to him and correct him yourselves alone?" In an attitude of being at the service of the word of God, Augustine anticipated what could disturb a member of the faithful who was not alert. In this regard, the two sermons provide a magnificent lesson in how to read the Scriptures; by underlining the difficulty in Sermon 82 of the two texts put together, Augustine put the congregation on its guard against the idea that the divine precepts might contradict each other. On the contrary, he saw in them a *perfect harmony* (*summam concordiam*), but it was now up to him to show this deep harmony and to convince those who were listening to him of it. This is what required that the orator use all of his talents. That his demonstration gave him an opportunity to take up the cudgels—in this case, it was against the Manichaeans—in the eyes of the preacher, this was part of the responsibility he had for the care that the pastor owed to the faithful.

In Sermon 83, Augustine fixed the attention of the faithful upon the number "seventy-seven;" to be sure, it was very high, how would someone be in a position to count that he had offended the same enemy seventy-seven times? Despite everything, we could imagine that this number offers a limit; this is why the orator himself formulated the transgression of this limit in a provocative way: "If you reach the seventy-eighth time, then prepare to avenge yourself;" but Augustine did not give up: "Is it in this way that the statement of the Lord is true, that it is to be understood?" With great elegance, he did not take the trouble to say 'No'; he went straight to the point, hitting it clearly: "I dare, I dare to say that, if your brother sins against you seventy-eight times, forgive him: And, if he sins a hundred times, forgive him. And, if he does so on countless occasions (*toties et quoties*)? Forgive him." Thus, after having affirmed the unity of the Old and the New Testament in the first part (82), he warned the faithful in the second part (83) not to fall into a literal interpretation of the Lord's words, which would contradict the spirit and the meaning of the gospel teaching (forgive *seventy-seven times* means to forgive always).

Binary Distinctions

After a very dense introduction, which announced the substance of the message that was to be discussed, Augustine set up several distinctions that would have the effect of placing his listener before the terms of a choice. Some of these binomials quite naturally, were taken from the gospel text, such as that of the splinter and the plank; others were the expression of a moral alternative or the consequences of an action, or of a sentiment. They functioned like beacons in the preacher's exposition, enabling him, from one distinction to the other, to recapture the attention of his listeners, who were not particularly well formed. Besides, they offered an ideal means of memorizing, so that they would be able later to remember the content and the nuances of a homily, which might have appeared to have endured for a very long time, had he not proceeded in this way. It is also true that taking up these semantic couplets in their chronological order would make it possible to reconstitute the totality of the bishop's preaching. Here are just a few examples: in sermon 82 "extrinsic-intrinsic, yesterday-today, poison-cure," in sermon 83, "seven times seventy times-seven times, being in debt to God-having someone in debt to you, crime-sin, one offering praise through words-having scorn in the heart ..."

The Thread Connecting Sermons 82 and 83

General Introduction: 82.1

The introduction to Sermon 82 prepared the content of the two interventions by means of a preliminary affirmation: God exhorts us not to neglect the sins we have committed towards one another, but he asks that we be attentive to what will help us to correct this. Correction is only possible if the eye is not encumbered by a plank. Augustine took his listeners at first off-balance; the duty to correct our brother was indeed something that God asks us to fulfil, but this was to be done without hatred. Hatred does not make it possible to correct a brother who is angry. How would the faithful be able to apply this warning to themselves? How would hatred concern them? Augustine compared hatred to the plank and anger to the splinter. How did he arrive at the plank? With great dexterity, the orator reversed the image in a way that would make you laugh: a splinter is the beginning of a plank, and we pass from one to the other by watering it; in other words, by feeding the anger (a further rhetorical reversal) by means of the suspicions which lead to hatred. The rhetoric was very well done; the faithful were thus led to consider the danger of falling into hatred as a real possibility, thus of having a plank in their eye and of being unable to fulfil the duty of correcting their brother. Why? Because hatred is a sentiment which is so excessive that no member of the faithful, listening to a sermon, could feel directly challenged by this warning; on the other hand, the suspicions, the process of worsening intentions, this is a daily threat to every community, which thus runs the risk of being divided. There would be no reason to think that the community at Mileve would be any exception. We could not exclude the possibility that the bishop had got wind of some difficulties, which might have been disturbing the community to which he was addressing himself. Whatever the case may be, Augustine, by capturing their attention from the start, opened up the possibility of developing what he had in his heart, namely, to explore the interiority of the human person in order to demonstrate that it needed to be visited by true charity.

The Interiority of the Act of Forgiving: 82.2 to 82.7

Ira et odium: anger and hatred

Anger and hatred[7] are two feelings that dwell in the heart of the human being, but there is nothing in common between the one and the other. Whereas the latter is always dark (*"Hatred is darkness,"* he would affirm later on), the former is ambiguous. Since, in the beginning, anger had this role of feeding the splinter and of transforming it into a plank, Augustine pointed out its positive function in the correction of children: he proceeded with a veritable *captatio benevolentiae*: do we not become angry when we are correcting our children? Hence, here there is not the slightest trace of hatred. It would be absurd to think differently. Better; this anger is at times necessary, when it is a case of saving the child who is running the risk of a mortal danger, wishing to bathe in a raging torrent, and even, paradoxically, "not to correct the child in anger would be to give him a witness of hatred," said Augustine. Thus, the faithful were led to consider how very little would be needed in the step they would be taking in being tempted to wish to correct others. The preacher could conclude this first point and could be understood: *"Above everything else, avoid hatred."*

Hatred is murderous, as the first letter of St John teaches, which Augustine took care to quote, in support of his condem-

---

7. The terms *ira* and *odium* are to be found often in the sermons; 72 times for the first and 245 times for the second. The topic of hatred is omnipresent in Augustine's preaching.

nation of sentiments of hatred, but it is something which turns against the person who shelters it in their heart. First of all, is prevents the person from seeing clearly, and it is for this reason that it does not make it possible for them to correct their brother. The real paradox of hatred lies in this: while it is spreading its activity of harming the other, it ignores the damage that it produces in the one who hates. What is more, this harm comes first. It is impossible for it to be otherwise, said Augustine: "Someone who hates his brother necessarily hates their own soul. That person behaves as the very real enemy of themselves." Vengeance is an external evil, which someone seeks to impose upon their enemy, but this evil has its first devastating effect first of all on the person themselves; the person who takes vengeance "loses their moral sense, becomes unjust, loses their innocence, and becomes at risk of perishing."

It remains for us to ask why the enemy cannot reach our interiority, in the eyes of St Augustine. An enemy does nothing other than to take away from us what we have or our good reputation; he has no leverage over the two goods which we possess and which it is not possible for us to lose against our will: our faith and our moral conscience. These, moreover, are the two most precious goods that we have. We do not lose anything essential, as long as our soul retains its integrity. The bishop's perspective remained resolutely that of salvation. How does it come about, then, he asked, that those who exact vengeance have no awareness of the fact that they are inflicting upon themselves great, interior harm? It is that, by acting in this way, they have lost their sense of morality. The loss of the sense of morality, for the bishop, is the greatest misfortune that a Christian could suffer, since this predisposes the person to do evil, in this way to lose his innocence and so to lose his very self.

Having said to the faithful everything he wanted to say on this point, Augustine gave the appearance of returning to the initial topic of correction; if we are minded to correct another person, let it be out of love for that person and not out of a desire to do him harm. It is in this that we find conduct that is excellent, one that makes it possible to gain a brother for salvation.

Taking seriously the gravity of the offence which has been committed

Once again, Augustine reversed the perspective:

> Of course, I have put you on guard against any kind of sentiment of hatred, which would prevent you from correcting your brother effectively. Therefore, so that those who have sinned against their neighbour should not feel themselves free of responsibility, to them too I have something to say.

In fact, in a very subtle way, Augustine continued to address himself to everyone, for, by quoting the first letter of St Paul to the Corinthians (1Cor 8:12), he spoke of the risk of clashing with brothers, of offending them, of a sick conscience. This is exactly what happens when we correct our brothers without love. "Let no one think that he has committed only a slight offence, for, if you wound your brothers, as the Apostle says, then you are sinning against Christ." In support of this affirmation, the preacher quoted explicitly the passage in St Matthew's Gospel (Mt 5:22) and he completed it with the verse that follows on the necessity of being reconciled with our brother before offering our sacrifice to God. By asserting that God cannot accept the sacrifice offered by someone who has damaged his brother, he suggested how serious the sin against others is: he prepared to condemn it forcefully. This passage (Mt 5:23), then, reinforced his argument. For Augustine, there was there the possibility of concentrating the attention of the faithful upon what was essential: to bring a sacrifice, that is a good thing; but what is better, is to make an offering of oneself, showing that we belong to God. Let us never lose sight of the fact that these words of Augustine were proclaimed precisely in the midst of the Eucharistic sacrifice. For Augustine, however, the most important thing remained to be said; in order to be reconciled with someone whom we have offended, we must still be ready to humble ourselves: Certainly, he remarks: "it is not so easy to ask forgiveness as it is to cause offence." To humble ourselves is undoubtedly to lower ourselves, and he adds ironically, "But you refuse to humble yourself, when already you are stretched out on the ground?" Here, it is understood, with respect to what it was that reduced you to this, namely, the evil you committed against your brother. You would not really lose anything by humbling yourself! Augustine could return now to the subject of correction.

Why and how to correct the offender

Now, it was a matter of trying to convince the faithful that fraternal correction is a duty. We could object that, for this duty, it means not to bear hatred towards our enemy; that is indeed exactly what the preacher had been saying up to this point and, in fact, Augustine rendered homage in this sense to forgetting the offences committed, which is a glorious act. However, with great firmness, the bishop denied the right of the Christian to forget the wound inflicted by his brother; the latter had inflicted great harm upon themselves by his offence. How, then, could such a wound be ignored? Nevertheless, it is very clear that this wound could not be considered less than the wound that could have been provoked by his wickedness. Now, someone who would neglect a wound of this kind would be even worse than his enemy. Here, his address was violent, and Augustine had chosen to mark this moment, which was the climax of his sermon by what was going to seem to the faithful to be a veritable verbal excess. So, it is always necessary to correct the one who is guilty? Yes, on all occasions where it is possible, but not under any circumstances whatsoever. That the one who corrects his brother be attentive not to humiliate him. The person who has been offended and who is correcting the guilty person is asked to show consideration (and compassion) for the self-respect of his adversary, not because of possibly causing an affront to the latter, but above all by reason of the foreseeable consequences of such a humiliation; the person might be tempted then to offer a justification for the wrong committed and to consider his sin as an act of justice. For this reason, it is good to follow the recommendation of the Lord in these verses of the evangelist: "If your brother sins against you, correct him face to face."

Must correction be public (82.8 to 82.15)?

It was time for Augustine to resolve the apparent divergence between the two readings, the Gospel of St Matthew (Mt 18:15) and the Book of Proverbs (Prov.10:10) and of which we have spoken above, in order to state what is the *supreme harmony* which unites them: there is no discordance between the Scriptural texts. Once again, the argumentation sought to come spiritually to the help of the faithful. There are two possibilities: either the offence was known only to the one who suffered it, or it was public. Why should the correction in the first case be secret? Could it not be thought that knowledge of such a correction might be helpful to others? Augustine did not deny this, even if he did not say so explicitly; for his concern lay elsewhere; he was addressing the one who claimed to correct the offender. Now, if someone wants to correct in public an offence, of which they alone know, there is room to ask about the nature of this desire: is it to correct a brother or is it to reveal to others the wrong which has been done? There was no hesitation on Augustine's part, being without illusions as to the heart of human beings: it would be indeed the pleasure of revealing to others the sin which had been committed. The preacher gave the example of Joseph, the just man, who wished only to repudiate in secret the wife who had been promised to him (82.10). As for the other type of offence, that which had been committed in public, it was appropriate to correct that in front of others. Why? Because the offence, in that case, had been committed against everyone. Augustine gave the example of the offence made in his presence to one of his brothers. He said that he could not consider that it had nothing to do with him. Thus, there is a discernment to be undertaken before revealing anything about sins committed by our brothers. There was a very specific example of a sin that Augustine wished to use, in order to show the importance of the discretion to be observed. It was that of adultery. How could the person guilty of that sin be reproached?

The case imagined by Augustine was the following: a bishop was the only person who had come to know of a crime that had been committed. It would be good for a public reprimand to have been made, but then someone would want to go to court.[8] At this point, Augustine used the first person: "I do not spread news of the sin, but I do not ignore it either." What did the bishop do then? Reproving the person in secret, he wished to make him aware of the gravity of his sin and would act in three ways in the bishop's place: I place before his eyes the judgment of God; I inspire terror in his wounded conscience, and I convince him to do penance.

The judgment of God upon the guilty person, which he evoked, was aimed at making the latter aware of the true gravity of their sin and of the importance of embarking upon a path of penitence. The fear of the divine court was the first point to be made, taking account of the crime committed. The preacher's second remark is interesting; he was not afraid of inspiring terror in the wounded conscience of the murderer. As bishop, was not only a master of doctrine, but was also responsible for the formation of consciences through his moral teaching. Now here,

---

8. It is necessary to be on our guard here against an anachronistic reading of this passage: if it seems quite normal to our contemporary sensitivities to bring someone before a court and *a fortiori* someone who might be guilty of a crime, we must keep before our minds the power that belonged to a bishop in the times of Augustine, not only that of hearing the plea, but even more of determining the sentence. In the Christian community, to call brothers to justice was considered to be a sin. In the example chosen by the preacher, the will to keep the crime secret was less from a desire to protect the guilty person (except, to be sure, on the hypothesis sustained by some, where it concerned a sacramental confession), than the will to preserve the one who might denounce the guilty person to the tribunal from the sin which he would commit by doing so.

the very strong expression must be interpreted strictly in the light of the end being pursued by the pastor, that of leading the assassin to repent of their sins in the strict sense of the term; not only that of being sorry for the sins in what the subsequent tradition would call sentiments of perfect contrition but above all and more immediately that of entering the Order of Penitents, persuading them to take this very public step.

Talking of homicide amounts to considering a case that is exceptional; the faithful could not but feel affected by this admonition. For this reason, Augustine would take up once more the other example, so banal that, in all likelihood, it would touch a much greater number of his listeners, that of adultery. He intended to awake in them the same torment of conscience, to evoke the same judgment of God, and more concretely to convince them also to undertake a path of penitence. Why this allusion to adultery? Simply because the sins in this matter, often remaining secret, were not always submitted to the purification of the *magna paenitentia*. However, they should not be underestimated. Did adulterers need to fear only that their blemished conduct might become known? They ought to be more afraid, affirmed the preacher with great force, of him who would be their judge. This allusion to adultery offered Augustine the opportunity to call all the faithful to conversion. All of them should have let themselves be corrected on that very day, not putting off taking this step until another day.

Following a reprimand of this sort, it was time to lighten the atmosphere, yet without losing the thread of what he was seeking, namely, to elicit the decision to correct their behaviour. Augustine made use of a play on words, in order to place in opposition to each other the genuine decision for conversion, which is always something immediate, and deferring it until tomorrow. Those who speak of tomorrow are like crows cawing because they keep on repeating *"Cras, cras"* (82,14). They would do better to prefer the murmuring of a dove to cawing like that! In Augustine's eyes, deferring conversion rested upon a kind of presumption; if it is true that God welcomes and will welcome the person who undergoes conversion, because he has promised to do this, he never promised to do this on any day whatsoever in the future.

The bishop had still not said everything he wished to say on that day; he would send the congregation away with one last appeal to conversion. The only thing that would bring him joy in the accomplishment of the mission entrusted to him by God was the resolution of the faithful; above all, it would not come from any applause on their part, which was not followed by that effect. There they were, then, furnished with a good subject for their meditation, in expectation of their meeting the next day.

The Ingratitude of the Unforgiving Servant and the Condition of All People (83.2)

The bishop called to mind the verses upon which he had commented the day before and referred to Peter's question to Jesus about the number of times we should forgive our brother. his preaching would move continually from this question, which all of those listening to him surely would pose to themselves, to the parable of the unforgiving servant. The parable which he had analyzed was without doubt as important here as the rest of the bishop's argumentation. He judged it necessary to warn the congregation: "Here we have a story that the Lord told, with the aim of bringing about our salvation."

How did St Augustine present this instruction? By identifying himself with those who were listening to him; every one of them, without exception, was in a position identical to that of this person in the parable. In fact, every human being is at one and the same time both debtor towards God and creditor towards his brother.

No one is exempt from sin and that is to be in debt towards God. At issue here is the meaning of sin, that is to say the meaning of one's personal sin. At the same time, each one has a brother or sister who is a debtor towards him, since everyone has already committed sins against his neighbour. Once this association with the unforgiving servant of the parable had been made, Augustine would start to reason on the basis of the demands of justice.

The rule here was the following: "Forgive and you will be forgiven, give and it will be given to you" (Lk 6:37–38). He evoked the two works of mercy: forgiving and giving.[9] Every person is a mendicant before God (*Dei mendicus*), to the extent that he address himself to God. He would be heard to the extent that he had himself been an almsgiver towards those in need; the bread given to the poor is a preparation for the living bread, Christ, which every person asks for when he turns to God.

Now, there is a prayer that everyone recites on a daily basis, it is the request: "Forgive us our sins, as we forgive those who sin against us." Very delicately, Augustine remarked that this establishes a rule;[10] the person who recites this prayer himself sets the conditions for the forgiveness of his own sins. To say this prayer means to enter into a pact with God. The effect produced in those listening to him was very powerful, since he could not retreat from the severe conditions that the Lord had set up (he who had forgiven everything, over and above any limit). In the setting of this very effective rhetoric, there was, undoubtedly, the concern of Augustine to offer an implicit invitation to Christians to reflect upon the words which they address, so often without much thought, to their God. It is they who set out the terms of the agreement.

---

9. As far as forgiveness is concerned, we have already seen that every person is in need of being forgiven by God and has at least someone who has offended them; as far as the second proposition is concerned, it happens to everyone that they are importuned by beggars, but who would think that the sole fact of praying would make of them a beggar before God?
10. His cleverness lies in the falsely naïve question which he poses like this: "When you say to God, 'Forgive us our trespasses ... of what sins are you speaking?' Of all your sins, or only of part of them? 'Of all,' you will reply. Well then, let it be the same with your debts towards your neighbor" (83.4).

Seventy-Seven Times: Without any Limits

Jesus's reply to Peter's question is an application of this *regula*, established by the Master, but the measure is used in reverse. Previously, it was a question of tracing the perspective of a forgiveness in the future, exercising mercy in this life towards those who have offended us. Now, Augustine would explain the meaning of the number given by Jesus, by evoking the example of mercy that he had given. It was that the Christian is called to imitate the Lord, as the Apostle, Paul, had invited the Christians at Colossae to do (cf. Col 3:13). Christ did not limit himself to a limited number, however elevated it might have been. The use of *septuagies septies* means precisely an unlimited number of times. In this way, Augustine formulated the absolute norm for forgiveness of injuries; there exists no sin that we must not forgive. How can we understand the spirit of this teaching? By returning to the parable: are not the ten thousand talents a figure for ten thousand sins? And the hundred denarii, do they not surpass the number of seventy-seven? Yet, what is there in common between the two debts? It is clear that, while insisting upon the colossal difference between the two sums, Augustine wanted to convince his listeners that there is no debt which is insignificant, in what relates to sin, since the smallest of debts in this regard surpasses very greatly the limit represented by the number indicated by Jesus.

Therefore, the quantitative aspect of this pastoral reminder from Augustine, the preacher, did not relegate to the second place the interior demand for forgiveness. The bishop evoked once more the moral quality of the act of forgiveness, which encompasses the entire interiority of the person: he must forgive from the heart, because God sees the conscience of the one who says: "I forgive." To correct someone is an act of charity, but it must be accompanied by gentleness.

The great Augustinian themes linked to the forgiveness of sins

The forgiveness of offenses, in Augustine, rests upon a certain number of theological principles, which are essential in his work. Some of these are obvious in Sermons 82 and 83; others are more explicit in other sermons. It is impossible to offer an exhaustive inventory of all of them, since that would amount to reconstructing the whole of the Augustinian theology of the Redemption. Nevertheless, it will be useful to bring together some of the exhortations of the pastor on forgiveness, in regard to questions which never ceased to occupy his apostolate and his teaching. We think that the sermons on the forgiveness of offences may profitably be considered as the pastoral expression of the great themes that follow.

In Sermons 82 & 83

Hatred (*odium*) refers to its contrary, charity (*caritas*), which is a perfect translation of Augustine's order.

The need to reestablish unity through reconciliation presupposes, by way of the request for forgiveness, for example, a personal commitment, which requires that the conditions of Augustinian *humilitas* be fulfilled

The correction of offences is a duty whose highest requirement is that of reestablishing the guilty person in his state of being reconciled and, in this way, of counting him once more among the number of our brethren. This presupposes, on the one hand, the reestablishment of justice in the relationship and, on the other, the concern for the eternal salvation of his brother (*iustitia* and *salus*).

The offence committed by a brother has provoked in him a greater harm than that inflicted upon his neighbour; the seriousness of this wound can only be understood in the light of the Augustinian conception of sin.

The need for conversion (*"today and not tomorrow"*) expresses two topics which here are linked together: that of the sovereignty of God over time and history, and that of the Augustinian *conversio*.

In the Totality of the Other Sermons

The person who has offended you is also your brother (16/A), your enemies are of the same nature as yourself (56); since you are a sinner, forgive the one who has sinned against you (114); this equality among debtors (114/A) reveals a solidarity of the members of the same body, in particular from the standpoint of the reception of the same gift: What do you have that you have not received? Grace received implies an act of thanksgiving.

This grace of Christ acts like a liberation; to be free from the old man, is to be freed from oneself, for each one of us is our own interior enemy—when we do not forgive (42).

To forgive our enemies is to imitate the Master, who forgave those who persecuted him the outrages they had perpetrated against him; the imitation of Christ is itself also a work of grace among us, an imitation of the Redeemer (56).

The link between almsgiving and forgiveness: if we consider the final end, remitting offences and giving to the poor out of compassion is to make a loan to God *with usury* (42), it is also to enter into a consideration of the final judgment and of final retribution (in the light of eschatology).

To forgive is a requirement of virtue; the obstacles to forgiveness are often the obstacles to a virtuous life (209).

Finally, martyrdom is the climax to which love of enemies can attain; it is also an imitation of Christ, and it is both the fruit (315) and the source of grace.

Let us take up once more some of the basic themes illustrated by the forgiveness of offences and by love of enemies.

Order and Charity

Order and charity cannot be considered apart from each other. For Augustine, *order* is what God had established, a harmony, a standard, a rule inscribed in every being. When the beginning of his ministry would lead him to specify the nature of good and of evil, to counter the errors of the Manichaeans, Augustine would give his thinking a systematic form. It was very important to him to be able to affirm that "there cannot be a nature which is bad, insofar as it is nature,"[11] because God is just and all goods, whatever their degree of being, share in that goodness which created them; thus, in every being there is a reason which presided over its creation, which makes it possible to see in it a certain degree of rationality; to understand the finality of a nature is to penetrate into its intelligibility. The human creature acts well when he goes in the direction of the rationality in which and through which he was created. Order, then, expresses itself at the concrete level as the work of reason.[12] This is indeed one reason why the human being must forgive his brother; it is God who has *ordered* him to do this.

From this then, it is clear that to refuse to forgive, or indeed to refuse to humiliate oneself in order to ask forgiveness from a brother, is in reality a form of conduct that is absurd or incongruous. Forgiving is a requirement of the *caritas Dei*, which has been at work in this way in our stead,[13] and which calls us to act in the same way. Every act of charity is inscribed within a conformity to the order which has been established by the charity of God. Moreover, the preacher addressed himself directly to the faithful, stimulating the charity in them, which would assist them, for example, in discerning when it would be appropriate to reprove someone in public and when in secret. All of the deeds accomplished by the Saviour in the economy of salvation are by definition an expression of his charity; in the same way,

---

11. St Augustine, *Enchridion de fide, spe et charitate*, I, cap. 4.
12. Thus, the term *ordo* designates both a rule of action, a measure of action, and, at the same time a style of life.
13. "The charity of Christ which has been poured into our hearts comes from a hidden principle: the depth of the divine will, the impenetrable judgment of mercy which has saved us in a completely gratuitous manner" (P.-M. Hombert, *Gloria Gratiae. Se glorifier en Dieu, principe et fin de la théologie augustinienne de la grâce* (Paris: IEA, 1996), 177.

every act of the disciple which aims to free his neighbour from his debt and to save him from perdition (through fraternal correction) is inspired by divine charity and, consequently, enters into that order which is willed by God.

We can understand, then, the real significance of the hatred, and of the anger that, at times, leads to it; hatred intends to withdraw our neighbour from the order of charity, which we cease to wish for him. It is irrational, because, by that same act, it excludes from that order the person whom it animates.

The Humility of Acting with Mercy: The Imitation of the Master

The humility of the Christian finds its foundation, its form, and its source in the redemptive humility of Christ. It has been emphasized quite rightly that the whole work of Augustine is to be understood on the basis of the mystery of the humility of the Incarnate Word; the humility of the Incarnation in the very first place, the humility of his life among us human beings, and the humility of his self-emptying on Calvary (*humilitas crucis*). Augustine's sermons naturally provide an echo of this theme, so propitious for the building-up of the faithful. He who had created us has come to us in great humility; "such a creature in our midst," said Augustine one day in the course of an episcopal ordination; on another occasion, commenting upon the birth of the Saviour, he said the same thing, but in a more oblique fashion: "For your benefit, the Creator made himself into a creature." One day, he would devote an entire homily to this topic, in which he would scold the faithful, but in a humorous way: "Who would lower themselves, to pass from the state of being a human to become an animal?" Hence, there can be no comparison: "The person who came to the point of doing that would still not have superseded the distance which God covered by lowering Himself to our level."

It can be understood that it is at its very root that Christ's humility is salvific, since it connotes every one of his deeds brought about for us. It acts like a medicine that heals the pride of sin; from then on, it acts as a sacrament, renewing the person from within, and rendering them capable of following the divine model.

Justice and Salvation (*Iustitia* and *salus*)

Justice, as the condition of salvation, is to be understood first of all in the interior sense of justification, as a work of grace. Augustine asked himself about the conditions necessary for obtaining this justice, which comes from God, when commenting, in sermon 179/A,[14] on the words of the letter of James: "If someone keeps the whole of the law, with the exception of one single point, he is still guilty of breaking the whole law" (Jas 2:10). How can we be sure in ourselves that we are keeping the law, in its entirety? By loving God with the whole of our being; that is the real foundation (*firmamentum*), it is towards this that it is worthwhile orientating ourselves, making of this our fortress and the house where we can find refuge. It is in the house of the Master that we can live in justice, because there we learn the morals of Christ, humble and merciful. The act of forgiving offences is, in the first place, an act of justice. To be sure, at times, the guilty person shows no sign of repentance; that person cannot be reinserted into the community of the brothers, if they persist in such an attitude.[15] Nevertheless, as we have said above, that does not dispense us from praying that one day they may be saved, as the preacher asked.[16] Augustine asked that forgiveness always be given, at least to the one who is sorry for having sinned and who asks for mercy.

To refuse forgiveness is to exclude ourselves from salvation. Augustine is very clear on this point: "If you, who are a human being, refuse to be human towards another human being, then

---

14. Cf. Wilmart, 2, see note 1, p. 421 above.
15. Augustine, *Sermon* 56, 16.
16. *Ibid.* 179/A. 4.

God will refuse divinity to you."[17] The unforgiving servant of the parable, at first, had been ungrateful, and his ingratitude had made him unjust. The gravity of refusing to remit the sin of a brother explains why, on one occasion, the Bishop of Hippo had shown consternation at discovering that the Christian community of which he had charge has refused, in his absence, to accept the return into its midst of a repentant Donatist. He reproached them vigorously. This case shows the extent to which Augustine was preoccupied by the injustice which had been committed by his people, having become a prey to doubt about the sincerity of taking such a step. How could they have judged the heart a person? The zeal of his brothers made the heart of the pastor sad and pounded him even to his entrails. He exhorted them, henceforth, to accept back the Donatists who repented; those who had not been Catholics before their entry into that sect were to be received in the normal way, those who had been Catholic before joining the Donatists, were to be admitted to penitence. The sermon, delivered in Carthage on the solemnity of Ss. Peter and Paul, offers a resounding, public demonstration of this superior justice: "What would make them seek reconciliation, if not their own will? For the moment, let us accept their infirmity and then we can test their will." This episode seems to us to be of very great importance, for it shows that, in the eyes of Augustine, mercy surpasses very considerably the sphere of the personal attitude of an individual; it has, and it must have, a communitarian and a social function.

Liberation from Sin and Conversion

To be merciful to an enemy is to give witness to the operation of grace; Augustine underlined the fact constantly that only forgiveness given from the depth of the heart is an act of charity. Charity gives us true knowledge of God, an interior presence which presupposes the liberating action of grace. It is impossible for there to be present in the same heart at the same time a de-

---

17. *Ibid.* 259. 3.

lectation for grace and an attachment to sin. The interior presence of sin is assimilated to the presence of an interior enemy. The sinful person is *his own enemy*. In the refusal to forgive, the following enemies were frequently denounced by Augustine: anger and hatred (sermon 82 has shown this), but also avarice, concupiscence, and pride, which leads people to consider the sin of our neighbour as worse than those which they might have committed themselves. With respect to an invitation to purify themselves by giving alms to the poor,[18] Augustine proclaimed the way in which God would free the sinner from himself. God "frees them from the anger" which disturbs them, he "forgives their sins," he "makes their life meritorious," he "gives them the strength" necessary to struggle against their evil desires; he "inspires virtue in them," and he "gives their spirit the taste of heaven" (*'donando caelestem delectationem'*). The person who refuses to reconcile himself with his brother by granting him forgiveness, is in the same position as the sinner who rejects it. Only a response to the call of God, an adherence to his merciful plans, makes it possible to enter into the action of *conversio*, which is proper to spiritual creatures. In a very profound way, *conversio* enables the creature to enter into the right position towards the Creator; hence, it presupposes the rediscovery of humility (which had been lost by sin), as well as giving praise and glory of God (*laus Dei*). The person, however unforgiving he may have been, who begins to dispose themselves to be able to forgive has begun by recognizing his position as debtor towards God and of being a mendicant of his mercy; "that person then enjoys the justice which their forgiveness has given to the brother whom they have found once more."

The Case of Martyrdom

Augustine's preaching on Christian martyrdom is so abundant that it would justify a study all of its own. There are several reasons for this: if it is a commonplace to say that the faith of the

---

18. *Ibid.* 42. 3.

Church has been built up on the witness of blood, this was a particularly sensitive point in the self-awareness of the pro-consular Church in Africa. The great basilicas of Carthage were dedicated to the great martyrs,[19] the liturgy made into a solemn occasion the day of the birth or of the death of the saint who had sacrificed his life. The feasts of St Cyprian or of St Stephen, for example, had given rise to demonstrations of popular joy, from which excessive entertainments of a profane nature were not always absent, as the Bishop of Hippo took care to denounce. For Augustine, there was a deeper reason; the martyr is the most perfect fulfilment in the person of the action of grace; he repeated often that no one could arrogate to himself this honour, and much less could they glory in it of themselves. The martyr places his trust in the power of God and not in his own strength. For this reason, it is in God alone that he should glorify, as the Apostle urges (1Cor 3:21). We know that this particular point had been decisive in the struggle against the sect of the Donatists.[20] Only a just cause makes the martyr.

Martyrdom finds its origin in the same source as the capacity to forgive offences. It is the forgiveness of offences itself brought to its highest point. Is not the very act of putting a Christian to death, from a certain standpoint, the greatest offence that could be committed against him? The preacher would go on to exclaim: "How many gifts has the devil given to us? he has offered to us all of the martyrs!"[21] However, for the victim, the nature of this act is transformed into a crown of glory. Augustine often underlined this aspect. The figure of the proto-martyr, St

---

19. The basilica of Ager Sexti was raised up in the place where St Cyprian, bishop of Carthage, was martyred. This is to be found in the Sermons under the denomination of Mensa Cypriani. At least 13 known homilies had been preached there by the Bishop of Hippo. Also, in the time of Augustine, a church was found in Carthage dedicated to St Peter (*Petri in regione tertia*), to St Paul (*Pauli regionis sextae*), St Faust, St Gratian. (cf. O. Perler, *Les voyage ... Excursus: Les basiliques chrétiennes de Carthage en rapport avec saint Augustin*, pp. 417–422.
20. Cf. Homber, *Op. cit.*, pp. 129–140.
21. St Augustine, *Sermon*, 315. 6.

Stephen, whose feasts had given rise to six sermons,[22] offered the preacher the occasion to exalt in him the love of enemies; if we follow his example (of martyrdom), we shall also receive the crown, *"but let us imitate above all his love for his enemies."* In Stephen, there was brought to fulfilment a perfect imitation of the Passion of the Lord; in both cases, there was false witness, which was the direct cause of their deaths, but, above all, there was the same interior attitude; to the forgiveness proclaimed by Jesus to those who were persecuting him, there corresponds the prayer of the disciple: "Lord, do not hold this sin against them." In particular, he imitated the suffering Christ. Augustine said that "Stephen had compassion for those who were stoning him and that it was for this reason that he prayed for them on his knees." On another occasion, Augustine made of Saul a wolf, whom the prayer of the deacon would transform into a sheep and then into a pastor.[23] Augustine always insisted upon Stephen's humility,[24] since it was in the capacity of a servant that the prayed in this way for those who were putting him to death. The bishop of Hippo was always attentive never to remove from God the glory manifested by his servants.

To God alone was adoration due. However, Augustine added, the altars built on the relics of the martyrs are pleasing to God, for "precious in the eyes of the Lord is the death of his faithful" (Ps 115:15), and these altars were altars erected to the glory of God. The pastor became very practical;[25] he called upon the community to imitate the example of the great witnesses in the

---

22. These sermons had all been delivered by Augustine between 416–417 and 425 (cf. A. Quacquarelli, "Introduzione," to *Discorsi*, vol. V (Rome: Città Nuova), VIII-IX.
23. St Augustine, *Sermon* 316. 4.
24. *Ibid*. 319. 7.
25. The pastor of souls sought very practically to encourage the faithful to interiorize the example and the teaching of the martyrs: the immediate effect of this had been to provoke a relapse into an excessive exaltation by the faithful on solemn occasions. Here, in the case of this homily, it was a question of welcoming the relics of St Stephen; we are in about 425, very probably, and the passage of these recently discovered relics

simple trials of everyday life, for example, by putting up with a serious illness without having recourse to magical rites, which would mean to be "nailed to the bed and at the same time be fighting in the ring." At times, his encouragement was expressed very nicely; thus, he said, the martyrs who had won their victory "have not cut down behind them the bridge which they have crossed, they have not blocked our passage."[26] Nothing of the sort with the Donatists, who honour the tombs of those who, according to them, have had the courage to die of their own initiative.[27] Martyrdom is a gift. Augustine comes back to this again and again. Mediating upon the death of St Cyprian, he affirmed very strongly his conviction that many of those who insulted him while he poured out his blood, bent his knee, and laid his neck on the block, were among those who subsequently became converts. "There is no reason to doubt it; we must believe it," he insisted,[28] for, in similar circumstances, the Lord's prayer could not be in vain: "Father, forgive them, for they know not what they do" (Lk. 23:34). And, in fact, as far as Cyprian was concerned, those who, impious as they were, had contemplated him in his death, came to believe in his Lord and "it could be that, in imitating him, they in their turn gave their blood for the name of Christ."

The passages on which we have been commenting constitute some particularly rich material, which helps us to appreciate the

---

had provoked an immense outburst of enthusiasm in the whole region of proconsular Africa; *Ibid.* 318. 2–3.

26. *Ibid.*
27. Augustine, the preacher, did not hesitate to enter into details, very realistic and such as to elicit an attentive ear from his listeners. Here, he scolded the Donatists, asking them why they did not make use of a rope to hang themselves, instead of throwing themselves into a ravine. This was because, according to them, the rope recalled Judas, the traitor. Augustine used this reference to Judas as a pretext for undertaking a long digression into forgiveness, of which no-one could despair: Judas himself would have had access to forgiveness, if he had wished it. Had not Jesus prayed for his persecutors on the wood of the Cross? (cf. *Ibid.* 313/E. 4, Guelf. 28).
28. St Augustine, *Sermon* 313/B. 4.

preaching of the bishop of Hippo. The forgiveness of sins and the love for our enemies have been so often addressed that we need not be afraid of counting them among the number of the most important topics of St Augustine's theology. In them, in fact, as we hope we have been able to show, the two major concerns of the pastor converge: the salvation of the souls entrusted to his care and the constant presence in his work of Christian charity. Charity is that action of the faithful which offers the most for a reflection upon the precise place of the creature in an order in which everything, being, grace, ransom, has been received from God. They are many who have underlined the constancy of the theme of charity in the work of Augustine. It is true that charity is the deep, underlying force of Augustinian thought; it develops the dynamic of love to encounter in it the moment of justice and of truth.

The texts that we have surveyed have shown also that St Augustine not only thought about charity, but that he put it into practice as a pastor. In this sense, we have in the *Sermones* thinking that is communicated through charity. This is not only an object of intelligibility in the Christian mystery, but it is also a principle of inspiration for the thought of the theologian and for the manner of communicating it. Quite obviously, Augustine considered his activity as a preacher as primordial, having before him the spirit of the prophet Ezekiel on the bad shepherds of Israel, those who did not push the sheep to conversion. Augustine wished to imitate the Good Shepherd, allowing the verse of the Song of Songs to rise before his faithful:

> Tell me, then, you whom my heart loves,
> Where will you lead the flock to graze,
> Where will you give them rest, at the mid-day hour (Sg 1:7)?[29]

---

29. *Ibid.* 46, 37.

The Heart of Christ

25 Gratitude and Grace[1]

"How can I give thanks to the Lord for his goodness to me?"

(Ps 115:12).

This verse of the Psalm expresses the very nature of gratitude, the sentiment of surprise, of amazement in the face of a gift that has not been earned.

What is not due to us enters easily into the category of gratuity. The amazement comes from the fact that the gift, above all if it comes from God, surpasses the measures of what is due. It is superabundant, and this incommensurate measure expresses precisely the paradox, for which we find an analogy already in the relationship between justice and mercy. Mercy surpasses what is due in terms of strict justice, but, at the same time, it is required because it is there is nothing more unjust than to content ourselves with only giving what is due. This conviction appeared even in the most well-proven sayings. The ancient *"Summum ius, summa iniuria"* could be understood also in this way. In other words, if we live only in relationships according to the measure of what is due, we become inhuman. The very fact that, in God, we cannot separate justice from mercy, under pain of denaturing both of them, helps us to understand why the appeal which Christ made of his disciples to be merciful was incessant: "Be merciful, just as your heavenly Father is merciful" (Lk 6:36). He refers them back to the mercy of God. This teaches human beings also that justice is truly itself only when it passes beyond itself into gratuity. The encyclical, *Dives in Misericordia*, gave a perfect illustration of this paradox:

1. "Gratitude and Grace" was published in G. Marengo, J. Prades López, G. Richi Alberti (ed.), *Sufficit Gratia Tua, Miscellanea in onore del Cardinale Angelo Scola per il suo 70° genetliaco* (Marcianum, Venezia, 2011), pp. 369–374.

> The experience of the past and that of our own time demonstrates that justice is not enough on its own, and even that it can lead to its own very negation and ruin, if we do not allow that deeper force, which is love, to fashion the human way forward in its various dimensions.[2]

We must not see here a denial of distributive justice but rather an affirmation that justice does not find within itself its own proper finality.

We must draw a conclusion from this, which concerns the deepest meaning of existence. The human being is made for gratuity. To remove gratuity from the tissue of human relations would mean to construct a society that was inhuman. The totalitarian systems of the last century have shown to what point endeavours of an absolute nature have led, in reducing what is human to its social dimension, starting from their exclusive relationship to the power of the State. Claiming to submit the whole of the existence of human beings to the authority that legislates, decrees, administers, controls and punishes, causes us to enter into a logic that leads to death. Everything that escapes from control is deemed punishable, since, to the extent that distrust and suspicion are dominant, the unknown of the other always constitutes a threat and a danger. Curiously, the first social categories at which a totalitarian power takes aim are artists and poets, intellectuals and religious, in short, all of those whose existence is devoted essentially to gratuity: the service of beauty, the research of science and of truth, and the worship of God, the source of every gift.

In the realm of conjugal love, there is also a gift without measure, since it is grounded upon the sacrifice of one person to another with the whole of their being. There are no limits in this gift, which embraces not only the whole of the bodily dimension but which encompasses also the future of each one of the two spouses; the absence of a temporal limit in their commitment signifies the sacrifice of their own liberty. No future any longer

---

2. John Paul II, *Dives in Misericordia*, § 12.

for the husband without the presence of the wife and no future any longer for the wife without the presence of the husband. The nuptial union is so paradigmatic of the vocation of every human being to gratuity that the institution that protects it comes rapidly to be excluded from the grip of totalitarianism. It is often forgotten that the very idea of divorce was born of the fever of French revolutionary spirits that had become incapable of continuing to conceive that the conjugal union could express anything other than an inequality between man and woman. In fact, the irrevocable character of the commitment between the spouses was denied by reason of the prejudice that it would constitute an obstacle to the rights of the woman.

Within the framework of the family, the dimension of gratuity is found once more in the welcome to human life. On the contrary, this is denied when, in a pregnancy, people see no more than a threat or a danger, thereby making impossible a welcome to life lived out in gratitude. Life is received gratuitously as a gift. For people to be sensitive to this means that they have not called into question its character as a blessing. Life is always an unexpected gift, which fills us with wonder and amazement. The whole mysterious reality of the family is expressed around this unknown; what form will the gift of God take? It is without any doubt Gabriel Marcel, who has expressed this dimension best in terms of philosophy:

> Beneath the abstract words of paternity ... I shall come to understand at least that, far from being endowed with an absolute existence, I am, and without initially have wanted or suspected this, I am the incarnation of a double response to a double call from beings who have launched themselves into the unknown and that, without having any doubts about it, have launched themselves beyond themselves, towards an incomprehensible power, which does not express itself except by giving life. I am this response, at first in an unformed way ...[3]

---

3. Gabriel Marcel, "Le mystère familial" in ID., *Homo viator* (Paris: Aubier-Montaigne, 1944), pp. 98–99.

The singular identity of the family is itself felt as a threat by totalitarian power. The latter always seeks to dismantle it, first of all by dividing its members one from the other. The way in which a communion of any kind is destroyed, but especially that of a family communion, is to instil suspicion within it. It is not by chance that the communists established a system of espionage destined to penetrate even to the last cell of the family. The system had an almost perfect efficacy: to create suspicion is deliberately to destroy what it is that cements together the interpersonal relationship at the heart of every communion, trust. Besides, trust of itself possesses a structure of gratuity because it is given gratuitously, *a priori*, something that did not escape the attention of the German philosopher, Gustav Siewerth. In his attempt to establish the outlines of a metaphysics of childhood, he had recognized what it is that cements the relationship between parents and children. In his reflection, he observed this transcendent dimension; trust is called "to be confident." We can see without any difficulty in what trust offers itself gratuitously; it calls irresistibly upon a gift of trust in return and only a reciprocity of trust which is offered is capable of enabling the growth of communion.

The paradox of gratuity appears naturally at the subjective level in the desires that inhabit the heart of the human person. Everyone is within their rights to expect relationships which are gratuitous, to wish for a great love or for great friendships. In this way, there is a natural expectation of an event, whose arrival may come upon us unexpectedly. In another context, in reality not so distant from this line of thought, it being a question of a sinner who is in expectation that his sin may be forgiven, we have called this paradox *waiting for the unexpected*. What goes for the sinner goes for the whole of their existence; a life without love or without friendship is simply a life that is inhuman; but, nevertheless, when this love or this friendship arises, it is still surprising. It is not something that is due to us, then, since its irruption on the scene is profoundly humanizing for human existence itself.

Gratitude and Grace

The gratuity inscribed in the heart of the human being is an illustration of that *capacitas Dei*, in which, for reasons which are understandable, emphasis has often been given to the relationship of the human being to God (the human being capable of conceiving the idea of the existence of God and of rendering worship to him), to the detriment of the gift which God himself has made of each of us and which causes the capacity of the human being to receive him with wonder arise. At the level of human interiority, a psychological fact reveals the paradoxical structure of the gift. When the human being receives what is due to him in justice, he is certainly satisfied; his legitimate expectation has been satisfied. It would appear, though, that he is not grateful. The victim who sees his rights vindicated in a court obtains satisfaction but finds no reason to be thankful for the fact that justice has been done to them. Entering into the logic of gift is to accept a justice that has escaped us in some respect and which, in some way, exercises an effect which is transcendent. The human being, then, accepts that he is not the measure of justice.

We can understand why certain philosophers have been tempted to deny any possibility that there could exist a gift that was gratuitous. The more serious temptation of denying the human gift in its essence comes from Marcel Maus. In the gift, he does indeed recognize a relationship of solidarity between the one who gives and the one who receives, but he recognizes also a relationship of superiority on the part of the donor with respect to the beneficiary. In his famous *Essai sur le don* that dates from 1929, Maus observed that many societies are structured around an economy of and a morality of gift, by reason of the fact that, in these societies, personal relationships have been predominant. According to him, individuals and groups have an interest in showing themselves to be disinterested. He affirms that people are pushed into making gifts because the action of giving places the beneficiary under an obligation. It is in this way that Maus thinks he can resolve the enigma of the gift. It is not without interest to note that, in him, this sort of invisible force which accompanies the gift, in which believers are rightly inclined to see the presence of a transcendence in the gratuitous act of generosity, is one in which the author forces himself to limit to a symbolic force. In categories that are his own, such a symbol is, structurally, of fundamental importance in interpersonal relations.

Contrary to Maus, other authors have wanted to rehabilitate gratuity, by giving it a central place in the metaphysics of in the human person. Many of them were attached to the idea of establishing gratuity as a reality, from Ebner to Buber, from Rosenzweig to Levinas. The attempt to inscribe gift in the original structure of the human being of characterizes the thought of Claude Bruaire; to speak of an *être de don* (a being of gift) to qualify the human person, is to express in philosophical terms what is a given of theology.

Everything that can be said about the relationship between persons takes on the dimensions of the infinite in the relationship with God, to the extent that every gift of God is accompanied by the gift that God makes of himself. Even the initial act of Creation is effected within the context of the gift of original holiness, in such a way that, except at the expense of remaining within a hypothesis in the abstract (such as pure nature), it is not possible to dissociate what God offers from the gift of his divine life.

There is a more radical aspect in the nature and in the expression of the divine gift, since it then touches upon our existence itself and also upon our eternal future. In fact, in the end, it is God himself who is united to the spiritual creature, who agrees to receive him.

It seems to me that the idea that God gives himself to those who are his own could be thought through usefully within the mystery of the sacrament of Order. Not only does God give himself to his "own," to those who are baptized, but he entrusts himself to some of them in the ordained ministry.[4] In every priest, in

---

4. Translator's note: this section clearly concerns only to those in priestly orders, not deacons.

every bishop, there exists a responsibility entrusted to that person of administering the gift of God; not only does God give himself, but he give himself over and entrusts himself into their consecrated hands, in order precisely to be able then to be given on to others. That word, which is at the same time an instruction, "Go and bear fruit that will last" (Jn 15:16) allows us to glimpse a mystery of fecundity, which specifies the existence of the minsters of Christ. God renders them capable of giving him on to others. He makes them mediators of a gift that remains.

The gratitude towards God, which was so well expressed by the verse which opened this reflection: "How can I thank the Lord for his goodness to me?" presents a dialectical tension analogous to that which has been illustrated in the gratitude to be found in the relationship between persons. We have a two-fold idea that is present in terms of a paradox. On the one side, there is present the requirement of giving back, in whatever form it may be, of what has been received; unfortunately, experience shows that this can never be done in a way which is sufficient. The gift of God places every human being under an obligation; finding himself in an impossible situation, that of not being able to render anything at all that might be commensurable to the gift which he has received, there remains quite simply (nothing but) gratitude. This is the sentiment that inspires a right relationship towards God and, to put it briefly, which is situated between praise of God and humility. Only the heart that is humble can praise God, since it is only outside of himself that each one recognizes the origin of the goods which he has received. And, from the other side, only the praise of God preserves the disciple in a condition of humility. St Augustine has seen perfectly how the binomial *laus-humilitas* alone could structure and characterize the life of the faithful. As it is not possible to give back something proportionate to the gift received, the sole manner of responding to God oneself is to bring a dimension of gratuity to what is given to him. The humble friendship of the disciple responds in this way to the friendship of the King of kings.

However, it is here that God transforms an exchange that clearly is also in the order of things. He makes his friends capable always of giving more in terms of gratitude. He makes himself into a petitioner before them, asking for their friendship. Love for love, friendship for friendship. This is the mystery of the Redemption (*redamatio*. The gratitude of the saints little by little becomes mad love, or the folly of love, if we wish; it is the creative folly of the saints in their manner of giving back to God. Gratitude appears as a special gift of the Grace of God.

Outside of the perspective of grace, it becomes impossible to think of gratitude towards God in an appropriate way. However, this structure, however just it may seem to be, never fails to clash with the refusal of the gift. Here it takes on the name of ingratitude. In some way, gratitude is due (that was the first term of our paradox); the refusal of gratitude defines the mystery of evil. Even the enigma of original sin could be expressed in these terms. The man and the woman had received everything—nature, life, and grace too—since they had been constituted in original justice. In the uncertainty brought about by temptation, the human being entered into a new way of looking upon the gift of God. God came to be regarded with suspicion in his action, instead of being praised. The words of the Tempter are revealing: "You will not die. But, God knows that the day that you eat (of the fruit of the tree), your eyes will be opened and you will be like the gods, who know good and evil." This amounts to saying: "What God has done for you is not a gratuitous gift. His Omnipotence is afraid that you, too, will become like the gods through this knowledge of good and evil, from which he seeks to exclude you." The Adversary sows suspicion about the gift of God.

Justice, mercy, sin, entire sections of theological explanation of the Christian faith find in gratitude a precious key for their reading. This extends to the apostolate and to missionary activity. In gratitude, there is included the call to give back to others.

Gratitude and Grace

It is through gratitude towards the Lord that we undertake evangelization. In fact, gratitude demands that the service of the Church never be reduced to the formalized fulfilment of what is demanded. In particular, the one who has received through sheer gratuity the capacity to transmit in his turn the divine gift to others cannot simply situate himself in the position of being his (good) administrator, not in the first place as a matter of moral, requirement, but by reason of the nature of the mysteries of which his is the servant; in reality, it is gratuity which is at the heart of the sacrificial dimension of the ministry. To abandon our apostolate would be to put ourselves in the situation of being unable to honour the gift of the Saviour, his glorious Cross.

26 The Mystery of the Heart According to St Bonaventure[1]

The contemporary understanding of the mystery of God today is entirely centred upon the *historia salutis*, to such a point that this term of Revelation indicates almost exclusively the unfolding of the events of salvation, such as they are manifested in the history of human beings, giving rise to a theological explanation which is the object of our treatises upon *De Revelatione*. On the occasion of the presentation of the second volume of the *Gesammelte Schriften* of Joseph Ratzinger at Castel Gandolfo, an edition containing for the first time the entirety of his *Habilitations* thesis, devoted to the theology of the history of St Bonaventure, Benedict XVI reminded us that the term *revelatio*, as commonly used in neo-scholastic and in medieval theology, did not mean the same thing in the Middle Ages as in modern theology. According to the author, only a vision of the totality of the several concepts, such as *manifestatio, doctrina, fides, apertio*,[2] and other terms, and also of their contents, makes it possible for us to have an idea of what Revelation could represent for the Seraphic Doctor.

With all of these terms, which could be multiplied further, we are able to contemplate objectively what God has revealed to all those who, through faith and by following the path, step by step, of a journey of purification, have made themselves available to the transforming Love of the Most Holy Trinity. The method of contemplation necessary is not one of a simple approach of

---

1. "The Mystery of the Heart according to St Bonaventure" was published in J. Mimeault, S. Zamboni, A. Chendi (ed.), *Nella luce del Figlio. Scritti in onore di Réal Tremblay nel suo 70° genetliaco*, EDB, Bologna, 2011), pp. 395–404.
2. Cf. J. Ratzinger, *San Bonaventura: la teologia della storia* (Florence: Nardini, 1991), pp. 126ff.

speculation. If everything has been given by the Creator, beginning from the Son, whose elevation upon the Cross, according to Réal Tremblay, represents *the fulfilment of the humanum*,[3] the participation of the human being in the mystery of the God-who-gives-himself can only be undertaken by the heart, which is capable of a loving understanding, which here is the only path which can be followed fruitfully. What follows here seeks to offer some reflections upon the mystery of the heart according to St Bonaventure.

Humility: The Condition for the Intelligentia per Cor

It was in 1244 that Bonaventure entered into the order of St Francis. The rapid development of the Franciscans in Italy and then in Europe, in particular in the towns, had the consequence of fostering a genuine renewal of theology and of spirituality. Without any doubt, Francis was the incarnation of a spiritual life, which was completely inspired by a passionate love for Christ and for the mystery of his Passion. In this sense, despite the novelty which the friars brought in their way of life and in their service of the poor, Franciscan spirituality, from one angle, could be inserted into the long history of the mendicant orders, centred upon a prayer characterized by a greater familiarity with the suffering Christ. At the theological level, the Franciscans introduced also a novelty in their manner of penetrating into the Christian mystery; their conception of God and of his relationship with human beings rested very radically upon the revealed love in the Person of Christ and thus upon the necessity for a loving response on the part of the Christian. Bonaventure would be at the beginning of this inspiration. His treatises, and in the first place his *Itinerarium*, had the express intention of showing the conditions for that extraordinary good, which is intellectual peace, which only love is able to obtain. At the centre of this

---

3. Cf. R. Tremblay, *L' «élévation» du Fils. Axe de la vie morale* (Fides, Quebec, 2001), pp. 69–78.

approach was to be found the search for true wisdom, which is possible only thanks to an experience of God. Contact with the divine is not limited to the joy of a discourse about God or to a speculative contemplation of his love; one of the conditions is humility. As with St Augustine, true knowledge is revealed to the humble person, because only the humble are able to discover beings in the truth of their being as creatures. Knowledge becomes a journey of the spirit in the sense that this latter term designates the highest or the deepest part of the heart. The *mens*, a term which Augustine had already used often to indicate the reality of the human heart, at the risk of imprecision at the metaphysical level, recognizes the presence of God at the end of a journey and of its various progressive stages. It is a question of an act of love, which neither eliminates nor eludes rational argumentation, but which incorporates this into a wider process, that of a loving and cordial search.

In St Augustine, humility was always linked to the worship of the Lord: For him, praise is fundamental because it brings the creature necessarily closer to the Creator. For the Bishop of Hippo, praise does not remain exterior; it is transforming, and it changes the human being interiorly. In other words, contemplation of the mystery makes it possible for love to arise in the creature, on condition that the latter remains in a state of humility. Contemplation on its own is not sufficient; it is praise that makes it possible to remain humble. Without any doubt, humility is the key for reading the thought of St, Augustine, as is witnessed by these famous antitheses: *amor-superbia, cor rectum-cor distortum, humiles cordis-superbi cordis, cor spiritualis-cor carnalis*. The Sermons of St Augustine offer us a long list of antithetical binomials.[4] Several of these terms arise also in the Seraphic Doctor.

---

4. On this point, we refer to our article "Pardon des offenses et Amour des enemies dans les Sermons de saint Augustin," *Anthropotes* 16 (2000), pp. 69–103; the English translation of «Le pardon des offences chez saint Augustin » ("The Forgiveness of Sins According to St Augustine") is Chapter 24 of this volume, pp. 487–515 above.

In St Bonaventure, humility is linked to desire, not a vague attraction towards the knowledge of God and to his hidden mysteries, but a desire at the limit of suffering, an imperious need to know. If knowledge were no more than an intellectual process, then desire would be confused with simple curiosity. To attain intelligence and wisdom, it is necessary to take up Bonaventure's expression of thirsting, according to the saying: *Sapientia similiter non habetur nisi a sitiente*. Thirst has its seat in the heart, to the extent that it is an experience at one and the same time metaphysical and sensitive. It is metaphysical because it signals something which is lacking: having a thirst to know God is to have an experience of his Being different and of his distance from us. But experience of this sort of thirst is also characterized by a disturbance at the sensitive level; to desire to know is also the profession of a love; only the person who desires can penetrate into the mysteries which are revealed to him, precisely because the disposition of his heart is an *affectus amantis*. We can understand that love is not situated only at the end of a search, as if it were the recompense desired from it, but it is located also at its beginning. It is, as it were, a methodological requirement of the search for God, since only the one who loves is capable of searching with perseverance for the one who is loved. The presence of desires in the heart is not only a privilege. Desires can be extinguished, or, on the other hand, they can be enkindled. Thus, there is a responsibility attaching to the one who searches authentically for God; namely, to be attentive, so that his own desires do not fade away. The Prologue of the *Itinerarium* teaches us that desires can be inflamed within us in two ways: first of all by the ardent prayer, which makes the heart shiver and groan, and then, by an attentive meditation, by which the spirit plunges itself into the rays of divine light.[5]

---

5. Cf. St Bonaventure, *Itinéraire de l'esprit vers Dieu*, text in the edition of Quaracchi; introduction, translation and notes by H. Duméry (Paris: Vrin, 1960), Prol, 3–4.

It is interesting to see that, in St Augustine also, desire formed part of the conditions for the knowledge and the thoughts which dwell in the heart, but in a negative way. For him, the activity of the heart and of the spirit requires that the *cogitatio* distance itself from all earthly desire. Nothing must distract the attention of the heart. The *attentive heart (cor attentum)* is placed in opposition to the *distracted heart (cor dispersum)*. We note that, in him, as later with Bonaventure, the attention of the heart remains primordial in the spiritual journey of the one who searches.[6]

The Cross at the Beginning and at the End of the Search for God

The spirit attains beatitude when it attains its end, which is peace, the order that presides over the relations between the Creator and his creatures. In this sense, peace is a characteristic of order; everything that is created is submitted to rules and to norms which are relationships which unite beings among themselves, according to a certain hierarchy and gradation. The spirit that contemplates this order finds itself at peace. Peace, in this sense, is an intellectual satisfaction not a psychological gratification. For Bonaventure, knowledge is an *ascesis*, it begins necessarily with a purification. The love which presides over and which accompanies the search (for God) dispenses neither with a rigorous exercise of the intelligence nor with ascetical practices of purification. The intuition of knowledge, as by degrees, was given to St Bonaventure by the ineffable, mystical experience of the vision of a seraphim, with six wings, which symbolized the degrees of a knowledge through which the soul is raised in successive stages to the point of mystical contemplation of divine love. The quite well-known text in which the theologian relates his experience deserves to be quoted:

---

6. Cf. St Augustine, *De quant. An.*, XXXIII, 75, PL, 32, p. 1076.

> Following Blessed Father Francis, while I was seeking that peace with an ardent spirit, I a sinner who, despite my unworthiness, am the seventh successor in the government of the order, it happened that thirty-three years after his death, by the will of God, I went to Mount La Verna, as to a place of quiet refuge, where I could search for peace of spirit; and there, when I was meditating on the possibility of the soul rising to God, there appeared to me among others this wonderful event lived in this place by Blessed Francis, namely, the vision of the winged seraphim in the form of a crucifix. On meditating upon this fact, I recognized suddenly that this vision was offering to me the contemplative ecstasy of Father Francis and, at the same time, the path which would lead to it.[7]

The seraphic vision introduced mystically the presence of the Cross from the beginning of the search. Bonaventure would never cease repeating that there was no access possible to the contemplation desired, without a very ardent love for Crucified Lord. The six wings are like are like illuminations which, starting from creatures, lead even to God, in the mystery which no one can penetrate other than through the Crucified One. It is a whole method of reflection and of spiritual and intellectual health which the Seraphic Doctor proposes, when introducing his itinerary. The groaning of the prayer of Christ on the Cross is necessary, he affirms, in order for the reader not to think that it would be sufficient to undertake a reading without anointing (*lectio sine unctione*), a speculation without devotion (*investigatio sine admiratione*), a consideration without being happy (*circumspectio sine exultatione*), a work without mercy (*industria sine pietate*), a science without charity (*scientia sine caritate*), an intelligence without humility (*intelligentia sine humilitate*), a study without divine grace (*studium absque divina gratia*), a mirror without wisdom (*speculum absque divina sapientia*). We can see that, from the beginning, Bonaventure gave priority to the work of grace. He saw all the

---

7. St Bonaventure, *Itinerarium*.

faculties of the human being as being orientated towards the gift of grace, which acts within them. We have, then, this common trait between Bonaventure and Augustine: there cannot exist a true autonomy of creatures in the search for the mystery of the Creator. We remember this idea of the Bishop of Hippo, who saw the human being affected by a sort of a *loss of equilibrium pressing him forward*, that is to say, his being orientated from his very origins towards grace.

We know that the itinerary progressed according to the following, perfectly inter-connected stages: starting from the universe in which the vestiges of the Creator are present, we reach the knowledge of God first of all through the traces which are his in the world of the senses. Then, the author attaches himself to the knowledge of God by means of his image impressed in the natural powers of the soul; this image, however, is renewed by the gifts of grace. It is only starting with Chapter V of the *Itinerarium* that God is considered in himself through the contemplation of his divine unity, by means of the being that is his principal name. The next step leads to knowing the Blessed Trinity in the name that is his: the Good. The whole of this process aimed, by way of a mental and mystical ecstasy, at calming the spirit and at the whole of its love being placed in God. It is above all the last chapter which is of particular interest to our purpose, since it indicates that, at a certain moment, true knowledge requires the suspension of the exercise of the intellect; it is no longer so much the manner of searching for God which is important, but it is more letting ourselves be encountered by him, once the heart (designated at times by *mens* and at times by *cor*) has come to know him. This knowledge is the knowledge proper to mystical experience. Thus, the purpose of knowledge is limited neither to appeasing the search of the spirit nor to filling the purified heart through *ascesis*, but it is to place the whole of our interiority and all of our affective and loving capacities in God. The seventh degree of knowledge presupposes repeating the preceding stages. In this degree, it is the Person of Jesus Christ who is the path and the gateway, the ladder and the motive force, but also the mercy seat placed on the ark of God. In reality, it is Christ on the Cross who is the rest for the soul: here we discover once more the mark of the symbolism of the experience of Francis:

> This state is mystical and very secret; the person who has not experienced it cannot know it, nor can someone receive it who has no desire for it, nor can someone desire it who is not profoundly inflamed by the fire of the Holy Spirit whom Jesus has sent upon the earth.

In his biography of St Francis, St Bonaventure identified the very essence of this experience. He described it by bringing out the dynamism of the affections of the heart: "His search, pure and free from all stain and penetrated by the secret of the mysteries and there where the science of the masters is excluded, he would enter with the affection of the lover (*affectu amantis*)." Mystical knowledge is not a substitute for the intellectual life; it rests upon it because it is a penetration into the truth that requires divine illumination. For the Seraphic Doctor, illumination does not mean simply a presence of light but more precisely the presence in the soul of the interior master. It is thus an intervention and an initiative of God. This is the reason why we cannot attain to the truth of love by way of abstraction but only by passing through all of the degrees of being by means of a loving penetration (*intelligentia per cor*) of that truth, which is made possible only by the illumination of the Word: *Ibi non intrat intellectus, sed affectus ... quia affectus vadit usque ad profundum Christi.*[8]

The Cross that accompanies every stage of the journey of the one who searches for God does not disappear with the peace of the heart which has been filled by the Master. It is never dissociated from Christ, for it is the place in which it is given to know the love of God for his friends. In the beautiful work already cited, Réal Tremblay writes: "It is the framework of the house which God inhabits and where, as a consequence, the noblest part of the human being, understanding its torment for the Infin-

---

8. St Bonaventure, *In Hex.* Coll. 2, 32.

ite, finds itself as satisfied."⁹ Then, Tremblay observes that many people have said that they love the Cross and that they have had an ardent desire for it. Among these, he cites the testimony of St Thérèse of the Child Jesus and of the Holy Face:

> I thank you, O my God! For all the graces that you have granted to me, in particular for having made me pass through the crucible of suffering. It is with joy that I shall contemplate you on the last day, bearing the sceptre of the Cross; since you have deigned to grant me a share in this so precious Cross, I hope in heaven to resemble you and to see shining forth in my glorified body the sacred stigmata of your passion.¹⁰

On the Life of Perfecton (De Perfectione Vitae)

In this small treatise, written in view of female religious, St Bonaventure consecrated a chapter to the memories of the passion of Christ.¹¹ Without doubt, it is a question of the text of the Seraphic Doctor in which his spirituality, centred upon the Heart of Christ, is most evident. The preacher recommended to the religious sisters to look often upon Christ in agony upon the Cross with the eyes of the heart. He compared the heart to an altar, on which the fire of devotion had to burn; the fire is kept going and is fed by the wood of the Cross of Christ. The ardour of the sentiments burning in the heart of the devout person is born of a loving contemplation of the one who consecrates all the efforts of their soul to this. In this sense, the heart burning with love is born of a heart that is attentive.

At one and the same time, Bonaventure encouraged the sisters listening to him to participate in the sufferings of Christ and he exhorted them to remain joyful. This latter element seems paradoxical, but it is part of a great tradition of the devotion in-

---

9. R.Tremblay, *L'élévation du Fils*, p. 74.
10. *Ibid.* p. 75.
11. Cf. St Bonaventure, *De la vie parfaite* in *Œuvres spirituelles*, vol. II (Paris: Librairie St François, 1931).

herited from the Fathers and of one which saw in the sufferings of the Cross the source of all joy: "Go to drink from the fountains of salvation, that is to say from the five wounds of Jesus Christ," he used to advise them. The sufferings of Christ become those of the friend introduced in this way into the dynamism of salvation. Those two dimensions of the devotion to the Heart of Christ appear here which are brought out in Pius XII's encyclical, *Haurietis Aquas*: the *reparatio* which consists in offering sacrifices for the reparation of sins and for the conversion of sinners, and the *redamatio*, the act by which an exchange is established with Christ, to whom the devout person offers love in return for love. From the time of St John the Evangelist, these two dimensions have not ceased to inspire all those who are inserted into this particular intimacy with the person of Christ, from St Gertrude to St Bernard and to St Catherine of Siena, from St Bonaventure to St John Eudes, from St Margaret Mary and from St Claude la Colombière to St Faustina Kowalska. The contact with the wounds of Christ is not an allegory; it is something as concrete as that of the Apostle, Thomas:

> Through the movements of your affections, come to meet Jesus pierced with the sword...With Thomas, look upon those marks, put your hand into his side, and enter completely through the door of his side, right up to the very Heart of Jesus.

We note that Bonaventure talks of the "open heart." According to St John's text, the sword opens the heart of Jesus, tracing out in this way the path that leads to his Heart. The open heart provides a direction to the disciple, a path that he may follow in order to discover in the Heart of the Master the essence of his deepest feelings. In his first encyclical, *Deus Caritas Est*, Benedict XVI identifies contemplation of the open side with the understanding of the fact that God is love: "It is there that this truth can be contemplated."[12] St Augustine had already written that,

---

12. Benedict XVI, *Deus Caritas Est*, § 12.

through the open side, in reality, the gateway to life (*vitae ostium*) had been opened.

The Seraphic Doctor made of the outpouring of blood and of water a personal gateway; it is a gift made to each one of us, and, in the context of this instruction, to each one of the religious sisters to whom this teaching was dedicated. He insisted on the fact that the sacrifice of the redemption had been offered for those who are devout. Consequently, it was an act of personal love on the part of Christ, an act which made his friends capable of a devotion which would be just as loving. Bonaventure makes this more explicit: Christ endured all of these things in order to inflame you with his love. Thus, we see that the reading of the redemption is an affective one, in the strong sense of the term (and not in a purely sentimental sense); this contemplation is an operation of all of the affective powers, which are, as it were, orientated towards this mystery. Finally, St Bonaventure asked the sisters not to be ungrateful for such as gift as this, which they had received. Any tepidness in love would be an act of ingratitude towards the Crucified One. When Christ makes himself known through a mystical experience, he does this often while formulating a reproach for the lack of gratitude of his friends. Numerous saints have had an experience of this pain, the effect of which has been then to set their hearts on fire (St Margaret Mary or, again, Blessed Elizabeth of the Trinity).

The Tree of Life (Lignum Vitae)

St Bonaventure broadened the extent of his contemplation of the Heart of Christ in his small work, *Lignum Vitae*. The side of Christ on the Cross displays also the mystery of the Church. The Church has been bought at a price, which, he says, is properly represented by the side torn apart and by the effusion of Blood and of water. It is from the Heart that the force that communicates the life of grace in the sacraments springs forth. There again, our author is situated with the long tradition that, across the centuries, had recognized in the Blood of Christ the birth of the sacraments, as also the gift of the Holy Spirit, and in the water the life of grace conferred by baptism.

In the *Tree of Life*, we find also this idea of the redemptive power present in the Precious Blood of the Savior, expressed in the following way: one single drop of this Blood could save the whole of humanity. The person who contemplates Christ on the Cross thereby becomes aware that he has offered the whole of himself by pouring out his Blood. Every possible part of the life that was in Christ has been given up. The abundance of blood (human life) and of water (regeneration) are expressions of the superabundance of the redemption.

The tree of life is opposed to the tree of death (*arbor mortis*), whose fruit in Genesis had been the vain wisdom of those who had wished to make themselves equal to God. By contrast, it is on the Cross of Christ that true wisdom is revealed. The crucified Word is an expression of the Trinity in its condescension. St Bonaventure shows how God broke the vicious circle of sin, which had enclosed us in ignorance and impotence. The fruit of the tree of life is the water that brings sanctification. St Bonaventure exploited once more the image of the fountain; the fecund waters of the Holy Spirit not only heal the sinner, but they transmit a river of graces: "And from his side there sprung forth a river of graces, which has the power to heal us."[13]

In the foregoing sections, it has emerged that the Heart of Christ transforms and structures the heart of the human being. "It is to the heart that the Word speaks," wrote Bonaventure in a sermon.[14] Contemplation, then, is an act of the heart, which alone is capable of a knowledge of love. Its recompense is the sweet and tasteful *suavitas* of God. The conversation with the one and only Master is necessarily a conversation of one heart to the Heart. It is in this deep place within the human being that the fulness of revelation is possible. The heart of the person is

---

13. St Bonaventure, *Les sept dons de l'Esprit Saint*, col. 1. 6.
14. Id. *Sermon* 1: The Birth of the Lord.

ceaselessly animated by a two-fold action, which leads it in successive stages outside of itself and which then enables it to gather within itself as a deposit what it had been able to contemplate, in order to make it its own:

> The life of the soul is two-fold, that from which it lives in the flesh and that from which it lives in God. In fact, there are two directions in the human being, the interior way of contemplation of the divinity, and the exterior way of the contemplation of humanity: And it is for this reason that God made himself man, in order to beatify in himself every human being, in such a way that, whether he enters within himself or whether he goes outside of himself, he finds his pasture in his author: outside is the pasture is the flesh of the Saviour, inside it is the divinity of the Creator.[15]

In the Heart of Christ, the human heart finds itself in a position to find nourishment in the two pastures of the flesh of the Saviour and in the divinity of the Creator.

---

15. Id.*Christus Unus omniumMagister*, VIIV.

27 Configuration to the Heart of Christ[1]

When we speak of the heart of Jesus, there arises immediately a simple question of intelligibility; what do we wish to signify by this expression? An anthropological reality that is easily understandable, a symbolic reality (and, in that case, what kind of symbol would it involve?), or a theological notion?

In tradition, there is a very rich anthropological patrimony, both philosophical and theological. We have the most complete and systematic elaboration of this in the synthesis of St Thomas Aquinas, which also underlies the collection of magisterial texts on the Heart of Jesus. For example, it could have been said of *Haurietis Aquas* that it is essentially a Thomistic encyclical, based upon the anthropology and the theology of Aquinas.[2] In the Thomist vision, the human being is seen in his substantial unity of body and spirit, and this is analyzed with the aid of the distinction between principles and faculties. Here, the heart means in the first place the vital organ, the seat or the principle of the movements of the body and the organ of the appetites of the senses; for St Thomas, the heart is also the natural symbol of love.[3] There is also another tradition, more attentive to the heart

---

1. "The Configuration of the Heart of Christ" is the text of a lecture delivered at Paray-le-Monial on 14th October, 1999, in the context of the international Congress on the theme *Pour une civilisation du Coeur* and published in the Acta of the Congress, edited by J-L-Bruguès and B. Peyrous (Emmanuel, Paris, 2000), pp. 235–248.
2. Cf. B. de Margerie, *Histoire doctrinale du culte au Cœur de Jésus*, I, *Lumières sur l'amour* (Paris: Mame, 1992), p. 125; cf. Pius XII, Encyclical Letter, *Haurietis Aquas* (1956).
3. Cf. St Thomas Aquinas, *Summa Theologiae*, IIa IIae, q. 44, a. 5. For an analysis of this passage, cf. E. Glotin, *Le Cœur de Jésus. Approaches*

as the place of experience, of life as lived at the affective and at the spiritual level. We are aware of the extent to which this renewed interest in human interiority has derived from the philosophical currents of thought of modern subjectivism; however, there have also been providential developments in terms of deepening our understanding of the mystery of the Heart of Jesus. The difficulty is that these two traditions have often been parallel, if not antithetical, to each other, rather than being truly interrelated. We may think of the old debates between the Franciscans and the Dominicans or again of the particular difficulty of the Church in its pastoral activity of locating itself with reference to contemporary subjectivism. Recently, efforts have been undertaken to reconcile the analysis of human interiority with Thomist realism. On the philosophical plane, we may think of a work such as Karol Wojtyla's *The Acting Person* or again of the reflection of authors as diverse as Guardini, Hildebrand and Ratzinger, on the concept of human experience, much to the honour of German phenomenology.

At the philosophical level, we could start from the presupposition that the human being has always perceived himself as endowed with a heart, through which he experiences his capacity to suffer and to love; but what meaning should be given to such an affirmation? Does the heart itself suffer or love, or is it only an expression of that suffering and of that love? The question remains. We can see that there is a need for these anthropological presuppositions, in order to be able to understand that Jesus had a heart. What we understand about the human heart, by means of an ascending analogy, will help us to give a simple consideration to the feelings and the choices of Jesus.

There is also a theological aspect to this enterprise. It is a matter of developing, by way of a descending analogy, a systematic theological understanding of the heart; if we have a theology of the Heart of Christ, this latter will become a light to enable us to grasp the nature and the destiny of the human heart. There is no

---

anciennes et nouvelles (Namur: Vie consacrée, 1997), pp. 70ff.

lack of sources. The heart is a given of the Bible; it belongs also to the spiritual tradition of the Church, and it is a given of the Magisterium. What follows here has the purpose of trying to take hold of these sources in such a way as to contribute to a doctrinal and theological elaboration of the heart; what does it mean for a human heart to be conformed and configured to the Heart of Christ? What does the Heart of Christ teach us about our own heart? Nevertheless, this undertaking requires us to say, even if only briefly, what it means when we speak of the human heart. It will be useful to start from a hypothesis; the heart, as it appears in the Scriptural, spiritual and magisterial sources, designates the person, symbolically, as the origin of his acts.

It seems that we could hold that the human heart designates the human person in his unity, insofar as it is the veritable origin of his acts. In this sense, the heart is the symbol of the person acting precisely as person, that is to say insofar as his master of his own actions. Here, we have two conjoined realities; on the one hand, the person acts in a fashion that is absolutely unique, putting to work the spiritual dynamisms which animate him, choosing to determine himself in relation to a good which has been glimpsed by his judgment, and each one of his deliberate actions bears the particular seal of his freedom. On the other hand, the person assumes parentage of his acts, since he is his author. When these acts are truly human acts and so when they have an impact upon the true good of the person, they will contribute to the making of that person, acting upon him, transforming him. This is what is expressed in current language when it is said that a person *realizes themselves*. Under the term *acts*, we understand, to be sure, those acts which intervene in the moral genesis of the person and which St Thomas designated by the expression the *actus humanus*, in order to distinguish them from *actus hominis*, acts undoubtedly produced by a person, but without the personal quality of being acts which are morally good or morally bad.

We need to make another specification, by reason of the difficulties that arise in regard to the term of symbol. To say *symbol* is to enter into the economy of signs, into a terminology that claims to refer back to some reality which is designated. However, the symbol of the heart has this particularity, that it concerns the human being, and his powers, in such a way that it moves to what is signified. There is nothing arbitrary about this, since the symbol relies upon a whole collection of primordial experiences which precede our intelligence and which structure that intelligence.[4] It presupposes the givens of the senses, which lie beneath the intelligible givens. It is clear that we include in these givens of the senses everything that touches upon affectivity, even if our purpose here will lead us to insist above all on voluntary acts.[5]

---

4. We may note that, in the understanding of Karl Rahner, who is without doubt the theologian who has reflected most of all on the symbolic dimension of the Heart, we do not find a clear affirmation of a distinction between the sensitive and the intelligible. The heart is an original word, an *"Ur-Wort,"* a term which cannot be deduced and whose definition cannot completely render the meaning of its content. The heart implies immediately human experience and it expresses the whole of the person as a sign which comprehends the material reality, while signifying something spiritual and *vice versa*. Rahner speaks of *Realsymbol*; in the notion of the heart, we discover in this way the internal and original unity of the signifying and of the signified, of what is named and of the one who names it (cf. K. Neufield, "Karl Rahner: Il cuore nel pensiero cattolico" in Giuseppe Beschin (a cura di), *Antonio Rosmini, filosofo del cuore? Philosophia cordis Theologia cordis nella cultura occidentale* (Morcellana, Brescia, 1995, p. 609); a complete theoretical analysis by the German theologian will be found in his fundamental article, Karl Rahner, "Zur Theologie des Symbols" in *Cor Iesu. Commentationes in litteras encyclicas 'Haurietis Aquas',* I, *pars theologica* (Roma: Herder, 1959), pp. 463–505.
5. On this subject, reference could be made to C. Bernard, *La théologie affective* (Cerf, Paris, 1984). On the importance of affectivity for pastoral care, cf. M. Gaidon, "Defensa de la afectividad. Elementos para una reflexión pastoral" in *Cor Christi* (Instituto Internacional del Corazón de Jesús, Bogotá, 1980), pp. 788–793.

Having outlined these presuppositions, it remains to explain the choice to ask about the human heart, starting from the Heart of Christ. It will suffice for this to recall those texts of the Second Vatican Council that grounded a whole theological anthropology. If it is true that *"the mystery of the human being does not become really clear except in the mystery of the Incarnate word,"*[6] then, necessarily, the heart of the human being cannot *be illuminated except in the mystery of the Heart of Christ.*

The Theologal Life as Meaning and Purpose of the Configuration of the Human Heart to the Heart of Christ

The Theologal Life: Gift of the Spirit and Gift of the Heart of Christ

The union of the word of God with human nature has introduced into this latter a new specification. The Council spoke of a dignity without equal.[7] It is obvious that this dignity has first of all a spiritual depth; through the gift of the Spirit of the Father and of the Son, human beings have become children of God, the Son of God has united himself in some way to each person, which is expressed for him or her through the revelation of their final vocation to live a life which is truly divine. They are called to become sons and daughters in the Son. But, it must be said that such a dignity has a moral significance, from which it cannot be separated. The union of every person with Christ is expressed and is necessarily translated in terms of good conduct. The great difficulty in expressing this reality, we can see, lies in avoiding a two-fold obstacle: on the one hand, that of a moral reductionism which would amount to identifying the moral good with the means of configuration to Christ, and on the other hand, that of conceiving of this latter as a kind of indistinct union with God, as a grace without commitment, as a transformation of our being without the participation of our acting

6. Vatican Council II, *Gaudium et Spes*, § 22.
7. *Ibid.*

freedom. To the first kind of figure are attached all forms of Pelagianism and of semi-Pelagianism, which debase and denature the Christian life, and to the second kind, all those manifestations of a spiritualism which is disincarnate, which imply always an abdication of personal responsibility. Neither, furthermore, is the actuation of this conformation to Christ to be sought in an equilibrium that would be a sort of just mean between the two obstacles that have been noted. To be conformed to Christ is a gift of the Holy Spirit, who comes to dwell within us; in us, means to say very precisely in that intimate place where we can welcome him and honour him, in our heart. This is what St Paul points out: "*We have received the Holy Spirit into our hearts, who cries out to the Father, 'Abba Father'*" (Gal. 4:6); to call out *Abba*, is to address ourselves to God, as to our Father, and to reproduce in this way the prayer of Jesus. We understand that such a prayer is not only vocal and that it is not just an exterior imitation of the words of Jesus. It is rich in a love, which is truly experienced through the commitment of every being towards the Father. Such a commitment was that which was lived by Jesus during his earthly life. The Apostle goes to the point of saying: "*It is Christ who lives in me*" (Gal. 2:20), the greatest expression of this configuration to the divine Master.

It is of great interest to contemplate from this perspective the mystery of Jesus's pierced heart. Without going into what has already been stated several times, let us observe that the blow from the sword of the Roman soldier constitutes both a verification of the fact that Jesus truly died and that this action provoked this effusion of water and of Blood, the source and the means of all his subsequent deeds. This gift of the Spirit upon the Cross (the water) was identical to the gift that Jesus made of his own life itself (the Blood), in conformity with the will of the Father. The Heart of Christ has made the human person capable of acting theologically, giving to his acts, henceforth, a supernatural significance. In the open Heart, the human being can contemplate the fact that only the presence of the Spirit can render his acts fruitful, beginning from the gift of his life. The presence of the Spirit in the person's own heart becomes the condition for being able to act in a way which is susceptible to resembling the action of Jesus himself and to pleasing the Father.

There is no need to be afraid of putting it in these terms: configuration to Christ is an authentic gift of the Heart of Jesus.

As a corollary, if this gift is made to people, so that they may welcome it in their hearts (cf. Gal. 4:6), in what way is the presence of the Spirit in the heart of a person itself decisive for their capacity to act? It would seem that here we could retrace the characteristics of the theologal life in terms of the heart to Heart with God. The outpouring of the Spirit into one's hearts is a gift of divine life. St John expresses the view that the union with God of people who believe, that is to say, in the context of the priestly prayer of Jesus, of those who have been consecrated by the Spirit in the truth, is analogous to the love which unites him, Jesus, to his Father: "As you, Father, are in me and I am in you, so may they also be one in us, so that the world may believe that it was You who sent me" (Jn 17: 21). To be in God, as the Father is in the Son and as the Son is in the Father, is to live to the highest degree this intimacy with God, a friendship that becomes the form of all the thoughts and of all the actions of a human being. Let us remark that only such a divine friendship, in the eyes of Jesus, was capable of attracting the adhesion of the world. Here, the world symbolized the totality of those who still did not believe and who did not yet recognize the One who was sent. Thus, only in the life of the disciple is the quality of the friendship that unites that person to God credible. How is it that the heart of the person, transformed in this way, is capable of attracting the world? Because in him, it is the Spirit himself who acts, the same Spirit who had acted in the Heart of the Divine Master.

For this reason, the grace of the Holy Spirit is redemptive; it is made for the hearts of sinners, whom it justifies and transforms. It is good to draw a parallel between this gift of the open Heart that gives, and the hardened heart of the sinner which receives, and which, in this way, is brought to open itself up. The divine friendship, which is thereby extended to the human being, from that moment onwards, unites two hearts, the first through the sword of the soldier, and the second through mercy. There, we are in the order of the redemption, which surpasses the order of moral perfection. Already,

> the Son of God, Jesus Christ, insofar as he was man, in the ardent prayer of his Passion, had allowed the Holy Spirit, who had already penetrated to the depths of his humanity, to transform that passion into a perfect sacrifice through the act of his death, as the victim of love on the Cross.[8]

Divine mercy inscribes into the heart of the sinner who has been forgiven the memory of his own redemption, in such a way that he becomes capable in his turn of offering his own sufferings for the salvation of human beings, uniting them to those of the Redeemer.

Charity: The Highest Exercise of the Gift of the Heart of Christ

It is clear that the theologal life is the work of God in this sense, that the spiritual faculties of the person do not of themselves make it possible for someone to place himself at such a level; to be able to share the very life of God himself. It is necessary that divine intervention, meaning clearly the action of the Holy Spirit, be operative at the root of our habitual capacity to understand and to will, specifically at this level of our spiritual faculties. More precisely, this assistance comes to afford to our actions a significance and an efficacy of grace which are radically new. This is what the theological tradition designates by the name of the theological virtues; by these, we mean both the destination and the origin of our actions, God himself. The end of

---

8. John Paul II, Encyclical Letter, *Dominum et Vivificantem* (1986), § 41. Besides, this passage has been noted by Margerie, *Op. cit*, II, *L'amour devenu lumière* (1999), p. 218.

Configuration to the Heart of Christ

our actions does not pose any particular difficulty for our understanding. It is natural to act for an end; that is simply true already of the moral life; we can conceive equally well, without any trouble, that the end of our theologal action is to be united to God and to participate in eternal beatitude. More complex, on the other hand, is the question of the origin. If God is also the origin of our acts, in what sense does such action remain ours? There again, the sole path to a possible understanding is to remain at the level of the action itself. The gift of the Holy Spirit is never a static gift; on the contrary, it introduces us into the dynamic of divine action. If the Spirit makes the gift to us of faith, he does not introduce into us a definitive understanding of the divine mysteries acquired once and for all, but he renders our spirit capable of welcoming and of giving our assent to these revealed mysteries. If he makes the gift to us of hope, he does not establish in us the security of being able to arrive at the port which we are able to glimpse, but, having identified this end very clearly, he renders our will firm both in its capacity to tend towards that end and in our hope, with the grace of God, of attaining that end. We can understand this; the greatest capacity that is given to us in this supernatural order is that of our loving union with God. This is the gift of charity.

Charity establishes the heart of the human being in God, animating it with a yearning of the whole of our being for him and not finding its rest except in him: "*You have made us for Yourself, my God, and our heart is restless until it rests in you,*"[9] was St Augustine's prayer. Charity establishes the friend of God in the heart to Heart with our divine Friend directly and to the highest degree. We shall see later on in which directions and towards which objects charity is exercised. However, let us note even now one of the traits of this love, which divine charity infuses into the heart of the human being, which is that of trust. We know that, when he was asking himself about the nature of charity, St Thomas noted that it established between God and the

---

9. St Augustine, *Confessions*, I.1.

human person a certain common good, since God grants us part in his beatitude. It is this *communicatio* that is the basis of that reciprocal benevolence, through which friendship is recognized.[10] Now, it is the certitude of the benevolence of the friend alone that is suitable for arousing trust in a relationship of friendship. Human trust, united to God, is without any doubt one of the distinctive features which connotes theological charity. Thus, we are enabled to see in the prayer of trust, addressed to the Heart of Christ, "*Cor Iesu, confido tibi,*" one of the purest expressions of the theologal life.

The Model

Before entering into the description of the heart configured to Christ, it remains now for us to ask in what sense we may speak of Jesus as a model. Grace conforms our heart to the Heart of Christ, which becomes the model for supernatural action, but how are we to conceive of this divine model? In Jesus, we have a divine identity, lived out in the symbolism of his Heart. The Trinitarian aspect of the identity of Christ will be examined in another paper.[11] Here, we are interested first of all in the manner in which this identity of Jesus expresses itself exteriorly, that is to say, in the flesh. The continuity between the earthly life of Jesus and eternity has been expressed clearly by *Haurietis Aquas*.[12] Jesus makes his origin perceptible, revealing his being through

---

10. St Thomas Aquinas, *Summa Theologiae*, IIa IIae, q. 32, a. 1: "When, then, there is a community of goods between the human being and God, since God enables us to participate in his beatitude, it follows that this sharing implies a friendship ... It is obvious, then, that charity is a certain kind of friendship between the human being and God."
11. Translator's note: this refers to another paper delivered at the international congress at Paray-le-Monial in 1999 and published in the *Acta* in 2000.
12. Pius XII, *Haurietis Aquas*, § 29: "It will be helpful for a moment to meditate upon the numerous manifestations of the divine and human affections of our Lord, Jesus Christ and to contemplate them, affections which were expressed by his Heart during his mortal life, which he expresses now and which he will express for all eternity."

the totality of his conduct: "Who is he, then, that the wind and the sea obey him?" (Mk 4:41). The power and the authority emanating from him led his interlocutors unceasingly to pose this question. The whole of the earthy life of Christ has been the object of this oscillation between a more and more specific revelation of what he was (up to the full revelation of the mysteries of his Heart on the Cross and in his Resurrection) and the mystery held by that divine secret which Jesus protected (*the messianic secret*). The gestures the words and the attitudes of Jesus made clear to the eyes of the people a resemblance to the gestures, words and attitudes attributed to God in the Old Testament. Jesus cast a look of anger upon the Pharisees, distressed by the hardness of their hearts (cf. Mk 3:5), but this gaze expressed love towards the rich young man (cf. Mk 10:21), mercy towards the sheep without a shepherd (cf. Mk 6:34), an echo of the words of compassion of God towards the sheep abandoned, in the judgment which fell upon the bad shepherds by the prophet, Ezekiel (cf. Ezek 34:11–16). There are numerous examples of this kind: Jesus' joy (cf. Lk 10:21), his profound distress (cf. Mk. 14:34), his burning impatience that all people be saved (cf. Lk 12:49–50): "I wish to cast fire upon the earth and how I wish that it were blazing already," attracting them to him (cf. Mt 11:28–30), his complaints and his groans for Jerusalem (cf. Lk 19:41–44), his anxiety faced with the imminence of his sacrifice (cf. Jn 12:27), all of these sentiments, these yearnings, these desires, which Christ expressed in his humanity are the object of authentic evangelical witness, constituting in effect a path of privileged access to the mystery of his Person, of his Love for us human beings, and of salvation.

In the life of Christ, God's unfathomable plan of salvation is expressed, in such a way that, moving in the opposite direction, the gaze of faith which people bring to bear upon this humanity of Jesus enables them to perceive the reality of this plan. *Haurietis Aquas* summarizes it in this way, that the Heart of Christ is the symbol of that Love: "Divine love and human love, spiritual and of the senses."[13] Reread according to this double movement, from the interior to the exterior (the visible expression of the identity of Jesus) and from the exterior to the interior (from the humanity of Jesus to the unfathomable design of the Father), these givens are inserted into movement of faith. It will be helpful first of all to pass from the sensible presence of Christ to the realm of humanity (words, feelings, and bodily attitudes), to the commitment of his human will, completely impregnated by charity, by which even the order of spiritual love, of which the encyclical speaks, can be recognized; and then to pass from this human gift of self to the divine Love which inspired it, manifested it and offered it up in sacrifice. In other words, in the symbolic dynamic of the Heart, we can see that these different loves are not perceived simply as juxtaposed one next to the other; the person of faith is led from one to the other. His gaze and his heart act like guides from the exteriority of Christ to the depths of intimacy in him, in short, towards his Presence and to the redemptive divine Love that animates it. Let us note, that here the totality of the dogma of the Council of Chalcedon is respected; the unique Person of the Son and his two natures, divine and human, *with neither separation nor confusion*, but, even if this not conceptualized, it is indeed the totality of the mystery of Christ to which the simple believer can adhere. It is interesting to note that the sole verse of the Gospel in which Jesus speaks explicitly of his Heart (Mt 11:29) is well situated within the context of an invitation made to the least and to "those who labour and are over-burdened" (Mt 11:25–28), to come to him, so that they may find rest for their soul. By approaching in this way Christ and the mystery of his Heart, they discover there the benevolence of the Father, who alone can reveal the Son, since he is the only one who knows him: "Everything has been given to me by my Father and no one knows the Son except the Father, and no-one knows the Father except the Son and those to whom the Son chooses to reveal him" (Mt 11:27).

---

13. *Ibid.* § 21–23, 27.

Configuration to the Heart of Christ

We were asking ourselves how to conceive of the divine model that the heart of Jesus offers us in the area of supernatural action. Jesus himself gives us the response in these verses from Matthew: "Learn from me, who am meek and humble of heart" (Mt 11:29). This school of the Heart of Jesus, if we may so designate it, teaches us not only the meekness and humility proposed by Jesus, but it unfolds the secrets of the salvific love of the Father, those that only the meek and humble Heart of the Divine Master could enclose and transmit.

Nevertheless, it remains for us to protect and to clarify the meaning of the idea of imitation, which is conveyed in the very word "model." Spiritualities founded upon devotion to the Heart of Christ (we may think of the major currents of the French School) have placed the accent often upon the Heart of Jesus as a source of inspiration for our action. This is a question of an imitation and of an appropriation of the interior attitudes of Christ, through which the Christian may little by little become conformed to the Master. In the light of what has gone before, it will be useful to insist on this particular point: this step is located within the realm of voluntary action. The disciple wishes to imitate Christ in his action. Jesus is a model in the dynamic sense of the term, the model of an action that is capable of pleasing the Father. It will be useful also to remember that, when we speak of interior attitudes of Christ, we are indicating movements of his Heart. Furthermore, appropriating to ourselves these attitudes of Christ is not a question of an exterior imitation, simply doing what Jesus did; this appropriation incorporates the affective order. We do not imitate Jesus' emotions, his compassion for the poor and for sinners, his anger in the face of the hypocrisy of the Scribes and the Pharisees or those buying and selling in the temple, his dereliction and his solitude in the Garden of Olives. These are attitudes of Jesus that become ours. It is Jesus who suffers and who loves in us, it is he who is patient in us, it is he who is meek and humble of heart. The relationship to the model is special. The affective appropriation, that is the welcoming of grace, but grace demands to be brought to another level, which remains supernatural. The action of the true disciple is animated by supernatural charity, which renders this imitation and this appropriation possible. This kind of spirituality makes it possible for the theologal life to become more specifically centered upon the person of Christ and attentive to the life of the Word Incarnate in the midst of humanity. Now, it is possible to specify the characteristics of a human heart that is configured to the Heart of Christ.

An Analysis of Theologal Action: The Stability of the Heart Configured to the Heart of Jesus

Following *Haurietis Aquas*, the Heart of Jesus has been readily presented as the seat of a triple love: sensitive, spiritual-human, and divine. It is clear that such a distinction aims to honor the Christological demands of the two dimensions of Love: Love for the Father and Love for humanity. It is for this reason that the Heart of Jesus is the most complete symbol, the *real symbol*, if we wish to use this Rahnerian expression, the source and the origin of every human love, of charity towards God and towards other human beings.

Revealed Paternity

The Love of Christ for his Father goes back to the mystery of the unfathomable Love which unites the divine Persons in the bosom of the Most Holy Trinity, and which is the object of the following paper. I shall not detain myself, then, with this here.[14] But, over and above the transcendence of this relationship between the Father and his only Son, Jesus reveals to us at the same time the fatherhood of God towards each human being; from the Heart of Christ, we learn that total and filial submission, which undoubtedly finds its highest expression in the chalice accepted because of the Father ("Father, if you will, take

---

14. Cf. note 10 above, p. 462.

this chalice away from me. Yet, not my will, but your will be done!"(Lk 22:42) and in his death, lived as a final offering to God ("Father, into your hands I commend my spirit." Lk 23:46). Each of the acts effected by Jesus was accomplished under the gaze of the Father, in order to do his will. Jesus often made explicit reference to this will of his Father: "My food is to do the will of the One who sent me and to do his work" (Jn 4:34). What occurred in the human conscience of the Lord, which had repercussions upon his physical Heart, to be reflected in his gaze, his voice, his gestures, is his revelation of divine and eternal love. Now, adhering to such love underpins all of Jesus's attitudes and it presupposes a costly victory over the burdens of the flesh, his tiredness, and his anxieties. Jesus had the terrible experience of this in his agony; the fulfilment of the Father's will would be made by way of an intense struggle against himself. Obedience to the will of the Father had led Christ to a lowering of himself, the first act of which had been his entry into the condition of being a servant: "He became as all men are" (Phil 2.6). The mystery of the Father in Jesus did not dispense him from having fully to confront the events, the meeting and the trials; it was the Father himself who never ceased to orientate him in this.

In this regard, the important point to underline, to be sure, concerns precisely the extent to which Jesus did love us human beings; his Passion on Calvary and his death on the Cross. Jesus's Passion illustrates and fulfils the words he himself had spoken to his disciples: "No one has a greater love than this, to lay down their life for their friends" (Jn 15:13). We learn from the Heart of Jesus the divine charity which is required of us; in other words, the double commandment of love. Let us note that it is indeed a question of a divine charity which is taught, not only because it was the Divine Master who transmitted it, but above all because, since the first object of charity is divine, only an infusion into us of divine love makes it possible for our faculties to proceed to their object. This is the meaning of the adage: *"Caritas fac-*

ultatem naturae excedit."¹⁵ At the same time, then, as the divine quality of this love is transmitted to human beings, it is the divine capacity to love that is transmitted to us also. "The Word of God," wrote Cardinal Muños Vegas, "together with the Spirit who is the personal, reciprocal love of the Father and of the Son, wanted to make his own a human reality, which would be the comprehensible expression of his love for human beings, and this is the human Heart of Jesus."[16]

Filial Charity

The charity of Christ is structured in a filial way and, as such, it is suitable for being configured to the human heart; the two dimensions of charity, of which we have spoken, teach people to love as children of God.

The filial heart of Jesus is not limited to being the centre of actions in conformity with the will of the Father. It is also, and in the first place, the receptacle for the charity of the Father: "My favour rests on him." The public revelation of the identity of Jesus: "This is my Son, the Beloved" (Mt 4:17), was also made in the midst of the revelation of the fatherly Love of God. Divine charity exercises an attraction upon the human heart, placed before the prospect of giving itself up. St Augustine saw very well this alternative of gift, when he exhorted the faithful in this way:

> Listen to what Charity says from the mouth of Wisdom: 'My Son, give me your soul.' It was in a poor position when it depended upon you, when it was yours, drawn as you were by the trifles and by so many culpable and dangerous affections. Pull yourself out of that! Where to take it, where to put it? Give me your heart, he said. That it may be mine and you shall not lose it! See, he wants to leave nothing in you that could still be of use to you ... The

---

15. St Thomas Aquinas, *Summa Theologiae*, IIa IIae, q. 24, a. 2.
16. Cardinal P. Munoz Vega, *La Declaración cristologica de la Conferencia de Puebla y la teología del Sgdo. Corazón de Cristo. Aportes latinoamericanos*, (Bogotá, Instituto Internacional del Corazón de Jesús, 1984), p. 199.

one who said to you: 'You shall love the Lord with all your heart, with all your soul and with all your mind" (Mt 22:37)...He who has made you wants you completely!'[17]

Let us remark in passing that this image of giving his heart to God is located in the context of a metaphysical anthropology, founded upon conversion.[18] The Augustinian *conversio* opens up access to the divine life because it is itself an action of God. It does not settle any right to be saved because, according to the bishop of Hippo, it is a restitution to God of his right over the creature who has been converted. If we admit that the Heart of Jesus is the symbol of the greatest sacrifice to the Father that could be effected by a human heart, we can gauge how far an anthropology of the heart is from being able to abstract from this dimension of *metanoia*.

The Heart of Christ gives to the heart of the human being, on the one hand, the power of being able to welcome the Love of the Father and, on the other hand, the power of giving to the Father the worship of the love of a son or daughter. In the Heart of Christ the person discovers that he or she is at the meeting point of these two loves, which at first sight seem to clash with each other, but, in fact, human beings love the Father by sacrificing their sufferings to the Heart of Christ, and they make the love of the Father known by making known the Heart of Jesus. We can see the issue at stake in such a perspective for evangelization; freed from every form of sentimentalism which would come to a halt at the Heart of Jesus itself, devotion to the Sacred Heart attracts hearts to God by giving witness to the Love of the

---

17. St Augustine, *Sermon* XXXIV; cf. also H. Seidul, «Sul concetto di cuore in s. Agostino» in G. Beschin, (a cura di), *Antonio Rosmini, filosofo del cuore? Philosophia cordis Theologia cordis nella cultura occidentale* (Morcellana, Brescia, 1995), pp. 93–102.

18. On this precise point, reference should be made to the work of P.-M. Hombert, *Gloria, Gratiae 1 Co. 1,31 et 1 Co. 4, 7 aux sources de la théologie augustinienne de la grâce* in Recherches des études augustiniennes, Institut d'Études augustiniennes, 1995, pp. 327ff.

Father: "The same heart of Christ which loves us "from the Father's side' loves the Father 'from our side as human beings.'"[19]

The Redemptive Union of Intention of God: The Mark of a Heart Configured to the Heart of Christ

The Heart of Christ teaches human beings how to love the Father, to unite ourselves to his redemptive intention. That intention had been lived out by Jesus, literally, as an order of mission, if we may say so. He appropriated to his human heart the divine intention of his Father.[20] The Heart of Jesus is indeed the Heart of the Saviour, the "perfect revelation of the mystery of the real Incarnation of God for the salvation of human beings."[21] For this reason, the heart devoted to the Heart of Jesus is necessarily united to the Church in its most intimate mystery, since it appropriates the same redemptive intention. We could even have spoken about the Sacred Heart as the Heart of the Mystical Body.[22] These two elements, joined together—the desire for the salvation of human beings and belonging to the ecclesial communion—paradoxically show each of us the presence of sin in our own heart. The Heart of Christ plunges our heart into his light in such a way that we become aware of the damage that our sin has inflicted upon the communion of the Church. It is the obedient love of the Son that reveals to us the significance of our disobedience. In fact, we could consider that the Heart of Jesus opened on the Cross is at the same time both

---

19. *Ibid.*
20. Cf. C. Folch Gomes, "El amor del verbo Encarnado hacia su Padre" in *Corazón de Cristo*.
21. J. Stirli, « Les valeurs dogmatiques et ascétiques de la dévotion au Sacré-Cœur » in *Le Cœur de Sauveur* (Salvator, Mulhouse, 1956), p. 241.
22. "The love which is symbolised is the redemptive love which has saved us, by incorporating us into the Mystical Body. The Sacred Heart becomes the Heart of the Mystical Body", G. Mathieu, *in Le Sacré-Coeur de Jésus et la doctrine du Corps mystique, Compte rendu du Congrès national du Sacré-Cœur, Paris, 14–17 juin, 1945* (Apostolat de la prière, Basilique du Sacré-Cœur de Montmartre, 1945), p. 74.

the point of convergence of all the sins of the world, since his death, proven by the sword, was, in the concrete, the work of those sins, and also the very place of their remission, since it was from the same opened Heart that, through water and Blood, the fountains of mercy sprung forth.

It teaches us also the limits of our own hearts. In fact, how could the heart of a human being unite itself to the universality of salvation willed by God?[23] Authentic union to the Heart of Christ, therefore, implies a much greater humility, which operates like an experience of kenosis, which brings us back to the self-emptying accepted by Christ. But, since the divine self-abasement, symbolized by the blow of the sword, which tore from the Heart of the Saviour his Blood, up to the very last drop, to take up the wonderful expression of Sirli, had been the fruit of an obedience *usque ad mortem*,[24] the self-emptying of the heart of us human beings is brought about in the recognition of our sin, of our personal rebellion. Given that the heart of the human being in the present state is necessarily that of a sinner, only the merciful compassion of God in Jesus Christ could reestablish that friendship and could recreate the conditions for a heart to Heart.

Effective Union Is a Union in the Present

In order to understand well the dynamism of the justifying action of God,[25] it is important to underline its character in the present, not in the sense of a vague relevance that could be attributed to this mystery. Devotion to the Heart of Jesus, from this perspective, would still be useful today, indeed important,

---

23. Vatican Council II, *Lumen Gentium*, § 16, which take sup 1 Tim 2:4, "*God wills that all people be saved*".
24. J. Stirli, *Art. cit.*, p. 242.
25. "By the justice of God, the interior person is renewed and becomes just. The justice of God, then, is the formal cause of the justification of human beings. The Heart of Jesus, in some way, is the turning plate on which sin is transformed into justice" (Rom 5: 8); R. Gutzwiller, "Caractère biblique de la litanie" in *La Coeur du Sauveur* (Salvator: Mulhouse, 1956).

but it would remain extrinsic to the mystery. It is appropriate, on the contrary, to affirm the present reality of the sacrifice of the Heart of Christ, since, in the course of history, men and women become his contemporaries.

The outrage done to God, which is expressed in the Passion of his Son and the bruise to his Heart of flesh, is not a reality that belongs only to the past. It is forever, just as the presence of the Lord among us in his mystical Body is for ever, until the consummation of the world.[26]

There is a contemporary aspect of the pierced Heart of Christ to men and women of all times and to which the religious person has access by way of the sacraments, which make it possible for them to hear the words of St John: "They will look upon the One they have pierced" (Jn 19:37). We must see clearly the requirement of Christology[27] that this presence presupposes; the heart of human beings does not have access to the Heart of Christ, suffering with us and merciful towards us, by way an affective union, in order to unite us to him in the mystery of the Cross, but that union issues forth from the transfixed Heart to all of the loving expression of this Heart in the course of the public ministry of Jesus. We could put it like this: the transfixed Heart alone makes it possible to understand in an appropriate way the thoughts, the words, and the actions of Jesus in the course of his earthly life; through the gateway of the side opened by the sword, the human person finds the most adequate way of uniting himself to the sentiments "which were those of Christ Jesus." It is interesting to note that, from a different perspective, a Rahner could have seen in acts of reparation the way to emerge through suffering, from that situation of the absence of God,

---

26. R. Marle, « La dévotion au Sacré-Cœur et le sens du péché» in *Le Cœur du Christ et le désordre du monde* (Le Puy: I. Mappus, 1958), p. 105.
27. On this point, see the work of the international colloquium at Lugano (June, 1996) on the theme: *Contemporaneità di Cristo all'uomo di tutti i tempi secondo il primo capitolo di Veritatis Splendor* - Stock, Rhonhieimer, Llanes, Tremblay, Melina, Pinckaers, Laffitte, Birot ... (Casale Monferrato: Piemme, 1996).

suffering united to that of the Son of God in Gethsemane and on Golgotha. And accepted in union with the apparently useless love of Christ for the sinful world.[28]

When this requirement of Christology is satisfied, the term "sentiments" ceases to be ambivalent. Every human heart that loves is then immersed in a sacrificial action, in which the artificial distinction *affectio-actio* is abolished. There is indeed an affective relationship with Jesus, but this is expressed in action. We can find the first signs of this intelligence of the heart (*intelligentia per cor*), so dear to St Bonaventure, which requires an orientation of the whole being towards God through the witness of life.[29] The heart is full of affections, and it acts. The more a person is affected in his depths, the more he is confronted by the necessity of giving a response of total commitment. The heart and human affectivity react in freedom. When the heart is passive and when it suffers, it is already inserted into a dynamism that causes it to pass from a passive compassion to an active compassion for Christ. The heart of the human being conformed to Christ would express this love in a bodily fashion by giving something to eat to the one who was hungry, to drink to someone who was thirsty, clothes to someone who was naked. It reproduces that love of Christ that goes from the interior of the Heart towards the exterior. We find this kind of Christian conduct in the saints, for example in a St Vincent de Paul, so concerned in his writings and in his life to unite affective love with an effective love in the service of the poor.[30]

In this way, Christian communion is established in all of its breadth. When St Paul says that it is Christ who acts in him, he expresses a union between the Heart of Christ and his own

---

28. Karl Rahner, « Quelques thèses pour une théologie de la dévotion au Sacré-Cœur » in *Le Sacré-Cœur du Sauveur*, p. 173.
29. Cf. C. Del Zotto, "La sistemizzazione della filosofia e teologia del cuore in St Bonaventura" in *Un filosofo del basso Medioevo*. (Brescia: Bonaventura in Pensatori religiosi, 1997), pp. 17–19.
30. St Vincent de Paul, *Correspondance, entretiens. documents* (Coste, Paris), I p. 241, XI, p. 291, XII, p. 264.

heart. Such a union of a human heart to the Heart of Jesus is extended to the hearts of other people through the same love of Christ.[31] If, after all that we have understood, the expression *one single heart* may designate symbolically the communion of persons, then we can understand that the Church is the place of a communion which is unlimited in its meaning and in its effects: the Heart of Jesus is an ecclesial heart; it is the Heart of the Church.

---

31. We have an example of this in the prayer of the Blessed Elizabeth of the Trinity: "O my Christ, crucified out of love, I would wish to be a spouse for Your heart ... I ask you to clothe me with Yourself, to identify my soul with all the movements of Your soul, to submerge me, to invade me, and to substitute Yourself for me, so that my life may be no more than a ray of Your Life;" Bl. Elizabeth of the Trinity, *Ô mon Dieu, Trinité que j'adore* in *Œuvres Complètes*, p. 199.

www.ingramcontent.com/pod-product-compliance
Lightning Source LLC
Chambersburg PA
CBHW021713300426
44114CB00009B/126